CLASSICAL DISCOVERY OF INDIA

CLASSICAL DISCOVERY OF INDIA

Contributions of the Ancient Greeks and Romans to the Discovery of History and Civilization of India

Volume-II

G.P. Singh

First Published, 2018

Published by

Gyan Publishing House
5, Main Ansari Road
Daryaganj, New Delhi-110002
Moble: 9811692060
Fax: 91-11-23285914
E-mail: books@gyanbooks.com

Printed at : G. Print Process, Delhi

Cataloging in Publication Data—DK
Courtesy: D.K. Agencies (P) Ltd. <docinfo@dkagencies.com>

Singh, G. P., author.
Classical discovery of India : contributions of the ancient Greeks and Romans to the discovery of history and civilization of India / G.P. Singh.
volumes cm
Includes bibliographical references.
ISBN 9788121214261 (set)
ISBN 9788121214285 (vol. 2)

1. India—History—To 324 B.C. 2. India—History—324 B.C.-1000 A.D. 3. India—Civilization. 4. Greeks—India. 5. Romans—India. I. Title.

LCC DS451.S56 2017 | DDC 934 23

To

My beloved wife

Kiran

Who sacrificed a lot

To enable me to

accomplish this work

OTHER BOOKS BY THE SAME AUTHOR

1. *The Kirātas in Ancient India: A Historical Study of their Life*, Culture and Civilization with Foreword by R. S. Sharma, Delhi, 1990.
2. *Political Thought in Ancient India*, Delhi, 1993.
3. *Early Indian Historical Tradition and Archaeology*, Delhi, 1994.
4. *Facets of Ancient Indian History and Culture New Perception*, Delhi, 2003.
5. *Ancient Indian Historiography: Sources and Interpretations*, Delhi, 2003.
6. *Republics, Kingdoms, Towns and Cities in Ancient India*, Delhi, 2003.
7. *Kingship in Ancient India: Genesis and Growth*, Delhi, 2008.
8. *Historicity of Rāma and Kṛṣna Literary, Historical, Archaeological and Scientific Perspectives*, Delhi, 2008.
9. *Researches into the History and Civilization of the Kirātas*, Delhi, 2008.
10. *Perspectives on Indian History, Historiography, and Philosophy of History*, Delhi, 2009.
11. *Historical Researches into Some Aspects of the Culture and Civilization of North-East India*, Delhi, 2009.
12. *Indian Historians and Historiography in the Twentieth Century*, Delhi, 2009.
13. *The Evolution of Historiographical Tradition in Ancient and Medieval India*, Delhi, 2011.
14. *Hinduism in Manipur*, Delhi, 2012.

Contents

Transliteration Chart xi
Preface xiii
Acknowledgements xv
Abbreviations xvii

VOLUME–I

Book One:
Introductory

1. Purpose, Scope, Method and Utility of the Work 3
2. Classical Sources and their Value: A Critical Estimate 11

Book Two:
Geography and Ethnography

1 Geographical Setting: Land and the People 71
2. Ariana – The Land of the Aryans 87
3. The Non-Aryan Races and Tribes: Their Settlement Patterns, Antiquity, Ethnology and Identification 95

Book Three:
Society and Economy

Preliminary Remarks 113
1. Social Divisions : Classes and Castes 117
2. Social Life, Customs, Traditions and Institutions 121
3. Positions and Status of Women in the Society 135
4. Agrarian and Agricultural System 139

5. Natural, Mineral and Commercial Products 145
6. Arts, Crafts and Indigenous Industries 155
7. Trade and Commerce: Internal and External 165

Book Four:
Political System: Polity and Administration

Introductory Remarks 215
1. Monarchical and Non-Monarchical Forms of Government 225
2. Administrative System 291

Index 311

VOLUME–II

Book Five
Religions and Philosophies

1. Religious Beliefs and Practices 331
2. Brahmanism, Buddhism and Jainism 337
3. Christianity in India 355

Book Six
Foreign Expeditions and Invasions

1. Pre-Persian Foreign Expeditions: Mythical and Historical Accounts 361
2. Persian Invasion and Domination (558 – 330 BCE) 375
3. Macedonian Invasion (327 – 325 BCE) 383

Book Seven
Kings and Kingdoms

1. The kingdom of Magadha from the Extinction of Nanda Rule to the Foundation of the Maurya Dynasty with Special Focus on the Rise of Candragupta and his Accession 437
2. Chandragupta Maurya and His Political Achievements 449
3. Kingdoms and Principalities 459

Book Eight
Foreign Rule and Influence

1. The Greek Rule in Bactriana, Ariana and Other Parts of India 477
2. The Rule of the Sakas in India 487
3. The Parthian Rule in North-West India 493

4. Foreign Influence on Indian Civilization and Indian Influence on Western Culture and Thought 501

Book Nine
Relations Between India and the West

1. Political Relations between India and Persia (Sixth to Fourth Centuries BCE) 523
2. Diplomatic and Friendly Relations between the Maurya Empire of Northern India and the Hellenic Kingdoms of Syria and Egypt (The Fourth and Third Centuries BCE) 529
3. Relations between India and the Roman Empire with Prime Focus on Indian Embassies to the Roman Emperors, Augustus to Justinian (First Century BCE – Sixth Century BCE) 537

Book Ten
Towns and Cities

General Remarks 549
1. Towns and Cities in North India 559
2. Towns and Cities in Eastern, Western, Central and Southern India 565
3. Growth and Decay of Urban Centres in Northern and North-Western India 585

Book Eleven
Splendour of Art

1. Evolution of Art 687
2. Architecture, Sculpture, Iconography and Painting 697

Book Twelve
Education, Palaeography and Chronology

1. Education and Learning 711
2. Evolution of the Art of Writing 717
3. Systems of Chronology 723

General Conclusions and Observations 727

General Bibliography 739

Index 765

Transliteration Chart

Classical Names of the Indian Rivers with their Equivalent Sanskrit and Modern Names

Classical	Sanskrit	Modern
Diamouna, Jomanes, Jobares, or Iomares	Yamunā	Yamunā
Indus, Sinthus of the author of the *Periplus, Sindus of Pliny, or Sindu of Kosmas*	Sindhu	Sindhu
Hyphasis, or Hypanis	Vipāśa	Biās, Beias, Beas, Byāsa or Vyāsa
Hydaspes (Bidaspes of Ptolemy)	Vitastā	Jhelum
Hydraotes, or Hyarotis	Paruūṣṇī, later Irāvatī	Rāvī (known to Ptolemy as Rhouadis or Rouadis)
Akesines	Asiknī, later	Cināb (called also "Chenāb")

This name has been inaccurately transformed by Ptolemy into Sandabal. It is an obvious error for Sandabaga.The Sanskrit Candrabhāgā has been correctly transliterated into the Greek as Sandrophagos by other writers.

Classical	Sanskrit	Modern
Hesidrus, hysedrus, sydrus, or Zaradrus of Ptolemy	Śutudrī, or Śatadru	Satalaj, Satlej, or Sutlej
Kophen, Kophes, or Koa of Ptolemy	Kubhā	Kābul
Khoaspes, or Khoes	Kunār	Kunār (a tributary of Kābul)
Souastos, Soastus, Svastos, or Ptolemy's Souastene	Suvāstu	Swāt, or Svāt
Gouraios, or Guraeus	Gauri	Pañjkora, which unites with the river Swāt to form, the Londai, a large affluent of the Kābul river.

Preface

My intense desire to bring to light the information embodied in the classics (the works of ancient Greek and Latin writers) relating to India prompted me to undertake this research work.

The object of this work is to highlight as far as possible the contributions of the ancient Greeks and Romans to the discovery of geography, ethnography, history, culture and civilization of India.

This work is based on my researches carried out into the subject over the past eight years. Overcoming the obstacles that off and on hindered the progress of my work, I pursued my investigation into the subject, and it is by the grace of the God that I became able to accomplish this work , which was really a *Herculean task* for me. I have tried to the best of my ability to do justice to the task. It is, however, for the reader to judge as to how far I have succeeded in achieving my object.

This work is divided into two volumes. The first volume contains Book One to Book Four and the Second one Book Five to Book Twelve.

The present author craves the indulgence of readers for any deficiency or omission that may have crept into the body of the volume. This work, I believe, will be useful to those who are inquisitive to familiarize themselves with the subject treated of here, and to those who intend to make a fresh disquisition into the subject as a whole or in any part of it.

G. P. Singh

Acknowledgements

First of all, I would like to express my gratitude to the learned members of the Expert Committee Constituted by the University Grants Commission (UGC) , New Delhi, for considering the topic, *Classical Discovery of India* , proposed by me, worthy of research , and for recommending the award of Emeritus Fellowship to me. No less grateful I am to the authorities, UGC, for offering me this Fellowship in History, in Feb. 2008.

I acknowledge my gratefulness to the librarian and staff, Asiatic Society library, Calcutta (now Kolkata) for their all help and cooperation to me in the course of my library work there from Dec.18-27, 2008, and again on Feb.10, 2009. I am also grateful to the librarian and staff, National Library Kolkata, for helping me to have access to all the books that I needed during my work period there from Jan.30 to Feb.09,2009. My special thanks go to Assistant Library and Information Officer Syed Abuzar, National Library, for taking pains to make some of very very rare books available to me for my use during the period of my work there. I cannot but offer my sincere thanks to the staff, National Library, for helping me to get Xerox of relevant portions of a very very useful book for me, *History of Ancient Geogrophy Among the Greeks and Romans from the Earliest Ages till the Fall of the Roman Empire* (vol.11), by E.H Bunbury, when I visited the library on Jan. 03, 2001.

I must acknowledge my indebtedness to Professor I.S.Mumtaza Khatun, Department of History, Guwahati University, Guwahati, for getting the first volume of the said Bunbury's book issued from the university library and sending me by post in Feb. 2003. I found both the volumes of Burbury's book useful for me. I have thoroughly used them in the present work.

I am extremely grateful to the library staff, B.R. Ambedkar Bihar University, Muzaffarpur, for making available to me the books I selected there in the library for my use during my stay there as UGC visiting fellow in the PG Department of History from Jan.15 - Feb. 28, 2002. The materials collected from those books have been used exclusively in the present work.

I embrace the opportunity of expressing my grateful thanks to the librarian and staff, Central University of Manipur, Imphal, for all kinds of help they extended to me in connection with my library work there during the period of my service at that university (from July 09, 1984 to Dec. 31, 2013) as a Professor of History.

I acknowledge my deep sense of gratitude to Dr S.K. Sharma, Professor of English, University of Allahabad, for taking trouble to send me the Photostat copies of the articles," India as known to the Early Greeks," JGRI XVII , 1-2, 1960-1961, pp. 1-41, and "Studies in Indian History and Geography Based on Early Greek Accounts," JGRI XVI, 3-4, 1959, pp. 265-306, both by B.C. Law, by post through one of his nearest and dearest, Akhilesh Kumar Shankhadhar, who is now Assistant Professor of Hindi at the University of Manipur, Imphal, and for whom I still have a great affection.

I am indebted to all those authors whose works I have utilized in this volume.

G.P. Singh

Abbreviations

ABORI	*Annals of the Bhandarkar Oriental Research Institute*, Puna.
AI	*Ancient India–Bulletin of the Archaeological survey of India*, New Delhi.
AICL	*Ancient India as described in Classical Literature*, by J.W.McCrindle.
AIHA	*Aspects of Indian History and Archaeology.*
AIHT	*Ancient Indian Historical Tradition.*
AII	*Ancient India Its Invasion by Alexander the Great*, by J.W. McCrindle.
AIIC	*Ancient India and Indian Civilization* by P. Masson-Oursel and others.
AIK	*Ancient India as described by Ktesias the Knidian*, by J.W. McCrindle.
AIMA	*Ancient India as described by Megasthenes and Arrian*, by J.W. McCrindle.
AISH	*Ancient Indian Social History.*
AIT	*Ancient India as described by Ptolemy*, by J.W. McCrindle (ed. With notes by S.N. Majumdar Sāstri).
Anab	*Anabasis (History of Alexander's Expeditions)*, by Arrian.
Ano.	*Geog. Expo. Comp. Anonymi Geographiae Expositio Compendiaria,* by an unknown writer who follows Eratosthenes and Ptolemy.
Antiq.	*Geog. Antiquite Geographique de I' Inde*, by M.D.' Anville

ApIAI	*Aspects of Political Ideas and Institutions in Ancient India.*
APP	*Ancient Peoples of the Punjab.* (Eng. trans, of two articles of J.P.rzyluski, pub. in French in the JA,1926 and 1929), by C. Sen.
Ar. Ant.	*Ariana Antiqua*, by H.W. Wilson.
Arch. Man. Disp.	*Archelai et Manetis Disputatio*
ARNWI	*Archaeological Reconnaissances in North – Western India and South Eastern, Iran*, by A. Stein.
Arth.	Arthasāśtra of Kautilya.
ASB	Asiatic Society of Bengal, Calcutta (Kolkata).
ASIAR	*Archaeological Survey of India, Annual Reports.*
As. Res.	*Asiatic Researches* (comprising History and Antiquities, the Arts, Sciences, Ethnology and Literature of Asia), Calcutta (Kolkata), now rept. Delhi.
ASWI (or *Arch.* S.W.I)	*Archaeological Survey of Western India,* Reports.
AV	*Atharvaveda.*
BCLS	Bohn's Classical Library Series.
BDCRS	*Bulletin of the Deccan Collage Research Society*, Puna.
Bh. Sāv. (or *Bh.Sv.*)	*Bhārata Sāvitrī* (An indepth historical study of the *Mahabhārata*), by V.S. Agrawala
Bib. Hist.	*Bibliotheca Historica*, called also *Bibliothekes Historikes* (Universal History or History of the World), by Diodorus Siculus.
Bibl.	*Bibliothēke.*
Bio Alex.	*Bios Alexandrou tou Makedōnos kai Prāxeis* (Romance History of Alaxander the Great of Macedon), by an anonymous Greek writer, Falsely ascribed to Kallisthenes and incorrectly called Pseudo Kallisthenes.
Biog. Appen.	Biographical Appendix.

BIS (or *Bibl. Ind.*)	Bibliotheca Indica Series (a collection of Oriental works), Asiatic Society, Calcutta (Kolkata).
BMD.	*Brahmāṇḍa Purāṇa.*
BORI	Bhandarkar Oriental Research Institute, Puna.
Br. Sam.	Bṛhat (Vārāhi) saṁhitā
BRWW	*Buddhist Records of the Western World* (Eng. tr. of the Chinese *Si-Yu-Ki* of Hiuen Tsang), by S. Beal
BSOAS	*Bulletin of the School of Orintal and African Studies*, London.
CAGI	*Cunningham's Ancient Geography of India.*
CAI	*Classical Accounts of India* (a compilation of the English translations of the Greek and Roman Accounts of Ancient India), by R.C. Majumdar.
CASE	*Coins of Alexander's Successors in the East*, by A. Cunningham.
CASR	*Cunningham's Archaeological Survey of India Reports.*
CCBM	*Catalogue of Indian coins in the British Museum, coins of Ancient India*, by John Allan.
CCBMG	*Catalogue of the coins of the Greek and Scythic Kings of Bactria and India in the British Museum*, by P Gardner.
CCIM	*Catalogue of the coins in the Indian Museum,* Calcutta, Vol. I, *Coins of Ancient India*, by V.A. Smith.
CCPM	*Catalogue of Coins in the Punjab Museum,* Lahore, Vol. 1, *Indo-Greek Coins*, by R.B. Whitehead.
CDGR	*Classical Dictionary of Greek and Roman Biography, Mythology and Geography*, by W. Smith, thoroughly revised and in part rewritten by G.E. Marindin.

CHI	*Cambridge History of India*, Vol. I, *Ancient India*, ed. E.J. Rapson.
CHLAG	*Critical History of the Language and Literature of Ancient Greece.*
CISSK (or CSSK)	*Coins of the Indo-Scythians, Śakas, and Kushans*, by Cunningham.
Class. Quart.	*Classical Quarterly.*
CLS	Classical Library Series.
CMI	*Coins of Medieval India* by Cunningham.
CNAIO	*Commerce and Navigation of the Ancients in the Indian Ocean.*
CNES	*Commerce and Navigation of the Erythraean Sea* (McCrindle's trans, of the *Periplus Maris Erythraei*, by an anonymous writer.
CO. An. Ind.	*Coins of Ancient India from the earliest times down to the seventh Century AD*, by Cunningham.
Coll. Rer. Memo.	*Collectanea Rerum Memorabilium* of Solinus.
Com. Hist. Ind.	*Comprehensive History of India.*
Contr. Jovin.	*Contra Jovinian.*
Corp. Ins. Graeco	*Corpus Inscriptionum Graecorum.*
CSARM	*Classical Studies in Ancient Races and Myths.*
CSS	*Classical Studies Series.*
Deip	*Deipnosophistae.*
DGRG	*Dictionary of Greek and Roman Geography.*
EAB	*Ethnology of Ancient Bhārata.*
EAI	*Ethnography of Ancient India.*
EB (or *En.Br.* or *Enc.Br.*)	*Encyclopaedia Britannica.*
Eccles. Hist.	*Ecclesiastical History.*
EHI	*Early History of India*, by V.A. Smith, revd. by S.M. Edwards, 4th edn. Oxford, 1924, rept, London, 1967.
EHIDS	*Early Hindu India : A Dynastic Study.*
EIC	*Encyclopaedia of Indian Culture.*

EIHTA	*Early Indian Historical Tradition and Archaeology*.
EIP	*Early India and Pakistan to Ashoka*, by M.Wheeler.
EP. Ind.	*Epigraphia Indica*, Delhi.
ESAI	*Ethnic Settlements in Ancient India*, by S.B. Choudhuri.
Etude	*Etude Sur La Geographie Grecque et Latine de L' Inde* (Geography of India as derived from the Greek and Latin Sources), by M.V. de St. Martin
Fact.dict. Memo.	*Facta et dicta Memorabilia*.
Fast. Hellen.	*Fasti Hellenici*.
FGH	*Fragmente der Griechischen Historiker* (A collection of the Fragments of the works of the ancient Greek authors on India), by F. Von Jecoby.
Fn.	Footnote.
Frag. Hist. Graeco.	*Fragmenta Historicorum Graecorum* (Fragments of the Historical works of the ancient Greek authors on India), ed. C. Müller.
GDAMI	*Geographical Dictionary of Ancient and Medieval India*, by N.L. Dey.
GDEP	*A Critical Study of the Geographical Data in the Early Purāṇas. Geographical Essays Geographical Essays : Relating to Ancient Geography of India*, by B.C. Law.
Geog. Graec. Mino.	*Geographi Graeci Minores* (on some geographical and Historical works of the ancient Greek writers on India), ed. C. Müller.
Geogr. Journ.	*Geographical Journal*, London.
GSH	*Geographical System of Herodotus*.
GTCP	*Glossary of the Tribes and Castes of the Punjab and North-West Frontier Province*, by H.A. Rose.

HA	*History of Antiquity*, tr. From the German of Max Duncker, by E. Abbott.
HAG	*History of Ancient Geography among the Greeks and Romans from the Earliest Ages till the Fall of the Roman Empire*, by E.H. Bunbury.
HAI	*History of Ancient India.*
HASA	*Historical Atlas of South Asia.*
HASL	*History of Ancient Sanskrit Literature*, by F. Max Müller.
HDAI	*Historical Disquisition Concerning Ancient India.*
Hell. Per.	*Hellados Periegesis* (Am Itinerary of Greece or Description of Greece), by Pausanias.
HGAI	*Historical Geography of Ancient India*, by B.C. Law
HHW	*Historian's History of the World* (A Comprehensive Narrative of the Rise and Development of Nations as recorded by the Great writers of all ages.)
HIC	*History of science, Philosophy and culture in Indian Civilization*, General Editor D.P. Chattopadhyaya.
HIL	*History of Indian Literature.*
Hist. Alex.	*Historiae Alexanderi Magni* (History of Alexander the Great), by Quintus Curtius Rufus.
Hist. Anc. Geog.	*History of Ancient Geography.*
Hist. Eccles.(or Eccles. Hist.)	*Historia Ecclesiastica* (*History Ecclesiastical*) or Ecclesiastical History.
Hist. Phil.	*Historiarum Philippicarum* (an Epitome of the lost work Historiae Philippicae of pompeius Trogus), by Justinus (Justin).
Hist. Philipp.	*Historiae philippicae* of Pompeius Trogus.
Historical Researches	*Historical Researchers into the Politics, Intercourse and Trade of the principal Nations of Antiquity.*

HOS	Harvard Oriental Series.
HPL	*History of Pāli Literature.*
HSL	*History of Sanskrit Literature.*
IC	*Indian Culture – Journal of the Indian Research Institute*, Calcutta (Kolkata).
IGI (or *Imp. Gaz. Ind.*)	*Imperial Gazetteer of India.*
IHC	Indian History Congress.
IHQ	*Indian Historical Quarterly*, Calcutta, now rept. Delhi.
IHR	*Indian Historical Review*, Journal of the Indian Council of Historical Research, New Delhi.
I IA	*Invasion of India by Alexander the Great as described by Arrian. Q. Curtius Rufus, Diodorus, Plutarch, and Justin*, by J.W. McCrindle.
Ind. Alt.	*Indische Alterthumskunde* (A German work on the History and Antiquities of India), by Chr. Lassen.
Ind. Ant.	*Indian Antiquary* (Journal of Oriental Research in Archaeology, History, Literature, Language, Folklore, etc.) Bombay (Mumbai).
Ind. Co.	*Indian Coins.*
Indian shipping	*Indian Shipping : A History of the Seaborne Trade and Maritime Activity of the Indians from the earliest times.*
Ind. Stud.	*Indi'sche Studien.*
IP	*India as Known to Pāṇini* (A study of the Cultural material in the Aṣṭādhyāyī), by V.S. Agrawala.
IPPH	*India Through the Ages: A popular and picturesque History of Hindustan.*
Itin. Alex.	*Itinerarium Alexandri Magni* (*Itinerary of Alexander the Great*), by Julius Valerius.
J A	*Journal Asiatique*, Paris.

JAHRS	*Journal of the Andhra Historical Research Society*, Rajahmundry.
JAOS	*Journal of the American Oriental society,* New Haven, Connecticut, USA.
JAS	*Journal of the Asiatic Society*, Culcutta (Kolkata).
JASB	*Journal of the Asiatic Society of Bengal*, Kolkata.
JASM	*Journal of the Asiatic Society of Mumbai*, Mumbai.
JBAS	*Journal of the Bombay Asiatic Society.*
JBBRAS	*Journal of the Bombay Branch of the Royal Asiatic Society*, Mumbai.
JBIAS	*Journal of the Bhāratīya Itihaāsa Adhyayan Sansthān*, Allahabad.
JBORS	*Journal of the Bihar and Odisha Research Society*, Patna.
JGIS	*Journal of the Greater India Society*, Culcutta.
JGRI	*Journal of the Gangānātha Jhā Research Institute*, Allahabad.
JHR	*Journal of Historical Research*, Jaipur.
JHS (or *Jour.Hell. Stud.*)	*Journal of Hellenic Studies or Journal of Hellenistic Studies.*
JIH	*Journal of Indian History*, Trivandrum.
JNSI	*Journal of the Numismatic Society of India*, Vārāṇasī.
Jour. As Soc. Bomb.	*Journal of the Asiatic Society of Bombay.*
JPASB	*Journal and Proceedinges of the Asiatic Society of Bengal*, Culcutta (Kolakta).
JRAS	*Journal of the Royal Asiatic Society of Great Britain and Ireland*, London.
JRASB	*Journal of the Royal Asiatic Society of Bengal*, Culcutta (Kolakta).
JRASB (L)	*Journal of the Royal Asiatic Society of Bengal, Letters*, Culcutta (Kolakta).

JRGS	*Journal of the Royal Geographical Society*, London.
JRSA	*Journal of the Royal Society of Arts*, London.
JUPHS	*Journal of the united Provinces Historical Society*, Lucknow.
LCL	Loeb Classical Library.
Lif. Alex.	*Life of Alexander* (as told by himself in his epistles), by Plutarch.
MAGK	*Memoir on Maps Illustrating the Ancient Geography of Kashmir*, by M.A. Stein.
MAHA	*Manual of Ancient History The Constitutions, the Commerce and the Colonies of the States of Antiquity.*
MAIMA	*McCrindle's Ancient India as described by Megasthenes and Arrian*, ed. R.C. Jain.
MAIT	*McCrindle's Ancient India as described by Ptolemy*, ed. R.C. Jain.
Mans. Parth.	*Mansiones Parthicae* (Parthian Stations).
Manu.	*Manusmrti.*
MASI	*Memoirs of the Archaeological Survey of India*, Calcutta.
Mat. (or *Mts*)	*Matsya Purāṇa.*
Mbh.	*Mahābhārata.*
Meg. Ind.	*Megasthenis Indica.*
Mkd.	*Mārkaṇḍeya Purāṇa.*
MMH	*Memoir of a Map of Hindustan*, by James Rennell.
MRI	*Martial Races of India.*
NAB	*Notes on Afghanistan and part of Baluchistan*, by G.H. Roverty.
Nat. Anim:	*Natura Animalium*, by Aelian.
Nat. Hist. (or *Hist. Nat.*)	*Naturalis Historia* (*Natural History* or *Historia Naturalis)* (*History Natural*) of Pliny.
NEB	*New Encyclopaedia Britannica.*

Num. Chron.	*Numismatic Chronicle and Journal of the Numismatic Society*, London.
OIB	*Original Inhabitants of Bhāratavarṣa.*
OUP	Oxford University Press.
Orb. Des.	*Orbis Descriptio*, A Latin version of the Greek *Periegesis*–Description of the whole world–, by Dionysius Periegetes.
PAHI	*Prehistoric Ancient and Hindu India.*
PAPDI	*Pre – Āryan and Pre – Dravidian in India* (Eng. trans. of articles in French, by Sylvain Levi, J.Przyluski and others), by P.C. Bagchi
PASB	*Proceedings of the Asiatic Society of Bengal*, Culcutta (Kolakta).
PDKA	*Purāṇa Text of the Dynasties of the Kali age.*
Pdm.	*Padma Purāṇa.*
Pent. Ind.	*Pentapotamia Indica* (Ancient Geography and History of India Based on Greek and Latin Sources) by Chr. Lassen.
Periplus	*Periplus of the Erythraean Sea* (Travel and Trade in the Indian Ocean) by a Greek Merchant (anonymous) of the first century, trans. from the Greek and annotated by W.H. Schoff.
PHAI	*Political History of Ancient India*, by H.C. Raychaudhari , 6th edn.
PIHC	*Proceedings of the Indian History Congress.*
PIOC	*Proceedings* (or Transactions) of the International Oriental congress.
PNEIHA	*Proceedings of North-East India History Association.*
POC	*Proceedings of the All India Oriental Conference.*
Praep. Evang.	*Praeparatio Evangelica* (Evangelical Preparation) of Eusebius.
PTOC	*Proceedings and Transactions of first Oriental Congress.*

PTS	*Pāli Text Society*, London.
QJAHRS	*Quarterly Journal of the Andhra Historical Research Society.*
RANIT	*Racial Affinities of Early North Indian Tribes.*
Rer. Ges.	*Rerum Gestarum* (History of the Roman Empire), by Ammianus Marcellinus.
Rom. Hist.	*Romaike Historia* (History of Rome).
RPGEA (or RTGEA)	*Researches on Ptolemy's Geography of Eastern Asia.*
RPICO	*Report of the Proceedings of the Second International Congress of Orientalists.*
SBA	*Sacred Books of the Aryans* Series.
SBE	*Sacred Books of the East*, Oxford.
SCD	*Smaller Classical Dictionary of Biography, Mythology and Geography*, A New ed. of W. Smith's larger Dictionary thoroughly revd. and in Part rewritten by G.E. Marindin.
SEHHW	*Social and Economic History of the Hellenistic World.*
SGAMI	*Studies in the Geography of Ancient and Medieval India.*
SHC	*Studies in History and Culture,* Journal of the PG Department of History, Berhampur University, Orissa (now Odisha).
SI	*Select Inscriptions Bearing on Indian History and Civilization.*
TAI	*Tribes in Ancient India.*
TOP. Chr.	*Topographia Christiana* (Christian Topography), by Kosmas Called also Cosmas.
Tot. Orb. Des.	*Totius Orbis Descriptio* (A Latin translation of a lost Greek Original, composed either at Antioch or at Alexandria between CE 350 and 353).
Var. Hist.	*Varia Historia* (A Collection of Miscellaneous History), by Aelian.

Vit. Alex.	*Vita Alexandri* (*Life of Alexander*, as told by Alexander himself in his epistles and as described by his companion and historian Aristoboulus in his Alexander's Indian Expedition), by Plutarch.
Vit. Apoll.	*Vita Apollonii* (*Life of Apollonius of Tyana*), by philostratus.
Vit. Const.	*Vita Constantinus* (Life of Constantine the Great), by Eusebious Pamphili.
Voy. Near.	*Voyage of Nearkhos*, from the mouth of the Indus to the head of the Persian Gulf, as described in the second part of the *Indika* of Arrian, trans. by McCrindle from C. Müller's edition as given in the *Geog. Graec. Mino*, Paris, 1855.
V.	Verse.
Vs	Vikrama Samvat.
Vsn.	*Vishnu Purāṇa.*
VV.	Verses.
VY	*Vayu Purāṇa.*
YCTI	*Yuan Chwang's Travels in India* (CE 629- 45), by Thomas Watters.

Book Five
Religions and Philosophies

1

Religious Beliefs and Practices

The ancient Greek and Roman writers transmit to us valuable information regarding Indian religions and philosophies. They give also accounts of the religious beliefs and practices of the Indians. They speak of polytheism in India.

Of all the classical authors, it was Ktésias of Greece who first noticed the worship of Sun and other deities in India. Giving an account of the manners and customs of the Indians, he states that they venerated the Sun and Moon as deities. They, he says, worshipped the former by performing his rites.[1] "This is perhaps the earliest reference to the existence of a Sun and Moon cult in ancient India," says D. Th. Vassiliades.[2]

The evidence produced by Ktésias with regard to the worship of the two deities, noted above, discredits the statement of E.A. Schwanbeck that "No writer before Alexander's time mentions the Indian gods."[3]

Weltheim relates that it was the region east of the Indus where the worship of the Sun god flourished in early times.[4]

The Greek traveller Apollonius, who accompanied by his Assyrian friend Damis visited India in CE 43-44, gives an eye-witness account of the subject under notice. He says that the Indian Brāhmaṇas called by him Sophoi, "whose country lay between the Hyphasis and the Ganges", worshipped the Sun in the day with hymns in praise and worshipped the fire in the night with religious but mysterious rites, as recorded by

Philostratus in his biographical work.[5] The Brāhmaṇas, as we are informed by Apollonius, used to adore the deities also in the temple.[6] He, in the course of his visit to Taxila city (in CE 44), saw outside its walls the temple of Sun with the image of the god, as we are told by Philostratus.[7] The Sun was worshipped there by the Brāhmaṇas.[8] Sun worship must have been one of the popular cults at Taxila.

It is in the fitness of things to mention here that one of the Apollonius' objectives of undertaking his travel to India was to make himself acquainted with the religious beliefs and practices, rites, and doctrines of both Brāhmaṇas and Buddhists.[9]

Speaking of brāhmanical religion and philosophy in his *Oeconomicus*, Hierokles says that the Brachmanes (Brāhmaṇas) "are philosophers dear to the gods, and especially devoted to the Sun," as we learn from Stephanus of Byzantium.[10]

The views of ancients are quoted by Colebrooke to show that the Brāhmaṇas worshipped the Sun.[11] The Indian Brāhmaṇas are described by more than one authority, especially the classical ones, as worshippers of the Sun.

Palladius, one of the ancient Greek authors, has focussed on the belief of the Indian Brachmans (Brāhmaṇas) in the worship of gods.[12]

Megasthenes describes the two principal deities of the Hindu pantheon – Śiva and Kṛṣṇa – under the names of Dionysus and Herakles respectively. He says, of the Indian philosophers (Brāhmaṇas) those who inhabited the mountains were worshippers of Dionysus, and those who lived in the plains worshipped Herakles.[13] "It seems probable that these two cults (Śaiva and Kṛṣṇa) took shape about the fourth century BC," says Charles Eliot[14], one of the noted authorities on Hinduism and Buddhism. The evidence furnished by Megasthenes is very valuable, says the same authority.

Arrian explicitly states that the Herakles (Hari, generally identified with Kṛṣṇa) was held in especial honour by the Sourasenoi (the people of Surasena kingdom), who possessed two large cities Methora and Kleisobora (Greek transliterations of Mathurā, and Kṛṣṇapura or Vrindāvana respectively) through whose territories flowed the river Jobares (Yamunā).[15] Arrian's evidence, according to B.N. Puri "is a true representation of Lord Krishna."[16] The popularity of both the cults of Hinduism – Śaiva and Vaiṣṇava – in early India can undoubtedly be proved on the combined testimony of the two Greek historians, Megasthenes and Arrian.

W.H, Schoff, translator and annotator of the Greek text *Periplus*, is absolutely correct in his assertion that "In Greek literature concerning India, Heracles is usually identified with Vishnu."[17] It is noteworthy that Kṛṣṇa being an incarnation or embodiment of the deity Viṣṇu is also known by this name.

It is worthy-recording here that the Greeks (Macedonians) who accompanied Alexander into India identified the gods they saw principally worshipped by the inhabitants with gods of their own country who possessed somewhat similar attributes or were worshipped with somewhat similar rites. Thus they identified Dionysus and Herakles, the gods of their own pantheon, with the Indian gods Śiva and Kṛṣṇa. They had no difficulty in deciding that Śiva was no other than Dionysus when the observed that the worship of the former was celebrated with rites in the Bacchi fashion. The Greek historians of both Alexandrian and post-Alexandrian times described Śiva and Kṛṣṇa under the names of Dionysus and Herakles respectively.

We learn from Curtius, one of the historians of Alexander's Indian campaign, that an image of Herakles (Kṛṣṇa) was carried in front of the army of the great Porus of the Punjab as he advanced against Alexander to provide incentives to make the soldiers fight well against the Macedonian invader.[18] This shows the veneration of Kṛṣṇa in India at the time of its invasion by Alexander the Great.

Clemens Alexandrinus (Clemens of Alexandria) also tells us that the Brachmans of India worshipped Herakles (Kṛṣṇa) and Pan (Viṣṇu) as deities.[19]

Aelian praised the Indians, for they had strong faith in God.[20]

W.W. Tarn says that the people of the city Nysa in Swāt Valley near Mount Meros, like their modern descendants worshipped some god ("Śiva!") who could be identified with Dionysus.[21] The people called Nysaeons by the Greek writers were settled at the time of Alexander's invasion of India to the west of the Indus, i.e., in the valley of the Kābul river near the Mount Meros and not in the Swāt Valley as held by some authorities.

The Kirāta tribe inhabiting the mountainous regions of India, called by the classical writers variously Skiratai, Kirrhadae, and Kirrhadia, were great worshippers of Śīva.[22] The Śivis, called in the classics Sibae, who occupied the territory between the Hydaspes and the Akesines, were also the devotees or votaries of the god Śiva. Mathurā, as already stated, was one of the great centres of the Kṛṣṇa or Viṣṇu cult.

A passage from Bardesanes' work (now lost) preserved by Stobaeus describes God Śiva in the form of Ardhanārīśvara (half man, half woman). This refers to the combined image of Śiva and Śakti. Such figures are to be found in the rock-cut temples in the region of Mahārāṣtra.[23] An androgynous image of the God Śiva must have been an object of adoration for the Brachmans or Brāhmaṇas of the Deccan.

From Bardesanes' account of the subject preserved by Stobaeus[24] it appears that along with the God Śiva other gods or deities were also worshipped by the Brachmans to invoke their blessings. From Porphyry[25] also we learn that the Indians, particularly Brachmans, believed in the worship of more than one god because of being ardent followers of polytheistic religion. They are also said to have inculcated the duty of worshipping the deities with pious reverence.

Strabo, on the testimony of historians, whose names he does not mention, states that the Indian worshipped *Zeus Ombrios* (the god Indra).[26] "Indra, the god of the firmament, who wielded the flaming thunderbolt, and sent down from the clouds the fertilising rains without which the crops would wither, the cattle perish, and all nature languish and die, was at the time of the Macedonian invasion the most popular of all the Nature –gods worshipped by the Indians. In this deity the Greeks readily recognised their own *Zeus Ombrios* (the *Jupiter Pluvius* of the Romans), who like Indra ruled supreme in heaven, wielding the thunderbolt, and sent down rain upon the earth," observes J.W. McCrindle.[27]

We are also told by Strabo that the Indians worshipped the river Ganges (Gaṅgā), and the indigenous deities of the country.[28] It is well known that purifying and supernatural properties are attributed to waters of the river Gaṅgā by the Hindus. They regard it as the stream that washes away all sin.[29]

Curtius says that "The Indians regard as gods whatever objects they value, especially trees, to violate which is a capital offence."[30] Certain trees, the pipal, for instance, are still held sacred and venerated by the Hindus in India.

Some of the Greek writers inform us that the Brāhmaṇas performed the sacrifices offered to the gods for the common benefit of the state or nation, as well as for the individuals. They performed other sacred rites when any religious ceremonies were held.[31] According to the established religious practices, anything sacrificed were offered to the diety.[32] Strabo relates on the authority of Megasthenes that sometimes the kings worshipped and supplicated the deity through the Brāhmaṇas.[33]

Clemens throws some light on the belief of the Sarmanai (Buddhists) in the worship of Buddha or their faith in the reverence for Buddha as their supreme God, and their practice of erecting *Stupa* (a solid dome-like structure of brick or stone resting on a round base on any of the relics of the Buddha's body, such as hair, nail, teeth, bones, or ashes) and worshipping it.[34]

Notes and References

1. *Indika*, Fragm.I, 8, in Photius, *Bibl.*, LXXII, pp. 144ff, AIK, pp. 12-13; also in Jacoby, FGH., No.688, Fragm. 45; see also Lassen's Review of the Reports of Ktésias concerning India (trans. from his *Ind. Alt.*, Vol. II, 2nd edn. 1874, pp. 641ff), in AIK, pp. 78-9.
2. The Greeks in India, p. 27.
3. *Meg. Ind.*, P.43
4. Cf. AIK, p. 12, note 26.
5. *Vit. Apoll.*, tr. by F.C. Conybeare, *The Life of Apollonius of Tyana*, Vol. I, III, 14 and 15, pp. 257 and 259 respectively; also Priaulx, Indian Travels of Apollonius of Tyana, in CAI, pp. 398 and 411.
6. Philostratus, *Vit. Apoll.*, tr. Conybeare, *Op. cit.*, III, 17, pp. 265-6.
7. *Op. cit.*, II, 24, pp. 180-81; also Priaulx, *The Indian Travels of Apollonius of Tyana*, p. 15; CAI, p. 388.
8. Priaulx, *op. cit.*, pp. 34ff.
9. See *Ibid.*, pp. 11-12.
10. Cf. AICL, p. 186.
11. *As. Res.,* IX, p. 298.
12. *About the Nations of India and the Brachmans*, in his *Lausiac Histories*, III, IX.
13. *Indika*, Bk. III, Frgam. XLI, in Strabo, *Geog.*, XV, I, 58; Hamilton and Falconer's tr. *The Geography of Strabo*, Vol.III, p. 108; see also E.R. Bevan, "India in Early Greek and Latin Literature," in CHI, I, pp. 376 and 379, also 437; Charles Eliot, *Hinduism and Buddhism An Historical Sketch*, II, p. 137; CAI, p. 273; W.W. Tarn, *The Greeks in Bactria and India*, p. 392.
14. *Op. cit.*, p. 138.
15. *Indika*, I, VIII; also Godolphin (ed), *The Greek Historians*, Vol. II, pp. 737-8; M. Elphinstone, "The Greek Accounts of India", rept. from his *The History of India* (ed. E.B. Cowell, London, 1911), in *Ancient India* (Delhi, 1983), p. 29, note 52.
16. *India as described by Early Greek writers*, p. 123.
17. *Periplus*, p. 238, note.

18. *Hist. Alex.*, VIII, 14.
19. *Stromateis*, III, 194; also AICL, p. 183, note 2.
20. *Var. Hist.*, II, 31.
21. *Alexander the Great*, I, p. 89.
22. For details see my work, *The Kirātas in Ancient India: A Historical study of their Life*, Culture and Civilization, pp. 243-44.
23. See Bardesanes, in Jacoby, FGH, No.719, Fragm. I; Stobaeus, *Physica* (or *Anthologium*), I, 3, 56; AICL, p. 173, and notes 1 and 3; CAI, p. 448, note 3; U.P. Arora, "Ancient India and Ancient Greece", in G.C. Pande (ed), *Life, Thought and Culture in India* (from c. 600 BC to c AD 300), Vol. I, pt.2 of HIC, p. 1064.
24. *Physica*, I, 3, 56.
25. *De Abstinentia*, IV, 17.
26. *Geog*. XV, I, 69; Hamilton and Falconer's tr. *The Geography of Strabo*, Vol. III, p. 117; see also E.R. Bevan, "India in Early Greek and Latin Literature", in CH 1, I, p. 379, note 3; J.T. Wheeler, "Greek and Roman India", rept. from his *The History of India from the Earliest Ages* (London, 1881), in *Ancient India* (Delhi, 1983), p. 109, note 22.
27. AICL, p. 74, note 4 which continues in p. 75.
28. *Geog*., XV, I, 69; H.L. Jones (tr.), *The Geography of Strabo*, Vol. VII, p. 121.
29. AICL, p. 75, note 1.
30. *Hist. Alex*., VII, 9.
31. Megasthenes, *Indika*, Book III, Fragm. XXXIII; Strabo, *Geog*., XV, I, 39; Arrian, *Indika*, I, XI.
32. Strabo, *Geog*., XV, I, 54.
33. *Ibid*., XV, I, 60.
34. *Stromateis*, I, 15, 71-72; III, 7, 60; III, 194; IV, 4, 17.

2

Brāhmanism, Buddhism and Jainism

Megasthenes divides the Indian philosophers into two sects, the Brachmanes and the Sarmanes[1]. They are called respectively Brachmanes and Garmanes (an erroneous transcription of Sarmanes) by Strabo[2], Brachmans, and Sammanaeoi or Samanaeans by Bardesanes[3], Brachmans and Samanaeoi by Alexander Polyhistor[4], Brachmanai, and Sarmanai, Samanaeoi or Semnoi by Clemens[5], Brachmans and Samanaioi by Origen,[6] and Sophoi and Sramanoi by Apollonius.[7] Ptolemy mentions only Brachmanai.[8] The Brachmanes, Brachmans or Brachmanai are represented by the Brāhmaṇa sages, and Sarmanes, Sarmanai, Samanaeoi or Sramanoi (Sanskrit Śramaṇas = Pāli Samanas) by the Buddhist ascetics or monks.

The followers of brāhmanical religion, culture and tradition are designated by the classical writers also as Gymnosophists (half-naked philosophers, dedicated to asceticism and meditation)[9] and Sophists (Teachers of Wisdom).[10]

It may be pointed out here that some of the classical accounts of the lives and philosophies of the Brāhmaṇas, Buddhists and Jains representing three principal religious sects are jumbled up to an extent that one can hardly be distinguished from the other. B.N. Puri aptly remarked: "The Greek historians failed to notice the distinction between Brāhmaṇism, Buddhism and Jainism."[11] The Sarmanes or Śramaṇas include both the

Buddhist and Jain ascetics, which can be supported by the statements of the authorities like H.G. Rawlinson,[12] M. Elphinstone[13], R.C. Majumdar[14], and R.C. Jain.[15]

The Brāhmaṇas and their Mode of Life, and Philosophical Doctrines

Of the Indian philosophers, the most honourable were the Brachmans (Brāhmaṇas). They held the supreme place of dignity and honour. They were held in higher estimation or in greater repute than the others, as they were more consistent in their opinions or doctrines.[16] They formed the "collective body of the philosophers".[17] They were a class by themselves. As philosophers, they maintained their distinct identity.

"The Brachmans", says Bardesanes, "are one family, the descendants of one father and mother, and they inherit their theology as a priesthood".[18] Porphyry also tells us that "The Brachmans form the leading sect, and succeed by right of birth to this kind of divine wisdom as to a priesthood."[19]

Palladius, whose account of the Brachmans is based on the narrative of a traveller who was no other than the Theban scholar (unnamed) who explored the land of the Indians, and contained in his small treatise *About the Nations of India and the Brachmans*, informs us that "The Brachman nation was not an order like that of the monks, which one could enter if he chose, but a society, admission into which was allotted from above by the decrees of God."[20]

Speaking of the Brāhmaṇa philosophers of India, Megasthenes says that they were exempted from all public duties. They were neither the masters nor the servants of others. Their services were employed privately by persons who wished to offer sacrifices to the gods, and also publicly by the kings. They were engaged by private persons also to celebrate the obsequies of the dead, for they were believed to be the most dear to the gods. These philosophers, who enjoyed pre-eminent dignity in the royal court, advised the king on all important matters for the welfare of the state and the people. To this calss of philosophers the knowledge of divination among the Indians was exclusively restricted, and none but a philosopher was allowed to practise that art. They also made predictions about any calamity which may befall the state. They lived upon the fruits which each season produced, and on the bark of trees.[21] Arrian also writes more or less to the same effect.[22] Bardesanes opines that "The Brachmans are so honoured by the Indians, that even the king will come to them to solicit their counsel in matters of moment, and their intercession with the gods when danger threatens the country."[23] Some of them, it is said, wore the muslin dress, and the turban. Some of their garments were dyed of bright colours.[24]

We are told by Megasthenes that some of the Brāhmaṇa philosophers resided in a grave in front of the city within a moderate-sized enclosure. They lived in a simple style. They were found lying on pallets of straw and on (deer) skins. They abstained from animal food and sexual pleasures; and occupied their times in listening to serious discourse and in imparting knowledge to willing persons. [25]

Megasthenes relates at some length different classes of the Brāhmaṇa philosophers and their life, practices and tenets. But he is clearly in error in placing them under the Sarmanes. He[26], as we learn from Strabo[27] and Clemens[28], says that of the Sarmanes, the most honourable are those called the *Hylobioi*. They neither live in cities nor even in houses. They rather live in the forests, subsist on leaves and wild fruits, wear garments made from the bark of trees, and abstain from wine and sex with women. They communicate with the kings who consult them by messengers regarding the causes of things, and who through them worship and supplicate the Deity.

The Brāhmaṇa philosophers described by Megasthenes as Hylobioi (forest-dwellers or hermits) were in that stage of their religious life which in ancient Indian brāhmanical tradition was called *Vanaprasthāśrama.*[29]

Curtius, one of the historians of Alexander, also informs us that of the Indian (Brāhmaṇa) philosophers one class was forest-dweller.[30] Giving description of the other class of the Brāhmaṇa philosophers, Megasthenes tells us that next in honour to the Hylobioi were the physicians. They applied philosophy to the study of the nature of man. Their food consisted of rice and barley-meal. By their knowledge of medicine they could make persons have a numerous offspring, and make also the children to be either male or female. They effected cures rather by regulating diet than by the use of medicines. Both the class and the other class of persons practised fortitude as well by undergoing active toil as by enduring suffering. Besides these, there were diviners and sorcerers, and those who were conversant with the rites and customs prevalent in the society. Those who were religious mendicants went about villages and towns begging. Those who were more cultured than these and mixed more with mankind inculcated which they thought conducive to piety and sanctity. Women studied philosophy with some of them, but they abstained from sexual intercourse.[31]

Megasthenes' descriptions applies to Brāhmaṇa ascetics rather than to Buddhists. "It is true", Max Duncker says, "that the Brāhmaṇs and the initiated of the Enlightened, the Śramaṇas, are confounded in the order of the sages; this is shown by the statement that any one could enter into this order… In the description of the life of the ascetics and wandering sages, the Brāhmaṇs and Bhikshus are again confounded… In the examination of the doctrines of the Indian sages, Megasthenes distinguished the Brāhmaṇs and the Buddhists, in as much as he opposes the less-honoured sects to the first, and declares the Brāhmaṇs to be the most important. From his whole account it is clear that at his date i.e. about the year 300 BC, the Brāhmaṇs had distinctly the upper hand. But, according to him, the Śramaṇas took the next place to the Brāhmaṇs among the less-honoured sects. Among the Buddhists Śramaṇa is the ordinary name for their clergy."[32]

Brāhmaṇism appears to have been the dominant religion in India in the time of Megasthenes. Brāhmaṇical religion and philosophy left so deep impression on his mind that he did not care much to know about other Indian religions. He knew very little about Buddhism.

There were various spheres of activities of the Brāhmaṇas. All Brāhmaṇas were not devoted to religious pursuits and other allied activities. Some of them took active part in politics. Giving an account of the Brāhmaṇa sages, Nearchus, who accompanied Alexander into India, says that "some of the Brachmanes take part in political life and attend the king as counsellors. The others are engaged in the study of nature. Women study philosophy along with them, and all lead an austere life."[33]

Clemens[34] relates on the authority of Megasthenes[35] that like philosophers of Greece, the Indian Brachmanes also possessed knowledge of nature.

Describing the Brachmans and their life, Bardesanes tells us that they were not subject to the authority of the king, and paid no taxes or tribute to the state. Of these philosophers, some lived on the mountains, and others on the banks of the river Ganges. The mountain Brachmans subsisted on fruits and cow's milk, curdled with herbs, while the dwellers of the Gangetic region lived on fruits of trees which grew in plenty near the said river. The eating of any other food, particularly animal food, was held by them to be the height of impurity and impiety. They set apart the whole day and greater part of the night for hymns and prayers to the gods. They were theists. They believed in the existence of gods. They worshipped the deities with pious reverence. Each of them had a hut of his own in which he passed as much time as possible in solitude, and much discourse. And they even frequently went on fast.[36]

Dion Chrysostom, while treating of the Brachmans, opined that they " ...live apart, absorbed in philosophic contemplation, subjecting their bodies to sufferings of astonishing severity, though no one compels them, and submitting to terrible endurances... They possess a remarkable fountain that of truth-by far the best and most divine of all..." "These statements," he himself says, "are not fictions, for some of those who come from India have now asserted them to be facts."[37] He met the Indians he speaks of possibly at Alexandria in Egypt which they frequently visited in connection with their commerce with that country. He says further that "The Indians have the Brachmans, who excel in self-control and in righteousness and their love of the Divine Being, whence they have a better knowledge of the future than other men have of the present."[38]

Giving a description of the mode of life of the Brachmans, Palladius says that they live in a state of nature near the river Ganges, and go about naked. They have no quadrupeds, no tillage, no iron, no house, no fire, no bread, no wine, no implement of labour, nothing tending to pleasure. They reverence the deity. They pray without ceasing. They subsist upon fruits and on wild herbs that grow spontaneously. They drink only water when they wander about in the woods, and they take their repose on pallets of the leaves of trees. They undergo hardships in life, and practise some sorts of religious austerities. They have self-control. They generally abstain from intercourse with their wives only for some part of their lives. Sometime they live with their wives and go for intercourse with them for their offspring. "Such is the body politic of the Brachmanas," says he.[39]

Speaking of the Brāhmaṇas and their philosophy, Pseudo-Origen states that "There is among the Brachmans in India a sect of philosophers who adopt an independent life, abstain from animal food, and subsist upon fruits of the trees. They hold that God is light. They members of this sect regard death with contemptuous indifference. They always pronounce the name of the Deity with a tone of peculiar reverence, and adore him with hymns. They neither have wives nor beget children."[40]

"The Brachmans neither eat anything having life nor drink wine, but some of them every day, like ourselves, take food, while others of them do so once in three days, as Alexander Polyhistor relates in his *Indika*.[41]

Clemens notices at some length the Brachmans (called Gymnosophists by him) and their life and philosophy. He says that "they do not use women, for they regard this as contrary to nature and unlawful; for which reason they keep themselves chaste." Some of the Brachmans, whom he mistakes for "Semnai," according to him, "observe closely the heavenly bodies, and, by the indications of futurity which these offer, make some predictions."[42]

"Those philosophers again who lead a civilised life in cities are said to observe the motions of the heavenly bodies, and to predict future events on scientific principles."[43]

Philostratus speaks very highly of Indian philosophers. He considers them nearer to the gods.[44]

The Greek traveller Apollonius, who visited India in CE 43-44, also describes the life of the Brāhmaṇas whom he calls Sophoi. "I have seen," he says, "Brāhmaṇs who dwell on the earth, and yet not on the earth; in places fortified, and yet without walls; and who possess nothing, and yet all things."[45]

St. Jerome, like other classical writers, also says that the Indian Brachmans subsist on the fruits of trees. He, however, adds that the king on coming to them worships them, and the peace of his dominions depends, according to his judgement, on their prayers.[46]

Hierokles in his *Oeconomicus* says that the Brachmanes abstain from all flesh meats and live out in the open air, and honour truth, as we learn from Stephanus of Byzantium.[47] Kedrenus makes an incidental reference to the Indian Brachmans and their temples.[48]

"It seems that the ideals of the gymnosophists concerning immunity to pleasure and pain and disregard of intellectual philosophy had reached Greece and were welcomed by sceptic and Cynic philosophers who shared similar aspirations," observes D. Th. Vassiliades.[49]

The Brāhmaṇa philosophers called Gymnosophists, according to Pliny, were "accustomed to remain in one posture with their eyes immovably fixed on the Sun from his rising till his going down, and to stand on the burning sands all day long now on one foot and then on the other..."[50]

Alexander the Great and his two companions and historians, Aristoboulus and Onesikritus, had an opportunity at Taxila (326 BCE) of witnessing with their own eyes the austerities practised by the Indian Gymnosophists (Brāhmaṇa sages) Kalanos and Mandanis (called also Dandamis) who were living there along with their disciples. The latter was the oldest and wisest of the sages.[51] These philosophers, as Arrian relates, through the interpreters told Alexander: "O king Alexander! every man possesses as much of the earth as this upon which we have stepped, but you… have traversed so much of the world troubling both yourself and others; and yet you must soon die and possess no more than the spot of earth which will suffice to bury you."[52]

Alexander heard that the Brāhmaṇa sages of Taxila were held in highest honour. He admired their patience in enduring hardships. He was desirous of knowing the wisdom and learning the doctrines of the two sages noted above. And thus he sent Onesikritus (an ardent votary of the Cynic school of philosophy founded by Diogenes of Greece) to converse with them, as we are told by the latter himself.[53]

Onesikritus conversed with Kalanos, one of the sages, who afterwards accompanied Alexander to Persia, and burned himself alive on a funeral pyre at Sousa (Susa).[54] "Kalanos, who had made great progress in philosophy, and was held in honour and esteem by Alexander, brought his life to an end in a most singular manner… Kalanos, following the rules prescribed by his philosophy, stepped with unflinching courage on to the summit of the pyre and perished in the flames which consumed it," says Diodorus Siculus,[55] one of the historians of Alexander's Indian campaign. He was on this account condemned by his fellow-Indian philosophers. But Mandanis was praised by other philosophers, for he did not got to meet Alexander in spite of threats of punishment if he refused to meet him. Onesikritus told Mandanis : "Hail to thee, thou teacher of the Brachmanes. The son of the mighty god Zeus (Jupiter), king Alexander, who is the sovereign lord of all men, asks you to go to him, and if you comply, he will reward you with great and splendid gifts, but if you refuse, he will behead you." Mandanis said, "Alexander was not the son of Zeus, for he was not so much as the master of the larger part of the world. Let Alexander, then, terrify with these threats, those who wish for gold and for wealth, and who dread death, for against us these weapons are both alike powerless, since the Brachmanes neither love gold nor fear death. For his part he wanted none of the gifts of a man whose desires nothing could satiate, and as little did he fear his threats, for while he lived India would supply him with food enough, and when he died he would be delivered from the flesh now wasted with age, and would be translated to a better and a purer state of existence."[56] The philosophical thoughts of Mandanis find expression in his assertion. Alexander, on receiving from Onesikirtus the report of his conversation with Mandanis, commended Mendanis and excused him from coming to him, and thereby showed his greatness.

We learn from Strabo that Mandanis called Onesikritus to him, and said that he praised the king (Alexander) because though he ruled over so great an empire, he nevertheless desired wisdom."[57]

We now turn our attention to the philosophical doctrines of the Brāhmaṇas. "Religion and philosophy," says B.N. Puri, "are related together as body and soul. Religion without a philosophical background is as ineffective as a philosophy divorced from a religious outlook. All philosophical ideas have a religious background with a view to make them effective on the popular mind. The Greek historians combined Religion with philosophy and it is only in their accounts on philosophical people and ideas that we find religious elements.[58]

The Brāhmaṇa sage of Taxila, Mandanis (noted before), while explaining his philosophical doctrines to Onesikritus in the course of his discourse with him, said that "the best doctrine was that which removed pleasure and grief from the mind; that grief differed from labour in that the former was an enemy and the latter a friend of man; for men exercised their bodies with labour in order to strengthen their mental powers, by which means they would put an end to dissensions, and would unite in giving good counsel to all, both to the public and to individuals." Mandanis having spoken to this effect, then enquired whether such doctrines were current among the Greeks. Onesikritus replied: "that Pythagoras taught a similar doctrine, and enjoined his disciples to abstain from animal food; and that Socrates and Diogenes (other two Greek philosophers), to whose discourses he had listened, held more or less similar views." Mandanis replied that in other respects he thought they entertained sound notions, but erred on one point by preferring custom to nature. He said also that they (his fellow Brāhmaṇa philosophers) busy themselves with enquiries concerning natural phenomena, prognostics, etc.[59]

We are informed also by Plutarch, a biographer of Alexander, that Onesikritus, a philosopher, who belonged to the school of Diogenes the Cynic, was sent by Alexander to confer with Mandanis, called Dandamis, the most renowned of the sages of Taxila. He tells us that when Dandamis was told by Onesikritus about Pythagoras, Socrates and Diogenes (The three noted Greek philosophers), he said, "they appeared to him to have been men of genius, but from an excessive difference to the laws had subjected their lives too much to their requirements."[60]

Alexander lived with Brāhmaṇa philosophers (Gymnosophists) of Taxila. He had a great desire to become acquainted with their doctrines and practices. The Brāhmaṇa sages instructed him in their philosophy, and failed not to impress upon him the superior grandeur of their view of life to his. An account is given at great length of these Brachmans in *The Romance History of Alexander the Great*,[61] by an anonymous Greek author, and not by Pseudo-Kallisthenes as held by some authorities.

Strabo, on the authority of Megasthenes,[62] says, "The Brachmanes do not communicate a knowledge of philosophy to their wives, lest they should divulge any of the forbidden mysteries to the profane, if they became depraved, or lest they should desert them if they became good philosophers; for no one who despises alike pleasure and pain, life and death, is willing to be subject to another; and this is the character both of a good man and of a good woman. Their discourse turns most frequently on death. They regard this life as the time, when the child within the womb becomes mature, and death as a birth into a real and happy life for those that are philosophers. On this account they undergo much discipline as a preparation for death. They consider nothing that befalls men to be either good or bad. Some persons would not be affected with sorrow and others with joy by the very same things."[63] With regard to ideas about physical phenomena, Strabo again quotes Megasthenes as his authority, and says that "they display great simplicity, for they are better in their actions than in their reasoning's, their belief being chiefly based upon fables. On many points, however, their opinions coincide with those of the Greeks, for the Brachmanes say with them that the world was created, and is liable to destruction, and that the Deity who made and governs it is diffused through all its parts. Concerning generation, the nature of the soul, and many other subjects, they express views similar to those of the Greeks. They wrap up their doctrines about the immortality of the soul and future judgement, and kindred topics after the manner of Plato."[64] This is the account which Megasthenes gives of the Brachmanes," says Strabo.[65]

"The Indian sages," Pausanias says, "have asserted that the soul of man is immortal."[66]

The Indian philosophers (Brāhmaṇas) – a class most eminent for their wisdom-had their own notion of death. They, because of their old age, poor health, worries and anxieties, or any disease, viewed the life as a burdensome, and liked to quit the world. They lost no time in freeing the soul from the body. They regarded death if waited for as a disgrace. They thought that it is glorious to die soon. They were guided by their beliefs that the soul after death exists, and that it is immortal. They ended their life by throwing or casting themselves into flames of a burning pyre amid the hymns of the assembled crowd resounding their praises. They after their death became immortal. Frequent references to this characteristic of the Indian philosophers are made by the classical writers.[67]

The brāhmanical practice of putting an end to life by resorting to immolation was based on the belief in the metempsychosis – transmigration of the soul (on death) into a new body – which is a doctrine of the Vedānta school of philosophy.

The brāhmanical doctrine of rebirth finds affirmation in the statement of Clemens. He says, "The Brachmans despise death, and set no value on life; for they are persuaded that there is a new birth."[68]

From Philostratus we learn that the Greek traveller Apollonius in the course of his Indian travels (time already noted) paid visit to the Indian philosophers with whom he stayed for four months. He learnt from their chief Iarchus that their views with regard to rebirth are similar to that of Pythagoras, the Greek philosopher.[69]

E.H. Bunbury opines that the doctrines and tenets of the Brāhmaṇa philosophers were regarded by Megasthenes and other Greek writers as having much resemblance with those of Pythagoras.[70]

"Indian Brāhmaṇ sages," Apollonius says, "like the Greek philosophers, believed in the philosophy of self-knowledge–the philosophy of knowing himself or oneself," as Philostratus records.[71]

"The account of religion and philosophy, though not quite adequate, offers a clue to form bigger and higher conceptions of religion and philosophy, which the Greek historians must have formed. The Greek historians should have been attracted much by the Religion and Philosophy of the Indians for which they were noted in the west, but only the historians of Alexander and Megasthenes contributed on this theme. If their full accounts were preserved, it is just possible that they would have acknowledged the superiority of Indian Religion and Philosophy in black and white," remarks B.N. Puri.[72]

The Buddhists and their Life and Philosophy

The Buddha, founder of the Buddhist doctrine, was known to classical writers by different names. He is called Boutta by Clemens[73], and Buddas by St. Jerome[74] and Archelaos.[75] It was the Greek writer Clemens who first perspicuously stated that "Among the Indians are those philosophers also who follow the precepts of Boutta (Buddha) whom they honour as a god on account of his extraordinary sanctity."[76] Apollonius describes the Indian ascetics (Buddhists) wise and divine, as we learn from Philostratus.[77]

Kuśinārā or Kuśinagara, which is celebrated as the place where Buddha obtained Nirvāṇa, was known to Nonnos as "Kusa".[78]

The Shamans or Samanaeans (Buddhists), Bardesanes says, are taken or collected from all classes of the Indians indifferently. They consist of persons who wish to devote themselves to divine wisdom[79] Speaking of this class of Indian philosophers, Apollonius says, "Their mode of election determined by ancestral and personal character points them out as Buddhists."[80]

We are told by Bardesanes that the Buddhists are selected or an elected body. Whoever wishes to be enrolled in their order presents himself to the city or village authorities, and there makes cession of all his property or his possessions. He then shaves his body, puts on the Buddhist robe, and goes to join the Buddhists, and never turns back to speak or look at his wife and children, if he has any, and never thinks of them anymore, but leaves his children to the king and his wife to his relations, who provide them with the necessaries of life. Describing the life of the Buddhists, Bardesanes says that they live outside the city, and spend the whole day in discourse on divine topics. Their houses and temples are founded by the king, and in them are stewards, who receive from the king a certain allowance of food, rice, bread, fruits, vegetables. etc for the support of the inmates of the convent (monastery). The Buddhists lead a strictly ascetic life in the convent. He tells us further that when the convent bell rings, all strangers there in the house withdraw, and the Buddhists enter and offer prayer. When prayer is over, the bell rings a second time, and they go for dinner. As soon as the dinner is over, they go out and betake themselves to their usual occupations. They are neither allowed to marry nor to possess property. They and the Brachmans are held in such high honour by the other Indians that even the king comes to them to solicit their prayers when the country is in danger or distress and their counsel in times of emergency. The peace of his dominions depends according to his judgement on their prayers.[81]

Kleitarchus, who accompanied Alexander into India, furnishes an account of a class of philosophers whom he calls pramnai, who may be identified with Sramanai, the Buddhist sect. "The Pramnai", to according Strabo, "are philosophers opposed to the Brachmanes, and are contentious and fond of argument. They ridicule the Brachmanes who study physiology and astronomy as fools and impostors."[82] "Possibly they may have been ordinary Buddhist monks, who scorned all pursuits excepting those connected with religion," says J.T. Wheeler.[83] He observes further that

"... Notwithstanding the supremacy of their moral tenets, they are a most disputatious sect... such was their character in the latter days of Sākya Muni (Buddha)..."[84] Some authorities, notably, M. Elphinstone,[85] H.H. Wilson[86] and E.R. Bevan[87], are of the opinion that Strabo considers the Pramnai as a separate class, but they were probably Brāhmaṇas themselves, attached to a particular school of philosophy. They derived their name from Prāmāṇika, a term applied to the followers of the logical school. Strabo, in fact, describes the Pramnai here as a separate Buddhist sect and not as a class of Brāhmaṇas.

Strabo says that the women live in the society of the Pramnai "without sexual commerce."[88]

Strabo's statement, that "the Pramnai of the mountains wear deer-skins and carry wallets filled with roots and drugs, professing to cure diseases by means of incantations, charms, and amulets",[89] no doubt applies to the Brāhmaṇas and not to the Buddhists.

Giving an account of the Buddhists called Semnoi, Clemens states that they "do not use woman, for they regard this as contrary to nature and unlawful; for which reason they keep themselves chaste."[90] He also tells us about the worship of *Stūpas* (pyramidal structures) by the Buddhists. He says, "Those Indian who are called Semnoi worship a kind of Pyramid (*Stūpa*) beneath which they think the bones (one of the relics of the body of some divinity (Buddha) lie buried."[91] This remarkable allusion to the Buddhist *Stūpa* is the earliest one in classical literature. This points to a unique feature of Buddhism.

We are also informed by Clemens that the Buddhists practised truth,[92] which was the keystone of their philosophy.

The Buddhists' notion of death was different from that of the Brāhmaṇas. The Buddhist doctrine was in contradistinction to the doctrine of the Brāhmaṇas, who sometimes committed suicide to liberate themselves from life's misery as stated before. The Buddhists, like the Brāhmaṇas, believed in the immortality of the soul, but they condemned suicide or self-immolation. Megasthenes statement, that "self-destruction is not a dogma of the philosophers, but that those who commit this act are regarded as foolhardy",[93] as recorded by Strabo,[94] applies more to the Buddhists than to the Brāhmaṇas. We learn from Bardesanes that those Buddhists who committed suicide were not liked by their nearest friends and relatives. "They", he says, "weep over themselves that they must continue to live, and deem him happy who has thus put on immortality. And among neither of the two sects (Shamans and Brachmans), as among the Greeks, has any sophist yet appeared to perplex them by asking, 'if everybody did this, what would become of the world."[95]

The Jains and their Way of Life, and Philosophy

Some of the classical writers notice, though not at length, the Jains and their life and philosophy. Herodotus was the first to mention them. He describes them as a special class of Indians, and says that they do not kill anything that has life, that they do have houses; and that they subsist upon herbs, and a grain that springs spontaneously from the earth which they gather and eat after boiling it. He says further that they are vegetarian and wandering ascetics.[96] Here there are some reflections on the doctrine of non-violence of the Jains, and on their life.

Strabo, while writing about the Pramnai (Sramanai), says that the Gymnetai, one of their sections, "in accordance with their name, are naked, and live generally in the open air practising endurance."[97] This description is obviously about Digambara Jains, who sat on penance in solitude, and observed certain austeric practices. One of the sections of the Sramanai, according to Strabo, lived in towns or cities and wore white muslin robes.[98] They were probably Śvetāmbara Jains. They, following their tradition and practices, were always clad in white dress.

Arrian's statement, that some "sages go naked, living during winter in the open air to enjoy the sunshine, and during summer, when the heat is too powerful, in meadows and lowgrounds under the shadow of large trees,"[99] is applicable to Digambara Jains. R.C. Jain also holds exactly the same view.[100] It may, however, be pointed out that Arrian erroneously includes the naked sages in the sophists.

Speaking of the Digambara Jains, Pseudo-Origen explicitly states that "throughout life they go about naked, saying that the body has been given by the Deity (God) as a covering for the soul."[101] Mixing them up with the Semnoi (holymen), Clemens says that "Those Indians, who are called Semnoi go naked all their lives."[102] His assertion, that the Semnoi practise truth,[103] applies to both the Buddhists and Jains. We do not have any other information in the classics about the Jain ascetics.

Notes and References

1. *Indika*, Bk. III, Fragm XLI.
2. *Geog.*, XV, I, 59; see also IIA, Note Hh, "Indian philosophers", p. 368. Dion Cassius' *Zarmanus* (Sarmanus) in his *Rom. Hist.* (LIV, IX) is the

Zarmanochegas (incorrect transliteration of Śramanācārya) of Strabo (*Geog.*, XV, I, 73).

3. In Stobaeus, *Physica*, I, 54; Porphyry, *De Abstinentia*, IV, 17; and St. Jerome, *Adv. Jovin.*, II, 14; II, 206.
4. In Clemens, *Stromateis*, III, 6, 60, 2.
5. *Stromateis*, I, 15, 71; I, 15, 68; I, p. 305, A,B and III, 194; see also AICL, p. 183, note 3.
6. *Contra Celsum*, I, 24.
7. See Priaulx, *The Indian Travels of Apollonius of Tyana*, pp. 22ff, 141-42, 145 f.

   For more information on the division of Indian philosophers into two classes see Arrian, *Anab.*, VII, 2, 5-9; Philostratus, *Vit. Apoll.*, III, 34; Eusebius, *Praep. Evang.*, IX, 6; Palladius, *De Brachmanes*, p. 14f; Cyrill, *Contra Julian*, IV, p. 133 E; Schwanbeck, *Meg. Ind.*, pp. 45ff; Lassen, *Ind. Alt.*, Vol. II, 2nd edn. p. 705.
8. *Geog.*, VII, I, 74.
9. Gymnosophists are called Gymnosophistai by Ptolemy, *Geog.*, VII, I, 51. For their accounts see also *Ind. Ant.*, VI, pp. 242-44; and JAOS, 82, 1962, pp. 21ff.
10. For Sophists see Arrian, *Indika,* I, XI.
11. *India as described by Early Greek Writers,* p. 125.
12. *Intercourse Between India and the Western World…*, p. 64.
13. "The Greek Accounts of India," rept. from his *The History of India* (ed. E.B. Cowell, London, 1911), in *Ancient India* (Delhi, 1983), p. 23.
14. CAI, *Introd.* XX, and p. 425.
15. MAIT, Conculturuum, XI. See also Colebrooke, *Observations on the sect of the Jains,* in AIMA, p. 105, note, and in AICL, p. 67, note 1 which continues in p. 68; E.R. Bevan, "India in Early Greek and Latin Literature," in CHI, I, p. 377.
16. Megasthenes, *Indika*, Bk. III, Fragms. XXXIII and XLI, in Strabo, *Geog.*, XV, I, 39; and XV, I, 59 respectively Arrian, *Anab.*, VI, 16; *Indika* I, XI.
17. Megasthenes, *Indika*, Bk. I, Fragm. I, "An Epitome of Megasthenes," in Diodorus, *Bib. Hist.*, II, 40.
18. Bardesanes' account of the subject is preserved in Porphyry's *De Abstinentia,* IV, 17, and in Stobaeus' *Physica (Anthologium)*, I. 54.
19. *De Abstinentia*, IV, 17.
20. *Lausiac Histories*, III, IX.
21. *Indika*, Bk.I, Fragm.I, "An Epitome of Megasthenes," in Diodorus, *Bib. Hist.*, II, 40, 1-3; *Indika*, Bk.III, Fragm. XXXIII, in Strabo, *Geog.*, XV, I, 39.

22. *Indika*, I, XI.
23. In Stobaeus, *Physica*, I, 54.
24. Megasthenes, *Indika*, Bk.III, Fragm.XLI, in Strabo, *Geog*., XV, I, 58.
25. *Indika*, Bk. III, Fragm. XLI, in Strabo, *Geog*., XV, I, 59.
26. *Ibid.*
27. Strabo, *geog*., XV, I, 60.
28. *Stromateis*, I, p. 305, A, B; also I, 15, 41-46.
29. See E.R. Bevan, "India in Early Greek and Latin Literature," in CHI, I, p. 377, and note 2; Schwanbeck, *Meg. Ind*., p. 46; H.F. Tozer, *Hist. An. Geog*., p. 152. W.W. Hunter ("The Greeks in India 327 to 161 BC," rept. from his *The Indian Empire*, London, 1882, in *Ancient India*, Delhi, 1983, p. 92, and note 17) says that Megasthenes draws a distinction between the Brachmanes and the Sarmanai, but the latter might also include the Brāhmaṇas in the third stage of their life as forest recluses. Weber (HIL, London, 1878, p. 28) also declines to identify the Sarmanai exclusively with the Buddhist Śramaṇas.
30. *Hist. Alex*., VIII, 9.
31. *Indika*, Bk. III, Fragm. XLI, in Strabo, *Geog*., XV, I, 60.
32. *History of Antiquity*, trans. from the German by E. Abbott, pp. 422-24.
33. Fragm.7, in Strabo, *Geog*., XV, I, 66.
34. *Stromateis*, I, p. 305 D; also I, 15, 22-26.
35. *Indika*, Bk. III, Fragm.XLII.
36. In Jacoby, FGH, No.719, Fragm.2; Porphyry, *De Abstinentia*, IV, 17; Eusebius, *Praep. Evang*., VI. 10; Stobaeus, *Physica*, I, 54.
37. *Oration,* XXXV, 434.
38. *Ibid*., XLIX, 538.
39. *About the Nations of India and the Brachmans*, in his *Lausiac Histories,* III, IX; also his *De Bragmanes* (called also *De Bragmanibus),* pp. 8, 20ff (based on Megasthenes' account of the subject in his *Indika*, (Bk. IV, Fragm. LV). See also Ambrosius (Ambrose), *De Moribus Brachmanorum*, pp. 62, 68ff (partly based on the testimony of Megasthenes, *op. cit*., Bk. IV, Fragm. LVB).
40. *Philosoph*., I, 24. He seems to have derived his authority from Megasthenes, *op. cit*., Bk. IV, Fragm. LIV.
41. In Clemens, *Stromateis*, III, 16, 60; III, 194.
42. *Op. cit*., III, 194.
43. Curtius, *Hist. Alex*., VIII, 9.
44. *Vit. Apoll*., VI, 11.

45. Priaulx, *Indian Travels of Apollonius of Tyana*, in CAI, p. 398.
46. *Adv. Jovin*, 14; *Epist*. 129; see also A.C. Perumalil, "Christian writers on Early India," JBORS, XXVIII, 4, 1942, p. 347.
47. In AICL, p. 186.
48. *Synopsis of History*, I, pp. 516-17. Valerius Maximums' *Fact dict. Memo.* (I, 8, 10; III, 3, 6), and Appian's *Roman History* (II, 154) are also useful for study of the Indian philosophers, including the Brāhmaṇas.
49. *The Greeks in India*, p. 49.
50. *Nat. Hist*., XVI, 17; also VII, 2.
51. Megasthenes, *Indika*, Bk. IV, Fragm. XLV; Arrian, *Anab*., VII, I, 5; VII, 2, 3; Onesikritus, in Jacoby FGH, No.134, Fragm.17, and in Strabo, *Geog*., XV, I, 63; Aristoboulus, in Jacoby, FGH, No.139, Fragm. 34, and in Strabo, *Geog.,* XV, I, 61; Strabo, *Geog*., XV, I, 64; see also F. Tola and C. Dragonetti, "India and Greece from Alexander to Augustus," in *Graeco-Indica* : *India's Cultural contacts with the Greek World,* ed. U.P. Arora, pp. 121-22; D.C. Velissaropoulos, "The Ancient Greek knowledge of Indian philosophy," in *Graeco-Indica,* ed. Arora, pp. 261-64.
52. Arrian, *Anab.,* VII, I, 5.
53. See Strabo, *Geog*., XV, I, 63.
54. Megasthenes, *Indika*, Bk. III, Fragm. XLIV; Strabo, *Geog*., XV, I, 64; XV, I, 68.
55. *Bib. Hist*., XVII, 107. For Kalanos and his immolation see also Arrian, *Anab*., VII, 3; Plutarch, *Lif. Alex*., Ch.69; Lucian, *De Morte Peregrini*, Ch.25; Aelian, *Var. Hist*., II, 41; V, 6; Athenaeus, *Deip*., X, 436f – 437a.
56. Arrian, *Anab*., VII, I, 5; Megasthenes, *Indika*, Bk. III, Fragm.XLIV, in Strabo, *Geog*., XV, I, 68; Megasthenes, *op. cit*., Bk. IV, Fragm. LV, in Palladius, *De Bragmanes* or *Bragmanibus*, pp. 8, 20ff; Megasthenes, *op. cit*., Bk. IV, Fragm.LV.B, in Ambrose, *De Moribus Brachmanorum*, pp. 62, 68ff.
57. *Geog*., XV, I, 64. The statement of Mandanis is held by T.S. Brown (JAOS, Vol. 80, no. 2, 1960, p. 92) with suspicion.
58. *India as described by Early Greek Writers*, pp. 126-27.
59. In Strabo, *Geog*., XV, I, 65; Hamilton and Falconer's tr. *The Geography of Strabo*, Vol. III, p. 114.
60. *Lif. Alex*., Ch. LXV; also his *The Parallel Lives,* ed. and tr. by B. Perrin, Vol. VII, *The Life of Alexander,* pp. 384-410.
61. Bk. III, Chaps. 11-17; see also *Bio. Alex*., Bk. III.
62. *Indika*, Bk. III, Fragm. XLI.

63. *Geog.*, XV, I, 59.
64. *Ibid.*
65. *Ibid.*
66. *Hell. Per.*, IV, 32, 4.
67. Bardesanes, in Porphyry, *De Abstinentia*, IV, 18; and in Stobaeus, *Physica*, I, 54; Pomponius Mela, *De Chorographia*, III, VII, 40; Curtius, *Hist. Alex.*, VIII, 9; Pliny, *Nat. Hist.*, VI, 19; VI, 22; VI, 66; also Megasthenes, *Indika*, Bk. IV, Fragm. LVI.B; Solinus, *Coll. Rer. Memo.*, 52, 6-17.
68. *Stromateis*, III, 194.
69. Priaulx, *The Indian Travels of Apollonius of Tyana*, pp. 22, 40, 50, 53. "Apollonius" story provides additional evidence of India's prestige in the Hellenistic world as a fountain of religious and philosophic knowledge," observes J.W. Sedlar, *India and the Greek World : A Study in Transmission of Culture,* p. 291.
70. HAG, Vol.I, p. 562.
71. *Vit. Apoll.*, tr. by F.C. Conybeare, *The Life of Apollonius of Tyana*, Vol. I, III, 18, p. 267.
72. *India as described by Early Greek writers*, p. 133.
73. *Stromateis*, I, 15, 72; I, p. 305, A.B.
74. *Contra Jovin.*, *Epist.* I, II, 26.
75. *Arch. Man. Disp.*, I, 97.
76. *Op. cit.*
77. *Vit. Apoll.*, III, 16.
78. *Dionysiaka*, Bk. XXVI, AICL, p. 197, and note 1.
79. In porphyry, *De Abstinentia*, IV, 7; Stobaeus, *Physica*, I, 54.
80. Priaulx, *Indian Travels of Apollonius of Tyana*, in CAI, p. 411.
81. See Porphyry, *De Abstinentia*, IV, 7; Stobaeus, *Physica,* I, 54; St. Jerome, *Adv. Jovin,* II, 14. Pliny also in his *Nat. Hist.* (VII, 21-30) describes the Buddhist monasteries of India.
82. *Geog.*, XV, I, 70.
83. "Greek and Roman India", rept. from his *The History of India from the Earliest Ages* (London, 1881), in *Ancient India* (Delhi, 1983), p. 126, note 59.
84. *Ibid.*, p. 136, note 77; *The History of India from the Earliest Ages*, Ch. IV, "Greek and Roman India," p. 204.
85. "The Greek Accounts of India," rept. from his *The History of India* (London, 1911), in *Ancient India, supra*, p. 20, and note 31; also his *The History of India*, App.III, "On the Greek Accounts of India," p. 234, and note 30.

86. *As. Res*., XVII, p. 279.
87. "India in Early Greek and Latin Literature," in CHI, I, pp. 378-79.
88. *Geog*., XV, I, 70.
89. *Ibid.*
90. *Stromateis*, III, 194.
91. *Ibid.*, III, 7, 60; III, 194; IV, 4, 17.
92. *Ibid.*, III, 194.
93. *Indika*., Bk. III, Fragm. XLIV.
94. *Geog*., XV, I, 68.
95. In Porphyry, *De Abstinentia,* IV, 18; and in Stobaeus, *Physica,* I, 54.
96. *Hist*., III, 100.
97. *Geog*., XV, I, 70.
98. *Ibid.*, XV, I, 71.
99. *Indika*, I, XI; also Godolphin (ed), *The Greek Historians,* Vol.II, pp. 739-40.
100. Ed. MAIMA, conculturuum, XLiii.
101. *Philosoph*. 24.
102. *Stromateis*, III, 194.
103. *Ibid.*

3

Christianity in India

It was the first century which marked the introduction of Christianity in India.

St. Thomas was one of the twelve Apostles (or disciples) of Jesus Christ. He was perhaps the only Apostle who went outside the Roman Empire to preach the Gospel of Christ. He is traditionally believed to have sailed to India in CE 52 to spread the Christian faith there. He is supposed to have landed at the ancient port of Muchiri, called by the Greeks Muziris, near Kodungalur or Kranganur (Cranganore), in the Malabar region of Kerala in south India. In CE 52 itself, he established seven Churches in Kerala which include those at Kodungalur, Kollam, Kokkamangalam, Kottakkayal and Palayoor.[1] In Malabar, a colony of Jews seems to have settled during the first century. Kottayam has one of the oldest Syrian Christian Churches in India.

St. Thomas was the first evangelist in India. He successfully converted the Indians to Christianity, especially by public preaching. We have little but valuable information in the classical literature about him and other Christian missionaries who came to India to propagate Christianity. Eusebius pamphilus (pamphili) in his *Ecclesiastical History*[2] quotes Origen[3] as having stated that "St. Thomas, an apostle of Jesus, is better known as missionary to India". The *Acta Thomae* (Acts of Thomas), composed between second and fourth century of the Christian era, also records that he visited Malabar and instructed the natives of that region in

Christian doctrine.[4] The tradition about St. Thomas in India was current as late as the time of St. Jerome (fourth century of the Christian era). He speaks of St. Thomas in India. Cosmas, a Christian monk of Alexandria, who visited India in the early sixth century, and whose work *Topographia Christiana (Christian Topography)* appeared some years before the middle of that century (between CE 535 and 547), speaks of progress of Christianity in Malabar. He explicitly refers to an early Christian Church of Malabar, called by him Male.[5] The Church of Malabar' largely cultivated the fellowship of the local people. Cosmas found Christianity making good headway in Ceylon and South India.

The South Indian tradition regarding the coming of St. Thomas to Malabar and the Church that was established there by him is still popular among the local Christian communities.[6]

St. Thomas went overland from Malabar to Madras[7] where he preached the message of Christ and brought some of its natives within the fold of Christianity. He was martyred at Mylapore near that place in CE 68.

The Christian Churches were established in South India during the first two centuries of the Christian era.

One of the earliest Christian missionaries to visit India in the second century of the Christian era was Pantaenus called also Pantainos. He seems to have been of Sicilian parentage. He was educated, if not also born, in Alexandria. The principles of Stoicism, which he first embraced, he abandoned for those of Christianity, in which, as we learn from Photius (Cod. 113), he was instructed by those who had seen the Apostles. In CE 181, he was appointed Head of the Catechetical School of Alexandria, an office in which he was succeeded by his illustrious pupil, Clemens Alexandrinus.[8] Pantaenus visited India sometime between CE 181 and 190, and propagated Christianity there. Clemens of Alexandria, one of the early Christian writers on India, derived much of his information from his tutor pantaenus about Christianity in India. The date of death of the latter is not known, but he was alive in CE 211, and the former died in CE 220.

We are indebted to Eusebius Pamphili for the notice of the mission of Pantaenus to India. Eusebius pamphili tells us that Pantaenus showed such a zeal for the divine word that he was consecrated to preach the Gospel of Christ to the nations of the East, being sent all the way to the Indians. There were even up till that time many "evangelists of the word" (Teachers of the Gospel) who, with a holy zeal of imitating the Apostles, sought to contribute to the spread and upbuilding of the divine word. One of these was pantaenus, who was sent to the Indians. There, report says, he found that the Gospel of St. Matthew had been introduced before his arrival, and was in the hands of some of the natives, who acknowledged Christ, and to whom Bartholomew, one of the Apostles, had preached, and left with them that Gospel written in the Hebrew character and preserved to the time of Eusebius Pamphili (CE 264 – 340), as the author himself says.[9] St. Zerome states that pantaenus, on returning from India to Alexandria, brought with him the Gospel of Matthew written in Hebrew. But Eusebius Pamphili does not say so. He merely says that the Gospel was in existence when pantaenus was in India.[10]

In the second century of the Christian era, Demetrius, Bishop of Alexandria, had sent forth the eloquent pantaenus to visit and instruct the native Christians of Malabar whose desire for further knowledge of the new Gospel was intense.[11] When pantaenus had visited India, he found that Jesus' disciple, Bartholomew, had preceded him there (in the second century itself), and founded a Christian Church in Malabar. It may be added here that the Christians of Malabar were under the rule of a king of the Cera dynasty.

Rufinus makes a mention of Frumentius of Tyros (Tyre)[12] who was the consecrated Bishop of Ethiopia CE 326. He is said to have been appointed the Bishop of India in CE 336. When Theophilus (mid-fourth century), the envoy of Roman Emperor constantinus (Constantine) II, visited India, he discovered a Christian community which claimed St. Bartholomew as its founder.[13]

The position of Christian community of the western coast of India during the second quarter of the sixth century is well reflected in the statements of Cosmas. He categorically states that at a place called Kalliana (Kalyāṇa in the Thane district, 33 miles north-east of Bombay, now called Mumbai) there was a Christian Church, and a bishop who was appointed from Persia. He tells us further that the Nestorian Christians of that place were governed by a Persian bishop. Among the rest of the Indians, and throughout the whole land of Persia, he says, there was no limit of the number of Churches with bishops and very large communities of Christian people.[14]

The Christian missionaries visited India from an early period. By the year CE 535 Christianity had spread in a number of places, especially in southern and western India. The Christian communities did not enjoy greater power and prestige at any point of time. It may, however, be admitted that they influenced the majority of the Hindus in their own way. Christianity has its own place in the religious history of early India. The classical writers no doubt contributed to the discovery of facts relating to its spread in India.

Notes and References

1. About the early Christian Church of Malabar, see Rev. J. Lobley's *The Church and Churches in southern India*, chap. IV.
2. III, 1.
3. Origen, one of the most eminent and most erudite of the early Christian writers, was born in Alexandria in CE 185 and died in CE 254. He wrote many works, notably the *Hexapla*, containing several copies of the old Testament, and some general information regarding Christianity.
4. See R. Sewell, JRAS, 1904, p. 611.
5. *Top. Chr.*, III, p. 169; J.W. McCrindle's tr. *The Christian Topography of Cosmos*, pp. 118-19.
6. See P.J. Thoma, "The South Indian Tradition of the Apostle Thomas," JRAS, 1924, pp. 203-23; W.R. Philipps, "The Connection of St. Thomas the Apostle with India", *Ind. Ant.*, 1903, pp. 1ff, 32.
7. See JRAS, 1917, p. 241; 1924, pp. 215 ff; *Ind. Ant.*, 1903, pp. 1ff, 145ff.
8. See AICL, p. 214, note 3.
9. *Eccles. Hist.*, V, 10.
10. AICL, p. 215, note 1.
11. See L.J. Trotter and W.H. Hutton, *History of India from the Earliest Times to the Present Day,* p. 34.
12. *Hist. Eccles.*, I, 9.
13. *Epitome of the Ecclesiastical History of Philostorgius,* in *Epitome of the Ecclesiastical History*, compiled by Photius, trans. by Edward Walford (London, 1855), pp. 437-46.
14. *Top. Chr.* III, pp. 169, 178-79, and XI, p. 337; McCrindle's tr. *The Christian Topography of Cosmas*, pp. 118-19 and 365.

Book Six
Foreign Expeditions and Invasions

1

Pre-Persian Foreign Expeditions: Mythical and Historical Accounts

The classical accounts of pre-Persian foreign expeditions into India are partly mythical and partly historical.

The history of the pre-Persian foreign expeditions into India is still enveloped in haziness because of manifold reasons. The primary reasons for this may precisely be attributed to conflicting, confusing and contradictory accounts of the classical and other writers. The history and mythology or facts and fictions have been jumbled up to such an extent that sometimes we are led to doubt the value of even credible and faithful accounts presented with accuracy, minuteness and precision.

It is further striking to note that some Greek historians in an attempt to minify the accomplishments of some of the pre-Persian rulers and the Persian monarch Cyrus and to magnify the success of the Macedonians went to an extent of distorting and falsifying the established historical truth. The avowed objective behind such exercise was to bring into light the mythical invasions and to push into background the real invasions of the pre-Alexandrian period. Thomas Maurice[1] has also dealt with this aspect of the subject.

The noted Greek historian Megasthenes tried to create an impression that before the Macedonian invasion led by Alexander, India was neither invaded nor conquered by any foreign power except by Herakles and Dionysus.[2] He (Megasthenes), as Strabo[3] says, "enjoins us to put no faith in the ancient history of India," which is really obnoxious. Arrian states that Alexander was the only conqueror who actually invaded the country. He tells us further that many traditions were current to the effect that Dionysus also made an expedition into India and subjugated the Indians before the days of Alexander.[4] Strabo says that the Assyrians and Persians did not invade India, but only approached its frontiers. He questions, how can any just confidence be placed on the account of India derived from such an expeditions as those of Sesostris of Egypt, Semiramis of Assyria and Cyrus of Persia?[5]

It is worthy of remark that Herakles and Dionysus are the two fictitious names. The stories about their expeditions into India are the figments of classical imagination. These two mythical figures have been misunderstood by Megasthenes and Arrian as historical personages. "Megasthenes and a few others think the stories of Herakles and Dionysus credible, but most writers, and among them Eratosthenes, regard them incredible and fabulous, like the Grecian stories," says Strabo.[6] It appears somewhat ridiculous that Arrian denies the same statement which he affirms with regard to the Assyrian invasion of India. He, however, maintains consistency in his statements pertaining to Persian invasion of India. Cyrus the Great of Persia, who was a historical figure and conquered some parts of northern India, has been recognized by him as a foreign invader. Cyrus was no doubt the most enterprising of Asiatic monarchs.

"The invasions of India by Semiramis of Assyria and Cyrus of Persia," observes J.W. McCrindle, "are as mythical as those which had been ascribed to Dionysus and Herakles".[7] "The Assyrians, says he, "extended their conquests into Ariana but neither they nor the Persians under Cyrus penetrated into India. The first invasion of India by the Persians was made in the days of Darius,"[8] There are some discrepancies in his statements. The invasions of India by Dionysus and Herakles are no doubt mythical, as noted before. But neither Semiramis of Assyria nor Cyrus of Persia was mythical figure. They were historical personages and both of them made expeditions into India. The greater portion of Ariana formed parts of north-western India before its occupation by the Persians. That was the Ariana which the Assyrians under Semiramis conquered before the Persians. The first Persian ruler to invade India was Cyrus, and not Darius. E.J. Rapson says, "There is no evidence that any foreign power of Western

Asia extended their political sway to the east as far as India until the time of Cyrus."[9]

The subject under notice attracted the attention of very few scholars, oriental or occidental, the reason for which is not far to discover. There is, however, a fair scope for making fresh attempt to deal with the subject in a very objective and dispassionate manner by placing our reliance on the statements furnished by some of the ancient Greek and Roman writers and modern authors relating to it. The distortions and confusions, whatever they may be should not be allowed to mar the prospect of historical reconstruction, wherever it may be deemed necessary. The classical accounts of the subject, supplemented and confirmed by the scholars of eminence, are relatively of greater value than other accounts.

We proceed now to examine the historical validity and veracity of the information supplied by the classical authors regarding the expeditions undertaken successively by the Egyptians under Sesostris and the Assyrians under Semiramis against the Indians before the time of Cyrus of Persia.

Herodotus, who inquired with the most persevering diligence into the ancient history of Egypt, and who received all the information concerning it which the priests of Memphis, Heliopolis and Thebes, could communicate, relates the history of Sesostris (the Greek name of the greatest of the early kings of Egypt) at some length. He does not mention his conquest of India.[10]

Diodorus Siculus in his Universal History calls Sesostris Sysoosis, and states that immediately after ascending the throne he collected an army consisting of 600,000 infantry, 24,000 cavalry, and 27,000 war chariots, and a fleet of 1,000 ships, and resolved to conquer the world. His enterprising ambition prompted him to undertake an expedition. He first conquered the Ethiopians and made them tributary, and then sent forth fleet of 400 ships in the Arabian Gulf to Subjugate the neighbouring nations. All the countries stretching along the Erythraean or Arabian sea to India were conquered by his commercial people with the help of naval power. He along with his army marched through Asia, and subjected to his dominion every part of it. He was everywhere crowned with victory. He not only invaded all those nations which Alexander, the Macedonian, afterwards subdued, but even others whose territories he did not enter. Diodorus records that Sesostris set out upon his Indian expedition about the fortieth year of his age. He and his victorious army reached eastward as far as India not only to its frontier but even to the land of the Ganges. They are said to have crossed that river and advanced to the Indian Ocean.

He spent nine years in this expedition and exacted no other tokens of submission from the conquered nations except the tribute which were being sent annually to Egypt. The primary purpose behind his expedition into India was an extension of maritime commerce. Diodorus gives an account of both the maritime and land expedition of Sesostris. We are further told by the former that on his return the latter installed pillars in the conquered countries with inscriptions attesting his victories, but these for the most part disappeared.[11] The efforts of Sesostris produced no permanent effect. Diodorus' statement, that the Egyptian Sesostris extended his conquests to all parts of the world, even beyond the Ganges, is absolutely unworthy of our credence.

What is described above is more or less a tale which was probably invented in the period between the age of Herodotus and that of Diodorus, from whom we receive a particular details of the Indian expedition of Sesostris. His account rests entirely upon the authority of the Egyptian priests who related everything with a desire to promote the honour of their country than to bring the truth into the light. Egyptian priests, as well as the Greek writers, differ widely from one another in the accounts they give of the actions of Sesostris. Though Diodorus asserts that in relating the history of Sesostris he had concentrated on what appeared to him most probable, and most agreeable to the monuments of that monarch still remaining in Egypt, the veracity of his narrative may nevertheless be suspected.

The narrative, which Diodorus admits to be very reliable of all the accounts circulated in Egypt, has been contradicted by the classical writers as well as other scholars because of some palpable discrepancy and extravagance on the face of it. Strabo and Arrian do not give any credence to the account given by Diodorus. Strabo[12] categorically states that Sesostris did not make any expedition into India. He says Megasthenes also does not consider Sesostris as one who approached India, and does not include him in the list of those who conquered India, Arrian[13] holds that Sesostris overran the greater part of Asia, but could not invade India. W. Robertson had discredited the account of Diodorus as an invention of the Egyptian priests. The whole account of Sesostris' expedition into India, according to Robertson, is fabulous.[14] According to one of the reliable sources,[15] Sesostris was a legendary figure in the history of Egypt. H.G. Rawlinson, while critically examining the reliability of the descriptions of the events that are said to have happened in the early ages of antiquity, doubts the historical authenticity of Diodorus' account of the expedition of Sesostris into India and his conquest of that country.[16]

Henry Beveridge, on the other hand, remarks that "To reject a statement thus supported because some flaws may be picked in particular parts of it is to strike at the foundation of humans testimony, and countenance the captious quibbling process under which all ancient history, sacred as well as profane, runs some risk of being converted into a myth. The fair conclusion concerning the Indian expedition of Sesostris seems to be that they really took place, but that in the accounts given of them, both the means which he employed and the extent of country which he subdued or traversed are exaggerated."[17] It has also been observed that "such vague traditions probably represent a racial memory of actual historical events, distorted of course, as to all details."[18]

In order to test the credibility and to judge the historical value of the information recorded in the classical tradition by Diodorus, we have to ascertain the views of those scholars also who have dwelt upon the subject to a considerable degree.

Montgomery Martin, while supporting the statement recorded by Diodorus, had clearly stated that Sesostris' expedition into India was successful but disastrous. His success, according to him, proved to be contrary to his expectation[19] Beveridge not only takes Diodorus' account preserved in his work as valuable but also confirms his statement.[20]

There are some evidence regarding the identification and historicity of Sesostris and the antiquity of his Indian expedition. He has generally been identified with Ramses the Great, the third king of the nineteenth dynasty of Manetho, the son of Seti, and the father of Menephthah, the pharaoh. Lepsius, however, from a study of the Tablet of Rameses II found at Abydos in Egypt (now in the British Museum) has been led to identify him with the Sesortasen or Osirtasen of the great twelfth dynasty.[21] Sesostris (Rameses II) was the king of Egypt about 1333 BCE, says H.L. Jones.[22] According to Wilkinson, he ruled from 1311 to 1245 BCE.[23] L.J. Trotter and W.H. Hutton observe that there is nothing "impossible in the story of a much more successful inroad, accomplished in the tenth century before Christ by the troops of the Egyptian Rameses II.[24] There is an epigraphic evidence which testifies to his existence as a historical personage. In an Egyptian inscription in the tomb of Khnumhotep II at Benihasen he finds mention as Sesostris II, but he is ascribed to 1900 BCE.[25] The period of his reign cannot be determined with certainty. Nor can we fix the exact date of his Indian expedition.

The plausible conclusion which we can derive from the foregoing details of the subject is that the expedition of Sesostris into India is not absolutely unfounded. It may be one of the mysteries of history. But it is very difficult to determine the location which was conquered and the year in which the event took place. The history we have of the Indian expedition of Sesostris is neither authentic nor trustworthy.

Semiramis of Assyria flourished towards the end of the eighth century or in the beginning of the ninth century before the Christian era. She ruled that country as queen mother for three years (811 – 808 BCE). Having learned that India was the greatest and richest country in the world, she resolved to make attempt to subjugate that country in order to prove her prowess and majesty. She took three years in assembling an immense army drawn from all the provinces of her extensive empire. After all preparations, she made an expedition into India in the year 808 BCE. Diodorus Siculus describes the historical facts about her Indian expedition with some myths and legends.

We learn from Diodorus about Semiramis and her rise. She, according to him, ascended the throne of Assyria on the death of her husband, King Ninus. She was of outstanding ability and courage. She accomplished many great deeds in her life.[26] After the conquest of Egypt and Ethiopia, she moved to India, and led her war against the Indians, says he.[27]

Diodorus gives an account of the Assyrian invasion of India on the authority of the *Assyriaka* of Ktésias the Knidian, who was a contemporary of the Greek historian Xenophon, and lived for about seventeen years in the courts of the Persian monarchs at Susa.

The great Assyrian queen Semiramis, Diodorus says, marched with large number of troops from her capital Nineveh towards India. She with the help of her army first took Baktriana, called also Baktria and Baktra (modern Balkh region in north Afghanistan). She started on her Indian expedition from there. All the provinces west of the Indus were made subject to her power. India was ruled at that time by a powerful king called Stabrobates, who was well equipped with innumerable hostes of soldiers, a great number of well trained elephants, and a naval force. On reaching the Indus, Semiramis found that the Indian king had sent no fewer than 4,000 vessels (boats made of reeds) to cover the river Indus to oppose her fleet of 2000 ships in that river, prepared his arms, and gathered a force greater than that collected by her. A great naval battle was fought upon that river. The victory was long undecided, but at long last it went in favour of the warlike queen possibly because of superior naval skill of the Phoenician and Cypriot sailors. The Indian king with the loss of a large portion of his fleet and an immense carnage of his soldiers was obliged to withdraw and leave the passage of the river free. The queen Semiramis immediately caused a bridge of boats to be constructed, and crossing that river with her whole army hastened forward with the hope of soon completing the conquest which she had so successfully begun. Stabrobates, however, had no idea of tendering his submission before the invader and stood prepared for her approach. We are further told by Diodorus that on the eastern bank of the Indus a fierce contest ensued between the Indian and Assyrian forces in which the latter had at first some advantage but were subsequently totally overthrown. Most of her army perished in the field or in attempting to regain the right bank of the Indus river. She was herself severely wounded during a personal encounter with the Indian king. She was eventually compelled to return to Baktra after losing two-thirds of her vast army, as Diodorus records.[28] She defeated the Indian king in a naval battle but was vanquished by him in the battle on land. She made her escape with shattered dream and humbled pride accompanied by a handful of troops to her own dominion. She dreamed no more of the conquest of India for crowning her fame. "The Bactrians who make a figure in Grecian history is not irreconcilable with the oriental traditions... Bacteria continued to be a dependency of the Assyro – Persic empire, and there, it is said, Semiramis fitted out her expedition against India, which notwithstanding the enormous extent of her preparations, terminated in her discomfiture," observes H.H. Wilson.[29] A.H.L. Heeren also says, "Bāhlika or Baktra in every age of Persian empire was important, but is continually interwoven in the traditions of the East with the accounts of the Semiramis and other conquerors."[30]

As Diodorus borrowed the account from Ktésias, who is said to have extracted it from Persian records, it is not improbable that its basis of fact has been overlaid with the embellishment which usually adorn a Persian tale. Some exaggeration is, of course, apparent in some parts of the narrative, particularly in case of an enormous army of the queen (3000,000 infantry, 500,000 cavalry, and 100,000 war chariots). That is why Walter Raleigh[31] regards the strength of her army more fictitious than real. It may be pointed out here that Ktésias is well-known for his characteristic style of presenting history with stories and fables. It is impossible to doubt that the whole account of the Indian expedition of Semiramis is highly coloured. Actually, the kernel of attested fact with later accretion of fabulous history created a lot of confusion.

It has been supposed that the form of the legend as it appears in Diodorus was not taken by him direct from Ktésias, but from Kleitarchus, who accompanied Alexander into India, and Diodorus modified the narrative of Ktésias to harmonize it with his better knowledge of the country. Even if it is accepted, we are sure that it will not cast any shadow on the historical character of the narrative of Diodorus. The German scholar Max Duncker in his *History of Antiquity* (Vol. IV) has questioned the historical validity of the narrative of Diodorus as it was excerpted from the said work of Ktésias. "The story itself, however… incredible in the shape traced out by the pens of Ktésias and Diodorus, need not perhaps be absolutely untrue."[32]

The accounts of Indian expedition of Semiramis given by other classical writers are also worthy of our attention.

Giving a faithful account of the subject, Arrian states that the two Indian tribes, the Assakenoi and the Astakenoi, inhabiting the regions beyond the river Indus on the west up to the river Kophen (Kābul) were in ancient times subject to the Assyrians, and then submitted to the Persians.[33] The Assakenoi (Assakenians) inhabited the Swāt valley, east of Nysa, and the Astakenoi (Astakenians) Gāndhāra in the lower region of the Kophes (Kābul). It is indeed a fact that the Indians between the river Indus and the river Kābul acknowledged the sovereignty of the Assyrians. The country on the right bank of upper Indus was also subject to Assyrian rule and paid tribute to them. We find that Arrian's statement contains some substratum of truth. The two tribes mentioned by him had been living in the regions, already indicated, since time immemorial. The mentions of Aśvakas (called Assakenoi by Arrian) in the *Mahābhārata*, the Purāṇas, and Pāṇini's *Asṭādhyāyī* (Aśvakānāmvataḥ, II, 2.31) amply substantiates the primeval antiquity of this group of tribe of northwest India. The numismatic evidence[34] also confirm the existence of this tribe in that part of India. It may reasonably be suggested that the tribes mentioned by Arrian might have played some role in repulsing the invasion of the Assyrian queen Semiramis under the leadership of their king Stabrobates, who has not yet been properly identified. A.K. Majumdar[35] has identified him with Sthavarpati, which seems to be hypothetical one. But he has, no doubt, supported the statements of the classical authors.

Justin asserts that no one invaded India, except Semiramis and Alexander.[36]

We learn from Pliny that Arachotus, a celebrated city (capital of Arachosia, Kandahār) was founded by Semiramis.[37] The authenticity of his statement cam be proved by an archaeological evidence brought to light by M. Court. The remains of the said city, according to him, were found on the Arghasan river, four farsangs from Kandahār, on the road to Shikarpur.

Strabo,[38] quoting Megasthenes as his authority, states that Semiramis meditated or contemplated India's conquest, but died before her enterprise was undertaken or the necessary preparations were made. Arrian[39] also deriving his authority from Megasthenes says that Semiramis took in hand an expedition against India, but died before she could execute her design. These statements are not reliable. Both Strabo and Arrian quote Megasthenes, whose account of the subject[40] is totally untrustworthy. Strabo quoted Megasthenes without showing any meticulous regard for the truth. Strabo, who is well known for his critical faculty, judicious and reasonable approach, and sound judgement in his presentation of history of India, appears to be hypercritical in his assessment of this expedition. His statement, that Semiramis and Cyrus did not invade India but only approached its frontier,[41] is far from the truth. Arrian's own views are based on the truth.

McCrindle's statement, that the invasion of India by Semiramis is mythical,[42] appears to be fallacious. And his statement, that the Assyrians extended their conquests to Ariana, but did not penetrate into India,[43] appears to be paradoxical. The fact remains that the greater portion of Ariana formed part of India before its occupation by the Persians.

Max Müller is of the view that "Sesostris and Semiramis, who were the conquerors of great antiquity did not disturb the peace of the Aryan settlers in north-western India."[44]

Semiramis is erroneously believed to have been a creation of Assyrian mythology. The ancient records of Assyria,[45] the *Encyclopaedia Britannica*,[46] recent discoveries of ruins, and decipherment of inscriptions prove her existence as an historical personage beyond doubt. An epigraphic record – Cuneiform Inscription of Nineveh – throws so much unexpected light on the ancient history of Asia. In this inscription, not only she but also her epoch distinctly figure. It is said that "the name of Semiramis is associated with classical imagination. It was Sammuramnat who was the real figure".[47] But this view is not supported or corroborated by any authority. Hence, this can also be disposed of. "Whatever be the real historical character of the expeditions of Semiramis and Cyrus, it is certain that their conquests on the Indus were only temporary acquisitions," observes St. Martin.[48]

Nearchus (Admiral of Alexander), who is generally acknowledged as the most scrupulous and honest in depicting the result of his exploration, is a principal authority on the subject. His memoirs have been lost, but their contents have been in great measures preserved in the works of Strabo and Arrian.

According to the account of Nearchus, as preserved by Strabo[49] and Arrian,[50] Alexander, when planning his march with his army through Gedrosia (Baluchistan) for going back his home, was told by the inhabitants that no one had ever before escaped with an army by this route excepting Semiramis, the far-framed Assyrian queen, and Cyrus of Persia, on their flight from India. They said (according to the tradition current till that time) that Semiramis escaped with only twenty men of her army, and Cyrus in his turn with only seven. Nearchus relates that Alexander having felt inspired by the exploits of his predecessors thought it would be a glorious achievement if helled his victorious army in safety through that part of India where Semiramis and Cyrus had suffered such great disasters. Alexander, while returning from India for his homeward journey went by the same route (Gedrosia), as told by all the historians of his Indian campaign. The information of Nearchus, transmitted to us by the two Greek writers, Strabo and Arrian, constitutes one of the classical testimonies of the Indian expeditions of Semiramis and Cyrus.

"Indian expedition of Semiramis and Cyrus through Mekran-barren region lying along the coast of Baluchistan," says H.J. Mackinder," may or may not be historical."[51] Their Indian expeditions were undoubtedly historical.

McCrindle's statement, that "Semiramis… was an entirely mythical personage, and it seems improbable that Cyrus even led an expedition through Gedrosia,"[52] can be disapproved of in view of the facts that Semiramis was a historical personage, and Cyrus, while returning from his expedition into India, followed the route of Gedrosia on his way back to Persia.

Semiramis is said to have erected a column, on which the immensity of her conquests was described, as extending from Niniveh or Nineveh (ancient Assyrian capital) to India eastward, upto Itamenes (river Yamenes or Jomanes = Yamunā).[53] "Fabulous as this pillar may be, and fabulous as the whole history of Semiramis may be," says W. Vincent, "there is still a degree of consistency in the fable, for the tradition is general that the Assyrians of Nineveh did make an incursion into India, and Semiramis returned through Gedrosia, the route which Alexander afterward pursued."[54]

Some competent authorities, like Beveridge,[55] Martin[56] and Heeren[57] are also of the view that the Assyrian invasion of India was a historical and not mythical event.

To sum up: The Indian expedition of a celebrated Assyrian queen Semiramis is no doubt a real historical event. She subjugated some parts of Afghanistan, and established her hold over the regions between the Indus and the Kābul. The two Indian tribes, the Assakenoi of the Swāt Valley, east of Nysa, and the Astakenoi of Gāndhāra in the lower region of the Kābul, acknowledged her political sway. The portion of India lying along the west bank of the Indus formed part of the Assyrian empire which was later overthrown by Cyrus the Great. As a sequel to this event, this portion became a satrapy or province of the Persian empire. This discovery should not be made an object of doubt. Greater doubt may reasonably be entertained about the historicity of Egyptian invasion of India, but the Assyrian expedition into India is beyond doubt, and hence it may be given due place in the pages of its ancient history.[58]

Notes and References

1. *Indian Antiquities or Dissertations of Hindustan*, Vol.I, pp. 138-39.
2. *Indika*, Bk. IV, Fragm. XLVI; Bk. IV, Fragm. LVII, in Polyaenus, *Strategemata,* I, 1, 1-3; AIMA, pp. 107-8 and 157-58; see also Arrian, *Indika*, pt. I, Ch.V; and Strabo, *Geog*., XV, I, 6.
3. *Geog*., XV, I, 6.
4. *Indika*, pt. I, Ch. V; also E.J. Chinnock's tr. of Arrian's *Indika*, p. 404; F.R.B. Godolphin (ed), *the Greek Historians*, Vol. II, pp. 735-6.
5. *Geog*., XV, I, 6; also Hamilton and Falconer's tr. *The Geography of Strabo*, Vol. III, pp. 74-75. See also M. Elphinstone, "The Greek Accounts of India," rept. from his *The History of India* (London, 1911), in *Ancient India* (Delhi, 1983), pp. 11-12, note 3.
6. *Geog*., XV, I, 7.
7. AICL, p. 10, note 4.
8. *Ibid.*
9. *Ancient India from the earliest times to the first century AD*. p. 43.
10. *Hist*. Bk. II, Ch.102.
11. *Bib. Hist*., Bk. I, Ch. 4, p. 64; see also J.T. Wheeler, *The Geography of Herodotus*, p. 20; G. Rawlinson, *History of Herodotus,* Vol. II, pp. 145 and 148; A.K. Majumdar, EHIDS, Vol. I, p. 29; Henry Beveridge, *A Comprehensive History of India*, Vol. I, pp. 22-24; R. Montgomery Martin, *The History of the Indian Empire,* Vol. I, p. 19.

12. *Geog.*, XV, I, 6; AIMA, p. 109; H.L. Jones (tr.) *The Geography of Strabo*, Vol. VII, p. 9; Hamilton and Falconer's tr. *The Geography of Strabo,* Vol. III, p. 75, note.
13. *Indika*, pt. I, ch. V; see also R.C. Jain (ed) MAIMA, App.5, p. 234.
14. *An Historical Disquisition Concerning Ancient India*, p. 6.
15. *Enc. Bk.*, Vol. XX, 1768, p. 262.
16. *Intercourse Between India and the Western World...*, Notes and Illustrations, Note I, pp. 289-91.
17. *Op. Cit.*, p. 24.
18. See Henry Smith Williams (ed), *The Historians History of the World*, Vol. I, p. 146.
19. *Op. Cit.*, p. 19.
20. *Op. Cit.*, pp. 22-24.
21. See AICL, p. 11, note 1; *Report of the Proceedings of the Second International Congress of Orientalists*, p. 44, cf. AIMA, pp. 108-9, fn; G. Rawlinson, *History of Herodotus*, Vol. II, pp. 143 and 151.
22. Tr.*The Geography of Strabo,* Vol. VII, p. 9.
23. *American Cyclopaedia,* XIV, p. 521 cf. B.N. Puri, *India as described by Early Greek Writers,* p. 2, note 3.
24. *History of India from the earliest times to the present Day*, p. 29.
25. *Periplus*, pp. 51, 192, notes.
26. *Bib. Hist.*, Bk. II, Chs.1 and 4-7.
27. *Ibid.*, Bk. II, Chs.14-16.
28. *Bib. Hist.*, Bk. II, Chs. 16-20; see also Pliny, *Hist. Nat.*, XVI, 37; AIT, p. 271. C.H. Oldfather says that Semiramis, a mythical figure, was made famous by Greek and Roman legend. He says further that she established her authority over all Asia with the exception of India. He refers to the account that Ktésias of Knidus has given about Semiramis, and quoting him says, "she passed away having lived sixty-two years and having reigned forty-two." Athenaeus and certain other classical and other historians, according to Oldfather, say that "she was a courtesan and because of her beauty loved by the king of the Assyrians – see his Eng. trans. of Diodorus' *Bib. Hist.*, Vol. I, pp. 356-57, note 2, and 417-18. The fact remains that Semiramis was not a mythical but a historical figure. She established her political hegemony over greater part of India to the west of the Indus. The other statements are unfounded.
29. *Ar. Ant.*, pp. 126-27.
30. *Historical Researches,* Vol. I, *Asiatic Nations* (2nd edn.), p. 424.
31. *History of the World*, p. 125.

32. See L.J. Trotter and W.H. Hutton, *History of India from the earliest times to the present Day*, pp. 28-29.
33. *Indika,* pt.I, Ch.I; also Godolphin (ed), *The Greek Historians*, Vol. II, p. 732; M. Elphinstone, "The Greek Accounts of India," in *Ancient India* (Delhi, 1983), p. 13.
34. A. Cunningham, *Co. An. Ind.,* p. 61, Pl.II, 17; V.A. Smith, CCIM, Vol.I, p. 157.
35. *Op. cit.*, Vol.II, pp. 367-68.
36. *Hist. Phil.*, I, 2, 9-10; see also E.A. Schwanbeck, *Meg. Ind.*, p. 13; CHI, I, p. 297.
37. *Hist. Nat.*, VI, 25, note 70; see also H.H. Wilson, *Ar. Ant.*, p. 157, note 2.
38. *Geog.*, XV, I, 6; H.L. Jones (tr.) *The Geography of Strabo*, Vol. VII, pp. 7 and 135.
39. *Indika*, pt. I, Ch. V.
40. *Indika* Bk. IV, Fragm. XLVI; also AIMA, p. 109 and fn.
41. *Geog.*, XV, I, 6.
42. AICL, p. 10, note 4.
43. *Ibid.*
44. *The Vedas*, p. 3.
45. *Ancient Records of Assyria and Babylon* (1127), ed. by D.D Luckenbill, Vol.I, pp. 731-45.
46. Vol. XX, 1768, pp. 207-8.
47. J.B. Bury, S.A. Cook and F.E. Adcock (ed), *The Cambridge Ancient History*, Vol. III, p. 27.
48. *E'tude,* p. 14.
49. *Geog.*, XV, I, 5; and XV, II, 5; Hamilton and Falconer's tr. *The Geography of Strabo,* Vol. III, pp. 74 and 122.
50. *Anab.*, VI, 24. See also Bunbury, HAG, Vol. I, p. 455; Rawlinson, *Intercourse Between India and the Western World…* p. 35; CNES, pp. 153-54, and 186-87; CHI, I, p. 296.
51. CHI, I, p. 26.
52. AICL, p. 84, note 3.
53. W. Vincent, CNAIO, Vol. II, *The Periplus of the Erythraean Sea*, pp. 62-63.
54. *Ibid.*
55. *Op. cit.*, pp. 24-27.
56. *Op. cit.*, p. 19.

57. *Historical Researches*, Vol.II, p. 211, and Vol. III, p. 387.
58. See G.P. Singh, "An Analytical and Critical Study of the Classical Accounts of Foreign Expeditions of North-Western India before the time of Cyrus (BC 558-530) of Persia," *Research Journal, Humanities and Social Sciences*, Manipur University, Imphal, IV, 1, 1987, p. 7.

2

Persian Invasion and Domination (558 – 330 BCE)

Cyrus the Great, the founder of the Achaemenian Empire of Persia, was one of those foreign invaders of ancient times who invaded India and conquered some parts of it. He ruled Persia from 558 to 530 or 529 BCE. He brought certain parts of northern and north-western India under his sway which can be proved on the testimony of some Greek and Latin authors.

Ktésias the Knidian in his *Persica*, (History of Persia) gives an account of Cyrus' campaign in India with details of the battles he fought with the Indian near the Indian frontier. He is said to have conquered Bactria (Bākhtri in old Persian inscription) in north Afghanistan, some portions of the Paropanisadae (Kābul valley), and Gāndhāra (west of the Indus). These Indian territories formed parts of his empire.[1] Xenophon, another Greek historian, also tells us that Cyrus brought under his rule the Bactrians and Indians.[2] The idea of some sort of suzerainty over northern India by him is well reflected in the account given by the same Greek author of an embassy sent to him by an Indian king.[3]

The Greek geographer and historian, Strabo, also records that "All the countries in the northern parts of the country (India), and Baktriana or all the countries in that direction, had been subject to the Persians."[4]

We learn from Pliny, the famous Roman geographer and historian, that Cyrus in the course of his expedition against India destroyed the city of Kāpiśī in the upper region of the Kophes (upper Kābul valley).[5] Historical tradition also attributes to Cyrus the destruction of this city, north of Kābul.

Arrian, one of the Greek historians of Alexander, informs us that the two Indian tribes, the Assakenoi (Assakenians of the Swāt valley) and the Astakenoi (Astakenians of Gāndhāra in the lower region of Kophes or Kābul) inhabiting the region beyond the river Indus on the west up to the river Kophen (Kābul) were in ancient times subject to the Assyrians, afterwards to the Medes, and finally they submitted to the Persians, and paid to Cyrus the tribute from their land that he had imposed on them.[6] The Persian domination in the territories to the west of the Indus has left more than one trace in the geographical nomenclature.

Nearchus, who accompanied Alexander into India, also presented an account of Cyrus' invasion of India which was preserved by Strabo and Arrian.

Both Arrian[7] and Strabo,[8] quoting Nearchus as their authority, tell us that in returning from his expedition into India, Cyrus escaped through Gedrosia (Baluchistan) with only seven men of his army. The classical evidence in this regard is supported by the tradition which was current up to the time of Alexander the Great.

"... even if there are just grounds for doubting that Cyrus actually invaded Northern India, there can be no question that he did campaign in the territories corresponding to the present Afghanistan and Baluchistan. It seems likely that Alexander's historians may have been inclined to minimise the accomplishments of Cyrus the Great, especially in the light of his apparent setback in Gedrosia in order to bring into greater prominence the achievements of the famous Greek invader," says A.V.W. Jackson.[9]

A Latin translation of a lost Greek original, composed either at Antioch or Alexandria between CE 350 and 353, bears an eloquent testimony to the fact that war was waged upon India to the west of the Indus, "India Minor", by the Persians.[10] J.W. McCirndle says, "India Minor lay to the west of the Indus- a quarter immediately exposed to attacks from Persia."[11]

Xenophon states that the empire of Cyrus was the greatest and most glorious of all the kingdoms in Asia. It was bounded on the east by the Erythraean sea (Indian Ocean).[12] There is a palpable exaggeration in his statements that Cyrus brought to subjection all the nations from Syria to the Erythraean sea, and that he had ruled all India to the eastern ocean.[13]

Darius I, the next powerful sovereign, ruled Persia from about 522 to 486 BCE. He conquered some parts of northern and western India during the period of his rule.

We are told by Strabo that some portions of the Ariane (also called Ariana) were subject to the Persians.[14] Here he speaks of the conquest of Aria (Herāt) and Arakhosia or Arachosia (Kandahār) – parts of Ariana by the famous Achaemenian emperor Darius. This can be testified to by the epigraphic evidence. These two places in Afghanistan in northern India are included in the lists of provinces conquered by Darius given in his two inscriptions, Persepolis (C. 518 – 515 BCE) and Naqsh-i-Rustam (C. 515 BCE). The former is called Haraivā and the latter Hara(h) uvatī or Haraouvati.[15] St. Martin has explicitly stated that "Darius had carried his arms to Arakhosia (south-west Afghanistan)... This was before he had achieved his well-known conquest of the valley of the Indus."[16] McCrindle also states that "Arachosia, a province of Persia, bordered on the north by part of the Paropanisos (also called Paropamisus) chain (Hindukush), on the east by the Indus..."[17]

Herodotus includes the Gandarioi (the people of Gāndhāra region) in his list of peoples that were subject to Darius. Gāndhāra, conquered by Darius, according to the said Greek historian, was the seventh satraphy (province) of the Persian Empire.[18]

In the Bahistān or Behistun Rock Inscription (*C.* 520-518 BCE), the people of "Gadārā" (Gāndhāra) appear among the subject peoples of the Persian Empire under Darius.[19]

Herodotus notices at length the Persian dominions in India in the time of Darius.[20]

Keeping in view the annexation of Sindh (the valley of the Indus) to his dominions, Darius sent his admiral Skylax, a native of Karyanda (in Greece), in 517 BCE on naval expedition to explore the Indus down to its mouth. Skylax and his companions embarked at the upper course of the river Indus (near its confluence with the river Kābul). They sailed down the river Indus towards the east to the sea, and then sailing on the sea westward arrived in the thirtieth month at that place where the king of Egypt despatched the Phoenicians to sail around Libya. After they had sailed round, Darius subdued the Indians and frequented the sea, as we are told by Herodotus.[21] E.J. Rapson's statement, that "Skylax was sent by Darius probably about 510 BC,"[22] is not worthy of acceptance. Skylax completed the voyage of discovery of the Indus valley probably in the latter half of 515 BCE. After the said discovery, Darius conquered Sindh and made it a part (province) of the Persian Empire. N.M. Chapekar is of the view that he "conquered the Punjab and Sindh in 512 BC."[23] James Douie also says that "In 512 BC, Darius pushed the boundary of his empire to the Indus then running in a more easterly course."[24] The legitimacy of the date 512 BCE, as suggested by both the learned scholars, is doubtful.

The evidence of Herodotus that Sindh (the western part of India) was incorporated into the Achaemenian Empire under Darius is attested by the inscriptions of the latter. The "Hidus" (Hindus, people of Sindhu or the Indus valley) are explicitly mentioned along with the Ga(n)dārians (Gāndhārians) in his Persepolis and Naqsh-i-Rustam inscriptions.[25] These peoples were subjugated by him. He annexed not only Sindh but also some parts of the Punjab to the Persian Empire. W.W. Tarn categorically states that "Darius I had ruled the Paropanisadae (Kābul valley) and Gāndhāra and had subsequently conquered Sindh and probably further parts of the Punjab."[26]

Herodotus relates that Darius on ascending the throne of Persia divided his empire into twenty governments called satrapies and fixed the amount of tribute which each of these should pay into his treasury. India, he says, was the twentieth, the richest and the most populous satrapy of the Persian Empire in the time of Darius.[27] Herodotus knew that India was one of the remotest provinces of the Persian empire towards the east, but of its extent and exact position he had no proper conception. Although the exact limit of the Indian satrapy cannot be determined, it can, however, be said with certainty that the whole of Sindh or most of the Indus valley and perhaps a considerable portion of the Punjab east of the Indus were included in it.[28] We are informed by Herodotus that the Indians paid to Darius an annual tribute proportionately larger than that of any other province of his vast empire. They paid to him 360 talents of gold dust,[29] equivalent to about £ 1290000[30] or £ 1078272. The tribute amounting to 360 talents of gold is also reckoned as equal to 4680 Euboic talents of Silver.[31] The tribute paid by the Indians to Darius constituted about one third of the total bullion revenue of the Asiatic provinces. We are also informed by Herodotus that the Indians obtained the great quantity of gold from which they supplied the dust to the Persian king.[32] The gold obtained from the mines in Dardistan found its way to the provinces west of the Indus. It is worthwhile to point out here that the Indian provinces on which the heavy tribute was levied by Darius were situated mainly to the west of the Indus. These provinces were under the sovereignty of the Persian Empire. The tributary

Indians to the west of the Indus were living in the territory of Kābul or in the neighbourhood of Bactria and Kābul. The Dominions of Darius never extended beyond the Punjab and the valley of the Indus.[33]

The Persian sway over northern India continued even in the time of Xerxes I (486 – 465 BCE), the son and successor of Darius I. This is proved by the presence of an Indian contingent, consisting of both infantry and cavalry, among the troops from the subject nations of the Persian Empire drawn upon by that monarch to augment the vast army of Asiatics which he marshalled to invade Greece. In his vast army of the Persian provinces of India were represented also the Gāndhārians (on the frontiers of India in Afghanistan to the west of the Indus). Xerxes at the head of a vast army which included the Indian troops, attacked Greece in 480 BCE, but was repulsed.

Herodotus has preserved a full account of the subject under notice. The Gāndhārians (Gandarioi) are described by him as bearing bows of reed and short spears. He described the equipment of the Indian infantry as follows: "The Indians, clad in garments made of cotton, carried bows and arrows of cane, the latter tipped with iron."[34] Regarding the Indian cavalry he says that they were "armed with the same equipment as in the case of the infantry, but they brought riding horses and Chariots, the latter being drawn by horses."[35]

Xerxes maintained the Indian satrapy intact as is clear from the Persepolis inscriptions, which included Gāndhāra and Sindhu in the list of his satrapies.

Strabo tells us that on one occasion the Persians summoned the Hydrakai (Oxydrakai, the Kshudrakas) from India (i.e. the Punjab) to serve as mercenaries.[36]

The Persian Empire rapidly declined after the death of Xerxes. But if Ktésias, who resided at the court of Artaxerxes II Mnemon (404-359 BCE), is to be believed, the Great king used to receive costly presents from India even in the fourth century BCE.[37] His two successors, Artaxerxes III (359 – 338 BCE) and Arses (338 – 336 BCE) were too weak to achieve anything worth-mentioning. The hold of the Achaemenians on the Indians in the various provinces on the frontier had grown very feeble about their times. However, the Persian domination in northern India continued up to the time of Darius III (336 – 330 BCE), the last Persian ruler of the Achaemenid dynasty.

We are told by Arrian that three distinct groups of Indians figured in the army of the Persian monarch Darius III – the Indians who were conterminous with the Bactrians and also the Bactrians themselves, the Arachotians (or Arakhosians), and the Mountainer Indians. These frontier troops were supplemented by a small force of elephants, about 15 in number, belonging to the Indians who lived this side of the Indus. We are further told by him that with these forces Darius fought his last Battle against Alexander the Great, king of Macedon, at Gaugamela, near the river Bumodus, about 600 stades distant from the city of Arabela, in 330 BCE.[38] The statements of Arrian have been called assumption and contradicted by some scholars.[39] But we find that Arrian has described the real historical event. With the conquest of Persia by Alexander and the death of Darius in the year 330 BCE, the Persian Empire ceased to exist.

Speaking of the extent of Persian Empire at the time of its overthrow by Alexander, McCrindle says, "The Persian empire when overthrown by Alexander the Great extended to the Indus, and even embraced territories lying eastward from that river."[40] It may indeed be questioned whether the Persians ever possessed any real sovereignty to the east of the Indus, which certainly formed the limit of the Persian dominions in India, or in this direction in the time of Alexander.

After the Persian conquest of Sindh, the river Indus formed the western boundary of India proper, but this geographical setting underwent change in the time of Sandrakottus, Candragupta, the founder of the Maurya Empire, as gleaned from the classical sources.

Kosmas says, "Sindu (Sindh) is the frontier country of India, for the river Indus, which empties into the Persian Gulf, separates Persia from India."[41]

Notes and References

1. Ktésias, *Persica*, ed. by J. Gilmore under the title, *Fragments of Ktésias' Persica*, Bk. X, Fragms. 33-34 and 37, pp. 127-29 and 133-35.
2. *Cyropaedia*, I, 1,4.
3. *Ibid*., VI, 2, 1-11.
4. *Geog*., XV, I, 26.
5. *Nat. Hist*., VI, 23.
6. *Indika*, Pt. I, Ch. I; also Arrian's *Indika*, tr. by E.J. Chinnock, p. 399.
7. *Anab*., VI, 24, 2-3; also Jacoby, FGH, No.133, Fragm. 3a.
8. *Geog*., XV, I, 5 and XV, II, 5; also Hamilton and Falconer's tr. *The Geography of Strabo*, Vol. III, pp. 74 and 122; Jacoby, FGH, No. 133, Fragm. 3b.

9. "The Persian Dominons in Northern India down to the time of Alexander's Invasion", in CHI, I, p. 298.
10. *Tot. Orb. Des*. Sec. 17.
11. AICL, p. 211, note 2.
12. *Cyropaedia,* VI, 19-23 and VIII, 1-4; *Cyropaedia,* ed. and tr. by W. Miller, Vol. II, pp. 421 and 439.
13. *Cyropaedia,* VIII, 6, 20-21.
14. *Geog*., XV, II, 1.
15. See D.C. Sircar (ed), SI, Vol. I, pp. 7-9.
16. *E'tude*, p. 14.
17. AICL, p. 199, note 2.
18. *Hist*., III, 91-93.
19. Sircar, *Op. cit*., pp. 4-6.
20. See his *Hist*., III, 88ff; also Rennell, *The Geographical System of Herodotus,* Vol.I, pp. 303-5.
21. *Hist*., IV, 44; also Jacoby, FGH, No. 709, Fragm. 3C.
22. *Ancient India from the earliest times to the first century AD*, p. 45.
23. *Ancient India and Iran*., p. 36.
24. *The Panjab, North-West Frontier Province and Kashmir*, p. 161.
25. Sircar (ed), SI, I, pp. 7-9.
26. *Alexander the Great*, Vol. I, pp. 85-86.
27. *Hist.* III, 89-96; see also G. Rawlinson's tr. of Herodotus' *Hist*., Vol. II, p. 403; Vol. IV, p. 207; Percy Sykes, *History of Persia*, pp. 179-80; H.F. Tozer, *Hist. Anc. Geog*., pp. 91-92; V.A. Smith, EHI, pp. 40-41.
28. H.G. Rawlinson, *A Concise History of the Indian People*, p. 48; Aurel Stein, *On Alexander's Track to the Indus*, p. 41; H.W. Bellew, *The Races of Afghanistan, Being a Brief Account of the Principal Nations Inhabiting that country,* p. 58.
29. *Hist.* III, 97; see also W.W. How and J. Well, *Commentary on Herodotus,* Vol.I, pp. 405-6.
30. B.N. Puri, *India as described by Early Greek writers,* p. 50; H.C. Raychaudhuri, PHAI, p. 241.
31. E.H. Bunbury, HAG, Vol. I, pp, 226, and 255, note A.
32. *Hist*., III, 98.
33. See J.W. McCrindle, AICL, p. 1, note 1; W. Vincent, CNAIO, Vol. I, *The Voyage of Nearchus from the Indus to the Euphrates,* p. 70; J. T. Wheeler, *The Geography of Herodotus*, pp. 299 and 306.

34. *Hist.* VII, 65; see also Rapson, *Op. cit.*, p. 46; Bunbury, HAG, I, p. 239.
35. *Hist.*, VII, 86.
36. *Geog.*, XV, I, 6.
37. *Ind. Ant.*, X, 1881, pp. ,304-10.
38. *Anab.*, III, 8, 3-6; also Chinnock's tr. of Arrian's *Anab.*, pp. 142-3.
39. IHQ, XXV, p. 153.
40. AICL, p. 161, note 9.
41. *Top. Chr.*, Bk. XI.

3

Macedonian Invasion (327 – 325 BCE)

The Invasion of India by Alexander the Great of Macedonia

Alexander the Great, son of king Philip of Macedonia, was one of the greatest conquerors the world has ever seen. His succession to the throne of Macedonia took place in 336 BCE. He succeeded not only to his sovereignty, but also to his supremacy in the affairs of Greece. In the year 334 BCE, the youthful monarch undertook the task of extending the frontier of the Macedonian empire by conquests. He made himself master of Asia Minor in that very year itself, reduced Syria to his subjection in 332 BCE, conquered Egypt also in the same year, established his hold over Babylon in 331 BCE and occupied Persia in 330 BCE. He then turned his attention towards India. We are told by Diodorus Siculus that the Macedonians (soldiers and generals) who had accompanied Alexander in his Indian expedition "surpassed all mankind in bravery and in arms."[1]

Alexander wanted to conquer India as far as the Gangetic region of Magadha with its capital Pāṭaliputra (called Pālibothra) and to make it also a part of his Asiatic Empire. Justin says he advanced towards India so that "he might make the remotest East the limits of his empire."[2]

If Alexander had found India united in arms to withstand his aggression, the star of his good fortune would have culminated with his passage of the Indus. But he found, on the contrary, the political condition of the country when he entered it eminently favourable to his designs. The whole of north-western India was parcelled out into separate states, some under kingly and others under republican governments; but all alike prevented by their mutual jealousies and feuds from acting in concert against a common enemy, and, therefore, it became all the more easy for Alexander to overcome them. There were some traitors who took the side of the Macedonian invader against India.

Alexander's invasion of India, which covered a period of about three years, 327-325 BCE, was one of the great events not only in the political history of ancient India but also in the history of the ancient world.

We proceed now to describe Alexander's campaigns in India on the combined testimony of his companions, his five historians, Arrian, Curtius, Diodorus, Justin and Plutarch, and other classical authors, notably, Strabo Polyaenus, Frontinus and Julius Valerius.

AFGHANISTAN

The Beginnings of Alexander's Indian Campaign

Alexander's Indian Campaign commenced in the spring (April) of the year 327 BCE. He crossed the Paropamisus (the lofty mountain range, now called the Hindukush) and entered India with 1,20,000 infantry and 15,000 cavalry, according to Plutarch.[3] He marched to Bactria (northern Afghanistan) and subjugated the Bactrians. From Bactria he led his army to conquer other Indians. He advanced to the Kābul Valley.[4]

Submission of the Nysaeans

The Nysaeans inhabited the city-state of Nysa, situated in the valley of the Kābul river near the Mount Meros, four or five miles west of Jalālābād.

They were republican tribe. They tendered their submission to the Macedonians without offering any resistance to them. Alexander permitted them to retain their autonomy.[5]

Revolt of Astes

At the time of Alexander's invasion, prince Astes (Hasti) ruled the territory near the confluence of the Souastene (Swāt) with the Kophen (Kābul) with capital at peukelaotis (Puṣkalāvatī, a city located on the eastern bank of the river Swāt, nearly seventeen miles north-west of

Peshawar, ancient Purūṣapura). The inhabitants of his principality and the surrounding region are called Astakenoi (Hāstināyana of Pāṇini, *Sūtra*, VI.4. 174[6]). Strabo relates that the regions between the two rivers, the Kophes (Kābul) and the Indus, were possessed by Astakenoi.[7]

The prince Astes was a true patriot. We learn from Arrian that he revolted against Alexander (in August 327 BCE). The city (Peukelaotis) to which he had fled for refuge was put under siege by the troops under Hephaistion (one of Alexander's generals) for full thirty days and finally captured by them. Astes himself fell fighting. Thus he lost both his city and his life. Sanggaios (Greek transcription of Sanjay, the earliest known Indian traitor), who had some time before fled from Astes and deserted to Taxiles (king of Taxila), a circumstance which guaranteed his fidelity to Alexander, was appointed governor of the city.[8]

Battles with the Aspasians and the Assakenians and their defeats – The fall of towns and cities after the resistance of their inhabitants – Siege and capture of Aornos.

In the winter (November – December 327 BCE), Alexander kept himself busy in subduing the fierce and warlike tribes of the mountainous regions on the north-western frontier of India. Aristoboulus, who accompanied Alexander into India as one of his historians, mentions two such tribes as Aspasioi (Aspasians) and Assakenoi (Assakenians).[9]

The Aspasioi or Aspasians of the Kunār valley were the first to bear the brunt of Macedonian attack. On hearing of the Macedonian soldiers' approach to their territory, they set fire to their city on the Khoaspes (Kunār river), and fled to the mountains. But Alexander's army chasing the fugitives as far as the mountains made a great slaughter of them before they could escape to other places. During the pursuit by Ptolemy (Alexander's general), their chief was killed. Alexander then crossed the mountains and came to a city at their base named Arigaion. He found that the inhabitants had burned the place and taken to flight. Some of them perished in the flight, while those taken alive were put to death by the Macedonians, who were enraged against them for having wounded Alexander by striking an arrow in his shoulder.[10] One of their fortified cities where they had fled for refuge called Andaka surrendered on capitulation.[11]

When the Aspasians saw the Macedonians advancing against them, they came down from the high ground which they had occupied into the plain below, and entered into a great pitched battle with them, but Alexander gained the victory. The Aspasians were the stoutest warriors, but they were driven from the hill by the Macedonians. Many were routed by Alexander's army. Ptolemy (one of Alexander's companions, generals and historians) states that the men taken prisoners were in all above 40,000, and that there were also captured more than 2,30,000 oxen, sent to Macedonia by Alexander to be employed in agriculture.[12]

Alexander marched thence to invade the territory of the Assakenians in the Swāt Valley, east of Nysa, then in eastern Afghanistan. We learn from Arrian that they were ready for battles with an army of 20,000 cavalry and more than 30,000 infantry, besides 30 elephants.[13] The strength of their infantry, according to Curtius, was 38,000,[14] but, according to Julius Valerius, it was 40,000.[15] Alexander passed through the territory of the Gouraians, crossed the river Guraeus or Gouraios (Sanskrit Gauri = modern Panjkora) below its junction with the Suastos (Swāt) and then entered the dominions of the Assakenians in the valley of the Swāt. Alexander with his army then proceeded to attack the Assakenians. When they saw the Macedonians invader approaching, they had not the courage to encounter him in the open field with their collective forces, and, hence, they dispersed to their several towns or cities, which they resolved to defend to the last extremity.[16]

Alexander marched first to attack Massaga,[17] which was the greatest city of the Assakenians in the northwestern parts of India. It was "strongly fortified both by nature and art". It was not only their main stronghold but also their metropolis. It was the seat of the sovereign power which controlled the whole realm. It was the royal residence. It was protected by a double ring of ramparts.[18] Arrian tells us that the Assakenians supported by a body of Indian mercenaries brought from a distance, and not less than 7,000 strong fought against the Macedonians in defence of this city. About 200 of them were killed, and the rest were shut up within the walls of the city. The city was assaulted.[19]

Highlighting the role of the Indians (Assakenians), men and women, in the defence of the city Massaga, the capital of their dominions, Diodorus says "Alexander pursued the mercenaries, and falling suddenly upon them made a great slaughter of their ranks. The Indians (Assakenians) foreseeing the danger ahead drew their ranks together in form of a ring, within which they placed the women and children to guard them on all sides against their assailants. They with valour and courage fought with the Macedonians. As the combatants were locked together fighting hand to hand, death and wounds were there... When many were thus wounded and not a few killed, the women, taking the arms of the fallen, fought side by side with the men, forcing them to be violent and to take an active part in the defence. Accordingly, some of them who had supplied themselves with arms, did their best to cover their husband with their shields, while others who were without arms did much to impede the enemy by flinging themselves upon them and catching hold of their shields. The defenders, however, after fighting desperately along with their wives were at last overpowered by superior numbers, and met a glorious death which they would have disdained to exchange for a life with dishonour. Alexander spared the unwarlike and unarmed multitude, as well as the women that still survived, but took them away under charge of the cavalry."[20]

We are told by one of Alexander's historians, Plutarch, that as the Indian mercenary troops consisting of the best soldiers found in the country flocked to the city (Mazaga) which Alkexander attacked, and defended it with the greatest vigour, he (Alexander) thus incurred serious losses, and accordingly concluded a treaty of peace with them; but afterwards, as they were going away, set upon them while they were on the road, and killed them all. "This rests as a foul blot on his material fame, for on all other occasions he observed the rules of civilized warfare as a king."[21]

We are informed by Arrian that the Assakenians continued with great vigour to maintain the defence of the city Massaga as long as the king Assakenus of that place was still living, but when he was struck by a missile from an engine and was killed by the blow, they surrendered, while some of themselves had fallen in the uninterrupted siege of the city, and most of them were wounded and disabled for fighting. The city now stripped of its defenders was taken by Alexander by storm.[22] Julius Valerius informs us that on the fourth day of the fighting, Assakenus, the sovereign of the place (Massaga) was slain.[23] He was slain in the course of the siege of that place by the troops of Alexander.[24] Curtius tells us that the city was under siege and captured by Alexander. He tells us further that the people of the city sent down envoys to the Macedonian king to sue for pardon, and surrendered their city.[25] Alexander, says Arrian, lost in the siege of the city from first to last twenty-five of his men in all.[26]

Thinking further resistance useless, king Assakenus' wife, Queen Cleophis, surrendered herself to Alexander, says Justin.[27] Alexander received the submission of this queen, and reinstated her in the possession of her kingdom. Curtius relates that the queen came with a group of noble ladies. The queen herself having placed her son, still a child, at Alexander's knees, obtained not only pardon, but permission to retain her former dignity, for she was styled queen.[28] She now ruled the city (Massaga) and the realm. In fact, this queen obtained the restoration of her kingdom by the sacrifice of her honour.[29] This finds the best expression in what Justin says: "Alexander marched to the dominions of Queen Cleophis, who, after surrendering her kingdom, purchased its restoration by permitting the conqueror to share her bed, thus gaining by her fascinations what she had not gained by her valour. The offspring of this intercourse was a son, whom she called Alexander, the same who afterwards reigned as an Indian king. Queen Cleophis, because she had prostituted her chastity, was thereafter called by the Indians the royal harlot."[30]

The city, Bazira, says Arrian, stood on a very lofty eminence, and was strongly fortified. The inhabitants here did not surrender. A sharp conflict between the Macedonians and the Bazirians took place in which 500 of the Indians were slain, and upwards of 70 taken prisoners.[31] Curtius tells us that Alexander left Coenus to besiege an opulent city which was called by its inhabitants Beira (Bazira).[32] The siege of the city, Ora, did not cost Alexander much labour, for he captured the place at the first assault. The inhabitants of this city fought against the Macedonian troops, but the Macedonians had no great difficulty in routing them, and driving them back within the walls of the city. The inhabitants of both these cities did not capitulate of their own volition but rather resisted the attempts of the Macedonians till the last moment as much as possible to defend their cities but ultimately they were forced to succumb to the Macedonians.[33] Julius Valerius informs us that from Massaga Alexander despatched Coenon (Coenus) to besiege Baziphara (Bazira) and Attalas to besiege the city Hora (Ora), under the belief that after the downfall of the Accae (Assakenians), their inhabitants would be brought to ready submission. Alexander himself captured both these towns or cities, in spite of a desperate resistance. After many had fallen, those who survived fled to a strongly fortified rock.[34] The fall of Massaga, Bazira and Ora marks the great victory of the Macedonians.

When the inhabitants of Bazira heard that Ora had fallen, they regarded their case as desperate, and at the dead of night fled from their city to the Rock, as all the other Indians were doing, for having left their cities they were fleeing to the rock in that land called Aornos,[35] which has been identified with Mount Mahaban.[36] Alexander's ardent desire was to capture the Rock Aornos for receiving the submission of all those people who had fled there for refuge. But before fulfilling his this desire, he reduced all the yet unconquered regions west of the Indus to his subjection. He took Peukelaotis (Puṣkalāvatī). He advanced up to the right bank of the

Indus till he reached Embolima, about eight miles distant from Aornos. Alexander was accompanied on this occasion by Kophaios (the ruler of the valley of the lower Kophen or Kābul river) and Assagetes (a transliteration into Greek of the Sanskrit Aśvajit), the local chief. On reaching Embolima, a city adjoining the rock of Aornos, he placed it under the control of the Macedonians for some time.[37]

Alexander then put rock Aornos under siege, and finally captured it, where many of the people had fled for refuge. The fugitives from the rock fled for shelter to the neighbouring mountains. He (Alexander), however, received the submission of all the tribes in that part of the country.[38]

Alexander built a fort upon Aornos, and placed its garrison under the command of Sisikottus (Śaśigupta, one of the Indian traitors of Alexander's time), who long before had in Baktra deserted from the Indians to the Macedonians, and after Alexander had conquered the Baktrian land served in his army and proved himself worthy of his full confidence. He sent messengers to inform Alexander that the Assakenians had revolted from him.[39] Alexander then set out from the rock Aornos and invaded the land of the Assakenians. That was the eastern part of their country. He had already reduced the western and the capital Massaga. He had been apprised that the brother of Assakenus, with a host of the Indians from the adjoining region, had fled for refuge to the mountains of that land. On reaching Dytra he found there were no inhabitants in the city itself or the surrounding district.[40]

The campaign westward of the Indus was brought to a close (in December 327 BCE) by the capture of a famous natural fortress known as Aornos which was deemed impregnable, and had been a place of refuge for a large number of defeated warriors. Alexander now began his campaign to the east of the Indus. In the year following 327 BCE, he marched eastward to the Panjab.

THE PANJAB

Surrender of the kingdom of Taxila to Alexander and friendly relations between him and Taxiles

When Alexander arrived at the river Indus (in January or February 326 BCE) he found a bridge already made over it by two of his generals, Hephaistion and Perdikkas, besides a great many small boats. He found also a present which had been sent by the then ruler of Taxila called Taxiles (father of Āmbhi). The present consisted of 200 talents of silver, 30 elephants, etc. The same king had also tent to his assistance a force of 700 horsemen.[41] The said Taxiles ruled his kingdom with its capital at

Taxila until he died. It may be noted here that Taxiles was a dynastic title which each sovereign of Taxila assumed on his accession to power. "The Taxiles," says Strabo, "ruled a vast kingdom between the Indus and the Hydaspes"[42] as a sovereign ruler. They, Plutarch says, ruled over a part of Indian which was as large as Egypt.[43]

Alexander crossed the Indus at Ohind (ancient Udbhāṇḍa or Udbhāṇḍndapura, the modern village of Und, 15 or 16 miles north of Aṭaka in Rawalpindi district) in March 326 BCE. He crossed this river to its other side, and then marching away from there arrived at Taxila, "a great and flourishing city, the greatest indeed of all the cities that lay between the river Indus and the Hydaspes."[44] He was received there by the inhabiutants of the city, the king Taxiles and his son, the prince Āmbhi, in a very hospitable or friendly manner.[45] Āmbhi has been called by Curtius correctly Omphis,[46] and by Diodorus less accurately Mophis.[47]

Curtius informs us that "Omphis received Alexander at Taxila. He had come with his army to meet Alexander that he might at once place at his disposal all the forces of his empire, without waiting to tender his allegiance through deputies".[48] We are further informed by him that "the prince Omphis had brought with him fifty-six elephants and those he gave to Alexander, with other valuable presents… Taxiles presented Alexander and all his friends with golden crowns, together with eighty talents of coined silver, while Alexander not only returned to Taxiles the presents he had given, but added a thousand talents with many banqueting vessels of gold and silver, etc."[49]

Plutarch records that Taxiles (Omphis) assured Alexander of his friendship. He said we should not fight with one another. Alexander was delighted with what he said. The friendly greetings were exchanged between the two.[50]

Arrian tells us that Taxiles surrendered into the hands of Alexander Taxila, the capital of his kingdom.[51] But Curtius informs us that it was his son Omphis (Āmbhi) who had urged him to surrender his kingdom to the conqueror.[52] Both father and the son can be included in the list of Indian traitors of Alexander's time.

After the death of Taxiles, his son (Āmbhi) had succeeded to the throne of Taxila, or to the government, as Diodorus says.[53] He recognised Alexander as his lord, and received from him an investiture as lawful successor of his deceased father, the king of Taxila, and called Taxiles.

We learn from Curtius that "Omphis, under Alexander's permission, and according to the usage of the realm, assumed the ensigns of royalty along with the name which his father had borne. His people called him

Taxiles, for such was the name which accompanied the sovereignty, on whomsoever it devolved."[54]

We are told by both Curtius[55] and Diodorus[56] that Taxiles' son (Omphis of the former or Mophis of the latter) surrendered himself and his kingdom to Alexander. Alexander, to mark his approbation of this conduct or as a pledge of good faith, gave back to him his kingdom and entrusted him with authority to rule it as an independent ruler, and confirmed him in his sovereignty. He was formally recognised as a king of Taxila. He thus assumed not only the sovereignty but also the dynastic title Taxiles. He, ever, afterwards, treated Alexander as a friend and ally. We know from Arrian[57] that he was rewarded by Alexander with an accession of territory.

The king Āmbhi (Omphis or Mophis) sent his forces to Alexander to help him in his fight against his rival, king Porus. This traitor also helped the Macedonian forces to reach the Hydaspes river, where Porus fought with them with all his strength on its other bank, but was defeated. "Alexander", says Arrian, "left a garrison in Taxila and then moved on towards the river Hydaspes with his own forces and 5000 of the Indians commanded by Taxiles, for he had learned that Porus with his army lay on the other side of that river resolved either to prevent him from making the passage or to attack him when crossing." [58]

Strabo, citing Aristoboulus as his authority, states that from the great city of Taxila the Macedonians went on to the Hydaspes and the land of Porus. They descended to Hydaspes and conquered Porus.[59]

Battle with Porus, his defeat and Submission, restoration of his kingdom with accession of another extensive territory, and his turning into an ally of Alexander

"One of the Indian kings called Porus", says Justin, "was remarkable alike for his personal strength and noble courage."[60] We are told by Julius Valerius that "Porus was the ruler of India, a man of astonishing stature, quite transcending that of other men, while in mental capacity he did not fall below the level of the endowments of his outward person."[61] The dominions of Porus, which were confined between the Hydaspes and the Akesines-a tract not more than 40 miles in width-contained about 300 cities.[62] Beyond the Hydaspes was the powerful kingdom of Porus, who held his sway as far as the Akesines.

Alexander, on reaching the Hydaspes (in May 326 BCE), found that Porus was ready with all his army and his array of elephants on the opposite side of the river for battle with him.[63] Alexander employed a stratagem for crossing to the other side of the river Hydaspes. During a dark and stormy night with torrents of rain, thunder and lightning, some of his soldiers had crossed over secretly by the bridge of boats. Alexander himself embarked on a thirty-oared galley, and went over accompanied by Ptolemy, Perdikkas, and Lysimachos, his body-guards, and by Seleukus, one of his companions and generals.[64]

Arrian tells us that Alexander took with himself nearly 6,000 foot-soldiers and about 5,000 horsemen. An encounter took place at the place of disembarkation on the other side of river between the Indians led by the son of Porus commanding 2,000 force and 120 chariots on the one side and Alexander and his troops on the other.[65] We are further, told by him that Alexander at first despatched against the prince the horse archers, and led the cavalry himself, under the belief that Porus was advancing against him with the whole of army. Four hundred of the horsemen of the Indians fell, and among them the son of Porus. Their chariots, moreover, were captured. The horsemen who had escaped from there reported one after another to the great Porus that Alexander himself had crossed the river with the strongest division of his army and that his son had been slain in the fight. Porus then took all his cavalry, 4,000 strong, all his chariots, 300 in number, 200 of his elephants, and 30,000 efficient infantry and marched against the Macedonians led by the king (Alexander) in person. Porus was himself mounted on an elephant attired as a warrior.[66] The strength of the army of Porus given by Arrian tallies with that given by Curtius.[67] But Diodorus says that "Porus had an army of more than 50,000 foot, about 3,000 horse, above 1,000 chariots, and 130 elephants."[68] And Plutarch says that the army Porus led amounted to 20,000 infantry and 2,000 cavalry.[69] Both sides were ready for battle with all preparations.[70]

A fierce battle was fought on the opposite bank of the Hydaspes. Alexander won a splendid victory. Porus was defeated. Losses were sustained by each side in this battle. The Indians killed fell little short of 20,000 infantry and 3,000 cavalry and all their Chariots were broken to pieces.[71] Two sons of Porus fell in the battle, and also some other Indians.[72] The drivers of the elephants and of the Chariots were also slain and the cavalry officers and the generals in the army of Porus all slain. On Alexander's side, there fell about 80 of the 6,000 infantry, who had taken part in the first attack, 10 of the horse archers who first began the action, 20 of the companion cavalry and 200 of the other cavalry.[73] According to Diodorus, more than 12,000 of the Indian fell, among whom were two of the sons of Porus, and his generals, and the most distinguished of his other officers. More than 9000 men were taken prisoners, and 80 elephants were captured. Of the Macedonians, he says, there fell 280 horsemen and more than 700 foot-soldiers.[74]

Porus was the first Indian sovereign who fought very bravely against the Macedonian's in defence of his kingdom. He had nobly discharged his duties throughout the battle, performing the part not only of a general, but also that of a gallant soldier. He continued to fight valiantly till he found himself wounded. He, being drained of blood by the number of his wounds, fainted away. A rumour having spread that their king was dead, the remnant of the Indians fled from the field, but many of them were slain in the field.[75]

Arrian informs us that Porus was protected to the last by his faithful elephants.[76] Plutarch,[77] who gives the account of Alexander's battle with Porus on the authorities of the former's epistles or letters and the writings of his companions and historians, and Aelian,[78] who is an authority on the Indian animals narrate that when the Indian king Porus was wounded in the battle with Alexander, the elephant on which he was mounted showed wonderful sagacity and care for him. It defended him against his assailants, and repulsed them. Though suffering itself from many wounds, it did nevertheless with gentleness and caution draw out or extract with its trunk the darts from the body of Porus. When it observed that its royal master (Porus) migh fall of its back because of excessive loss of blood from his wounds, it lowered him slowly and gently, and stood still with its knees bent in such a way that he descended on the ground quiet safely. He recovered from his wounds.

Arrian says, Alexander, perceiving that Porus was a great man and valiant in fight, decided to save his life, and for this purpose he sent to him messenger after messenger with request to conduct him without delay to meet him. Porus ultimately agreed to meet him.[79] He tells us further that "he was then conducted to Alexander. He advanced to meet him as a brave man would meet another brave man after gallantly contending with another king in defence of his Kingdom".[80] Then Alexander requested Porus to say how he wished to be treated. Porus said in reply." "Treat me O Alexander! as befits a king." Alexander, being pleased with his answer, replied that "O Porus, you shall be so treated." Alexander not only appointed Porus to govern his own kingdom, but added to his original territory another of still greater extent. Alexander thus treated this brave man as befitted a king, and he consequently found him in all respects faithful and devoted to his interests. Alexander made Porus his firm friend and ally.[81] This was, according to Plutarch, "Alexander's noble treatment of Porus." [82]

Diodorus says that "Alexander appointed Porus, in consideration of the courage and valour he had displayed, to be king of the country over which he had formerly ruled."[83] Justin also states that "Alexander, out of respect for his valour, restored him in safety to his sovereignty."[84] Julius Valerius tells us that the "king Porus was admitted into the circle of Alexander's friends, and on account of his distinguished merits, had the administration of his kingdom restored to him…"[85] Plutarch relates that Alexander not only reinstated Porus in his kingdom with authority to govern it but added a large province to it, subduing the inhabitants whose form of government was republican. This country contained 15 tribes, 5000 considerable cities, and villages without number. He subdued, besides, another district three times as large, over which he appointed Philippos to be Satrap (ruler).[86]

Alexander is said to have founded two cities, one on the battlefield, and the other at the point where he had started to cross the river Hydaspes. The former he called Nikaia in honour of his victory over the Indians, and the other Boukephala in memory of his horse Boukephosalos, which died there. The ancient Greek and Roman writers are not in agreement about the place where the city called Boukephala was built.[87]

One of the great battles the Indians fought with the Macedonians was that of the Hydaspes. Plutarch remarks: "The battle with Porus depressed the spirits of the Macedonians and made them very unwilling to advance farther into India.[88]

Conquest of the territories, including that of the Glausai, and delivered to Porus to rule-Reconciliation between Porus and Taxiles

Alexander advanced himself against the Indians whose "country" lay next to the dominions of Porus. Aristoboulus says that the name of the nation (people) was the Glaukanikoi, but Ptolemy calls them the Glausai. Alexander invaded their "country" with his army. The people everywhere surrendered on terms of capitulation. In this manner, he took thirty-seven cities the smallest of which contained not fewer than 5,000 inhabitants, while many contained upwards of 10,000. He took also a great many villages which were not less populous than the towns; and this "country" (of Glausai) he gave to Porus to rule, as we learn from Arrian.[89]

"Other writers", says Strabo, "affirm that the Macedonians conquered nine nations situated between the Hydaspes and the Hypanis (Hyphasis); and obtained possession of 500 cities, and that Alexander after having conquered all this country delivered it up to Porus."[90]

Alexander effected a reconciliation between Porus and Taxiles. He then sent Taxiles home to his capital, as we are told by Arrian.[91]

Embassies from Abisares to Alexander and his submission to him-Envoys from some other Indians to Alexander

The name of Abisares was derived from that of his kingdom, Abhisāra, which designated the mountainous country to the east of the Indus. He was the ruler of a hill country between the upper Hydaspes and the Akesines. Above Taxila, says Strabo, among the mountains lie the dominions of Abisares.[92] He was a potentate on a level with Taxiles and Porus.

We are informed by Arrian that while Alexander was at Taxila, Abhisāra, the king of the Indians of the hill country, sent him an embassy which included his own brother and other grandees of his court. Alexander appointed Philip satrap of the Indians of that district.[93]

Abisares was in alliance with Porus and was ready with his army to fight on the side of Porus. But before Abisares joined Porus in his fight with Alex, he sent envoys, including his brother, to Alexander with money and forty elephants as a present, and the envoys surrendered to him all that their master possessed. After pledges of good faith had been interchanged, they were sent back to their sovereign.[94]

After the defeat of Porus, Abisares sent an embassy to the conqueror with presents and proffers of submission. Arrian tells us that the envoys came from Abisares to say that their king surrendered himself and his whole realm to Alexander.[95] Abisares was permitted by Alexander to retain his kingdom and govern it.[96]

Regarding Abisares' embassies to Alexander before and after the battle with Porus, Curtius informs us that "Abisares, who had sent envoys to Alexander before the battle with Porus, had come off; now (after Alexander's victory in the battle) sent others to assure him that he was ready to do whatever he commanded, provided only he was not obliged to surrender his person; for he could neither live without having the power of a king nor have that power if he were to be kept in captivity."[97] It was probably after this that he was allowed by Alexander to retain his kingdom and govern it. We learn from Curtius himself that Alexander made Abisares satrap (ruler) of his own kingdom, and when he died appointed his son to succeed him. He ascended the vacant throne and ruled the kingdom.[98]

Envoys also arrived from the independent Indians to Alexander. There came also envoys from Sisikottos, the satrap of the Assakenians, reporting that these people had slain their governor and revolted from Alexander. Against these he (Alexander) sent Philippos and Tyriaspes to quell the insurrection and restore tranquility and order to the province.[99]

Submission and Revolt of younger Porus, the handing over of his dominions to great Porus, and the placing of all the conquered independent Indian tribes bordering on the banks of Hydraotes also under his rule-Resistance and surrender of some Indians beyond the Hydraotes

The Indian ruler called younger Porus was the nephew of great Porus. He was sovereign of the territory situated between the Akesines and Hydraotes.

The younger Porus had sent envoys to Alexander offering to surrender into his hands both his person and the kingdom over which he ruled. But suddenly he quitted his kingdom and fled to the "nation of the Gandaridai." Alexander, while marching to overtake him, arrived at Hydraotes. He then despatched Hephaistion with a body of troops into the "country" of that Porus who had revolted. He received orders to hand over the kingdom to the other (great) Porus, who was on his side.[100]

Alexander reduced all the independent Indian tribes bordering on the banks of the Hydraotes and placed them also under the rule of other Porus. He himself then crossed the river Hydraotes. When he was advancing into the country beyond the Hydraotes, he found most of the natives willing to surrender on capitulation, while some met him in arms, and others were captured when attempting to escape and reduced to submission.[101]

Resistance and Surrender of the Adraistai

The accounts of the historians of Alexander are at variance regarding the Adraistai. Arrian tells us that Alexander, after crossing the river Hydraotes, arrived in the territory of "an Indian race called the Adraistai", who voluntarily surrendered themselves and their city named Pimprama on terms of capitulation.[102] But Curtius says that Alexander captured this town by a general attack, and having received hostages, imposed a tribute upon the inhabitants.[103] Diodorus relates that Alexander subdued the Adrestai, and reduced some of their cities which offered resistance, and persuaded others to surrender.[104] Justin informs us that Alexander conquered the Adrestae after defeating their armies.[105]

Battle with the Kathaians and their neighbouring tribes, their defeats, and capture of the city of Sangala

The Kathaians, settled in a territory situated to the east of the river Hydraotes, and other independent Indian tribes were preparing to meet Alexander in battle if he invaded their "country", and were inviting the neighbouring tribes, which were independent like themselves, to cooperate with them. Alexander had already learned about their preparations to fight against him. He learned also that the city near which they meant to engage him was strongly fortified and was called Sangala. The Kathaians themselves enjoyed the highest reputation for courage and skill in the art of war, and the same warlike spirit characterised the Oxydrakai and Malloi (two other independent Indian tribes). They could not make a united front against the Macedonian invader. The Kathaians were supported only by their neighbouring tribes in their fight against that invader. Alexander advancing beyond the Hydraotes reached the city of Sangala, where the Kathaians and their neighbouring tribes that had joined them were ready for battle with him.[106] Ptolemy, Alexander's general, advanced against them with his troops. Ptolemy, with his men fell upon those who were going to take the refuge in the city, and killed them one after another. Upon this the Indians fled back once more the city for refuge, and as many as 500 of them were slain in the retreat. Meanwhile, the great Porus also arrived bringing with him a force of 5000 Indians to help his ally Alexander in his military operation against the Kathaians. But the Macedonians took the city by Storm. In the capture of the city, 17,000 of the Indians were slaughtered, and more than 70,000 were captured, together with 300 waggons and 500 horsemen. The loss in Alexander's army during all the siege of the city was somewhat under 100 killed, but the proportion of the wounded to the number killed was higher than usual, for there were 1200 wounded, including, some army officers.[107] Arrian's numbers of the Indians killed and captured seem to be grossly exaggerated. Curtius tells us that the Macedonians in their battle with the Indians at Sangola killed all the men that offered resistance. The enemy (Indians) after a loss of 8000 men withdrew into the town.[108] None of the independent Indians who had voluntarily surrendered themselves had received any ill-treatment at the hands of Alexander. When they were informed of the King's (Alexander's) clemency to the submissive and his severity if opposed, they surrendered. But they had already learned that Sangala had been stormed by Alexander, and being terrified by the news had left the cities and were in flight. Those who were left behind in the retreat when their strength failed were taken by the troops and slaughtered to the number of about 500. The city of Sangala, metropolis of the Kathaians, was razed to the ground. The land belonging to it Alexander made over to those Indians who had formerly been independent but who had voluntarily submitted to him. He then sent

Porus with his own forces to the cities which had submitted to introduce garrisons within them.[109]

Submission of Sophytes

One of the petty Indians kings, Sophytes, is called Sopeithes by Arrian,[110] Diodorus[111] and Strabo[112], and Sopithes by Curtius.[113] The name transliterates Sanskrit Saubhūtu or Saubhūta. He was a neighbour of the Kathaians, whose territories were situated to the east of the Hydraotes, and were famous for their republican institutions.

Diodorus[114] and Curtius[115] place the dominions of Sophytes between the Hydraotes and the Hyphasis. Some writers, Strabo says, place Kathaia (Kathaians) and the kingdom of Sopeithes in the tract between the two rivers (the Hydaspes and the Akesines); others, he says, again place them on the other side of the Akesines and of the Hydraotes.[116] Arrian relegates the kingdom of Sopeithes to the regions of the Hydaspes and places its capital on the opposite side of that river.[117]

We are told by Diodorus that "The king Sopeithes came forth from the city where his palace was, and on surrendering himself and his kingdom to Alexander was reinstated in his authority by the clemency of the conqueror. Speithes with the utmost cordiality feasted the whole army in splendid style for several days."[118]

Curtius also informs us that after the capture of the city Sangala Alexander entered the dominions of king Sopithes who received him with great hospitality. Alexander came with his army before the palace in the capital of the kingdom of Sopithes. At that time he was himself there in his palace. "The Indian King", he says, "with two grown-up sons came to meet Alexander. He surrendered into his hands his children and his kingdom. Alexander, therefore, leaving Sopithes in possession of his kingdom, advanced to the river Hyphasis."[119]

Submission of Phegeus, information supplied by him to Alexander about the Prasians and the Gaógâridai and their king Dhanananda – Alexander's advance to the Hyphasis and his address to his soldiers to advance beyond it to the Ganges – The refusal of soldiers to do so – The erection of Altars on the Hyphasis – the Retreat of Alexander – The Conquest of the Gangetic kingdom of Magadha, an unfulfilled dream of Alexander

Alexander, leaving Sopithes in possession of his kingdom, advanced with his army towards the river Hyphasis to conquer the Indians who dwelt beyond it.[120] Before reaching his destination, Alexander led his army into the dominions of Phegeus[121] which lay between the Hydraotes and the Hyphasis, or adjoined the latter. Here the natives welcomed the presence of the Macedonians, and the prince Phegeus came out with many gifts or presents to meet them. After the submission of that prince, Alexander allowed him to retain his principality, and then enjoyed along with his army the noble hospitality of prince for two days during which he obtained information from him about the strength of the army of his contemporary Indian king and his enemy, Dhanananda, called Agrammes by Curtius[122] and Xandrames by Diodorus.[123] He was the last king of the Nanda dynasty. He was then ruling the kingdom of Magadha with its capital at Pāṭaliputra, called Pālibothra.

Keeping in view his goal of unfurling the banner of his victory beyond the Hyphasis, and extending the eastern limits of his empire up to the Gangetic region by conquering Magadha kingdom, Alexander wanted to know the military strength of the ruler of that kingdom. He was informed by Phegeus that the king Dhanananda "kept in the field for guarding the approaches to his country (kingdom) 200,000 infantry, 20,000 cavalry, 2,000 four-horsed chariots, and 3,000 or 4,000 trained elephants, the most formidable force of all."[124] Alexander got the credibility of his information confirmed by his faithful ally, the elder Porus, called also the great Porus. The King (Dhanananda) of the Praisiai (Prasians) and the Gaṅgāridai (the people of the eastern Gangetic kingdom of Magadha), according to Plutarch, was waiting for Alexander with an army of 80,000 horse, 200,000 foot, 8,000 war-chariots, and 6,000 fighting elephants. The opposite banks of the Ganges, he says, were covered all over with armed men, horses, and elephants.[125] Justin also tells us that "Alexander's enemy awaited him with 200,000 cavalry."[126] This was actually the strength of his infantry and not of cavalry.

On reaching the river Hyphasis (in early September 326 BCE), Alexander ordered his soldiers to advance beyond it to the Ganges and cross it over for facing the standing army of Dhanananda on its opposite banks. But they did not give assent to his proposal and refused to proceed even beyond the Hyphasis as they were completely exhausted in strength (especially after battles with Porus and the Kathaians) and depressed in spirit. They became tired of continued wars. They were also afraid of mighty forces of Magadhan king. Alexander addressed the soldiers and their officers to enthuse and embolden them to do what he desired, but they remained firm on their decision not to advance farther into India. They did not budge an inch from their stand till the last moment. Alexander ultimately decided to retreat from the Hyphasis.[127]

"Alexander at first in vexation and rage withdrew to his tent, and shutting himself up lay there feeling no gratitude towards those who had thwarted his purpose of crossing the Ganges; but regarding a retreat as tantamount to a confession of defeat. But being swayed by the persuasions of his friends, and the entreaties of his soldiers who stood weeping and lamenting at the door of his tent, he at last relented, and prepared to retreat," as told by one of his own historians.[128] Thus, his dream of conquering the Gangetic kingdom of Magadha with its capital Pāṭaliputra and making it a part of his Asiatic Empire got shattered and battered.

Diodorus, like other historians of Alexander, except Justin, asserts that "Alexander did not undertake an expedition against the Gaṅgāridai (the inhabitants of the Gangetic region, i.e. Magadha) being deterred by the multitude of their elephants"[129], the most formidable force of all kept by their king Dhananānda. Justin's statement, that Alexander conquered the Praesidae (Prasians) and the Gaṅgāridae along with others after defeating their army,[130] appears to be a mere supposition or a fanciful notion, and hence it can unhesitatingly be disposed of. The assertion of Krateros, who was one of Alexander's most distinguished generals, and next to Hephaistion, that "Alexander advanced as far as the Ganges"[131] is also untenable. Megasthenes has rightly pointed out that the Gaṅgāridai has never been conquered by any foreign king.[132] Arrian also correctly states that in an eastern direction, Alexander did not penetrate beyond the river Hypahsis,[133] and that his progress was arrested by that river.[134] Palladius' statement, that "Alexander, the king of the Macedonians, did not make his way to the Ganges,"[135] is also worthy of our notice. Lassen observes that "Alexander, the Macedonian, after conquering all Asia, did not make war upon the Gaṅgāridai when he learned that they possessed four thousand elephants well trained and equipped for war."[136]

Before Alexander retreated with a heavy heart from the Hypahsis, he had ordered his army to erect twelve altars of square blocks of stone on its banks as a monument of his Indian expedition and to mark the limits of his advance eastward. Besides altars, other memorials were also raised there to mark his presence.[137] Palladius tells us that Alexander erected a stone pillar with the inscription: "Alexander, the king of the Macedonians, reached this place."[138] Both Pliny[139] and Solinus,[140] on the authority of Megasthenes (*Indika*, Bk. I, Fragm. XXB, and Bk. IV, Fragm. LVI B respectively) stated that in India the river Hypanis (Hyphasis) formed the limit of Alexander's march, as the altars set up on its banks testify. Pliny also says that "Alexander acquired a very extensive and accurate knowledge of that part of India."[141] In his incidental notices of India, Strabo observes: "Alexander erected altars as boundaries of his Indian campaign in those parts of Indies (India) he arrived at, which were situated farthest towards the east."[142]

A pillar, which was erected on the Hyphasis possibly after the retreat of Alexander from there, remained in an excellent state of preservation till about the middle of the first century of the Christian era. The Greek traveller Apollonius and his Assyrian companion Damis, who visited India in CE 43-4, saw, as they approached the Hyphasis, the altars which Alexander had built there, and also a bronze pillar with this inscription: "Here Alexander halted," as we learn from Philostratus.[143] He conjectures that this pillar was erected by the Indians out of joy for Alexander's return homeward.

It is only Plutarch who tells us that the altars erected on the Hyphasis were afterwards held in veneration by the Praisian (Prasian) kings; and that they crossing the river, used to go there to offer sacrifices upon them in the Hellenic fashion.

The events that took place between September and December in 326 BCE are described here under the following three sub-headings:

Alexander's treatment of Porus and Taxiles-Submission of Arsakes

Alexander, before leaving the Hyphasis (towards the end of September 326 BCE), "committed all the country (territories) west of that river to the government of Porus, and then he marched back to the Hydraotes," says Arrian.[144] After crossing this river, Alexander retraced his steps to the Akesines. He reached the river Akesines and reconciled Porus and Taxiles. Curtius informs us that "Alexander left Porus and Taxiles, the Indian kings who had been disagreeing and raking up old feuds, in friendly relations with each other, strengthened by a marriage alliance; and as they had done their utmost to help him forward with the building of his fleet, he confirmed each in his sovereignty."[145] Alexander treated both Porus and Taxiles, permitting them to retain the power and dignity which they had previously enjoyed as independent ruler. Here lies the greatness of Alexander.

Alexander recrossed the river Akesines, and reached the Hydaspes. We learn from Arrian that "he assembled the companions and all the ambassadors of the Indians who had come to him, and in their presence appointed Porus king of all the Indian territories already subjugated – seven nations in all, containing more than 2,000 cities."[146] This is another glowing testimony of Alexander's greatness.

"At this time Arsakes, ruler of the country adjoining the dominions of Abisares, together with the brother of Abisares and his own relatives came to Alexander, bringing presents such as the Indians consider the most valuable, and some thirty elephants sent by Abisares. Alexander, readily believing that such was the case, made Abisares satrap of his own dominions, and moreover placed Arsakes under his jurisdiction."[147]

Resistance of the Sibi or Siboi[148] to Alexander, operation against them, and their submission

Arrian tells us that after reaching the Hydaspes, "Alexander made himself an inroad into the territories of the Sibi (called also Siboi) who refused their submission."[149] We are told by Diodorus that on coming to the place where the Hydaspes and Akesines join each other, Alexander landed his troops, and led them against the Siboi. Alexander encamped near their capital, and thereupon the citizens, who filled the highest offices came forth to meet him. They presented him also with magnificent gifts. Alexander was so gratified by their professions of goodwill that he permitted their cities to remain in the enjoyment of their freedom.[150] Justin also informs us that Alexander received the submission of the Silei (Sibi).[151]

The Agalassians : Their Resistance to and Battle with Alexander, and their Sacrifices

The people called Agalassians were the next neighbours of the Siboi.[152] We are informed by Diodorus that Alexander, with his troops, advanced against them, and finding that they had mustered an army of 40,000 foot, and 3,000 horse, he gave them battle, put the greater number of them to the sword, and thus emerged victorious. The rest, who had fled for safety to the adjacent towns, but were soon captured, he condemned to slavery. He seized 20,000 of the remainder of the inhabitants, who had taken refuge in a large city, which he stormed. The Indians, however, having barricaded the narrow streets, fought with great vigour from the houses, so that Alexander in pressing the attack lost not a few Macedonians. This enraged him and he set fire to the city, burning with it most of its defenders. He gave quarter, however, to 3,000 to the survivors, who had fled for refuge to the citadel and sued for mercy.[153]

Curtius' account of the subject under notice is at little variance with that of Diodorus. "Alexander", Curtius says, "laid the country of the Sibi's neighbours (Agalassians) waste, and took its capital town by an assault made against the walls all round. The nation, consisting of 40,000 foot-soldiers, had been drawn up along the bank of the river (Hydaspes, near its junction with the Akesines) to oppose his landing, but he nevertheless crossed the stream, put the enemy to fight, and having stormed the town, compelled all who were shut up within its walls to surrender. Those who were of military age were put to sword, and the rest were sold as slaves."[154] He tells us further that "Alexander laid siege to another town, but the defenders made so gallant a resistance that he was repulsed with the loss of many of his Macedonians. He persevered, however, with the siege till the inhabitants, despairing of their safety, set fire to their houses, and cast themselves along with their wives and children into the flames. War then showed itself in a new form, for while the inhabitants were destroying their city by spreading the flames, the enemy (Macedonains) were striving to save it by quenching them. The citadel of the town had escaped damage, and Alexander accordingly left a garrison behind it."[155] Justin holds that the Hiacensanae (Agalassians) submitted to Alexander.[156]

Alexander subjugated a number of Indian tribes, kings and princes between January and September in the year 325 BCE the details of which are furnished here under separate sub-headings.

Joint preparations of the Oxydrakai and Malloi to fight together against the Macedonains – Alexander's sudden attack on the Malloi, their defeat and submission – surrender of the Oxydrakai

Alexander first subjected the Indians who lived near the Hydaspes to his authority, some having surrendered on terms of capitulation, and such as resorted to arms, having been subdued by force. He then sailed rapidly to the "country" of the Oxydrakai and Malloi, because he had ascertained that they were the most numerous and warlike of all the Indian tribes in those parts. The news had reached him that they were chalking out their plans and making their preparations for battle with the Macedonians. He advanced against them. He reached the junction of the Hydaspes and Akesines.[157]

The accounts of the historians of Alexander bear testimony to the fact that the two republican communities, Oxydrakai[158] (Kṣudrakas), who occupied a part of the territory on the Hydaspes above its confluence with the Akesines, and the Malloi[159] (Mālavas), who were settled in the region situated between the lower Hydraotes and the Akesines extending up to the junction of the later with the Indus[160], sank their mutual differences and formed a confederacy to fight unitedly against their common enemy, Alexander. We know from Diodorus that "Before Alexander's coming they had been at feud with each other, but on his approach had settled their differences, and cemented an alliance by intermarriage, each nation taking and giving in exchange 10,000 of their young women for wives."[161] There are some variations in the accounts of Alexander's historians with regard to the combined strength of their forces. Their army, Curtius says consisted of 90,000 foot-soldiers, 10,000 cavalry, and 900 war chariots.[162] According to Diodorus, they had a force of 80,000 foot, 10,000 horse, and 700 chriots.[163] Justin says, they had an army of 80,000 foot, and 60,000 cavalry.[164] Their combined forces under the command of an experienced general elected or selected from the Oxydrakai community were almost ready for "war" against the Macedonians. But Alexander with his army suddenly fell upon the Malloi who were more superior to their neighbours (Oxydrakai) in fighting, to thwart their purpose and frustrate their plans.[165] They were prevented from giving each other mutual help. The Malloi alone had to bear the brunt of all attacks of the Macedonians.

Alexander invaded the territories of the Malloi, called by Arrian "a race of independent Indians." We are informed by him that at a distance of about 400 stadia from the river Akesines, Alexander arrived with his army before a city to which many of the Malloi had fled for refuge. He thus fell upon them unexpectedly, and slew most of them without their even turning to offer resistance, since they were unarmed. He came to another city of the Malloi into which many of the Indians of that district had fled for refuge. He made an assault upon the wall, many had been killed during the siege. The others were disabled for fighting by reason of their wounds. They fled into the citadel, which being seated on a commanding height and difficult of access, they continued to defend for some time. As the Macedonians vigorously pressed the attack at all points, the citadel was stormed, and all the men who had fled to it for refuge were put to the sword to the number of 2,000.[166] The place described here has been identified by Cunningham with Kot-Kamālia, "a small but ancient town situated on an isolated mound on the right or northern bank of the Hydraotes."[167] Perdikkas, Alexander's general, meanwhile reached the city from where the inhabitants had not long before fled from it. He followed them with troops. Some of the fugitives he overtook and killed.[168] This city has been identified by Cunningham with Harapa on the opposite bank of the Hydraotes, about sixteen miles to the east or south-east of Kot-Ka-Mālia.[169]

Alexander arrived at the river Hydraotes. There he learned that many of the Malloi had already crossed to the other bank, but he fell upon others who were in the act of crossing and slew many of them during the passage. He crossed the river and closely pursued the fugitives. Many of these he slew and he captured others, but most of them escaped to a nearby place of great natural strength which was also strongly fortified. Alexander's army attacked the stronghold, captured it at the first assault, and made slaves of all who had fled into it, except, of course, those who had fallen in the attack.[170] The fortified place mentioned here has been identified by Cunningham with Tulamba, situated on the left bank of the Rāvī at a distance of about 52 miles to the northeast of Multan (ancient Mulasthānapura).[171]

Alexander himself next led his army against a certain city of the Brachmans (Brāhmaṇas)[172] because he had learned that many of the Malloi had fled thither for refuge. On reaching there, all parts of the walls were undermined. The inhabitants fled to the citadel, and began to defend themselves from thence. They killed twenty-five of the Macedonians. Upon this Alexander ordered his men to apply the scaling ladders to the citadel on all its side, and to undermine its walls. Alexander was seen to be the first man to scale and lay hold of the wall. Upon seeing this, the rest of the Macedonians ascended the wall at various points, and quickly had the citadel in their hands. Some of the Indians set fire to their houses, in which they were caught and killed, but most part fell fighting. About 5,000 in all were killed, and, as they were men of spirit, a few only were taken prisoners.[173]

On the opposite bank of the Hydraotes, the Indian (Malloi) fought stoutly, being about 50,000 in number. As they were threatened at once with so many dangers, they fled to the strongest of all the cities that lay near their chief stronghold or capital, now called Multan. Alexander killed many of them in the pursuit, while those who escaped to the city were shut up within its walls.[174] Alexander himself with his army assaulted the wall of the city. Upon this the Malloi without waiting to receive the attack of the Macedonians, abandoned the walls and fled for refuge to the citadel. Alexander and his troops, therefore, burst open a small gate and entered the city. The Malloi were still in possession of the citadel, and many of them were drawn up in front of it to repel the attack. The Macedonians endeavoured to force their way into it, some by sapping the walls, and others by applying the scaling ladders wherever that was practicable. Alexander placed one of the ladders against the wall, and began to ascend. Alexander, while standing on the wall, was then assailed on every side from the adjacent towers, for none of the Indians had the courage to come near him. He was assailed also by men in the city, who threw darts at him from no great distance off. He then perceived that if he remained where he was he would be exposed to danger without being able to achieve anything noteworthy. He did not like to die ignobly, but after performing great deeds worthy of being remembered by the posterity. Having so resolved, he leaped down from the wall into the citadel. Then, supporting himself against the wall, he slew with his word some who assailed him at close quarters, and in particular the governor of the Indians, who had rushed upon him too boldly. The Indians standing around assailed him from all quarters with whatever missiles they carried.[175]

Those Macedonians who succeeded in reaching the top of the wall of the citadel of the city of the Malloi before the ladder broke, leaped down and began fighting in front of their king (Alexander). But there Abreas (one of the Macedonains) fell, pierced in the forehead by an arrow. Alexander himself was also struck by an arrow which pierced through his cuirass or corselet into his chest above the pap, causing wound along with the blood. He was severely wounded, but even while he was fainting from the loss of blood, he continued fighting till he slew the man by whom he had been wounded. He, however, was about to die or "very nearly lost his life".[176] Arrian clearly states that this accident befell Alexander among the Malloi, "an independent Indian nation"; that the city belonged to the Malloi' and that the man who wounded Alexander was a Malloi.[177] In the fight within the citadel, many soldiers and generals of Alexander were also wounded.[178] Alexander was mortally wounded within the citadel of the capital city of the Malloi in his war with them; he was about to lose his life; and he lost some of his distinguished military officers. These facts have been brought to light not only by Alexander himself,[179] by one of his companions,[180] and by his historians[181] but also by other classical writers.[182] Some Macedonian soldiers, being enraged after finding that Alexander was wounded, made their way into the citadel and began to kill the Indians, and in the massacre spared none, neither old men, women, nor children.[183] "It was the climax of Alexander's conquest of India", says J.F.C. Fuller.[184]

It was Critobulus who extracted arrow from the chest of Alexander and saved him.[185] Alexander's wound was healing. In due course of time, he fully recovered from his wound.[186] His army became joyful on seeing him after recovery.[187] The Macedonians, seeing the magnitude of the loss they suffered in their battles with the Malloi, and the insignificance of the gain, advised their king (Alexander) not to risk his life anymore but to return to Babylon.[188]

When Alexander was in his camp at the confluence of the Hydraotes and the Akesines, "envoys came to him from the Malloi who still survived, tendering the submission of the nation; and from the Oxydrakai came the leading men of their cities and their provincial governors, besides 150 of their most eminent men, entrusted with full powers to conclude a treaty. They brought with them those presents which the Indians consider the choicest, and, like the Malloi, tendered the submission of their nation. Their error in so long delaying to send an embassy was, they said, pardonable, for they were attached more than others to freedom and autonomy, and their freedom they had preserved intact from the time. Dionysos came to India until Alexander's arrival. They sent 1,000 men, their best ("the flower of the nation") and tallest as hostages to Alexander together with 500 chariots and their charioteers though these were not demanded. The hostages he sent back, but he kept the chariots. Alexander appointed Philippos as satrap (ruler) over that nation and over the Malloi who still survived."[189] After the Oxydrakai and the Malloi fell apart, their confederacy dissolved.

Subjugation of the Abastanoi, Xathroi, and Ossadioi

Alexander, after the submission of the Oxydrakai and the Malloi to him, sailed down the Hydraotes and Akesines to the Indus. Arrian informs us that "There at the confluence of the Akesines and the Indus Alexander waited until the general Perdikkas arrived with his forces. This general, in the course of his march, had subjugated a number of independent Indian tribes, including the Abastanoi, the Xathroi and Ossadioi.[190]

We learn from Curtius[191] and Diodorus[192] that the Abastanoi were very powerful and brave warriors. They had a democratic form of government. Their army consisted of 60,000 foot-soldiers, 6,000 cavalry and 500 chariots. They had elected three generals renowned for their valour and military skill. Alexander with his army invaded their dominions. But being afraid of battle with invincible warriors – the Macedonians – they could not face them. They followed the advice of their elders not to fight with them, and therefore sent on an embassy consisting of fifty of their foremost citizens to surrender their "whole nation" to Alexander.

We are told by Arrian that Alexander had received the submission of also the Xathroi; and that from the Ossadioi also came envoys offering the submission of their nation. Alexander then fixed the confluence of the Akesines and Indus as the boundary of the satrapy of Philip (generally called Philippos).[193]

SINDH

The historians of Alexander have transmitted brief but valuable accounts of his campaign in the valley of the Indus.

UPPER SINDH

Submission of Sogdoi, Sodrai and Massanoi

On reaching Sindh, Alexander first met the Sogdoi and then their two neighbours, Sodrai and Massanoi. These three people were settled on the banks of the Indus. They had little inclination for fighting with the Macedonians. And thus they also submitted to Alexander.[194]

Submission, Revolt, and Execution of Mousikanus–Campaign against Oxykanus (or Portikanus) – Conquest of their kingdoms

After the submission of Sogdoi, Sodrai and Massanoi, Alexander reached the dominions of Mousikanus in Upper Sindh.[195] That sovereign met him and offered to surrender both his kingdom and himself. Alexander, therefore, granted him a full pardon on account of his submission and penitence, expressed much admiration of his capital and his realm, and confirmed him in his sovereignty. Krateros was then ordered to fortify the citadel which protected the capital. A. Garrison was placed in the fortress, which he thought suitable for keeping the surrounding tribes in subjection. On hearing the news that Mousikanus, being instigated by the Brachmans (Brāhmaṇas), revolted against the Macedonians, Alexander despatched Peithon against him with force, while he marched himself against the cities which had been placed under the rule of Mousikanus. Some of these he razed to the ground after reducing the inhabitants to slavery; into others he introduced garrisons and fortified their citadels. Mousikanus, was captured by Peithon and executed (or crucified) by Alexander's orders.[196]

Alexander next invaded the territories under the sway of the king called Oxykanus by Arrian, Portikanus by Curtius, Diodorus and Strabo, and Pekanus by Julius Valerius.[197] At the first assault Alexander with the help of his army took by storm the two largest cities under the rule of that king, in the second of which the king with a few others offered resistance and entered into a battle with the Macedonians, but was defeated, taken prisoner, and slain. The other cities subject to his sceptre or rule surrendered without attempting resistance, or were captured and razed to the ground. The territories of that king passed under the sway of Alexander.[198]

Middle Sindh

Campaign against Sambos, and conquest of his principality

The prince Sambus or Sambos (Śambhū) was the ruler of the mountainous region west of the Indus, having Sindimana or Sindomana, for the capital.[199] Alexander marched into the territories of that prince, where he, according to Klitarchus (one of Alexander's companions), destroyed most of his cities, put upwards of 80,000 Indians to the sword, and sold numerous prisoners as slaves. And the rest sued for mercy. Alexander punished the most guilty and acquitted the innocents. Sambus escaped the danger with which he was menaced by taking flight from his capital city with thirty elephants into the country west of the Indus.[200] Curtius in particular says that "The prince Sambus had but lately surrendered himself to Alexander."[201] The principality of Sambus was conquered by Alexander.

Uprising of the Brachmans

The Brachmans (Brāhmaṇas), called both philosophers and gymnosophists by the historians of Alexander, not only themselves raised the banner of revolt against the Macedonians but instigated others also to rise against them. Plutarch records that "The philosophers gave him (Alexander) no less trouble than the other Indians, because they reviled the princes who declared for him (Alexander), and encouraged the free states to revolt from his authority. On this account he (Alexander) hanged many of them."[202]

Arrian tells us that Mousikanus (a sovereign whose dominions lay in Upper Sindh) had revolted against the Macedonians after being instigated by the Brachmans. But he was taken prisoner by Peithon, and executed. Mousikanus, he says, was hanged in his own country together with all those Brachmans who had instigated him to revolt.[203]

The Brachmans also instigated Sambos against Alexander to fight, but that prince fled from his capital and did not offer any resistance to him. In this regard, we are informed by Plutarch that "He (Alexander) captured ten of the Indian gymnosophists who had been principally concerned in persuading Sabbas (Sambos) to revolt and had done much harm otherwise to the Macedonians." One of the captured Brāhmaṇas, according to him, was asked by Alexander, "For what reason he induced Sabbas to revolt?" He answered, "Because I wished him to live with honour or die with honour." Alex put some of them to death, but how many, is not recorded by this author.[204] Diodorus also informs us that "The nation (people) called the Brāhmaṇoi were involved in like calamities. In the kingdom of Sambos thousands of the Indian were put to sword, including the Brāhmaṇoi."[205]

We learn from the historians of Alexander that he sailed down the river Indus to a city that lay at the very extremity of the kingdom of Sambus.[206] The people of the city refused to obey Alexander, and had even closed their gates against him. Alexander in person with his troops entered into a fight with them. The fighting was there with the result that out of the 3,000 Indians, mostly the Brāhmaṇas, who were in the action (or took the arms), 600 were killed, 1000 taken prisoners, and the rest driven back into the city. But this victory did not end so happily, for the Brachmans had used poisoned swords. The poison quickly spread to the vital parts of the body through the bloods of the affected parts, and caused a death of fearful agony. Those who had been severely wounded soon afterwards died. With this deadly weapon the Brachmans killed great numbers of the enemy (Macedonians). Ptolemy (Alexander's companion and general) was dangerously wounded by a poisoned sword, but recovered soon. The Indians had been in hopes that Alexander might be in this way cut off, but it was only by sheer good luck that he escaped untouched. Alexander then laid siege to the capital city of the Brāhmaṇas called Harmatelia. The Brāhmaṇas finding themselves disappointed of their hopes, surrendered themselves and their city.[207]

Arrian expressly states that "Alexander captured a city of the Brachmans, which had at this time revolted, and he put to death all those Brachmans who had instigated the revolt."[208] The city itself was called Brāhmaṇa, which, according to Cunningham, is identical with Brāhmaṇabad, whose ruins are situated near an old bed of the Indus at a distance of 47 miles to the northeast of Haidarabad.[209]

Alexander could only overpower the opposition instigated by the Brāhmaṇas by means of their wholesale massacres and executions.

Lower Sindh

Surrender of the Ruler of Patala

Patala, a republican city-state, was situated at the apex of the Indus Delta.[210] Its inhabitants are called the Patalians. Alexander sailed down to the mouth of the Indus and reached Patala. There, Arrian says, came to him the ruler (one of the two chiefs) of that state and surrendered himself and his whole realm. Alexander sent him back to his government.[211] Curtius informs us that one of the chiefs of Patala was Moeres, but he had abandoned the town and fled for safety to the mountains. Alexander then took possession of the place, and ravaged the surrounding country.[212] Strabo states that in Sindh last of all Alexander reduced Patalene which contained a city, Patala.[213]

We are told by Arrian that Alexander instructed Peithon to put colonists into the cities, which had just been fortified, to suppress any insurrection which the Indians might attempt, to introduce settled order among them, and then to join him at Patala.[214]

We learn from Justin that near the mouth of the Indus Alexander fixed the frontiers of his empire; that he also erected altars there; and that on departing left one governor of the maritime Indians.[215]

The author of the *Periplus* (sec. 41) tells us that in the regions adjoining the Indus mouths there were preserved even to his very day (the first century) memorials of the expedition of Alexander.

West of the Lower Indus, and Gedrosia (Baluchistan)

The Fleeing of the Arbitai to escape their subduing –Resistance and Surrender of the Gedrosians and Oritians

Alexander set out from Patala and advanced with his army to the river Arbaios (now called Purali) near which were settled an independent Indian tribe called both Arbitai and Arabitai. Their territories extended from the western mouth of the Indus to the river Purali. They fled into the neighbouring desert of Gedrosia when they learned that Alexander was marching against them to subdue them. Thereafter, Alexander reduced the whole of their territory to submission. He, after crossing the Arabios, entered the dominions of the Oritae or Oreitai, called also Oritians, another independent Indian tribe and the neighbours of the Arbitai. All who turned to offer resistance to him were cut off by the sword, and many were taken prisoners.[216] We are informed by Strabo that some of the Oritai entered into a fierce battle with the Macedonians. They attacked them with their poisoned arrows. Ptolemy was in the danger of losing his life from a wound inflicted by one of these arrows. Later, the Oritai surrendered to Alexander.[217]

Alexander next advanced towards Gedrosia. The combined forces of the Oreitai and the Gedrosoi (Gedrosians), "the free people," were lying encamped on the frontiers. They resolved to prevent Alexander and his troops from entering their territories. But when they were apprised of Alexander's approach, most of them deserted the posts they were guarding and fled from there. Then the leaders of the Oreitai came to Alexander to surrender themselves and their "nation." The Gedrosians also agreed to surrender to him and they surrendered voluntarily to him.[218]

Diodorus relates that "When Alexander was on the march through Gedrosia, some of the Oritai, having attacked the troops commanded by Leonnatos and slain a good many men (Macedonians), escaped scatheless into their own country."[219] But Arrian tells us that "In this part of the country, Leonnatos, who had been commissioned by Alexander to reduce the Oreitai and settle their affairs, defeated that people and their allies in a great battle, wherein all the leaders and 6,000 men were slain, the loss of Leonnatos being only 15 of his horse, besides a few foot-soldiers, and one man of note Apollophanes, the satrap (ruler) of the Gedrosians."[220]

Departure of Alexander from India for his native country

Alexander's "remarkable campaign lasted from April 327 BCE to October 325 BC when he started from Sindh on his march homeward through Gedrosia…", says James Douie.[221]

After his nineteen months of campaign in India (east of the Indus), Alexander departed from there for his native country in the beginning of October 325 BCE. He started his journey from Sindh, and then marching through Gedrosia arrived at its capital Poura (Bāmpur) early in January 324 BCE. In February 324 BCE, he had advanced into Karmania (western frontier) from where he reached Susa (in Persia) towards the end of April or in the beginning of May 324 BCE. From Susa he came to Babylon where he breathed his last in June 323 BCE.[222]

The Role of the People of North-West India in Anti-Alexander Resistance Movement

The role played by some of the tribes, princes, kings and rulers, and some others, including the Kṣatriyas and Brāhmaṇas, in anti-Alexander resistance movement in north-western part of the country need to be separately highlighted here. Not only the men but also the women offered their resistance to the Macedonians and fought against them.

The first Indian to revolt against Alexander was prince Astes (Hastī) of Puṣkalāvatī. In his fight against him and his army, he fell fighting. He lost not only his life but also his city.[223]

The tribes of the mountainous regions on the north-western frontier of India strongly resisted the attempt of Alexander to subdue them and conquer their territories. The two warlike tribes, the Aspasians of the Kunār valley and the Assakenians of the Swāt Valley (then in Afghanistan), fought against the Macedonians in a very organised way. More than forty thousand Aspasians took part in the resistance movement. They fought tooth and nail against Alexander and his troops. But all of them were taken prisoners. The Assakenians offered a stubborn resistance to them. A large number of people joined the movement, but a great many of them lost their lives.[224] The women fought side by side with the men in defending the city Massaga, the capital of the dominions of the Assakenians.[225] The people of several cities, like Bazira and Ora, also raised their voice against the Macedonian invader.

The battle Porus fought with Alexander and his troops on the opposite side of the Hydaspes was one of the great battles of Indian history. In that battle, Porus lost not only two of his sons, but also many soldiers and generals. More than twelve thousands of the Indians lost their lives in the battle of Hydaspes. The great Porus of the Panjab was the first Indian monarch to fight valiantly against a foreign invader. He fought till he was completely exhausted and severely wounded. In consideration of his valour and courage, Alexander restored his kingdom to him with accession of another extensive territory entrusting him with the authority to govern it.[226]

The younger Porus, the nephew of great Porus, revolted against Alexander but eventually surrendered to him. Some Indians beyond the Hydraotes also resisted Alexander and took the arms against him, but they were reduced to submission.[227]

The Adraistai also offered resistance to Alexander and entered into battle with him, but were conquered.[228]

The Kathaians (Kṣatriyas), and other independent Indian tribes in their neighbourhood, fought a great battle with Alexander and his army at Sangala city, and resisted till the last not to capture their city and territories. But they were defeated; a great many of them were killed; and lost their city which was their metropolis. Their bravery was a source of inspiration for other Indian in their fight against the Macedonians.[229]

The resistance of the Sibi or Siboi to Alexander was very feeble. They refused their submission but at last submitted to him.[230]

The resistance of the Indian people called Agalassians to Alexander, their battle with him, and their sacrifices will ever remain memorable. They stubbornly offered resistance to the Macedonians. They left no stone unturned to defend their towns. A large number of them were put to sword by the Macedonian soldiers. Having no way for their safety, some of them set fire to their houses and cast themselves along with their wives and children into the flames.[231]

The Malloi (Mālavas) fought battle after battle with Alexander and his army and struck blow after blow to them. At the same time, they also suffered a lot. Several thousands of the Malloi were put to sword in resisting their advance in their territories. About 50,000 of the Malloi said to have fought against the Macedonians stoutly. In one of the fiercest fighting with them in their capital city, they killed a number of Macedonian soldiers. They made Alexander wounded within the citadel of their capital. He was in the danger of losing his life. Alexander lost quite a good number of soldiers and some of his distinguished generals in his fight with the Malloi. The Malloi at last tendered their submission to Alexander.[232]

It may also be added here that the Malloi after being defeated by Alexander's army on the right bank of the lower Hydraotes fled to one of the towns or cities on the other side of the river for better security. This town or city belonged to the Brachmans (Brāhmaṇas) of the southern Panjab. Alexander and his troops hotly pursuing them reached the said city and besieged it. According to Arrian, about 5,000 Brachmans left the pen for the sword and defended their city to the last drop of their blood. They displayed exemplary courage but eventually fell or died fighting during the siege, and a few were taken prisoners or came alive into the enemy's hands. Some abandoned the city and fled to the castle, which being stormed they set fire to their houses and perished in the flames.[233] Curtius[234] and Diodorus[235] have also dealt with the subject, but the latter author specifically points out that there were 20,000 defenders of the city of whom, 3,000 only escaped by taking refuge in the citadel, where they capitulated on certain stipulated conditions. Cunningham affirms that "the ruined mound of Atari has a very good claim to be identified with the strong city of the Brāhmaṇas which made so stout a defence against Alexander."[236]

In almost all parts of the Panjab, the people took part in anti-Alexander resistance movement. In Sindh also, the people rose in open revolt against Alexander.

Mousikanus, the sovereign of Upper Sindh, revolted from the authority of Alexander, but was captured and executed by the orders of the latter.[237] The other sovereign of Upper Sindh Oxykanus with a few others offered resistance to and entered into a battle with the Macedonians, but was defeated, taken prisoner, and slain.[238]

The Brāhmaṇas, designated by the classical historians both as Brachmans and as Brachmanoi, and located by them in middle Sindh, played the most effective role in anti-Alexander resistance movement. They not only themselves raised the banner of revolt against Alexander but persuaded others also to rise against him. They kindled the spark of patriotism in the hearts of the populace and potentates of Sindh. They inspired them to fight unitedly against the Macedonian invader, to expel the Macedonians from their dominions, to throw off the ignominy of foreign thraldom, and lead free life. From Arrian's account of the subject they appear to have possessed separate villages and towns as early as the time of Alexander; to have already assumed the military character on occasions and to have defended themselves with great valour.[239] "Their military traditions continued up to the time of Alexander whose invasion they resisted with patriotic heroism", says V.S. Agrawala.[240] Their perfect sense of independence, warlike character, patriotic feelings, and loyalty to the nation in Alexander's time are indeed remarkable. Chinnock, on the authority of Arrian, states that the Brāhmaṇas were very influential in Sindh. They were "the main agents in bringing about an uprising of the people against the Macedonian invader."[241] M. Elphinstone observes that the Brāhmaṇas "defended themselves with that fury and desperation which sometimes still characterises Hindus."[242]

The entire responsibility for political awakening of the people of the Indus valley to shake off the yoke of servitude of Macedonians from their necks was heaped on the Brāhmaṇas by Alexander himself. "These philosophers", says Plutarch, "were specially marked down for revenge by Alexander as they gave him no less trouble than the others. They reviled those who did not take up the arms against Alexander, and encouraged the free states to revolt from his authority. On this account Alexander hanged many of them."[243]

Mousikanus, the sovereign of Upper Sindh, first submitted to Alexander but after being instigated by the Brachmans revolted against him. Mousikanus was hanged in his own "country" together with all those Brachmans who had instigated him to revolt.[244]

The Brachmans also persuaded the prince Sambos of middle Sindh to revolt against Alexander. In the course of Alexander's operations against Sambos, a large number of Brachmans were killed near Sindomana.[245] Alexander seized some of the Brachmans whom he suspected of having instigated Sambos to raise his voice against him. We learn from Arrian that Alexander wreaked his vengeance by putting to death "as many of the Brachmans as fell into his hands, having eharged them with being the authors of the rebellion."[246] This goes well in accord with the statement of Diodorus: "Alexander was satisfied with punishing those who advised the resistance and pardoned all others."

Plutarch tells us that Alexander captured ten of the revolutionary Brāhmaṇas who were principally involved in persuading Sambos to revolt and put some of them to death.[247] In the kingdom of Sambos, thousands of the Indians, including the Brāhmaṇas, were put to sword.[248] Alexander resorted to wholesale massacres and executions of the Brāhmaṇas who played the role of rebels. In fact, they were both instigators and fighters.

In a fight with 3,000 Indians in a city of the Brāhmaṇas at the very extremity of the kingdom of Sambos, Alexander and his troops killed six hundred, mostly the Brāhmaṇas. The Brāhmaṇas also killed great numbers of the enemy (Macedonians) and wounded many of them by using poisoned swords. But lastly they surrendered themselves and their capital city to Alexander.[249] Arrian expressly states that "Alexander captured a city of the Brachmans which had at this time revolted, and he put to death all those Brachmans who had instigated others to revolt."[250]

The Brāhmaṇas appear to have incited the kings and the people of the whole Indus valley to rise in open revolt against Alexander. They offered stoutest resistance to the foreign invader.

Arrian, while assessing the role of the Brāhmaṇas in anti-Alexander resistance movement, unequivocally states that "these philosophers were the leaders of the patriotic movement in lower Sindh. They were hanged on a gibbet by Alexander, whose task was becoming more and more ardous on account of the patriotic movement inspired by them."[251]

The Brāhmaṇic opposition to a foreign invader in Sindh in the fourth century before the Christian era has its own importance in the political history of ancient India. "The Europeans in the country along the Indus had more implacable enemies than the native princes. The power behind the throne was the Brāhmaṇ community, and here for the first time we come upon an opposition inspired by the conception of a national religion, the only germ to be found in ancient times of the idea of Indian nationality. It was the philosophers (Brāhmaṇas) who denounced the princes, if they submitted to the foreigner, and goaded the free tribes into revolt", observes E.R. Bevan.[252]

"The suppression of Brāhmaṇical opposition could not have been an easy task for Alexander since the Brāhmaṇs were not only respected throughout the land, but they were themselves… 'men of spirit'. The taking up of arms by the meek Brāhmaṇs must not be regarded as a strange phenomenon or a mere figment of Greek imagination… The country was menaced with a calamity during the Macedonian avalanche, and so the Brāhmaṇs valiantly rose to defend their honour and their hearth and home," says R.S. Tripathi.[253]

The Brāhmaṇas of the Indus valley laid down their lives in defence of freedom, religion and culture, and by their heroic deeds and supreme sacrifices presented one of the earliest examples of patriotism.[254]

One of the independent Indian tribes, Oritai or Oreitai, settled within the territorial limits of Baluchistan, called by Alexander's historians Gedrosia, stubbornly resisted the advance of the Alexander in their dominions. But many of them were put to sword by Alexander's army.

Some of the Oritai entered into a fierce battle with the Macedonians and wounded some of them.[255] When Alexander was on the march through Gedrosia, some of the Oritai attacked the Macedonian troops and slew a good many of them.[256] But they and their allies were defeated by Leonnatos, the commander of Macedonian troops, in a great battle. Their all the leaders and 6,000 men were slain.[257]

The mutual jealousies and hostilities of the Indian rulers, their disunity, and their enmity with the neighbouring autonomous or independent tribes did not enable them to stand together and fight unitedly against the Macedonain invader, Alexander, as a result of which he succeeded in conquering the greater part of northwest India. Had the people of northwest India offered their resistance unitedly to him, the star of his fortune would have changed, and the history of India of his time would have become different. "A disunited people could not long resist the united forces of the Hellenic world led by the greatest captain of ancient Europe."[258]

Results of Alexander's Invasion of India

Alexander's invasion of India proved to be a boon for the country from the commercial, political, historical and cultural points of view to a considerable degree.

It was Alexander who removed the barrier between East and West and thereby paved the way for the establishment of trade contacts between the two. A new era in the history of commercial intercourse between the two began. J. B. Bury also opines that "Alexander began to carry out schemes which he had formed for breaking down the barrier which divides the East from the West."[259]

We learn from Arrian that "on his return to Patala, Alexander ordered his general Hephaistion to prepare what was required for the fortification of the harbour, and the construction of a dockyard, for here at the city of Patala, which stands where the river Indus bifurcates, he meant to live behind him a very considerable navals squadron."[260] The harbour and dockyard at Patala facilitated the trading activities. Justin tells us that as a monument of his achievements, Alexander founded at the mouth of the river Indus the city of Barce.[261] Both Patala and Barce (Barbarei of Ptolemy, *Geog*., VII,I, 59, and Barbarike of the author of the *Periplus*) were ports on the principal mouth of the Indus. They became emporiums of the trade especially in the first century of the Christian era. The latter also served the purpose of an entrepot. These two ports became helpful in promoting the ancient commerce of the East with the West.

"Patala", M.L.W. Laistner says, "was designed by Alexander to become a far-eastern counterpart of Alexandria (a seat of commerce) in Egypt."[262] W.W. Tarn also observes that "At Patala Alexander began to build a great harbour and dockyard to secure sea connection with the west."[263]

Alexander discovered a new world. He despatched a naval expedition under Nearchus from the mouth of the Indus up the Persian Gulf to the mouth of the Euphrates.[264] Nearchus set out on his voyage on September 21, 325 BCE and completed it in February 324 BCE. His voyage opened up a new line of communication by sea. This sea-route was used for India's commerce with the western world. The voyage of Nearchus was, no doubt, a discovery of new sea-route.[265] "Alexander's primary object seems to have been to develop for commercial purposes a direct searoute from the estuary of the Indus to the Euphrates," observes Laistner.[266]

Arrian informs us that "Alexander ordered a city to be founded there at the confluence of the Akesines and Indus; and that he ordered also the construction of dockyards."[267] We are further informed by him that "Alexander, near the capital of the Sogdoi (who were settled on the banks of the Indus), founded a city and fortified it, and constructed other dockyards".[268] These dockyards were used for trade purpose.

Alexander's invasion promoted the political unification of the country. At the time of Alexander's invasion, some of the Indian tribes as well as kings were at war with each other. After Alexander's invasion, they realised their mistakes and felt the necessity of maintaining unity. In the words of H.C. Ray Chaudhri, "Alexander's invasion produced one indirect result. It helped the cause of Indian unity by destroying the power of the petty states of north-west India, just as the Danish invasion contributed to the union of England under Wessex by destroying the independence of Northumbria and Mercia."[269]

The most significant outcome of Alexander's invasion of India was the discovery of its geography and history. Alexander was accompanied on his Indian expedition by some learned men, including Nearchus, Onesikritus, Aristoboulus, Kleitarchus, Kallisthenes, and Ptolemy. These six presented eye-witness accounts of the geographical boundary of India, and of the history and culture of the people of north-western part of the country in their respective works, which were later utilised by Alexander's historians, Arrian, Curtius, Diodorus, Justin and Plutarch, and some other classical writers, notably, Strabo in their writings on India. The companions and historians of Alexander discovered many such facts relating to India which are not recorded elsewhere. They no doubt made great contributions to the enrichment of our knowledge of the geography and history of India. In absence of their writings on our country, there would have been several vacuums in our knowledge of especially the ancient history and civilization of northwest India. It may also be pointed out here that had Alexander not invaded India there would have been no writings either by his companions or by his historians either about his invasion of India or about history and culture of northwest India. And as such, Indian history would have been barren of the chapters which are found today on these topics.

The Greeks first became acquainted with the Indians after the discovery of India by Alexander the Great. It was the Macedonian invasion which brought India to the full view of the Greek world. The Greeks possessed but very limited knowledge of India before its invasion by Alexander. Alexander had with him a number of Greeks who recorded their impressions of India. Alexander's invasion brought a vast increase in the knowledge of the Europeans about India.

"The only permanent result of Alexander's campaign was that it opened up communication between Greece and India and paved the way for a more intimate intercourse between the two," says B.C. Sinha.[270]

One of the important results of Alexander's invasion was the cultural interaction between the Greeks and the Indians. In every town or city founded by Alexander, the Indians and Macedonians inhabited together for some time and learned from each other about their art, culture and philosophy. We know from Diodorus that Alexander founded near the river Indus the city of Alexandreia in which he planted a colony of 10,000 men.[271] Alexander established Greek colonies in all the towns or cities founded by him in India. "They became centres of Greek culture and of inter-communication between India and Greece."[272]

"Alexander", H.G. Rawlinson says, "had shattered for ever the barrier between East and West. The two great civilization were engaged in mutually borrowing ideas and principles which had been separately evolved by either."[273]

"Alexander in pursuance of his usual policy sought to secure the permanence of his Indian conquests by founding cities. Commerce was promoted, wealth increased, and the administration of justice improved," observes J.W. McCrindle.[274]

Laistner says, "The effect of Alexander's conquest was to change the world. It made possible the spread of Hellenism (a new culture compounded of Greek and oriental elements, an extension of Greek culture to orientals, or the continuation of the pure line of the older Greek civilization) in all its aspects over Asia. Greek ideas and customs were diffused far and wide during the following centuries."[275] He tells us further that Alexander's policy was to fuse East and West.[276]

"The Indian expedition of Alexander the Great in BC 327-326 was, so far as our knowledge extends, the first occasion of close conscious contact between East and West," V.A. Smith[277] says. But his statements, that "India remained unchanged; that India was not Hellenized' and that she continued to live the life of splendid isolation, and soon forgot the passing of the Macedonian storm,"[278] can fairly be disputed.

Alexander's Indian expedition, says one of his historians, Plutarch, was a "civilizing mission". Alexander promoted the contact between East and West; united all mankind, and changed their very ways of life; and paved the way for a synthesis of the cultural elements of the Indians and the Greeks, he says.[279]

Notes and References

1. *Bib. Hist.*, XVII, 105. In the third book of *The Romance History of Alexander the Great* by an anonymous author, he is represented to have entered India after overcoming the reluctance of his army to encounter toils and dangers anew after the conquest of Persia. See *Bio. Alex.*, Bk. III.
2. *Hist.* Phil., XII, 7, In *The Sikandar Nama E Bara* (on Alexander the Great, relating to his adventures and conquest, by Shaikh Nizami, trans. from the Persian Manuscript into English by H.W. Clarke, Canto XLV, pp. 562-64 also it is stated that "Sikandar (Alexander) wished for the conquest of Hindustan. And, hence, he marched to that country."
3. *Vit. Alex.*, (*Lif. Alex.*), Ch. LXVI.
4. See Arrian, *Anab.*, IV, 22; Arrian's *Anab.* Tr. by E.I. Robson under the title *History of Alexander,* Vol.I, p. 413; Strabo,*Geog.* XV, I, 26; Hamilton and Falconer's tr. *The Geography of Strabo,* Vol. III, pp. 88-9.
5. Arrian, *Anab.*, V, 1 and 2; Arrian's *Anab.* tr. by E.J. Chinnock, pp. 244-47; Curtius, *Hist. Alex.*, VIII, 10; Justin, *Hist. Phil.*, XII, 7; Plutarch, *Vit. Alex.* (Lif. Alex.), Ch. LVIII.
6. IP, p. 456.
7. *Geog.*, XV, I, 27; also Hamilton and Falconer's tr. *The Geography of Strabo,* Vol. III, p. 90; AICL, p. 33, note 1.
8. *Anab.*, IV, 22; see also IIA, Biog. Appen., p. 381.

9. Cf. Strabo, *Geog.*, XV, I, 17; Hamilton and Falconer's tr. *The Geography of Strabo*, Vol. III, pp. 82-83. Pāṇini designates the Aspasiol as Āśvāyana (*Sūtra*, IV.1.110) and the Assakenoi as Āśvakāyana (*Nadadi gana*, IV.1.99). These tribes were cavaliers.
10. Arrian, *Anab.*, IV, 23-24; Robson, *Op.cit.*, p. 417; Chinnock, *Op.cit.*, pp. 228-31; Curtius, *Hist. Alex.*, VIII, 10; Julius Valerius, *Itin. Alex.*, secs. 104 and 105; Plutarch, *Moralia*, De Alexandri Fortuna, 327, 2. Arigaion, situated to the east of the Khoaspes, is perhaps now represented by Naoghi, a village in the province of Bajore. See IIA, p. 64, note 1.
11. Arrian, *Anab.*, IV, 23.
12. *Ibid.*, IV, 25.
13. *Anab.*, IV, 25.
14. *Hist. Alex.*, VIII, 10.
15. *Itin. Alex.*, sec. 106.
16. Arrian, *Anab.*, IV, 25; Robson, *Op. cit.*, p. 427; Chinnock, *Op. cit.*, p. 232; Julius Valerius, *Itin. Alex.*, sec.106; see also IIA, Note C, pp. 333-34.
17. The celebrated city Massaga is called by the classic authors variously Massaka, Mazaga and Masoga. Its Sanskrit name is Maśakāvatī. At the time of Alexander's invasion, it was situated on or near the river Swāt. It is now represented by a ruined site called Mashanagar at a distance of twenty-four miles from Bajaur. For details of this city see AICL, p. 33, note 2; IIA, Note D, pp. 334-35; Aurel Stein, *On Alexander's Track to the Indus*, p. 44; Thomas Holdich, *The Gates of India Being an Historical Narrative,* p. 105. Tucci *(East and West*, new series, XIV, 1-2, p. 27) holds that Massage of the classical literature was somewhere near Chakdarra in the Swāt region.
18. See Arrian, *Anab.*, IV, 26; Cirtius, *Hist. Alex.*, VIII, 10; Strabo, *Geog.*, XV, I, 27; Hamilton and Falconer's tr. *The Geography of Strabo*, Vol.III, p. 90; Arrian *Indika*, Pt.I, Ch-1; Julius Valerius, *Itin. Alex.*, sec.106.
19. *Anab.*, IV, 26; Robson, *Op. cit.*, pp. 427-28; Chinnock, *Op. cit.*, pp. 233-34; see also V.A. Smith, EHI, pp. 57-59; AICL, p. 151, note 8.
20. *Bib. Hist.*, XVII, 84.
21. *Vit. Alex.*, Ch. LIX.
22. *Anab.*, IV, 27; Robson, *Op. cit.*, pp. 427-28; Chinnock, *Op. cit.*, pp. 233-35.
23. *Itin. Alex.*, sec.106; see also AIMA, p. 180, fn.
24. AICL, p. 22, note 1; IIA, Biog. Appen. p. 381.
25. *Hist. Alex.*, VIII, 10.

26. *Anab.*, IV, 27.
27. *Hist. Phil.*, XII, 7. The Assertion of Arrian (*Anab.*, IV, 27) and Curtius (VIII, 10) that Cleophis was the mother of the sovereign Assakenus, is not tenable.
28. *Hist. Alex.*, VIII, 10.
29. See also J.T. Wheeler, "Greek and Roman India", rept. from his *The History of India from the Earliest Ages* (London, 1881), in *Ancient India* (Delhi, 1983), pp. 102-3.
30. *Hist. Phil.*, XII, 7.
31. *Anab.*, IV, 27; on Bazira see IIA, Note E, p. 335.
32. *Hist. Alex.*, VIII, 10.
33. Arrian, *Anab.*, IV, 27; Robson, *Op. cit.*, pp. 431-33; Chinnock, *Op. cit.*, pp. 235-37.
34. *Itin. Alex.*, sec.107. Aurel Stein identifies Bazira as the ancient stronghold marked by the ruins on Bir-Kot hill. Ora, he considers, lay farther up the Swāt valley, and identifies it with udegram, seven to eight miles north of Bir-Kot. See his *On Alexander's Track to the Indus,* pp. 46-48, 59-60. See also W.W. Tarn, *Alexander the Great*, Vol.I, p. 90; E.H. Bunbury, HAG, Vol.I, pp. 442-43; Holdich, *The Gates of India Being Historical Narrative*, p. 106.
35. Arrian, *Anab.*, IV, 28; Robson, *Op. cit.*, pp. 435-36; Chinnock, *Op. cit.*, pp. 237-38.
36. See IIA, p. 73, note 2; IIA, Note F, pp. 335-38; AICL, p. 152, note 3.
37. Arrian, *Anab.*, IV, 28; IIA, p. 72, note 4. For Assagetes see IIA, Biog. Appen. p. 381. The place Embolima lay opposite to Aṭak, called also Attak. See IIA, p. 72, note 5.
38. Arrian, *Anab.*, IV, 29-30; Curtius, *Hist. Alex.*, VIII, 11; Diodrus, *Bib. Hist.*, XVII, 85; Justin, *Hist. Phil.*, XII, 7; Julius Valerius, *Itin. Alex.*, sec. 108.
39. Arrian, *Anab.,* IV, 30. For Sisikottus see IIA, Biog. Appen., p. 410. For some time he was the chief of Gāndhāra. It was he who had informed Alexader that Āmbhi of Taxila was eager to meet him and to help him against his neighbour Porus with whom his relation was hostile.
40. Arrian, *Anab.*, IV, 30; Chinnock, *Op. cit.*, pp. 239-41. "Dyrta probably lay to the north of Mahāban, near the point where the Indus issues from the mountains." – IIA, p. 76, note 3.
41. Arrian, *Anab.*, V, 3.
42. *Geog.*, XV, I, 28.
43. *Vit. Alex.*, Ch. LIX. About Taxiles see also Plutarch's *The Parallel Lives*, ed. and tr. by B. Perrin, Vol.VII, p. 384.

44. Arrian, *Anab.*, V, 3 and 8; also Strabo, *Geog.*, XV, I, 28; Hamilton and Falconer's tr. *The Geography of Strabo*, Vol. III, pp. 90-91.
45. Arrian, *Anab.*, V, 8; Curtius, *Hist. Alex.*, VIII, 12; Strabo, *Geog.*, XV, I, 28; IIA, Biog. Appen, pp. 412-13; see also V.A. Smith, *The Oxford History of India,* revd. by H.G. Rawlinson, p. 49; A. Stein, *Archaeological Reconnaissance's in North-Western India and South-Eastern Iran*, p. 10.
46. *Hist. Alex.*, VIII, 12.
47. *Bib. Hist.*, XVII, 86. The Greek Omphis was first identified by S. Levi with Āmbhi. See JA, 1890, pp. 234-36.
48. *Hist. Alex.*, VIII, 12.
49. *Ibid.*
50. *Vit. Alex.*, Ch. LIX.
51. *Anab.*, V, 3.
52. *Hist. Alex.*, VIII, 12.
53. *Bib. Hist.,*XVII, 86.
54. *Hist. Alex.*, VIII, 12.
55. *Ibid.*
56. *Bib. Hist.*, XVII, 86.
57. *Anab.*, V, 8.
58. *Ibid.*, see also Chinnock, *Op. cit.*, pp. 258-59.
59. *Geog.*, XV, I, 17; Hamilton and Falconer's tr. *The Geography of Strabo,* Vol.III, pp. 82-83.
60. *Hist. Phil.*, XII, 8.
61. *Itin. Alex.*, Sec. 111.
62. Strabo, *Geog.*, XV, I, 29; Hamilton and Falconer's tr. *The Geography of Strabo*, Vol.III, pp. 91-92.
63. Arrian, *Anab.*, V, 9; Chinnock, *Op. cit.*, p. 260.
64. *Ibid.*, V, 10-13; Chinnock, *Op. Cit.*, pp. 261-62; Curtius, *Hist. Alex.*, VIII, 13; Plutarch, *Vit. Alex.*, Ch. LX; Polyaenus, *Strategemata,* IV, 3, 20-21; Sextus Julius Frontinus, *Strategematica*, I, IV, 9.
65. Anab., V, 14; Chinnock, *op. cit.*, p. 266.
66. *Ibid.*, V, 15; Chinnock, *op. cit.*, p. 267.
67. *Hist. Alex.*, VIII, 13.
68. *Bib. Hist.*, XVII, 87.
69. *Vit. Alex.*, Ch. LXII.

70. Arrian, *Anab.*, V, 16; Chinnock, *op. cit.*, pp. 267-68; Justin, *Hist. Phil.*, XII, 8.
71. Arrian, *Anab.*, V, 17-18; Chinnock, *op. cit.*, pp. 270-71; Curtius, *Hist. Alex.*, VIII, 13-14; also Strabo, *Geog.*, XV, I, 29.
72. Arrian, *Anab.*, V, 18; see also IIA, p. 107, note 2.
73. *Ibid*; Chinnock, *op. cit.*, p. 272; see also IIA, p. 108, note 1.
74. *Bib. Hist.*, XVII, 89.
75. See Arrian, *Anab.*, V, 18; Diodorus, *Bib. Hist.*, XVII, 88; Justin, *Hist. Phil.*, XII, 8; IIA, Note L, pp. 345-6; C. Pearson, "Alexander, Porus and the Panjab" *Ind. Akt.*, XXXIV, 1905, pp. 253ff. H.F. Tozer (*Hist. Anc. Geog.*, p. 138) opines that "In the neighbourhood of Hydaspes-probably near the modern city of Jelalpur-the famous battle was fought in which the Macedonian monarch defeated the powerful Indian prince Porus."
76. *Anab.*, V, 18.
77. *Vit. Alex.*, Ch. LX.
78. *Nat. Anim.*, VI, 37.
79. *Anab.*, V, 18.
80. *Ibid.*, V, 19. In the light of the facts stated above on the authority of Arrian, the statements of Strabo (*Geog.*, XV, I, 30; Hamilton and Falconer's tr. *The Geography of Strabo*, Vol.III, pp. 92-93), Plutarch (*Vit. Alex.*, Ch. LX; *On the Fortune of Alexander,* Oration I, 11), Justin (*Hist. Phil.*, XII, 8), and Julius Valerius (*Itin. Alex.*, sec. 111), that Porus was taken Prisoner by Alexander, and the former was led as a captive to the latter, can be disposed of. The statement of Aurel Stein, that Porus was forced to surrender (*The Site of Alexander's passage of the Hydaspes and the Battle with Porus*, reptd. from the *Geog. Jour.*, LXXX, 1, July 1932, p. 35), can also be dismissed as unworthy of credence. "The statement recorded in *The Romance History of Alexander the Great,* by an anonymous author, that Alexander was opposed by Porus, whom he slew in single combat (Bio, Alex., Bk. III), can outrightly be rejected.
81. See Arrian, *Anab.*, V, 19; Chinnock, *op. cit.*, pp. 274-75; Curtius, *Hist. Alex.*, VIII, 14; Plutarch, *Vit. Alex.*, Ch.LX; and *On the Fortune of Alexander*, Oration, I, 11.
82. *Vit. Alex.*, Ch. LX.
83. *Bib. Hist.*, XVII, 89.
84. *Hist. Phil.*, XII, 8.
85. *Itin. Alex.*, sec. 111.
86. *Vit. Alex.*, Ch. LX. It may be noted here that the number of cities conquered by Alexander has been exaggerated by his historians to magnify his exploits. See Bunbury, HAG, Vol.I, p. 453.

87. See Arrian, *Anab.*, V, 19; Curtius, *Hist. Alex.*, VIII, 14; Diodorus, *Bib. Hist.*, XVII, 89. Plutarch, *Vit. Alex.*, Ch. LXI; Justin, *Hist. Phil.*, XII, 8; IIA, Note R; Strabo, *Geog.*, XV, I, 29.
88. *Vit. Alex.*, Ch. LXII.
89. *Anab.,* V, 20.
90. *Geog.*, XV, I, 3.
91. *Anab.*, V, 20.
92. *Geog.*, XV, I, 28; Hamilton and Falconer's tr. *The Geography of Strabo*, Vol. III, pp. 90-91; see also AICL, p. 34, note 2; IIA, Biog. Appen. p. 375.
93. *Anab.*, V, 8.
94. Arrian, *Anab.*, V, 20; Chinnock, *op. cit.*, pp. 276-77; Curtius, *Hist. Alex.*, VIII, 12-14; Diodorus, *Bib. Hist.*, XVII, 87 and 90.
95. *Anab.*, V, 20.
96. *Ibid.*, V, 29.
97. *Hist. Alex.*, IX, 1.
98. *Ibid.*, X, 1.
99. Arrian, *Anab.*, V, 20.
100. Arrian, *Anab.*, V, 21; Diodorus, *Bib. Hist.*, XVII, 91.
101. *Ibid.*
102. *Anab.*, V, 22. The Adraistai appear to be the people called in the *Periplus*, the Aratrioi. They are identical with the Āraṭṭa of the *Mahābhārata.* Orosius (History, III, 19) calls them the Adrestae. Their capital Pimprama has not yet been identified with certainty. It was probably "eight leagues" distant from Lahore towards the south-east.
103. *Hist. Alex.*, IX, 1; see also IIA, p. 217, note 4.
104. *Bib. Hist.*, XVII, 91.
105. *Hist. Phil.*, XII, 8.
106. Arrian, *Anab.*, V, 22.
107. *Ibid.*, V, 24; Chinnock, *op. cit.*, pp. 279-82; see also Diodorus, *Bib. Hist.*, XVII, 91; Justin, *Hist. Phil.,* XII, 8; IIA, pp. 347-8.
108. *Hist. Alex.*, IX, 1.
109. See Arrian, *Anab.*, V, 24; Curtius, *Hist. Alex.*, IX, 1; Diodorus, *Bib. Hist.*, XVII, 91.
110. *Anab.*, VI, 2.
111. *Bib. Hist.*, XVII, 91 and 92.
112. *Geog.*, XV, I, 30.
113. *Hist. Alex.*, IX, 1.

114. *Bib. Hist.*, XVII, 91.

115. *Hist. Alex.*, IX, 1.

116. *Geog.*, XV, I, 30.

117. *Anab.*, VI, 2, 2; see also IIA, p. 133, note 2; IIA, Biog. Appen., p. 411.

118. *Bib. Hist.*, XVII, 91.

119. *Hist. Alex.,* IX, 1.

120. Alexander advanced to the river Hyphasis, according to Arrian (*Anab.,* V, 24), after defeating the Kathaians and razing their city Sangala to the ground, but, according to Curtius (*Hist. Alex.*, IX, 1), after the surrender of king Sopithes to him. The latter's view is preferable to that of the former.

121. Curtius, *Hist. Alex.*, IX, 1 and 2; Diodorus, *Bib. Hist.*, XVII, 93. He is called more correctly phegelas by Arrian. The name is Greek transliteration of the Indian name Bhagala. See M. Sylvain Levi, JA, 1890, p. 239.

122. *Hist. Alex.*, IX, 2.

123. *Bib. Hist.*, XVII, 93.

124. Curtius, *Hist. Alex.*, IX, 2; Diodorus, *Bib. Hist.*, XVII, 93.

125. *Vit. Alex.*, Ch.LXII. Plutarch is clearly in error in conducting Alexander as far as the Ganges. The author of the *Periplus* (sec. 47) made the same egregious blunder by stating that "Alexander penetrated to the Ganges."

126. *Hist. Phil.*, XII, 8.

127. See Arrian, *Anab.*, V, 25-28; Curtius, *Hist. Alex.*, IX, 2-3; Diodorus, *Bib. Hist.*, XVII, 94; Plutarch, *Vit. Alex.*, Ch. LXII; Justin, *Hist. Phil.*, XII, 8.

128. Plutarch, *Vit. Alex.*, Ch. LXII.

129. *Bib. Hist.*, XVIII, 6.

130. *Hist. Phil.*, XII, 8.

131. Cf. Strabo, *Geog.*, XV, I, 35.

132. *Indika*, Bk. I, Frag.I, in Diodorus, *Bib. Hist.*, II, 37 (An Epitome of Megasthenes).

133. *Indika*, pt.I, Ch. II.

134. *Ibid.*, pt. I, Ch. IV.

135. *Lausiac History,* III, 7.

136. *Pent. Ind.*, p. 16; see also *Ind. Ant.*, V, p. 87.

137. Arrian, *Anab.*, V, 29; Curtius, *Hist. Alex.*, IX, 3; Diodorus, *Bib. Hist.*, XVII, 95; Plutarch, *Vit. Alex.*, Ch. LXII; Justin, XII, 8; see also IIA, "Alexander's Altars on the Hyphasis," pp. 348-49.

138. *Lausiac Histories*, III, 7.
139. *Hist. Nat.*, VI, 21.
140. *Coll. Rer. Memo.*, 52, 6f.
141. *Hist. Nat.*, VI, 17.
142. *Geog.*, II, V, 5.
143. *Vit. Apoll.*, II, 43; Its trans. by Conybeare, *The Life of Apollonius of Tyana,* Vol. I, p. 229; also AICL, p. 193; Priaulx, *The Indian Travels of Apollonius of Tyana,* pp. 25-26; CAI, pp. 393-94; J. Charpentier, *The Indian Travels of Apollonius of Tyana,* p. 58.
144. *Anab.*, V, 29.
145. *Hist. Alex.*, IX, 3.
146. *Anab.*, Vi, 2.
147. Arrian, *Anab.*, V, 29. Arsakes was the ruler of a small kingdom called Urśā, the hill tracts between the upper Hydaspes and the Indus comprehending almost the whole of the present Hazara district, which adjoined the dominions of Abisares between the upper courses of the Hydaspes and the Akesines. See also IIA, p. 380.
148. They were the inhabitants of the Shorkot region in the Jhang district of the Panjab at some distance above the confluence of the Hydaspes and the Akesines. The ancient Sibipura, identified with modern Shorkot, was their capital. (*Ep. Ind.*, XVI, 1921, p. 16; also V.A. Smith, EHI, p. 97). Strabo (*Geog.*, XV, I, 33) says, "The Śivis inhabited a district between the Hydaspes and the Indus." "Their capital stood at a distance of about thirty miles from the Hydaspes above its confluence with the Akesines." – IIA, Note Ee, p. 366.
149. *Anab.*, VI, 5.
150. *Bib. Hist.*, XVII, 96.
151. *Hist. Phil.*, XII, 9.
152. St. Martin (*E'tude,* p. 115) says that the Agalassians were very close to the Siboi on the eastern side. See also IIA, Note Ff, "The Agalassians," p. 367.
153. *Bib. Hist.*, XVII, 96.
154. *Hist. Alex.*, IX, 4.
155. *Hist. Alex.*, IX, 4.
156. *Hist. Phil.*, XII, 9.
157. See Arrian, *Anab.*, VI, 4; Curtius, *Hist. Alex.*, I. IX, 4; Diodorus, *Bib. Hist.*, XVII, 98.

158. The Oxydrakai of Arrian and Strabo are called Sudracae by Curtius, Sydracae by Pliny, Syrakousai by Diodorus, and Sigambari by Justin.
159. The Malloi of Arrian, Strabo, Diodorus and Plutarch are called Malli by Curtius, and Ambri by Justin.
160. For location of the territories of both Oxydrakai and Malloi see Arrian, *Anab.*, VI, 4; Arrian, *Indika*, pt. I, Ch.4; AICL, p. 40, note 1; IIA, p. 350-51.
161. *Bib. Hist.*, XVII, 98.
162. *Hist. Alex.*, IX, 4.
163. *Bib. Hist.*, XVII, 98.
164. *Hist. Phil.*, XII, 9.
165. See Arrian, *Anab.*, VI, 11; and Curtius, *Hist. Alex.*, IX, 4.
166. *Anab.*, VI, 6.
167. CAGI, p. 175; see also E.H. Bunbury, HAG, Vol.I, Note Ss, p. 514.
168. Arrian, *Anab.*, VI, 6.
169. CAGI, p. 177.
170. Arrian, *Anab.*, VI, 7.
171. CAGI, pp. 189-91.
172. Cunningham (CAGI, pp. 192-93) identifies the Brachmans' city with the old ruined town and fort of Atari, twenty miles from Tulamba on the road to Multan, from where it is thirty-four miles distant. The remains consist of a strong citadel. On two of its sides are to be found the remains of the old town. Of its history there is not even a tradition, but it was definitely a place of considerable antiquity.
173. Arrian., *Anab.*, VI, 7.
174. *Ibid.*, VI, 8. For details of the capital of the Malloi see IIA, p. 145, note 1, and pp. 351-52, Note; CAGI, p. 200.
175. Arrian, *Anab.*, VI, 9; Curtius, *Hist. Alex.*, IX, 4; Diodorus, *Bib. Hist.*, XVII, 98; Plutarch, *Vit. Alex.*, Ch. LXIII; also Plutarch, *The Parallel Lives,* ed. and tr. by B. Perrin, Vol. VII, p. 384 ff; Justin, *Hist. Phil.*, XII, 9; Julius Valerius, *Itin. Alex.*, sec. 115.
176. Arrian, *Anab.*, VI, 10-12; Curtius, *Hist. Alex.*, IX, 5; Diodorus, *Bib. Hist.*, XVII, 98-99; Plutarch, *Vit. Alex.*, Ch. LXIII; also his *On the Fortune of Alexander*, Oration, I, 2; II, 9; II, 13; Justin, *Hist. Phil.*, XII, 9; Julius Valerius, *Itin. Alex.*, sec. 116. Plutarch in particular says that this was Alexander's eighth and most dangerous wound. The other seven he lists including an arrow wound in the shoulder among the Aspasians, and an arrow wound in the leg among the Gandridae. – *Moralia, De Alexandri Fortuna,* 327, 2.
177. *Anab.*, VI, 11; also Arrian's *Indika,* pt. II, Ch. XIX.

178. Curtius, *Hist. Alex.*, IX, 5.

179. See Plutarch, *On the Fortune of Alexander,* Oration, I, 2.

180. Aristoboulus, in Plutarch, *op. cit.*, Oration, II, 9.

181. Arrian, *Anab.*, VI, 10-12; Curtius, *Hist. Alex.*, IX, 5; Diodorus, *Bib. Hist.*, XVII, 99; Plutarch, *Vit. Alex.*, Ch. LXIII; Justin, *Hist. Phil.*, XII, 9.

182. Strabo, *Geog.*, XV, I, 33; also Hamilton and Falconer's tr. *The Geography of Strabo,* Vol.III, pp. 94-5; Julius Valerius, *Itin. Alex.*, sec.116; *Biog. Alex.*, III, IV. See also CAGI, p. 201.

183. Arrian, *Anab.*, VI, 11; Curtius, *Hist. Alex.*, IX, 5; Diodorus, *Bib. Hist.*, XVII, 99; Julius Valerius, *Itin. Alex.*, sec.116; see also T.A. Dodge, *History of Alexander and His Art of War,* Vol.II, pp. 602-5.

184. *The Generalship of Alexander the Great,* p. 263.

185. Curtius, *Hist. Alex.*, IX, 5.

186. *Ibid.*, IX, 6; Diodorus, *Bib. Hist.* XVII, 100.

187. Arrian, *Anab.*, VI, 13.

188. Julius Valerius, *Itin. Alex.*, sec. 117.

189. Arrian, *Anab.*, VI, 14; see also Curtius, *Hist. Alex.*, IX, 7-8. It may be noted here that the city from which the representatives of the Oxydrakai came to meet Alexander was no other than Uccha lying forty miles to the north-east of the confluence of the united streams of the Panjab and the Indus at Miṭhānkoṭ The city is chiefly distinguished by its ruins which are very extensive and attest the pristine prosperity of the locality. See St. Martin, *E'tude,* pp. 124-25.

190. *Anab.*, VI, 15. The Abastanoi (Greek transliteration of Sanskrit Ambaṣṭha), called Sabarcae by Curtius, Sambastai by Diodorus, and Sabagrae by Orosius, were settled on the lower Akesines. The modern Khatrīs of the Panjab are regarded as the descendants of the ancient Xathroi or Xathri. Ossadioi appears to be a close transcription of the Yaudheya, settled along the banks of the lower Satlej, but their location does not show that they are the same people mentioned in the classics. In the Ossadioi we have the Vasāti of the *Mahābhārata.*

191. *Hist. Alex.*, IX, 8.

192. *Bib. Hist.*, XVII, 102.

193. *Anab.*, VI, 15.

194. See Curtius, *Hist. Alex.*, IX, 8; Diodorus, *Bib. Hist.*, XVII, 102; The Sogdoi have been identified with the Sohda Rajputs who now occupy the south-east district of Sindh about Amarkot, but who in former times held large possessions on the banks of the Indus to the northward of a city called Alor. This city, according to St. Martin, was the Sogdian capital. Cunningham, however, places the capital about midway between Alor and Uccha, at a village which appears in old maps under the name

of Sirwahi, and which, he says, may possibly represent the Seori of Sindh history. They Sogdian capital was near Bhakar. About Sogdoi see IIA, Note R, p. 354; St. Martin, *E'tude*, pp. 150-61; CAGI, pp. 249-56. Sodrai of Diodorus is a closer transliteration of the Sūdras of Sanskrit literature. They represent the servile class or the lowest of the four cates. In Alexander's time, they were settled on the opposite bank of the Indus. See Lassen, *Ind. Alt.*, II, p. 174; St. Martin, *E'tude*, pp. 150-61. Cunningham (CAGI, p. 254) inclines to believe that the Massanoi of Diodorus are the Musarnoi of Ptolemy, whose name, he says, still exists in the district of Muzarka to the west of the Indus below Mithankot.

195. Mousikanus' dominions lay along the banks of the Indus. Alor, which was anciently and for many ages the metropolis of the rich and powerful kingdom of Upper Sindh, was the capital of that king. See also AICL, p. 41, note 2.

196. Arrian, *Anab.*, VI, 15 and 17; Chinnock, *op. cit.*, pp. 315-16 and 319; Curtius, *Hist. Alex.*, IX, 8; Diodorus, *Bib, Hist.*, XVII, 102; also Strabo, XV, I, 33; IIA, Biog. Appen., p. 395.

197. It is not easy to determine where the dominions of the said king lay. Cunningham places them to the west of the Indus in the "level country" around Larkhana (also called Larkana) which, though now close to the Indus, was in Alexander's time about forty miles distant from it. Their capital he identified with Mahorta, a place about ten miles north-west from Larkhana or Larkana, where there are remains of an ancient fortress on a huge mound. (CAGI, pp. 259-62). Lassen (*Ind. Alt.*, II, p. 177) and St. Martin (*E'tude*, p. 165) place the realm of that king to the east of the Indus. It may be added here that Curtius designates the people under the rule of Mousikanus Musicani, and calls the subject of Portikanus the Praesti.

198. Arrian, *Anab.*, VI, 16; Chinnock, *op. cit.*, pp. 317-18; Curtius, *Hist. Alex.*, IX, 8; Diodorus, *Bib. Hist.*, XVII, 102; also Strabo, *Geog.*, XV, I, 33; Julius Valerius, *Itin. Alex.*, sec. 112. For both Mousikanus and Oxykanus see also J. Rennell's MMH, pp. 129ff (based on M.D. Anville's account of Alexander's invasion of India given in his *Antiq. Geog*) and W. Vincent's CNAIO, Vol. I, *The Voyage of Nearchus from the Indus to the Euphrates,* pp. 122-23.

199. The said capital has been satisfactorily identified with Sehwan, which stands on a site of very high antiquity, past which now flows the Indus. In Alexander's time, however, the river pursued a course from which Sindomana lay at a considerable distance westward. See AICL, p. 40, note 2; IIA, Note S, pp. 354-5; also IIA, Biog. Appen., p. 404.

200. See Arrian, *Anab.*, VI, 16; Curtius, *Hist. Alex.*, IX, 8; Diodorus, *Bib. Hist.*, XVII, 102; Strabo, *Geog.*, XV, I, 33.

201. *Hist. Alex.*, IX, 8.
202. *Vit. Alex.*, Ch. LIX.
203. *Anab.*, VI, 17.
204. *Vit. Alex.*, Ch. LXIV. See also H.H. Wilson, *Ar. Ant.*, p. 205.
205. *Bib. Hist.*, XVII, 102.
206. He is called Ambigerus by Justin (*Hist. Phil.*, XII, 10). In Orosius (*Hist.* III, 19) the name is transcribed as Ambiraren.
207. For details see Curtius, *Hist. Alex.*, IX, 8; Diodorus, *Bib. Hist.*, XVII, 103; Justin, *Hist. phil.*, XII, 10. For identification of the city called Harmatelia by Diodorus see IIA, Note T, pp. 355-6; CAGI, pp, 226-27; Vincent, CNAIO, Vol.I, p. 136.
208. *Anab.*, VI, 16.
209. CAGI, pp. 225-32; see also JBBRAS, V, pp. 413-17.
210. For Patala city see IIA, Note U, pp. 356-7.
211. *Anab.*, VI, 17.
212. *Hist. Alex.*, IX, 8.
213. *Geog.*, XV, I, 33.
214. *Anab.*, VI, 17.
215. *Hist. Phil.*, XII, 10.
216. Arrian, *Anab.*, VI, 21; Chinnock, *op. cit.*, p. 324; Curtius, *Hist. Alex.*, IX, 10; Diodorus, *Bib. Hist.*, XVII, 104 and 105.
217. *Geog.*, XV, II, 7.
218. Arrian, *Anab.*, VI, 22; Curtius, *Hist. Alex.*, IX, 10; Diodorus, *Bib. Hist.*, XVII, 104.
219. *Bib. Hist.*, XVII, 105.
220. *Indika.*, pt. II, Ch. XXIII, J.B. Bury (*A History of Greece to the Death of Alexander the Great,* p. 813) states that the Macedonian conqueror subjugated the Oritae, a warlike people. A.H.L. Heeren (*Historical Researches,* Vol. I, *Asiatic Nations,* p. 297) also speaks of Alexander's conquest of Arabitae and Oritae, who were of Indian descent.
221. *The Panjab, North-West Frontier Province and Kashmir*, p. 161.
222. For details of Alexander's return journey from India to Babylon see Arrian, *Anab.*, VI, Chs. XXII – XXVIII; Curtius, *Hist. Alex.*, IX, Ch.X; Diodorus, *Bib. Hist.*, XVII, Ch. CV; Plutarch, *Vit. Alex.*, Chs. LXVI – LXVII; Justin, *Hist. Phil.*, XII, Ch. X; Strabo, *Geography,* XV, II, 4 and 7; AICL, p. 83 note 3; also IIA, pp. 357-58 (for Alexander's march through Gedrosia only).
223. Arrian, *Anab.*, IV, 22.

224. *Ibid.*, IV, 24-26; Curtius, *Hist. Alex.*, VIII, 10; Julius Valerius, *Itin. Alex.*, 105 and 106.

225. Diodorus, *Bib. Hist.*, XVII, 84.

226. For details see Arrian, *Anab.*, V, 9-19; Diodorus, *Bib. Hist.*, XVII, 87-89; Curtius, *Hist. Alex.*, VIII, 13-14; Plutarch, *Vit. Alex.*, Chs. LX and LXII; Justin, *Hist. Phil.*, XII, 8; Julius Valerius, *Itin. Alex.*, sec. 111.

227. Arrian, *Anab.*, V, 21; Diodorus, *Bib. Hist.*, XVII, 91.

228. *Ibid.*, V, 22; Diodorus, *op. cit.*, Curtius, *Hist. Alex.*, IX, 1; Justin, *Hist. Phil.*, XII, 8.

229. Arrian, *Anab.*, V, 22 and 24; Curtius, IX, 1; Diodorus, XVII, 91; Justin, XII, 8.

230. Arrian, *Anab.*, VI, 5; Diodorus, XVII, 96; Justin, XII, 9.

231. Diodorus, XVII, 96; Curtius, IX, 4; Justin, XII, 9.

232. Arrian, *Anab.*, VI, 6-12; Diodorus, XVII, 98-99; Curtius, IX, 4-8; Plutarch, Ch. LXIII; Justin, XII, 9; also Arrian, *Anab.*, VI, 14.

233. *Anab.*, VI, 6-7.

234. *Hist. Alex.*, IX, 4.

235. *Bib. Hist.*, XVII, 98.

236. CAGI, p. 193.

237. Arrian, *Anab.*, VI, 15 and 17; Curtius, IX, 8; Diodorus, XVII, 102.

238. Arrian, *Anab.*, VI, 16; Curtius, IX, 8; Diodorus, XVII, 102.

239. *Anab.*, VI, 7.

240. IP, p. 51.

241. See his trans. of Arrian's *Anab.*, p. 319.

242. "The Greek Accounts of India", rept. from his *The History of India* (London, 1911), in *Ancient India* (Delhi, 1983), p. 20.

243. *Lif. Alex.*, Ch. LIX.

244. Arrian, *Anab.* VI, 17.

245. *Ibid.*, VI, 16.

246. *Ibid.*

247. *Lif. Alex.*, Ch. LXIV

248. Diodorus, *Bib. Hist.*, XVII, 102.

249. *Ibid.*, XVII, 103; Curtius, *Hist. Alex.*, IX, 8; Justin, *Hist. Phil.*, XII, 10.

250. *Anab.*, *Anab.*, VI, 16.

251. *Ibid.*

252. "Alexander the Great", in CHI, Vol. I, p. 339.

253. HAI, p. 140.
254. For details see G.P. Singh, "The Role of the Brāhmaṇas in Anti-Alexander Movement in North-West India 326-325 BCE," SHC, 3, 1, 1995, pp. 1-7.
255. See Arrian, *Anab.*, Vi, 21; Curtius, IX, 10; Diodorus, XVII, 104-105; Strabo, XV, II, 7.
256. Diodorus, XVII, 105.
257. Arrian, *Indika.*, pt. II, Ch. XXIII.
258. H.C. Raychaudhuri, PHAI, p. 261.
259. *A History of Greece to the Death of Alexander the Great,* p. 815.
260. *Anab.*, VI, 20.
261. *Hist. Phil.*, XII., 10.
262. *A History of the Greek World from 479 to 323 BC*, p. 314.
263. *Alexander the Great*, Vol. I, p. 105.
264. See Arrian, *Anab.*, VI, 19; Curtius, IX, 10; Diodorus, XVII, 104.
265. See also W. Robertson, *An Historical Disquisition concerning Ancient India*, pp. 19 and 28-29; A.H.L. Heeren, MAHA, pp. 219-20.
266. *Op. cit.*, pp. 314-15.
267. *Anab.*, VI, 15.
268. *Ibid.*
269. PHAI, p. 263.
270. *Studies in Alexander's Campaigns,* p. 62.
271. *Bib. Hist.*, XVII, 102. The city, Diodorus speaks of, lay according to St. Martin (*E'tude*, pp. 150ff), in the vicinity of Alor or at Rori. See also IIA, Note R, p. 354.
272. F. Tola and C. Dragonetti, "India and Greece from Alexander to Augustus", in *Graeco-Indica*, ed. by U.P. Arora, p. 120. see also W.W. Hunter, "The Greeks in India", rept. from his *The Indian Empire* (London, 1882), in *Ancient India* (Delhi, 1983), p. 89.
273. *Bactria from the Earliest times to the Extinction of Bactrio-Greek rule in the Punjab,* pp. 140-141.
274. IIA, Introd. Pp.4-5.
275. *op. cit.*, p. 319.
276. *op. cit.*, pp. 321-22.
277. JASB, LVIII, I, 1889, p. 108.
278. EHI, p. 117; see also A.V. Williams Jackson (ed), *History of India*, Vol. II, *From the sixth century BC to the Mohammedan conquest including the invasion of Alexander the Great*, by V.A. Smith, p. 102.
279. "On the Fortune of Alexander", in his *Moralia,* 329 b-c.

Book Seven
Kings and Kingdoms

1

The Kingdom of Magadha from the Extinction of Nanda Rule to the Foundation of the Maurya Dynasty with Special Focus on the Rise of Candragupta and his Accession

The last Nanda monarch, his pedigree, and the contemporary events of his times, and the role of Candragupta in the liberation of India from the foreign rule, and his rise to power also received the notices of the classical authors.

The last king of the Nanda dynasty, Dhanananda, called Xandrames by Diodorus,[1] and less correctly Agrammes by Curtius,[2] was the son of Mahāpadma Nanda (of Śūdra origin),[3] the founder of the dynasty, which had succeeded to that of Śiśunāga. At the time of the invasion of India by Alexander the Great, Dhanananda was ruling over the great Gangetic kingdom of Magadha with its capital at Pāṭaliputra, called both Pālibothra and Pālimbothra[4] by the ancient Greek and Latin writers.

Alexander, while advancing towards the Hyphasis, met a chief named Phegeus,[5] whose territory adjoined that river, and obtained information from him about the country beyond it, as we learn from the two noted classical authors. He was told by that Chief that "Next came the Ganges, the largest river in all India, the farther bank of which was inhabited by two nations, the Gaṅgāridae and the Prasii,[6] whose king Agrammes kept the formidable force," as recorded by Curtius.[7] Diodorus puts it little differently but more correctly: "Beyond the river Ganges were situated the dominions of the nation of the Praisioi and the Gaṅgāridai, whose king Xandrames" had powerful force.[8] The description given by Phegeus of the Ganges beyond the Hyphasis which these two classical authors have preserved, distinctly shows that the kingdom of Magadha in the eastern Gangetic region of India was inhabited by the people called Prasii or Praisioi, and Gaṅgāridai, who combined together constituted "a united nation", and were under the rule of a single sovereign, the said Nanda king.

Alexander suspected the veracity of what he had heard from Phegeus, and he, therefore, asked his faithful ally, Porus, whether the account was true? He assured Alexander in reply that, "as far as the strength of the nation and kingdom was concerned, there was no exaggeration in the reports, but that the presents king (Dhanananda) was not merely a man originally of no distinction, but even of the very meanest condition. His father was in fact a barber, scarcely staving off hunger by his daily earnings, but who, from his being not uncomely in person, had gained the affections of the queen, and was by her influence advanced to too near a place in the confidence of the reigning monarch. Afterwards, however, he treacherously murdered his sovereign; and then, under the pretence of acting as guardian to the royal children, usurped the supreme authority, and having put the young princes to death begot the present king (Dhanananda) who was detested and held cheap by his subjects, as he rather took after his father than conducted himself as the occupant of a throne," as we are told by Curtius.[9]

We are also informed by Diodorus that Porus, while telling Alexander about Dhanananda and his antecedents, added that "the king of the Gaṅgāridae was a man of quite worthless character, and held in no respect, as he was thought to be the son of a barber. This man – the king's father – was of a comely person, and of him the queen had become deeply enamoured. The old king having been treacherously murdered by his wife, the succession had devolved on him who now reigned."[10] Plutarch tells us that "… the king (Dhanananda) was hated and despised by his subjects for the wickedness of his disposition and the meanness of his origion."[11]

Dhanananda was, no doubt, an unworthy ruler. He did not do anything substantial either to promote the welfare of his subjects or for the stability and prosperity of his kingdom. He levied heavy taxes on his subjects that made him very unpopular among them. They were fed up of his oppressive and tyrannical rule. He himself was rolling in luxury and leading a voluptuous life at the cost of their sufferings. He was an avaricious king, and hence amassed enormous wealth. He regularly exacted tributes from his subjects. The Nanda dynasty was tottering.

The year 326 BCE was not only a momentous epoch but also an eventful in the political history of ancient India. In that very year, a new power had arisen in India. Candragupta,[12] a promising young man of twenty-two (a flowering stage of his life), met Dhanananda at Pāṭaliputra, the seat of his government and advised him to rule his kingdom keeping in view the future of Magadha which was then the nucleus of power in northern India. They had heated exchanges. Candragputa was the Commander-in-Chief or general of the Nanda forces and as such he formed a plot in league with Cāṇakya to overthrow the last Nanda ruler, but his plot failed. Dhanananda saw in Candragupta a potential source of danger to him and thus banished him out of his capital. He soon afterwards fled from there for his safety.

We are told by Justin that "Sandrocottus (Candragputa) was born in humble life, but was prompted to aspire to royality by an omen significant of an august destiny. For when by his insolent behaviour he had offended Nandrum[13] (Dhanananda) and was ordered by that king to be put to death, he sought safety by a speedy flight." [14] Candragupta incurred the displeasure of the reigning king of Magadha, Dhanananda, a contemporary of Alexander the Great, also because of the boldness of his speech, and was forced to go into exile.

It was in February or March 326 BCE that Candragupta fled from the Magadhan capital pataliputra to Taxila (in the western Punjab) [15] where he remained in exile for eight years. It is Plutarch who informs us that "Androkottos (Candragupta) himself who was then but a youth saw Alexander himself and afterwards used to declare that Alexander could easily have taken possession of the whole country (the Gangetic Magadha kingdom then under the rule of the Nanda king) since the king was hated..."[16] The fact brought to light by Plutarch that Androkottos met Alexander (in 326 BCE) has a place in the classical discovery of India from a chronological point of view. In fact, Candragupta met Alexander at Taxila and persuaded or induced him to invade the kingdom of Magadha ruled by his powerful rival Dhanananda and dislodge him from power so as to enable him to establish his rule there. His persuasion to a foreign invader, who had crushed the liberty of his fellow-countrymen, to undertake an expedition against a kingdom which he himself was aspiring for, does not cast any aspersion on his lack of sense of patriotism. He actually wanted Magadha and its inhabitants to get rid of a worthless ruler.

After being swayed by the persuasion of Candragupta, Alexander made up his mind to attack Magadha. He collected the information from the said chief Phegeus regarding the strength of the army of the reigning monarch Dhanananda, the most powerful among the contemporary Indian sovereigns. He was told by him that the king of the Prasians kept in the field for guarding the approaches to his country 200,000 infantry, 20,000 cavalry, 2000 four-horsed chariots, and a troop of 3000 or 4000 elephants well-trained and equipped for war, the most formidable force of all.[17] These statements seemed to the Macedonian king to be incredible, and he therefore questioned Porus as to their accuracy. Porus assured him to the correctness of the information transmitted to him. It is Plutarch who expressly states that the king of the Gaṅgāridai and the Praisiai was waiting for Alexander with an army of 200,000 foot, 80,000 horse, 8000 war chariots, and 6000 fighting elephants. The farther (opposite) banks of the Ganges were covered all over with armed men, horses, and elephants. This was not an exaggeration, he himself says.[18] Justin says that Alexander's enemy (Dhanananda) awaited him with 200,000 cavalry.[19] This was the strength of his foot-soldiers and not of his cavalry.

We are informed by Arrian,[20] Curtius,[21] Diodorus,[22] Plutarch,[23] and Justin[24] that Alexander on reaching the Hyphasis (Sept. 326 BCE), asked his soldiers to move beyond it, and advance to the Ganges and cross it over to defeat the forces of Dhanananda and occupy his kingdom. He addressed the soldiers to animate or embolden them to do so, but they most resolutely opposed Alexander's proposals and refused to advance even beyond the Hyphasis. Alexander's troops refused to advance beyond the Hyphasis to the Ganges to cross it for fighting against the forces of Dhanananda' because they were war worn; the place was too far distant for them to reach; it was not possible for them to cross the Ganges; and they were scared for facing the forces of that Nanda king who were ready on the other side of the Ganges to fight them, as gleaned from the classical sources.

Alexander ultimately renounced his contemplated enterprise. His purpose of crossing the Ganges along with his army was thwarted. And his ambition of conquering the Gangetic Magadha kingdom then under the rule of Dhanananda and making it a part of his empire was not fulfilled.

Diodorus unequivocally states that Alexander did not undertake an expedition against the Gaṅgāridai (the inhabitants of the Gangetic Magadha), being deterred by the multitude of their elephants, the most formidable force of all, kept by their king.[25] Justin alone of all the historians of Alexander asserts that he conquered the Praesidae and the Gaṅgāridae after defeating their army.[26] This can be dismissed as unfounded and baseless. He made their remark perhaps to glorify his exploits.

The last Nanda Monarch (Dhanananda) continued to rule his kingdom till he was overthrown by Candragupta in concert with Cāṇakya.

I proceed now to describe the political events that took place in Alexandrian and post-Alexandrian times leading to a revolt or movement led by Sandrakottus for the liberation of the Punjab and Sindh from the Greek rule.

The departure of Alexander from India for his native country in the beginning of October 325 BCE left a political vacuum. He had left India placing it under the rule of Philip, who is called by Arrian "the satrap (governor) of the Indian country."[27] We are told by him that the confluence of the Akesines and the Indus was fixed by Alexander as the boundary of his satrapy.[28] Philip was ruling the Punjab with his capital at Taxila. Alexander, on his way to his native country, arrived at Poura (Bāmpur), the ancient Gedrosian capital early in January 324 BCE. When he was advancing into Karmania (western frontier of India) in February 324 BCE, he received the report that Philip, the satrap of India, had been treacherously assassinated (at Taxila) by the Greek mercenaries under his command. His murder was a blow to Greek rule in India. In fact, he was the "pillar of Greek imperialism in India." We are informed by Arrian that "On learning what had occurred, Alexander sent a letter addressed to Eudemus, commander of the Greek troops in the Punjab, and Taxiles (king Āmbhi of Taxila) directing them to assume the administration of the province previously governed by Philip until he could send a satrap to govern it."[29] As Alexander could not send a successor to Philip because of his sudden demise in 323 BCE, Eudemus and Taxiles governed temporarily his Indian conquests.

On the murder of Perdikkas (one of Alexander's generals), 321 BCE, Antipater became supreme regent of Alexander's empire, and made a new division of its provinces without much disturbance of the previous arrangement. We are informed by Diodorus that Peithon (the son of Agenor), whom Alex had appointed governor of the lower Indus Valley (Sindh), was now removed, and placed in charge of the provinces which bordered on the Paropanisadai (Kābul Valley), west of the Indus, and that the native kings Porus and Āmbhi were given the charge of Sindh and the Punjab respectively, for it was impossible to remove these two.[30] Eudemus retained his authority as the military governor of the Punjab.

The Punjab, even six years after the death of Alexander, was under Greek vassalage, and ruled as formerly in civil matters by Omphis (Āmbhi) of Taxila and the great Porus, while the military administration had passed into the hands of the Greek governor Eudemus. We learn from Diodorus that it was Eudemus who having decoyed the great Porus into his power treacherously murdered him (317 BCE), soon after which he left India with 3000 infantry, 500 cavalry, and 120 elephants, which belonged to Porus, to join Eumenes in his war against Antigonus.[31] Eudemus led away with him a great part of the troops by which the Punjab was held in subjection. The departure of Eudemus was fatal to Greek power. It was a blow to the Macedonian attempt to establish a Greek empire in India. The people of the Punjab and the Indus valley, who longed for freedom, and were greatly incensed and exasperated by the brutal murder of their greatest king Porus, rose in open revolt in 317 BCE itself against the Greek rulers. Sandrakottus, who headed this movement, overthrew the existing government, expelled the remainder of the Greek garrison from the Punjab, and finally installed himself in the sovereignty of the Punjab and of all the lower valley of the Indus. He virtually made himself master of all the Indian provinces Alexander had conquered.[32]

Justin tells us that having collected a band of robbers (rebels or revolutionaries ready to rise in revolt against the foreign power), Sandrocottus stirred up or instigated the Indians to overthrow the existing government (that of the Macedonains). When he was thereafter preparing to a attack Alexander's prefects (governors), a wild elephant of monstrous size approached him, and kneeling submissively like a tame elephant received him on to its back and fought vigirorously in front of the army.[33] He tells us further that "India after Alexander's death, as if the yoke of servitude had been shaken off from its neck, had put his prefects to death. Sandrocottus was the leader who achieved their freedom, but after his victory he forfeited by his tyranny all title to the name of liberator, for he oppressed with servitude the very people whom he had emancipated from foreign thraldom."[34]

"The Greek withdrawal from India was not an automatic process. It was forced by a revolution, a war of independence declared by Chandragupta as its leader... Chandragupta was the hero of this Indian war of Independence," says Radha Kumud Mookerji.[35]

"After Alexander's death in 323 BC, the empire which he had founded quickly dissolved, and by 317 BC, nearly all traces of Greek rule had vanished," observes H.G. Rawlinson.[36] It is also said that "... almost everything he (Alexander) did in India was wiped off the map within seven years of his death, and the whole of his Indian dominions fell into the hands of Chandragupta."[37]

After liberating the Punjab and Sindh from the Greek rule in 317 BCE, Sandrakottus soon rose to power.

"After the departure of Alexander", observes R.S. Tripathi, "there arose on the political firmament of India a new star that soon eclipsed the rest by its brilliance."[38]

Candragupta along with Cāṇakya returned from the Punjab with a powerful force, which they had organized there, to Magadha. On reaching its capital Pāṭaliputra, they entered into a battle with Dhanananda and his forces in which the Nanda monarch was defeated and killed. Nay, all the members of his family were put to death. The Nanda dynasty was uprooted. The rule of the Nandas became extinct. Candragupta founded the Maurya dynasty, and ascended the throne of Pāṭaliputra.[39] The details of the overthrow of the Nanda rule are conspicuous by their absence in the classics. We are, however, told by Justin that Sandrocottus had won the throne of India after the war of liberation (317 BCE).[40] Mrs. C. Speir also states that after the revolt of 317 BCE he acquired the kingdom of Magadha.[41] P.L. Bhargava is of the view that having conquered the Punjab, and vanquished and killed the Nandas, he ascended the throne in 317 BCE.[42] W.W. Hunter places his accession in 316 BCE.[43]

The accession of Candragupta to the throne of Magadha took place in 315 BCE, eight years after Alexander had passed away, as stated by no less an authority than McCrindle.[44] This date is also based on classical chronology. A.K. Majumdar[45], H.G. Rawlinson[46], A.A. Macdonell[47], and Cunningham[48] are also of the view that his accession took place in 315 BCE. Max Müller says that "he became king about 315 BC." [49]

It may be noted here that the date of accession of Candrapgupta Maurya in three different traditions – Purāṇic, Buddhist, and Jain – on the whole ranges from 322 BCE to 312 BCE. The dates suggested by some authorities in the light of classical testimony vary from 317 to 315 BCE. Some historians of ancient India, presuming that the expulsion of the Greeks from the Punjab and the Indus valley and the overthrow of the Nanda rule in Magadha by Candragupta took place within two or three years of Alexander's death, place his accession in 321 BCE, which in the light of the evidences furnished by the ancient Greek and Roman authors and some modern authorities appears to be unworthy of credence. Some scholars believe that the conquest of Magadha preceded the overthrow of the Macedonian power in the Punjab.

Of all the dates we have of the accession of Candragupta, 315 BCE appears to be the most reliable.

Notes and References

1. *Bib. Hist.*, XVII, 93.
2. *Hist. Alex.*, IX, 2.
3. Traditions differ regarding his origin. According to Purāṇic evidence, he was the son of Mahānandin (one of the Magadhan kings of Bimbisarian dynasty) by a woman of Śūdra or Servile class. [See G.P. Singh, EIHTA, p. 170.) In one of the Jaina texts (Hemacandra's *Pariṣiṣṭaparvan*, VI, 231-32), he is described as the son of a barber by a courtesan Śūdra women.
4. Pālibothra or Palimbothra is a transcription of ancient Magadhan capital Pāṭaliputra.
5. He is also called Phegelas, which is transliteration of the Sanskrit Bhagala.
6. The Prasii of Curtius (*Hist. Alex.*, IX, 2,3) and Pliny (*Hist. Nat.*, VI, 22, 68), Prasioi of Strabo (*Geog.*, XV, I, 36), Praisioi of Diodorus (*Bib. Hist.*, XVII, 93), Praisai of Plutarch (*Vit. Alex.*, LXII, 2), Praesidae of Justin (*Hist. Phil.*, XII, 8,9), or Prasians of Arrian (*Indika*, I, 10), Aelian (*Nat. Anim.*, XV, 7). Solinus (*Coll. Rer. Memo.*, 52, 6-17) and Nonnos (*Dionysiaka,* Bk. XXVI) correspond to the Sanskrit pracyas, i.e. the Magadhas. They have been transcribed with perfect accuracy as the Prasians. They together with the Gaṅgāridae are designated by the Greek and Roman historians as the people of Magadha of which Palibothra on the Ganges was the capital. (see also AIMA, pp. 57 and 205, fn; IIA, Note Dd, pp. I, 365-6), Ptolemy describes in his *Geography* (VIII, 53) a kingdom, which he locates in the Gangetic region and calls Prasiake (Sanskrit Prācyaka), i.e. eastern Gangetic kingdom of Magadha inhabited by the Prasii. (See also AIT, pp. 132-3.) Prasiaca also finds mention in the *Bio. Alex.*, (Bk. III). H.F. Tozer (*Hist. Anc. Geog.*, p. 147) says that "At the time of Alexander's invasion of India, there existed on the banks of the Ganges a powerful monarchy, that of the Prasians…"
7. *Hist. Alex.*, IX, 2.
8. *Bib. Hist.*, XVII, 93.
9. *Hist. Alex.*, IX, 2.
10. *Bib. Hist.*, XVII, 93. It is worthy of note that the reigning monarch, who was murdered by his wife in collusion with Dhanananda's father Mahāpadma Nanda, of whom she had become enamoured, was no other than Kālāśoka

or Kākavarṇa of the Śaiśunāga dynasty. Having put all his ten sons to death, Mahāpadma usurped the throne and then begot a son, Dhanananda (from that queen), who became his successor. The Śaiśunāga dynasty was supplanted by the Nanda. See also G.P. Singh, *op. cit*., pp. 162 and 168.

11. *Vit. Alex*., Ch. LXII.

12. He is variously called by the classical writers Sandrakottas, Sandrakottus, Sandrakottos, Sandrokottos, Sandracottus, Sandrocottus, Sandrocoptus, Sandrokuptos and Androkottos. See Schlegel, *Bibl. Ind*., I, p. 245; Schwanbeck, *Meg. Ind*., p. 12, note 6.

    It was William Jones, a distinguished orientalist and indologist, who established the identity of Sandrocoptus with Candragupta. (*As. Res*. IV, p. 11.) Radha Kumud Mookerji (*Chandragupta Maurya and His Times*, p. 3) calls it "One of the greatest discoveries of Indian history." "The discovery that the Sandrokottos of the Greeks was identical with the Chandragupta... was the means of ... supplying for the first time a date to early Indian history which had not a single chronological landmarks of its own," says J.W. McCrindle, AIMA, p. 7, fn. See also IIA, *Biog. Appen*., p. 404; E.J. Rapson, *Ancient India from the earliest times to the first century AD*, p. 53.

    F. Max Müller categorically states that "Everything in Indian chronology depends on the date of Chandragupta". (HASL, p. 245). He further observes: "... although it is impossible to identify any of the historical events, related by Alexander's companions, with the historical traditions of India, one name has fortunately been preserved by classical writers... This is the name of Sandracottus or Sandrocyptus, the Sanskrit Chandragupta." (*Ibid*, p. 246). There are some coincidences and differences between the classical accounts of Sandrocptus and Indian accounts of Chandragupta, he says (*Ibid*, pp. 248-51). The classical description of the celebrated Indian king Candragupta (the founder of the Maurya dynasty of Magadha) as Sandrakottus, Sandrokottos, Sandrocoptus, or Androkottos, a contemporary of Alexander the Great, is of great importance from a chronological point of view. The date 326 BCE, which marks not only the invasion of India by Alexander but also his meeting with Candragupta at Taxila, may be taken as sheet-anchor of ancient Indian chronology. This date, no doubt, constitutes a chronological landmark in the history of ancient India. The chronology of most of the events that took place posterior of this date can be determined with accuracy. The dates (with few exceptions) in ancient Indian history anterior to this date are either tentative or hypothetical. They are not fully authentic or perfectly accurate.

13. Justin by mistake calls Nandrum Alexandrum The former has, therefore, been substituted here for the latter which is the common reading. See IIA, p. 327, note 1, and Biog. Appen. therein, p. 405.

14. *Hist. Phil*., XV, 4.

15. Candragupta was accompanied by Cāṇakya, who was also humiliated by Dhanananda and expelled by him from his court following his differences

with him over the matter relating to the governance of the kingdom. Cāṇakya had advised the Nanda king to rule his kingdom as a benevolent king and not as a tyrant. He vowed to take revenge of his humiliation and expulsion by uprooting the Nanda dynasty. The flight of both Candragupta and Cāṇakya together, the inspiration of the latter to the former to put the Greek rule in the Punjab to an end, and his role in the overthrow of Dhanananda and in the ascendancy of Candragupta seem to have escaped the notices of the classical authors.

J.W. McCrindle states that "Sandrokottos was a native of the Punjab from where he had gone to Magadha to seek his fortune, but after he incurred the displeasure of Dhanananda or committed some offence against him, he quitted his dominions and returned to the Punjab"; and that "Cāṇakya, a Brāhmaṇa, had come from the great city of Taxila in the Punjab to Pāṭaliputra where he resided at that time." (AICL, p. 43, note 1; IIA, Biog. Appen., pp. 405-6, 408). H.G. Rawlinson (*Intercourse Between India and the Western World from the Earliest times to the Fall of the Rome*, p. 37) also says that "Candragupta had originally lived in the Punjab. He then went to seek his fortune at the court of the Nanda king of Magadha, and there he met with a fellow-countryman, the crafty Brahmin minister Cāṇakya from Taxila. Becoming implicated in a plot which Cāṇakya had made against his master, he was forced to flee to his former home." The fact remains that both Candragupta and Cāṇakya originally belonged to Magadha from where they had fled to the Punjab for the reasons already explained.

16. *Vit. Alex.*, Ch. LXII.
17. Curtius, *Hist. Alex.*, IX, 2; Diodorus, *Bib. Hist.*, XVII, 93.
18. *Vit. Alex.*, Ch. LXII.
19. *Hist. Phil.*, XII, 8.
20. *Anab.*, V, 25-28.
21. *His. Alex.*, IX, 2-3.
22. *Bib. Hist.*, XVII, 94.
23. *Vit. Alex.*, LXII, 94.
24. *Hist. Phil.*, XII, 8.
25. *Bib. Hist.*, XVIII, 6. He tells us also that "the Ganges form the eastern boundary of the Gaṅgāridai, a nation which possesses a vast force of the largest-sized elephants. Owing to this, their country (Magadha) has never been conquered by any foreign king." (*Ibid.*, II, 37) Lassen (*Pent. Ind.*, p. 16) also says that "Alexander, the Macedonian, did not make war upon the Gaṅgāridai when he learned that they possessed four thousand elephants well trained and equipped for war".
26. *Hist. Phil.*, XII, 8.

27. *Anab.*, VI, 27.
28. *Ibid.*, VI, 15.
29. *Ibid.*, VI, 27.
30. *Bib. Hist.*, XVIII, 39.
31. *Bib. Hist.*, XIX, 14. Eumenes was captured and killed by Antigonus in 316 BCE. After the fall of his chief (Eumenes), Eudemus was also put to death by him. See Diodorus, *Bib. Hist.*, XIX, 27 and 44.
32. See also HA, IV, p. 442; A.K. Majumdar, EHIDS, II, p. 511; AIIC, p. 36; Cunningham, CASE, p. 8 (a separate section towards the end of the book); E.H. Bunbury, HAG, I, p. 554; John Marshall, *Taxila*, I, p. 83; R.G. Bhandarkar, *A Peep into the Early History of India*, p. 5; H.G. Rawlinson, *Intercourse Between India and the Western World…* pp. 36-38; *A Concise History of the Indian People*, p. 33; H.F. Tozer, *Hist. Anct. Geog.*, p. 148.
33. *Hist. Phil.*, XV, 4.
34. *Ibid.* – "*Post mortem Alexandri, Velut cervicibus jugo servitutis excusso praefectos ejus occiderat ... populum quem ab externa dominatione vindicaverat, ipse servitio premebat.*" See also J.S. Watson's Eng. trans. of Justin's *Hist. Phil.*, p. 142.

    "Candragupta, it is true, held "India for the Indians', against all comers, especially the Greek from the West," says H.G. Rawlinson, *Bactria from the Earliest times to the Extinction of Bactrio-Greek Rule in the Punjab,* p. 141.
35. *Chandragupta Maurya and His Times*, pp. 31-32.
36. "India in European Literature and Thought", in *The Legacy of India,* ed G.T. Garratt, p. 9.
37. W.W. Tarn, *The Greeks in Bactria and India*, p. 168.
38. HAI, p. 146.
39. See *Mudrārākṣasa* of Viṣākha Datta, Act I, 11-13; Act II, 13-15 and 23; *Milindapañho*, IV.8.26, also its tr. In SBE, XXXVI, pp. 147-8; Raj Bali Pandey, *Bhāratiya Itihāsa Kā Paricaya* (Introduction to Indian History), p. 54; *Ind. Ant.*, 1914, p. 124, note.
40. *Hist. phil.*, XV, 4.
41. *Phases of Indian Civilization : A Historical and Cultural Outline*, p. 214.
42. *Chandragupta Maurya : A Gem of Indian History*, p. 5.
43. "The Greeks in India (327 – 161 BCE)", rept. from his *The Indian Empire : Its Peoples, History and Products* (3rd edn. London, 1882), in *Ancient India*, a collection of Articles from various scholars (Delhi, 1983), p. 90.
44. AICL, p. 43, note 1; IIA, Biog. Appen. p. 409.
45. EHIDS, II, pp. 514-15.

46. *Intercourse Between India and the Western World*... p. 38.
47. HSL, pp. 413-14.
48. CASE, p. 88.
49. HASL, p. 267.

2

Candragupta Maurya and His Political Achievements

Candragupta Maurya occupies a distinguished place in the galaxy of the great emperors of India. He has been called by two classical writers, Arrian[1] and Aelian[2], the greatest Indian king. According to McCrindle, "Sandrokottos, with the exception perhaps of his grandson, Aśoka, was the greatest ruler ancient India produced."[3] Radha Kumud Mookerji, the Chief authority on Candragupta Maurya, says that he "ranks as one of India's greatest rulers... He figures as the first historical emperor of India in the sense that he is the earliest emperor in Indian History." [4]

There are some classical notices of the personal life, royalty, kingly duties, the conquests, and political achievements of Sandrakottus, the great Maurya emperor. His administration has already been covered in the fourth book of this work.

In the typical oriental tradition, Candragupta is called by the historians a liberal or benevolent despot. But this cannot be denied that he was a true autocrat; and that the rule he followed for governing his kingdom was regarded as unduly strict by the people. These are the reasons why he lived in constant fear of assassination. He took all precautions for his personal safety. He kept himself under strict security. Strabo, on the authority of Megasthenes (*Indika,* Bk. II, Fragm. XXVII), states that inside the palace the care of the king's person was entrusted to women, who also were bought from their parents. The bodyguards and the rest of the soldiery were posted outside the gates. A woman who killed a king when drunk was rewarded by becoming the wife of his successor. The sons succeeded the father. The king generally did not sleep during the daytime, and at night he was obliged to change his couch from time to time to defeat plots against his life.[5] Strabo states further that the king left his palace in time of war to personally direct the operations on the battlefield with a view to encourage his soldiers, and for the purpose of sitting in court to try cases. He usually remained in court for the whole day without allowing the business to be interrupted, even though the time arrived for attending to his person. He continued hearing cases. Another purpose for which he left his palace was to offer sacrifice. He used to go out of his palace for hunting also. This was in a sort of "bacchanalian fashion". Crowds of women surrounded him, and on the outside were spearmen. The road was marked off with ropes, and it was death for a man or even for a woman to pass within the ropes. Men with drums and gongs led the procession. The king hunted in the enclosures and shot arrows from a platform. At his side stood two or three armed women. If he hunted in the open grounds, he shot from the back of an elephant. Of the women, some rode in Chariots, some on horses, and some even on elephants, and they were equipped with all sorts of weapons, as if they were going on a military expedition.[6]

Curtius informs us that when the king condescended to show himself in public his attendants carried in their hands silver censers, and perfumes with incense all the road by which it was his pleasure to be conveyed. He was carried in a golden palanquin garnished with pearls, and he was robed in fine muslin embroidered with purple and gold. Behind his palanquin followed men-at-arms and his bodyguards.[7]

Describing the royal processions at Indian festivals in the Maurya capital Pāṭaliputra in the time of Candragupta, Strabo tells us that in the processions at their festivals, many elephants adorned with gold and silver were in the train, as well as four-horsed chariots. Then followed a great host of attendants in their holiday attire, with vessels of gold, such as large basins and goblets, drinking cups and lavers all made of Indian copper, and set many of them with precious stones – emeralds, beryls, and Indian garnets-garments embroidered and interwoven with gold.[8] Kleitarchus, one of the historians and companions of Alexander, also describes the pageantry of a court festival. He mentions that four-wheeled carriages were also brought in the processions.

For the defence of his vast dominions, Candragupta maintained an army so numerous, well-organized and well-disciplined. Pliny, deriving his authority from Megasthenes (*Indika*, Bk. IV, Fragm. LVI), says he maintained 600,000 infantry, 30,000 cavalry, 9,000 elephants and a multitude of war-chariots (about 8000)[9]. But Solinus relates that the king of an extremely powerful Prasian nation with its capita at Pālibothra kept at all times 60,000 foot-soldiers, 30,000 horses and 8,000 elephants.[10] His statement is also based on the testimony of Megasthenes (*Indika*, Bk. IV, Fragm. LVI B).

The army, to which Candragupta owed his throne and empire, was maintained at enormous numerical strength so organized, equipped, and administered as to attain a high degree of efficiency, as judged by an oriental standard.

We are told by Plutarch that "Androkottos overran and subdued the whole of India with an army of 600,000 men."[11]

We turn now to Seleukus Nikator, who originally belonged to Macedon, accompanied Alexander the Great on his Asiatic expedition as one of his generals, distinguished himself as the most powerful of all his successors, undertook an Indian expedition, waged war with Sandrakottus and entered into an alliance with him.

In the second partition of Alexander's empire among his great/leading generals made in 321 BCE at a place in upper Syria called Triparadeisos (not much different from the former one made at Babylon soon after his death there in 323 BCE), the rich and important province of Babylonia fell to Seleukus' share. He became its governor, but six years later (i.e. in 315 BCE) was dispossessed of it by his rival Antigonus, and fled to Ptolemy of Egypt, whom he instigated to oppose him. After three years in exile, he recovered it (i.e. in 312 BCE) from his ambitious rival, and established himself there as a crowned king. He now devoted himself to the consolidation and extension of his power in western Asia. "Sandrocottus", says Justin, "having thus won the throne was reigning over India when Seleucus was laying the foundations of his future greatness."[12] In 312 BC itself, Seleukus founded the Greek Kingdom in Syria. He is also called "the founder of the Syrian monarchy." He became more famous as king of Syria than as a ruler of Babylonia. He ruled Syria as a Greek king from 312 BCE till his death in 280 BCE. He attacked and subjugated the Bactrians in BCE 306, and formally assumed the regal title. He made Bactria (on the Oxus), in the extreme north of Afghanistan, a dependency of the Syrian kingdom. He afterwards reduced to his power all the eastern dominions conquered by Alexander. The eastern provinces of his realm extended to the borders of India. By 305 BCE, he brought under his rule all the countries as far as the Indus. Appian says that he virtually made himself master of the whole region from Phrygia to the Indus.[13]

"Seleucus Nicator", observes Justin, "waged many wars in the east after the partition of Alexander's empire among his generals. He first took Babylon, and then with his forces augmented by victory subjugated the Bactrians. He then passed over into India." [14]

Since no attempt was made to recover Alexander's Indian conquests within ten years of the rule of Sandrokottus, he employed that interval in consolidating his power in northern India. His antagonist, Seleukus, on the other hand, was engaged during that period in establishing his supremacy in western Asia.

Seleukus along with his army led an expedition on into India in 303 BCE, and not in or about 305 BCE as held by some authorities, with a view to recover the territories conquered by Alexander in northwestern India and to rule over them. In pursuit of his object, he crossed the river Indus which marked the northwestern boundary of the Maurya empire at that time. It is difficult to say as to how far he advanced into India. A passage from Pliny: "*Reliqua Inde Seleuco Nicatori peragrata sunt*" [15] seems to imply that he himself had penetrated as far as Pālibothra on the Ganges, the chief seat of his enemy's power. That he himself had carried his arms to the regions of the Ganges may reasonably be doubted or refuted.[16] The veracity of Pliny's description of his journey from the Indus to the Ganges or to the city of Pāṭaliputra by traversing several stages[17] on his way is also not beyond suspicion.

Appian, one of the classical historians, and an authority on the Syrian king Seleukus, however, makes a convincing statement: "Having crossed the Indus, he (Seleukus) warred with Androkottos, the king of the Indians, who dwelt about that river, until he entered into an alliance and a marriage affinity with him.[18]

The war between the forces of Seleukus and Sandrakottus, no doubt, took place in 303 BCE on this side of the river Indus or on its banks in which the former was defeated at the hands of the latter or accepted the defeat and submitted to him, and then entered into a treaty with him. Sandrakottus defeated the most powerful foreign king Seleukus who held all western Asia under his sway, and was trying to establish his hold in India up to the Indus.[19] The incidents of war between these two mighty potentates are not recorded in detail in the classics. The particulars of the treaty of peace and friendship concluded between them are, however, given therein.

In 303 BCE itself, a treaty of peace was concluded between the Syrian monarch Seleukus and the Indian sovereign Sandrakottus in accordance with the provisions of which the former ceded to the latter the satrapies of Aria (Herāt), Arachosia (Kandahār) and Paropanisadae (Kābul valley), all three in Afghanistan, and the satrapy of Gedrosia (Baluchistan)[20] and received in return, a present of five hundred elephants from him.[21] The four provinces west of the Indus, which Sandrakottus received from Seleukus, were the main constituents of Greater Ariana[22], but after the treaty formed parts of the Maurya empire. Ariane (Ariana), which, according to Strabo, lay immediately to the west, was subject to the Persians, but in later times the Indians occupied a great part of Ariane which they received from the Macedonians.[23] Strabo here refers to the cession of the provinces westward of the Indus by Seleukus to Sandrakottus.[24] Strabo relates further that "The territories lying along the Indus possessed by the Indians belonged formerly to the Persians. Alexander took them away from the Arianoi (the people of Ariana region) and established in them colonies of his own. Seleukos Nikator gave them to Sandrokottos, and received in exchange 500 elephants." [25] Arianoi, according to Strabo, inhabited the territories which formed parts of the Ariana region called by him Ariane. He includes in Ariana Paropamisadai (Kābul) at the base of the Paropamisus range (Hindukush), Arachotia, also called Arachosia (Kandahār), and Gedrosia (Baluchistan), which were ceded by Seleukus to Sandrakottus. All the territories between the Indus and the Paropamisus, which were formerly under the sway of the Macedonians, were ceded by the former to the latter. Candragupta no doubt extended his conquests far beyond the eastern limits of Magadha. After the conclusion of the treaty, he ruled an empire extending westward from the river Indus to the southern slopes of the Hindukush. "The range of the Hindukush mountains... became the frontier between Candragupta's provinces of Herāt and Kābul on the south and the Seleukidan province of Bactria on the north. The first Indian emperor (Candragupta)... thus entered into possession of that 'Scientific frontier'..."[26] It is also to be added here that as a mark of friendship and amity Seleukus entered into a matrimonial alliance with Sandrakottus,[27] according to which, he gave him his daughter (Atheni or Helena) in marriage. The friendly relations seem to have subsisted ever afterwards between the two sovereigns.

Having formed an alliance with Sandrakottus in 303 BCE, Seleukus left for Babylonia. Justin says, "Seleucus having made a treaty with him and otherwise settled his affairs in the east, returned home to prosecute the war with Antigonus. [28]

The celebrated Candragupta Maurya built up an empire such as no Indian king had before possessed. M. Wheeler also points out that it was the greatest empire India had ever produced.[29] In the times subsequent to the Macedonian invasion of India, his empire extended from the mouths of the Ganges to the regions beyond the Indus. He was thus able to combine into one great empire the regions both of the Indus and the Ganges. H.G. Rawlinson has aptly remarked that "He had thus built up for himself a far vaster Empire than India had ever before seen, stretching as it did from the Ganges to the Hindukush mountains." [30] He restored the geographical position that India had attained before its invasion by the Persians and Macedonians. He liberated the Punjab and Sindh from the foreign rule. The political unification of northern India has been taken by the classical authors as well as some modern authorities as the greatest of his all achievements. "History can show few greater political achievements," observes V.A. Smith.[31]

Candragupta gained recognition as the paramount sovereign in the whole of India. He was one of those few great men who transformed the destinies of nations.

Forming an estimate of Candragupta, V.A. Smith writes: "In the course of some eighteen years, Chandragupta had expelled the Macedonian garrisons from the Punjab and Sindh, repulsed and humbled Seleucus the conqueror, and established himself as undisputed supreme lord of at least all Northern India and a large part of Ariana. These achievements fairly entitle him to rank among the greatest and most successful kings known to history.[32]

Throwing light on Candragupta and his political achievements, Radha Kumud Mookerji opines that "He is the first Indian king who established his rule over an extended India, an India greater than even British India. The boundaries of this Greater India lay far beyond the frontiers of modern India along the borders of Persia. Chandragupta is again the first of the Rulers of India to be able by his conquests to join up the valleys of the Indus and the land of the five rivers with the eastern valleys of the Ganges and the Jumna (the Gaṅgā and the Yamunā) in one Empire that sretched from Aria (Herāt) to Pāṭaliputra. And he is also the first India king who followed up his political unification of Northern Indian by extending his conquests beyond the barriers of the Vindhyas so as to bring both North and South under the umbrella of one paramount sovereign. Earlier in his career, he was again the first Indian leader who had to confront the distressing consequences of a European and foreign invasion of his country, the conditions of national depression and disorganization to which it was exposed, and then to achieve the unique distinction of recovering his country's freedom from the yoke of Greek rule . . . Candragupta was able to rid the country… Chandragupta was able to rid the country of all traces of Greek occupation… Very few rulers of India have to their credit the accomplishment of so much within the short time of his reign… To crown all, Candragupta, as the founder of the imperial Maurya dynasty, gives to India for the first time a continuous history as well as a unified history… The political unity of India attained under the Maurya emperors was not maintained by their successors. . ." [33]

About six years after the withdrawal of Seleukus from India, Candragupta abdicated the throne (298 BCE) and handed on the imperial succession to his son Bindusāra.

The history of India in the time of the last Nanda ruler, the contemporary of Alexander the Great, and also the history of the rise of Candragupta after the liberation of the Punjab and the Indus valley from the Greek rule and of his political achievements can be reconstructed to a considerable extent with the help of the evidence adduced by the classical writers.

Notes and References

1. *Indika*, I, 5.
2. *Nat. Anim.*, XIII, 18, 1.
3. IIA, Biog. Appen., p. 404.
4. *Candragupta Maurya and His Times*, p. 1. see also V.A. Smith, *The Oxford History of India,* revd. by H.G. Rawlinson, p. 52.
5. *Geog.*, XV, I, 55. Kautilya's statement, that the king was under the protection of female guards (*Arth.* I. 21; II, 3), goes in harmony with that of Megasthenes.

   From Curtius (*Hist. Alex.*, VIII, 9) we learn that the food eaten by the king was prepared by women. Women also served him with wine, and, when he fell into a drunken sleep, carried him away to his bedchamber, while invoking the gods of the night in their native hymns.

   Curtius represents the king as so engaged within the palace at the metropolis. The palace, he says (*Hist. Alex.*, VIII, 9), is open to all corners. It is there that he gives audience to public and ambassadors, and administers justice to his subjects.

6. *Geog.*, XV, I, 55.
7. *Hist. Alex.*, VIII, 9.
8. *Geog.*, XV, I, 69; see also AIMA, p. 208, fn.
9. *Nat. Hist.*, VI, 22, see also VI, 19 and VI, 68.
10. *Coll. Rer. Memo.*, 52, 6-17.
11. *Vit. Alex.*, Ch. LXII.
12. *Hist. Phil.*, XV, 4; also J.S. Watson's Eng. trans. of Justin's *Hist. Phil.*, p. 143.
13. *Roman History*, Vol. II.
14. *Hist. Phil.*, XV, 4.
15. *Nat. Hist.*, VI, 17.
16. See Lassen, *Pent. Ind.*, p. 61; Schwanbeck, *Meg. Ind.*, pp. 12-18.
17. *Nat. Hist.*, VI, 21.
18. *Syriake*, XI. 55; see also Schwanbeck, *Meg. Ind.,* pp. 13-14; *Ind. Ant.*, VI, p. 114.
19. H.T. Prinsep (*Historical Results from Bactrian Coins : Discoveries in Afghanistan*, pp. 22-23) also admits that "In 303 BCE, Seleucus crossed the river Indus to make war on Sandracottus… Seleucus made, however, a hasty peace with Sandracottus…" H.G. Rawlinson (*Bactria from the Earliest times to the Extinction of Bactrio-Greek Rule in the Punjab*, p. 37) relates that "Chandragupta ("303 BC") brought Seleucus Nicator to his knees, and forced the 'ever-victorious' monarch to cede the provinces west of the Indus." V.A. Smith says, "About 305 BC he (Seleukus) crossed the Indus with the intention of subduing the country. But Chandragupta was too strong for him, and Seleukos was obliged to retreat, surrendering all claims to the satrapies or provinces west of the Indus. Those provinces passed under the sway of Chandragupta, who thus ruled the countries now called Baluchistan and Afghanistan, as well as Northern India." (*The Oxford History of India*, p. 52). See H.G. Rawlinson (*A Concise History of the Indian People*, pp. 33, 47, 60), H.F. Tozer (*Hist. Anct. Geog.*, p. 148), R.G. Bhandarkar (*A Peep into the Early History of India*, pp. 5 and 6), R.S. Sharma, *India's Ancient Past,* p. 170), and R.B. Pandey (*Bhāratiya Itihāsa Kā Paricaya*, p. 54) regarding the war between the two rival powers, Sandrakottus and Seleukus, the victory of the former and defeat of the latter, and the treaty between the two. Rawlinson in particular ascribes "305 BC" to these events. Cunningham has quite different view. He says, "A year or two later than BC 306 Seleukus conducted an expedition against Sandrokottus. He crossed the Indus, and according to some authors, advanced as far as the Ganges. Sandrokottus

hastily assembled an army of sixty thousand men, with his elephants to oppose him, and presented so bold a front that Seleukus thought it prudent to enter into an alliance with him." (CASE, p. 8, a separate section towards the end of the book). H.H. Wilson's statement, that Seleucus Nicator's invasion of India took place some time between BC 312 and 306, according to the authors of the Ancient Universal History" (*Ar. Ant.*, p. 216, note 1), is misleading.

20. Pliny, *Nat. Hist.*, VI, 69.
21. Plutarch, *Vit. Alex.*, Ch. LXII.
22. See V.A. Smith, EHI, Appendix F, "The Extent of the cession of Ariana by Seleukos Nikator to Chandragupta Maurya", pp. 158-60; Schwanbeck, *Meg. Ind.*, pp. 29, 30, note 24; Lassen, *Pent. Ind.*, p. 42.
23. *Geog.*, XV, I, 10.
24. See AICL, p. 15, note 4.
25. *Geog.*, XV, II, 9; see also H.L. Jones' trans. *The Geography of Strabo,* Vol.VII, p. 143; Hamilton and Falconer's trans. *The Geography of Strabo*, Vol.III, pp. 78 and 125.
26. V.A. Smith, EHI, p. 126.
27. Strabo, *Geog.*, XV, II, 9; Appian, *Syriake,* XI, 55.
28. *Hist. Phil.*, XV, 4. Antigonus was defeated and slain by Seleukus in the battle that took place at Ipsus in 301 BCE. After 301 BCE, the empire of the Syrian king Seleukus became the most extensive of those which had been formed out of Alexander's conquests. The whole of Asia to the Indus and Jaxartes passed under his rule. In the beginning of the year 280 BCE, he crossed the Hellespont to possess himself of the throne of Macedonia which had fallen vacant by the death of Lysimachos, but he was soon afterwards assassinated by Ptolemy Keraunus. He had then reigned for thirty-two years (312-280 BCE).
29. *Early India and Pakistan to Ashoka*, p. 172.
30. *Intercourse Between India and the Western World…*, p. 38.
31. *Aśoka,* p. 104.
32. *EHI,* p. 126.
33. *Chandragupta Maurya and His Times*, pp. 2-3.

3

Kingdoms and Principalities

The Indian kingdoms and principalities described by the classical writers are given below with all relevant details thereof. The kingdoms under monarchic rule have already been treated of in the fourth book of this work, and hence they are not included here.

The Kingdom of Gāndhāra

Of all the ancient Indian kingdoms, Gāndhāra was of the highest antiquity. It was known to the Greeks as early as the times of Hecataeus, who, as we learn from Stephanus of Byzantium, in his *Periodos Ges* (Fragm. 178) mentions the "country of the Gandarri." He designates Gāndhāra as Gandaria or Gandarie and the people who inhabited it as Gandarians or Gandaraeans (Fragm. 179)[1], whom Herodotus calls Gandarioi,[2] and the author of the *Periplus* Gandaraei.[3] Strabo describes this kingdom under the name Gandaritis, which according to him, lay between the Khoaspes (Kunār) and the Indus and along the river Kophes (Kābul).[4] He does not locate it only west of the Indus in the valley of the Kābul river, as some authorities hold . "The Gandarians or Gandaridae of the Greeks," says H.W. Bellew, "formerly occupied the tract of the country enclosed between the Kābul and the Indus rivers."[5] McCrindle also states that the seats of the Gandaridai, the people of Gāndhāra, "were in the neighborhood of the Indus and the Kophen or Kābul river."[6] The Greek geographer Ptolemy places the territory of the Gandarai "between the Souastos (Swāt) and the Indus."[7]

The Gāndhāric territory lay on both sides of the Kābul river immediately above its confluence with the Indus. In very early times, however, it extended even to the country east of the Indus.[8] Its eastern capital Takṣaśilā, a great and flourishing city, generally written as Taxila by the classical authors, was situated to the east of the Indus, about twenty miles northwest of Rawalpindi. Ptolemy alone of all the ancient Greek writers calls it Taxiala, and places it between the Indus and the Bidaspes (Hydaspes)[9]. With regard to its position, he is in perfect agreement with Strabo.[10] The city called Poclais by the author of *Periplus*[11], Proklais by Ptolemy,[12] Peukolaitis by Strabo,[13] Peukelaotis or Peukelaitis by Arrian,[14] a transliteration or transcription of the Sanskrit name Puṣkarāvatī or Puṣkalāvatī, of the Pāli form Pukhalaoti, or of the Prākṛit Pukkalaoti, was its western capital. It was situated to the west of the Indus Ptolemy has fixed its position with great accuracy, as being on the eastern bank of the river of Souastene or Swāt at a distance of about seventeen miles northwest of Peshawar (ancient Purūṣapura). It is said that "Puśkalāvatī and Taxila were the two chief cities of Gāndhāra."[15] It appears that this kingdom extended from the Kābul valley to Taxila, the former to the west and the latter to the east of the Indus. McCrindle observes that in early times the Gāndhāric territory lay on both sides of the river Indus, though in subsequent times it was confined to the western side.[16]

"Gāndhāra", according to V.S. Agrawala, "extended from Takshaśilā, its eastern capital, to the river Kunār, its western boundary, and from the river Kābul in the south to Swāt in the north."[17]

Gāndhāra was the largest of all kingdoms in northwest India in pre-Alexandrian times. It included the region stretching from the Kābul to the Indus, modern Peshawar and Rawalpindi districts, the Kābul valley and the regions still further west.[18]

It is worthwhile to note here that the kingdom of Gāndhāra has not been mentioned either by any of the writers who accompanied Alexander into India and recorded his deeds in their works or by any of the historians of his Indian campaign.

The Principality of Astes

At the time of Alexander's invasion, an Indian prince named Hastī, called Astes by Arrian[19], ruled a principality near or a little above the confluence of the Swāt with the Kābul river, with the capital at Peukelaotis (Puṣkalāvatī).[20] Arrian distinctly calls him "a prince of the land of Peukelaotis."[21] He was invested with sovereignty or supreme power to rule his territory or dominions. The people who inhabited his principality and the surrounding region have been called the Astakenoi (Astakenians) by Strabo[22]. They are identical with Hāstināyana of Pāṇini (mentioned in *Sūtra*, VI. 4.174). The capital city of Hasti or Astes has been fixed by some oriental scholars at a place called Hashtnagar, on the north bank of the Kābul river, near its junction with the river of Swāt[23]. This situation goes well in accord with the expression of Arrian.

The Kingdom of the Younger Porus

The younger Porus, the nephew of the great Porus, was one of the Indian sovereigns of Alexander's time. He ruled over a small kingdoms, which, according to Arrian[24], was situated between the Akesines and the Hydraotes. McCrindle has rightly pointed out that he was "sovereign of a territory situated to the east of the Hydraotes." [25]

The Kingdom of Arsakes

Arsakes, like his brother Abisares (Abhisāra), derived his name from that of his kingdom, which Ptolemy calls Arsa, and places it between the Indus and the Bidaspes (Hydaspes).[26] The people of Arsa are called the Arsanians by Nonnos.[27]

Arrian tells us that Arsakes was the "ruler of the country adjoining the dominions of Abisares,"[28] which is in strict accordance with truth. He was the ruler of a kingdom called Urśā or Uraśa – the hill tracts between the Hydaspes and the Indus comprising almost the whole of the present Hazara district – which adjoined the dominions of Abisares lying between the upper courses of the Hydaspes and the Akesines.[29]

Some authorities are of the opinion that this kingdom included all the hill country between the Indus and Kaśmīr as far south as the boundary of Aṭak (also spelt Aṭṭak or Attock).[30]

The Kingdom of Phegeus

Phegeus[31], as we learn from Curtius, was the the king of the nearest nation to the river Hyphasis.[32] Diodorus says that his dominions adjoined the Hyphasis.[33] McCrindle is of the view that he was "chief of a territory which lay between the Hydraotes and the Hyphasis."[34]

Principalities in Sindh

The principalities in the rich and populous province of Sindh in the west were distinguished from the kingdoms in the north. H.A. Rose has pin-pointed that in Sindh there were a group of principalities.[35]

The Principality of Oxykanus or Portikanus

The prince Oxykanus, mentioned by Arrian[36], is called Portikanus by Strabo[37], Diodorus[38] and Curtius[39], but by Julius Valerius Pecanus.[40] From the accounts given by these classical writers of the subject under notice it appears that the territory which he ruled was adjacent to that of king Mousikanus of upper Sindh[41], but its exact position or boundaries cannot be ascertained. We have, however, some positive evidence regarding its location. H.H. Wilson says that it "lay on the west of the Indus, opposite to that of Musikanus, or to the south-east of Alor (capital of Upper Sindh)."[42] Some authorities like McCrindle,[43] Cunningham,[44] and Bunbury[45] are more or less at one in placing the territory of the prince Oxykanus or Portikanus to the west of the Indus in the level country around Larkāna, which, though, now near the Indus but not close to it, was in Alexander's time about forty miles distant from it eastward, and in identifying his capital with Mahorta, a place about ten miles north-west from Larkāna, where there are the remains of an ancient fortress on a huge mound. But Lassen[46], followed by St. Martin[47], places the dominions of the said prince to the east of the river Indus. The Alexandrian writer Julius Valerius, noted before, makes an incidental notice of his "wide dominions,"[48] but without giving any details thereof.

The Principality of Sambos

The Prince Sambos (Śambhu), mentioned by Arrian[49] and Diodorus[50], is called Sambus by Curtius[51], Sabos by Strabo[52], and Sabbas by Plutarch.[53] He was the ruler of the mountainous region west of the Indus adjoining the kingdoms of Mousikanus.[54] Arrian in particular mentions the principality of Sambos (which was in Middle Sindh) with its metropolis Sindimana,[55] called Sindomana by Strabo.[56] His capital Sindimana or Sindomana, has been identified with Sehwan – a city on the Indus. The city stands on an ancient site.[57]

The names of the Princes of Sindh mentioned by the ancient Greek and Roman historians can be recognized under their native forms in the Sanskrit literature still extant which is indeed a strong confirmation of the accuracy of the information transmitted by them in this regard. St. Martin has correctly stated that all peoples, kings, and chiefs or princes of the Lower Indus Valley are of Indian origion.[58]

The Kingdom of Kaśmīr

One of the ancient kingdoms of India of very high antiquity was that of Kaśmīr on the Hydaspes, one of the tributaries of the Indus. "Kashmir has been a regular kingdom for a period that transcends the limits of legitimate history," says H.H. Wilson.[59]

Of all the classical writers, the Greek geographer Ptolemy was the first to mention Kaśmīr as a kingdom. He designates it as Kaspeiria.[60] The value of Ptolemy's notice of Kaspeiria lies mainly in the fact that it presents us with an accurate transcription of the ancient Sanskrit name Kaśmīr (modern Kashmir).[61] The name Kaspeiria and its position concur in indicating this to be the valley of Kaśmīr.

In the time of Ptolemy, Kaśmīr was the most powerful and extensive kingdom, which was according to him, watered by the Bidaspes (Hydaspes or Jhelum), the Sandabal (Candrabhāgā or Cināb), and the Adris (Rāvī).[62] "The dominions... embraced, together with the extensive mountain region wherein the great rivers of the punjab had their sources, a great part of the Punjab itself," says McCrindle.[63] The valley proper of Kaśmīr was the region watered by the Bidaspes in the upper part of its course. Ptolemy assigns to it (to Kaśmīr) also the sources of the Sandabal and of the Adris, and thus includes within it the provinces of the lower Himālayan region that lay between Kaśmīr and the Satlaj. Masson[64], Lassen[65] and St. Martin[66] are almost in agreement with each other in suggesting that the statement of Ptolemy refers to a period when the power of the dynasty ruling over Kaśmīr actually extended over the wide territories, as indicated above. The sovereigns of this kingdom in Ptolemy's days had, no doubt, extended their rule far beyond the limits of the present state of Kaśmīr. It is said that they had extended their rule as far eastward as the regions of the Yamunā.[67]

"Kashmir in its palmy days", observes Wilson, "comprehended great part of the Punjab, and extended as far as, if not beyond, the Indus."[68] V.A. Smith also states that its earlier extension was wider.[69] It is really striking that Kaśmīr attracted the notice of also the German scholar, Max Duncker, who calls it the "mightiest kingdom", and says further that its potentates "had extended their territory over the mountains in the south and the land of the Abhisara."[70]

The French scholar St. Martin observes: "To the south of the mountains, in the Panjab, Ptolemy indicates under the general name of Kaspiraei an extension genuinely historical of the Kaśmirian empire... Kaśmīr ... appertains itself to the region which traverses more to the north, the Tibetan portion of the Indus 'above the point where the ancients placed the sources of the Indus')".[71] The latter part of the observation more or less corresponds with the present Laddakh region of Kashmir.

St. Martin takes without any hesitation Ptolemy's Asmiraia (VI, 16, 6) to be identical with Kaśmīr itself.[72]

The people who inhabited Asmiraia have been called Asmirae by the ancient Roman historian Ammianus Marcellinus.[73]

The capital of Kaspeiria (Kaśmīr) is called Kaspeira by Ptolemy[74] which lies at the sources of the Hydaspes. And the Kashmirians are called by him the Kaspeiraioi.[75] The two Greek writers of the later period, Dionysius of Samos, and Nonnos, in their respective works, the *Bassarika*[76], *Dionysiaka*[77], have made incidental notices of the people of (Kaśmīr– the Kashmiris. The former calls them Kaspeiroi, and the latter Kaspeiri.

The Sātavāhana Kingdom

On the combined testimony of Ptolemy and the author of the *Periplus*, fresh light can be thrown on some phases and facets of the Sātavāhana kingdom in the Deccan.

The author of the *Periplus*, while speaking of Dachinabades or Dakinabades[78] (Deccan), refers to Paethana as situated towards the south of Barygaza (now Broach) at a distance of twenty days' journey[79] which was known to Ptolemy as Baithana, placed by him in Ariake.[80]

Paethana of the *Periplus* or Baithana of Ptolemy is identical with Paithan of the present day on the north bank of the river Godāvāri in the Aurangabad district of Mahārāṣṭra.[81] In ancient times, it was popularly known as Pratiṣṭhāna or Pratiṣṭhānapura. It was the western capital of the Sātavāhana kingdom. It was the seat of government of some of the early Sātavāhana rulers as well as the later Sātavāhanas.

We learn from the *Periplus*[82] that the elder Saraganus[83] (Ariṣṭa Śātakarṇi), one of the early Sātavāhana kings (*circa* CE 44-69) had previously governed Kalliena (modern Kalyāṇa in the Thane district at a distance of about 33 miles northeast of Bombay, now called Mumbai), which was the western part of the kingdom,[84] and then extended his sway over its eastern part in Āndhradeśa. We are informed by W.H. Schoff (translator of the Greek text *Periplus Maris Erythraei*, and annotator) that his court was held at his eastern capital, Dhānyakaṭaka,[85] and that to the author of the *Periplus* who landed on the west coast, "he was no more than a name, and the visible authority was vested in the western viceroy."[86]

The next great king of the Sātavāhana dynasty is called Sandares or Sandanes by the author of the *Periplus*[87], and Sadinon or Sandineis by Ptolemy.[88] Schoff has correctly identified him with Sundara Śātakarṇi, who according to him, ruled in CE 83-4,[89] "but before his accession to the throne, while as one of the heirs presumptive he was acting as viceroy at Paethana, towards the end of the reign of Arishta Śātakarṇi, the elder Saraganus", as told by him.[90] It is recorded in the *Periplus* itself that he had ruled Kalliena (Kalyāṇa). More or less the same fact has been highlighted by Ptolemy but in different fashion. He states that he ruled over Ariake, which included Kalyāṇa. The territory of Ariake was in Ptolemy's time divided among three potentates, one of whom was Sadineis or Sandanes. Having made himself the master of Kalyāṇa, which had formerly belonged to the house of the elder Saraganus, he ruled the prosperous trading communities that occupied the seaboard. His dynasty further ruled Kalyāṇa about which nothing has been told to us either by the author of the *Periplus* or by Ptolemy.

One of the later Sātavāhana kings called Siro Polemaios by Ptolemy[91] is identical with Śrī Pulumāyi II of the Nāsik cave and Amarāvātī Stupa inscriptions. He ruled the kingdom with his capital at Baithana (Paethana or Paithan), which Ptolemy refers to as "royal seat".[92] He was the son of Gautamīputra Sātakarṇi (CE 106-30).[93] He ruled from CE 130 to 154 or 155. He was the great monarch of the Sātavāhana dynasty. He extended the Sātavāhana sway over Āndhradeśa (between the rivers Kṛṣṇa and Godāvārī). By the middle of the second century, Āndhra had become a part of the Sātavāhana kingdom. His successors continued to rule the kingdom till about the end of the first quarter of the third century of which we do not have any classical account.

On the testimony of the classical authors and that of W.H. Schoff, the history of the Sātavāhanas can be reconstructed to a considerable extent.

The Kingdoms of South India

All the three Tamil kingdoms – the Coḷa, the Cera, and the Pāṇḍya – that existed from a fairly remote antiquity were known to the classical geographers and historians.

The Coḷa Kingdom

Of the three kingdoms, the largest, richest and most flourishing was that of the Coḷas, who were known to Aelian[94] and Ptolemy[95] as Soras. The former calls them men of royal extraction. This kingdom, which constituted the northern portion of Tamilkaṁ or Tamildeśa, is described by the author of the *Periplus* as the "Coast country" [96] It, at his time, as he states, was the most prosperous.

The kingdoms of the Coḷas (the traditional *Coḷamanḍalaṁ*) was bounded on the north by the river Pennar and on the south by the river

Vellāru (Vellar), or in other words extended along the eastern coast from Nellore to Pedukotta. It roughly comprised the modern districts of Tanjore and Trichinopoly.

Ptolemy's Orthoura, called by him the royal city of Sornagos (Soras or Coḷas)[97], or Argaru of the *Periplus*[98] is undoubtedly Uraiyūr, two miles from Trichinopoly, which was "the most ancient historical capital" of the Coḷa kingdom.[99] It was also known by the name of Uragapur. This city was built by the great Coḷa king Karikāla Peravaḷattan. Tañjāvūr (now Tanjore) was one of the later capitals of the kingdom.

The Cera Kingdom

The Ceras were known to the author of the *Periplus* as Cerobothras (Ceraputras) [100] and to Ptolemy as Kerobothros (Keralaputras).[101] Pliny says: "At the time I was writing this Caelobothras was the sovereign of that country".[102] It has been correctly stated by McCrindle that "The King here called Caelobothras belonged to the Keralaputra dynasty."[103]

The Cera kingdom, which constituted one of the three traditional divisions of southern India, corresponded closely with the modern district of Malabar and the states of Travancore (northern part) and Cochin. The Coimbatore or Koimbatur district originally was included in this kingdom. "This was the western Tamil kingdom which in its greatest extension", says Schoff, "reached from Cape Comorin (called "Cape of Comari" in the *Periplus*, sec. 58) to Kārwār point. At the time of the *Periplus*, the northern part had separated, while the southern end had passed to its neighbour, the Pāṇḍya kingdom; leaving Kerala nearly coterminous with modern Malabar and Cochin district..."[104]

From Ptolemy we learn that the capital of the Ceras was Karoura,[105] which has been identified with karūr, an important town in the Coimbatore district[106] originally included in the Cera kingdom, as noted before. Ptolemy's word Karoura "represents the Tamil name of the place with perfect accuracy".

The Pāṇḍya Kingdom

The Pāṇḍya kingdom was of high antiquity. The kingdom is mentioned by the author of the *Periplus*, by Pliny, by Ptolemy, by Strabo, and also by Megasthenes and Arrian.

The author of the *Periplus* distinctly refers to "The Pandian kingdom".[107] The kings, who ruled the kingdom, have been designated as "Pandion" by both Pliny[108] and Strabo.[109] Ptolemy uses "Pandion"[110] for both kingdom and the kings. Here too, as in the case of Cera kingdom, the name is used by the Greek and Latin authors for the kingdom and as a dynastic title. "A dynasty of Rajas, known as the Pāṇḍyana dynasty, appears to have reigned over a kingdom also called Pāṇḍya..."[111] The kingdom called Pandian was Pāṇḍya, the southernmost, and traditionally the earliest of the three Tamil kingdoms.

The Pāṇḍyas ruled the southern extremity of the Indian Peninsula along the east coast. Their kingdom comprised the modern districts of Tinnevelley and Madurai, and also southern Travancore. It extended northward as far as the highlands near the Coimbatore or Koimbatur gap. On the west it was bounded by the Southern Ghāts and on the east by the sea. At the time of the *Periplus*, it extended beyond the Ghāṭs and included Travancore.[112]

The author of the *Periplus*[113], and Ptolemy[114], both mention a place called Kolkhoi, which is identical with Korkai (Kolkai) on the Tāmraparṇī river in Tinnevelly. This was the original capital of the Pāṇḍyas.[115] Their second capital was Madura, called by Pliny Modura[116], and by Ptolemy Modoura[117]. The latter mentions it as "the royal city of Pandion."[118] The site of ancient Madura is situated at a distance of six miles to the south-east of the modern Madurai on the northern banks of the river Vaigai.

Women rule in the realm of the Pāṇḍyas was first noticed by Megasthenes.[119] Arrian[120], Polyaenus[121], Solinus[122], and Phlegon[123], they all, on the authority of Megasthenes, transmit to us more or less the same information with regard to the authority of women to rule the Pāṇḍya kingdom. Pliny categorically states that this was the only kingdom in India which was governed by female sovereigns (queens).[124]

Notes and References

1. See also C. Müller (ed), *Fragm. Hist. Graec.*, I, p. 12; St. Martin, *E'tude*, pp. 364 and 376-8.
2. *History,* III, 91.
3. Sec. 47; also CNES, p. 121.
4. *Geog.*, XV, I, 26; also Hamilton and Falconer's tr. *The Geography of Strabo*, Vol. III, pp. 88-9.
5. *The Races of Afghanistan, Being A Brief Account of the Principal Nations Inhabiting that country,* pp. 60-61.
6. IIA, Note Cc, p. 364.
7. *Geog.*, VII, I, 44. B.N. Mukherjee is absolutely right in stating that the Gandarai or Gandaridai were the people of Gāndhāra in north-western

India. ("The Territory of the Gaṅgāridai-Reappraisal of Classical and Chinese Sources," in *Graeco – Indica: India's cultural contacts with the Greek world*, ed. U.P. Arora, pp. 58, 61, Ref. 9)

8. AICL, p. 31, note 4; *Periplus,* Notes, pp. 183-4.
9. *Geog*., VII, I, 45.
10. *Geog*., XV, I, 28; also Hamilton and Falconer's tr. *Op. cit*., p. 90.
11. Sec. 47.
12. *Geog*., VII, I, 44.
13. *Geog*., XV, I, 27.
14. *Anab*., IV, 22; *Indika*, I, 4 (respectively). Dionysius Periegetes (*Orb. Des*., vv.1080-1164) refers to the seats of the "Gargaridae". McCrindle (AICL, p. 189, note 10) points out that speaks of the Gandaridae whose seats lay to the west of the Indus in Afghanistan. The former writer calls the people of Peukelaitis the Peukalensians.
15. See IHQ, 1953, pp. 14-15.
16. AIT, p. 115.
17. IP, p. 49, see also p. 50.
18. See also J. Douie, *The Punjab, North-West Frontier Province and Kashmir,* p. 160; H.W. Bellew, *op. cit.*
19. *Anab*., IV, 22.
20. See V.S. Agrawala, *India as known to Pāṇini,* p. 456; "Geographical Data in Pāṇini's Asṭādhyāyī," JUPHS, XVI, 1, p. 18.
21. *Anab*., IV, 22; also E.J. Chinnock's tr. of Arrian's *Anab.,* p. 228; H.H. Wilson, *Ar. Ant*., p. 185; IIA, *Biog. Appen.,* p. 381.
22. *Geog*., XV, I, 27; AICL, p. 33, note 1.
23. St. Martin, *E'tude*, p. 37. For details of the position of the ancient city of Puśkalāvatī see IIA, p. 59, note 5; AIMA, pp. 180-81, fn; B.N. Puri, *India as described by Early Greek Writers,* p. 55; E.H. Bunbury, HAG, I, p. 440, and Note Cc, pp. 498-9; CAGI, pp. 42-3; B.C. Law, "Studies in Indian History and Geography Based on Early Greek Accounts," JGRI, XVI, 3-4, 1959, p. 298, note 218.
24. *Anab*., V, 21; see also Diodorus, *Bib. Hist*., XVII, 91; HA, Vol. IV, p. 399.
25. AICL, p. 9, note 4.
26. *Geog*., VII, I, 45.
27. *Dionysiaka,* AICL, p. 199, and note 7.
28. *Anab*., V, 29.

29. See IIA, Biog. Appen., p. 380; H.A. Rose, GTCP, I, p. 27, note 2; J. Hutchison and J. PH. Vogel, *History of the Punjab Hill States,* I, p. 42; V.A. Smith, EHI, p. 62, and note 1; A.V. Williams Jackson (ed), *History of India*, Vol. II, *From the sixth century BC to the Mohammedan Conquest Including the Invasion of Alexander the Great,* by V.A. Smith, pp. 75-6.
30. IIA, p. 129, note 3; AIT, p. 118; CAGI, p. 87.
31. He has been called Phegelas and taken to be identical with the Sanskrit Bhagala, mentioned in the *Gaṇapātha* on Pāṇini (IV.2.80). He belonged to a royal Ksatriya family. See JA, XV, 1890, p. 239 (for view of Sylvain Levi), and IIA, p. 221, note 1 (by McCrindle).
32. *Hist. Alex.*, IX, 1.
33. *Bib.Hist.*, XVII, 93; see also IIA, p. 121, fn.
34. IIA, Biog. Appen., p. 401.
35. GTCP, I, p. 29.
36. *Anab.*, VI, 16.
37. *Geog.*, XV, I, 33.
38. *Bib. Hist.*, XVII, 102.
39. *Hist. Alex.*, IX, 8.
40. *Itin. Alex.*, 112, AICL, p. 153, and note 4.
41. See IIA, Biog. Appen., p. 399.
42. *Ar. Ant.*, p. 204.
43. AICL, p. 40, note 3; IIA, p. 158, note 1 (only notes by him).
44. CAGI, p. 219.
45. HAG, I, Note Uu, pp. 517-18.
46. *Ind. Alt.*, II, p. 177.
47. *E'tude,* p. 165.
48. *Itin. Alex.*, 112.
49. *Anab.*, VI, 16.
50. *Bib. Hist.*, XVII, 102.
51. *Hist. Alex.*, IX, 8.
52. *Geog.*, XV, I, 33.
53. *Vit. Alex.*, Ch. LXIV; also IIA, p. 313, note 1.
54. Strabo (Geog., XV, I, 33) informs us that "Near Patalene (which the Indus forms by splitting into two branches) lies the country of Mousikanos, that of Sabos, that of Portikanos, and other chiefs whose dominions lay along the banks of the Indus." Actually, the dominions of the three chiefs here mentioned lay higher up the Indus than Strabo has indicated.

55. *Anab*., VI, 16.
56. *Geog*., XV, I, 33.
57. IIA, Note S, pp. 354-5, and Biog. Appen., p. 404; AICL, p. 40, note 2; Wilson, *Ar. Ant*., p. 205; CAGI, pp. 222-25; W. Vincent, CNAIO, I, *The Voyage of Nearchus from the Indus to the Euphrates,* p. 135.
58. *E'tude*, pp. 116-22.
59. HHK, Ch. IV, "Remarks on the History and Chronology of Kashmir:, p. 76.
60. *Geog*., VII, I, 42; see also Wilson, HHK, App. VIII, "The Ancient Names of Kashmir in Classical Writers", p. 116.
61. The original designation of Kaśmīr, according to Wilson, was Kaśyapapura, named after its founder, the great sage Kasyapa. Wilson was the first oriental scholar to strongly advocate the identification of Kashmir with this name. (*Ar. Ant*., pp. 136-137; HHK, App. VIII, pp. 114-15; *Miscellaneous Essays*, p. 117). He seems to have been guided by the oriental tradition which still supports the identification of Kaśmīr with its original name Kaśyapapura. See also Lassen, *Ind. Alt*., I, p. 142; II, pp. 631, 635; and Humboldt, *Asie Centrale,* I, p. 102.
62. *Geog*., VII, I, 42.
63. AIT, p. 109.
64. *Various Journeys,* Vol. III, p. 164.
65. *Ind. Alt*., II, p. 898.
66. *M'emoires de L'Acade'mie des Inscriptions, sav. e'trang, Ire S'erie., t.v.* p. 330.
67. IIA, p. 194, note 1.
68. *Ar. Ant*., p. 137.
69. EHI, pp. 32, 37-8.
70. IIA, IV, p. 391.
71. *E'tude*, p. 414 cf AIT, pp. 301-2.
72. See AIT, p. 305.
73. *History,* Bk. XXIII.
74. *Geog*., VII, I, 49; see also AICL, p. 199, note 5; St. Martin, *E'tude*, p. 226; AIT, Notes, p. 360.
75. *Geog*., VII, I, 47; see also R.C. Jain (ed), MAIT, App. 4.
76. A lost poem, but some of passages from it are preserved in the work of Stephenus of Byzantium, first noticed by D' Anville. See M.A. Stein, MAGK, p. 10.
77. XXVI, 165.

78. Sanskrit Dakṣiṇāpatha = Pāli Dakkhiṇāpatha = Prākrit Dakkhinābadha
79. *Periplus*, sec.51, p. 43; CNES, p. 125; CAI, p. 304.
80. *Geog*., VII, I, 82. Ariake (Aparānta or Aparāntika) corresponded more or less with the region what was known subsequently as Mahārāsṭra.
81. *Imp. Gaz. Ind*., XIX, p. 317.
82. Sec. 52, p. 43; CNES, p. 127; CAI, p. 305.
83. The name signifies Śātakarṇi - a dynastic name borne by many of the Sātavāhana monarchs.
84. See *Periplus*, pp. 198 and 294.
85. Dhānyakataka or Dhāṇakataka, now Dharaṇīkota, about 20 miles above Vijayawādā on the river Kṛṣṇā, was an extensive town. It was the eastern capital of the Sātavāhana kingdom. The remains of an ancient township, about one-and-a half miles west of Amrāvatī, in all probability represents Dhānakaṭaka of the inscriptions.
86. *Periplus*, p. 294.
87. Sec.52, p. 43; CNES, p. 128; CAI, p. 305.
88. *Geog*., VII, I, 6; see also L. Renou (ed), *La Geographie de Ptolemee, L Inde*, pp. 3-4. Regarding Ptolemy's Ariake Sadinon (VII, I, 6), D.C. Sircar (SGAMI, p. 229) observes that "Ptolemy's representation of Ariake as the land of the Sadenoi is justifiable..."
89. *Periplus*, pp. 198 and 294. It is worth-nothing here that in the list of thirty Sātavāhana kings given in one of the Purāṇas (*Matsya*, 273, 1-17) Sundara Śātakrṇi figures as the twentieth one. It is also stated therein that he ruled for only one year, which agrees perfectly with the regnal year given by Schoff. The Purāṇic evidence further shows the validity of the identification of the said king by him. For the details of the Purāṇic evidence concerned see G.P. Singh, *Early Indian Historical Tradition and Archaeology*, p. 184.
90. *Periplus*, p. 294.
91. *Geog*., VII, I, 82.
92. *Ibid*., see also L. Renou (ed), *La Geographie de Ptolemee, L'Inde*, p. 35; CAI, p. 381, note 82.
93. See also JBORS, XVI, p. 288.
94. *Nat. Anim*., XV, 8; see also AICL, p. 143, note 5.
95. *Geog*., VII, I, 68; AIT, p. 162; CAI, p. 381, note 68.
96. *Periplus*, sec. 59, p. 46.
97. *Geog*., VII, I, 91; CAI, p. 381, note 91.
98. Sec. 59.

99. *Periplus*, Notes, p. 241; V.A. Smith, EHI, p. 480, and note 2; R.S. Tripathi, HAI, p. 457.

100. *Periplus*, sec. 54, p. 44.

101. *Geog.*, VII, I, 86.

102. *Hist. Nat.*, VI, 23(26)

103. AICL, p. 112, note 1.

104 .*Periplus*, Notes, p. 208.

105. *Geog.*, VII, I, 86.

106. CAI, p. 381, note 86; CNES, p. 133, comm; *Periplus*, Notes, p. 208. B.C. Law ("Studies in Indian History and Geography Based on Early Greek Accounts," JGRI, XVI, 3-4, 1959, p. 282) holds that the capital of the Ceras was originally Vañji ("now Tirukarur on the Periyar river near Cochin"), but later Tiruvañjikalam near the mouth of the Periyar."

107. *Periplus*, sec .54, p. 44 sec.59, p. 46. We are informed by Schoff that the author of the *Periplus* in the first century sojourned among "the sister nations three, Cholas, Cheras, and the Pāṇḍyas dwelling by the southern sea." - *Periplus*, Notes, p. 281.

108. *Hist. Nat.*, VI, 23 (26)

109. *Geog.*, XV, I, 4.

110. *Geog.*, VII, I, 11; VII, I, 89. "By Ptolemy's time, the classical geographers knew of the three Tamil kingdoms... their capital cities and sources of their wealth; they knew other smaller dynasties..", observes Thomas Mcevilley, *The Shape of Ancient Thought: Comparative studies in Greek and Indian philosophies*, p. 391.

111. J.T. Wheeler, "Greek and Roman India", rept. from his *The History of India from the Earliest Ages* (London, 1881), in *Ancient India* (A collection of articles from the works of some foreign scholars), Delhi, 1983, p. 137, note 80.

112. See R.C. Jain (ed), MAIT, App.3; AIT, pp. 59-60, and Notes pp. 351-52; AICL, p. 112, note 3; *Periplus*, Notes, p. 211.

113. CNES, Secs. 58 and 59, pp. 139-40; *Periplus*, sec. 59 and Notes, pp. 211 and 237.

114. *Geog.*, VII, I, 10; also AIT, pp. 57-58.

115. See AICL, p. 144, note 3; *Periplus*, Notes, p. 211; V.A. Smith, EHI, pp. 468-69; R.S. Tripathi, HAI, p. 481; B.C. Law, HGAI, (2nd revd. Edn. Paris, 1967), pp. 215-16; E.H. Warmington, *The Commerce Between the Roman Empire and India*, p. 59.

116. *Hist. Nat.*, VI, 23 (26).

117. *Geog.*, VII, I, 89.

118. *Ibid.*

119. *Indika*, Bk. IV, Fragms. LI, LVI, LVI, B and LVIII.

120. *Indika*, I, 8 and 9; also F.R.B. Godolphin (ed), *The Greek Historians,* Vol.II, pp. 737-39; E.J. Chinnock's tr. of Arrian's *Indika*, pp. 408-9.

121. *Strategemata,* I, 3.4.

122. *Coll. Rer. Memo*., 52, 6-17.

123. *Mirab.* or *on Marvels*, 33, cf Fragm XXX. 6.

124. *Hist. Nat.*, VI, 23; see also H.H. Wilson, HHK, App. III, "The Pandaea Regio of the classical writers", pp. 94-95.

Book Eight
Foreign Rule and Influence

1

The Greek Rule in Bactriana, Ariana and Other Parts of India

The ancient Greek and Roman writers provide us with valuable information regarding the foundation and rise of the Greek kingdom of Bactria, the Greek rule in different parts of India, the fall of the power of the Indo-Greek kings, and the extinction of Greek rule in the East.

Bactria, called also Bactriana (the region of north Afghanistan, bounded on the north by the river Oxus)[1], was one of the provinces of the Seleucid empire of Syria in Western Asia. Its Greek Governor Diodotus revolted from the Seleucid emperor Seleucus II, the great-grandson of Seleucus Nicator[2], declared the independence of Bactria, and proclaimed himself the kings, as we learn from Justin.[3] He founded the independent Greek kingdom of Bactria and ruled over it as an independent monarch.

The notice of Pompeius Trogus is limited to the fact that the Bactrian kingdom was founded by Diodotus[4], who is called Theodotus by Justin. We are told by him that Theodotus, governor of Bactria, revolted and assumed the title of king.[5]

Strabo says that "Those who were entrusted with the government of Syria first caused the revolt of Bactriana."[6] He gives the name of Diodotus (the leader of the revolt) in another passage.[7] He tells us further on the authority of Apollodorus that "the Greeks made Baktriane revolt from the Syrian kings, who succeeded Seleukus Nikator."[8]

The revolt that Justin speaks of took place in 246 BCE immediately after the death of Antiochus II Theos and the accession of Seleucus II, the former grandson and the latter great-grandson of the Syrian king Seleucus Nicator. Diodotus, Governor of Bactriana, took advantage of the disturbances which followed the death of Antiochus II to make himself independent.[9]

The establishment of the Greek kingdom of Bactria in the third century before the Christian era was a landmark in the political history of northern India. "The birth of the new kingdom of Bactria (in 246 BCE)", observes G. Macdonald, "was an event of first-rate political importance."[10]

The founder of the Graeco-Bactrian monarchy was Diodotus.[11] He was the first Greek king of Bactria. He ruled it from 246 BCE[12] till he was succeeded by his "son Diodotus II".[13]

Diodotus II ruled Bactria from about 245 to 220 BCE. According to testimony of Polybius[14], he was deposed and put to death by Euthydemus (about the year 220 BCE). Strabo says that "Euthydemus and his party occasioned the revolt of all the country near the province of Bactriana."[15]

Euthydemus, the successor of Diodotus II, was the founder of the greatness of the Bactrian kingdom. He reigned fairly for a long period (*c.* 220 – 189 BCE) over an extensive territory. He first consolidated his position as a ruler of Bactria. And then he extended his sway over Aria (Herāt), Arachosia (Kandahār), Paropanisadae (Kābul valley), Gāndhāra, and other parts of north-western India.

The Seleucid sovereign, Antiochus III the Great of Syria (223 – 187 BCE), marched eastward in the year 212 BCE to recover the province of Bactria which had been wrested from Syria in the reign of his grandfather Seleucus II (246 – 226 BCE) and not his father (Seleucus III, 226 – 223 BCE), as held by McCrindle.[16] In this regard, we are told by Polybius that the Syrian king Antiochus III waged a war with the contemporary Bactrian monarch Euthydemus (212 BCE) to attain his goal. The former after realising that he was not able to offer any effective resistance to the latter, his adversary, and to assert his supremacy over the kingdom of Bactria concluded the treaty of peace with him (in 206 BCE), practically acknowledged his independence and his sovereignty on Bactria and as a mark of friendship promised to give the hand of one of his daughters to his son Demetrius, then a young prince, whom he found worthy of royal power, and conceded the royal title to his father. We are further told by

Polybius that Antiochus the Great then crossed the Hindukush (in 206 BCE itself) and renewed his alliance with the Indian king Sophagasenus[17] (Greek transcription of the Sanskrit Subhagasena)[18], then reigning in the Kābul valley.[19] Antiochus returned to Syria in the year 205 BCE.

The departure of the Syrian monarch from India thus left the Bactrian Greeks free to pursue their schemes of consolidation and extension of their rule in this country.

The man who established Greek supremacy on Indian soil was Euthydemus' son Demetrius. He succeeded his father in 189 BCE and ruled till about 175 BCE. He held sovereignty in India to the south of the Hindukush called Paropamisus. The city founded by him in Arachosia (southern Afghanistan) which was included in his dominions, was named after him Demetriaspolis, as we learn from Isidore of Charax.[20] He reconstructed the city of Sangala destroyed by the Macedonians in the course of Alexander's invasion of India and gave the name Euthydemia in honour of his father Euthydemus. The city, which was in the Punjab, was also included in his dominions. The city is identical with Sagala of Ptolemy called by him erroneously Euthymedia.[21] Nonnos, however, gives the name more correctly than Ptolemy. The name given by him is Euthydimeia.[22]

Demetrius established his sway over the Kābul valley, the eastern part of Gedrosia (Baluchistan), Gāndhāra, the western Punjab, Lower Sindh and Taxila. He seems to have conquered the territories both to the west and to the east of the Indus. Strabo speaks of the extension of the territories of this Indo-Greek king.[23] Justin designates him "king of the Indians."[24]

"Diodotus laid the foundation of the Graeco – Bactrian kingdom. But the growth and consolidation of their power was largely due to the achievements of Euthydemus and his son Demetrius," says A.K. Narain[25], one of the authorities on the subject.

One of the most powerful of the Graeco – Bactrian kings was Eucratides. He ascended the throne of Bactria in the year 181 BCE and reigned till about 155 BCE. Aelian categorically states that he "governed the Bactrians."[26] He succeeded in extending his dominions in India. He proceeded from Bactria to conqueror the Indian territories. He occupied the Kābul valley, Kandahār, Herāt, Gāndhāra and other parts of north-western India before 162 BCE and brought them under his rule. He was undoubtedly the sovereign of the country west of the Indus.

Apollodorus informs us that "Eucratides had a thousand cities which acknowledged his authority." This is perhaps the basis on which he asserts that "the Baktrians had subjected to their rule a greater portion of India than the Macedonians."[27]

It is worthwhile to mention here that there were two separate Greek principalities in the East, ruled by the rival houses of Euthydemus and Eucratides. Some parts of north-west India conquered and ruled by the later were formerly under the rule of the former and his son Demetrius.

We know from Justin that Eucratides was engaged in many wars which he prosecuted with great vigour. He with the help of his 300 soldiers defeated his rival Demetrius, the king of the Indian, although he had 60,000 strong force. He then made India subject to his power. When he was returning home from his Indian campaign, he was assassinated on the way by his son whom he had made the partner of his throne.[28] The patricide was his eldest son Plato. He was slain by him about 155 BCE.

The murder of Eucratides struck a fatal blow to the fortunes of Graeco - Bactrians.

Eucratides was succeeded by his second son Heliocles about 155 BCE. We do not know the exact period of his reign. He ruled Bactriana from about 155 BCE till he was driven out of that place by the Scythians or Śakas in or about 135 BCE.[29] He was the last Greek king of Bactria or Bactriana. His rule in India lasted for some years more after that date. After the loss of Bactria, he established his rule in the upper Kābul valley, in central and southern Afghanistan, and also in Puṣkalāvatī. This was no doubt the transference of Greek rule from one part of India to its other parts.

Demetrius II (*Circa* 175 – 165 BCE) made some headway in eastern part of Gāndhāra and occupied Taxila, temporarily. It was not part of his kingdom.

The greatest and the most famous of the Indo-Greek rulers was Menander, called Menandrus. He belonged to or was intimately associated with the house of Demetrius II. The period of his reign cannot be fixed with certainty. He ruled from 165 to 145 BCE or till his death in 130 BCE.

Menander ruled in India south of the Paropanisus or Hindukush. His dominions included the Paropanisadae or Kābul valley, the eastern portion of Arachosia or Kandahār and Gedrosia or Baluchistan, the western part of Gāndhāra, and North West Frontier province. He ruled also the western Punjab with his capital at Śakala (modern Sialkot). The Lower Indus Valley with its capital at Patala was also under his rule. He established his hold over Surāṣṭra or Kāthiāwād region of Gujarat. His kingdom extended from Kābul in the north to Kāthiāwād in the west. He penetrated into the Indian heartland. He extended his sway as far as the Yamunā Valley.[30] The river Yamunā is variously called in the classics Isamus, Iomanes, Iobares, Jomanes, and Jobares. It may be added here that before the Lower valley of the Indus passed to the Indo – Scythian or Śaka it was under the rule of the Greeks – Demetrius, the son of Euthydemus, and Menander.[31]

We are informed by Plutarch that Menander (as a ruler) was noted for his justice, and enjoyed great popularity with his subjects.[32]

Strabo, citing Apollodorus as his authority states that "The Greeks who effected the revolt of Bactra (Bactria) became so powerful by means of its fertility and advantages of the country that they became masters of Ariana (Paropanisadae or Kābul Valley, Aria or Herāt, Arachosia or Kandahār, and Gedrosia or Baluchistan) and India." "These conquests", says Strabo "were achieved partly by Menander, partly by Demetrius, son of Euthydemus, king of the Bactrians. They got possession not only of Patalene (so called from its capital Patala, in Lower Sindh, was the delta at the mouth of the Indus) but of the kingdom of Saraostus (Surāṣṭra, i.e., Kāthiāwād) and Sigerdis (probably Sāgaradwipa); which constitute the remainder of the coast. Their (Greeks') chiefs, particularly Menander, if he really crossed the Hypanis (Hyphasis) to the east and reached Isamus (Jomanes or Yamunā river), conquered more nations than Alexander."[33] The discovery of coins of Menander in the neighbourhood of this river[34] testifies to the extension of his sway as far as the Yamunā valley.

"The Great period of Greek rule in India from Demetrius' conquest to the death of Menander is the most notable," observes W.W. Tarn[35], the chief authority on the subject.

Pompeius Trogus describes Apollodorum (Apollodotus) and Menandrum (Menander) as Greek kings of India.[36]

The author of the *Periplus* tells us that up to his time (*Circa* 60-80 CE, or about the third quarter of the first century) ancient *drachmae* (coins) were current in Barygaza (Broach), bearing inscriptions in Greek letters, and the devices of those who reigned after Alexander, Apollodotus and Menander.[37] The Broach region of Gujarat possibly formed part of the dominions of these two Greek kings during their rule in India. Their sway must have extended to western India.

In the early part of the second century before the Christian era, Taxila had become a province of Graeco – Bactrian monarchy. Antialcidas, who belonged to the house of Eucratides, was reigning between 115 and 90 BCE at Taxila.

During the first half of the first century BCE Afghanistan and Gāndhāra were in the possession of princes of the Eucratidian house. Those princes who were ruling in the western part of Gāndhāra with their capital at Peucalaotis (Puśkalāvatī) include Diomedes, Artemidorus and Peucolaus. The Eucratidian princes of Puṣkalāvatī and Taxila regions were outsed by the Śakas of the Lower Sindhu Valley under their king Maues about the beginning of the first century of the Christian era.

Another Branch of the house of Eucratides was represented by Amyntas and Hermaeus who appear to have held sway over Kābul region. Hermaeus, who flourished about the second quarter of the first century of the Christian era, was the Last Greek king of the Kābul valley which soon passed to the Parthians. With the end of his reign ended the Greek rule in India.

The Greeks established their rule in Bactriana, Ariana region (Aria or Herat, Paropanisadae or Kābul valley, and Arachosia or Kandahār in Afghanistan), Baluchistan (Gedrosia), the North Western Frontier Province, Gāndhāra (including Puṣkalāvatī), Taxila, the Punjab, Sindh and other parts of India which became Hellenized to a considerable extent.

It is worthy of remark that the Greek rulers in India belonged to different houses. There was political rivalry among them for supremacy. The Greek dynasties ruled north-western India on parallel lines at one and the same time. The Greeks, who were successors of Alexander, occupied a large part of India. But they failed to establish united rule in this country.

We gather from the coins[38] the names of thirty-eight Greek kings and two Greek queens who ruled in India.

There were various factors that led to the fall of the Indo-Greek kingdom. One of the important factors was the rise of two new powers, the Parthians and the Śakas. Their frequent attack proved to be detrimental to the stability of the Greek rule in India. The Parthians conquered some parts of Ariana region in the second century BCE. They expelled the Greeks from the Upper Kābul Valley about the second quarter of the first century. By the end of the third decade of the first century the Śakas conquered the Paropanisadae, Arachosia, and Gāndhāra, including Taxila, from the Greek rulers. They had already expelled the Greeks from Bactria in or about 135 BCE.

We are told by Justin that the Bactrians were so harassed by various wars that they lost not only their sway over the dominions but even their liberty or independence. For when they had been broken by the wars which they had waged with the Indians and others, they at last feebly succumbed to the once weaker power of the Parthians.[39]

Precisely stating the facts, weakened by internal feuds or dissensions and by the drain on their resources caused by the Indian conquests, and due to attack of the Parthians and the Śakas, the Greeks could not continue their rule in India for long.

The Graeco – Bactrian empire, after having subsisted for about two centuries and a half, was finally overthrown by the invasion of different hordes of the Śaka tribe. The Greek rule in India was supplanted by that of the Śakas.

Notes and References

1. Bactria lying between the Hindukush and the Oxus (or south of the latter) was rich, fertile, and thickly populated province. Pliny [*Nat. Hist.*, VI, 16 (18)] places it at the back of Mount Paropanisus (the Hindukush mountains). Apollodorus of Artemita, the author of the *Parthicae* (History of Parthia) calls it "the ornament of all Ariana," as we know from Strabo (Geog., XI,11, 1).
2. It may fairly be stated here that Seleucus Nicator laid the foundations of the Syrian monarchy in 312 BCE. He also conquered Bactria and made it a dependency of the Syrian kingdom which he had founded. He ruled Syria maintaining his sway over Bactria from 312 to 280 BCE. Bactria remained under the control of his successors (called the Seleucid sovereigns) until its governor Diodotus threw off his allegiance to Seleucus II, declared his independence and became master of Bactria. Thus Bactria became independent of the Syrian monarchy. Those Bactrian Greeks who had declared themselves independent were the descendants of Alexander's colonists in Bactria. The Greek rulers in India are known as Alexander's successors in the East. It may also be mentioned here that they are called in ancient Sanskrit literature Yavanas and in Pāli Yonas (old Persian Yaunas). They were known to the Persians also an Ionians.
3. *Hist. Phil.*, XLI, 4.
4. "In Bactrian is autem rebus ut a Diodoto regnum constitutium est." – *Hist. Philipp.*, XLI.
5. "Eodem tempore etiam Theodoto mille urbium Bactrianarum praefectus defecit, regemque se appellari jussit, quod exemplum secuti." – *Hist. Phil.*, XLI, 4.
6. *Geog.*, XI 9, 2.

7. *Ibid.*, XI, 9, 3.
8. *Ibid.*, XV, I, 3; H.L. Jones (tr.), *The Geography of Strabo*, Vol. VII, p. 5, also Vol. V, p. 273; Hamilton and Falconer's tr. *The Geography of Strabo,* Vol. III, pp. 73-74.
9. See also R.S. Tripathi, HAI, pp. 202-3. Cunningham has also placed the said revolt in 246 BCE (CASE, pp. 85-87, and 111). In one place (*Ibid.*, pp. 79-80), he says that it was about 250 BCE, which is evidently a paradoxical statement. Authorities differ regarding the date of the revolt of Bactrian Greeks under Diodotus for their independence from the Syrian rule. H.T. Prinsep (*Historical Results from Bactrian Coins : Discoveries in Afghanistan*, p. 23), H.H. Wilson (*Ar. Ant.*, p. 216) and J.W. McCrindle (AICL, p. 8, note 1) assign it to the year 256 or 255 BCE. H.G. Rawlinson (*Intercourse Between India and the Western World from the Earliest times to the Fall of Rome,* p. 70; *Bactria from the earliest times to the Extinction of Bactrio – Greek Rule in the Punjab*, p. 48), E.H. Bunbury, (HAG., Vol. II, Note A, p. 102), Clinton (*Fast. Hellen.*, Vol. III, p. 18), E.J. Rapson (*Ancient India from the Earliest times to the first century AD*, p. 62) and J. Marshall (*Taxila*, Vol. I, p. 83) have fixed it "in or about 250 BCE" or "a few years later" Rapson in his another work. (*Ind. Co.*, p. 4) has placed it in 248 BCE. All the dates (except 246 BCE) are conjectural or hypothetical. All those who have suggested the date 256, 255 or 250 BCE or a few years later are of the opinion that the revolt took place in the reign of the Seleucid monarch Antiochus II (261-246 BCE). But the fact remains that the revolt broke out immediately after the death of Antiochus II in 246 BCE and the accession of Seleucus II in the same year, as noted before. McCrindle (AICL, p. 100, note 6) states that "Diodotus revolted from Syria in the latter years of the reign of the third prince of the Seleucidan dynasty, Antiochus II, who died in BC 246." In the light of the fact stated above this may be taken as unworthy of credence. Some writers have placed the date of the foundation of the independent Bactrian kingdom in or about the middle of the third century BCE. See V.A. Smith, *The Oxford History of India*, revd. by H.G. Rawlinson, p. 62; H.C. Raychaudhuri, PHAI, p. 379; and *Imp. Gaz. Ind.*, Vol. II, p. 137.
10. "The Hellenic kingdoms of Syria, Bacteria, and Parthia", in CHI, I, p. 391.
11. R.G. Bhandarkar, *A peep into the Early History of India from the Foundation of the Maurya Dynasty to the Downfall of the Imperial Gupta Dynasty*, p. 22.
12. G. Macdonald (*op. cit*) says that "The formal accession of Diodotus took place about 250 BC."
13. Justin, *Hist. Phil.*, XLI, 4.
14. *History*. XI, 39.
15. Hamilton and Falconer's tr. *The Geography of Strabo,* Vol. II, p. 251.

16. AICL, p. 209, note 3.
17. *History*, XI, 34, also X, 49; B.N. Puri, *India as described by Early Greek Writers*, pp. 16, 68-69.
18. See Lassen, *Ind. Alt*., II, p. 273.
19. Some historians are of the view that Subhagasena was the ruler of Gāndhāra with its capital at Taxila. See also JIH, LVI, I, 1978, p. 48.
20. *Mans. Parth*., tr. by W.H. Schoff, *Parthian stations of Isidore of Charox*, p. 19, see also pp. 8ff; JRAS, 1915, p. 830.
21. *Geog*., VII, I, 46; AIT, pp. 122 and 124; also *Ind. Ant*., 1884, pp. 349-50.
22. *Dionysiaka,* Bk. XXVI; and AICL, p. 200, note 2.
23. *Geog*., XI, 11, 1.
24. *Hist, Phil*., XLI, 6.
25. *The Indo-Greeks,* p. 19.
26. *Nat. Anim*., XV, 8.
27. Cf. Strabo, *Geog*., XV, I, 3, Ptolemy mentions Eucratidia (*Geog*., VI, 11, 8), which received its name from Eucratides, by whom it was founded (AIT, p. 274). Its site cannot be identified.
28. "Multa tamen Eucratides bella magna virtute gessit quibus attritus cum obsidionem Demetrii regis Indorum pateretur cum CCC militibus LX millia hostium assiduis eruptionibus vicit. Quinto itaque mense Liberatus India in protestatem redegit." – *Hist. Phil*., XLI, 6; Watson's trans. of Justin's *Hist. Phil.,* p. 277. See also H.G. Rawlinson, *Bactria, the History of a Forgotten Empire,* pp. 155-6; Cunningham, *Num. Chron*., 1869, p. 241; Rapson, JRAS, 1905, p. 783; W.W. Tarn, "Hellenism in Baktria", *Jour. Hells. Stud.* 1902, p. 272. M. Elphinstone, "The Greek Kingdom of Bactria", rept. from his *The History of India* (ed. E.B. Cowell, 9th edn. London, 1911), in *Ancient India* (Delhi, 1983), pp. 34-35.
29. See also Hamilton and Falconer's tr. *The Geography of Strabo*, Vol. II, pp. 245-46.
30. See Rawlinson, *Bactria from the earliest times*…, pp. 134-35; Wilson, *Ar. Ant*., p. 281; Bunbury, HAG, Vol. II, p. 46.
31. See AIT, pp. 139-40.
32. *Moralia*, p. 821 D – E, LCL edn. X, pp. 276-9.
33. *Geog*., XI, xi, 1; see also H.L. Jones (tr.) *The Geography of Strabo*, Vol. V, pp. 279-80; Hamilton and Falconer's tr. *The Geography of Strabo*, Vol. II, pp. 252-53; Jacoby, FGH, No. 779, Fragm. 7a; Bunbury, HAG, Vol. I, p. 571; M. Elphinstone, "The Greek Kingdom of Bactria", rept. from his *The History of India* (London, 1911), in *Ancient India* (Delhi, 1983), p. 35; B.C. Law, HAGI, pp. 297 ff; and TAI, pp. 347-48; *Ind. Ant*., 1884, p. 354.

34. See Wilson, *Ar.* Ant., p. 281; AICL, p. 100, note 8. According to the testimony of the *Yuga Purāṇa* of the *Gārgī – Saṁhitā* (11, 22-26), the Yavana forces having occupied Sāketa (Ayodhyā), Pañcāla and Mathurā reached Puspapura (Pāṭaliputra). See A.K. Narain, *op. cit.*, pp. 82-83, and App. IV, pp. 174-79; and K.P. Jayaswal, JBORS, XIV, 1928, p. 402. Patanjalli in his *Mahābhāṣya* (III, 2, 111) also mentions that the Yavana forces besieged Sāketa. See B.N. Puri, *India in the time of Patañjali,* pp. 28-29. Menander is generally identified with the Yavana invader who carried his arms as far as the Gaṅgā – Yamunā doab.

35. *The Greeks in Bactria and India*, p. 361.

36. *Hist. Philipp.*, Bk. XLI.

37. *Periplus*, sec. 47, and p. 185, note; CNES, pp. 121-22; see also Wilson, *Ar. Ant.*, pp. 280-81 and 288; *Ind. Ant.*, Vol. VIII, p. 143.

38. For details see R.B. Whitehead, CCPM, Vol. I, *Indo – Greek Coins*, pp. 9-86; Whitehead *Num. Chron.*, 1923, pp. 300-1; 1940, p. 104, pl. VIII, 2; CHI, I, pp. 417-19, and pls. III and IV; Cunningham, CASE, pp. 126-276; E.J. Rapson, *Ind. Co.*, pl. I, 9, 10, 12, 16 and 18; Wilson, *Ar. Ant.*, pp. 222ff, 228ff, 236-37, 288ff; P. Gardner, CCGBM, pl. I, 9, pl. II, 9-12, pl. III, 3, pl. V, 7, Pl. IX, 8-13, pl. XXX, 3; J. Allan, CCBM, pl. XXXII, 21; *Num. Chron.*, 1869, pp. 136, 217; 1887, p. 177; and 1943, pp. 57-8; Rapson, *Num. Chron.*, 1940, pp. 319-21.

39. *Hist. Phil.*, XLI, 6, 3. Throwing light on the end of Greek rule in Afghanistan and other parts of northern India, P. Sykes *(A History of Afghanistan,* Vol. I, p. 101) opines that "The fall of the dominion exercised by the Greeks in provinces east of Hindukush coincided with the establishment of the Roman Empire by Augustus."

2

The Rule of the Śakas in India

The tribe known to the ancient Indians as Śaka is called Sacae (Śakae) by the classical writers.[1] The author (anonymous) of the *Periplus*[2], and another unknown writer[3], who follows Eratosthenes and Ptolemy, call the Śaka also Scythia. The word Sacae is used loosely of all Scythians by the ancient Greek and Roman geographers and historians. It may also be added here that Sakai is the Persian equivalent of Śakae, or Skythai (the Scythians) of the ancient Greeks and Romans.[4]

We are indebted to the classical authors, for our knowledge of the early history of the Śakas and of their rule in India.

The Śakas called Sacae belonged to the family of the Scythians that played an important role in the history of Asia. We learn from Strabo that these Śakas originally lived in the vast plains of the Jaxartes (now Syrdaryā), on its other side, in Central Asia.[5] About 165 BCE they were driven out of their original homeland by the Yueh-Chi tribe, who after being turned out of their native place in north-western China by a rival horde migrated to Central Asia, overpowered them, and established their hold.[6] One section of the Scythians or Śakas went to Iran, and the other came to India who became known as Indo-Scythians.

The Śakas on their way to India first crossed the Hindukush (Mount Paropamisus or Paropanisus of the classical geographers) and then moving further south of the Oxus river entered Bactria (north Afghanistan), drove the Indo-Greek king Heliocles out of this place in or about 135 BCE and occupied it. The Śaka occupation of Bactria is noticed by Strabo.[7] Justin also makes an incidental notice of the "overthrow of the Graeco-Bactrian empire by the Sacae."[8] The Śakas ruled Bactria till they were expelled from there by the Yueh-Chi tribe from central Asia in 126 BCE. E.H. Bunbury observes that this was the final extinction of the Greek kingdom of Bactria in this part of Asia.[9]

From Bactria the Śakas moved further in search of a new land to settle down. They could not move through Kābul valley as the area was ruled by powerful Indo-Greeks. And hence they moved through Arachosia (Kandahār, in southern Afghanistan). Then they came to Baluchistan (Gedrosia of the historians of Alexander) and settled in its southern part. The place of their settlement became known as Śakasthāna (the abode of the Śakas), which was called Śakasthene first by Isidore of Charax and then by Stephanus of Byzantium. The Śakas settlement there can also be confirmed by the statement of W.H. Schoff, the translator and annotator of the *Periplus*[10]. The aforesaid place was afterwards called Seistan.[11] They remained there for a considerable period of time. From there they finally came to Sindh and took possession of its lower valley. It has been rightly stated by one of the authorities that "shortly before the Christian era the Śakas held possession of the country on the western bank of the Indus.[12] The place of their settlement in the lower valley of the Indus became known as Śakadvīpa to Hindu writers and Indo-Scythia to Greek writers. The Indo-Scythians or Śakas established their rule in Lower Sindh some time between 30 and 20 before Christ and ruled it from that period onwards till about the close of the sixth decade of the first century of the Christian era. In the first century itself, the Indo-Greek rulers had been dispossessed of lower Indus region by the Śakas. From this base the latter established their settlements in several parts of India and ruled there.

The author of the *Periplus* informs us that in his time (the first century of the Christian era) the wide tract which was watered by the river Indus called Sinthus (transliteration of the native name of it-Sindhu) in the lower part of its course was called Scythia (the territory of the Śaksas); and that Minnagara (city of the Min or Scythians, Śakas), which lay inland (on or near the banks of the Indus) behind Barbaricum an entrepot on the principal mouth of the Indus) was the metropolis of Scythia.[13]

Minnagara of the *Periplus* is Minagara of Ptolemy[14], the Greek geographer, who flourished about the middle of the second century of the

Christian era. Binagara of the latter[15] is a less correct form than Minnagara. Scythia of the *Periplus* is Indi-Scythia (or Indo-Skythia) of Ptolemy.[16]

The city called Minnagara by the author of the *Periplus* was no other than Patala (skt. Prasthala) at the mouth of the Indus. It was the metropolis of Scythia or Indo-Scythia (the Śaka kingdom in the Lower Indus valley).[17]

We know from Dionysius Periegetes also that in the orient (India) dwelt the Scythians (Śakas) of the south, on the banks of the river Indus.[18]

The Śakas ruled Lower Sindh from about 25 BCE till they were dislodged by the Indo-Parthians about CE 60.

The Śaka rulers, who ruled in the north-western parts of India, were from eastern Iran.

The first Iranian Śaka to rule in India was Maues (*circa* 20 BCE – CE 22). Puṣkalāvatī (Peukelaotis of the Greeks), a very large and populous city, situated to the west of the river Indus, came under the Śaka rule during his reign. His dominions included also Taxila. Gāndhāra and other adjacent lands formerly under the Greek rule came under his possession. He ruled Lower Indus Valley about the beginning of the first century of the Christian era. He extended Śaka suzerainty over large parts of north-western India. It appears that he established his rule both to the west and to the east of the Indus. He was succeeded on the throne of Gāndhāra by Azes I in CE 22 who put an end to the remnant of Greek rule in the eastern Punjab. He extended the Śaka rule over eastern part of the Punjab during his reign (CE 22-30). The Roman historian Orosius specifically refers to the Scythians' or Śakas' rule in the Punjab.[19]

After Azes II the Śaka territories passed under the sway of the Indo-Parthian ruler Gondophernes. The Śaka domination in north-western India was followed by that of the Parthians. There are, however, some classical evidence regarding the expansion of Śaka rule in other parts of India.

The Śaka Kṣatrapas, who ruled in Gujarat and Mahārāṣṭra in western India and in west Mālavā region in central India, were independent rulers.

The author of the *Periplus* transmits to us valuable information regarding the Śaka rule in western India. He says, "Beyond the gulf of Baraca (Cutch) is that of Barygaza and the coast of the country of Ariaca, which is the beginning of the kingdom of Nambanus… the coast is called Syrastrene… The metropolis of this country is Minnagara, from which much cotton cloth is brought down to Barygaza."[20]

From the preceding Greek account of the subject it is quite evident that in the time of the author of the *Periplus* Syrastrene (Sanskrit Surāṣṭra

= modern Saurāṣṭra Kāṭhiāwād), Barygaza (modern Broach or Bharoch, situated about 30 miles from the sea on the north side of the river Narmadā called Namados), and the territories on the Gulf of Cutch and on both sides of the Gulf of Cambay in Gujarat (Ariaka in the text, and Larike of Ptolemy, VII, I, 62) were under the rule of the Śaka Kṣatrapa Nambanus (Nahapāna), who belonged to the Ksaharata dynasty founded by Bhūmaka in western India. The metropolis of the Śaka kingdom that Nahapāna ruled from about 24 to 70 CE was apparently Surat, which is is called in the text Minnagara as it was the city of the Śakas. Syrastrene, which extended form the mouth of the Indus to the Gulf of Cutch, was one of the three divisions of Indo-Scythia in Ptolemy's time. It may also be added here that a large part of Mahāraṣṭra (Sanskrit Aparantikā = Greek Ariaka) was also under the sway of Nahapāna. He must have wrested this region from the early Sātavāhana rulers. By about 70 CE both Gujarat and Mahāraṣṭra might have formed parts of the Śaka kingdom of western India which was ruled by Nahapana.[21]

Ptolemy tells us that in his time "Ozene (Ujjayini) was the capital of Tiastanes."[22] This name is a Greek transcription of Caṣṭana, the famous Śaka ksatrapa. He was the son of Yasamatika or Ysāmotika.

Caṣṭana ruled the Śaka kingdom in western Mālavā region with his capital Ujjayini (Ujjain) in the second quarter of the second century of the Christian era. The earliest known date of his rule is CE 130.[23]

Ujjayini remained the capital of Caṣṭana's successors or descendants till their overthrow by Candragupta II about the close of the fourth century.

The Śaka rule in western and central India finally came to an end towards the close of the fourth century.

Notes and References

1. Herodotus, *Hist.,* VII, 64; Strabo, *Geog*., XI, 8, 2 and 4; Pliny, *Nat. Hist*., VI, 19; Ptolemy, *Geog*., VII, I , 1; *Ano. Geog., Expo. Comp*. (by an unknown writer, who follows Eratosthenes and Ptolemy), VI, 24; Justin, *Hist. Phil*., XLI, 6; Nonnos, *Dionysiaka*, Bk. XXVI, tr. by Priaulx, pp. 206-9, in AICL , p. 200. It is also stated in *Enc. Br*. (Vol. 19, p. 928) that the Śaka, a Scythian tribe, is identical with the Sacae of classical literature.
2. Sec. 38.
3. *Ano. Geog. Expo. Comp*., VI, 24.
4. See AICL, p. 200, note 5.
5. *Geog*., XI, 8, 2.
6. See H.G. Rawlinson, *Bactria from the earliest times to the extinction of Bactrio-Greek Rule in the Punjab,* p. 94.

7. *Geog.*, XI, 8, 2; XI, 8, 4; Hamilton and Falconer's tr. *The Geography of Strabo*, Vol. II, pp. 245-46; also H.H. Wilson, *Ar. Ant.*, p. 139.
8. *Hist. Phil.*, II, 3.
9. HAG, I, p. 570, note 5.
10. p. 166, note.
11. Seistan, called Śakastan, is now a province of eastern Iran – *Ind. Ant.*, 1909, p. 24. For details see F.W. Thomas, "Śakastana, where dwelt the Śakas named by Darius and Herodotus", JRAS, 1906, pp. 181ff, and 204-14.
12. JBAS, IX, p. 139.
13. *Periplus*, sec. 38, and pp. 165-66, notes; CNES, Sec. 38, and pp. 107-8, comm.; also W. Vincent, CNAIO, Vol. I, *The Voyage of Nearchus from the Indus to the Euphrates,* p. 141; Vol. II, *The Periplus of the Erythrean sea,* pp. 345 and 349; H.G. Rawlinson, *Intercourse Between India and the Western World from the Earliest times to the Fall of Rome,* p. 114; CAGI, p. 246; CISSK, pp. 36-37.
14. *Geog.*, VII, I, 63; also AIT, p. 156.
15. *Ibid.*, VII, I, 61; also *Ibid.*, p. 152.
16. *Ibid.*, VII, I, 62 and VII, I, 55; see also AIT, pp. 136, 139 and 272; *Ep. Ind.*, VIII, p. 36f.
17. McCrindle (AICL, p. 187, note 3) has correctly stated that "the Lower Indus was called Indo-Scythia – a name derived from the Scythian tribes."
18. *Orb. Des.*, Lines 1080-1165.
19. *Roman History*, V, 4.
20. *Periplus,* sec.41; also CNES, sec.41, and pp. 113-14.
21. See *Periplus*, pp. 174-76, 180, 198, notes, and p. 294; AIT, pp. 136, 140 and 153; Rawlinson, *Intercourse Between India and the Western World…*, p. 118, Rapson, JRAS, 1904, p. 371; D.C. Sircar, SGAMI, p. 226.
22. *Geog.*, VII, I, 63.
23. See AIT, p. 155; *Periplus*, p. 188, note; CAI, pp. 373, and 381, note 63.

3

The Parthian Rule in North-West India

Parthia played an important role in the history of Persia and India. It was a part of Persia. It was originally a province lying to the south-east of the Caspian sea. The two modern provinces, *viz.* Khurasan and Astravad of Iran, constituted Parthian kingdom.

Parthia, once the predominant power in western Asia, was at the last reduced to the province of Syria. We have the classical notices of Parthia, which was one of the provinces of the Seleucid empire of Syria of revolt of the Parthians under Arsaces (or Arsakes) against the Seleucid overlord, establishment of an independent kingdom of Parthia by him, and of the rise of the Parthians and their rule in north-western parts of India.

"According to one account," says Strabo, "Arsaces was a Bactrian, who withdrew himself from the encroachments of Diodotus (founder of the Greek Kingdom of Bactria) and established Parthia as an independent state."[1] Arsaces was no doubt a native of Bactria. He had fled to Parthia, because the rival Diodotus had prevailed in his native city. One coin bearing his name has also been discovered in Afghanistan.[2]

Justin, the chief authority on the subject, tells us that the Parthians were under the rule of Seleucus Nicator, the Greek king of Syria (312-280 BCE), and then under his two immediate successors, Antiochus I Soter

(280 – 261 BCE) and Antiochus II Theos (261 – 246 BCE). It was from Seleuchus Nicator's great-grandson Seleucus II that they (the Parthians) revolted (in 246 BCE – the year of his accession to the throne of Syria). We are further told by him that Arsaces, a man of uncertain origin but of undaunted courage and valour, arose at this period. He had report that Seleucus had been defeated and worsted by the Gauls in Asia. Feeling himself free from his fear of him and safe from his interference, Arsaces invaded Parthia with a band of brigands, defeated and killed Andragoras, the governor, declared the independence of Parthia and took the reins of government into his own hands.[3] This occurred after the death of Antiochus II and the succession of Seleucus II in 246 BCE at the time when there was a commotion or internal disturbance in Syria. Seleucus was not in a position or powerful enough to put down the Parthian revolt. It was the period of decline of the Seleucid power. Parthia, like Bactria, became independent of the Syrian monarchy. Justin unequivocally calls Arsaces "king of the Parthians."[4] Strabo informs us that all the Parthians were called Arsakai[5] after the name of Arsakes, the founder of the kingdom of Parthia and of the dynasty of Parthia called Arsacid dynasty.

Appian places the revolt of the Parthians in 246 BCE, as we learn from Clinton[6], a trustworthy authority on the history of Syria under the Greek sovereigns. Cunningham, citing Justin (XLI, 4) as his authority, states that the Parthians revolted under Arsakes in the reign of Seleucid sovereign Seleucus II, the great – grandson of Seleucus I, but mistakenly places the revolt in or about the year 250 BCE.[7]

In the light of the testimony of Justin (brought forth before), the statements of some authorities, notably, Eusebius[8], H.G. Rawlinson[9], J.W. McCrindle[10], H.T. Prinsep[11] and John Marshall[12], that Arsaces revolted from Syria in the reign of the Seleucid monarch Antiochus II in or about the year 250 BCE, can be disposed of. Some writers place the revolt about 249 or 248 BCE.[13] The two distinguished historians of ancient India, R.S. Tripathi and E.J. Rapson, are also at variance with each other regarding the date of the revolt or uprising. The date suggested by the former is "about 248 BCE"[14] and by the latter is "about 250 BC or a few years later".[15] All the aforesaid dates (except 246 BCE) are based purely on speculation and not on any original evidence. "... the revolt of Parthia took place almost simultaneously with the revolt of Bactria, although probably a year or two later," says G. Macdonald.[16] He has also not given any specific date of the revolt of either Parthians or the Bactrian Greeks against the Seleucid sovereign.

Arsaces ruled Parthia from 246 to about 230 BCE. He was succeeded by his brother Tiridates, afterwards called Arsaces II. We are informed by Justin that Seleucus II of Syria tried to reassert his authority in Parthia (some time between 230 and 226 BCE). He led two expeditions into Parthia. But he was ultimately defeated by Tiridates.[17] After his triumph over Seleucus, Tiridates recovered his dominions, and extended and consolidated the Parthian monarchy between 220 and 214 BCE. He was, in fact, the real founder of the Parthian empire. He was succeeded by Artabanus I, who ruled Parthia from about 214 BCE to 191 BCE.

It is worthy of note that originally the Parthians lived in eastern Iran from where they moved to India. The Parthian rulers in India are called Indo-Parthians. They are described in some of the ancient Indian Sanskrit texts both as Pārthavas and Pahlavas. They established their rule in north-western parts of India.

The Parthian rule in India began in the second century before the Christian era and continued down to the first century of that era.

Mithridates I (171-138 BCE) was the first powerful Parthian monarch to bring north-west India under his rule. He ruled over eastern Iran as well as over India. "Two great men", Justin says, "Mithridates and Eucratidas, began to reign almost simultaneously, the one over the Parthians and the other over Bactria. Fortune was more propitious to the Parthians under their king, who conducted them to supreme power..."[18]

Strabo tells us that the Parthian king (Mithridates) deprived Eucratides by force of arms a part of Bactriana and incorporated it in his empire. He tells us further that he took away from Eucratides (in 159 BCE) two Bactrian satrapies – Aria (Herāt in western Afghanistan) and Arachosia (Kandahār in southern Afghanistan) – which formed parts of Ariana.[19] Arachosia in particular passed from the Greeks to the Parthians in the reign of Mithridates I himself. Speaking of Parthian dominions in north-west India, Isidore of Charax categorically states that "Arachosia was a part of Parthian province."[20] Mithridates conquered the provinces of Sindh and the Punjab in or about 150 BCE. The Parthian power extended up to the lower Indus region during his reign, about the middle of the second century before the Christian era. The Parthian king penetrated into India even beyond Sindh. Orosius, one of the ancient Roman historians, makes a definite statement to the effect that Mithridates subdued the nations between the Indus and the Hydaspes.[21] The Parthian occupation south of the Hindukush was, however, not permanent. Justin expressly says that this range of mountains was the limit of his kingdom to the East.[22] It is, however, not the absolute truth. He ruled some parts of north-western India even beyond this limit. But he could not establish his hold there permanently.

It was during the reign of Mithridates' successor Phraates II (138 – 128 BCE) that Śaka invasion took place which swept over Bactria. But Phraates II failed to put them down.[23] In the struggle with the Śakas he was killed in 128 BCE. In Śaka invasion Artabanus II (128 – 123 BCE) also lost his life in 123 BCE.

"The Parthians", says Strabo, "conquered Bactria from the Scythians (Śakas), and gradually occupied the north-western parts of India where they left their impact for posterity."[24] Here he refers to the period of Mithridates II the Great (123 – 88 BCE), who defeated the Scythians and dislodged them from the western parts of Bactria of which they were in possession. But we have no evidence to show how long he continued to possess those parts of Bactria. He established his rule also in Seistan (southern part of Baluchistan, called Gedrosia) and Gāndhāra. He, no doubt, reasserted the Parthian power.

Isidore of Charax also relates that Seistan was ruled by the Parthians.[25] Pliny says that the dominions of the Indians, Scythians, Bactrians, and all the eastern nations were comprehended in the vast empire of the Parthians.[26] The Parthians ruled those dominions which they subjugated in north-western parts of India.

It may be noted here that the Śaka – Pahlavas ruled over this country on parallel lines for some time.

The Parthian rule in some parts of Afghanistan was established even after Mithridates II.

Strabo refers to a Parthian king named Phraates[27], who, according to McCrindle, was contemporary with Strabo.[28] He ruled Parthia probably in 26 BCE. Nothing can be said of him for want of details.

Strabo speaks of the extension of the Parthian monarchy as one of the sources of increased geographical knowledge in his day (i.e. 31 BCE – 21 CE).[29]

Gondophernes (CE 21-51) was the most eminent Parthian ruler in India. Originally, he was a ruler of Arachosia (Kandahār region in southern Afghanistan). He gradually extended his power in different directions and became an emperor. He ousted Hermaeus, the last Greek king of the upper Kābul valley, about the second quarter of the first century and established his rule there. Isidore of Charax does not include that region in the list of eastern provinces of the Parthian empire[30] which shows that Kābul valley was brought under the Parthian rule posterior to his time. He ruled also western Gāndhāra. He ruled not only to the west of the Indus but also to its east. He occupied the eastern Gāndhāra region, and established his capital at Taxila. He ruled over the western Punjab. The parthain supremacy in the Punjab was established by the middle of the first century. The coins of Gondophernes have been found from the Kābul valley, Gāndhāra, Seistan, and Sindh which bear testimony to the fact that he ruled over a large part of northwest India. He ruled in India for about thirty years. He died in CE 51.

The Parthian prince Phraotes was not only independent of the Parthian emperor Vardanes (*Circa* CE 39-47) but was himself powerful enough to exercise suzeraign power over the satrapy of the Sindhu Valley. It appears that Phraotes was for some time the semi-independent Governor of Gāndhāra under Gondophernes. He soon became independent ruler of Gāndhāra region with his capital at Taxila.

It is said that Phraotes "threw off the Śaka sovereignty in parts of Gāndhāra."[31] The Śaka sovereignty in Gāndhāra was supplanted by that of the Parthians.

We learn from the Greek historian Philostratus that the Greek traveller Apollonius of Tyana in course of his visit to Taxila in CE 44 found that it was under the rule of Phraotes, "apparently a Parthian, but an Indian King." We also know from him that Taxila was the capital of a sovereign (Phraotes) who ruled over what was formerly the kingdom of Porus.[32]

After the death of the greatest Indo-Parthian monarch Gondophernes in CE 51, his empire split up into smaller principalities. Pacores (or Pakores), the successor of Gondophernes, ruled over portions of southern Afghanistan (Kandahār region), and the western Punjab.

The author of the *Periplus* informs us that Minnagara (Patala), earlier the metropolis of Scythia (the Śaka kingdom in the Lower Indus Valley), was governed in his time by the Indo-Parthian princes who were constantly at feud with each other for the supremacy.[33]

W.H. Schoff, the translator and annotator of the text *Periplus*, says that the political conditions described in the text were probably those that followed the death of Gondophernes, the last powerful Indo-Parthian ruler in the Punjab.[34] "Parthian princes were at war with each other probably within the decade following the death of Gondophernes, which occurred 51 AD."[35]

J.W. McCrindle comments that "The Parthians must therefore have subverted a Scythian (Śaka) dynasty (in Lower Sindh) which must have been that which was founded between the years 30 and 20 BC."[36] Pliny also tells us that the dynasty of Parthian kings than that of the Śakas ruled Lower Indus.

The statement of the author of the *Periplus* that Parthian rulers succeeded the Scythians in the lower valley of the Indus is confirmed by the Parthian coins found everywhere in this part of the country.[37]

"Evidence of the ousting of Śaka rule by the Parthians in the Lower Indus Valley is furnished by the author of the *Periplus* in whose time ("about 60 to 80 AD") Minnagara, the metropolis of Scythia (i.e "the Śaka kingdom in the Lower Indus Valley"), was subject to Parthian princes, who were constantly driving each other out", says H.C. Raychaudhuri.[38]

Like the Greeks and the Śakas, the Parthians also ruled in different parts of north-west India.

The Parthian power began to decline from CE 64 onwards. It appears that by CE 79[39] the Parthians were overthrown by the Kuṣāṇas. The latter must have become absolute masters of large parts of north-western India after the end of the Parthian rule in this country. The Parthian rule in Afghanistan, Gāndhāra, Sindh and the Punjab was supplanted by that of the Kuṣāṇa dynasty.

Notes and References

1. *Geog.*, XI, 9, 3.
2. H.T. Prinsep, *Historical Results from Bactrian Coins : Discoveries in Afghanistan,* pp. 24-25, 30.
3. *Hist. Phil.*, XLI, 4-5: "… Arsaces, Vir, Sicut incertae originis, ita virtutis expertae, … cum Praedonum manu Parthos ingressus, praefectum eorum Andragorum oppressit sublataeque eo, imperium gentis invasit."
4. *Hist. Phil.*, XXXVI, 1.
5. *Geog.*, XV, I, 36; Hamilton and Falconer's tr. *The Geography of Strabo*, Vol. III, pp. 97-98.
6. *Fast. Hellen.*, Vol. III, p. 20.
7. CASE, pp. 79-83 and 85.
8. *Chronicle,* II, p. 32.
9. *Bactria from the earliest times to the extinction of Bactrio – Greek rule in the Punjab*, pp. 47-48.

10. AICL, p. 44, note 1. "... the rise and spread of the Parthian power... interposed as a barrier to prevent communication between Syria and her provinces in the East which had revolted from her authority in the reign of Antiochus II," observes he (*Ibid.*, Introd. xvii).
11. *Op. cit.*, pp. 23-24 and 30.
12. *Taxila*, I, p. 83.
13. See PHAI, p. 451, note 1.
14. HAI, p. 202.
15. *Ancient India from the earliest times to the first century AD*, p. 62.
16. "The Hellenic kingdoms of Syria, Bactria and Parthia", in CHI, I, p. 394.
17. *Hist. Phil.*, XLI, 4; see also Clinton, *Fast. Hellen.*, Vol. II, *Kings of Syria.*
18. *Hist. Phil.*, XLI, 6.
19. Hamilton and Falconer's tr. The Geography of Strabo, Vol. II, pp. 251-53.
20. *Mans. Parth.*, in C. Müller (ed), *Geog. Graec. Mino.*, Vol.I, pp. 244-56.
21. *Roman History*, V, 4; see also Diodorus Siculus, *Bib. Hist.*, p. 597.
22. *Hist. Phil.*, XLI, 6, 8.
23. Justin, *Ibid.*, XLII, 1-2.
24. *Geog.*, XI, 9, 2.
25. *Mans. Parth.*, tr. by W.H. Schoff, *The Parthian Stations of Isidore of Charax,* p. 18.
26. *Nat. Hist.*, XVI, 37 (65).
27. *Geog.*, XV, I, 36.
28. AICL, p. 44, note 1.
29. *Geog.*, II, 5, p. 118.
30. *Mans. Parth.*, ed. and tr. by Schoff, *The Parthian Stations of Isidore of Charax*, p. 17.
31. B.N. Puri, *India as described by Early Greek Writers,* p. 71.
32. *Vit. Apoll.*, II, 12; II, 23 and 26; Eng. trans of the Greek text *Vit. Apoll.*, by F.C. Conybeare, *The Life of Apollonius of Tyana*, Vol.I, pp. 147 and 185; also AICL, p. 192; Priaulx, *Indian Travels of Apollonius of Tyana*, in CAI, pp. 387-88.
33. *Periplus,* sec.38; CNES, p. 108; also AIT, pp. 139 and 152.
34. *Periplus*, p. 167, note.
35. *Ibid.*, p. 294.
36. CNES, p. 110.
37. *Ibid.* and AIT, p. 139.

38. PHAI, p. 453.
39. R.C. Jain is of the opinion that "By the fourth quarter of the first century AD they (Parthians) were driven out by the Kushanas." – MAIT, Conculturuum, XI.

4

Foreign Influence on Indian Civilization and Indian Influence on Western Culture and Thought

The ancient Greeks and Indians were mutually influenced by each other in various fields through their contacts and interactions. There are some positive evidence in the classics regarding the influence of Greek town-planning ideas in India, the Greek influence on Indian, art, coinage, language and literature, influence of Indian religions – Buddhism and Hinduism – on the Greeks in India, influence of Indian philosophical ideas on the thought of the Greek philosophers of both pre- and post-Alexandrian age, and the influence of Indian science of medicine on the Greek medicine.

It may specifically be mentioned here that the Greek influence on the art of India was first seen in the time of Alexander the Great. In post-Alexandrian times, there was Hellenistic influence on that art. The influence of Hellenism was witnessed in north-western parts of India during the rule of Alexander's successors (Bactrian Greeks)[1]. "If certain, statements of classical authors were true", says G.N. Banerjee, "Hellenism in India flourished exceedingly."[2] He further observes that "Greece has played a part, but by no means a predominant part, in the civilization of ancient India."[3]

V.A. Smith opines that the Indian expedition of Alexander the Great in BCE 327-326 was the first occasion of close conscious contact between East and West. The diffusion of Hellenistic culture to which Alexander devoted attention was in different directions in India. He relates further that post-Alexandrian influence was the most obvious in the domain of Indian art and architecture. He asserts that influence on the development of the Indian arts of architecture and sculpture was not only Hellenistic but also Roman.[4]

The contact between the Greeks and the Indians, established in the time of Alexander, was maintained till the end of Greek rule in India. During their contacts, they had exchange of ideas, cultural interactions, and transmission of knowledge.

During the Greek rule in India for over two centuries and a half, the Greeks and the Indians came into close contact and greatly influenced each other. The Greeks had left some marks on Indian civilization and *vice-versa*. Their rule resulted in a certain amount of mutual borrowing in the cultural field. Dwelling upon interaction between two ancient civilizations, the Greek and the Indian, W.W. Tarn writes, "Two peoples (Greek and Indian) could hardly live side by side in the same country for a long period without a certain amount of mutual borrowing."[5]

"... We are beginning to realize the innumerable contacts, throughout the course of history, between East and West, and their mutual indebtedness in language, literature, art, and philosophy. As time goes on it will be increasingly realized that a knowledge of the history and culture of India is essential to the foundation of a proper understanding of the origin and growth of Western civilization," says H.G. Rawlinson.[6]

Stating that the effects produced by Greek ideas on the Indian mind can be traced in a variety of spheres, such as religion, poetry, philosophy, science art and architecture, J.W. McCrindle remarks that "Scholars now rather incline to believe that whatever may be the exact degree of the indebtedness of India to Greece, the ancient civilization of India was much less original and self-contained than it was at one time supposed to be."[7]

It will not be appropriate to say that there was no foreign influence on ancient Indian civilization, and that there was only Indian influence on western culture and thought. In fact, it was a two-way traffic.

"Whenever countries come into intimate contact with one another, they are bound to be influenced by each other. It cannot be contended that India was altogether impervious to the influence of the west; likewise it is ridiculous to maintain that Indian civilization was a by-product of the Macedonian or Achaemenian cultures."[8]

"The contacts between India and the Greek world continued throughout their ancient history. It is, therefore, possible both to identify the nature of the links and to trace their dynamics from epoch to epoch. The results of the cross-fertilization between the two cultures in the domain of religion and mythology, art and architecture, fable and folklore, science and philosophy, coins and metallurgy, language and literature, have attracted the attention of scholars, but they require a still deeper investigation…", observes U.P. Arora.[9] The subject under discussion has no doubt received the notices of some authorities, but still there is a fair scope to make further historical disquisition into it on the basis of classical testimony.

We begin with Greek influence in ancient India. The Greek traveller, Apollonius of Tyana, and his Assyrian companion Damis in the course of their visit to Taxila city in CE 44 found that it was laid out on Greek plan. They tell us that it was fortified fairly well after the manner of a Greek city; and that it was well-planned, and divided up into narrow streets and well arranged in the same manner as is Athens.[10]

In the early part of the second century BCE, Taxila became a province of the Graeco-Bactrian monarchy. The Bactrian Greeks laid the foundations of a new city about 180 BCE at a site called Sirkap which was visited by the said two travellers. Speaking of the Greek influence on Indian culture in the Hellenistic age, M.I. Finley says that Alexander's successors (Bactrian Greeks) "founded new cities modelled on the Greeks."[11]

There is an archaeological evidence to corroborate and supplement the Greek account of the town of Taxila planned like a Greek town. The excavations conducted by John Marshall at Taxila reveal that the town Sirkap was well built here according to a typically Greek lay-out.[12]

"It is not inconceivable that Greek town-planning ideas may have been introduced into India."[13] The planning of the town at Sirkap was decidedly Hellenistic in effect.

It is said that Taxila city in northern India was "a meeting place of Indian, Iranian and Greek cultural influence."[14]

The Greek artists of both Alexandrian and post-Alexandrian times left their stamp on the sculptural art of India. The Greek sculptors from Greece as well as from Graeco-Bactria contributed to the development of particularly Indian art of sculpture.

The Greek ideal of beauty in art may possibly have been brought direct to India by the artists who accompanied Alexander the Great in his Indian expedition.[15]

We are told by philostratus that Apollonius and Damis (already noted) in the course of their visit to Taxila city saw outside its walls a beautiful temple of shell marble with a shrine and many columns. They found that around the shrine were hung pictures engraved on copper tablets representing the feats of Alexander and Porus. There were many other sculptured or carved objects, and other works of art, which were comparable to the productions of the Greek artists. Philostratus distinctly refers to "Greek reliefs" (reliefs showing the Greek method or style of carving) in temple at Taxila. It was not till after the death of Alexander the Great that Porus placed all the works of art in the temple.[16] All sculptural works preserved in the temple of Taxila were the productions of either the Greek artists of Alexander's time or the Indian artists of that time bearing the Greek influence. Indian artists of Taxila might have borrowed some ideas from the Greek artists relating to the art of sculpture.

It may be added here that all the sculptured objects and other works of art of Alexander's time were placed by Porus in the temple (containing a shrine) at Taxila built by him during his rule over the kingdom of Taxila which he received from Alexander as a gift shortly before his departure from India in the beginning of October 325 BCE. All sculptured or carved objects and other works of art of Alexander's time, placed later by Porus in a temple with shrine at Taxila, were in the excellent state of preservation till the visit of the said two travellers to that city in the first century.

"Taxila has supplied a few pieces of Greek sculpture, and various small objects of art..., some with Greek engravings...", says Tarn.[17]

"Classical culture had acted as ferment to revive the native qualities of the Indian artists, without robbing them of their originality and subtlety."[18] It is true that Greek art lived on in India for many years longer; but it finally became absorbed and lost all resemblance to its former self in the hands of the Indian."[19]

The Hellenistic influence on Indian architecture and sculpture in the post-Maurya age cannot be denied. The transmission of Hellenistic art and culture into north-western India during the Greek rule in the second century before the Christina era has been acknowledged by some renowned authorities.[20]

The Greek rule is also memorable on account of the introduction of Hellenistic art features in the north-west frontier of India, giving rise to the Gāndhāra art. The Gāndhāra territory was the principal seat of Hellenic culture in India.[21]

The Greek artists (sculptors) at Gāndhāra evolved a new method of making the figure of Buddha. The figures of Buddha in the base-reliefs of Gāndhāra bore the impression of Greek art. The artists of Gāndhāra applied the Hellenistic methods to the portrayal of scenes from the life of the Buddha, and more especially to the delineation of the Master (Buddha) himself. The Greeks, no doubt, left an indelible mark on the Buddhist art of Gāndhāra.

Marshall attributes the Gāndhāra sculptures to the workmanship of Bactrian Greeks.[22] Rawlinson has rightly observed that "It is by their wonderful influence upon Indian art that the Bactrian Greeks will ever be known to the world."[23] He has pin-pointed that Indian architects and sculptors took many ideas from the Greeks.[24]

"The Gāndhāra sculpture and architecture exhibit the strongest classical influence."[25] "The art represented by the Gāndhāra sculptures is the result of the union of the older Indian art and Hellenistic art as it was known in Bactria."[26]

"The Gāndhāra sculpture is an offshoot of the Hellenistic art of Asia Minor and of that of the Roman Empire. It is, therefore, called the Indo-Greek or the Graeco-Roman art. It owes its origin and development to the patronage of the Greek rulers of Bactria and North-West India. The technique of the Gāndhāra art is definitely Greek; but art itself is essentially Indian in form and content. The Gāndhāra sculpture… 'had the head of a Greek, but the heart of an Indian."[27] Some authorities have focused especially on the Roman influence on the art of the Gāndhāra school.[28]

The Gāndhāra school of Sculpture no doubt flourished under the Kuṣāṇs, but their art was predominantly Hellenistic in nature. It has been observed that the influence of Roman arts and ideas in India was at its height during the Kuṣāṇa period[29], but its legitimacy is not beyond question. Priaulx categorically states that "… between India and the Roman empire there never existed any interchange of thought."[30]

The Greek influence on Indian coinage can be traced back to the fourth century before the Christian era. An Indian monarch, who ruled a kingdom situated in the tract between the rivers Akesines and Hydaspes in the Punjab from about 330 to 303 or 300 BCE, struck a silver coin of fine Greek workmanship in 305 BCE bearing his name Sophutou, which was a Greek form of his original name Saubhāta[31], called variously Sopeithes, and Sopithes (sophytes) by the classical writers.[32] He struck his coins after the Greek fashion. His coins contained Greek legends. His coins in all probability were copied from those of his Greek contemporary, Seleucus Nicator.

Sophytes' coins "may be regarded as a very direct memorial of Greek influence in India", observes G. Macdonald in his note on "Ancient Greek coins in India."[33]

The Indians learnt much from the Indo-Greeks about the coinage. Prior to their advent, the punch-marked rude coins were current in India, but they introduced the practice of using regular coins, better shaped and stamped. The coins were often with bilingual legends written in Greek and in Kharoṣṭhi. "In the sphere of arts and crafts", says Marshall, "the Greeks made many valuable contributions to the material culture of the North-West (India). It was they who introduced a vastly superior type of coin, bearing the name and usually the portrait of the ruling sovereign stamped upon it in relief, with the legend repeated in the Indian as well as in the Greek script."[34]

"Until the beginning of the second century BC no extensive modification of the native Indian coinage had been caused by foreign influence. It was during the Greek rule of Bactria that there came eventually the influence which completely changed the form and character of the coinage of north-western India."[35]

The Indians acquired the craft of minting gold coins from the Greeks and Romans. India definitely owes to the West in respect of coinage system. The beautiful coinage of the Greeks and Romans were initiated by the Indians.[36]

We now come to the influence of Greek language and literature in India. We take up first the former. During Indo-Greek rule, the Greeks popularized the Greek way of life, including the language which had become the *lingua-franca* in north-west India. In the Greek dominions in that part of the country, the Greek language was understood, spoken, and employed by the non-Greeks. The Indian populace and potentates in the north-west made use of the Greek language to a considerable extent. We are informed by the Greek historian Philostratus that an Indian king, Phraotes of Taxila, conversed with the Greek traveller Apollonius in Greek when he visited his city in CE 44.[37] We are also told by him that an Indian village, where all the inhabitants spoke Greek, was visited by Apollonius (some time between CE 43 and 41).[38] Some Indians were indeed remarkably well acquainted with the Greek language and literature.

It may also be added here that the Greek word *Drachmae* found its way in the Indian language in Sanskrit as *Drachma*. By the end of the first century, the Roman word *Denarius* was adopted into Sanskrit as *Dināra* and in Prākrit as *Damma* (now Dāma, used in the modern Indian languages).[39] It is said that the Roman influence had generally made its mark on south India, particularly in those places and areas which were accessible by sea.[40]

The Indians were influenced also by the Greek literature, as gleaned from the Greek sources. Some of the educated Indians were familiar with the Greek epics, poetry, drama, etc.[41] The Greek writers provide us with valuable information regarding the interaction of Greek and Indian literary traditions.

Dion Chrysostom tells us that "the poetry of Homer was sung by the Indians, who had translated it into their own language and modes of expression... so potent was the influence of what one man had sung."[42] The Indians whom Chrysostom met in Egyptian capital Alexandria may have given him the information he transmits to us.

Aelian's statement[43] goes well in accord with that of Chrysostom.

Plutarch informs us that by Alexander's means Asia was civilized and Homer read there, and that the tragedies of two noted Greek playwrights, Euripides (480-406 BCE) and Sophocles (496-406 BCE) were read and staged by the Gedrosians (native of Baluchistan) and others.[44]

We are told by Philostratus that an Indian king Phraotes of Taxila, informed the Greek traveller Apollonius when he visited that city in CE 44 (as noted before), that he had read the Greek play *Herakleidai* of Euripides.[45]

We know from H.G. Rawlinson that the Greek dramas were performed in India during the Greek rule. During Euthydemid dynasty's rule in north-west India, the tragedies were performed at Peshawar and other places.[46]

Examining critically the extent of the influence of Greek language and literature in India during the Greek rule, V.A. Smith remarks that the Greek language must have been more or less familiar to the officials at the king's court, and that the literature of Greece was known slightly to some of the native officers, who were obliged to learn their masters' language. But that language was not widely diffused, and the impression made by Greek authors upon Indian literature and science is hardly traceable.[47]

We now turn to Indian influence on the West in the realm of religion and philosophy. We first take up here the influence of Indian religions-Buddhism and Hinduism – on the Greeks in India.

Menander (*c.* 165-145 or 130 BCE), the greatest of the Indo-Greek kings, and ruler of the Central Punjab with his capital at Sāgala (or Śakala), embraced Buddhism after coming under the influence of a Buddhist scholar and monk Nāgasena. After his conversion to Buddhism his name was changed to Milinda, and he became an *Arhat* (Buddhist ascetic).[48] A great many of his followers also came within the fold of Buddhism.

We learn from Plutarch that Menander, who had reigned with equity and justice, died in camp during a campaign. On his death, the states or cities of his realm or under his sway joined together in celebrating his obsequies (funeral rites), but over the relies of his body a dispute arose among them which was settled upon after they agreed that each was to take back an equal share of his ashes so that memorials (*Stūpas*) might be set up over them to preserve his memory.[49]

There are also umismatic and epigraphic evidence to show that the Greek king Menander was a converted Buddhist. Some of his coins throw a little light upon his faith in Buddhism. On one of his coins appears the "Wheel of the Law", the "*Dharma-Chakra*", a favourite emblem of the Buddhists.[50] His other coins contain interesting inscriptions which may testify to his Buddhist leanings.

"The conversion of Menander to Buddhism is as dramatic as that of Aśoka", says Rawlinson.[51]

By the time of Menander the Bactrian Greeks had become thoroughly Indianized. The process of their Indianization further continued after c. 100 BCE or about the beginning of the first century BCE which is without parallel in Hellenistic history. The Greeks in India adopted Indian religions – Buddhism and Hinduism.[52] Before adoption of Indian culture they were followers of western culture and way of life.

The influence of Indian religion – Buddhism – in the West can also be traced out. Several religious leaders of the West, because of being deeply influenced by the doctrines of Buddhism, adopted the name "Boutta" (Buddha).

The Alexandrians (the Greeks of Alexandria, ancient Egyptian capital, the seat of learning and commerce) must have been well acquainted with the Buddha and his teachings by the third century of the Christian era. The Greeks might have learnt about him from the Indians who often visited Alexandria in connection with their commerce with Egypt.

We are told by Archelaos that Terebinthus (an Alexandrian), who proclaimed himself learned in all the wisdom of the Egyptians, assumed a new name, "Buddas" (Buddha),[53] perhaps after his Enlightenment (attainment of spiritual insight, in Buddhism).

Antialcidas, the Greek king of Taxila (*c.* 115-90 BCE), sent Heliodorus, the son of Dion, as his envoy to the court of Bhāgabhadra, called also Bhāgavata (114-82 BCE), the last but one Śunga ruler of Besnagar (Vidiśā, eastern Mālavā), in the fourteenth year of the reign of the latter (i.e. 100 BCE). There the Greek envoy came under the brāhmanical influence, embraced the Vaiṣṇava cult of Hinduism, and proclaimed himself a "Bhāgavata" (worshipper of Viṣṇu). In honour of the god Viṣṇu, he erected a monolithic pillar surmounted with Garuda (supposedly the vehicle of that god) on the top at Besnagar. The inscription on it in early Brahmi records the facts stated above. The English translation of the inscription follows: "This Garuda – column of Vasudeva (Vishnu), the god of gods, was erected here by Heliodorus, a Bhāgavata (worshipper of Vishnu), the son of Diya (Dion), and an inhabitant of Taxila, who came as Greek ambassador from the Great King Antialcidas to king Kaśiputra Bhagabhadra, the saviour, then, reigning prosperously in the fourteenth year of his kingship."[54]

The conversion of Menander to Buddhism and that of Heliodorus to Hinduism are the two notable examples of the influence of Indian religions on the Greeks in India.

The influence of Indian philosophical ideas on the thought of the Greek philosophers of pre- and post-Alexandrian age received the special attention of the classical authors.

Pythagoras (*circa* 580-493 or 568-493 BCE) was the first Greek philosopher to be influenced by the Indian philosophical idea of metempsychosis – transmigration of the soul (on death) into a new body. Its doctrine was originally enunciated by the Indian philosophers of the Brāhmanic and Upanishadic age. His belief in this doctrine in *c.* 540 BCE can fairly be attested to by the statement of a Greek historian and philosopher Xenophanes. He possessed the knowledge of this doctrine before his visit to Egypt about 500 BCE. In the light of the facts stated here, the veracity of the statements of some scholars, that he borrowed this doctrine from the Egyptians, and that the Indians transmitted their knowledge of the transmigration of soul to the Egyptians from whom he derived his knowledge, can be suspected.

The ancient Greek and Roman writers as well as the modern authorities are divided in their opinion about the subject under notice. It was the famous Greek historian Herodotus who first asserted that the Greeks borrowed the doctrine of metempsychosis from the Egyptians.[55] But the other two Greek authors, Alexander Polyhistor, and Philostratus[56] held the opinion that Pythagoras acquired his knowledge from India and not from Egypt. Philostratus, on the other hand, records that he adopted the doctrine of soul from the Egyptians who had learned it from the Indians.[57]

The Greek traveller Apollonius in the course of his visit to India (in CE 43-44) learnt from Iarchas, the Chief of the Brāhmaṇa philosophers called Sophoi (teachers of wisdom), that the views of latter are similar to that of Pythagorus.[58] Iarchas imparted to the Greek philosopher Apollonius all his wisdom. Apollonius also found that Iarchas was quite conversant even with the most abstruse doctrines of Greek philosophy as well as with the nature of Greek institutions.[59]

It was upheld by the classical authors of the Roman period that India and not Egypt was a source of philosophical knowledge of the Greek philosophers. Lucian related that "philosophy had first visited India, from there to Ethiopia, then to Egypt and other countries."[60]

Some authorities have strongly advocated that the theory of metempsychosis ascribed to Pythagoras is of Indian origin.[61] J.W. McCrindle says that the doctrine of Pythagoreans bears too close resemblance to that of the Indians to favour the supposition that it was directly borrowed from India.[62] J.W. Sedlar connects the doctrine of metempsychosis in Greek philosophy with the common philosophical heritage of India. He speaks of possible influence in both directions and asserts that exchange of philosophical ideas had started between Greece and India much before Alexander. He is in favour of India as a source of Pythagorean philosophy.[63] A.N. Marlowe has admitted that some mystical ideas such as those professed by the Pythagoreans probably came from India.[64] G.N. Banerjee has also pointed out that "philosophical ideas such as the Indian doctrine of the transmigration of souls found their way to Greek territory."[65]

"India is the source from which not only the rest of Asia but the whole Western world derived their knowledge and their religion," says A.H.L. Heeren.[66]

Rawlinson categorically states that "it is extremely doubtful whether the Egyptians did actually believe in transmigration of the soul. It is more likely that Pythagoras was influenced by India than by Egypt. Almost all the theories, religious, philosophical, and mathematical, taught by the Pythagoreans were known in India in the sixth century BC."[67] "Indian philosophy", says he, "was acquiring a growing reputation in the Hellenistic schools of Asia Minor and Egypt."[68] In one of his another works, he first states that the Pythagorean philosophy owes something to India, and that there are some resemblance between Pythagorean schools and Indian beliefs.[69] And then he contradicts his own statements by relating that "If Pythagoras, Plato or any other Greek philosopher before the days of Alexander borrowed anything from India, we find no mention of the fact in contemporary Greek literature."[70] "Egypt, not India, was the source, if any, from which Greece borrowed her early philosophy. Egyptians were the first to propound the theory of the transmigration of the soul. Nor did this doctrine of transmigration come through Egypt from India."[71] The statements he has made in his two different works are not consistent rather contradictory.

Examining at length the question of Indian influence on the philosophy of Pythagoras, A.B. Keith comes to the conclusion that there is no evidence of the Indian influence on Pythagoras or his "Doctrine of Transmigration."[72] But the fact remains that there are both classical and non-classical evidence in this regard. Indian influence on the philosophical thought of Pythagoras can hardly be doubted. The theory of metempsychosis plays almost as great a part in Greek as in Indian philosophical thought.

"... the Greeks in India were deeply involved in cultural interaction with Indians, in the fields of art and astronomy surely, and probably in the fields of literature... and philosophy as well... Greek influences on Indian culture was a profound and historic as the penetration of Indian ideas into Greek thought in the pre-Socratic period", observes Thomas McEvilley.[73]

In *c.* 315 CE, Eusebius recorded a tradition, preserved by Aristoxenus[74] (330-300 BCE), a disciple of Aristotle (384-322 BCE), that certain learned Indians actually visited Athens and conversed with Socrates (469-399 BCE). They asked him to explain the object of his philosophy and when he replied, "an inquiry into human affairs", one of the Indian philosophers reacted and asked, "How could a man grasp human things without first knowing the Divine."?[75] Socrates was greatly influenced by the idea of Indian philosopher. It is said that the Greeks had vague knowledge of some of the teachings of the Indian philosophy.[76]

Megasthenes was the first Greek writer to note the similarity between the views of the Brāhmaṇa philosophers of India and the philosophers of

Greece concerning the nature of the soul, and many other subjects. He expressly states that the Brachmanes (Brāhmaṇas) wrap up their doctrines about the immortality of the soul after the manner of Plato[77], an eminent Greek philosopher, who belonged to the period 427-348 or 428-347 BCE.

The later Greek writer, Pausanias, informs us that Plato was well-acquainted with Indian wisdom. He was influenced by the Indian philosophers. He borrowed his doctrine of the immortality of the soul from them. He says the Indian philosophers were the first to say that the soul of man is immortal, which was followed by some of the Greeks, particularly by Plato, the son of Ariston.[78] The doctrine of *Karma*, which is the keystone of the philosophy of Plato, is also of Indian origin. Rawlinson opines that "Plato never mentions Indian philosophy or India at all in all his writings."[79] However, Indian influence on both of his doctrines (noted above) cannot be negated. Plato had travelled to Egypt after Socrates' death in 399 BCE, but it is not yet known whether he required any knowledge of Indian philosophy there.

We learn from Plutarch that Alexander, while at Taxila (in 326 BCE), sent Onesikritus, his companion, and a philosopher of the school of Diogenes the Cynic, to the Indian gymnosophists (Brāhmaṇa philosophers) for philosophical discourse with them. When Dandamis (called also Mandanis), the wisest of all the philosophers of Taxila, was told about Pythagoras, Socrates and Diogenes, he said, they appeared to him to have been men of genius but nevertheless criticized them for subjecting their lives too much to the requirements of their laws.[80] This evidence shows that the said three Greek philosophers were known to Dandamis. It may be added here that Alexander himself was keen enough to know of Indian philosophy. Strabo tells us that Mandanis told Onesikritus, "he praised the king (Alexander) because though he ruled over so great an empire, he nevertheless desired wisdom, and was the only philosopher in arms that he had ever seen."[81]

Megasthenes says, "All that has been said regarding nature by the ancients is asserted also by philosophers out of Greece, on the one part in India by the Brachmanes."[82]

There are evidences to show the influence of Indian philosophy on Democritus[83] and Lycurgus[84], both Greek philosophers.

The Greek philosophers Clemens, who flourished about the third century of the Christian era, says that the influence of Eastern philosophy was chiefly felt in Alexandria when he was there. In his *Stromateis*, he remarks that "the Greeks stole their philosophy from the Indians."

Plotinus (CE 204-269 or 270), originally the Greek philosopher, was the real founder of the Neo-Platonic school of philosophy. He was greatly influenced by Indian philosophy. He says, "souls after being detached from the body will pass into the world of Being and reality". His thought was principally based on Vedānta and Sāṁkhya philosophy. The Neo-Platonic philosophy embodies Brāhmanic ideas in many respects. Plotinus arrived in Rome in CE 245. His followers became popularly known as Neo-Platonist. Porphyrios, called also Porphyry (CE 233-305), was one of the chief exponents or expositors of the doctrines of Neo-Platonism which he had learned in Rome from Plotinus. The former, who is also one of the classical authors, in his *Life of Plotinus* claims that his master (Plotinus) taught him the doctrines of the Indians while he was in Alexandria. Rawlinson is absolutely correct in his assertion that Indian philosophy exercised a great influence on the development of Neo-Platonism.[85]

The ancient Greeks started acquiring knowledge of Indian philosophy since the time of Megasthenes. They continued this practice more or less till the third century.[86]"

"The cultural and ideological contacts between the two peoples (Greeks and Indians) enriched their spiritual heritage and played a significant part in their intellectual development. The parallel search for philosophical truth and understanding made a diffusion of ideas possible... The vast gap that divided East and West for millennia was bridged and the world took yet another notable turn in its vast and intricate destiny", says Demetrios Th. Vassiliades.[87]

We are told by Kedrenus that "during the reign of Constantine (the Roman Emperor, fourth century) Metrodorus, a Persian by birth, joined by his friend Meropius of Tyre and his companions Frumentius and Aedisius journeyed to India to study the science and philosophy of Hindus. He led a strict ascetic life and won the respect and reverence of the Brāhmaṇas".[88]

The statement of St. Jerome may be placed here by way of a digression. He tells us that the Christians of his time (CE 342-420) imitated the mode of life of the Indian gymnosophists (Brāhmaṇa philosophers) to some extent.[89]

Regarding the influence of Indian science of medicine on Greek medicine, it may first be mentioned here that for the first time Greeks and Indian met each other in the courts of the Persian kings and embraced the opportunity to exchange their knowledge of the science of medicine. The

Greek physicians employed in the Persian courts met Indians from the north-western parts of India.

In his treatise *Gynaikeia* (The Diseases of Women), Hippocrates prescribed an ingredient which was the Indian medicine for the treatment of eyes (Greek peperi = Sanskrit pippali). The Hippocratians (460-333 BCE) became familiar with that Indian medicine.

Arrian, on the authority of Nearchus, who had accompanied Alexander the Great in his Indian expedition, tells us that Alexander had all the most skilful of the Indians in the healing art collected around him. They were able to cure not only snake bite, which the Greek physicians were unable to do, but also other diseases and bodily pains. The Greeks acquired some knowledge of Indian drugs used for medical treatment.[90]

Dioskorides, the Greek author of the first century of the Christian era, in his *Materia Medica* (Herbal) specifically mentions that the following plants were brought from India for medicinal purposes : Kardamomum (I. 5), i.e., Sanskrit Kardama and English Cardamom, Kostos (I. 15), Sanskrit Kuṣṭha, Bdellion (I. 80), Sanskrit guggula and English bdellium, a fragrant gum, etc.[91] Theophrastus in his *History of Plants* (IX, 19, 4)[92] refers to pepper (Indian product) as a medical drug. Another Indian product camphor is mentioned in the Syrian book of medicine of the Greek Medical School of Edessa (third-fifth centuries CE).[93]

Indian influences (or "Hindu influence") on Greek medicine has been acknowledged by both Indian[94] and foreign[95] authorities.

Notes and References

1. E.H. Bunbury (HAG, Vol. II, p. 46) has rightly pointed out that the Hellenization of a large part of Asia had followed rapidly upon the conquests of Alexander.
2. *Hellenism in Ancient India*, p. 14.
3. *Ibid.*, p. 26.
4. For details see his article, "Graeco-Roman Influence on the civilization of Ancient India", JASB, LVIII, I, 1889, pp. 108-97; also same article, JASB, LXI, I, 1892, pp. 54f; JASB, LXII, I, 1893 (supplementary Note), pp. 84-87.
5. *The Greeks in Bactria and India*, p. 375.
6. "India in European Literature and Thought", in *The Legacy of India*, ed. G.T. Garratt, p. 37.
7. IIA, Introduction, p. 5, note 2, and p. 6 (continuation of same note).
8. K.C. Sagar, *Foreign Influence on Ancient India*, p. 9.

9. "Ancient India and Ancient Greece", in *Life, Thought and Culture in India,* (from *c.* 600 BC to *c.* A 300), ed. G.C. Pande, Vol. I, pt.2 of HIC, p. 1065.
10. Philostratus, *Vit. Apoll.*, II, 20 and 23; Eng. tr. of *Vit. Apoll.* by F.C. Conybeare, *The Life of Apollonius of Tyana,* Vol.I, pp. 169 and 181; also Philostratus' *Life of Apollonius of Tyana*, in AICL, pp. 191-92; Priaulx, *The Indian Travels of Apollonius of Tyana,* pp. 13-15; Priaulx's *Indian Travels of Apollonius of Tyana,* in CAI, pp. 387-89; B.N. Puri, *India as described by Early Greek writers,* pp. 146-49; G.P. Singh, "Early History of North-West India as described by the Greek and Assyrian Travellers", JIH (Platinum Jubilee volume), 2001, pp. 45-48.
11. *The Ancient Greeks*, p. 174.
12. For details see *Taxila*, Vol. I, pp. 12, 140-41, 198, pl. 24.
13. R.A. Jairazbhoy, *Foreign Influence in Ancient India*, pp. 50-51.
14. NEB, XVII, (Chicago, 1980), p. 1082.
15. See W.W. Hunter, "The Greeks in India", rept. from his *The Indian Empire : Its Peoples, History and Products* (London, 1881), in *Ancient India* (Delhi, 1983), p. 95.
16. *Vit. Apoll.*, II, 20; Conybeare's tr. *The Life of Apollonius of Tyana,* Vol. I, pp. 168-71; Philostratus' *Life of Apollonius of Tyana,* in AICL, p. 192, see also p. 22, note 2; Priaulx, *The Indian Travels of Apollonius of Tyana*, pp. 13-14; CAI, p. 388; B.N. Puri, *India as described by Early Greek Writers,* p. 147; G.P. Singh, "North-West India as described by the Greek and Assyrian Travellers of the first century", JASM (new series), vols. 77-78, 2002-2003, p. 176; J. Marshall, *Taxila*, I, p. 227.
17. *Op. cit.*, p. 361.
18. G.N. Banerjee, *op. cit.*, p. 26.
19. Banerjee, *India as known to the Ancient World,* p. 15.
20. Jairazbhoy, *Foreign Influence in Ancient India*, p. 109; V.A. Smith, "Graeco-Roman Influence on the civilization of Ancient India", JASB, LVIII, I, 1889, pp. 108-9; Banerjee, *Hellenism in Ancient India*, pp. 37-38; H.G. Rawlinson, *A Concise History of the Indian people,* p. 58; Marshall, *Taxila*, I, p. 19; also his "The Monuments of Ancient India", in CHI, I, pp. 563-584. Marshall is absolutely right in stating that Hellenistic art in spite of its diffusion in northwest India never dominated the Indian art. See his "The Monuments of Ancient India", in *op. cit.*, p. 588.
21. Regarding the essentials or fundamentals of the Hellenistic culture and its fusion and diffusion see M. Hadas, *Hellenistic Culture : Fusion and Diffusion,* pp. 15f.
22. JRAS, 1909, pp. 1060f.

23. *Bactria from the earliest times to the Extinction of Bactrio-Greek Rule in the Punjab*, p. 144.
24. *Intercourse Between India and the Western World…*, p. 167; *A Concise History of the Indian People*, p. 58.
25. Banerjee, *Hellenism in Ancient India*, p. 61.
26. *Ibid*., p. 76.
27. S.B. Mookherji, *India's Empire of Mind,* p. 109.
28. Jairazbhoy, *Foreign Influence in Ancient India*, p. 109; V.A. Smith, "Graeco-Roman Influence on the civilization of Ancient India", LVIII, I, 1889, p. 159. E.B. Havell (JRAS, April 1909, pp. 541f) repudiates the idea that Indians art owes anything to Graeco-Roman influence. M. Elphinstone ("The Greek Kingdom of Bactria", rept. from his *The History of India*, London, 1911, in *Ancient India*. Delhi, 1983, p. 34) holds that the Greek kingdom of Bactria had very little influence on India.
29. JRAS, Jan. 1903, p. 56.
30. *The Indian Travels of Apollonius of Tyana,* p. 159.
31. See Cunningham, "Coin of the Indian prince Sophytes, a contemporary of Alexander the Great", CASE, I, (last section), pp. 1-3 and 12; Num. Chron., 1866, pp. 220f; E.J. Rapson, *Ancient India from the Earliest times to the first century AD*, App. D, "Coins of Ancient India", p. 97, and pl. II, 6; D.C. Sircar (ed.) SI, Vol. I, p. 83, and note 2; E.J. Rapson, *Indian Coins,* p. 3, and pl. I, 8; V.A. Smith, CCIM, Vol. I, *Coins of Ancient India*, p. 7, and note 1, and pl. I, 1 (facing p. 8); CHI, 1, pp. 333, 348, 564-65, pl. 1, 17 (facing p. 684), and pl. XIII, 34; P. Gardner, CCGBM, pp. XIX-XX, and pl. I, 3; R.B. Whitehead, *Num. Chron*., 1943, pp. 60-72.
32. Strabo, *Geog*., XV, I, 30 and 31; Arrian, *Anab*., VI, 2, 2; Diodorus, *Bib. Hist*., XVII, 91 and 92; Curtius, *Hist. Alex*., IX, 1.
33. CHI, I, p. 348.
34. *Taxila,* I, p. 40.
35. Banerjee, *Hellenism in Ancient India*, p. 130; see also *Imp. Gaz. Ind*., II, pp. 137 - 38.
36. See Rawlinson, *Intercourse Between India and the Western World…*, p. 102; *A concise History of the Indian People*, p. 59.
37. *Vit. Apoll*., tr. by Conybeare, *The Life of Apollonius of Tyana,* Vol. I, p. 185.
38. *Vit. Apoll*., III, 12.
39. See Sagara, *Foreign Influence on Ancient India*, pp. 69, 238, and note 5.
40. *Ibid*., p. 246.
41. See Arora, "Metamorphosis in Myth", in *India and Greece – connections and parallels,* ed. S. Doshi, pp. 48-52.

42. *Orationes* (Orations), LIII, 554-555.
43. *Var. Hist.*, XII, 48.
44. "On the Fortune of Alexander", in his *Moralia*, I, 328 D.
45. *Vit. Apoll.*, II, 27 and 32.
46. For details see his "Foreign Influence in the Civilization of Ancient India, 900 BC - 400 AD." JRAS (1908-1913), pp. 217-38.
47. *EHI,* p. 256.
48. See *Milindapañha,* VII. 7.21; also its trans. by T.W. Rhys Davids, SBE, XXXV, I, p. 6.
49. "De Republicae (or Reipublicae) Gerendae Praecepta", in his *Moralia*, 821 D-E; also *Moralia*, ed. Bernardakis, Vol. V, p. 119. The passage from Plutarch is quoted in full in the *Num. Chron.*, 1869, p. 229. See also G. Woodcock, *The Greeks in India,* p. 95; and James Prinsep, JASB, 1833, p. 409.

    The information transmitted to us by Plutarch is a reminiscence of the story relating to the dispute among the Buddhists over the distribution of relics of the body of the Buddha after his funeral. There was definitely some impact of the Indian Buddhist tradition in this regard on the subjects of Menander. According to the *Mahāparinibbāna Sutta* (VI, 51-57; also Pāli text with parallel Hindi trans. ed. by S.G. Prajñanand, Lucknow, 1981, pp. 281-97; SBE, XI, pp. 131-33), after the funeral of the Buddha a dispute arose among the Buddhists from eight different places, including Magadha, over the distribution of the relics of his body. The bones (relics) of his body were divided into eight equal parts which were taken back by those Buddhists to build memorials over them. Eight *Stūpas* were built over the relics in eight different parts of northern India.
50. Cunningham, *Co. An. Ind.* p. 101, C; Gardner, CCGBM, XII, 7.
51. *Intercourse Between India and the Western World…*, p. 162.
52. See *Ibid*., and also Tarn, *op. cit*., pp. 351, 390 and 393.
53. *Arch. Man, Disp*., I, 97; See also AICL, p. 185, note 1; Rawlinson, *Intercourse Between India and the Western World…*, pp. 138, 142, and note 1; JRAS, XX, p. 267.
54. See J. Marshal, JRAS, 1909, p. 1055; H.C. Raychaudhuri, JASB, XVIII, 1923, pp. 269-71; Vogel, ASIAR, 1908-9, p. 126; IHQ, VIII, 1932, p. 610; E.J. Rapson, *Ancient India from the Earliest times to the First century AD,* pp. 71 and 100.
55. *Hist.,* II, 123.
56. *Vit. Apoll*., (*The Life of Apollonius of Tyana*), VIII, 7.
57. *Ibid*., III, 19; see also VI, 10-11.
58. Priaulx, *The Indian Travels of Apollonius of Tyana,* pp. 22, 40, 50, 53.
59. Philostratus' *Life of Apollonius of Tyana*, in AICL, p. 194.

60. *Drapetai,* VI and VIII.
61. See Schroeder, *Pythagoras und die Inder* (Leipzig, 1884); R. Garbe, *The Philosophy of Ancient India*, p. 39; H.G. Rawlinson, *India : A Short Cultural History,* p. 55; Gomperz, *Greek Thinkers,* Vol. I, p. 127; S. Radhakrishnan, *Eastern Religion and Western Thought,* pp. 142-43.
62. AIMA, p. 122, fn.
63. *India and the Greek World : A Study in Transmission of Culture,* pp. 22, 24, 31-32, 124-25, 129, 131.
64. "Hinduism and Buddhism in Greek Philosophy", in *Philosophy East and West*, 4, 1954, pp. 3-38; see also G.P. Conger, "Did India influence Early Greek Philosophy"? *Philosophy East and West,* 2, 1952, pp. 102-128, especially p. 123.
65. *India as known to the Ancient World...*, p. 20.
66. *Historical Researches,* Vol. II, p. 45.
67. "India in European Literature and Thought", in *The Legacy of India*, ed. G.T. Garratt, p. 5.
68. *Ibid.*, p. 18.
69. *Intercourse Between India and the Western World...*, p. 156.
70. *Ibid.*, p. 157.
71. *Ibid.*, p. 158.
72. JRAS, 1909, pp. 569f.
73. *The Shape of Ancient Thought : Comparative Studies in Greek and Indian Philosophies,* p. 392.
74. For Aristoxenus see C. Müller (ed), *Frag. Hist. Graeco.*, Vol. II, Fragm. 31, p. 81.
75. *Praep. Evang.*, XI, 3. J. Filliozat ("Ancient India and Graeco-Roman World", *Proceedings of the Fifth World Sanskrit Conference,* p. 928) considers the tradition recorded by Eusebius to be reliable. See also Sagar, *Foreign Influence on Ancient India*, p. 69.
76. See Dimitraos C. Velissaropoulos, "The Ancient Greek knowledge of Indian philosophy", in *Graeco-Indica : India's cultural contacts with the Greeks world*, ed. U.P. Arora, pp. 260-61.
77. *Indika.*, Bk. III, Fragm. XLI, Cf. Strabo, *Geog.*, XV, I, 59.
78. *Hell. Per.*, IV, XXXII, 4.
79. *Intercourse Between India and the Western World...*, p. 157.
80. *Vit. Alex.* (Life of Alexander the Great), Ch. LXV.
81. *Geog.*, XV, I, 64.
82. *Indika*, Bk. III, Fragm. XLII Cf. Clemens, *Stromateis,* I, p. 305 D.

83. Aelian, *Var. Hist.*, IV, 20.
84. Plutarch, *Lycurgus*, Ch. 4; also C. Müller (ed), *Frag. Hist. Graec.*, Vol. IV, p. 332.
85. *Intercourse Between India and the Western World*..., pp. 142 and 175; also his "India in European Literature and Thought", in *The Legacy of India*, ed. Garratt, pp. 18-19. See also A.B. Keith, "Plotinus and Indian Thought", in *Indian Culture*, 2, 1936, p. 130; A.H. Armstrong, "Plotinus and India," in *Class. Quart.*, 30, 1936, pp. 22-28.
86. See J. Przyluski, "Indian Influence on Western Thought before and during the third century AD". JGIS, Jan. 1934, pp. 1-10, especially, p. 5.
87. *The Greeks in India: A Survey in Philosophical understanding, p. 89.*
88. *Synopsis of History, I, pp. 516-17.*
89. *Epist.,* 129; see also A.C. Perumalil, "Christian writers on Early India", JBORS, XXVIII, 4, 1942, p. 347.
90. *Indika*, XV.
91. See R.T. Gunther, *The Greek Herbal of Dioskorides,* New York, 1959.
92. Cf. Athenaeus, *Deip.*, II, 66, e, f.
93. Schoff, JAOS, XLII, p. 359.
94. Jairzabhoy, *Foreign Influence in Ancient India*, pp. 77-78; Arora, *Greeks on India*, pp. 85-87.
95. J. Filliozat, *The Classical Doctrine of Indian Medicine,* trans. by D.R. Channa from the French, pp. 254-5, 263.

Book Nine
Relations Between India and the West

1

Political Relations between India and Persia (Sixth to Fourth Centuries BCE)

The three Greek historians who have thrown some light on the relations between India and Persia (in Western Asia) include Xenophon, Kte'sias and Herodotus. The accounts of the subject given by the former two (contemporary) are relatively of greater value than that of the latter. Besides, there are also some incidental notices of Indo-Persian contacts in the classics. There was undoubtedly some sort of political relationship between the two countries during the period from the sixth to fourth centuries BCE. H. G. Rawlinson says, "Persia was in close contact with India for nearly two centuries"[1]. He further observes: "....there was an early intercourse between Persia and India, of which hardly any trace remains in history"[2].

We learn from Xenophon that the Persian monarch Cyrus the Great (558-530 BCE) sent an embassy to an Indian King (Pushkarasarin of Gāndhāra, included in the Achaemenian empire) for borrowing money. The Indian King sent an embassy and a letter of friendship to Cyrus (sometime after 539 BCE).

The members of the Indian embassy not only conveyed a large sum of money (possibly in payment of tribute) for which the Persian King had asked but also served him in the delicate matter of organizing espionage before he started his war against Crosesus and campaigns in Asia Minor[3]. Thus, Indian King of Gāndhāra helped the Persian King not only financially but also politically.

Giving an account of Indo-Persian relations at the time of Cyrus, Xenophon says that an Indian King took interest in the establishment of peace between Persians and Assyrians and sent a delegation to visit both kings and resolve their dispute. "And when the Indians came in they said that the king of India had sent them with orders to ask on what ground the Medes and Assyrians had declared war against the Persians". "And he (Indian King) has ordered us", they said, "when we have heard your statement to go also to the Assyrians and ask him the same question and finally, he made us say to both of you that the king of India declares that when he has weighed the merits of the case, he will side with the party wronged". Cyrus replied, "tell the king of India that we propose, in case the Assyrian says he has been wronged by us, to choose the king of India himself to be our arbitrator"[4]. This shows that Cyrus held the contemporary Indian king in high esteem.

The expansion of the powerful Persian Empire eastwards to the Indus at the end of the sixth century before the Christian era gave a new turn to Indo-Persian relations.

Herodotus informs us that Indian soldiers were recruited in the army of the famous Achaemenian Emperor Xerxes I (486-465 BCE), the son and successor of Darius I (522-486 BCE), to assist him in his fight against the Greeks. The army with which Xerxes invaded Greece included an Indian contingent from northern India consisting of both infantry and cavalry. Indian soldiers, he says, were clad in garments made of cotton, and armed with bows made of cane and arrows of cane tipped with iron[5]. These Indian soldiers were predominantly tribes living near Bactria on the Oxus in North Afghanistan and near the Indus. It is likely that the Persians mobilized a large number of Indian soldiers from the land which they occupied in northwest India after Darius' conquest of the Indus Valley. Herodotus also tells us that a number of tribes who inhabited the Indo-Iranian borderland in the time of Darius were represented in the army of Xerxes as well, namely, the Bactrians, Ar(e)ioi (of Aria=Herāt), Gandarioi (of Gāndhāra), Paktyes (Pakhtuns of Afghanistan) and the Mykoi of Baluchistan[6]. Regarding the Indian cavalry, that assisted Xerxes in his fight against the Greeks, he says that horses and chariots drawn by horses were brought and used[7].

Herodotus tells us further that Indian troops formed part of the army of Xerxes I and fought against the Greeks in the battles of Thermopylae (480 BCE) and Plataiae (479 BCE)[8]. The military assistance provided by the Indians to the Persian king was facilitated by their close and constant political contacts.

Kte'sias has given an eye-witness account of political relations between India and Persia during his own time. He resided at the royal court (at Susa) in Persia for seventeen years, of which the first eleven years (415-404 BCE) were spent under Darius II, and the remaining six (404-398 BCE) under his successor Artaxerxes II (also called Artaxerxes Mnémón)[9]. During his time in Persia, he met Persian officials who had visited India on the king's service or on state business and also the Indian envoys who came to the Persian court with presents and tributes from the rulers of various provinces of northern India, which was then subject to Persian rule[10]. Kte'sias categorically states that he had himself seen Indian men and women of fair complexion who attended the Persian court[11]. We are informed by Pausanias that Kte'sias had seen the presents, including a tiger, sent from India to the Persian king[12]. It has been said on the testimony of Kte'sias that the Great King of Persia used to receive costly presents from India even in the fourth century BCE[13].

In his "Review of the Reports of Kte'sias concerning India," Lassen also admits that in the time of Kte'sias the Persians and Indians used to visit each other's country for political purposes[14]. Their political contacts, Kte'sias says, continued till the beginning of the fourth century before the Christian era. Rawlinson, on the authority of Lassen, states that Kte'sias had ample opportunities to question Persian officials who had been to the Punjab, and that he met certain Indians who had come on an embassy to Persia[15]. Persian officials, says Rawlinson, had served in India[16]. Embassies from kings of Kābul, Gāndhāra, and Taxila, (the capital of western Punjab) which were the satrapies or provinces of Persian Empire, were sent to Persian court in the time of Kte'sias.

Those Achaemenian Kings, "who had political relations with India," include not only Xerxes I (486-465 BCE)[17], but also Darius II (424-404 BCE) and Artaxerxes II (404-359 BCE).

The political contacts between the two countries (India and Persia) was beneficial to both in several respects. The Indians extended all possible help to Darius III (336-330 BCE), the last king of Achaemenid dynasty, in resisting the invasion of Persia by Alexander of Greece. We are told by Arrian that the Indians of Bactriana and Arachosia (Kandahār) and of mountainous region fought along with Persian forces against the Greek invader. Besides the Indian troops of frontier region, the Indians who lived west of the Indus also helped the Persian king with a small force of elephants. The Indian and Persian forces fought together against the Greeks at Gaugemala (in 331 BCE) and at Arabela (in 330 BCE)[18].

One of the classical sources of the exceptional value–a Latin translation of a lost Greek original–also contains a notice of contacts of the Indians west of the Indus with the Persians during the time of Darius III. It is clearly stated therein that "The inhabitants of India have elephants without number, which they dispose of to the Persians. Their country is traversed in fifteen days"[19].

Strabo asserts that "The Persians did indeed summon the Hydrakai to attend them as mercenaries"[20]. The Hydrakai, or Sydracae of Pliny[21] are identical with the Ksudrakas of the Punjab. The Indian soldiers, who helped the Persian monarchs, belonged to not only the north-western part of the country but also to the Punjab.

The political tie between Persia and India finally snapped after 330 BCE.

Notes and References

1. *Intercourse between India and the Western World from the earliest times to the fall of Rome,* p. 160.
2. *Ibid.*, p. 292, note 1.
3. *Cyropaedia*, III, 2,28-30; V1, 2, 1, 3 and 9-11; also Eng. trans. by Walter Miller, Vol. I, p. 265.
4. *Cyropaedia*, II, 4, 1-8.
5. *History*, VII, 65.
6. *Ibid.*, VII, 64-68.
7. *History*, VII, 86.
8. *Ibid.*, VII, 186.
9. See Diodorus, *Bid. Hist.*, I, 1; II, 32, 4; and XIV, 46, 6; Tzetzes, *Chiliads*, I, 1, 82.
10. See J.W. McCrindle, AIK, Introduction: "The Life and Writings of Ktésias", pp. 3-4; also AICL, p. 18, note 2; B N Puri, *India as described by Early Greek Writers,* p. 7.
11. *Indika,* Fragm. I, in Photios, *Bibl.*, LXXII.
12. *Hell. Per.*, IX, 21.
13. *Ind. Ant.*, X, 1881, pp. 304-10.

14. *Ind. Alt.*, Vol.II (2nd edn. 1874), pp. 641 ff; also AIK, pp. 78 and 90.
15. *Intercourse between India and the Western World...*, App. p. 29.
16. *Ibid.*, p. 24 and note 4.
17. N.M. Chapekar, *Ancient India and Iran*, p. 36.
18. *Anab.*, III, 8, 3-6; also its trans. by Chinnock, pp. 142-43.
19. *Tot. Orb. Des.*, section 18.
20. *Geog.*, XV, I.6.
21. *Nat. Hist.*, XII, 6.

2

Diplomatic and Friendly Relations between the Maurya Empire of Northern India and the Hellenic Kingdoms of Syria and Egypt (The Fourth and Third Centuries BCE)

The conclusion of peace treaty between the Indian Sovereign Candragupta Maurya (Sandrakottus) and the Syrian Monarch Seleukus Nikator in 303 BCE resulted in the establishment of diplomatic and friendly relations between the Maurya Empire of northern India and the Hellenic kingdom of Syria in Western Asia. For a considerable period after this date these relations were maintained between the two and their successors. It has been rightly pointed out by J.W. McCrindle that "The alliance thus formed between the kingdoms of India and Syria was maintained not only while these two kings lived, but even for many years afterwards, when their thrones were filled by their successors"[1]. "This was the beginning of a long, intimate and fruitful intercourse between the Greek and Indian courts, which was continued by Candragupta's son and grandson, Bindusāra and Aśoka. Ambassadors from the Greek Monarchs of the West resided at Pāṭaliputra, the Maurya capital. The intercourse between the Indian and Syrian courts was not confirmed to the interchange of occasional courtesies...", says H.G. Rawlinson.[2] The Maurya Empire was acknowledged in the West as one of the great powers; and ambassadors both from Syria and from Egypt were deputed to the Maurya court at Pālibothra (Pāṭaliputra), as we know from the classical authors. Rawlinson states that the Mauryas adopted extraordinarily an enlightened policy towards the Greek Monarchs of Syria and Egypt and kept in close touch with them.[3] "The interest in the Greeks', remarks G. Woodcock, "certainly did not exist in India before the establishment of the Mauryan Empire".[4] It was no doubt the age of the Mauryas which marked the opening of a new chapter in the history of relations between the East and the West.

We learn from the ancient Greek and Roman writers that the Maurya Emperors of India maintained both diplomatic and friendly relations with their contemporary Hellenic kings of the West in the fourth and third centuries before the Christian era.

Deriving his authority from a Greek historian of the third century, Phylarchus (Fragm. 28), Athenaeus informs us that among the presents, which Sandrokoptos (Candragupta), the king of the Indians, sent to Seleukus, after the conclusion of the treaty of friendship between the two, were certain powerful aphrodisiacs.[5] There was also an exchange of gifts between the two.

Megasthenes was the first Greek ambassador to visit India. He himself tells us, he resided at the court of Sandrakottus, the king of India.[6]

Alexander Polyhistor states that Megasthenes remained for some time with the Indian kings and wrote a history of Indian affairs; and that he handed down to posterity a faithful accounts of all that he had witnessed during his stay at the court of Sandrakottus.[7] Clemens says that Megasthenes, the historian, who lived with Seleukus Nikator, visited Pālibothra.[8] Pliny also relates that Megasthenes was one of those Greek authors who resided with Indian king.[9]

Strabo affirms that Megasthenes was sent on an embassy by Seleukus to Sandrakottus at Pālibothra.[10]

We learn from Arrian that Megasthenes lived with Siburtius, the satrap (governor) of Arachosia (Kandahār, Afghanishtan)[11] "during 320-316 BC"[12], and later he resided with him there as a representative of Seleukus by whom he was sent from there to Pāṭaliputra.

Megasthenes came by the royal road that ran from Peucolatis (Puṣkalāvatī) in the West to Pālibothra (Pāṭaliputra) in the east.[13]

Strabo relates on the authority of Megasthenes (*Indika*, Bk. III, Fragm. XXXIV) that a separate board consisting of five members was set up in the time of Sandrakottus to take care of the foreigners, including the ambassadors or diplomats, who came on their visit to the Maurya court at Pālibothra.[14]

Megasthenes was accredited by the Greek king of Syria, Seleukus (312-280 BCE), in 302 BCE as his ambassador to the imperial court of Sandrakottus at Pālibothra (Pāṭaliputra), where he resided for five years, i.e. up to 298 BCE, which marked the end of his reign. He was sent after the treaty had been struck and friendship had sprung up between the two sovereigns. He set out for Pāṭaliputra in 302 BCE and not before.[15] "In order to maintain the friendly relations which were now set on foot, an ambassador was sent by Seleukus to imperial court at Pālibothra who was Megasthenes, the Greek, who made the best use of the facilities which his position furnished for the study of the country and its inhabitants," observes H. F. Tozer.[16]

Arrian tells us that Megasthenes often visited Sandrakottus, the king of the Indians.[17] This does not mean that Megasthenes was sent on frequent embassies to Sandrakottus but that during his embassy he had frequent interviews with him.[18] We are also told by Arrian that Megasthenes resided at the court of Sandrakottus, the greatest king in India and also at the court of Porus, who was still greater than he.[19] A slight emendation of the reading restores the passage to sense making Arrian say that Sandrakottus was greater even than Porus.[20] Megasthenes visited only the court of Candragupta and not of Porus who died, long before his visit, in 317 BCE.[21]

Strabo states that Deimachus or Daimachus (of Plataea) was sent by Seleukus as ambassador to the court of Sandrakottus' son and successor Allitrochades (Bindusāra), the king of Pālibothra.[22] Athenaeus, who is more trustworthy authority than Strabo on the subject, says that Deimachus was sent by Seleukus' son and successor, Antiochus I Soter (280-261 BCE), as his ambassador to the court of Bindusāra (298-273 BCE) called by him Amitrochates,[23] which is a Greek rendering or transcription of Sanskrit Amitraghāta (slayer of foes), another name of the said Maurya king. Deimachus also, like Megasthenes, wrote an account of his sojourn in India.

Bindusāra, like his illustrious father, maintained cordial relations with contemporary Hellenic rulers of the West. He strengthened the bond of friendship with them.

Athenaeus, citing Hegesander (middle of the second century of the Christian era) as his authority, tells us that Amitrochates (Bindusāra), the king of India, wrote to Antiochus (the king of Syria) requesting that king to buy and send him sweet wine, some figs and a sophist (philosopher) to teach him how to argue. Antiochus replied : "We will send you the wine and figs with great pleasure, but not the sophist, as it is against the law in Greece.[24]

We learn from Pliny that Dionysius (284-262 BCE) was sent (from Alexandria) by Ptolemy II Philadelphus, the Hellenistic king of Egypt (285-247 BCE), as an envoy to the court of an Indian king[25], who was no other than the great Maurya Emperor Aśoka (273-232 BCE).[26] He was sent to put the truth to the test by personal inspection and observation. He, like other envoys to the Maurya court at Pāṭaliputra, wrote an account of his experiences in India which was still available to Pliny in the first century of the Christian era.

Aśoka, "the Constantine of the Buddhist faith", also maintained diplomatic and friendly relations with contemporary Greek kings of the West. From his thirteenth Rock Edict it appears that he despatched missionaries and ambassadors to Antiyoka (Antiochus II Theos of Syria, 261-246 BCE), Tulamaya (Ptolemy Philadelphus of Egypt, 285-247 BCE), Antekina (Antigonus II Gonatas of Macedonia, 278-239 or 277-239 BCE), Maka (Magas of Cyrene, 285-258 BCE), and Alikyaśudala (Alexander II of Epirus, 272-240 BCE) not merely to promulgate Buddhism but also to establish world peace.[27]

With the death of Aśoka in 232 BCE, the intercourse between the Mauryas and the Greeks of the West almost came to an end.

The three Greek ambassadors, who had the privilege of visiting the Maurya court at Pāṭaliputra, were Megasthenes and Deimachus from the Syrian court and Dionysius from the Egyptian. They resided at the royal court for a certain period of time during which they learnt about India and its people, history, geography, culture and civilization and presented accounts thereof whatsoever in their respective works. The evidence furnished by the ancient Greek and Latin writers in this regard testifies to the diplomatic and friendly relations of the Maurya Emperors of India with their contemporary Greek sovereigns of Syria and Egypt.

The constant relations were maintained between India and the West during the period of the Maurya empire.[28]

Notes and References

1. AICL, p. 44, continuation of note 1 of p. 43.
2. "India in European Literature and Thought", in *The Legacy of India*, ed. by G.T. Garratt, p. 10.
3. *Intercourse between India and the Western World from the earliest times to the Fall of Rome*. pp. 160-61.
4. *The Greeks in India* p. 56.
5. *Deip*., I, 32, p. 18 D.
6. *Indika,* Bk. I, Fragm. II, Arrian, *Anab*., V, 6, and *Indika*, I, 5.
7. *Indika*, ch. 60.
8. *Strōmateis*, I, p. 305 D.
9. *Nat. Hist.,* VI, 17, 3 ; VI, 21, 3.
10. *Geog.,* XV, I, 36; also II, I, 10.
11. *Anab*., V, 6; see also Diodorus, *Bib. Hist.,* XVIII, III, 3.
12. B.A. Saletore, *India's Diplomatic Relations with the West*, pp. 116-18.
13. Schwanbeck, *Meg. Ind.,* p. 21; Rawlinson, *Intercourse between India and Western World...*, pp. 42 and 46. For details of the so-called royal road leading to the city of Pāṭaliputra see Pliny, *Nat. Hist.,* VI, 21 and Megasthenes' *Indika*, Bk.I, Fragm. IV.
14. *Geog.* XV, I, 51. Let this be said by way of a digression that the Greek traveller Iamboulus, who came to India subsequent to Alexander's Indian expedition (towards the end of third century before the Christian era), once remarked that the kings of Pālibothra (the Mauryas) were not only friendly to the Graecians (Greeks) but also had regard for them. See Diodorus, *Bib. Hist.,* II.60.3.
15. V.A. Smith (EHI, p. 126) and Rawlinson (*Intercourse between India and the Western World ...*, p. 40; *A Concise History of the Indian People*, p. 47) are of the view that Megasthenes came to India in or about 302 BCE. Clinton (*Fast. Hellen*., Vol.III, p. 482) asserts that "he came to the Indian king a little before BC 302". J. Douie (*The Punjab, North-West Frontier Province and Kashmir*, p. 162) says that he came to India in 303 BCE. E.J. Rapson (*Ancient India from the earliest times to the first century AD,* p. 90) states that he visited the court of Chandragupta Maurya, "*c.* 300 BC". R.C. Majumdar (CAI, p. 461) opines that "He must have been in India shortly before 300 BC". R.D. Banerji's statement, that he might have visited India "sometime between 305 and 297 BC"(PAHL, p. 84), is not in approximation to the truth but a far-fetched imagination.
16. *Hist. Anct. Geog.,* p. 148.
17. *Anab.,* V, 6.
18. IIA, p. 88, note 1; Schwanbeck, *Meg. Ind.,* p. 23.
19. *Indika,* I, 5; also E.I Robson's tr. of Arrian's *Indika,* Vol. II, p. 319.

20. See IIA, p. 405, note 1; Lassen, *Pent. Ind.*, p. 44.

21. See Diodorus, *Bib. Hist.,* XIX, 14.

22. *Geog.,* II. I. 10. Placing their reliance on the statement of Strabo, McCrindle (AICL, p. 32, note 3), Rawlinson (*Intercourse between India and the Western World...*, p. 39), E.H. Bunbury (HAG, Vol.I, p. 568), E.H. Warmington (*The Commerce between the Roman Empire and India,* p. 35) and John Marshall (*Taxila,* Vol. I, pp. 22 and 83) write to the same effect. But the fact remains that neither Seleukus sent any ambassador to nor did he enter into any correspondence with Bindusāra. No diplomatic or amicable relations between the two was ever maintained. The view of L.J. Trotter and W.H. Hutton, that Chandragupta's son Bindusāra "renewed the treaties with Seleucus" (*History of India from the earliest times to the Present Day,* p. 33), is not tenable.

23. *Deip.*, IX, p. 394; see also Jacoby, FGH, No. 716, T. 1; H. L. Jones (tr.) *The Geography of Strabo*, Vol. I, pp. 257 and 263; Rawlinson, "India in European Literature and Thought", in *The Legacy of India*, ed by G.T. Garratt, p. 10; P. Masson-Oursel and others, AIIC, p. 37; A Cunningham, CASE, p. 8 (a separate section after p. 278); E.J. Rapson, *Ancient India*, p. 55; R.A. Jairzabhoy, *Foreign Influence in Ancient India*, p. 62; J.W. Sedlar, *India and the Greek World; A study in Transmission of Culture*, p. 90; V.A. Smith, EHI, pp. 129-30; F.Tola and C. Dragonetti, "India and Greece from Alexander to Augustus", in *Graeco-Indica*: *India's cultural contacts with the Greek World,* ed. U.P. Arora, p. 127; U.P. Arora, "Ancient India and Ancient Greece", in *Life, Thought and Culture in India*, ed. G.C. Pande, Vol. I, pt. 2 of HIC, p. 1056; R.S. Tripathi, HAI, p. 161; H.C. Raychaudhuri, PHAI, p. 299; Radha Kumud Mookerji, *Chandragupta Maurya and His Times*, p. 38; G. Macdonald, "The Hellenic Kingdoms of Syria, Bactria and Parthia", in CHI, I, *Ancient India*, ed. E.J. Rapson, p. 389.

    It may be pointed out here that Seleukus ruled Syria jointly with his son Antiochus I from 289 BCE onwards till 280 BCE to manage the eastern affairs. After the latter became an independent king of Syria in 280 BCE after the death of his father, he sent his ambassador Deimachus to the court of Bindusāra. Memnon (cf. C. Müller, ed., *Frag. Hist. Graeco*., Vol. III, p. 533, 12, 1) and Pausanias (*Hell. Per.,* I, 16, 2) clearly state that Antiochus, for some time, had his powers as co-regent. He had under his care the whole of Asia as a co-regent.

24. *Deip.*, XIV, 67, pp. 652 F and 653 A; see also C. Müller (ed), *Frag. Hist. Graeco*., Vol. IV, Fragm. 43, p. 421.

25. *Nat. Hist*., VI, 17, 3; VI, 21, 3; and VI, 58; see also Jacoby, FGH., No. 715, T.1.

26. Some authorities are of the opinion that it was Bindusāra, who towards the end of his reign entertained an ambassador (Dionysius) sent by Ptolemy

Philadelphus to his court. V. A. Smith (EHI, p. 156) observes: "It is uncertain whether Dionysius presented his credentials to Bindusāra or to his successor Aśoka".

27. D.C. Sircar, *Inscriptions of Aśoka,* pp. 40, 54, 78,81, 83; V.A. Smith, *Aśoka*, p. 43; D.R. Bhandarkar, *Aśoka*, p. 33f; also Lassen, *Ind. Alt.,* II, p. 256 f; Rawlinson, *Intercourse between India and the Western World...,* p. 39; JRAS, XII, p. 225.

    Aśoka's relations with the Greek kings of the West seem to have escaped the notices of the classical writers.

28. See also Rawlinson, *Bactria from the Earliest Times to the Extinction of Bactrio-Greek Rule in the Punjab*, pp. 141-42.

3

Relations between India and the Roman Empire with Prime Focus on Indian Embassies to the Roman Emperors, Augustus to Justinian (First Century BCE – Sixth Century BC)

The establishment or formation of the Roman Empire in 31 BCE under the leadership of Augustus was an epoch-making event in the history of the ancient world. The greatness of the Roman power had made a deep impression on the Indian mind. The Indian sovereigns greatly felt the Roman influence. Their intense desire to enter into alliances with the Roman Emperors and to maintain friendly relations with them provided an impetus or gave fillip to Indo-Roman diplomatic relations that commenced in the age of Augustus and continued down to the time of Justinian covering on the whole the period from the first century before the Christian era to the sixth century of that era. Some of the classical historians have supplied us with valuable information regarding diplomatic relations between India and the Roman Empire during the period.

Indian embassies were frequently sent to the courts of the Roman Emperors either at Rome or at Constantinople.

It is said that various Indian rulers were desirous of sending embassies to the Romans.[1]

The accession of Augustus to the throne of Rome in 29 BCE was in itself a historic event. Several Indian states sent embassies to Rome in honour of his accession, an honour never bestowed before on any western prince.[2] He himself says that Indian embassies came to him "frequently", as evidenced by his monumentar record at Ankara.[3] Dion Cassius also says that numerous embassies came to him.[4]

Many embassies from India came to Augustus, the first powerful Roman Emperor, during his reign (29 BCE-14 CE).

The Greek historian Nikolaus, surnamed Damaskernus (being a native of Damascus, in Syria), flourished in the days of Augustus and wrote his biography. He has given an eye-witness account of the first Indian embassy to Augustus at Rome in his biography of that Emperor. His account is preserved in the *Geography*[5] of Strabo and in the works of others.[6]

Nikolaus says that at Antioch (then in Syria)[7] he met with the Indian ambassadors who had been sent to Augustus Caesar. They were on their way to Rome. It appeared from the letter he saw that their number had been more than merely th three. The rest had died chiefly in consequence of the length of the journey. The letter was written in Greek on parchment and imported that Porus was the writer,[8] and that though he was the sovereign of six hundred kings, he nevertheless set a high value on being Caesar's friend and was willing to grant him a passage wherever he wished through his dominions and to assist him in any good enterprise. Such, he says, were the contents of the letter.[9] Porus, like other Asiatic princes, had the desire to secure a powerful ally from the western world and to form an alliance with him.

The ambassadors sent by an Indian Prince Porus came to the Roman Emperor Augustus as early as 26 BCE. Hieronymus in his translation of the *Canon Chronicon* of Eusebius just notices an Indian embassy to that Emperor and places it in the third year of the 188th Olympiad = 26 BCE. Some incidental notices of India in the classics also throw light on the embassies sent to him. Horace, a contemporary of Augustus, in his *Odes*[10] (composed in or about 24 BCE) alludes to this Indian embassy.

The Indian embassy to Augustus is mentioned by Suetonius in his Life of that Emperor. He informs us that the Indians were greatly attracted to the fame of Augustus' moderation and virtues. One of their kings (Porus) through ambassadors solicited the friendship of the Emperor as well as of the Roman people.[11] We learn from Orosius that an Indian embassy reached Augustus while he was residing in the city of Tarraco or Tarragona, in Spain. He received the embassy during his stay there, 27-24 BCE. He also received gifts from the Indians.[12] This embassy, according to E.H. Warmington, was received by Augustus in Spain in 26 or in 25 BCE.[13]

Strabo's own account of Indian embassy to Augustus is of great value. He says: "From one place in India and from one king, Pandion,... there came to Caesar Augustus gifts and an embassy....".[14] The king called here Pandion was a Pāṇḍya king who ruled the kingdom situated on the southern extremity of the Indian Peninsula with its capital at Madura (Modoura of the classical writers).[15]

It was Madaranjeral Irumporai, the most famous king of the Pāṇḍyas, who sent an embassy to the great Roman Emperor Augustus. The Pāṇḍyas of the south were then the only people in India to perceive the advantages of an alliance with the Romans.

Strabo says that an embassy from the Pāṇḍya king was "accompanied by the Indian sophist (philosopher) who committed himself to the flame at Athens".[16] He proceeded to Athens probably to learn something of Greek philosophy. Strabo tells us further: "He thought it necessary to depart to avoid some unexpected calamity that should befall him if he lives longer in the world. He therefore with a smile leaped upon the pyre naked and anointed and wearing a girdle round his loins. On his tomb was this inscription, 'zarmanochegas, an Indian from Bargosa (now Broach on the western coast at the mouth of the river Narmadā) having immortalised himself, according to the custom of his country, lies here".[17] Dion Cassius also relates that one of the Indians, Zarmaros or Zarmanus, having resolved to put an end to his life, burned himself after the manner of his country on a funeral pyre in presence of the Athenians and Augustus who was then in Athens.[18]

Dion Cassius notices at length the embassies which were sent from India to Augustus. He says that one of the Indian embassies (from the Pāṇḍya King) came to him (at Samos, BCE 21) and that the Indians entered into a league of amity or concluded a treaty of alliance with him and presented him some gifts, which the Romans and even the Greeks as well saw for the first time.[19] Florus speaks of the same embassy. He states that the Indian ambassadors after finishing the length of their journey in four years came to him for alliance. They also brought with them some presents for the Emperor which included pearls and precious stones[20] for which the Pāṇḍya Kingdom was very famous.

Rawlinson categorically states that an embassy from the Pāṇḍya king of Madurā left Barygaza (Broach, noted before) in 25 BCE and came to Augustus at Samos four years later, in 21 BCE. The ambassadors brought for him many presents and gifts. The leader of the embassy, he says, was a monk (from Broach).[21] This embassy was received by Augustus at Samos in 21 BCE, according to Warmington[22] also, but, accordingly to Priaulx[23] and R.C. Majumdar,[24] in 22 or 20 BCE. Some authorities are of the view that this embassy was sent by King Pandion to Augustus in or about 20 BCE.[25]

The Greek merchants who visited Barygaza (Broach) in the course of their commerce with India offered a passage in their ship for the ambassadors and for their presents which they carried with them for the Roman Emperor Augustus. In due course, the embassy from India arrived at Alexandria (in Egypt). The ambassadors went with Alexandrians with presents to the court of that Emperor.[26] It may be added here that Egypt became a Roman province in 30 BCE.

The embassies sent from India to the courts of the Roman Emperors during the first four centuries of the Christian era are also noticed in the classics.

We learn from Pliny that in the reign of the Emperor Claudius (CE 41-54) ambassadors came to his court from Taprobane (Ceylon)[27] in "South-East India". Priaulx calls it "the Indian Embassy", which according to him, was sent to Rome in CE 41. He says that the members of this embassy may have been Tamils, not natives.[28] Rawlinson also includes the embassy from Ceylon to Claudius in the Indian embassies sent to Rome.[29]

Dion Cassius informs us that an Indian embassy came to the court of Trajan (CE 98-117) after he had arrived in Rome and that the Emperor treated its members with the utmost courtesy and distinction giving them the seats of Senators at the theatre to watch a show or some spectacles or to witness the celebration of his recent triumph over the Dacae.[30]

This embassy was dispatched by the Kuṣāṇa King Kadphises II to Rome in CE 99 to congratulate Trajan on his accession.[31]

The Emperor Hadrian (CE 117-38) was on good terms with the Indians. The envoys from the Indian and the Bactrian Kings visited his court and solicited his friendship.[32]

Some Indian ambassadors went to Rome to pay homage to the virtue of the Emperor Antoninus Pius (CE 138-61), as stated by Aurelius Victor also called Aurelian Victor.[33]

Bardesanes says he met the members of an Indian embassy at Antioch in Syria in CE 218. They were on their way to Rome to represent India on the occasion of the accession of the Emperor Heliogabalus (also called Elagabalus) and welcome him. His accession took place in CE 218 and he reigned from that time onward to 222. The chief of this embassy, Bardesanes says, was Sandanes or Dandamis. Bardesanes' account is now lost but some of its fragments are preserved in the works of Johannes Stobaeus (also called Stobaios)[34] and Porphyry[35] and in other works.[36] The chief of this Indian embassy (already noted) belonged to the Śātkarṇī dynasty that ruled Kalliena (now Kalyana, in the Thane district, 33 miles north-east of Bombay). The legitimacy of the statement of Rawlinson, that the embassy led by Sandanes or Dandamis was from the Deccan[37], cannot be questioned. McCrindle has also rightly pointed out that "The part of India from which this embassy came may be inferred from the name borne by the Chief who conducted it, namely sandanes of Maratha country (Mahārāṣṭra) called by Ptolemy Ariake...".[38]

The ambassadors from India and other countries visited the court of the Emperor Aurelian (CE 270-75) at his triumph in CE 274.[39]

We are told by Eusebius Pamphilus (Pamphili) that ambassadors from the Indians of the East visited the court of the Emperor constantinus (Constantine the Great). They brought presents to the Emperor as an acknowledgment that his sovereignty extended to their ocean. They told him that Indian princes had dedicated pictures and statues in his honour in token that they recognised him as their king.[40] "This embassy", says McCrindle, "reached Constantinople in the last year (of the reign/life) of the Emperor Constantine the Great, 337 AD".[41]

This may be noted here that the embassies were sent from India to the imperial courts at both Rome and Constantinople before the division of the Roman Empire in CE 364. In most of the cases, the names of Indian kings, who sent their representatives on a diplomatic mission, representatives and which parts of the country they belonged to, are not mentioned by the classical writers.

Regarding the friendly relations between the Roman Emperor Constantine and the Indian king (unnamed), Kedrenos tells us that in the time of the former Metrodoros, a Persian by birth, on pretence of philosophy went off to India. He received also from the king of the Indians presents to carry to the Emperor.[42]

That the communication between the East and West in the fourth century was frequent and regular may be gathered from the Roman writers. We learn from Ammianus Marcellinus that the Indian ambassadors came to Rome to congratulate the Emperor Julian on his accession to the throne (in CE 361). They also brought some presents to the Emperor. This can best be qualified in his own words: "*Inde nationibus Indicis certatim cum donis optimates mittentibus ante tempus abusque Divis et Serendivis*".[43] The Emperor reigned from CE 361 to 363. Sextus Aurelius Victor's *Epitome* (XVI) also contains a notice of the Indian ambassadors sent to that Emperor, who, according to him, was well known for his justice.

"These are but scant memorials of petty diplomatic courtesies and scattered over nearly five hundred years to illustrate the intercourse between Rome and India, which during the first half of these long centuries reached its highest point of development", remarks Priaulx.[44]

In CE 364, the Roman Empire was divided into two parts – Eastern Roman Empire and Western Roman Empire. The capital of the former was Constantinople and that of the latter Rome. After the fall of Rome in CE 476, Constantinople rose into prominence.

Two embassies were sent from India with presents and gifts to the court of the Emperor Justinianus (Justinian) at Constantinople, one in CE 530 and the other in CE 552.[45] Justinian was one of the greatest of the Emperors of Constantinople. He was the Emperor from CE 527 to 563 and died in 565.[46]

The diplomatic relations between India and the Roman Empire were maintained from the time of Augustus down to the time of Justinian which constitute a very important phase in the political history of ancient India. We do have sufficient evidence in the classics regarding the Indian embassies to the Roman Emperors, but we do not find any testimony therein as to whether those Emperors in turn sent their diplomats or ambassadors to the courts of Indian kings during the period under notice.

Notes and References

1. See B.A. Saletore, *India's Diplomatic Relations with the West*, pp. 216f, 220 f.
2. Monum, *Ancyranum*, 36; *Corp. Ins. Graeco*., V. 4040 cf R.A. Jairzabhoy, *Foreign Influence in Ancient India*, p. 110.
3. M. Wheeler, *Rome Beyond the Imperial Frontiers*, p. 133.
4. *Rom. Hist*., IX, 58.
5. XV, I, 73.

6. C. Müller (ed), *Fragm. Hist. Graeco.*, V, Fragm. 91, p. 419; Jacoby, FGH, No. 90, Fragm. I00.

7. Antioch was the capital of the Greek kings of Syria from 312 to 150 BCE. Syria became a Roman province in 64 BCE. It was under the rule of the Romans during the period of the Empire. There was land route from Antioch in Syria to Rome.

8. This Porus was, in all probability, one of the descendants of the Great Porus of the Western Punjab of Alexander's time and belonged to the most illustrious family. He was a contemporary of Augustus in the first century BCE. The letter written by him in Greek shows that the Greek language was still used in the first century BCE in north-west India. A.H.L. Heeren (*Historical Researches*, Vol. II, p. 107) says: "Parchment was material used for writing on in India. The letter was written on parchment and in the name of Porus and in Greek". The letter, according to W.W. Hunter ("The Greeks in India", rept. from his *The Indian Empire : Its Peoples, History and Products,* London, 1882, in *Ancient India*, Delhi, 1983, p. 96), contained the names or credentials of the Indian ambassadors sent by Porus to Augustus.

9. Strabo, *Geog.*, XV, I, 73; H.L. Jones (tr.), *The Geography of Strabo*, Vol, VII, pp. 125, 127; Hamilton and Falconer's tr. *The Geography of Strabo*, Vol. III, pp. 118-19; see also Priaulx, T*he Indian Travels of Apollonius of Tyana and the Indian Embassies to Rome from the Reign of Augustus to the Death of Justinian,* pp. 65-67; "Indian Travellers, Life of Apollonius of Tyana, and Indian Embassies to Rome", JRAS, XIX, p. 294 f; B.N. Puri, *India as described by Early Greek Writers,* p. 136; J.T. Wheelers, "Greek and Roman India", rept. from his *The History of India from the Earliest Ages* (London, 1881), in *Ancient India* (Delhi, 1983), pp. 137-39.

10. I, 12, 56; III, 29, 27-8; IV, 14, 41-3; IV, 15, 23.

11. *Vita Augusti*, 21.

12. *Roman History*, VI, 12.

13. *The Commerce between the Roman Empire and India*, p. 36.

14. *Geog.*, XV, I, 4; H.L. Jones (tr.), *The Geography of Strabo*, Vol.VII, p. 5; Hamilton and Falconer's tr. *The Geography of Strabo*, Vol.III, p. 74.

15. See Priaulx, *The Indian Travels of Apollonius of Tyana and the Indian Embassies to Rome from the Reign of Augustus to the Death of Justinian,* p. 78; H.G. Rawlinson, *Intercourse between India and the Western World from the earliest times to the Fall of Rome*, p. 107; J.T. Wheeler, *The History of India from the Earliest Ages*, Ch. IV, "Greek and Roman India", p. 206, note 80; McCrindle, AICL, p. 9, note 3; Warmington, *op. cit.,* pp. 37 and 60; K.A. Nilakanta Śāstrī (ed), *Foreign Notices of South India*, p. 46f; L.J. Trotter and W.H. Hutton, *History of India from the Earliest Times to the present day*, p. 34.

16. *Geog.*, XV, I, 4.

17. *Geog.*, XV, I, 73.

18. *Rom. Hist.*, IX, 58; LIV, 9; also Plutarch, *Vit. Alex.*, Ch. LXIX. Strabo's *zarmanochegas* (a somewhat incorrect transliteration of Sanskrit Śramaṇācārya – teacher of Śramaṇas, Pāli shamans) or Dion's *zarmanus* (sarmanus) was a Buddhist ascetic. He was a spiritual guide or preceptor. See AICL, pp. 78, note 1, 79; IIA, Biog. Appen., p. 389. His death, according to the Hindu custom of his country, generated controversy among the authorities regarding his identity. J.T. Wheeler ("Greek and Roman India", rept. from his *The History of India from the Earliest Ages, Supra,* in *Ancient India, Supra*, p. 138, note 80 of p. 137 and p. 139; *The History of India from the Earliest Ages*, pp. 206, note 80, 207 and 208, note 83) says that he was either a Brāhmaṇa sage, or a Śramana (Buddhist ascetic) or a Hindu philosopher from Broach who accompanied the embassy from the paṇḍya king of Madura to Augustus. Warmington (*op. cit.*, p. 37) calls him "the Buddhist monk". Rawlinson is of the opinion that "he was a Jain, as Jainism looks upon Voluntary immolation as a laudable act". ("India in European Literature and Thought", in *The Legacy of India*, ed. G.T. Garratt, pp. 14-15) see also *Ind. Ant.*, XIV, p. 305.

19. *Rom. Hist.,* IX, 58; also IX, 73.

20. *Epitome of Roman History*, IV, 12.

21. "India in European Literature and Thought, in *The Legacy of India*, ed. G.T. Garratt, pp. 14-15; and *Intercourse between India and the Western World*, pp. 108-9.

22. *Op. cit.,* p. 36.

23. *Op. cit.,* pp. 68-69.

24. CAI, App. II, "On the Indian Embassy to Augustus", pp. 475-6.

25. Merivale, *History of the Romans under the Empire*, IV, pp. 118, 175 cf. V.A. Smith, EHI, p. 471; R.S. Tripathi, HAI, p. 482.

26. Priaulx, *op. cit.*, p. 86.

27. *Nat. Hist.*, VI, 22; VI, 24.

28. *Op. cit.,* pp. 92-93.

29. *Intercourse between India and the Western World*, p. 109.

30. *Rom. Hist.*, LXVIII, 156; see also Rawlinson, *Intercourse between India and the Western World*, pp. 127-28, 164; Priaulx, *op. cit.*, p. 125; Warmington, *op. cit.,* pp. 95, 139.

31. Rawlinson, "India in European Literature and Thought", in *The Legacy of India,* ed. G.T. Garratt, p. 15; *Intercourse between India and the Western World*, p. 109; V.A. Smith, EHI, p. 238; *Periplus*, p. 187, note by W.H. Schoff. Rawlinson observes that the Indian embassies were sent also from

the Kuṣāṇa Kings to the Roman Emperors. (BSOAS, 1960, pp. 47-55; JA, 1958, p. 395.)

32. *Historia Augusta, Hadrian*, 21; also Warmington, *op. cit.*, p. 99.
33. *Epitoma* (Epitome), XVI.
34. *Physica (*or *Anthologium*), 1, 54; 1, 3, 56; Jacoby, FGH, No. 719, Fragms 1 and 2.
35. *De Abstinentia*, IV, 17-18.
36. *Historia Augusta, Elagabalus*, 23-4, 26-33; Dion Cassius, *Rom. Hist.*, LXXIX, 9; see also Warmington, *op. cit.,* p. 137.
37. *Intercourse between India and the Western World*, p. 146.
38. AICL, p. 172, note 1.
39. *Historia Augusta, Aurelian*, 33, 41 also 29 and 45; Warmington, *op. cit*., p. 138.
40. *De Vita Constantinus*, IV, 7, 50; also Warmington*, op. cit*., p. 139.
41. AICL, p. 214, note 2.
42. *Synopsis of History*, I, pp. 516-17.
43. *Rer. Ges*., XXII, 7, 10; see also Priaulx, *op. cit*., p. 234; Warmington, *op. cit*., pp. 124 and 139.
44. *Op. cit*., 126.
45. J. Malala, *History,* p. 477; Priaulx, *op. cit*., pp. 126, 132 and 237.
46. CDGR, pp. 464-65.

Book Ten
Towns and Cities

General Remarks

The towns and cities, including the urban centres, of India received the notices of classical writers of both the pre- and post-Christian era. They have provided us with valuable information regarding the urban culture that flourished in the country in ancient times. The classical writings on the subject may undoubtedly be regarded as significant contribution to the enrichment of our knowledge of the urban history of ancient India.

The Greek and Roman accounts of both the small and large towns and some capital cities in northern, north-western, eastern, western, central and southern parts of India are worthy of our notice.

The Greek and Roman writers have also thrown light on town-planning, architectural designs of the cities, urban life of the people, the patterns of urban settlement, and urban growth and decay.

The information supplied by the celebrated classical historians, geographers and travellers belonging to the period extending from the fourth century BCE to the sixth century CE regarding the towns and cities in different parts of India are of inestimable value.

The noted classical authorities on the subject under notice are Arrian, Diodorus Siculus, Quintus Curtius Rufuṣ, Justin and Plutarch,-the five well known historians of Alexander's Indian campaign, – Megasthenes, Strabo, Pliny, anonymous writer of the *Periplus*, Ptolemy, Aelian, Solinus, Philostratus, Dionysius Periegetes, Ammianus Marcellinus, Julius Valerius and Kosmas Indikopleustes.

The study of the subject is primarily based on the original sources (in the form of translations of the Greek and Latin texts preserving the narratives, extracts and fragments of the works of various classical authors). But just to supplement and support them we have utilized some of those works which are purely based on the classical writings on the subject. It is worthy of remark that some of the classical authors have applied their sound judgment in providing accurate picture of the subject. They have presented very trustworthy and intelligible accounts distinguished by their conspicuous merits. However, their authenticity have been examined in the light of the facts recorded in different sources. In order to identify the place-names and determine the exact geographical location and position of old and forgotten towns and cities situated in northern, eastern, western, central and southern parts of the country, in the hills and valleys of Afghanistans, in the plains of the northern, western, central and southern Punjab, in the upper, middle and lower valley of the Indus and in some parts of Baluchistan (called Gedrosia) with accuracy and precision, we have placed our reliance on the combined testimony of both classical and non-classical sources. The classical accounts of the subject have also been corroborated and confirmed by the literary sources, the archaeological evidence (coins, inscriptions, and remains or ruins of the cities), the Chinese account of Hiuen Tsang (CE 629-45), and the statements of the explorers and travellers (who discovered the remains of towns or cities described in the classical treatises) and some chroniclers and geographers, wherever necessary.

Blindly relying upon the traditions regarding Dionysos current among the Indians, Megasthenes says that the men of greatest learning among the Indians relate that in the most primitive times, when the people of the country were still living in villages, Dionysos made his appearance coming from the regions lying to the west, and at the head of a considerable army overran the whole of India, as there was no great city capable of resisting his arms. He was the founder of larger cities. He also showed the people how to worship the deity, and introduced laws and courts of justice. He was the founder of no small number of cities. He built therein many sumptuous palaces, and settled within its walls a numerous population.[1] The traditions recorded by Megasthenes are purely based on fanciful notion. Deriving his authority from Megasthenes Arrian also states that "the Indians in old times had neither the towns nor temples of the gods. Dionysos, however, when he came and had conquered the people, founded cities and gave laws to these cities."[2] These two Greek historians, however, have not denied the existence of cities in India. They have rather brought to light some of the cities that existed in the country. It is undeniable that some Greek writers do not make mention of the towns and cities, temples, palaces and other large buildings that existed in India. It is, however, a fact to be reckoned with that temples were hardly found in India before the dawn of the fourth century before the Christian era, but the towns and cities very much existed in the country preceding the century Megasthenes belonged to. Moreover, Dionysos was a legendary figure. His historicity is yet to be proved. The towns were too numerous to be reckoned, and they were close to each other. As a matter of fact, some of them had already come into existence before the Persian invasion of the north-west in the sixth century before the Christian era. Some of them were founded later. In north-west India, towns and cities were mostly situated in the valleys of Kābul, Kunār, Swāt and the Indus, and in different parts of the Punjab. A large number of towns and cities were discovered there by the companions or followers of Alexander in the course of his Indian campaign between 327 and 325 BCE. Alexander himself founded some of the towns in that part of the country. Many of them were destroyed during the period, but some were found in existence up to the first century of the Christian era, and some continued to exist beyond that period.

Arrian, on the authority of Megasthenes (*Indika*, Bk. II, Fragm. XXVI), says that it is not possible to record with accuracy the number of Indian cities on account of their multiplicity. He tells us further that for the construction of buildings in the cities in India it was the usual practice to use wood where floods were common, and brick and clay where there were elevated places. This can best be expressed in his own words: "Of the cities of the Indians it is said that the number is so great that it cannot be stated with precision, but that such cities as are situated on the banks of rivers or on the sea-coast are built of wood, for were they built of brick they would not last long-so destructive are the rains, and also the rivers when they overflow their banks and inundate the plains; those cities, however, which stand on commanding situations and lofty eminences are built of brick and mud."[3] Curtius also informs us that in the fortifications of the towns in the regions west of the Indus, wooden beams were used to prevent the superstructure from sinking, and that unburnt or sundried bricks and moist clay were employed for making houses.[4]

The four cardinal factors, – demographic, political, economic and defensory, - were greatly responsible for urbanization in ancient India as appears from some of the classical (Greek and Latin) sources. From the classical description of the subject it is quite evident that the towns and cities were densely populated. The administrative centres or seats of government evolved into the capital cities. In north-west India in particular, the free cities were generally without chief or king. The cities with chiefs were the seats of sovereign power. Each city-state had its own political institutions, including assembly or council, and laws and army. Each citizen owed allegiance to his city. The citizens possessed all real property, exercised all political rights and performed all military duties. Most of the capital cities of the tribal states, which broadly fall within the two categories, monarchical and oligarchical or republican-gradually developed as urban centres. Some of them assumed the character of small city-states. The large, populous and extensive cities, including the metropolis, in India were well protected by defensive walls, forts and fortifications and ramparts of formidable strength. They also served as strongholds or acropolis. Many cities were founded in north-western parts of India for defensive purpose in the sense of offering the stout resistance to the Macedonian invaders. The Indian people were by and large agricultural communities. The higher agricultural production and the economic prosperity of the people facilitated the growth of commercial activities. The commercial or trade centres developed into township. The people with surplus production played an active role in the growth of trade and commerce. Many towns and cities developed as great emporium of trade. It is striking to note that all important market towns and port towns, besides small towns, large cities, provincial capitals, royal capitals, fortified cities, inland cities, and coastal towns, in India have been brought to light by the author of the *Periplus*, and by Ptolemy.[5] Many of them have been identified but some are not identifiable. The numerous commercial cities and ports mentioned in the *Periplus* attest the progress of the Indians in the field of external trade and show the advanced state of the country. Some towns and cities also developed as religious and educational centres. Some of them contained temples, and some were seats of learning.

The classical sources bear eloquent and glowing testimony to the existence of a large number of towns and cities in India which can further be substantiated by other reliable evidences. The entire details are not available because many towns and cities passed into oblivion because of their decay or destruction for some reason or the other. However, a number of towns and cities received the notices of classical writers. Those cities which were explored and discovered also became the object of attraction for them.

The evidence adduced by some Greek and Roman writers regarding the cities in the Punjab and the Indus Valley deserve our attention. Deriving his authority from previous Greek writers (unnamed), Strabo says “We know from previous writers that the Macedonians conquered nine nations situated between the Hydaspes and the Hypanis (Hyphasis) and possessed 5000 cities, not one of which was less than KosMeropis and Alexander after having reduced all this country delivered it over to Poros".[6] Pliny also relates that "In this country (India) the nations and cities are numberless should one attempt to reckon them all up ... The companions of Alexander the Great have written that in that tract of India, which he subdued there were 5,000 towns, none less than Cos (=two miles) - that its nations were nine in number.-"[7] He says further that "In India Alexander conquered five thousand towns of more than two thousand population each".[8] On the basis of a thorough scrutiny of data available in the classical sources, we do not find the number of towns stated above by Strabo and Pliny as worthy of our credence. The number of cities or towns between Hydaspes and Hyphasis is given 5,000, which is obviously an error for 500.[9] Strabo himself admits that "... the number seems to be exaggerated."[10] Apollodorus states that there were between the Hydaspes and Hypanis 1500 cities.[11] Strabo tells us that the dominions of Elder Porus which were confined between the Hydaspes and the Akesines - an extensive and fertile tract not more than forty miles in width - contained three hundred cities.[12] Arrian affirms that the Indian territories -seven nations in all, containing more than two thousand cities- subjugated by Alexander were placed under the rule of Porus.[13] Plutarch, on the other hand, says that Alexander reinstated Porus in his kingdom adding a large province to it which contained 5,000 considerable cities, and innumerable villages.[14]

The companions and historians of Alexander have exaggerated the number of cities with a view of magnifying the exploits of the great conqueror.[15] The accounts transmitted by the Greek historians of the wealth and populousness of the provinces of India, which were traversed by Alexander and temporarily annexed to his dominions, are very remarkable. There can be no doubt that they were in most instances derived from native information, and deeply tinged with oriental exaggeration, to give us a high opinion of the flourishing condition of the country and of the comparative advance in urban civilization. The number of cities is grossly exaggerated which may be a figment of classical imagination. The urban and semi-urban centres, fortified places and villages not less populous than towns are included in the cities as gleaned from the classified sources. The classical concept of a city appears somewhat different from that of the modern time. The Punjab in those days was indeed one of the richest provinces of India, abounding in villages and towns. It was economically prosperous and developed. In the territories of the Malloi, Oxydrakai and others there were as many as 500 cities. We are informed by Arrian that the Glausai (free clan or republican tribe) had as many as 37 towns in their territory the smallest of which contained not less than 5,000 inhabitants, while many contained upwards of 10,000.[16] Max Duncker has rightly pointed out that the northern and north-western parts of India with numerous towns and cities were known to the Greek writers.[17]

Vasudeva Sharana Agrawala on the basis of his comparative study of Pāṇinian and classical tradition, which are complementary to each other in respect of towns and cities of India, has correctly observed: "That ancient India possessed a large number of flourishing centres of population in the form of cities or towns is also attested to by Greek writers. According to them, the Panjab was full of towns, centres of industry and economic prosperity. Many of these figured as forts or centres of defence ... Both Pāṇini and Greek geographers depended on a common source of tradition..."[18] It has been further stated by him that the cities, five hundred in number, between the Jhelum and the Beas (the Vāhika region), as recorded by the historians of Alexander's Indian campaign almost tallies with the figures given by Pāṇini in his *Aṣṭādhyāyī* (*Sūtras* and *Gaṇa-Pāṭha*).[19] In the lists of towns attached to the two *gaṇas* (IV.2.75 and IV.2.80), we have about 500 names. These may further be augmented if we add the testimony of other *gaṇas*. This gives us a substantial list of about 750 towns in Pāṇini.

Aristoboulos (the companion and historian of Alexander), as we learn from Strabo,[20] saw a tract of land on the banks of the Indus deserted which earlier contained more than a thousand cities with their villages. We are told by McCrindle that in the Indus valley, "The towns being but very slightly built are seldom of more than ephemeral duration, and if, as often happens they are destroyed by inundations, every trace is lost of their ever having existed. The river besides frequently changes its course and leaves the towns which it abandons to sink into decay and utter oblivion".[21]

Rufinus (CE 330-410) in one of his Latin works has unravelled a mystery of history by stating that the philosopher Metrodoros, a Persian by birth, had penetrated into India for the purpose of seeing its various towns and cities.[22]

The urban centres (towns or cities) that existed in northern and north-western India, which include mainly Afghanistan and the Punjab, and Sindh and Baluchistan, respectively, attracted the notices of historians of Alexander's Indian campaign. They have given trustworthy accounts of their growth and decay. They have focused on almost all the towns or cities to the west and the east of the Indus. Most of the towns lost their existence in the course of Alexander's invasion of India, but some continued to flourish even in post-Alexandrian age.

The classical writers have also taken notices of the towns and cities in the neighbourhood of Purūṣapura and Swāt (Souastos) valley in Afghanistan. The former represented by Peshawar, and the latter, became parts of North West Frontier Province carved out in 1901 during the viceroyalty of Lord Curzon (1899-1905) which now forms part of Pakistan.

Some of the towns or cities in Afghanistan and the Punjab were well-planned with beautiful designs, architectural beauty and fortifications. The famous Massaga city in the realm of the Assakenians was built up as a fort commanding great natural advantages on an eminence inaccessible on all sides against steep rock, deep stream, and a great rampart guarded by a deep moat. Curtius (*Hist. Alex.*, VIII, 10) gives a picturesque description of the planning of that city. The Kathaians had a strongly fortified city called Sangala with its walls made of brick. The Malloi had also many walled cities with citadels on commanding heights. The walls had towers for defensive purpose. The city of Taxila was laid out on a symmetrical plan. Philostratus in his *Life of Apollonius of Tyana* (II, XXIII) has portrayed a vivid picture of the planning of that city with all relevant details. There wee some splendid structures of artistic beauty. The architectural styles of some of the urban centres, particularly in Gāndhāra region (the Kābul and Swāt valleys and Purūṣapura in Afghanistan, and Rāwalpiṇḍī district in the northern Punjab), underwent profound changes because of the successive rule of the Persians, Macedonians, Graeco-Bactrians, Śakas and Kuṣāṇas there between the sixth century BCE and the first century CE. In most of the parts of north-western India, the towns and cities belonged to the tribal people. Besides the tribal towns and cities, there were some other urban centres including the brāhmaṇical cities in the Lower Sindh. However, it cannot be denied that some of them were no better than the early urban centres in the Gangetic valley (ascribed to the earlier half of the first millennium BCE) with mud huts the circumference of which formed a protective wall of no great height or thickness. Some were, of course, of enormous size which flourished as centres of urban culture. The cities were, on the whole, both large and small. Their construction, location and fortifications give us some idea of the system of town-planning then in vogue.

The foundation of most of the cities in north-west India may reasonably be ascribed to the indigenous people. U.P. Arora is also of the view that the "early Greek accounts of India corroborated by archaeological evidence lead us to believe that the North-Western urbanization was an indigenous evolution."[23] However, there were some urban centres which bore the stamp of Hellenic cities because of being transformed with a new Greek name or enlarged by Alexander effecting the settlements of the native people and the Greeks or Yavaṇas. A few ancient cities of indigenous origin received new names from the Macedonian conqueror. Alexander was not only the destroyer but also the builder of the cities. In pursuance of his policy to secure the permanence of his Indian conquests by founding cities, he built some new cities in north-west India and fortified and garrisoned them with large body of troops to overawe and hold in subjection the tribes in their neighbourhood. He planted colonies in the places concerned with the Greek and Indian settlements. The civil administration was entrusted to native chiefs while the executive and military authority was wielded by Macedonian officials.[24] Some of the large and important towns of native urban communities were converted by him into military and non-military colonies dominated by Greek population in oriental environment. According to Plutarch, seventy Asiatic cities at the least owed their origin to Alexander out of which forty can still be traced.[25] But this cannot be accepted as a well ascertained fact. Grote is of the view that the number is exaggerated, and disparages their importance.[26]

The transformation of some place-names in north-west India from the Sanskrit to Persian and then on to the Greek because of the Persian and Greek rule there for sometime between the sixth and the first century before the Christian era has really made our task of identifying them in the geographical setting very difficult. Moreover, the lack of uniformity in the system followed by different authorities for transcribing and transliterating the classical appellations sometimes makes the confusion worse confounded. Thus, all the available evidence have been harmonized together for piercing through the haziness enveloping the subject with particular reference to the identification and geographical locations of the towns and cities in north-west India. Some of the towns described in classical literature (Greek and Latin) also find mention in Indian literature (Sanskrit and Pāli). Some of the towns or cities in Afghanistan, the Punjab and Sindh mentioned by the Greek and Roman writers find mention in the *Aṣṭādhyāyī* of Pāṇini bearing the original Indian names. Their respective identity can be established by applying the laws of transcription.

The towns and cities in general described by the classical authors have been identified and their geographical position and location determined with the help of literary, epigraphic and numismatic evidences, annotations and commentaries of the translators of the Greek and Latin texts, the information transmitted by the authorities who have dealt with the subject and other relevant sources.

Notes and References

1. *Indika*, Bk. I, Fragm., I, cf An Epitome of Megasthenes, Diodorus, *Bib. Hist.,* II, 38-39, AIMA, pp. 36-39.
2. *Indika*, I, 7, AIMA, p. 199.
3. *Indika*, I, 10, AIMA, pp. 68 and 204; Arrian's *Indika*, tr. Chinnock, p. 410; Godolphin, *The Greek Historians*, II, p. 739; see also B.C. Law, "India as known to the Early Greeks", JGRI, XVII, 1-2, Nov. 1960-Feb. 1961, p. 7;Mrs. C.Speir, *Phases of Indian Civilization -A Historical and Cultured Outline*, p. 219.
4. *Hist. Alex.*, VIII, 10, 23.
5. It has been claimed by E.H. Johnson (JRAS, 1941, pp. 208ff) that for the towns in the interior of India Ptolemy used a Purāṇic text available in a Greek translation. Some of the towns mentioned by him are, of course, described in Purāṇas.
6. *Geog.*, XV, I, 3; XV, I, 33; see AICL, pp. 9, 39-40; Hamilton and Falconer (tr.), *The Geography of Strabo*, III, pp. 73-74, 94-95.
7. *Nat. Hist.,* VI, 17 (21); see AICL, pp. 107-08; CAI, p. 340.
8. *Ibid.*, VI, 59.
9. See IIA, p. 112, note 1.
10. *Geog.*, XV, I, 33.
11. M. Elphinstone, *The History of India*, App. III, "On the Greek Accounts of India", pp. 238-39.
12. *Geog.*, XV, I, 29; see AICL,p.35.
13. *Anab.*, VI, 2; IIA, p. 133; *Anab.*, tr. Chinnock, p. 296; see also A.V. Williams Jackson (ed) *History of India*, Vol. II, *From the Sixth Century BC to the Mohammedan Conquest Including the Invasion of Alexander the Great,* by V.A. Smith, pp. 76-77.
14. *Vit. Alex.*, ch. LX, IIA, p. 309.
15. See also E.H. Bunbury, HAG, I, p. 453.
16. *Anab.*,V. 20; IIA, p. 112; *Anab.*, tr., Chinnock, pp. 276-77.
17. HA, Vol. IV, p. 408.
18. IP, pp. 75-76.
19. *Ibid.*, 496-97.
20. *Geog.*, XV, I, 19; AICL, p. 25; AIT, p. 137, note 24; Hamilton and Falconer, *op.cit.,* p. 84.
21. AIT, p. 137.
22. *Hist. Eccles*, I,9; see also AICL, p. 185; D. Th. Vassiliades, *The Greeks in India,* p. 78; Priaulx, *The Indian Travels of Apolloniuus of Tyana…*, pp. 179-80. Metrodoros is believed to have visited India during the reign of Roman emperor Constantine I (CE 306-337).

23. "Ancient India and Ancient Greece", in HIC, Vol. I pt. 2, *Life, Thought and Culture in India* (from c. 600 BC to c. AD 300), ed. G.C. Pande, p. 1050; see also his *Greeks on India*, p. 107.
24. IIA, Introd. pp. 4-5; William Robertson, HDAI, p. 27.
25. IIA, p. 5, note 1.
26. See his *History of Greece*, Vol. XII.

1

Towns and Cities in North India

Of the towns and cities in north India known to the classical writers, notably, Megasthenes, Arrian, Pliny and Ptolemy, mention may first be made of those in the Gaṅgā-Yamunā valley. It is Ptolemy who has described the towns of both lower and upper Gangetic region. He refers to the Pauravas as Porouaroi or Porvaroi who reigned over the realms between the upper Gaṅgā and Yamunā.

Describing the towns and cities of upper Gangetic Doāb, Ptolemy clearly mentions Pandoouoi (Pāṇḍavas) and their capital cities Hastināpura on the upper Gaṅgā[1] and Indabara (Indraprastha) on the Yamunā in the neighbourhood of Delhi.[2] The Prākṛt form of the latter name is Indrabaṭṭha.[3] The inhabitants of Indraprastha city have been called Indaprathai by Ptolemy.[4]

Ptolemy's Kosamba[5] is identical with Kauśāmbi, a famous city founded by Kuśāmba (one of the kings of Puru dynasty) on the river Yamunā, which became the Pāṇḍū capital after Hastināpura had been swept away by the Gaṅgā. He distinctly refers to this city as a capital of the Porouaroi (Pauravas). It was, according to Cunningham, "one of the most celebrated places in ancient India, and its name was famous amongst Brāhmaṇs as well as Buddhists".[6] It was one of the great cities of the time of the Buddha. In his time, it was an entrepot or emporium of trade. Kosamba of Ptolemy, says McCrindle, was a seat of Buddhism.[7] Cunningham was the first archaeologist to locate Kauśāmbi's extensive ruins lying near the village Kosam on the right bank of the Yamunā, about 30 miles south-west of Allahabad.[8]

Ptolemy gives a list of 33 towns by way of supplement to those situated along the Gaṅgā. He includes in it Kassida[9] which is evidently identical with Kāśī situated on the north bank of the Gaṅgā at the junction between it and the river Varaṇāvatī or Varaṇā. It is the older name than Vārāṇasī (now Banāras)[10], which he describes as Erarasa and calls it a metropolis.[11] St. Martin takes this name as an addition of the Roman copyists.[12] It was one of the principal cities of the mid-Gaṅgā valley. It was once the capital of the Kāśī kingdom.

Ptolemy distinctly mentions the Passalae (Pañcālas) of lower Gangetic Doāb and their northern capital Adisdara[13] which has been satisfactorily identified with Ahicchatra, a city of great antiquity. It was situated north of the Gaṅgā. It was the capital of north Pañcāla kingdom in the first millennium BCE. The ruins of Ahicchatra are situated about half a mile to the north-east of the village of Rāmnagar and about seven miles to the north of Aonla town in Bareilly district of Uttar Pradesh. Ahicchatra was visited by Hodgson in 1833. He found the ruins of an ancient fortress several miles in circumference, which had 34 bastions, and was known in the neighbourhood by the name of the Pāṇḍu's fort.

On the combined testimony of Megasthenes,[14] Arrian[15] and Pliny[16] it can fairly be stated that the Sourasenoi (Śūrasenas- the people inhabiting the territory of Śūrasena kingdom) possessed two large cities – Methora (Mathurā) and Carisobora or Cleisobora (Kṛṣṇapura identical with Vrindāvana) – on the Yamunā (Jobares of Arrian, Jomanes of Pliny, and Diamouna of Ptolemy). Ptolemy designates Mathurā as Modoura and calls it the city of the gods.[17] It is higher up than Agra from which it is 35 miles distant. It was the capital of Śūrasena kingdom in the age of the Buddha (sixth and fifth centuries BCE). Lassen transcribes Carisobora as Kṛṣṇapura.[18] Cunningham has correctly identified the city of Klisobora (Cleisobora) with Vrindāvana, 6 miles to the north of Mathurā.[19] Wilkins' identification of Clisobora with Kalisapura[20] can be disposed of.

Ptolemy's Sageda, called the metropolis,[21] is transcription of Sāketa. He mentions the same city under the name Sagoda.[22] McCrindle,[23] Pargiter,[24] Cunningham[25] and Csoma de Koros[26] take it as identical with Ayodha on the Sarayu (Sarabos of Ptolemy), a city of vast extent. In fact, they were the twin capital cities of Kośala kingdom. They were "adjoining cities like London and Westminster". The site of Saketa has been identified with the ruins at Sujān Koṭon the river Sai in the Unnāo district of Uttar Pradesh.

The town called Kalinipaxa[27] is transliteration of ancient Kānyakubja, a famous city in the Gangetic Doāb of great antiquity. It has been identified with modern Kanauj situated on the bank of the river Kālindī also known as Ikṣumati (Oxymagis of the Greeks), a branch of the Gaṅgā, in Farrukhābād district of Uttar Pradesh.[28] Ptolemy's Kanagora is little identical with Kanauj.

Ptolemy's Sambalaka[29] can also be identified with some certainty. The name represents Sambhal, a town of Rohilkhand.[30] It is about 30 miles distant from Ahicchatra. It is the name of several other towns in India.

A very ancient city Sthāṇiśvara or Sthāṇeśvara called by Ptolemy Ostobalasara[31] has been identified by St. Martin with modern Thāṇeśvara (in Haryana).[32]

Notes and References

1. *Geog.*, VII, I, 46, AIT, pp. 121-22. Hastināpura in the upper Gaṅgā valley was the earlier capital of the Kuru Kingdom. It was Bharata's fifth successor Hastin, the son of Suhotra in the Paurava line of the Kings, who founded this city on the river Gaṅgā, about sixty miles north-east of Delhi, and made it his own capital. It was evidently so named after him. It was the most magnificent of all the cities existing during the pre-Bhārata war period. It continued to be the chief capital city of the Kauravas until their annihilation in the Great Bhārata battle. In the post-Bhārata war period, it came into possession of the Pāṇḍavas who ruled over the kingdom with its capital at Hastināpura for nearly thirty-six years – the period during which it had attained all the paraphernalia of a prosperous city. It continued to exist as a great city upto the time of an illustrious Paurava king Adhisīmakṛṣṇa. It was his son and Successor named Nicakṣu who abandoned the city because of being washed away by heavy floods in the Gaṅgā and shifted his capital therefrom to Kauśāmbi. The transfer of the capital from Hastināpura to Kauśāmbi took

place sometime after 800 BCE or between 800 and 600 BCE which can archaeologically be also proved. However, the former was rebuilt sometime in the early sixth century before the Christian era and continued to flourish in the succeeding period. It has been identified with a ruined site (about eight km long and over one km wide, still called Hastī kā nagara) on the old bed of the Gaṅgā, about 22 miles north-east of Meerut in Uttar Pradesh.

2. *Geog*., VII, I,49, AIT, pp. 126,128-29, and 367 note; see also R.C. Jain (ed), MAIT, App. 3, p. 439. Indraprastha, Ptolemy's Indabara, another great city founded in the pre-Bhārata war period on the Yamunā, was the later capital of the Kuru kingdom. Dhṛtarāṣṭra, Kaurava king, in order to avoid the rivalry or conflict between the two branches of the Kuru family divided the kingdom and ceded half to Pāṇḍavas assigning to them the small principality of Khāṇḍavaprastha, a part of Khāṇḍavavana, on the bank of Yamunā, and retaining Hastināpura proper with him to continue his rule over it. The Pāṇḍavas led by Yudhiṣṭhira left Hastināpoura for destination. After clearing the jungle called Khāṇdvavana by settling it on fire, they established a colony, built a palace and made it their new capital which became popularly known as the city of Indraprastha. It was well fortified with deep moats, a high rampart and numerous gateways and towers. The descendants of Pāṇḍavas at Indraprastha continued to rule there long after the destruction of their principal metropolis Hastināpura and migration of the older line of Kuru Kings to Kauśāmbi. Hastināpura and Indraprastha were the two great cities of the epic fame. B.C. Law ("Hastināpura and Indraprastha in Ancient India", *Jour. As. Soc. Bom.*, New series, XXX, 1, 1955, pp. 9-16; "Studies in Indian History and Geography Based on Early Greek Accounts", JGRI, XVI, 3-4, 1959, pp. 276-77; HGAI, p. 86) has rightly pointed out that the former was the earlier as well as the later capital of Kuru kingdom and it was one of the nineteen great cities of ancient India, while the latter was the capital of the Pāṇḍavas or later capital of the Kuru kingdom founded by Pāṇḍavas on the bank of Yamunā, two miles south of modern Delhi. Indraprastha now called Indrapat is archaeologically identified with ancient mound on which stands the Purāṇa Qila (a fort of the sixteenth century) at Delhi.

3. Lassen, *Ind. Alt.,* III, p.151.

4. *Geog*., VII, II, 21, AIT, p. 222, also p. 391, note.

5. *Ibid*., VII, 1, 17, *Ibid*., p. 70.

6. CAGI, p. 330.

7. AIT, p. 72.

8. CASR, Vol. I (1871), pp. 302-03; CAGI, p. 332.
9. *Geog.*,VII, II, 22, AIT, p. 225.
10. See AIT, pp. 228, 391-92, note.
11. *Geog.*, VII, I, 50, AIT, pp. 126 and 129; R.C. Jain (ed), MAIT, App. 3, p. 439.
12. Cf. AIT, p. 129.
13. *Geog.*, VII, I, 53, AIT, p.131, see also pp. 133-34 and 368-69, note.
14. *Indika*, Bk. IV, Fragm. LVI, AIMA, pp.139, and 140, note.
15. *Indika*, I, 8, AIMA, p. 201; see also E.J. Chinnock (tr.), *Indika* of Arrian, p. 408-09; F.R.B. Godolphin (ed.), *The Greek Historians* (Chinnock's trans. of Arrian's *Indika*), Vol. II, pp. 737-8; R.C. Jain (ed), MAIMA, App. 3, p. 229; IIA, p. 89; E.R. Bevan, "India in Early Greek and Latin Literature", in CHI, I, ed. E.J. Rapson, p. 367; H.H. Wilson, *Ar. Ant.*, pp. 195-96; J.E. Schwartzberg (ed), HASA, pp. 169-70; B.C. Law, "Studies in Indian History and Geography Based on Early Greek Accounts", JGRI, XVI, 3-4, 1959, pp. 268, and note 9, and 269, note 10; and his IETBJ, p.103.
16. *Hist. Nat.*, VI, XXI, 22; see also CAI, p. 343.
17. *Geog.*, VII, I, 50, AIT, p.126, see also pp. 98, 129, and 367, note.
18. *Ind. Alt.*, I, p. 127, note 3.
19. CAGI, p. 316.
20. *As. Res.*, V, p. 270; see also *Ind. Ant.*, VI, p. 249, note.
21. *Geog.*, VII, I,71, AIT, p.164.
22. *Ibid.*, VII, II,22, *Ibid.*, p. 225.
23. AIT, pp. 165-66, 228-29.
24. PDKA, p. 53.
25. CAGI, p. 341; CASR, I, p. 318.
26. *As. Res.*, XX, p. 442.
27. Megasthenes, *Indika*, Bk. IV, Fragm, LVI, AIMA, p. 129; R.C. Jain (ed) MAIMA, App. 3, p. 229; Pliny, *Hist. Nat.*, VI, 21, 11.
28. See Lassen, *Ind. Alt.*, I, 2nd edn., p. 760; St. Martin, *Ětude*, pp. 271-78; B.C. Law, "Studies in Indian History and Geography Based on Early Greek Accounts", JGRI, XVI, 3-4, 1959, p. 282.
29. *Geog.*, VII, I, 53, AIT, p. 131.
30. AIT,p.133.

31. *Geog.*, VII, I, 48, AIT, p. 125.
32. Cf. AIT, p. 128, see also p. 367, note.

2

Towns and Cities in Eastern, Western, Central and Southern India

Eastern India

The towns and cities in eastern India described by the classical writers include those of Bihar, Bengal and Orissa (ancient Odradeśa, now Odisha).

The city usually called Pālibothra by the classical writers is transcription of Pāṭaliputra. It has been designated less properly as Pālimbothra by Arrian and Ptolemy. It was situated at the confluence of the Ganges (Gaṅgā) with another river the Sonus (Son) also called Erannoboas.[1] It was the greatest city in Gangetic India. It was the ancient capital of Magadha kingdom in the Prācya (eastern) region transliterated in Greek as Prasi or Prasii whose inhabitants including those of the said city have been called Prasioi or Prasians by Strabo, Pliny and Arrian. It rose into prominence as an imperial capital of the Mauryas. In the time of Candragupta (Sandrakottas of the Greeks), the great Maurya emperor, it became famous as the metropolis of Maurya empire which extended from the mouth of the Ganges to the regions beyond the Indus.

Megasthenes has given an eye-witness description of Pāṭaliputra city (called Pālibothra) where he had resided for five years (302- 298 BCE) as a Greek ambassador of Seleukus Nikator during the reign of Candragupta Maurya. His description of the city can best be put in his own words: "This city stretched in the inhabited quarters to an extreme length on each side of eighty stadia (9 ½ or about 10 miles), and its breadth was fifteen stadia (about 2 miles); a ditch (moat) encompassed it all round, which was six hundred feet in breadth and thirty cubits (about 60 feet) in depth, and the wall (wooden palisade) was crowned with five hundred and seventy towers and had sixty-four gates".[2] He was highly impressed by the immense size and splendour of the city. The wooden wall he speaks of continued to exist till about the beginning of the fifth century.

The extracts from the writings of Megasthenes about Pāṭaliputra city are preserved by later classical writers. The city of Pālimbothra in the dominions of the Prasians, says Arrian, was the greatest in India. It was situated near the confluence of the streams of the Erannoboas (Son) and the Ganges (Gaṅgā).[3] His further description of the city[4] is exactly the same that Megasthenes has given in his *Indika* (Bk. II, Fragm. XXVI), as noted before. Arrian seems to have derived his authority from the former for his description of this city.

Patlibothra was "a very large city", says Strabo.[5] He, on the authority of Megasthenes,[6] states further in his *Geography*[7] that it was eighty stadia in length and fifteen in breadth. It was of the shape of a parallelogram, and was surrounded by a wooden wall or palisade, pierced with loopholes for the discharge of arrows (by archers against a besieging force). It had a ditch in front for the purpose of defence and for receiving the sewage of the city. The people in whose country this city was situated were the most distinguished in all India, and were called the Prasioi. The king in addition to his family name adopted the surname of Pālibothros, as Sandrakottas, for instance, did.

In the third book of his *Geography*, Eratosthenes, as cited by Strabo,[8] refers to the city of Pālibothra. Artemidoros distinctly places this city in the eastern Gangetic region.[9]

The capital city of Pālibothra also attracted the notice of Diodorus Sculus.[10] In his epitome of Fragm. I of Book I of the *Indika* of Megasthenes, he tells us that it was the most renowned and the greatest of all the cities. It was adorned with many sumptuous palaces, and within its walls a numerous population were settled. It was a fortified city with trenches of notable dimensions which were filled with water introduced from the river.[11] We are told by Pliny that the people of Prasii surpassed in power and glory every other people, not only in this quarter, but in all India, and their capital Pālibothra was a very large and wealthy city, after which some called the people itself the Pālibothri, nay, even the whole tract along the Ganges.[12] Solinus, who derived nearly all his materials from the works of Megasthenes and Pliny, calls the city Pālibothra. Borrowing a passage from the former, he relates that it was the capital of the Prasian nation, which was extremely powerful, and that some called the nation itself the Pālibothri.[13] In the third book of the *Bios Alexandrou tou Makedonos Kai Práxeis* (The Romance History of Alexander the Great), by an anonymous author, Pālibothra being in eastern Gangetic region (Prasi) has itself been designated as Prasiaca (=Sanskrit Prācyaka) and called the "Capital of India".

Ptolemy includes Pālimbothra in the towns on the river Ganges in the east. He also refers to its royal residence.[14] The great city contained many stately buildings. The most splendid one in this city was the palace of Maurya emperor Sandrakottas (Candragupta) which, according to Megasthenes, surpassed or excelled in splendour the Persian palaces of Susa and Ekbatana. Aelian, who is believed to have derived his authority from the former in this regard, also informs us that the said royal palace was more magnificent than the said two Persian palaces.[15] The said imperial palace probably stood close to the modern village of Kumharar on the outskirts of modern Patna. Mortimer Wheeler's remark, that the ancient Pāṭaliputra city was modelled on the famous Persian city of Persepolis, and his impression that there was Persianisation of the urban pattern in the Gangetic valley[16], can unhesitatingly be dismissed. Nihar Ranjan Ray in his famous article "Rural–urban dichotomy in Indian tradition and history" has also expressed the view that Pāṭaliputra city was a prototype of Achaemenian model. But at the same time he has reasonably doubted the transplantation of Achaemenid craftsmanship at this place.[17] We do not have much positive evidence to show the impact of Persian urban tradition on urbanization process of the Maurya period. Nor do we have any clue to show its impact on the pattern of Gangetic urbanization. The Gaṅgā valley, in fact, had its own urban tradition which does not bear stamp of any Persian influence.

In the times of Candragupta and the kings of his dynasty, Pālibothra (Pāṭaliputra) was the capital of the great Maurya Empire. For about eight centuries after the time of the former, the said capital continued to be a great and flourishing city, adorned with a magnificent palace, many temples and monuments and other public buildings of great splendour. It was not only a seat of government, but also a great and opulent seat of commerce, which increased its wealth and prosperity. It being an administrative, commercial, religious and educational centre rapidly grew into a big city. It was the largest of all the cities in the middle Gangetic plains.

Fa-hian visited the imperial city of Pāṭaliputra called *Pa-lian-fu* about the beginning of the fifth century of the Christian era. He is believed to have stayed there for about three years (CE 406-08). He was so much impressed by the glory and splendour of the city. He calls it the greatest of all the cities in Madhyadeśa. According to him, the inhabitants of the city were rich, prosperous and righteous.[18] At the time of his visit, the city was in a excellent state of preservation. The wooden wall by which it is said to have been surrounded was seen still standing by the said Chinese pilgrim. The fall of the city was accomplished by the year 632. The place where the splendid metropolis had once stood, Hiuen Tsang found there nothing but heaps of ruins and a village containing about two or three hundred miserable houses. At the time of his visit, the city wore a deserted look. According to him, "South of the Ganges … was an old city about 70 li (about fourteen miles) in circuit the foundations of which were still visible although the city had long been a wilderness."[19]

The ruins of Pāṭaliputra city witnessed by the Chinese traveller Hiuen Tsang remained lying buried deep below the foundations of modern Patna till its discovery in 1876. It was in this very year that the workmen employed in digging a tank in Sheikh Mithia Ghari between the market-place of Patna and its railway station discovered at a depth of some twelve or fifteen feet below the swampy surface of the ground the remains of a long brick wall with a line of palisades of strong timber running near and almost parallel to it, and slightly inclined towards it. The wooden wall by which the city was defended, as we learn from Megasthenes, was in reality a line of palisades running in front of wall of brick.[20] L.A. Waddell had remarked as far back as 1892 that "nearly the whole of the site of the city is intact; much lies below Patna, Bankipur and the E.I. Railway, being buried at a depth of ten to twenty feet. The old city was on the north bank of the old Sone but it was several miles distant from the Ganges which shifted later to the south".

The excavations, which were carried out at the site of the village Kumharar at the outskirts of Patna by L.A. Waddell in 1896, brought to light the wooden fortifications of the city of Candragupta Maurya's time.[21] D.B. Spooner, who carried out the excavations at the same site in 1912, remarked on the basis of his findings that "Judging from the timbers that have been preserved for us it is clear that the woodwork of the superstructure and room must have been extremely solid and massive".[22] M. Ghosh, while carrying out excavations at Bulandibag (a suburb of Patana) in 1926-27, also discovered the remains of defensive wooden palisade of fourteen to fifteen feet height (belonging to the latter part of the fourth century BCE) and some other antiquities.[23]

The archaeological rediscovery of wooden structures at the Maurya capital city confirms the veracity of Megasthenes' as well as Strabo's statements about it.

Tamalites, which distinctly figures in a list of towns given by Ptolemy,[24] represents ancient Tāmraliptī, identical with modern Tamluk situated on the western bank of the river Rūpanārāyaṇa, 12 miles above its junction with the Hughli mouth of the Ganges.[25] The Pāli form of the Sanskrit name Tāmraliptī was Tāmalitti, and this accounts for the form in Greek. Pliny mentions a people called Taluctae belonging to this part of India, and the similarity of the name leaves little doubt of their identity with the people whose capital was Tamluk. Tāmraliptī was one of the famous port towns of ancient India. St. Martin calls it the old port of the Ganges.[26] It was the great emporium of the trade between the Ganges and Ceylon. Being a commercial centre, it developed into a township. And it acquired a place in Ptolemy's list of chief nineteen towns of Gangetic India.

The town called Souanagoura by Ptolemy[27] is a transcript of Suvarṇanagara, according to St. Martin. In this name, he recognizes that of one of the ancient capitals of erstwhile Eastern Bengal,

Suvarṇagrāma,[28] now Sonārgāon, about 12 miles from Ḍhākā, near the right bank of the lower Brahmaputra. The town, in ancient times, was a centre of trade and commerce.

Pliny mentions the town of Dandaguda or Dandagula, which, according to him, was situated 625 Roman miles (574 British miles) from the mouth of the Ganges.[29] It is identical with Dantapura which can fairly be attested to by epigraphic evidence[30] and on the authority of Cunningham.[31] It was the ancient capital of Kalinga (Calingae of Pliny).[32] It was an emporium of trade. It has been identified with the ruins of the fort of Dantapura, situated on the southern bank of the river Vaṃśadharā, three miles from Chicacole road station.[33]

The royal city of Calingae (Kalinga) is called Parthalis by Pliny. He also gives the military strength of its king. He says, 60,000 foot-soldiers, 1000 horsemen, and 700 elephants keep watch over their king and ward in precinct of war.[34] The city has been identified with Pateli, some eight or ten miles from Puri and at more or less same distance from Chilk.[35]

Tosalei, called a metropolis by Ptolemy,[36] is identical with city of Tosali. Archaeological discoveries have led to the finding of the name in Dhauli Rock Inscription of Aśoka. "Vestiges of a larger city have been discovered not far from the site of this monument, and there can be no doubt that the Tosali of the inscription was the capital in Aśoka's time of the province of Orissa, and continued to be so till at least the time of Ptolemy. The city was situated on the margin of a pool called Kōsalā- Gaṅgā, which was an object of great religious veneration throughout the country".[37] The name of Tosala-Kōsālakas, which is found in the *Brahmāṇḍa Purāṇa*, has been connected with the Tosalei of Ptolemy by Wilford.[38]

A city called Sambalaka of the Mandalai by Ptolemy[39] may perhaps be Sambalpur on the upper Mahānadi, the capital of a district of the same name.[40] It is included in the list of ancient towns in eastern part of India.

Western India

The towns and cities of Gujarāt and Mahārāṣṭra in western India also received the notices of the classical writers.

We are informed by Ptolemy that in Larike (Lāṭadeśa or Lārdeśa) - the ancient name of the territory of Gujarāt - there was a large city of Barygaza. It was, according to him, a mart of commerce.[41] It is so often mentioned in the *Periplus*[42] as a market town. Nikolaos Damaskenos, as cited by Strabo,[43] calls the same city Bargosa. The Greek name Barygaza or Barugaza is a transcription of the Sanskrit Bhṛgukaccha and Prakṛt Bharukaccha,[44] which is identical with modern Broach (also called Bharoch), situated about thirty miles from the sea on the north side of the river Narmadā (called Nammadus by the author of the *Periplus* and Namados by Ptolemy). In ancient times, it was a famous sea-port town.[45] During the early centuries of the Christian era, it was the greatest seat or an emporium of trade and commerce in western India. It was, in fact, an entrepot- a centre for import and export.

Syrastrēnĕ of the *Periplus*[46] and of Ptolemy[47] represents the Sanskrit Surāṣṭra, and Syrastra[48] of the latter the Prakṛit Sorath. Both the names have been used for the modern name Surat in Kathiawar on the Gulf of Kutch.[49] Pliny mentions the Horatae,[50] which is an incorrect transcription of Soratae - the name of the people of Sorath-who have, he says, a fine city, defended by marshes. Orrhotha is used by Kosmas as the name of a city in the west of India. He includes it in the list of the most famous commercial marts in India.[51] "Orrhotha seems to have been a port on the western coast of the Gujarāt peninsula", observes McCrindle.[52] Orrhotha of Kosmas is undoubtedly identical with Sorath, which, as noted before, is the name of Surat, a place of great antiquity and historical interest. It has been a commercial centre since ancient times. It has been famous as a centre of indigenous textile industry. Ptolemy distinctly includes it in the list of towns in Larike (Gujarāt).

Pliny, while speaking of the people and cities of Gujarāt, refers to a city of Automela and calls it an emporium of trade.[53] This city cannot be identified with absolute certainty, but St. Martin conjectures it may have been the once famous Vallabhī, which was situated in the peninsular part of Gujarat at a distance of about twenty-four miles from the Gulf of Cambay or Khambhāt.[54] It was once a seaport on the western shore of this gulf. It was not only a prosperous commercial centre but also a seat of learning in western India. Vallabhī, now known as Vallabhīpura, was situated at Wala at a distance of about eighteen miles north-west of Bhaunagar also called Bhavanagar.

Describing the towns and cities of Dachinabades also called Dakhinabades (=Sanskrit Dakṣināpatha= Prākrit Dakkhinābadha =Deccan), the author of the *Periplus* refers to Paethana calling it the greatest city in that part of the country. It was, according to him, situated towards the south of Barygaza at a distance of twenty days' journey.[55] Ptolemy calls it Baithana and describes it as one of the cities in Ariake[56] (Aparānta = western region = Mahārāṣṭra). Paethana of the *Periplus* or Baithana of Ptolemy is identical with Paithana of the present day on the north bank of the river Godāvarī in the Aurangābād district of Mahārāṣṭra. Paithana is the Prākrit form of the Sanskrit Pratiṣṭhāna which was also known as Pratiṣṭhānapura in ancient times.[57] It is called "one of the oldest cities in the Deccan".[58] Paithana or Pratiṣṭhāna was the western capital of the Sātavāhana kingdom. It was the seat of government of both early and later Sātavāhanas. Ptolemy has rightly called it the capital of Siroptolemaios or Siropolemaios,[59] a name, which represents the Sanskrit Śrī-Pulumāvi, Pulumāyi II of the Nasik cave and Amarāvatī stupa inscriptions.[60] He was one of the later Sātavāhana kings. He ruled from CE 130 to 154. Paithana or Pratiṣṭhāna continued to flourish as the capital city of the later Sātavāhanas from about the middle of the second century till about the end of the first quarter of the third century. In the *Periplus*,[61] it has been called a market town. It was an important centre of the textile industry.[62]

Another very great city, Tagara, is mentioned in both the *Periplus*[63] and the *Geography* of Ptolemy.[64] Ptolemy places it to the northeast of Baithana (Paithana) and the *Periplus* to the east of it at a distance of ten days' journey. It has been identified by J.F. Fleet with the modern Ter, which is about 95 miles southeast of Paithana.[65] It agrees substantially with the distance and direction given in the *Periplus*. The actual distance from Paithana to Ter by road is 104 miles. Ter of today is at the distance of 12 miles north of Osmanabad. There are some archaeological evidence of the existence of the ancient city of Tagara. Some very interesting remains of this city were discovered by H. Cousens.[66] The name of the city is found in inscriptions under the form Tagarapura which can be testified to by an epigraphic evidence.[67] Paithana and Tagara were two very important seats of commerce in Dakhinabades or Deccan.

The two famous towns in the Deccan were known to the author of the *Periplus* as Suppara and Calliena (Kalliena).[68] The former is called

Soupara by Ptolemy and placed by him in Ariake[69] (Aparānta, i.e., the Thane region, northern Konkan). Suppara or Soupara is identical with modern Sopārā in the district of Thane, 37 miles north of Bombay (now Mumbai) and about 5 or 6 miles northwest of Vasai (Bassein). It appears to have been from very early times an important centre of trade and commerce where merchants from different parts of the country used to flock with their merchandise. It has been distinctly mentioned in the *Periplus*[70] as one of the market towns of the Deccan. It is said to have been the capital of Konkan between 500 BCE and 1300 CE.[71] Among its ruins have been preserved some monuments, which are not only of historical interest but also attest its high antiquity.

Calliena or Kalliena is now represented by Kalyāṇa, on the eastern shore of the harbour of Bombay. It is in the Thane district at the distance of 33 miles northeast of Bombay. It was the principal port during the periods when the Sātavāhanas established their hold over the west coast. We learn from the *Periplus*[72] that in the lifetime of the elder Saraganus (probably Ariṣṭa Śātakarṇi, one of the early Sātavāhana kings, who reigned about CE 44-69) it became a lawful market town. It was raised to the rank of a regular mart during his rule over it. It is also recorded in the same text (*Periplus*)[73] that after it came into the possession of Sandares or Sandanes (called Sadinon, Sadenoi or Sadineis by Ptolemy[74]), who is none other than Sundara Śātakarṇi of the Sātavāhana dynasty who ruled in CE 83-4, its economic prosperity gradually began to decline as the port was much restricted. He virtually ruled over Ariake. After having made himself master of Kalliena or Kalyāṇa, he imposed the severest restrictions on its trade. He ruled the prosperous trading communities that occupied the seaboard. Its old fame as a commercial town was, however, revived by the end of the fifth century of the Christian era. In the sixth century, Kosmas found it one of the five chief commercial marts of western India which he speaks of in one of his monumental works.[75] Its political fortune also changed. It became the capital of the powerful Cālukya kings.[76] Kalyāṇa is at least reminiscent of similar names on the western shores of the Erythraean sea.

Simylla (also called Semulla) has been mentioned in both the *Periplus*[77] and the *Geography*[78] of Ptolemy as one of the market towns beyond Kalyāṇa. It has been identified with Chaul, a seaport (in the Thane district), 23 miles south of Bombay.[79] It was one of the chief ports of western India. But Bhagvanlal Indraji "suggests Chimūla in Trombay island at the head of the Bombay harbour; and this is curiously supported by one of the Kanheri inscriptions in which Chemūla is mentioned, apparently as a large city, like Supārā and Kalyāṇa in the neighbourhood".[80]

A town named Hippokoura has been mentioned by Ptolemy as a seaport to the south of Simylla.[81] A town of the same name mentioned by him[82] lay inland, and was the capital of the southern parts of Ariake, as Paithaṇa was the capital of the northern. Its position is uncertain. Yule places it doubtfully at Kalyāṇa, a place about half a degree to the west of Bidar, and at some distance south from the river Mañjirā. Ptolemy calls it the royal seat (capital) of Baleokouros, which has been identified by Bhandarkar and others with Vilivāyakura, a name found upon two Āndhra coins discovered at Kolhapur.[83] There is no other clue to its identification. What Lassen says[84] in this regard is not of any use for us.

The town called Byzantium by the author of the *Periplus*[85] has been identified with Vijayadurga,[86] which is described as being one of the best harbour on the western coast.[87] In the first century of the Christian era, it had great commercial importance. It was also called Vaijayanti or Vaijayantipura.

The town, Nāsika, mentioned in Ptolemy's *Geography*,[88] says McCrindle, "has preserved its name unaltered to the present day, distant 116 miles N.E. from Bombay. It was one of the most sacred seats of Brāhmaṇism. It has also important Buddhistic remains, being noted for a group of rock-temples."[89] It is "on the upper valley of the Godāvarī river."[90] It is the Nāsikya of the *Mahābhāṣya* of Patañjali.[91]

Central India

The city called Ozene by the author of the *Periplus*,[92] and by Ptolemy,[93] represents ancient Ujjayini (modern Ujjain) on the river Śiprā. It was one of the seven sacred cities of the Hindus. According to a Purāṇic evidence, it was adorned with magnificent buildings, strong boundary walls, entrances gates, market-complex and trade centres.[94] In the age of the Buddha (sixth and fifth centuries before the Christian era), it was the capital of Avanti kingdom (western Mālavā). In the first century before the Christian era, it was the capital of the celebrated Vikramāditya, who having expelled the Scythians (Śakas) and thereafter established his power over the greater part of India, restored the Hindu monarchy to its ancient splendour. The author of the *Periplus* tells us that Ozene was "formerly a royal capital".[95] We are further told by Schoff, the translator and annotator of this text, that at the time of the *Periplus* it was no longer a capital but a great commercial centre.[96] It was famous as an emporium of trade. It has been rightly pointed out by McCrindle that "... about a century and a half after Vikramāditya's era (57 BCE) Ujjain was still a flourishing city, though it had lost something of its former importance and dignity from being no longer the residence of the sovereign".[97] Ptolemy informs us that in his time it was the capital of Tiastanes.[98] This name transliterates Chashtana- the founder of the Kshatrapa (Śaka Satrap) dynasty of western India.[99] The ancient city no longer exists but its ruins can be traced at the distance of a mile from its modern successor.

Tewar, near Jabalpur, the capital of the Cedi, a people of Bundelkhaṇḍ is also included in the list of towns mentioned by Ptolemy, as we are told by some scholars.[100]

Southern India

The towns and cities of south India described by the classical writers, mainly Ptolemy, belong to its all four parts- Tamiladeśa, also called Tamilakam, Āndhradeśa, Karṇāṭadeśa and Kerala.

The city, Argaru, mentioned in the *Periplus*[101] appears to be a Greek transcript of its Sanskrit name Uragapura found in the *Mahābhārata*[102] and in one of the works of Kālidāsa.[103] It was situated on the south bank of the Kāverī. It is identical with the modern Uraiyūr ("city of habitation") near Trichinopoly. It was the ancient capital of the Coḷa kingdom. It was known to Ptolemy as Orthoura, which he calls the royal city of Sornagos (Coḷas).[104] It was both an administrative and a commercial centre. It was in a very flourishing state in the third century of the Christian era. "The capital grew up around a fortress, built on the summit of the Rock of Trichinopoly, which rises abruptly out of the plain to a height of 340 feet above the old city, which nestles picturesquely at its foot".[105] Even after its destruction about the seventh century, it retains traces of its former grandeur.

Of the eight inland cities named as belonging to the maritime territory of the Sórétai, only two- Abour and Orthoura[106]- have been identified. The former is Āmbūrdurg in north Arkat, and the latter Uraiyūr, the capital of the Coḷas, as noted before. "The Soringae", observes Cunningham, “are most probably the Syrieni of Pliny with their 300 cities, as they occupied the coast between the Pandae and the Derangae or Dravidians”.[107]

The city called Modura by Pliny[108] and Modoura by Ptolemy[109] is identical with ancient Madurā, situated at the distance of about six miles southeast of the modern Madurai on the northern banks of the river Vaigai. It has a very high antiquity. It was the capital of the Pāṇḍyan kingdom. Ptolemy’s perfect knowledge of this celebrated city as a capital of the Pāṇḍyas is proved by his saying that it was the “royal city of Pandion”.[110] The dominions of the Pāṇḍyas included principally the modern districts of Madurā and Tinnevelly. “Modura” says McCrindle, “has retained its name almost unchanged, being now called Madurā. It is an inland town in the south … The land of Pandion, of which it was the capital, included most of Tinneveli and extended northward as far as the highlands near the Koimbatur gap. On the west it was bounded by the Southern Ghats and on the east by the sea…”[111]

In one of his lists of towns of south India, Ptolemy includes Peringkarei, Tainour, and Tangala or Taga.[112] Peringkarei has preserved its name almost without change, being now known as Peruṅgari, on the river Vaigai, about 40 miles lower down its course than Madurā. Ptolemy places a town called Tainour at the distance of less than a degree to the north-east of Peringkarei. The direction would suit Tanjor, but the distance is more than a degree, Ptolemy has, however, placed his Peringkarei quite in a wrong position with regard to Madurā. There can be little doubt that Tangala or Taga is now represented by Diṇḍugal, an important and flourishing town lying at a distance of 32 miles north by west from Madurā.[113]

The other towns mentioned by Ptolemy are Bideris, Pantipolis, and Aloe.[114] Bideris is perhaps Erod Yirodu in the district of Koimbatur near the Kāveri. Pantipolis, according to Yule, represents the obsolete name Pantiyapura, which he places at Hangal, in the Dhārwād district of Karṇāṭaka.[115] Aloe may be Yellapur, a small town in north Kanara, in lat. 14^{0}56' long. 74^{0}43'.[116]

Ptolemy further goes on to mention some more towns. His Bata[117] may perhaps be Pattukóṭṭa, a small town not very far inland from the northern end of the Argolic Gulf. As Pudukóṭṭa is the capital of the

Tondiman Rāja, Lassen has suggested its identity with Bata. It is upwards of 20 miles farther inland than Paṭṭukóṭṭa.[118]

Ptolemy speaks of Pikendaka, and Malanga- "the royal city".[119] Pikendaka may have been Pennakonda, the name of a town in the district of Balāri. Malanga was located near Elur (or Eluru), a place some distance inland about half way between the Kṛṣṇā and Godāvarī towards their embouchures and in the neighbourhood of which are the remains of an old capital named Veṅgi.[120] In Yule's map, Malanga is placed conjecturally about two degrees farther south at Velur near the mouth of Pennar.[121]

The two other great cities mentioned by Ptolemy are Koroungkala and Pityndra. The latter has been called by him the metropolis.[122] The former appears to be the place now known as Warangal, which was in early medieval period the capital of the Kākatīyas of Teliṅgānā. It has but few tokens remaining to attest its former grandeur. Pityndra, according to Ptolemy, was the capital of Maisoloi or Maisolia. D.C. Sircar regards it as the capital city of the Brihatphalayana dynasty that ruled in the Masulipatam regions.[123] The said capital city was not very far from Vijayapurī of the Nāgārjunakoṇḍa inscription, Amarāvatī and Bezwada (now called Vijayawādā) in the heart of the ancient Āndhradeśa. Pliny informs us that the Andarae (people of Āndhra) possessed numerous villages, and thirty towns defended by walls and towers.[124] Some of the towns representing the settlements of the Sātavāhana period excavated in the modern Teliṅgānā region may be identical with those mentioned by him.

The city designated Banaouasei by Ptolemy[125] is no doubt identical with the modern Banavāsī on the river Varadā (a tributary of the Tuṅgabhadra) in the Sirsi Taluk of north Kānārā district. It is at the distance of fourteen miles from Sirsi town. It was the capital of the district of the same name mentioned in the *Mahābhārata*, the Purāṇas, and the *Bṛhat Saṁhitā* of Varāhamihir. It was one of the capitals of the Kadambas (CE 300-1200) whose territory comprised the north-western parts of Mysore and portions of north Kānārā.[126] It has been wrongly identified by some scholars with Byzantium also called Vaijayanti or Vaijayantipura,[127] a town on the west coast already noted before. Byzantium of the *Periplus* and Banaouasei of Ptolemy represent two different towns, one in the west and the other in the south.

Ptolemy mentions with perfect accuracy Karoura as "the royal seat of Kerobothros".[128] Karoura, says Caldwell, is mentioned in Tamil traditions as the ancient capital of the Cera (called Chera) or Kerala kings, and is generally identified with Karūr, an important town in the Koimbatur district, originally included in the Cera kingdom. It is situated on the river Kāverī, near a large fort now in ruins.[129]

Notes and References

1. As the sands of the river son contained the particles of gold, the river has been called in Sanskrit Hiraṇyavāha (carrying gold) or Hiraṇyabāhu (having golden arms). The Sanskrit name has been transliterated by the Greek writers as Erannoboas. The city Pālibothra (Pāṭaliputra) lay on the southern bank of the Gaṅgā at the point where up till 1379 CE it received the waters of the Erannoboas, now the Son river. The city is now represented by Patna.

2. *Indika,* Bk. II, Fragm. XXVI, AIMA, p. 68; see also E.R. Bevan, "India in Early Greek and Latin Literature", in CHI, I.P. 369. J. Rennell (MMH, pp. 49-50) opines that the city described by Megasthenes has been ranked by Europeans among the wonders of the world.

3. *Indika*, I, 2 and 10, AIMA, pp. 184, 204-05; see also *Indika* of Arrian, tr. Chinnock, pp. 400-01 and 410; Godolphin, *The Greek Historians*, II, pp. 732-33 and 739.

4. *Indika*, I, 10, AIMA, p. 205.

5. *Geog*., XV, I, 13, AICL, p. 19; see also Hamilton and Falconch (tr.), *The Geography of Strabo*, III, pp. 80-81.

6. *Indika*, Bk. II. Fragm. XXV, AIMA, p. 66.

7. XV, I, 36; AICL, pp. 42-43; H.L. Jones (tr), *The Geography of Strabo*, VII, pp. 17 and 125; Hamilton and Falconer (tr.), *op.cit.,* pp. 97-98; see also J. Talboys Wheeler,. *India from the Earliest Ages,* Vol. III of *The History of India,* Ch. IV, "Greek and Roman India", p. 180; and H.F. Tozer, *A History of Ancient Geography*, p. 150.

8. *Geog*., XV, I, 11, AICL, p. 16.

9. Cf. Strabo, *Geog*., XV, I, 72, AICL, p. 77.

10. *Bib. Hist.,* I, 11, 12.

11. *Bib. Hist*., II, 39; AIMA, p. 39; AICL, p. 42, note 3; CAI, p. 236; see also *Ind. Ant*., V, pp. 89-90; F. Wilford, "An Essay on the sacred Isles in the West with other Essays connected with that works", Essay II, *As. Res*., IX, 1807 (Delhi, 1979), pp. 33, 36, 46; "Chronology of the Hindus", *As.*

Res., V (Delhi, 1979), pp. 270, 273-74 (for description of the city by Diodorus Siculus, Strabo and Pliny).

12. *Nat. Hist.*, VI, 21, 22; CAI, p. 342; and also cf. Megasthenes, *Indika*, Bk. IV, Fragm, LVI, AIMA, p. 139.
13. *Coll. Rer. Memo.*, 52, 6-17; see also CAI, pp. 457-58; and Megasthenes, *Indika*, Bk. IV, Fragm. LVI B, AIMA, p. 155.
14. *Geog.*, VII, I, 73, AIT, p. 167. G.E. Gerini, the chief authority on Ptolemy's *Geography* mentions the town in his RTGEA (p. 28) under the name of Pālibothra and not Pālimbothra.
15. *De Nat. Anim.,* XIII, 18; see also AICL, pp. 141, and 142, note 1; CAI, pp. 414-15, and 421, note 3.
16. See his EIP, pp. 176-77.
17. ABORI, LVIII-LIX, 1977-78, pp. 873-74.
18. J. Legge (r.), RBK, pp. 77-78; H.A. Giles (tr.), RBK, pp. 45-47.
19. YCTI, II, p. 87.
20. See AIMA, p. 207, fn; and AICL, p. 43 (continuation of note 3 of p. 42).
21. For details of his findings see his *Report on the Excavations at Pāṭaliputra* (Calcutta, 1903), pp. 1-35.
22. ASIAR (Eastern Circle), 1912-13, pt. 1, p. 63.
23. *Ibid.*, 1926-27 (Calcutta, 1929), pp. 135ff; see also M. Wheeler, *op.cit.*, p. 177, pl. 48.
24. *Geog.*, VII, I, 73, AIT, p. 167.
25. See also AIT, pp. 169-70; G.E. Gerini, RTGEA, p. 527, note 3; CAGI, p. 425; N.L. Dey, GDAMI, p. 203.
26. *E'tude*, pp. 271ff.
27. *Geog.*, VII, II, 22, AIT, p. 225.
28. *E'tude*, p. 351.
29. *Nat. Hist.*, VI, 21, 23; see also Megasthenes, *Indika*, Bk. IV, Fragm. LVI, AIMA, p. 141.
30. Jiringi plates of Gaṅga king Indravarman, *Ep. Ind.*, XXV, VI, April 1940, p. 285.
31. CAGI, p. 436.
32. *Ibid*; JASB, 1837, p. 860.

33. JBORS, XV, I and II, p. 112; Law, HGAI, p. 149.
34. *Nat. Hist.* VI, 21, 22.
35. QJAHRS, II, I, pp. 22-23.
36. *Geog.*, VII, II, 23, AIT, p. 225.
37. AIT, p. 230.
38. *As. Res.* VIII, p. 344.
39. *Geog.*, VII, I, 73, AIT, p. 167.
40. AIT, p. 169.
41. *Geog.*, VII, I, 62, AIT, p. 152; VII, I, 5, AIT, p. 38; CAI, p. 373; L. Renou (ed.), *La Geographiĕ de Ptolemĕe l' Inde*, pp. 28-29.
42. Sec. 14, p. 27, and secs. 51 and 52, p. 43; see also CNES, secs. 41-43, pp. 112, 116-17.
43. *Geog.*, XV, I, 73.
44. *Periplus*, p. 180, note.
45 See AICL, p. 78, note 2; AIT.p. 153; Gerini, RTGEA, p. 400, note 2; Law, HGAI, pp. 277ff; "Studies in Indian History and Geography Based on Early Greek Accounts", JGRI, XVI, 3-4, 1959, p. 284.
46. Secs. 41 and 44, pp. 39-40.
47. *Geog.*, VII, I, 2, AIT, pp. 35 and 140.
48. *Ibid.*, VII, I, 3, *Ibid.*, pp. 33 and 37.
49. *Periplus*, p. 176, note; Law, *op. cit.*, JGRI, XVI, 3-4, 1959, p. 283; E.J. Rapson, *Ancient India*, p. 85.
50. *Nat. Hist.*, VI, 20.
51. AICL, p. 161; see also AIMA, p. 146 fn.
52. *Ibid.*, 161, note 10.
53. *Nat. Hist.*, VI, 21, 23.
54. Cf. AIMA, p. 146, fn; see also Lassen, *Ind, Alt.*, I, 2nd. edn. p. 760.
55. *Periplus*, sec. 51, p. 43; CNES, p. 125; CAI, p. 304.
56. *Geog.*, VII, I, 82, AIT, p. 175.
57. *Padma Purāṇa* (Uttarakhaṇḍa, 180, 2-7) also refers to "Godāvarītīre Pratiṣṭhānaṁpuraṁ".
58. *Imp. Gaz. Ind.,* XIX, p. 317.

59. *Geog.*, VII, I, 82; L. Renou(ed), *La Geographiĕ de Ptolemĕe l' Inde,* p. 35.
60. See AIT, pp. 176-77; *Periplus*, p. 195, note; CAI, p. 381, note 82.
61. Sec. 51, p. 43.
62. *Periplus*, p. 196, note.
63. Sec. 51, p. 43; CNES, p. 125; CAI, p. 304.
64. VII, I, 82, AIT, p. 175; L. Renou, *op. cit.*, p. 35.
65. "Tagara: Ter,", JRAS, 1901, pp. 537ff.
66. ASIAR, 1902-03, p. 195.
67. See JRAS, IV, p. 34.
68. *Periplus*, sec. 52, p. 43; CNES, p. 127; CAI, p. 305.
69. *Geog.*, VII, I, 6, AIT, p. 39.
70. Sec. 52, p. 432.
71. *Periplus*, p. 197, note.
72. Sec. 52, p. 43; CNES, p. 127; CAI, p. 305.
73. *Ibid*; CNES, p. 128.
74. *Geog.*, VII, I, 6; also AIT, p. 39; L. Renou (ed) *La Geographiĕ de Ptolemĕe l' Inde,* pp. 3-4.
75. *Top. Chr.*, p. 337.
76. *Imp. Gaz. Ind.,* XIV, p. 322.
77. Sec. 53, p. 43; CNES, pp. 128-29.
78. VII, I, 6, AIT, p. 39.
79. AICL, p. 161, note 11; AIT, pp. 42, and 346, note; CNES, pp. 128-29; D.C. Sircar, SGAMI, p. 226.
80. Cf. CNES, p. 128, McCrindle's comm. on sec. 53 of the *Periplus*.
81. *Geog.*, VII, I, 6, AIT, p. 39.
82. *Ibid.*, VII, I, 83.
83. Sec. AIT, pp. 176, 178-79; D.C. Sircar, SGAMI, p. 226, note 2.
84. *Ind. Alt.*, III, pp. 179, 185.
85. Sec. 53, p. 43.
86. *Periplus*, p. 201, note; CNES, p. 129; U.P. Arora, "Classical Accounts on India- Some Observation", in *Graeco-Indica: India's Cultural Contacts with the Greek World,* ed. by himself, p. 93.

87. *Imp. Gaz. Ind.*, XXIV, p. 310.
88. VII, I, 63, AIT, p. 152.
89. AIT, p. 156.
90. *Ibid.*, p. 374, note.
91. See *Ind. Ant.,* 1893, p. 113; 1894, p. 28.
92. Sec. 48, p. 42; CNES, p. 122.
93. *Geog.*, VII, I, 63, AIT, p. 152; L. Renou (ed). *La Geographiĕ de Ptolemĕe l' Inde*, pp. 28-29.
94. *Brahma Purāṇa*, 43, 24-35; see also V.S. Agrawala, "Brahma Purāṇa mein Ujjayini", in *Itihāsa-Darśana* (collection of his papers), ed. by P.K. Agrawala, pp. 157-60.
95. *Periplus*, sec. 48, p. 42.
96. *Ibid.*, pp. 187-88, note.
97. AIT, p. 155.
98. *Geog.*, VII, I, 63.
99. AIT, pp. 155, 373, note; see also Lassen, *Ind. Alt.*, III, p. 171.
100. For details see AIT, p. 166.
101. Sec. 59, p. 46.
102. *Sabhā Parva*, 24, 18-20.
103. Raghuvaṁśa, VI, 59; see also *Ep. Ind.,* X, p. 103.
104. *Geog.*, VII, I, 91, AIT, 184; see also CAI, p. 381, note 91.
105. *Periplus*, p. 242, note.
106. Ptolemy, *Geog.*, VII, I, 91.
107. See AIT, pp. 185-86.
108. *Nat. Hist.*, VI, 23 (26).
109. *Geog.*, VII, I, 89, AIT, p. 183.
110. *Geog.*, VII, I, 89, AIT, p. 183.
111. AICL, p. 112, note 3; see also AIT, pp. 351-52, note.
112. *Geog.*, VII, I, 89, AIT, p. 183.
113. See AIT, pp. 183-84.
114. *Geog.*, VII, I, 86, AIT, p. 180.
115. *AIT*, p. 182.

116. *Ibid.*, p. 181.
117. *Geog.*, VII, I, 90, AIT, p. 183.
118. AIT, p. 184.
119. *Geog.*, VII, I, 92, AIT, p. 185.
120. AIT, p. 186.
121. *Ibid.*, p. 187.
122. *Geog.*, VII, I, 93, AIT, p. 185.
123. *The Successors of the Sātavāhanas*, p. 48 cf. CAI, p. 381, note 93.
124. *Nat. Hist.*, VI, XXI, 22. The Andarae were settled originally in the Dekkan, also called Dekhan, between the middle part of the courses of the Godāvarī and the Kṛṣṇā rivers.
125. *Geog.*, VII, I, 83, AIT, p. 176.
126. See AIT, pp. 179, and 385 note; B.C. Law, "Studies in Indian History and Geography based on Early Greek Accounts", JGRI, XVI, 3-4, 1959, p. 281; also his *Tribes in Ancient India*, p. 382.
127. See D.R. Das, *Economic History of the Deccan from the first to the sixth century AD,* p. 147; E.J. Rapson, *Ancient India*, p. 90; M.R. Singh, GDEP, p. 272.
128. *Geog.*, VII, I, 86, AIT, p. 180.
129. Quoted by McCrindle, AIT, p. 182; see also CAI, p. 381, note 86; AIT, p. 352, note.

3

Growth and Decay of Urban Centres in Northern and North-Western India

The classical accounts of the urban centres (towns and cities) of northern and north-western India are also worthy of our notice.

The first discovery of a city in north-west India is ascribed to Skylax of Karyanda, a Greek explorer and voyager, who undertook a naval expedition sometime about 517 BCE under the direction of the Persian king Darius I (522-486 BCE) to explore the course of the Indus. He found a city named Kaspatyros in the "Gāndhāra country" somewhere near the upper course of the Indus where he embarked. He set out on his voyage from this city down the Indus towards the east and to the sea as described by him in his own narrative,[1] which became the source of information for the later Greek writers. There has been some controversy among scholars in the past over the exact location of this place. According to A.V. Williams Jackson, "the town may have been situated near the lower end of the Cophen (Kābul) river before it joins the Indus".[2] M.A. Stein, while making an attempt to identify the exact site of Kaspatyros, suggests that this city must have been situated near Jahangira, a place on the left bank of the Kābul river, some six miles above the confluence of the latter with the

Indus at Attock from where Skylax and his companions started on their voyage. He refers to many ruined sites near Jahangira, and near Alladher closeby on the Indus.[3] The geographical position assigned to this city by him has also been supported by other scholars.[4]

Hecataeus of Miletus, who derived his authority from Skylax, called this city Kaspapyros. He speaks of it as a city of the Gandaraeans or Gandarians.[5] He has preserved some extracts from the narrative of Skylax in his geographical work, the *Periodos,* which appeared before 500 BCE. Herodotous, borrowing the ideas from his predecessors, placed the city, Kaspatyros, in the land of Pactyice or Pactyes (Afghanistan).[6] Though Herodotus had very vague and hazy knowledge of the territorial settlements of the people in the towns and cities to the west of Indus as indicated by J. Rennell,[7] we may resonably infer from his statement that the northern Indians who dwelt near the said city and the country of the Pactyes, Paktyike or Pashtus (represented by the ethnic name Pakhtūn or the Pathān) were no other than the hill-tribes of the Upper Kābul valley whose mode of life resembled that of the Bactrians. M.A. Stein has made it quite clear that "Kaśpatyros or Kaspapyros, whichever form may be more accurate, must have been situated in that territory where the Indus first becomes navigable, i.e., in the ancient Gāndhāra, the present Peshawar District".[8]

The author of the *Periplus* refers to this city as "Caspapyrene" also called "Caspapyra". W.H. Schoff, translator and annotator of this text, has categorically stated that it was from this town that Skylax began his voyage of discovery at the command of the Persian king Darius. It could not have been far above the modern Attock [33^{0}53'N, 72^{0}15'E]. In view of the fact that the *Periplus* distinguishes it from Gāndhāra, he prefers to fix its location in that direction.[9]

Ptolemy designates Kashmir as "Kaspeiria", but he has, however, misplaced it. He describes Kaspeiria as situated below the sources of the Bidaspes (Jhelum), the Sandabal (Cenāb) and the Adris (Rāvī).[10] The geographical position assigned to it by Ptolemy in his map would bring Kaspeiria close to the junction of the Hydaspes (Jhelum) and Zaradros (Sutlej), i.e., the neighbourhood of Multān. This is obviously an error in the latitude implied by him to fix its position. In fact, it was watered by the Bidaspes in the upper part of its course. Kaspeira has been called the capital of Kaspeiria (Kashmir).[11] Some scholars have rightly identified Kaspeiria with Kashmir. Masson observes that in the time of Ptolemy Kashmir was the most powerful and extensive kingdom which was watered by Jhelum, Cenāb and Rāvī. It included within it provinces of the lower

Himālayan region that lay between Kashmir and the Sutlej.[12] Lassen[13] and V. De St. Martin[14] are almost in agreement with each other in suggesting that the Ptolemy's statement refers to a period when the power of the dynasty ruling over Kashmir actually extended over the wide territories, as indicated above. J.W. McCrindle also affirms hat Kaspeiria of Ptolemy corresponds with Kashmir or the Sanskrit name Kaśyapapur which has been used in different forms by some classical writers by a slight contraction. Its sovereigns in Ptolemy's days had extended their rule far beyond the limits of the present kingdom of Kashmir.[15] Kaspeiria, according to Burnouf, is a contraction of Kaśyapamira which is said to be Kaspapyrus of old geographer Hecataous and Kaspatyros of Herodotus.[16] M. D'Anville does not support its identification with Kashmir. He rather takes it as a city mentioned by Hecatacus and Herodorus.[17] Stephanus Byzantinus (or Stephanus of Byzantium) in his *Geographical Dictionary* (in which an extract from the work of Hecatacus is preserved) refers to it as a Gandaric city.[18] B.C. Law asserts that Kashmir, the Kaspeiria of Ptolemy, was included in the Gāndhāra kingdom in the dim past.[19] But at the same time he is disposed to accept it as a Kaspapyros city of Gāndhāra.[20] Ptolemy's Asmirae or Asmiraia[21] also stands for Kashmir, as pointed out by Ammianus Marcellinus,[22] supported by St. Martin.[23]

Dionysios of Samos in his *Bassarika* (a lost poem whose fragment is preserved in the work of Stephanus of Byzantium and first noticed by D'Anville,[24] and Nonnos is his *Dionysiaka* (xxvi, 165)[25] have made incidental notices of the people of this city as Kaspeiroi and Caspeiri respectively. They were among the Indian tribes who rose in open revolt against Bacchos in remote past. No clear picture, however, emerges from their explanations.

E.H. Bunbury is of the firm opinion that Caspapyrus of Hecataeus or Kaspatyrus of Herodotus was one of the capital cities of Gāndhāra.[26] A.H.L. Heeren[27] and Mannert[28] place it in the vicinity of Kābul. James Rennell has fixed its location on the upper part of the Indus above Attock from where Scylax set out to explore the Indus.[29] Wilford has identified it with Kashabpur, a modern town near Jhelum,[30] which is merely based on his supposition. Wahl places it with confidence at the fort of Kuttver,[31] which is also hypothetical. It will not be reasonable to entertain such hypothesis.

H.H. Wilson was the first oriental scholar to strongly advocate the identification of Kaspapyrus or Kaspatyrus with Kaśyapapura, a city being named after Kaśyapa, a great sage and the first coloniser of the country.

This was, according to him, the original designation of Kashmir which in its palmy days comprehended great part of the Punjab and extended as far as the Indus. In support of this identification he has advanced the argument that no such place as Kaspatyrus has been traced westward of the Indus in Afghanistan. Alexander and his generals met with no such city in that direction.[32] He seems to have been guided by the oriental tradition which still supports the identification of Kashmir with its original name Kaśyapapura. But this should be borne in mind that this city may be distinguished from that of the Greek writers concerned. The philological derivation of Kaśyapapura or Kashmir from Kaspapyros is based on Wilson's fanciful etymological interpretations of the latter name. Kaśyapapura (Kashmir) on the Jhelum has been mistakenly identified by some authorities with Kaspapyros of Hecatacus.[33]

It is curious to note that Alberuni,[34] A. Foucher,[35] W. Vincent[36] and A. Cunningham[37] have identified Kaśyapapura (Kaspeira of Ptolemy) with Multān situated on the old bank of the Ravi which is unworthy of acceptance. In the opinion held by Lassen[38] and Humboldt[39] it is taken to be Kashmir. V.A. Smith, on the one hand, doubts the connection of the name with Kashmir of the present day, but, on the other hand, seems to be little inclined to associate it with the same assuming that its earlier extension was wider.[40] However, M.A. Stein rejects the identification of Kaspatyros or Kaspapyros with Kashmir.[41] The contradictions in the statements of scholars concerned which are very much apparent here, no doubt, widen the scope of speculation about the identification of the city described by classical writer. But in view of the fact that the knowledge of three early Greek writers, Skylax, Hecataeus and Herodotus, did not advance much beyond the frontiers of the Indus constituting as one of the remotest provinces of the Persian empire towards the east, it will not be reasonable on our part to approve of the identification of this city with ancient Kashmir. This town must have been situated in Gāndhāra region or near Kābul whose sovereigns in all probability by the middle of the second century of the Christian era might have extended their rule far beyond the limits of their kingdom to Punjab and Kashmir. We may further assume that as Kashmir formed part of ancient Gāndhāra, the people from the former place settled down in the city which came to be known as Kaspatyros or Kaspapyros.

According to the division of the Greek geographers, Gāndhāra was the country below Kābul, while Kaśyapapura was the adjoining district in India proper.[42] H.A. Rose has conjecturally stated that Kaspatyros or Kaspapyros (called Kaśyapapura) was a dependency of Gāndhāra.[43]

Placing their reliance on the information transmitted by Herodotus (*Hist.* III, 102 and IV, 44) that Kaspatyros was situated in the country of Paktyike, J.T. Wheeler[44] and H.G. Rawlinson[45] have identified it with a city on the Kābul river. The former says that it was situated at the upper course of the Indus[46] which is in perfect harmony with the view of H.F. Tozer.[47]

Taking the city Kaspapyros and Kaspatyros of the Greek geographer Hecataeus and historian Herodotus respectively as identical, St. Martin has placed it in the basin of Kābul to the west of the Indus.[48]

Kaspapyros called by Hecatacus (*Periodus*, Fragm. 179) a city of the Gandaraeans (Gāndhārians) was "a frontier city of Gāndhāra".[49]

Kaspapyros, according to Olaf Caroe, is transliteration of Paskapuros, which is identical with the ancient city of Puruṣapura (modern Peshawar).[50]

Before providing the detailed description of other towns and cities of Afghanistan in northern India, here it will be worthwhile to note that its greater part (Eastern Ariana) beyond the Indus remained in the possession of the Indians for several centuries both anterior and posterior to the Macedonian invasion.

The city called by Pliny Capisa or Capissa[51] and by his copyist, Solinus, Caphusa can easily be identified with Pāṇini's Kāpisī (IV, 2, 99), the ancient capital of the kingdom of Kapiśa, Kapisene of Ptolemy or *"Ka-pi-shih"* of Yuan Chwang.[52] The said kingdom included the whole of modern Kohistan-Kafiristan as well as the two large valleys of Ghorband and Panjshir.[53] Ptolemy places the town of Kapiśa amongst the Paropanisade 2½ degrees to the north of Kabura or Kābul[54] which is nearly 2 degrees in excess of the truth. Arrian *(Indica,* I, 3) has also incidentally referred to the city of Kapiśa. St. Martin,[55] A. Foucher[56] and R.D. Banerji[57] have placed this city in the upper region of the Kophes or Kābul. According to Pliny, this famous city was destroyed by the Achaemenian emperor Cyrus (558-530 BCE)[58] in the course of his invasion of north-west India. The historical tradition also attributes the destruction of this city to the Persian invader. In the Behistun Rock Inscription (520-518 BCE) of Darius (522-486 BCE), king of Persia, Capisa figures as Kāpisa-kāni which signifies merely a stronghold.[59] The Kaspioi of Herodotus *(Hist.,* III, 93; VII, 67, 86) were the people of Kapiśa who have been located in the wild tract of Kafiristan to the north of the Kābul river.[60] There are some missing links in the classical accounts of this urban centre in the upper Kābul valley which can be restored with the help of other sources.

The city, Kapiśa, is identified with modem Begrām, about 50 miles north of Kābul, on the ground of an epigraphic evidence, i.e., a Kharoṣṭhi inscription found there naming the city,[61] the ruins of which are described in a memoir by Charles Masson.[62] A. Cunningham, on the basis of the routes followed by Hiuen-Tsang in the course of his visits to the capital of *Ka-pi-shih* in CE 630 and again fourteen years later in CE 644,[63] has fixed the position of the said capital city at Opian near Begrām.[64] This place was visited by Mr. Masson sometime between 1833 and 1836. He describes it as "distinguished by its huge artificial mounds, from which, at various times, copious antique treasures have been extracted".[65] He further observes that "it possesses many vestiges of antiquity; yet, as they are exclusively of a Sepulchral or religious character, the site of the city, to which they refer, may rather be looked for the actual village of Malik Hupian on the plain below, and near Charikar".[66] Begrām, which is the city *par excellence,* lies about 6 or 7 miles to the "E.N.E. of Charikar and Opian", Opiane of Hekataeus and Stephanus of Byzantium and Opianum of Pliny. According to the traditions of the people, "Begrām was a Greek city, which was overwhelmed by some natural catastrophe.[67] The name of Opian is certainly as old as the fifth century BCE as Hekataeus places a tribe called the Opiai to the west of the upper course of the Indus where there was a royal town or fort.[68] This is what Stephanus has also mentioned in his *In Voce Alexandria.* B.N. Puri's supposition that Opiai do not represent any tribe[69] can very well be disposed of.

The city of Kāpiśi at Begrām near Kābul after being destroyed by Cyrus in the sixth century BCE in all likelihood might have been rebuilt bearing the same name either in its neighbourhood or at Opian sometime between the third and the second century BCE because the professed historians of Alexander do not mention this city. It might have come into existence during the time of Aśoka. In the post-Maurya age, it fell under the rule of Eukratides (181-160 BCE), the Greek ruler of Bactria, after Appollodotus I was deprived of the kingdom of Kapiśa by him. In the age of the Kuṣāṇas, the city gained popularity as a centre of trade and commerce. It is said to have formed part of the Kuṣāṇa empire of Kaniṣka in the first century CE.[70] The city continued to flourish down to the eighth century CE. In the seventh century CE, Hiuen-Tsang found the kingdom of Kapiśa in a very flourishing state with towns, temples, etc.[71] The city remained as capital of Afghanistan till CE 792-93 – the year in which it was sacked by the Arabs in their desperate bid to conquer Afghanistan. The city gradually began to decay because of desertion of the people after Kābul took its place as a new capital.

The existence of towns or cities within the confines of the kingdom of Kapisene or Kapiśa can also be proved with the help of evidences available in classical literature.

The city founded by Alexander in 329 BCE (two years before his actual campaign) in the land of the Paropamisadai (Kābul) or at the foot of the Paropamisos range called Indian Caucasus (Hindukush) and named after him Alexandria, as stated by Strabo,[72] Pliny,[73] Arrian[74] Curtius[75] and Julius Valerius,[76] is identified with the city the vast ruins of which in all probability lay at Opian or Houpian in the neighbourhood of the village of Charikar situated in the beautiful valley of the Koh-Daman where the three roads leading from Baktra into Afghanistan converged.[77] The city occupied a commanding position in the plain of Koh-Daman, "about forty miles in length by sixteen or eighteen in breadth. It stretches to the very foot of the Hindu-Kush, and gives exit at its northern end to four several routes, by which that chain may be passed".[78] It is believed that Alexander after the conquest of some parts of Afghanistan to commemorate the victory founded in the land of the Paropamisadai a city named Alexandria. The city at the foot of the Kaukasos or Central Hindukush, which forms the northern frontier of Kābul, was more or less a military colony. Pliny's *Alexandrian Opianes*[79] is interpreted by Philemon Holland (who translated his work in CE 1601) as "the city of Alexandria in Opianum".[80] Stephanus also places it in "Opiane"[81] which agrees exactly with the site of the present Opian near Charikar. According to the measurement recorded by Pliny, the city was situated at 50 Roman miles, or 45.96 English miles distant from the city of Ortospana (or Kābul).[82] According to W.W. Tarn, the city called Alexandria stood on the west bank of the united Panjshir and Ghorband rivers near the confluence facing Kapiṣa on the east bank. It is represented by the modern Begrām.[83] In July 1833, Charles Masson left the city of Kābul to explore the districts north of it at the base of the Hindukush with the primary object of identifying the site of "Alexandria and Caucasum", and after his continuous researches of four succeeding years he discovered numerous interesting objects and the ruins of an ancient city of immense extent on the plain now called Beghrām or Begrām, 25 miles N. 15 E. from the modern city of Kābul. In a square plain of nearly six miles in each direction, situated at the north-east point of the level country of the Kohistan, in an angle formed by a ridge of Hindukush, he found fragments of pottery, lumps of iron, and other indications of a numerous population, coins, seals, rings, and other signs of habitation, some few fragments of sculpture, but no vestiges of buildings were discovered, except, at the depth of three or four feet, where lines of cement which seem to be the remains of foundations, and a large unburnt bricks forming mounds of considerable extent, which have been supposed to indicate the walls of the city, were found. He has suggested other localities, of which Perwan might be preferred, as being eight miles north-west of Begrām, and so much nearer to the Caucasus. He has also given indications of extensive sites of ancient cities in the Kohistan and the Koh-Daman. In the valley of the latter, he discovered two very important sites, which unquestionably refer to the capital cities of ancient times. At the second of these, about sixteen miles from Begrām, was found some important structure – a palace or a citadel. Many important vestiges of antiquity are said to be discoverable. The distances would nearly correspond as to Charikar in the plain of Begrām and to Ghorband in the valley of that name. In the course of his investigations between 1833 and 1836, he collected above thirty thousand coins including those of Greek and Indo-Scythic princes.[84] From his discoveries no conclusive opinion can be formed as to a preferable site for so-called Alexandria city. Nor can we draw any positive conclusion from the statements of two other renowned travellers, A. Burnes[85] and Mr. Vigne,[86] and the celebrated geographer, C. Ritter,[87] with regard to the identification of this city with Bamian. Its reputed antiquity and the excavations in its vicinity are some of the chief arguments in its favour. But this fact cannot be lost sight of that it is about eighty-five miles distant from Kābul. Hence Bamian cannot be Alexandria. The same objection may be urged against the place – Sighan, – as proposed by M. Court. Although there may be the ruins of a fortress attributed by the natives to Alexander, yet it is still farther beyond the summits of the Caucasus than Bamian.[88]

From the data available to us we can simply deduce that there were some urban centres in and around Opian, Charikar or Begrām, north of Kābul. One of them, which was already in existence near either of the former two places, might have been taken over by Alexander after his advent into India and converted into a city of Greek type or the Yavaṇa colony. It might have been further enlarged with the settlements of the people of the land and the Macedonians. The work of making a city of Greek type was carried through under the supervision of Nicanor, a Macedonian of high rank. The so-called Greek City Alexandria (near Kāpiśī) was capital of the province of the Paropanisadae or upper Kābul valley in Alexander's time.

The exact position of the town or city founded by Alexander at the foot of the Paropamisus or Hindukush (known to the Macedonian Greeks by the name of Indian Caucasus), named after him Alexandria, cannot be determined with certainty. Its site, according to V.A. Smith, may be marked by the extensive ruins at Opian or Houpian, near Charikar, some thirty miles northward from Kābul.[89] A. Cunningham has identified it with Opian, 36 miles to the north of Kābul.[90] M. Elphinstone has placed it at Begrām, 25 miles N 15 E from Kābul,[91] the ruins of which are described in a memoir by Mr. Masson.[92] Its population was recruited by fresh settlers from the surrounding or adjoining regions. This city, according to E.H. Bunbury, "continued for more than two centuries to be the centre of Greek civilization in these remote and mountainous regions".[93]

There were other towns at the foot of the so-called Indian Caucasus or in the immediate vicinity of Alexander's city. Pliny has assigned exactly the same position to the town of Cartana (Kartana),[94] which may be identified with Ptolemy's Karsana, placed by him on the right bank of a river that comes from the vicinity of Kapiśa and Niphanda (or Opian), and joins the river of Lokharna or Logarh, nearly opposite Nagara. According to A. Cunningham, it was situated on the right bank of the United Panjshir and Ghorband rivers, immediately at the foot of the Kohistan hills, and within 6 miles of Opian or Alexandria Opiane, which corresponds with the locality of Begrām. He accepts this identification on the ground that Parwan and Kushan (Ptolemy's Baborana and Kapiśa respectively), the two ancient places in the neighbourhood of Opian, are both on the left bank of the Ghorband river.[95] Karsana and Opian, the two distinct places, like London and Westminster are said to have "approached each other as they increased in size, until at last they virtually became one large city". The coins of the earlier Greek kings of Ariana -- Euthydemus, Demetrius and Eukratides – bear the monograms of both cities, "but after the time of Eukratides, that of Opaina disappears altogether, while that of Karsana is common to most of the later princes. The contemporary occurrence of these mint monograms proves that the two cities were existing at the same time; while the sudden disuse of the name of Opian may serve to show that during the latter period of Greek occupation, the city of Alexandria had been temporarily supplanted by Karsana".[96]

Cartana was a walled town, noted for its rectangular precision. The city called Cadrusi or Cadrusia is placed both by Pliny and Solinus close to the Caucasus or in close proximity to Alexandria.[97] Philemon Holland, the translator of Pliny's work, renders the passage concerned thus: "Upon the hill Caucasus Standeth the town Cadrusi, built likewise by the said Alexander".[98] But, according to the commentators, Pliny's Cadrusi was the name of a people whose city was called Alexandria.[99] It has been rightly pointed out that "As a general rule, the Greeks... designated the various peoples whom they encountered by the names of their principal towns". Like "Kabura (Kābul) and the Kabolitae, Drepsa and the Drepsiani, Taxila and the Taxili or Taxiles, Kaspeira and the Kaspeirae,... there was most probably also a town named Cadrusia, whose inhabitants were called Cadrusi".[100] Cunningham seem to be disposed to identify the city of Cadrusi with the old site of Koratas, which Masson discovered under the hills of Kohistan, 6 miles to the north-east of Begrām, and on the north bank of the Panjshir river. There are the usual remains of an old city, consisting of mounds covered with fragments of pottery, amongst which old coins are frequently found. There are also remains of masonry works about the hills, which the people call Kafir-kot or the Kafir's fort.[101]

Alexandria, Cartana and Cadrusi became famous as three Greek towns. Both Curtius[102] and Diodorus[103] are in perfect agreement with each other about the settlements of 7000 of the people of the land in the new towns as their citizens with those of Alexander's mercenaries who established themselves in the region 2800 miles away from their old home. Plutarch's[104] categorical statement, that there were Hellenic cities in the neighbourhood of Kaukasos, goes as a corroboration of the assertion of Diodorus, that Alexander built other cities, each distant a day's journey from Alexandria.

The cities of Kapisene received the notice of only Ptolemy. The names of peoples as well as their towns are recorded by him. His Parsioi, Parsii or Parsyetai were the people of the Panjhir or Panjshir Valley. And their two towns Parsia and Parsiana are identified with capital of Parsii called Farzah and Panjhir respectively.[105] A town named Panjhir is also mentioned by the early Arab geographers.

Ptolemy in his *Geography* has supplied a long list of towns. The towns not already noticed are Barzaura in the north and Drastoka and Naulibis in the south.[106] The first of these may be Bazarak, a large town in Panjshir valley, the second was most probably a town in one of the daras or valleys or the Koh-Daman, and the last may be Nilab of Ghorband.[107]

The towns and cities situated within the boundaries of Aria, Arachosia and Paropanisadae to the west of the Indus in Afghanistan are also worthy of our notice. These three formed important parts of Ariane or Ariana which, according to Megasthenes and Pliny,[108] belonged to India (i.e., Greater India). Their inhabitants in common have been called in the classics Areitanians of Ariainoi.

From Strabo's and Ptolemy's description of the extent of the boundaries of different parts of Ariana it appears that Aria was bounded by Baktriana on the north, by Drangiana on the south, and by Paropamisadai on the west.[109] According to Strabo, Aria was two thousand Stadia (two hundred and twenty-nine miles) in length; and only three hundred Stadia (or little more than thirty-four miles) in breadth in the level country.[110] If these measurements be correct, Aria will be restricted to the tract from about Meshed to the neighbourhood of Herāt[111] – a position well enough reconcilable with what Strabo relates of Aria. Ptolemy has enumerated no fewer than thirty-five towns belonging to the small province of Areia.[112] (Arii of Herodotus, *Hist*, Bk. VII, 61-62). It is not possible to verify his long list of cities because of absence of details thereof and for want of authentic data in regard to their identifications. However, a number of small towns, as H.H. Wilson[113] points out, existed on the road from Meshed to Herāt and thence towards Kandahār or Kābul. The Aria, Arii, Arioi or Areia of the classical authors is believed to be the ancient capital city called by oriental writers Hera or Heri (=*Harōiva* in the *Avesta* = *Harāiva* in the old Persian inscriptions = Skt. *Sarova* = mod. Herāt) situated on the river Arius or Arias (=Ṛgvedic Sarayū or Hariyupiya = mod. Hari Rūd) in north-western Afghanisthan. In the Elamite version of the Behistun inscription it is called Arriya. According to the local tradition, as recorded by Wilson, "Herāt unites the claims of the ancient capital and the city built or rather repaired by Alexander".[114] Ptolemy (*Geog*., VI, 17, 7) calls Areia (Herāt) a city. It is said that "Hari was founded by Lohrasp, extended by Gushtasp, improved by Bahman, and completed by Alexander".[115] The capital of Aria, according to Strabo[116] and Arrian,[117] was Artakoana (also read Artakakana), the identity of which with Herāt on the west or its immediate vicinity cannot be ruled out. Artakoana is believed to have contained the royal palace. Strabo specifies as other cities, Alexandria[118] and Akhaia.[119] The cities mentioned by Isidore of Charax include Artakauna and Alexandria.[120] Ptolemy not only mentions Areia or Hera, but two other cities, Artakaudna and Alexandria.[121] Ptolemy (*Geog*., VI, 17, 6) places Artakaudna (Artakoana), the ancient capital of the province of Aria, on the banks of the Areian lake about two-thirds of a degree north-west of his Alexandreia of the Areians. Ammianus Marcellinus says: "Aria possesses a great many towns, of which the most distinguished are Bitaxa (or Bitana), Sarmatina, Sotera, and Nisibis and Alexandria".[122] We do not have any source-material at our disposal to identify them except for the last one. According to Strabo, Alexander after having reduced to his authority the people called Arianians founded a city in their country – Arioi, – which he called Alexandria,[123] which is reasonably taken as Herāt.[124] Strabo quoting from the *Geog.* of Eratosthenes (xi, 48) gives the distance from Alexandria in Ariis to Bactria at 3870 stadia (387 English miles).[125] Further, Strabo in his incidental notices of India (XI, viii, 9), quoting Eratosthenes, assigns the distance from the Kaspian Gates to Alexandreia in the country of the Arioi (identified with Herāt) at 4,530 stadia (518 miles).[126] The total distance from the Kaspian Gates to Alexandria in Ariis is reckoned at six thousand four hundred stadia or seven hundred and thirty-one miles. Alexandria in Ariis, according to another source, is said to be situated at six thousand stadia from the Kaspian, or above six hundred and eighty miles, which is as nearly as possible the distance of Herāt from Asterabad.[127] The distance from the Kaspian Gates to Alexandria is in favour of the identification of that city with Herāt, and its traditional attribution to Alexander may not be wholly unfounded. Artakoana could not, however, have been very distant from it. According to Barbie de Bocage, it was situated at a place called Fusheng,[128] the Busheng or Pusheng of Ibn Haukil, one stage from Herāt, on the borders of Heri river. M. Court proposes to place it at Obeh or Oba, ten farsangs from Herāt. He refers to a town called Ardekoun, which is valuable testimony for the genuineness of the appellation Artakoana.[129] According to Pliny, the river flowed by Artakoana, which will apply either to Herāt or Pusheng. Ptolemy places Artakaudna on the banks of the Areian or Arian lake, about two-thirds of a degree north-west of his Alexandria.[130] M. Jacquet seems to have attached weight to the position of the latter, as assigned by Ptolemy.[131] In Heeren's estimation, Alexandria and Artakoana are almost identical. His statement, "that Arrian does not inform us of the foundation by Alexander of any new city in this country. . . Several ancient cities received new names from the Macedonian conquerors",[132] seems to be absolutely justified. This also confirms the traditon. "It seems not unlikely that Artakoana, Alexandria, and Aria are aggregated in Herāt".[133]

The people of Aria called Arioi (or Arii), according to Strabo, were situated beside the Drangai (the people of Drangiane or Drangiana) both on the north and on the west, and nearly encompassed them[134] because of their contiguity or geographical proximity to each other. The metropolis or ancient capital of Drangiana, according to Strabo,[135] Pliny[136] and Ammianus Marcellinus,[137] was Prophthasia, called by Isidore of Charax Phra,[138] which is identified with much probability with modern Furrah or Farah (in Afghanistan), one hundred and thirty miles south of Herāt, and generally accepted as the northern capital of the province now called

Seistan.[139] "There can be no reasonable doubt", says Bunbury, "that Phra, which is described by Isidore of Charax as the largest town in the district immediately north of Drangiana, is the same name with the modern Furrah, and we are distinctly told by Stephanus of Byzantium, on the authority of the historian of Charax, that Phrada was the name of the city which was called by Alexander Prophthasia ...[140] But, according to Plutarch, Alexander founded the city, or at feast converted an insignificant village into a town of note. Prophthasia, a city of Drangiana, has been mistakenly placed by him in Sogdiana.[141] The ancient capital Prophthasia (the Persian Peshawaran), according to Eratosthenes, as quoted by Strabo *(Geog.,* XI, viii, 9, p. 514), was 1,600 stadia (183 miles) distant from Alexandria in Aria (Herāt),[142] which considerably exceeds the actual distance from Herāt to Furrat, but he himself adds that others only give it as 1500 stadia. D'Anville proposed Parra or Phurrah for the site of Alexandria which is not convincing at all. It is not supported by any evidence either. Pliny, in one place, calls Prophthasia the capital of the Zariaspae.[143] Arrian refers to the royal city of the Zarangaei (Drangae), which is recognised in Zarang, an ancient name for the capital of Seistan.[144] It is worthy of note that up to seventh century CE Drangiana's capital, situated between the river Helmund and the lake Zarah, still retained the name of Zaranj. Dushak, the capital of Seistan, is supposed to be Zaranj or Zarang, and in this name the Zarangae of antiquity is unquestionably preserved. In, the neighbourhood of Dushak the remains of several ancient cities were seen by Captain Christie. About half-way between Dushak and Furrah he found the relics of a very large city named Peshawarun, about twenty-seven miles north of the former, as pointed out by H.H. Wilson.[145] Ibn Haukil has mentioned the city of Zaranj as Ram-Shehristan, a curious compound of Indian and Persian appellatives.[146] Ammianus Marcellinus has categorically stated that besides other cities, the Drangiani, who lived in close vicinity to the hills contiguous to Aria, had "two of which they proudly boast, Prophthasia and Ariaspe, on account of their opulence and renown".[147] Ptolemy calls Ariaspa the second city of Drangiana. The people of this city called Ariaspae or Aryaspae represented, according to Wilson, the Indian "Aryaśva" – "the rearers or riders of excellent horses".[148]

The Arachotoi or Arachotus of Eratosthenes,[149] Arachotoi of Strabo,[150] Arachotae of Pliny,[151] Arachotia or Arachosia of Ariian,[152] Curtius,[153] Dionysios,[154] Polybios,[155] Ammianus Marcellinus[156] and an unknown writer who follows the geographies of Eratosthenes and Ptolemy (*Anonymi Geographiae Expositio Compendiaria*),[157] Arachotes of Megasthenes[158] and Nonnos[159] or Ptolemy's or Arakhosia or Arakhotes[160] represents the city as well as the province.

Arachosia extended westward beyond the meridian of Kandahār. It was bounded on the north by the Paropanisos mountain (the western section of the Hindukush), on the east by the Indus, on the west by Drangiana, and on the south by Gedrosia. It was situated to the south of Paropanisadai. It was a rich and populous province (or kingdom) and acquired early importance as one of the main routes by which Persia communicated with India. It was watered by the Helmund and its tributaries. The river Urghundab or Arkandab passed through it. It comprised the greater part of south-western Afghanistan and a considerable portion of Eastern Afghanistan.[161] Its Zend name (as given in the *Avesta)* was *Harahvaiti*[162] and its old Persian name (as recorded in the inscriptions) *Hara(h)uvati.*[163]

The city called by Ptolemy Kandaroi[164] and by Isidore of Charax Kandake[165] can be identified with modern Kandahār, which was probably one of the capitals of Arachosia. The people called Arachosii in the *Periplus,* according to W.H. Schoff, "occupied the country around the modern Kandahār".[166] The identification of Arachosia itself or its capital with Kandahār (in south-eastern Afghanistan) has been generally accepted by the scholars.[167] The claims of Kandahār to antiquity has been doubted by H.H. Wilson.[168] But in the light of the references to it in classical literature under different denominations, such doubt can be dissipated. The distance from Prophthasia to the "city Arachotoi" or "Arachotus", as given by Eratosthenes, was 4,120 stadia (about 469 miles),[169] which, in a direct line, would bring us to the Indus. The measurement given here supports Rawlinson's identification of Arachotos with a site at Ulān-Robāt, where there are ruins of a city of a very remarkable character.[170] Keeping in view the distance of Arachotus city from Ortospana (Kābul), which was, according to Eratosthenes, two thousand stadia,[171] or about two hundred and twenty-eight miles, Wilson has identified the city of the Arachoti with a small town – Arkandab or Urghundab-situated on the river of the same name, which is said to be two hundred and twenty miles from Kābul.[172] Placing his reliance more on the recent measurements, as given by different perambulators, which have placed the city of Kandahār on the south-west at the distance of three hundred and nine miles[173] or three hundred and thirteen miles from Kābul[174] than on the ancient measurements, as recorded by the classical writers, he has rejected the identification of Arachosia directly with Kandahār.[175] There may be some inaccuracies in the classical measurements derived by Eratosthenes, Strabo and Pliny from the itineraries of Alexander's marches based on the details of his two surveyors, Diognetes and Baiton; and it is also true that their exactitude cannot be ascertained because of being taken by different routes. However, the identification of the city of the Arachosians with Kandahār cannot be denied.

The Arachotus is also celebrated as the site of a city. It is said to have been founded by Semiramis (the far-famed Assyrian Queen, who appears to have flourished in the eighth century BCE),[176] the remains of which, M. Court says, are to be seen on the Arghasan river, four parasangs from Kandahār, on the road to Shikarpur. This appears somewhat incompatible with the Arachotus being the Urghundab.[177] The Arachotus being the chief city is considered to be the capital of Arachosia.[178] Ptolemy (*Geog*., VI, 20, 5) refers to Arachotus as a town which was no doubt one of the capitals of Arachosia. The aforesaid name of the capital is preserved in Arokhaj or Rokhaj (also called Roh-Kaj) of the Arab geographers (who derived the term possibly from the Greek), as pointed out by J. Rennell,[179] H. Rawlinson[180] and Wilford.[181] H.H. Wilson, getting clues from the *itineraries* of Ibn Haukil (tr. by Sir William Ouseley),[182] and *Geography of Al-Edrisi,*[183] places Arachotus somewhere to the north of Rokhaj (fifty-six miles distant from Bost on the Helmund, at the confluence of the Urghundab) and south of Ghazni in Afghanistan.[184] We find some discrepancies in Wilson's statements, for in one place he has placed the people called Arachoti near Kandahār and the Arkandab river.[185]

A. Cunningham[186] and M.de St. Martin[187] have identified one of the two capitals of the Arachosia of classical writers with modern Ghazni. But the validity of this identification can be questioned on the basis of the distance of the latter from Kābul, which is only eighty-eight miles, which falls short of the distance of the former from Kābul, i.e., two hundred and twenty-eight miles, as given by the classical geographers. St. Martin has identified Arachosia with Kandahār too.[188] But Cunningham has identified the other capital with *Guzar* or *Guzaristan,* which is the chief town on the Helmand of the present day, and with *Ozola* of Ptolemy, which he places in the north-west of Arachosia, the Position of which is reconcilable with *Guzaristan.*[189]

Dionysios in his *Bassarika* (a poem in hexameter verse) and Nonnos in his *Dionysiaka* (a Greek epic poem in hexameter verse) refer pointedly to the impregnability of a place called *Gaza.* Dionysios calls it "As stern in war as if it was made of brass",[190] and Nonnos observes: "They fortified, with a net-like enclosure of interlacing works, Gazos, on immovable bulwark of Ares, and never has any armed enemy breached its compact foundations".[191] Stephanus of Byzantium has also quoted the *Bassarika* of Dionysios as his authority for this Indian town. The evidence recorded in these two classical works pertaining to the place concerned seems to have prompted Cunningham to identify the Arachosian capital with Ghazni. But it is very difficult to determine as to how far the appellation *Gazos* or Ptolemy's Gazaka (which has been misplaced amongst the Paropamisadae to the north of Kābul, instead of to the south of it) corresponds with modern town of Ghazni. The statement of Stephanus of Byzantium, that "the towns or cities named Arakhosia and Arakhoti were near the country of the Massagetae, or near Śakastene –the country of Śakas, who were of the same race as Massagetae–",[192] is wholly inadmissible.

Ammianus Marcellinus has expressly stated that "Among the cities of the country, Arachosia, the most important are Alexandria and Arbaca and Choaspa".[193] The identification of the said cities except the first one is uncertain. Alexandria also figures in the list of towns enumerated by Ptolemy. Alexander, after subduing the Indians bordering on Arachosia in the southern part of Afghanistan, constructed a city after the manner of the Yavanas at a point commanding the roads which marked the celebration of his victory. The Macedonians and some thousands of the native people settled side by side in the newly built city. The city called "Alexandria–among–the–Archosians" has been located at the old site of Kandahār.[194] In fact, like many other cities this too was given the name of the conqueror. "It was only one of the chains of cities which marked the track of conquering Hellenism".[195] Isidorus names it Alexanropolis.

The people called by Starbo Paropamisadai are more correctly denominated by Ptolemy the Paropanisadai. They are exactly the same whom Ammianus Marcellinus calls the Paropanisatae. They, according to these three classical authorities, were bounded on the west by Aria, on the north by Bactria, on the east by the Indus and on the south by Arachosia. The tribes comprehended under this name were located along the southern and eastern sides of Paropamisos or Paropanisus range.[196] (Avestan Upāirisaena) or the Central Hindukush (Avestan US-Hindava), and thus occupied Kābulistan and a considerable part of Afghanistan. They belonged to the province of the same name called by Pliny Paropamisadae[197] and by an unknown writer (who follows Eratosthenes and Ptolemy) Paropanisadae,[198] which comprised the Kābul valley (east Afghanistan) and the country north of the Kābul river now known as Lamhman or Larrighan (= Skt. Lampaka), Kohistan and Kafiristan (Kapiśa).

The existence of Kābul in the second century of the Christian era as the capital of the province or "country" (Afghanistan) can be testified to by the evidence of Ptolemy. He calls it Karura (Karoura) or Kabura (Kaboura) which, according to him, was situated on the Lokharna or Logarh river[199] whose ruins are still available on the right bank of the same river. This was one of the principal cities of the Paropanisadae. The inhabitant of the city has been called by him Kabolitae. The same city has been called by him,[200] Strabo,[201] Pliny,[202] Eratosthences[203] and Ammaianus Marcellinus[204] Ortospana, which Cunningham has identified with "the ancient city of Kābul and its citadel or high fort, the Bala Hisar".[205] The distance from the city of Arachotus to Ortospana on the three roads from Bactra, according to Eratosthenes (Strabo, XI, viii, 9) was 2,000 stadia (228 miles), as has been already stated. The said three roads, which include "the north-east road, by the Panjshir valley and over the Khawak pass to Anderab", "the west road, by the Kushan valley, and over the Hindukush pass to Ghori" and "the south-west road, up the Ghorband valley, and over the Hajiyak pass to Barman", diverged at Opian near Charikar. Ortospana or Pliny's Orthospanum because of being on the high road to Bactria has been conjecturally equated by H.H. Wilson with Orthostana (= the Sanskrit Ūrddhasthāna or Ūrdhvasthāna), i.e., high place or lofty city. This also applies to the elevated plain on which Kābul was situated.[206] Foucher (one of the most reliable French authorities on the subject) is also of the opinion that both Kabura and Ortospana stand for Kābul, and perhaps Ortospana was situated in the immediate vicinity of Kābul.[207]

The names of many towns in the Kābul valley (Paropanisadae) are recorded by Ptolemy as well as by the historians of Alexander's Indian campaign.

It is significant to note that after the destruction of Kapiśi, the first capital of Afghanistan, by Cyrus, Kābul shot into prominence as its second capital, which was also known as Òrtospana. By the seventh century of the Christian era its popularity as the capital seems to have declined. Because Hiuen Tsang in place of the city of Kābul mentions *Hu-pi-na* (Opian or modern Hupian, situated to the north of Charikar) as the capital,[208] which, according to V.A. Smith, was that of the Kābul territory.[209] Cunningham's view that Kābul was included within the territories of Opiai[210] is no longer tenable in view of the fact that both Kābul and Opian near Charikar were two different urban centres with their respective territory at the distance of about 50 miles from each other. Further, in ancient times Kābul remained in existence as the city at its original place (at Logarh river) till its occupation by the Saffarid ya'qub ibn Laith in H. 256 = CE 870-71. After the Arab conquest of the place the new city of Kābul came into being in the early medieval period which was situated on the Kābul-Rūda. It continued to exist as a chief city. Besides the chief city of Kabura or Ortospana, some towns were also located in the territories of the Paropanisadae along the Kophes or Kābul river. The most notable of these is Naulibis or Naulibus, as mentioned by both Ptolemy[211] and Ammianus Marcellinus.[212] The name bears a closer affinity to Nilab, an important town situated to the south of the Kophes or on the Ghor, an affluent of the Kābul river. This may be the probable site of this town. We have no data for determining the locations of either Agazaca of Marcellinus[213] or Arguda or Argandi of Ptolemy,[214] which is almost identical with Argante of Hekataeus who has mentioned it in his *Geography* as the Indian city juxtaposed to Gandarii (the people of Gāndhāra).[215] The town of Bagarda, as mentioned by Ptolemy, has been placed in the valley of Wardak or Logarh valley in the province of Kābul, inhabited by the Wardak tribe of Afghans.[216]

Hecataeus also describes a "royal town" amongst the Opiai. The details thereof are provided by Stephanus of Byzantium in his *In Voce Alexanderia.*

Strabo has rightly pointed out that in the country of Paropamisadae the towns were numerous, well supplied with everything, except oil.[217]

Here it may be added that Aria, Arachosia and Paropanisadae (with their respective capitals at Herāt, Kandahār and Kābul) remained in the possession of Persians from about the middle of the sixth century before the Christian era to the time of Alexander's invasion. The latter wrested them from the former and established in them colonies of his own. But, subsequently, Seleukos Nikator ceded them to Sandrokottos (Candragupta Maurya) following a treaty of peace ratified in 303 BCE.[218] And, consequently, they formed parts of Maurya empire, and remained as integral parts of northern India till about the end of the ninth century.

The Greek Bactria (=Skt. Bāhlīka = Avestic Bakhdhi = Old Persian Bākhtri), a principal part of Ariana or in the words of Apollodoros "the ornament of all Ariana,"[219] is placed on the river Oxus (=Skt. Vaṃkṣu) in the northern part of Afghanistan. Strabo, observes: "Baktriane is coterminous on the north both with Aria and the Propamisadai".[220] Both Pliny[221] and Ptolemy[222] place it at the back of Mount Paropanisus, but the latter erroneously places the city of "Bactra" in Sogdiana.[223] G.E. Gerini (a distinguished authority on Ptolemy's *Geography)* has also mistakenly placed it in Arakhosia.[224] Both the views are quite inconsistent with the information recorded by the historians of Alexander. As a matter of fact, this city was situated between the Oxus and the Paropamisus (Hidukush).

Bactra or Baktra, which once stood on the river Oxus in north Afghanistan, was one of the the greatest cities of the ancient world. It was the capital of Bactriana (or Baktriana) region. Of all the classical writers, it was Strabo who first described it as a city.[225] He also speaks of its great fertility and wealth which enabled the Grecian rulers to become powerful and to extend their sovereignty to other countries. Arrian mentions it as one of the two chief cities of the Bactrians.[226] Ptolemy describes it as a capital city. He unequivocally refers to its royal residence.[227] Curtius categorically states that "Baktra itself, the capital city of that region, is situated under mount Paropanisos (Hindukush). The river Bactrus passed by its walls; and gave the city and the region their name"[228] Ammianus Marcellinus also took notice of the city Baktra, "which", he says, "is both the capital and the name of the nation".[229]

"Baktra", says McCrindle "figures very early in history. Its capital indeed Baktra ("now Balkh") is one of the oldest cities in the world".[230] Bactria was known to Greece partly from its commercial importance. It was the chief seat of commerce between the east and west of Asia. It was destined by nature to be the first place of exchange for the productions of India. Heeren writes: "The city of Baktra must be regarded as the commercial entrepot of Eastern Asia; its name belongs to a people who never cease to afford matter for historical details from the time they are first mentioned. Not only does Baktra constantly appear as a city of wealth and importance in every age of the Persian empire, but it is continually interwoven in the traditions of the East with the accounts of Semiramis and other conquerors. It stood on the borders of the gold country, 'in the road of the confluence of nations'... and the conjecture that in this part of the world the human race made its first advance in civilization seems highly probable".[231]

H.G. Rawlinson, the principal authority on Bactria, indentifies it with Bāhlika which is of Vedic antiquity. He says "... there is immense antiquity of the advanced type of civilization in Bactria" ("Bāhlika of the Hindus").[232] It was, according to him, "the great commercial entrepot of the East".[233]

Rawlinson has transmitted to us very valuable information regarding the city called Bactra or Baktra by classical writers. According to him, the great city of Bactra standing on the high road between east and west was a meeting place of the nations. It was situated in the midst of the fertile foothills of the Paropamisus with its almost impregnable Acropolis and its famous shrine. It was a meeting point of the two civilizations.[234] "The ancient city of Baktra", observes he, "like Constantinople or Alexandria, was destined by its geographical position to play a leading part in the history of the world".[235]

The city of Bactra was at the height of its glory during the Vedic age. It was in the flourishing state between that age and the sixth century before the Christian era as reflected in the accounts of the Hindus. Bebween the sixth century BCE and the third century CE Bactria was under the Persian, Greek, Śaka and Kuṣāṇa rule. It was the principal capital of the Huṇas from about the middle of the fifth century to about the middle of the sixth century. The capital must have been built over with fresh materials. It might have been destroyed by the Turks after their occupation of Afghanistan in CE 870. The new city of Balkh might have been built in early medieval period after the destruction of the old city of Baktra or on its ruins.

Rawlinson has explicitly stated that the modern travellers find no remains of the ancient glories of the city of Bactra in the rambling town of modern Balkh. All traces of the old Iranian and Greek cities are hidden under a mass of medieval Muhammedan ruins.[236] General Ferrier was impressed with the size of the ruins of the old Baktra city of the classical writers. But he refers to medieval and not ancient remains. However, he appears to have seen some inscribed bricks among them.[237] "Baktra, the chief city of the land", says J.B. Bury, "preserved its old site but has changed its name to Balkh".[238] The name of the old city mentioned by classical writers is not preserved in modern Balkh as generally supposed. The ancient Bactra and modern Balkh represent two different cities. Some modern authorities still consider the two names identical with each other.

Starbo has mentioned Adrapsa or Darapsa as a principal Baktrian city where Alexander, according to him, reached on the fifteenth day after leaving the city Alexandria he had founded at the foot of Kaukasos. He first crossed over the summits of the mountains and then marching through the territory of the Paropamisadae entered into Baktriana.[239] The same city has been mentioned by Pliny,[240] Arrian,[241] and Ptolemy[242] with a slight change of name, i.e., Zariaspa, Drapsaca, Drepsa, etc. According to Arrian, it was one of the first cities taken by Alexander after crossing the mountains. It has been identified with Anderab of the present day, but it is said that "this identification rests on very slender ground". Further, its identity has been established with Kunduz[243] which is probably more correct. Ptolemy has mentioned various cities of Bactria including those founded and destroyed by the Macedonian conqueror (between 329 and 327 BCE - the period during which he was occupied in reducing that province) but no satisfactory indication has been offered about their locations. Hence, I refrain from entering into further details.

Despite the fact that the Persians, the Greeks, the Indo-Scythians and the Kuṣāṇas – all ruled over Bactria between the sixth century BCE and first century CE as a whole - the site of the capital remained unchanged and the city continued to flourish. In the seventh century CE, the capital was known as "Little Rājagṛha City", as revealed by Hiuen Tsang.[244]

The geographical transformation of the frontiers of Bhāratavarṣa from the times of the Persian invasion to the fourth century BCE, sometimes creates difficulty in our way in fixing their limits. However, the elucidation of the subject in the contemporary geographical setting is a guiding factor in ascertaining the exact position of the towns and cities situated within the boundaries of India which successively fell under the occupation of foreign powers.

From the accounts of classical authorities it transpires that the towns and cities lying between the great mountain ranges of the Hindukush (called Paropanisos), on the northern frontier towards the west (in the north-east of Kābul), and in the region of the Indus - so-called eastern frontier - were all Indian at the time of Alexander's invasion.

An old Indian city transformed with a new Greek name, Nicaea, Nikaea or Nikaia, was situated somewhere between Alexandria and the Kābul river. According to Arrian, Alexander from this city advanced towards the Kophen or Kābul.[245] Julius Valerius, while clarifying the position of this city, has fairly stated that Alexander marching from Bactra forthwith recrossed Caucasus or mountain rampart and reached Alexandria. "After passing through the country of the Parapapisamides (Paropanisadae) he directed his march towards the Indus by way of the city of Nicaea and the river Cophoen (Kābul)".[246] In the course of the march, many tribes were put to the sword, and their towns were captured. According to Nonnos *(Dionysiaka,* xvi, last three lines), Bacchus built a stone city, named Nikaia, near a lake which he also called *Indophon* in remembrance of his victory over the Indians on this spot. The conspicuous absence of authentic details of this city in the classical texts sparked off a lot of controversy among scholars in the past over its exact geographical position and identification. According to Wilson, "the Greek name does not imply a Greek city, and it was probably a translation of some such appellation as Jayapur, "the city of Victory."[247] Elphinstone during his Kābul mission in 1808 found tribes speaking language closely allied to Sanskrit and not Greek. One such village-tribe was Nisa, similar to Nikaia. General Abbott identified the city with Nangnihar - five miles west of modern Jalālābād.[248] H.G. Raverty,[249] Burnes,[250] V.A. Smith[251] and J. Hutchinson and J.Ph. Vogel[252] have also located the city to the west of Jalālābād. Wilson has fixed its location on the plain of Begrām at a spot with ruins, about 18 miles distant from Houpian[253] which is also favoured by Bunbury.[254] Thirlwall supposes that Nikaea was a new name given to the city otherwise called Ortospana or Kabura, the site of the modern Kābul.[255] This can also be corroborated by statement of Cunningham.[256] Ritter, Droysen[257] and T.H. Holdich[258] also put it at Kābul. M. Jacquet infers that it was situated at some distance from the Kophen.[259] The evidence adduced, particularly by Arrian, that Alexander proceeded to that river from the city of Nikaea, invalidates the assumptions with regard to its location at Kābul. Foucher discovered the ruins of this city on the spot where the roads to Mandaravara and Carabaga diverged.[260]

After having a deeper insight into the classical sources we find that between the Kophen or Kābul river and the Indus there were a large number of towns and cities. There stood also the famous ancient Indian city of Nysa. The earliest reference to this city occurs in Homer's *Iliad* (Bk. VI, 130-40). But the description thereof is more fictional than historical. However, the city was not a fiction of the poet but a historical reality. The existence of this city in pre-Alexandrian period can be proved by the evidences furnished in both the classical and non-classical sources. Megasthenes,[261] Pliny,[262] Strabo,[263] Arrian,[264] Curtius,[265] Justin,[266] Plutarch[267] and others have also mentioned this city with some variations in their presentation of accounts of the subject. The foundation of this city has been ascribed to a mythical hero, Dionysos, by both Megasthenes[268] and Arrian[269] on fabulous ground and under the erroneous impression that in the most primitive times the people of India were living in the villages, and they had neither the towns nor cities. It was Dionysos who came along with other Greeks at the head of the considerable army and conquered the country, settled therein and converted the villages into large cities and gave laws to them. One of the cities named Nysa or Nyssa was founded by him at the foot of the mountain called Meros. Arrian says "the city of Nysa is no mean monument with Mount Moms".[270] The Nysaeans or Nysaioi, according to them, were not an Indian race but the descendants of the Greeks. Diodorus has also narrated more or less the same story.[271] The evidence relating to Dionysos has been partly quoted by Strabo.[272] Diodorus in particular ascribes the foundation of the city to another mythical figure, the Greek Bacchus. He is said to have built many cities in India one of which he called Nysa in memory of that (Nysa) in Egypt where he was brought up. At this Nysa in India he is believed to have planted ivy which continues to grow here. Besides many other marks of his visit left there, he got his statue carved as lasting monument of his expedition.[273] About the middle of the first century of the Christian era, Apollonius with his fellow-traveller, Damis of Assyria, after crossing the Kophen (the Kābul river) entered the city of Nysa ruled by a king (Akouphis), and "saw the peaked summit of Mount Nysa, where was a circular space fenced with a hedge of laurels, vine and ivy planted by the hands of Bacchus himself, whose statue in white stone adorned the centre of this rustic temple". This can be confirmed by Philostratos' statements recorded in his biographical work, *Life of Apollonius of Tyana.*[274] The sense underlying the narratives or legendary accounts of the classical writers concerned leads us to warrant the belief that this city was founded by the Greek colonists long before the invasion of Alexander. It is, however, very difficult to ascertain the truth contained in their statements. Alexander personally saw many towns and cities between the Kābul and the Indus Doab. According to Curtius (VIII, 10), he visited the flourishing city of Nysa too. He attacked it and, consequently, the Nysaeans offered their submission to him. The city was eventually claimed to be the Greek or Ionian colony.[275] This city is generally placed near Mount Meros on the opposite bank of the river Kābul or in the valley of Kābul. Pliny (*Hist. Nat.*, VI, 21) explicitly states that the city Nysa and mountain Meros belonged to India.

According to St. Martin[276] and Bellew,[277] the existing Nysatta village situated near the northern bank of the river Kābul, six miles below Hashtnagar or Puṣkalāvatī preserves the vestige of the ancient city of Nysa. The city was actually situated to the west of the Indus (above Attock). Holdich, whose knowledge of the Indian frontier is unsurpassable, has fixed its location on the lower spurse of the three-peaked Koh-i-Mor,[278] wliich is also supported by Smith.[279] The Nysaeans have been placed on the "well-watered slopes of those mountains which crown the uplands of Swāt and Bajour, where they cultivated the vine for generations". The city called Nagara by Ptolemy in his *Geography* [VII, I, 43] is identified with Nagarahāra, an ancient capital of a kingdom of the same name, the ruins of which have been traced four or five miles to the west of Jalālābād.[280] St. Martin states that, Udayanapura was an old name of Nagarahāra.[281] The popular tradition also affirms it. Cunningham has fixed the position of the said capital at Begrām, about two miles to the west of Jalālābād.

He also admits that Nagara was situated midway between Kabura (Kābul) and the Indus.[282] In the beginning of the fifth century CE, this city was called *Na-kie* or Nagara by Fa-hien. It was then an independent state governed by its own king.[283] The same city was called by Hiuen Tsang *Na-ka-lo-ho* (Nagara or Nagarahāra) when he visited it in CE 630. It was then without a king, and subject to Kapisene or Kapiśa with its dependency city of Hi-lo or Hidda, situated near Peśāwar south of Udayana.[284] The mention of this city by the Chinese pilgrims not only testifies to its existence but also strengthens the classical evidence. In the post-seventh century CE, this city probably followed the fortunes of the sovereign state, and became successively a part of the brāhmaṇa kingdom of Kābul and of the Mohammedan empire of Ghazni. It may be noted here that the city of Nysa is often confounded with Nagara of Ptolemy. But the fact remains that both were two different cities and not the same as held by some scholars.

Strabo makes a mention of small town, Plemyrion. He adds that the river Khoaspes (Kunār) falls into the Kophes (the Kābul river) near it after passing by another city, "Gorys" (the city of Gauraeans or Gauraioi situated on the bank of the river "Guraeus" or Gauri, modern Panjkora).[285] "Plemyrion must have been situated at or near where Jalālābād now stands".[286] The city called "Gorys" is identified with "Gorydale"[287] on the eastern bank of the Khoes (the Kunār or Kameh river) or in the valley of the Kābul river which was also taken by the Macedonians.

The towns and cities situated in the region between two rivers, the Khoaspes or Kunār (a tributary of the Kophes or the Kābul river) and the Indus, received the notices of not only the professed historians of Alexander but other classical writers too.

The town called by Arrian Arigaion[288] or Arigacum,[289] which is absolutely identical with Argacum of Julius Valerius,[290] was situated to the east of the river Khoaspes. It was one of the walled towns. According to Arrian, it was fortified by double wall. The weight of the evidence is in favour of its identification with Bajour or Bagawar, the capital of the province of the same name.[291] According to some other evidence, it is represented by Naoghi or Nawagai, a village in the modern province of Bajour.[292] It is further suggested that "Arigaeum may be found in Arichand",[293] but since this is on the east of the Landai river, the validity of this identification may be doubted. However, in this direction besides the town of Bajour, there are several ruins, and some of these may be the relics of Arigaeum. The name of the place is apparently Indian –"Arijaya" or "Arinjaya", "the foe-vanquishing city"[294] which is comparable with "Ārjunāva" of the *Kāśikā* on Pāṇini (IV, 2, 69).[295] The town mentioned by the Greeks is said to have "commanded the road between the Kunār and the Panjkora valley".[296] This capital town belonged the Aspasians or Aspasioi[297] "(Sanskrit Aśvakas = Āśvāyana of Pāṇini, *sūtra* IV, 1, 110,[298] or Cavaliers) of Alishang-Kunār or Chitral-Bajour valley. They were the eastern branch of the Aśvakas – the indigenous hill-tribes that occupied the mountainous regions to the north of the Kābul river. They are represented by the Pashtus, probably the ancestors of the modern Afghans. The said town was very populous, opulent and prosperous.

The Aspasians, on perceiving Alexander's approach after he had crossed the Kunār river to subjugate them, set their town on fire having thought it hopeless to save from his onslaught, abandoned it and retired to an inaccessible mountains. But the latter took care to have rebuilt on account of its commanding position or because of its advantageous site.[299] It was recolonised by a number of the native people and the war-worn Greeks. The strength of the inhabitants of the town from the demographic point of view is strikingly illustrated by the fact that 40,000 of them were taken captive in course of their pitched battles with Alexander.[300] The Aspasians besides the principal city, Arigaeum, had another town called Andaka by Arrian[301] and Akadera by Curtius.[302] Alexander took possession of this town and then garrisoned. It is identified with the present town named Adrek, not far from the confluence of the Alishang with the Kābul river.[303] Here it is to be added that the name of Apasians' chief is not mentioned by any classical writer. There were many other walled cities belonging to the Aśvaka tribes.

The towns and cities situated within the Gāndhāric territory lying on both sides of the Kābul river, immediately above its confluence with the Indus at Ohind (mod. Peshawar dist.) about 16 miles north of Attock, also deserve our notice. The ancient name of Ohind was Udabhāṇḍapur, the place of transhipment of goods across the Sindh. It is equivalent to Hiuen Tsang's *U-to-kia-han-cha,* which is transcribed as Utakhaṇḍa.

A city called by the classical authors variously Massaga, Massaka, Mazaga, and Masoga was situated on the bank of the river Souastos or Swāt or near the Guraeus or Panjkora river. This celebrated city, which was strongly fortified, was the capital of the kingdom of the Assakenians, Assakenos or Assakenoi (the Aśvasenīs, "those fighting on horeseback") of the valleys of Swāt and Buner. It was very large, populous and prosperous city. It had great defensive walls and magnificent gates.[304] Strabo in his faithful account of the subject calls it "the chief city of the country (the realm of the Assakanos) and the royal residence".[305] According to Curtius, it occupied a very strong position and was surrounded by a wall of stone thirty-five stadia in circumference. Thirty eight thousand infantry were deployed to defend the city against Alexander's invasion.[306] Julius Valerius, while adding to this information, has revealed that the walls of the towns of the Accae (Assakenian) tribes were of "most formidable strength and equipped with every means of defence... the town was protected by a double ring of ramparts".[307] The city of Massaga was the citadel for the hill-people and was impregnable because of a fortress which stood on a precipitous mountain. Arrian (*Anab.*, IV, 26) says that Massaga was the greatest city in the dominions of the Assakenians.[308]

Curtius has provided a picturesque description of Massaga – the capital city of the realm of Assakenus or Assakenians - which can best be put in his own words (translated ones): "The city was strongly fortified both by nature and art… The city was surrounded with a wall (rampart) 35 stadia (= about four miles) in circumference which had a basis of stone-work supporting a superstructure of unburnt sun-dried bricks. The brick-work was bound into a solid fabric by means of stones so interposed that the more brittle material rested upon the harder, while moist clay had been used for mortar. Lest, however, the structure should all at once sink, strong beams had been laid upon these, supporting wooden floors which covered the walls and afforded a passage along them".[309]

The exact location of the city called Massaga or Massaka has not yet been ascertained in a conclusive manner. However, there was a town called Mashanagar (as mentioned by Babur in his Memoir) on the river of Swāt.,[310] with which the identity of this city can incontrovertibly be established. Rennell also identified Massaga of Alexander's historians with this city.[311] M. Court states that at a distance of twenty-four miles from the town of Bajour on the river Swāt a ruined site of ancient city exists which is called Massangar (Massanagar) or Mashkine.[312] He further holds that the ancient remains of the city called Maha-gram or Ma-gram are observable near a hill called Mount Maram.[313] Pāṇini identified the warlike people called Assakenoi with the Āśvakāyanas (*Naḍādi-gaṇa,* IV, 1, 99) of the Swāt valley (Suvāstu, IV, 2, 77 = ancient Uddiyāna = Udayana of the Buddhist literature) and their capital with Maśakāvatī which is mentioned in the *Mahābhāśya* as the name of the river (IV, 2, 71), which denotes that portion of the river Swāt in its lower reaches where the town of the same name or Massaga or Massanagar was situated on it.[314] Aurel Stein also located it in the lower Swāt valley.[315] St. Martin in his map of the basin of the Kophes has placed it near the river of Swāt in 34^{0}40'N. Lat.[316] Some traces of its name are still to be found in the regions which must have been subject to the authority of its sovereign. The Sanskrit name of the city must have been Maśaka. In the *Mahābhārata* exactly the same name figures as one of the four important towns of the north-west.[317] This proves the remote antiquity of the urban settlement in this region. Various names have been given to this city in Sanskrit, Greek and Latin literatures. M. Elphinstone is of the firm opinion that the names of the towns and cities of north-west India can be found in the Sanskrit sources.[318] Olaf Caroe proposes the Katgala site for Massaga of the Greek historians.[319] G. Tucci has located it somewhere near Chakdarra in the Swāt region.[320] Holdich connects it with a place called Matkanai near the Malakand Pass situated on the south bank of the Swāt.[321] This is also called a "Pakhtoon city".[322] This was perhaps one of the greatest cities of Gāndhāra in eastern Afghanistan or the largest among the tribal cities that belonged to the Āsvakas of that region. Plutarch has rightly called Massaga a city of the Gandridai (Gandarians).[323] The river Swāt (Souastene of Ptolemy, VII, 1, 42) with its western tributary, the Gauri, flowed through Gāndhāra the basins of which were inhabited by them. This capital city of the tribal kingdom was apparently in the territory of Kābul. The Assakenians were the western branch of the Aspasians or the Aśvakas.[324] They were separated from each other by the territory of the Guraeans. They were ethnically connected. It is because of their propinquity that they are considered the kindred tribes. They relied for their defence on the fortifications of their towns. The Assakenians dominion seems to have been "encompassed by the Swāt on the north, the Landai on the west and the Kābul on the south".[325] The Massaga city was besieged and razed to the ground during the operation of Alexander. The reigning king at the time called Assakenos was slain in the course of its siege by the troops of Alexander. The latter after sometime found the walls of the city deserted and the city burned down by its inhabitants, who had dispersed in quest of safer hiding-places.[326] This city seems to have been the seat of sovereign power which controlled the whole realm. The wife of the deceased king, Queen Kleophes (Justin, XII, 7, 10-11), mistakenly called the mother by Curtius (VIII, 10, 35), was restored to the throne and ruled for sometime over her own kingdom comprising many towns and cities.

We have also some archaeological evidence to prove the close commercial relations of the said tribal people of the Swāt region with Taxila as well as their settlements in this region sometime between the fourth century BCE and the second century BCE. A few inscribed copper coins of the Aśvaka tribe bearing the legends in early Brāhmī characters were discovered by Cunningham in the neighbourhood of Taxila. One of these coins (No. 13) bears the legend "Vataśvaka",[327] which both V.A. Smith,[328] and Buhler[329] have taken as equivalent to Sanskrit Aśvaka. The tribe designated in the legend may no doubt be identified with the Aśvakas of Indian literature and the Assakenoi of the classical literature. The legend may be interpreted as meaning Aśvakānāmvataḥ = Vataśvakah. The coin has been assigned to 350 BCE by Smith,[330] whereas, on the other hand, Rapson[331] and J. Allan[332] have assigned the coins in general to the third century BCE and the early second century BCE respectively. Whatever may be the fact, the possibility of the shifting of the Assakenians from the Swāt valley to Taxila region because of their territorial proximity after the occupation of their towns and cities by Alexander as well as in the later period cannot be precluded. The archaeological discoveries made in the Saidu Sharif region (Swāt State) by Italian archaeological mission also help us establish the age-old connection of the Aśvakas of the Swāt valley as well as those of the Taxila coins with the horse.[333]

The territory of the Assakenians, besides its metropolis (Massaga), was adorned with two other small fortified towns, which have been called by Arrian Bazira and Ora,[334] by Curtius Beira and Ora,[335] and by Julius Valerius Baziphara and Hora.[336] The former also finds mention in the Buddhist literature as a city of Uttarāpatha. In the Pāli Chronicle, *Dipavamsa* (p. 27), and the text, *Buddhavaṁsa* (XXVIII, 8), it figures as Vajirā and in the Sanskrit Buddhist text, *Bodhisattvāvadāna Kalpalatā* (p. 4), as Vajrāvatī. In one of the epigraphic records (the Sanskrit inscription discovered in Barikot in upper Swāt valley ascribed to an illustrious ruler of Kābul of Shahi dynasty, Jaipal Deva, who ascended the throne in CE 960) also it figures as Vajirā or Vajirāsthāna.[337] Aurel Stein, who undertook an archaeological exploration of North-West Frontier of India in 1926, identified Bazira with the ancient stronghold marked by the ruins of Bir-Kot hill - the castle of Bir (called Beira by Curtius, VIII, X, 22) in the Swāt Valley now represented by Barikot.[338] M. Court has identified it with a place named Bāzār, situated on the southern face of the Koh-Gaṅgā mountain, where are very extensive ruins.[339] Cunningham relying upon the traditional belief identified the site of the original town of Bazira with Bāzār, a large village situated on the bank of the Kalpan or Kālī-pānī river, and quite close to the town of Rustam, built on a very extensive old mound.[340] The position is said to be an important one, as it stands just midway between the Swāt and the Indus rivers. It was apparently a market-town and great centre of trade. It has been "from time immemorial the entrepot of trade between the rich valley of Swāt and the large towns on the Indus and the Kābul rivers".[341] Judging by the importance of the place,

Curtius (VIII, 10) called it an opulent city. Rennell conjecturally identified it with Bajour, which lies midway between the river of Kunār and Landai.[342] But there is nothing beyond the similarity of the two names to subscribe to this view.

The town of Ora has been placed by Stein farther up the Swāt valley and identified with Ude-gram situated at a distance of seven or eight miles north of Bīrkot.[343] M. Court has identified it with a town called Oora that still exists in the district of Buner.[344]

Both the towns mentioned above were besieged, stormed and ultimately captured by the generals of Alexander. Thereafter, those who survived fled out of their cities in the dead of night to a strongly fortified rock called Aornos for safety. The information supplied by Arrian[345] and Julius Valerius[346] in this regard are almost identical. As a matter of fact, after the fall of Massaga, Bazira and Ora in the hills of Swāt and Buner the inhabitants deserted their towns and took shelter in a mountainous fortress on the left bank of the Indus. Valerius has categorically stated that Alexander "on coming to that locality, seized a great many cities.[347] This locality was near the fort of Aornos (Varaṇā of Pāṇini, IV, 2, 82) in the domain of the Āśvakāyanas. The identification of this celebrated hill fort has been one of the most perplexing problems of Indian archaeology. The accounts of Arrian,[348] Strabo,[349] Diodorus,[350] Justin,[351] Philostratus[352] and Valerius[353] are discrepant. The other views are equally conflicting. However, Strabo has given an indication that the foot of Aornos was washed by the Indus near its source[354] which, according to the ancient belief, was at a distance of some 70 miles above Attak or Attock. Court was the first man to suggest that "... it is probably the castle which was opposite Attak, and the vestiges of which we see upon the summit of the mountain". Its foundation is attributed to Raja Hodi.[355] Cunningham relying chiefly on the classical accounts of the subject took it as Varnos and placed it in the country of the Varni. He has identified it with the fort of Raja Vara, whose name, according to him, is till attached to all the ruined strongholds between Hashtnagar (Puṣkalāvatī) and Ohind (Udbhāṇḍa). The old hill-fort and the city of Takhti-Bahai, 15 miles to the north-east of Hashtnagar is said to have been the residence of Raja Vara. Some ruins of his fort at the foot of the hill are called Raja Vara's stables. He has also connected it with the ruined fortress of Rānī-gat situated immediately above the small village of Nogrām, about 16 miles to the north of Ohind.[356] General Abbott identified the "Aornos of history" as the Mahāban hill on the western bank of the Indus,[357] which concurs with Arrian's view.[358] Bellew in his work, *Ethnography of Afghanistan,* suggests that the Greek name Aornos is a transformation of the native word *Aranai* (a common Hindi name for hill-ridges in that part of the country), adding that there is an *Aranai* spur of Mahāban, near Charorai in the Chumla valley. He seems to have identified the rock with the modern Malka near the summit of Mahāban.[359] Aurel Stein in the course of his tour in the Upper Swāt District in 1926 located the site of this mountain fortress on the left bank of the Indus. He later identified it with old remains at Pir-sae in the Swāt valley.[360] It was the refuge of all the neighbouring tribes. Valerius, while highlighting the importance of this place, has asserted that "a thousand peasantry had full scope for their industry".[361] This stronghold was assaulted and captured by Alexander.[362] While elaborating on the subject, Arrian has candidly stated that he also built a fort there and placed it under the command of the Indian chief (king of Gāndhāra region) named Sisikottos (Śaśigupta).[363] In a different context, he has pointed out that "he placed a garrison in the castle of Aornos".[364]

A small town in the realm of Assakenians called by Arrian Dyrta, lying to the north of Aornos or Mahāban, was also occupied by Alexander.[365] It has been identified with Dhyr (Dir).[366] However, the information available about this town is too meagre to present a clear picture of it.

Another small town called Embolima by Arrian,[367] Ptolemy[368] and Curtius[369] was not far from Aornos. Arrian relates that Alexander after taking possession of Peukelaotis (which I have described here later quite separately) captured other small towns on the river Kophen, and arrived at last at Embolima, a city seated not far from the rock Aomos.[370] Curtius' statement vindicates the truth that when he had finished his campaign, the west of the Indus, by the capture of Aornos, he proceeded towards Embolima.[371] Ptolemy has fixed its position near the junction of the Kābul river with the Indus[372] which agrees with the accounts of Alexander's historians. It represents the combination of two neighbouring places called Amb-Balimah. Abbott has identified the town with these two on the Indus, 8 miles to the east of Mahāban or Aornos,[373] which exactly corresponds with what Arrian says: "Aornos was only one day's march from Embolima" (*Anab.,* IV, 28). Cunningham has identified it with modern Ambar-Ohind at a distance of two miles from each other.[374] Court proposes Ambar, a town not far from the west bank of the Indus, for Embolima,[375] or it may be Amb, higher up. This identification seems to be incontestable. The two forts of Amb and Balimah are now in ruins on the spur of the Mahāban, which preserve to this day the traditions of the inhabitants of these two urban centres.[376] Ritter takes Embolima opposite Attock.[377] It is said to be about 60 miles above Attak or Attock.[378] Many small towns situated on the western bank of the Indus along with it were occupied by the said invader. The town of Orobatis (perhaps Oroppa) west of Puṣkalāvatī was fortified and garrisoned by Alexander's generals.[379] We do not have any concrete evidence about its identification.

Elphinstone has correctly observed that an extensive tract comprehending the valleys of Kunār, Kābul, Panjkora, Swāt, Buner, and Chumla were occupied by various divisions of the Yusuf-Zai tribe of Afghans, "in which there are some considerable towns, and in many places of which there are extensive vestiges of ancient population and prosperity".[380]

It is striking to note that the towns and the surrounding places after being occupied by Alexander were abandoned by the inhabitants, who were mainly the hill-tribes. They crossed the Indus and took refuge in Abhisāra country in the hills between the upper Jhelum and Cenāb.

One of the two chief cities of Gāndhāra has been called by Strabo Peukolaitis,[381] by Pliny Peucolaitis or Peucolaitae,[382] by Arrian Peukelaotis, Peukelaitis or Peukelas,[383] by Ptolemy Proklais,[384] and by an anonymous author of the *Periplus* Poclais[385] or Proklais,[386] which is a transliteration of Pukkalaoti, the Pāli form of the Sanskrit Puṣkaravatī or Puṣkalāvatī. It was the western capital of the kingdom of Gāndhāra (Gandarioi of Herodotus, Bk, iii, c, xci; Gandaritis of Strabo, XV, i, 26: Gandarai of Ptolemy or Gandaraei of *Periplus,* sec. 47). The people inhabiting the city have been called Peukalensians or Peukalei (transcript of Pāli Pukkala) by Dionysios Periegetes.[387] According to Arrian, it was a fortified, very large, populous and prosperous city, seated not far from the river Indus.[388] It was indeed a splendid structure of magnificent size. In early times, it was a great emporium of commerce.[389] It was also a centre of Buddhism. At the time of Alexander's expedition it was the capital of a chief or king named Astes (Hāsti).[390] This city was also named after him Hāstinagara or Hashtnagar. As stated by Arrian, the city was captured after a siege of thirty days by Hephaestion and its chief was killed in the defence of one of his strongholds. His successor Sangaeus (Skt. Sañjay) was then allowed by Alexander to become governor (Hyparch) of the city.[391]

The Peucolaitae of Megasthenes *(Indika,* Fragm. LVI, *AIMA,* 1st edn., p. 151) probably stands for the dwellers of Puṣkalāvatī city.

The city, Peukolaitis, belonged to the people called Astakenians or Astakenoil[392] (Hāstināyana of Pāṇini, *sūtra* VI, 4, 174).[393] They along with other indigenous tribes of Gāndhāra like Aspasioi, Assakanos, etc., have been placed by both Arrian[394] and Strabo[395] in the regions between the river Kophes and the Indus. Ptolemy has correctly fixed the position of the city on the eastern bank of the river Suastene or Swāt.[396] According to archaeological and other evidence, modern Parang and Chārasadda, situated 17 miles to the north-east or north-west of Peśāwar (Purūśapura) near the junction of the river Swāt with the Kābul, preserve the vestiges of the ancient city of Puṣkalāvatī.[397] The two large towns of Parang and Chārasadda are said to have formed part of Aṣṭanagar or eight cities, that are seated close together on the eastern bank of the lower Swāt river now called the Landai. The other six towns are Tangi, Shirpao, Umrzai, Turangzai, Usmanzai and Rajur[398] for which we do not have equivalent words in the classical sources. The rulers of all the eight cities together inclusive of Astes were called Aṣṭakarāja. Puṣkala is still represented by the modern Pakholi in the neighbourhood of Peshawar. The remains of Puśkalāvatī city in the vicinity of above-mentioned two large towns constitute the mute evidence to its glorious past.

Court placed the fort of Hisār standing on a mound above the ruins of the old town of Hashtnagar opposite Rajur.[399] "All the suburbs", he says, "are scattered over with vast ruins".[400] The archaeological excavation carried out at Chārasadda in 1958-59 under the guidance of Sir Mortimer Wheeler also testifies to the existence of a group of small towns there. Bala-Hisar (high fort) was first occupied by the Persian in the latter half of the sixth century BCE. The site is said to be a memorial to the Pax-Persica. To the east of it a line of rampart was unearthed, which represents the part of the town besieged by the troops of Alexander. The excavations at the different site of Gāndhāra have brought to light a radical change in the town-planning in the second century BCE after the establishment of the rule of the Indo-or Bactrian Greeks. They abandoned the old site (Bala-Hisar) and rebuilt a new city as Shaikhan (at Puśkalāvatī) in conformity with the Graeco-Parthian plan.[401] However, the popularity of the ancient city of Puṣkalāvatī did not decline till the dawn of the seventh century. Hiuen Tsang found this city, which he calls *Pu-se-ka-lo-fa-ti,* in a flourishing condition. It was about fourteen or fifteen *li* (1 *yojana* = 8 miles or 4 *krosas*) in circuit, well peopled and decorated with gates, temples, etc,[402] whereas, on the other hand, in *Pu-lu-sha-pu-lo* (Purūṣapura) he found that the royal family was extinct, the towns were desolate and the inhabitants were very few.[403] Puṣkalāvatī had all the characteristic features of an urban centre in the latter half of the first millennium BCE in NBPW phase. It was an administrative, religious and commercial centre which led to its growth as a city. It remained an urban centre till the end of the Gupta rule. It began to decline from about the middle of the seventh century onwards.

Various small towns in the lower Kābul valley or those lying between Puṣkalāvatī and the Indus were occupied by Alexander with the help of two local chiefs named Kophaios (or Cophaeus) and Assagetes (Aśvajit).[404] The former was the king of the region about Puṣkala near the Kophen and the latter the king of the Assakenoi (successor of the king killed in Massaga).[405]

In very early times, the frontier of the kingdom of Gāndhāra extended even to the country east of the Indus, where was situated its famous eastern capital called by the Greeks Taxila (Skt. Takṣaśilā = Pāli Takkasilā, or Takhasilā, as found in a copper-plate inscription,[406] = Takṣaśilā of Pāṇini, iv, 3, 93). This great capital was, no doubt, one of the most ancient cities of India. It was built of the material like most other cities of India. According to the Purāṇic evidence (*Vy*., 88. 188-91), it was named after Takṣa, the son of Bharat. The name of the city is generally taken to mean either "the Rock of the Takkas", the tribes, or "the Rock of Takṣaka", the great Nāga king. It also means the hewn stone or cut rock. Pomponius Mela in his *De Chorographia*, a Compendium of Geography (iii, 7), written about CE 42, had rightly pointed out that various legends were invented to account for the name. It is stated that "The Takkas, a Turanian race, the earliest inhabitants of Rawalpindi District gave their name to the town of Takshaśilā or Taxila".[407]

The classical writers are unanimous in their accounts of the position, size and wealth of Taxila. Aristoboulos (who accompanied Alexander on his eastern expedition and wrote a history of his wars) was the first to mention it as "the great city".[408] Megasthenes was the next to state that Taxila was a famous city of the Taxillae *(Indika,* Fragm LVI), which was visited by Alexander the Great. According to Strabo, "Taxila, a large city between the Indus and the Hydaspes, was governed by good laws. The surrounding country was densely populated and extremely fertile".[409] Arrian describes it as the most populous, wealthy and flourishing city. It was, according to him, the capital of Taxiles. He further adds that it was the greatest of all Indian cities, which lay between the Indus and the Hydaspes."[410] As a city it was indisputably unequalled in whole northern India. Plutarch observes: "Taxiles ruled over a part of India (Taxila) which was as large as Egypt".[411] But Strabo says that according to some, it "was larger than Egypt".[412] Pliny calls it "a famous city" of Amanda (Gāndhāra), which, according to him, was situated in a level country where the hills unite with the plains. It was, according to him, Capital of Taxillae people who were to the east of the Indus.[413] According to Diodorus Siculus, the region, which was well watered by rivers and highly renowned for its prosperous and happy condition, contained along with many other kingdoms the realm subject to Taxiles.[414] Julius Valerius has also recorded that Taxiles held sway over the vast dominions situated between the Indus and the Hydaspes.[415] The inhabitants of the city were known as "Taxilans", as stated by Dionysios periegetes.[416] And the dynastic title of the ruling class was Taxiles. Ptolemy has fixed the position of the city called "Taxiala" at 125^0 32 .15' between the Indus and the Bidespes (Hydaspes).[417] Pliny, citing Diognetos and Baeton, the perambulators or measurers of Alexander's marches, recorded that Taxila to the east of the Indus was only 60 Roman, or 55 English, miles distant from Peucolaitis or Hashtnagar to the west of the Indus, which would fix its site somewhere on the Haro river to the west of Hasan Abdal (in the Attock Dist.) or at just two days march from the Indus.[418] The actual distance between Puṣkalāvatī and Taxila, the two famous capital cities of the Gāndhāra kingdom, according to A. Cunningham, was 74 miles (English), 19 in excess of Pliny's estimate. But, according to the recent measurements, the distance from Chārasadda (the site of the ruins of Puṣkalāvatī) to Shah-ḍheri (the site of Taxila's ruins) is 80 miles. Cunningham, "the father of the Indian archaeology" undertook the excavations at Taxila in 1863-64 and 1872-73.

The great city of Taxila has a chequered history. In order to get a very graphic picture of this city within a chronological framework, we have combinded the classical and archaeological evidence together. It is worthy of note that the site has been extensively excavated by several excavators between 1913 and 1950. These excavations have brought to light the existence of a. number of ancient cities built at or near Taxila between the sixth century BCE and the first century CE Sir John Marshall has presented an illustrative account of archaeological excavations carried out at the site for over two decades at regular interval between 1913 and 1934. The vast ruins of Taxila bespeak its past glory as a city.

Cunningham was the first archaeologist to discover the ruins of the city Taxlia, described by the classical writers concerned. He found the ruins of this ancient city in the vicinity of Shāh-ḍherī, just one mile to the north-east of a town called Kāla-kā-Sarāi (between Attock and Rāwalpiṇḍī), or at the distance of a three-days' journey to the east of the Indus. The extensive ruins of a fortified city abounding with *stūpas,* monasteries, temples, etc., are scattered over a wide space extending about three miles from north to south, and two miles from east to west. They lie about eight miles to the south-east of Hasan Abdal and about twenty-two miles north-west of Rāwalpiṇḍī in northern Punjab.[419] The ruins of the city indicate its size and show its past glory. The discovery of these ruins and their identification as those of Taxila is one of the great services which Cunningham has rendered to the cause of Indian archaeology. Excavations have shown that the Bhir mound on the west side towards the rock-seated village of Shāh-ḍheri was the most ancient of all the urban sites at Taxila. In fact, it stands for a small village of Bir or Bhir which stands on the great mound. Through the midst of the ruins flows a stream called the Tabrā or Tamrā Nālā, which is identical with a river called variously in different MSS of the *Pseudo-Kallisthenes* the Tiberoboam, Tibernābon, etc. Here we have some idea of town-planning in ancient India. According to Cunningham, "The remains of the walls can be traced only in a few places both on the east and west sides; but the whole surface is covered with broken stones and fragments of bricks and pottery".[420] Haitāl – a strong fortified position – is immediately to the north-east of the Bhir Mound. Sir John Marshall, one of the excavators of the site, says that till 326 BCE "the town had no architecture worthy of the name. With rare exceptions its buildings were a rambling conglomeration of ill-aligned and ill-built walls of plastered rubble resembling rather the slum of a poverty-stricken sub-urb than the central lay-out of a capital city. The only architectural feature . . . is the occasional use of untidy stone pedestals designed to carry wooden roof-posts".[421] The general culture of the city was of the same inferior order. Only at the end of the fourth century or shortly after the arrival of Alexander there was spectacular improvement. He further observes that before the arrival of the Indo-Greeks in the second century BCE the layout of the first city was irregular and haphazard. There were streets and lanes "... for the convenience of the traffic and other purposes, small open squares were provided. Further, to protect the corners of houses from damage by passing carts and chariots wheel-guards were set up by erecting rough stone pillars at the corners of building".[422] The houses were also irregular in plan, the principle underlying their design was of an open court with rooms on one or more sides. There were two such courts in well-to-do houses and they had probably more than one storey. The rooms were about fifteen to twenty in number. Their walls were mud-plastered and white-washed with lime and provided with wooden balconies and flat roofs".[423] There was also drainage system for the city. The earliest urban settlement at Bhir mound was little earlier than the invasion of the Persian king, Darius I (522-486 BCE). After the end of the Achaemenian rule over Taxila it probably attained independence.

Between the fifth and second century BCE this city was thrice destroyed and thrice rebuilt at higher levels. This was the site where the palace of the Taxiles was located. Beneath the Bhir mound lies the ruins of the old city which Alexander visited in 326 BCE.[424]

At the time of the Macedonian invasion, Taxila (the site of Bhir Mound) was a very rich and flourishing city, and it continued to be so for many centuries thereafter. The material prosperity of its people was reflected in the presents received by Alexander in 326 BCE from the king Āmbhi called Omphis by Curtius[425] and Mophis by Diodorus.[426] According to the former, "Taxiles presented Alexander and all his friends with golden crowns, together with eighty talents of coined silver, while Alexander not only returned to Taxiles the presents he had given, but added a thousand talents with many banqueting vessels of gold and silver, a vast quantity of Persian drapery…".[427] According to Arrian, the present sent by Taxiles to him consisted of 200 talents of silver.[428] We learn from Plutarch that it was Alexander who gave 1000 talents in coined money to Omphis. The archaeological discovery of several bent-bar silver coins of about 300 BCE from Bhir Mound[429] lends credence to the classical description of the subject. There is a striking similarity between the two. While establishing the link between the two, Allan has emphatically asserted that the presents consisted of silver bar coins, found in the Bhir Mound at Taxila.[430] Kallisthenes, who accompanied Alexander, has also remarked that Taxila was very populous and possessed of incredible wealth.[431] The king called Taxiles surrendered himself and his kingdom with its capital at Taxila unreservedly to the great conqueror in 326 BCE. In the third century BCE, it formed the part of the Maurya empire. The great Aśoka made it his place of residence while he held the vice-royalty of the Punjab during the lifetime of his father, Bindusāra (298-273 BCE). After the death of Aśoka, the great king Subhagasena (227-202 BCE) called Sophagasenus by Polybios[432] established his sway over Taxila. He has been wrongly identified with Jaloka (one of the Aśoka's sons)[433] or Samprati (Aśoka's grandson in the line of Kuṇāla).[434] He was most probably the descendant of Virasena of Gāndhāra who was the great grandson of Aśoka.[435] The importance of this city as an emporium of trade in the age of the Mauryas has been highlighted in the *Periplus*.[436] Its reputation as a centre of trade and as a seat of learning had already been established between the sixth and the fourth century BCE. It was also the seat of the government. These were the three primary factors which led to its growth as an urban centre in northern India.

In the early part of the second century BCE, Taxila became a province of the Graeco-Bactrian monarchy. The Bactrian Greeks laid the foundation of a new city at a site called Sirkap, which successively remained in occupation of the Greeks, the Scythians (Sacae or Śakas), the Parthians or Pahalavas and the Kuṣāṇas altogether for nearly three centuries during their rule. The new city of Sirkap was well fortified. It was defended on all sides – by the lofty citadel of Hatiāl on the south, by the Tamra Nālā on the west, and by the Gau-Nālā on the east and north sides. The streets and buildings were laid out by the Hellenistic town-planner on the typical Greek Chess-board pattern. Kacha-koṭ or the mud fort lies to the north of Sirkap.[437] The coins of the Greek rulers of Taxila[438] bear witness to their rule during the period concerned. In 126 BCE, this city was wrested from the Greeks by the Indo-Scythian Sus or Abars with whom it remained for about three quarters of a century. They in thier turn were dispossessed of it by another branch of the Śakas, Maues (Moa or Moga), who sometime between 20 BCE, and CE 22 established his sway over both Puṣkalāvatī and Takṣaśilā to the west and the east of the Indus respectively. His name figures in the Taxila copper-plate grant[439] as well as in the coins.[440] The Greek city originally built sometime between 183 and 175 BCE lay buried under the mound of Sirkap which has been thoroughly excavated but very little has been discovered from here. The city of Sirkap was remodelled by the Śaka-Parthians.

By the middle of the first century of the Christian era the rebuilt city of Sirkap reached the pinnacle of its glory. It was a well-planned city. This is the city which Apollonius of Tyana and his Assyrian companion, Damis, visited in CE 44 when it was under the rule of Phraotes, apparently a Parthian but an Indian King. After having crossed the river Indus they reached Taxila and stayed there for three days. They saw a city about the size of Nineveh (the great Assyrian capital city of by-gone ages), walled like a Greek town (Athens), and the residence of a sovereign (who ruled over what had formerly been the kingdom of Poros). Taxila, according to them, was the "greatest city in India". Outside the walls they found a beautiful temple of shell marble with a shrine and many columns. Round the shrine were hung pictures on copper tablets representing the feats of Alexander and Poros. The various figures were protrayed in a mosaic of Orichalcum, silver, gold and oxydized copper, but the weapons in iron. The metals were so ingeniously worked into one another that the picture which they formed were comparable to the productions of the most famous Greek artists. Apollonius waited in this temple till he was invited by the king Phraotes to enter the gates of the city and present himself at the palace.

There he was received by the king (who spoke Greek). They were taken to the palace, which was considerably large and well built. "It was no less magnificent an architecture and the male chamber and the porticos and the whole of the vestitute was very chaste in style." "The palace was, however, no distinguished by any superior splendour from the residence of the wealthier citizens, and within its precincts there were no trace of courtly pomp, no sentinels, no guards, and but very few attendants." They found the city divided by narrow streets and well arranged. It reminded Apollonius of Athens. He says that the city planning was Hellinistic in style. The houses were so connected that from outside they appeared to be a single storied but there were underground rooms equal in length to the chambers above. The large buildings and other dwelling houses pleased the travellers more than all the pomp of Babylon. They also saw the temple of the sun, which stood outside the walls of the city, and in it statues of Alexander and Poros, the one of gold and other of bronze. Its walls were of red marble, but glittering with gold, and the image of the god was of pearls. They also saw a temple in front of the wall about 100 ft in length and built of steel like stone. The above description of the city is based on the eye-witness accounts of the travellers, as recorded by Philostratos in his biographical work.[441] The said work is primarily based on the narrative of the journey preserved in the *Journal* of Damis, which is a trustworthy record of their visit to this city. The classical account of this city can be partly corroborated and supplemented by an archaeological evidence. John Marshall in the course of his excavation at the site also discovered some remains of almost identical nature. According to him also, the city was well-planned. The buildings were like that of the modern city of the Near and Middle East. There were streets with a row of shops. The private dwelling-houses of the citizens were small and single-storey structures. The large houses belonged to the rich. The royal palace was planned on a bigger scale and with more spacious courts and rooms. It was decorated with gates. Near the palace the houses were rather carefully planned and furnished with layer courts. There were separate houses for the governing classes living with attendants and slaves. There were houses for the soldiers who guarded the ramparts. He found it a walled city. It was adorned with shrines, temples and various other religious structures.[442] Some other monuments and antiquities of great historical and archaeological importance were also discovered by him. We find that a Kuṣāṇa king, identified with Wima Kadphises, occupied this city in CE 77 or 78.

In the first century of the Christian era, probably after CE 78, the celebrated Buddhist king Kaniṣka built another city at Taxila which is at present represented by the remains of Sir-Suk or Sir-Sukh. It remained under the sway of the Kuṣāṇas till the early third century. It was also a fortified city. But very little has been explored at this site. Cunningham, while providing the detailed description of Taxila, has concluded that each city built there including that of Sirkap and Sir-Suk was "nearly as large as Shah Jahan's imperial city of Delhi".[443] Some ruins of the city of Taxila especially massive walls of stone have also been found in the vicinity of Mānikyāla[444] at a distance of eight days journey from Hashtnagar or few miles away from Shāh-ḍherī. Bhir Mound, Sirkap and Sir-Sukh, the three important sites of urban settlements, formed parts of a large Taxila city. The city remained in existence from NBPW phase till its fall in early Gupta period.

The Taxila city was visited by the Chinese pilgrims Fa-hian in CE 400[445] and Hiuen Tsang in 630 and afterwards in 643. According to latter, the district of *Ta-cha-shi-lo* (Takṣaśilā or Taxila) was 2000 *li* (or 333 miles) in circuit and its capital above ten *li* in circuit. He did not find the city in a flourishing condition. The inhabitants were very few. The royal family had become extinguished.[446] It appears that between the sixth century BCE and the third century CE at least four to six cities were built here. Like Bāhlika, Kāpisī, Kābul and Bamian or Bamanpur this city also underwent metamorphosis. The history of north-west India is replete with several examples of destruction and construction of the cities at or near these sites. After the seventh century of the Christian era, the city, Taxila, disappears altogether from history, and we know neither how nor when its ruin was accomplished. However, we have every reason to believe that this city might have been destroyed by the Hūṇas in the fifth or sixth century of the Christian era, and was never re-built. The extensive ruins of this great city comprising all its different parts built at different periods of history now covers an area of more than six square miles.

H.D. Sankalia, while dealing with evlution of urban culture and antiquity of some towns and cities in north-west India, has expressed the view that both the cities, Takṣaśilā and Puruṣapura, had come into existence about 2300 years before from 1981.[447] But in absence of any corroborative evidence we can neither confirm nor deny it. Cunningham's statement that the mounds of ruins found in all directions in Afghanistan constitute the mute evidence of the existence of a number of flourishing towns there in ancient past[448] seems to be reliable. The impact of Persian and Hellenic urban tradition on the planning, patterns and designs of the towns and cities of the indigenous people of particularly Gāndhāra region during their contacts with them cannot be denied.

We would also like to examine the relevance of an identical statement of the two classical authors, Appollodoros (author of the *History of Parthia)*[449] and Justin.[450] According to them, Eukratides (one of the most powerful Greek monarchs of Bactria) conquered India and became "lord of a thousand cities, which acknowledged his authority." It is true that he occupied Bactria, the Kābul valley, Ariana (Arachosia and Aria), Kapiśa, Nicaea, Gāndhāra with its eastern capital at Taxila, and some other parts of western Punjab sometime between 181 or 175 and 160 BCE. But we are not in a position to ascertain the exact number of cities, which were in his possession. We very often come across such exaggerated statement in the classical sources.

The classical notices of Sangala, one of the principal cities in northern Punjab, are confined to the two historical accounts of Arrian and Curtius, and a passing mention by Diodorus. Curtius simply calls it "a great city defended not only by a wall but also by a swamp".[451] Arrian, while describing the city, observes that it was strong both by art and nature, being protected by brick walls and covered by the lake. It was adorned with the gates, rampart etc. There was a low hill close to the city walls,[452] which was possibly the abandoned mound of earlier cities. Diodorus has incidentally referred to the city without providing a description thereof.[453] This fortified city, according to them, was the capital of the Kathaians or Kathaeans (Skt. Kaṭhas), who belonged to the warrior class or ksatriya tribe. They were one of the independent tribes of Punjab. They inhabited the regions lying to the east of the Hydraotes. Some writers, however, as Strabo informs us, have placed the "Kathaia" in the tract between the two rivers, the Hydaspes and the Akesines,[454] but this view is manifestly wrong. According to the narrative of Arrian, their capital, Sangala, was situated between the Hydraotes and the Hyphasis, which is absolutely correct. It is on this basis that some authorities have placed this city in the Gurdaspur district (about 50 miles N.E. from Amritsar) not far from Fathgarh[455] and some at Jaṇḍiala to the east of Amritsar.[456] It is generally placed either near Lahore or between Lahore and Multān or in the Amritsar district.[457] It has not yet been ascertained where this city actually stood. But the Kathaians must have been situated to the east of the river Rāvī and may probably have been nearly if not altogether co-extensive with what we now call the districts of Lahore and Amritsar. C. Masson has proposed "Haripa" (Harappā), which was quite close to the Rāvī, as the site of Sangala.[458] The topographical features of the place, the hill or rising ground and a swamp with the remains of a brick fort, suit very well with the description of Arrian. It is said to have been the site of a very extensive and ancient town. It is very difficult to determine the exact location of the city which was attacked and destroyed by Alexander's troops. At the time of Alexander's invasion, it was, no doubt, a large city with more than 12,000 populations. The administration of the city was controlled by them and not by any king or chief. According to Arrian, 17,000 Kathaeans defended their city, while it was stormed by the Macedonians. They all lost their lives and the city was razed to the ground.[459]

Pāṇini's Sānkala *(Gaṇa-Pāṭha,* IV, 2, 75),[460] according to the laws of transcription, has been identified with Sangala of the Greeks.[461]

The Sagala of Ptolemy's *Geography* (VII, 1, 46)[462] orresponds exactly with the Sanskrit Śākala (as mentioned in the *Mahābhārata* and the Purāṇas) and the Pāli Sāgala, a city of great note in ancient times. It was situated between the rivers Hydraotes and the Akesines. It occupied the district of Siālkoṭ Saint Martin takes it as royal city in the north of India.[463] Here it must be made specifically clear that it was situated to the west of the Hydraotes,[464] and Sangala on the east bank of that river.[465] Some Savants regardless of the laws of transcription have attempted to establish the identity of both,[466] but the fact remains that they were two different cities in two different directions of two different periods.

Cunningham has also mistakenly taken Sangala of the classical writers and Śākala of the *Brāhmaṇas,* Sāgala of the Buddhists or Sagala of Ptolemy as identical.[467] But this identification is no longer tenable. There are some reasons, mainly philological, which go against his hypothesis. He found a site for the city concerned at Sangalawala-Tiba, a small rocky hill or Sangala Hill (in the Jhang district) with ruins upon it and a large swamp at its base, situated between the Rāvī and the Cenāb at a distance of about sixty miles to the west of the former river or Lahore. On the north-eastern side of the hill he found the remains of two large buildings. He found the plain on the north and west sides of the hill strewn with broken pottery and fragments of brick gathering the impression that the town once must have extended in both of those directions. The remains covered an area of about 1½ miles.[468] However, this could not have been the site of the Grecian Sangala, because all the historians place that city between the Rāvī and the "Beas". It was probably the site of Śākala or Sāgala[469] in Central Punjab. As regards the settlement of this important site, question has lately been considerably advanced by the researches undertaken by the Punjab Government at Sanglawala-Tiba with the positive result of showing that no such large fortified city as Sangala could have ever existed there.

Ptolemy's Sagala, Pāli Sāgala or Śākala of Sanskrit writers roughly corresponds to the modern Siālkoṭ and the surrounding regions between the Rāvī and the Cenāb. It was situated to the west of the Hydraotes or Rāvī at a distance of about sixty miles from Lahore. It was the capital of the Madras.[470] It is believed that the city passed under the sway of Alexander in 326 BCE who placed it under the Satrap of the adjacent territory between the Jhelum and the Cenāb. One of the Greek kings, Euthydemos (220-190 BCE), the founder of the greatness of the Baktrian kingdom, held eastern Punjab with its capital at Śākala (Siālkoṭ), and the city was thereafter named after him as Euthydemia. This is the city called by Nonnos "Euthydimeia".[471] We do not have any positive evidence to prove the historical authenticity of the conventional statement that his son Demetrios (190-165 BCE) rebuilt the city, having been destroyed by the Macedonians, and called it Euthydemia in honour of his father Euthydemos.[472] It has also been rejected by Tarn on both historical and textual grounds.[473] But we have positive proof to show that it became the capital of the most famous Indo-Greek ruler, Menander or Milinda (165-145 BCE).[474] This city, situated in a delightful country, well watered and hilly, abounding in parks and gardens, groves and lakes, tanks, well-laid out streets, cross-roads and market-complex, wore a beautiful look. It was adorned with splendid and magnificent buildings, various strong towers and ramparts, defensive walls, superb gates, entrance archways and with the royal citadel in its midst, white-walled and deeply moated. It was crowded with peoples of all castes, brāhmaṇas, kṣatriyas or nobles, vaiśyas or traders and śūdras or servants, and the leading men of each of the different sects. It was a great centre of trade end commerce. The shops were filled with innumerable sorts of costly merchandise. There were some shops for the sale of Benares muslin, other clothes of various kinds, jewels and other costly articles. The guilds of traders displayed their goods in the bazaars. The city was full of money, and of gold and silverware, of copper and stoneware, indicating its wealth and prosperity.[475] Later, in the early part of the sixth century of the Christian era, it became the capital of the Hūṇa conqueror, Mihirakula, who not only destroyed it but also subdued all the neighbouring provinces. In CE 630, Hiuen Tsang found the walls of the city called *She-kie-lo* (Śākala) completely ruined, but their foundations still remained, showing a circuit of about 20 *li* or 3 ½ miles. In the midst of the ruins he saw a small portion of an inhabited old city, which was only 6 or 7 li or just one mile in circuit. He also found the other neighbouring towns in dilapidated condition.[476]

After having investigated all the available sources we find that the Greek writers' Sangala identical with Sāṇkala of Pāṇini was different from Śākala or Sāgala. The former was situated between the Rāvī and the "Beas" and the latter between Rāvī and the Cenāb. The former was situated to the east and the latter to the west of the Rāvī.

The city of Pimprama, situated on the eastern side of the Hydraotes, according to Arrian,[477] Diodorus[478] and Justin,[479] belonged to Adraistai called by Ptolemy Adraistoi or Adeisathra[480] (Araṭṭas, Adhṛṣṭas, or Aristas of Pāṇini, VI, 2, 100; *Gaṇa-Pāṭha,* IV, 2, 80) who were independent tribes not being subject to authority of any king. The city was located in sub-urban area, which was not well-equipped with all necessary paraphernalia of urbanism. It was eight leagues or *yojana* distant from Lahore towards the south-east. After it was captured by Alexander, the inhabitants deserted it which gradually led to its decadence. Some more important towns or cities of northern Punjab are described below.

Strabo affirms that the dominions of the great Porus confined between the Hydaspes and Akesines – an extensive and fertile tract (not more than forty miles in width) – contained about 300 cities.[481] Their exact number cannot be determined with any amount of certainty. However, it cannot be denied that at the time of Alexander's invasion numerous towns existed within the limits of the kingdom of Porus the details of which are, of course, wanting in the classics with few exceptions. In other sources as well, the details of only a few towns of the contemporary peroid are available.

One of the principal towns called the town of Jhelum is said to have been "situated on the west bank of that river, 30 miles to the north-east of modern Jalālpur, and exactly 100 miles to the north-west of Lahore. The remains of the old towns consist of a large ruined mound to the west of the present city, about 1300 feet square and 30 feet high, which is surrounded by fields covered with broken bricks and pottery".[482] The city remained in existence even later than the first century BCE. The ancient Girjak or Girivraja, the capital of Kekaya kingdom, which very much formed the part of the dominion of Porus, can also be taken as one of the cities of that time. This name remained in use until the time of Akbar when it was changed to Jalālpur. This town is situated on the west bank of the Jhelum at the point where the Kandar ravine joins the old bed of the river. Cunningham has observed that "the town might formerly have been about three or four times its present size".[483] He has identified Girjak with the remains of walls on the top of the Mangal-De hill, which rises 1100 feet above Jalālpur. He says that "there is no doubt that the city did once extend to the westward for some considerable distance, as the ground on that side is thickly strewn with broken pottery for about half a mile. Its antiquity is undoubted, as the coins which it yields reach back to the times of Alexander's successors. But . . . it is much older; as its favourable position at the south-east end of the lower road would certainly have led to its occupation at a very early period".[484]

The ruined city near Dārāpur (ancient Udamnagar or Udinagar) is said to have been situated on the west bank of the river, 20 miles below Jhelum, and 10 miles above Jalālpur.[485] Court, while including these ruins under that of Gagirakhi (Gir-Jhāk or Girjak), observed that they extended along the banks "of the Hydaspes from near Jalalpur to Darapur".[486] According to this account, the ruins covered an area of not less than 6 or 7 miles in length. Cunningham identified Girjhāk with an old ruined fort on the top of the hill to the north of Jalalpur, about 8 miles from Dārāpur.[487] Burnes also describes the old city as extending "for three or four miles".[488] It is said that "the ruins consist of two large mounds just half a mile apart, with two smaller mounds about midway between them". On the south, mound Dilāwar (Udinagar) is situated, and on the north, mound old Dārāpur stands. Between these mounds the fields are covered with broken bricks and pottery, and the whole place is said to be the ruins of a single city.[489] Many old coins including those of Indo-Scythians have been collected from the site, which must have been reoccupied in the post-Alexandrian period as early as the second century before the Christian era. The headquarters of Porus must have been about Muhābatpur, 4 miles to the south-west of present town of Mong and 3 miles to the south-west of modern Jalālpur.

We learn from Strabo,[490] Arrian,[491] Megasthenes and Pliny,[492] Diodorus,[493] Justin[494] and Plutarch[495] that Alexander after having crowned himself with victory in the battle with Porus built two memorable cities – one called Boukephala, Boukephalia or Boukephalas and the other Nikaea or Nikaia, a "city of victory". The former was built on the western bank of the Hydaspes in memory of his horse and the latter on its eastern bank, the site of the battle, in commemoration of his victory. According to some reliable evidences, either Jalālpur or Dilāwar at the distance of 10 miles from each other was the site of the first city. Jalālpur is said to be 30 miles higher up the river Jhelum. The second city is now represented by Mong (founded by Rājā Moga), 6 miles to the east of Jalāpur or at the same distance to the south of Dilāwar. If the two cities were built on the same plan, which is not improbable, then Dilāwar would have the preferable claim to represent the first city, as its ruined mound is of the same size and height as that of Mong. It may be added here that the battlefield was near Pakral, about 3 miles to the north of Sukchenpur.[496] The absence of details of the monolithic structure of the said two cities in the classics raises doubts in our mind about their construction by Alexander himself. The original sites of the cities of indigenous origin might have received new names in a Hellenised form which was not very unusual at the time of Alexander's invasion. Some rudimentary walls were, of course, erected on the Hydaspes by his army to mark the new cities. The possibility that Bugiād or Bugiāl, the name of the district in which Dilāwar is situated, might have been transformed with new Greek name, Boukephala, cannot be precluded. This Greek city can also be identified without much hesitation with the modern town of Jhelum. The new cities, however, rose into prominence and seem to have flourished for centuries. The author of the *Periplus* refers to the first city as Bucephalus Alexandria also called Boukephalos Alexandreia (sec. 47). Schoff, the translator and annotator of the text, has correctly stated that "Its position is marked by an extensive mound west of the present settlements. The mound is known as Pindi, the town, and yields large ancient bricks and numerous Graeco-Bactrian coins. Its position at a ferry on the high-road from the west to the Indian interior gave it great commercial importance".[497] Here have been found some old coins, but not earlier than those of the Indo-Scythian period, and three iron tripods of Greek firms. Ptolemy in his *Geography* (VII, I, 46) has also located it at the Jhelum (Bidespes) and highlighted its importance.

Nonnos has also mentioned Nicaea[498] as a city founded by Alexander. According to Pliny (VI, 21), it was the "chief of three cities which belonged to the Asini" (or Asene, one of the Indian tribes).

The total urban population of the dominions of Poros (also called Porus) on the basis of available indications could be estimated not less than fifty thousand. From the accounts of Arrian (*Anab.*, V, 18) and Diodorus *(Bib. Hist.,* XVII, 89) it appears that more than twenty thousand people lost their lives in the battle of Porus with Alexander.

An older native town on the bank of Akesines was rebuilt and fortified on Hellenic principles (Arrian, *Anab.,* V, 29, 3) where Wazīrābād now stands from where one road goes to Jalālpur and other to Jhelum. It is known as sixth Alexandria.[499]

According to Arrian, a large tract lying to the west of the Akesines and coterminous with the dominion of Porus included as many as thirty-seven towns, "the smallest of which contained not fewer than 5,000 inhabitants while many contained upwards of 10,000".[500] These belonged to the free tribe called Glaukanikoi by Arrian and Aristoboulos and Glausai by Ptolemy. They have been identified with Glaucukāyanakas of the *Kāśikā* on Pāṇini (IV. 3, 99).[501] It is said that their territories were situated in the fertile and densely populated regions lying in the south of Kāśmir (the Bhimber and Rajauri districts) between the upper courses of Jhelum and the Cenāb and the Rāvī.[502] From the statement of Arrian it is quite evident that the towns were both small and large. He says *(Anab.,* V, 20, 21) that Alexander took them and handed over to Porus thereby adding much to what he had before possessed. R.S. Sharma (*APIAI*, p. 225) has rightly pointed out that urbanism was an important element in the state of Elder Poros and in that of a people called Glauganikai, whose tract lay to the west of the Chenab and bordered the dominion of Poros.

Strabo deriving his authority from previous writers (names not mentioned) has categorically stated that "the Macedonians conquered nine nations situated between the Hydaspes and Hypanis (generally called in the classics the Hyphasis), and possessed 5,000 cities not one of which was less than Kos Meropis (or simply Kos) and that Alexander after having reduced all this country delievered it over to Poros".[503] But Strabo himself says that "the number seems to be exaggerated".[504] Pliny's statement based on the writings of the companions and historians of Alexander the Great exactly tallies with that of Strabo with regard to the number of nations and their towns, which were subdued by the Macedonians.[505] Apollodorus states that there were 1500 cities between the Hydaspes and Hypanis.[506] Arrian has also postulated that seven nations in all (seven territorial units of the Punjab) conquered by Alexander contained more than 2,000 (two thousand) towns.[507] V.A. Smith has supported this number without assigning any valid reason therefor.[508] Plutarch refers to 5,000 cities.[509] These figures are obviously imaginative, fabricated and factually incorrect. The number of towns, i.e., "5,000", as specified by Strabo, Pliny and Plutarch, is evidently a mistake for "500", which can be authenticated by the statment of McCrindle.[510]

It is worthy of remark that the historians of Alexander presented a distorted and magnified picture of the subject with reference to the number of towns or cities in the Punjab only to glorify his deeds. Bunbury has also pointed out that "the Greeks were misled by the exaggerated reports so common with all orientalists, and so greedily swallowed by the historians of Alexander with a view of magnifying the exploits of the great conqueror".[511] However, it is a fact to be reckoned with that the so-called seven or nine nations (territorial units) lying between Hydaspes and Hyphasis contained some considerable cities whatever their number may be. Alexander after having subjugated all the territories concerned returned them along with the towns to Porus in presence of all the ambassadors or representatives of the people who assembled after his defeat, and thus he not only reinstated him in his kingdom but also added a large province to it in honour of his valour he displayed. As a matter of fact the vanquished Porus was restored to his sovereignty through the clemency of victorious Alexander. The above statement can be confirmed by the unanimous testimony of Plutarch *(Life of Alex.* Ch. LX), Justin *(Hist. Phil.,* XII, 8), Arrian *(Anab.,* VI, 2) and Onesikritos, one of the companions of Alexander.

Here it must be made clear that the towns, which are said to have been delivered by Alexander to Porus, not only included those of lying between the Jhelum and the "Beas", and between the Jhelum and the Cenāb (the territory of Porus), but also those which belonged to the Kathaioi, Glausai and other independent tribes of northern Punjab. These towns seem to have flourished for centuries as centres of urban culture. The period and causes of their decay are not known to us. Many other flourishing and prosperous villages which were no less populous than the towns are also included in the figures shown above. The towns enumerated, particularly by the Greek writers, actually comprise both the urban and semi-urban areas. And sometimes it becomes difficult to distinguish between the two. In fact, the classical concept of a town or city was totally different from that of modern time.

The capital of Sophites, Sopeithes or Sophytes (Saubhūta of Pāṇini, *Gaṇa Pātha,* IV, 2, 67 and 75, or Saubhūti), one of the petty kings of the western Punjab, according to Arrian, was situated on the left or eastern bank of the Hydaspes or on its opposite bank,[512] which Cunningham has identified with an ancient city whose ruins in the form of an extensive mound lay in the neighbourhood of Ahmedabad or at Jobnāthanagar at some distance from Nikaea or Mong where Alexander defeated Porus.[513] Thus, it was very close to the kingdom of Porus. It was a semi-urban centre. Strabo has placed his dominion in the tract between the two rivers, the Hydaspes and Akesines.[514] But Curtius has located it on the west of the Hyphasis.[515] It seems that there is no agreement among the classical authors with regard to the position of the kingdom and its capital, which belonged to an independent sovereign called Sopeithes. However, we learn from Diodorus[516] and Curtius[517] that his cities were governed by the good laws in highest degree with admirable political system. He struck coins in 305 BCE with his name in Hellenised form, "Sophutes" or "Sophutou", which is a transliteration of Saubhūta.[518] The inscribed silver coins concerned, according to R.B. Whitehead,[519] do not belong to him. But his view is not acceptable. It may be added here that the capital city remained in excellent state of preservation till much later date. We do not have any definite information about its destruction.

The two of the famous ancient cities in the Punjab were Labokla and Amakatis or Amakapis, as mentioned by Ptolemy.[520] The identification of the first one (also known as Lohawar) with the great city of Lahore was first made in Kiepert's *Map of India,* as stated by Lassen.[521] It has since been confirmed by the researches of T.H. Thornton, the author of the *History and Antiquities of Lahor.* This is the city which has been the capital of the Western Punjab for nearly one thousand years. The second one has been placed by Ptolemy himself to the west of the Hydraotes or Rāvī, and in the immediate neighbourhood of Labokla or Lahore.

The town called Ambakapi or Amakatis is actually represented by the two ruined mounds known as Amba and Kapi. The mound of Amba lies upwards of 9 miles to the south of Shekohpura. It is said to be "900 feet-square, and from 25 to 30 feet in height; but as the whole of the surrounding fields, for a breadth of about 600 feet, are covered with broken pottery, the full extent of the ancient town may be taken at not less than 8000 feet, or upwards of 3 miles in circuit. The mound itself is covered with broken bricks of large size", amongst which Cunningham discovered several pieces of carved brick. He also found one piece of grey sandstone, and piece of speckled iron ore, similar to that of Sangala.[522] The distance of the mounds from Lahore is about 25 miles. According to the local tradition, the town was founded by Raja Amba about two thousand years ago or just about the beginning of the Christian era which synchronises with the rule of the Indo-Scythians and the Pārthians or Pahalavas in the Pubjab. The small mound of Kapi is 2½ miles to the east of Amba on the old high-road to Lahore. Ptolemy's Daidala can be identified with Depālpur, which was on the Sutlej to the south of Labokla and Amakatis.

The Sibis (Skt. Śivis) called Sibae by Megasthenes[523] and Ptolemy,[524] Sibai by Arrian,[525] Strabo,[526] Dionysios Periegetes[527] and Nonnos,[528] Sobii by Curtius,[529] and Siboi by Diodorus[530] and Justin,[531] inhabited a district between the Hydaspes and the Indus and their capital stood at a distance of about thirty miles from the former river, or, as appears from Diodorus, at some distance above its confluence with the Akesines.[532] According to Curtius, they occupied the region between the Hydaspes and Akesines. Arrian locates them between the Indus and the Akesines. Their territories were actually situated to the west of the Cenāb below its junction with the Jhelum. They were free tribes numbering about fifty to sixty thousand.

According to an epigraphic evidence, they were the inhabitants of Shorkot region in the Jhang district lying between the Rāvī and the Cenāb in the central Punjab, and the ancient name of their capital was Śibipura,[533] which is identical with Śivapur of Patāñjali *(Mahābhāṣya,* IV, 2, 2). Ariṣṭapura of Pāṇini *(Sūtra,* VI, 2. I00),[534] Pāli Ariṭṭhapura or Aristobothra of Ptolemy may be another city.

A huge mound of ruins of Shorkot marks the site of the chief city or town called Śibipura. It was visited by Burnes, who describes the place as "a mound of earth, surrounded by a brick wall, and so high as to be seen for a circuit of six or eight miles".[535] He adds that it is much larger than Sehwan (a city of Sindh which I have described here separately along with other cities of that region). According to the measurement of De la Hoste, "it is 1200 feet long, by 750 feet broad".[536] The presence of a wall of large-sized bricks, irrefutably, proves the high antiquity of the urban settlement at this place. It is much smaller but loftier than Harappā. Burnes assigns its downfall to Alexander himself. But we find that it was enlarged and strengthened by Philip whom Alexander left behind as governor of the Oxydrakae and Malli. Shorkot was in the direct line of Alexander's route, from the junction of the Hydaspes and Akesines to the capital of the Malli. Shorkot may be the "Alexanderia Soriane" of Stephanus Byzantinus. The antiquity of Shorkot may be ascertained approximately by the coins which have been found in its ruins. A single copper piece of Apollodotus was obtained by Burnes. It leads us to warrant the belief that the town must have been reoccupied by the Greek kings of Ariana and the Punjab. It was in the flourishing state during the sway of the Indo-Scythians which can by evidenced from the discovery of their copper coins in large numbers. It continued to thrive from 126 BCE down to CE 250, or perhaps later. The local tradition relates that this town had been destroyed by some king of the westward, about 1400 years ago. We can, thus, attribute its destruction to the White Hūṇas who must have entered the Punjab from the westward during the sixth century CE. But the discovery of some coins of the brāhmaṇa kings of the Kābul valley and the Punjab leads us to surmise that the place was either deserted thereafter or remained in a very decayed state for sometime and it was again occupied by one of these brāhmaṇa kings in the tenth centurry.

One of the free tribes called by the historians of Alexander the Malli or Malloi (Mālavas) occupied an extensive territory situated between the lower Hydraotes and the Akesines. Their territories as a whole not only comprehended the modern Doāb of the Rāvī and Cenāb but also extended to the junction of thc Indus and the Akesines. They occupied the fertile valley of the lower Hydraotes on both sides of the river. They also inhabited the lower reaches of the Indus. Thus, their dominions comprised the greater part of the modern Multan district and some parts of the Montgomery and Jhang districts. They had in their possession several fortified towns besides their capital city, and they were all densely populated. Their towns were mostly situated on the north of the confluence of the Hydraotes and Akesines and the capital to its south.[537] Their towns or cities were situated both along the Cenāb and the Rāvī in the central and southern Punjab.

Here mention may first be made of those towns which were located in the central Punjab. Their first city, according to Arrian, was 400 stadia (or 46 miles) distant from the Akesines. He described it as a walled city with a castle or citadel which was captured by assault by Alexander in his campaign against the Malli.[538] Curtius *(Hist. of Alex.,* IX, 4, 10) places it at 250 stadia, or 28 3/4 miles from the junction of the Hydaspes and Akesines. It is identified with Koṭ Kamāliā, a small but ancient town situated on an isolated mound on the right or northern bank of the Rāvī. It is 44 miles to the south-east of the junction of the Hydaspes and Akesines, and 35 miles to the east or south-east of Shorkot. It possesses an ancient mound of burnt brick ruins. It owes it origin to the Malli tribe which still exists in this part of the country.[539]

Arrian relates that there was "another city of Malli, into which a great body of Indians had fled for safety".[540] When Alexander despatched Perdik as to blockade the city, its inhabitants deserted the place and took refuge in the neighbouring marshes near the Rāvī. This town has been identified with Harappā, which is situated 16 miles to the east-south-east of Koṭ Kamāliā, and on the opposite high bank of the Rāvī.[541] The great mass of ruins is on the western side, where the mound rises to 60 feet in height in the centre. At this point there are several massive walls built of large bricks, which are, no doubt, the remains of some extensive building.[542] Burnes estimated the extent of the ruins as "about three miles in circumference"...[543] But this comprises only the remains of the walled town. Masson, relying on the tradition, recorded that Harappā once extended on the west as far as Chichawatni, a distance of 12 miles, which confirms the belief of the people as to the former site and importance of their town.[544] Saint Martin's identification of the "Mallian capital" with Harappā[545] seems to be absolutely baseless. Tradition attributes the destruction of both Koṭ Kamāliā and Harappā to the western king of the sixth century, i.e. the White Hūṇas who overthrew Shorkot. The coins found in the ruins of Harappā are similar to those discovered at Shorkot.

Thus, all these towns must have experienced the same fortune. Harappā remained uninhabited for several centuries.

Arrian refers to a "town well fortified both by the art and nature" *(Anab.,* VI, 3), the art being the brick walls, and the nature, the enormous mounds of earthen ramparts. This is the town which he perhaps includes into the "strongest cities" *(ibid.,* VI, 4). Curtius' account, that on the bank of the Rāvī there was a strong fort *(Hist. of Alex.* IX, 4, 10), agrees with that of Arrian. It was one of the towns of the Malli which was captured by Alexander. This town was first identified by Rennell with the present town of Toulumba or Tulamba (in the southern Punjab). He adds that it was on the opposite side of the Cenāb in the neighbourhood of the Malloi.[546] Cunningham has also identified it with the same town which, according to him, is situated on the left bank of the Rāvī, at a distance of about 52 miles to the north-east of Multan. He says, `The antiquity of Tulamba is vouched for by tradition, and by the large size of the bricks, which are similar to the oldest in the walls and ruins of Multān..."[547] Masson has suggested that it represents either "the capital of the Malli or the fort held by Brāhmaṇs, whose defence was so obstinate and so fatal to themselves, and which was evidently contiguous to the capital of the Malli".[548]

Arrian *(Aanb.,* VI, 7*)* specifically makes a mention of the strongly fortified "city of the Brachmans (brāhmaṇas)" in the territory of the Malloi, which was captured by Alexander in his campaign against the latter. The Garrison "abandoned the city and fled to the castle" which being stormed they set fire to their houses, and perished in the flames. Several thousands of the brāhmaṇa population lost their lives. Curtius *(Hist. of Alex.,* IX, 4*)* and Diodorus *(Bib. Hist.,* XVII, 98-99*)* have also presented very faithful accounts of the city of the brāhmaṇas with special reference to the loss of the human lives. It is said that there were two towns of the brāhmaṇas near the Rāvī, which were taken by Alexander, and some of the occupants burnt themselves out of panic and consternation.[549] Arrian's city of the brāhmaṇas has been identified with the old ruined town and fort of Atari (in the southern Punjab) which is situated at the distance of 20 miles to the west-south-west of Tulamba and 34 miles to the north-east of Multān. "The remains consist of a strong citadel 750 feet square and 35 feet high with a ditch all round it, and a tower in the centre 50 feet high. On two sides are the remains of the town forming a mound 20 feet high, and 1200 feet square, the whole being a mass of ruin 1800 feet in length, and 1200 feet in breadth".[550] The large size of the bricks points to the high antiquity of the place.

Arrian quite separately refers to "the capital city of the Malli" where "many of the inhabitants of other cities had fled for their better security". He adds that it had the greatest number of defenders, 50,000, and it was the largest city, situated on the south of the confluence of the Hydraotes and the Akesines. Alexander after having captured and destroyed several towns, north and south of the Rāvī, came to this city.[551] It was not only the largest but also the "Strongest city".[552] Julius Valerius, while providing a picturesque description of this place, observes: "There was a city in India into which many had fled for refuge, -one that was of immense size and of impregnable strength".[553] It was surrounded by walls of great height. It had ramparts and gates. This is the city which Alexander besieged and brought its whole population to subjection. Strabo calls it "a small town of the Malloi in the capture of which Alexander received a wound".[554] From the narrative of Arrian (based on the account of Aristoboulos, the companion and historian of Alexander, and the materials supplied by Ptolemy, who accompanied Alexander) also it is quite evident that this "city belonged to the Malli".[555] Plutarch calls the inhabitants of the city both the Mallotes and the Malloi.[556] They also figure in the *Journal of Voyage* of Nearkhos, as described by Arrian in his *Indika* (pt. II, chs. XVIII, f).[557]

The famous metropolis of the Malloi has been identified with the ancient Mūlasthānapura or modern Multān (the capital of the southern Punjab), which in Alexander's time was situated at the distance of fifteen miles above the confluence of the Rāvī and the Cenāb. And now it is about thirty miles below the junction of that rivers, and about 34 miles from the brāhmaṇa city of Atari. In the first half of the second century of the Christian era, it was situated on the bank of the Rāvī, but now on the Cenāb perhaps because of the change of the course of the rivers concerned. Multan comprises nearly the same territories as those occupied by the Malloi of the Greek historians. This city owes its name to the Malloi.[558] Burnes, one of the chief protagonists of its identification with this place, has revealed that it is still called by the native people "Mallithān, the place of the Malli".[559] V.A. Smith does not accept this identification. He is of the view that this place has no etymological connection with the name Malloi. Their stronghold or the chief city, according to him, was "situated somewhere near the boundary of the Jhang and Motgomery Districts, 80 or 90 miles to the north-east of Multān".[560] But there are many other considerations in favour of its identification with the place shown above.

Cunningham, while firmly establishing the link of the Mallian capital with Multān, has stated that "… it consists of walled city and a strong fortress, situated on opposite banks of an old bed of the Rāvī ... The original site consisted of the low mounds not more than 8 or 10 feet high... It had 46 towers or bastions, including the two flanking towers at each of the four gates. The walled city, which envelops the citadel for more than two-thirds of the curve, is 4200 feet in length, and 2400 feet in breadth... Altogether the walled circuit of Multān, including both city and citadel, is 15,000 feet or very nearly 3 miles, and the whole circuit of the place, including its suburbs, is $4^{1/2}$ miles".[561] Thirlwall has also pointed out that the Malloi had numerous towns and cities with ramparts and fortresses.[562]

The capture of the capital of the Malloi at the hands of Alexander and his army[563] compelled its inhabitants to desert it and take refuge in the neighbouring area. It really marked the beginning of the decline of their city. According to Hiuen-Tsang, this place called *"Mou-lo-san-pu-lu"* (Mūlasthānapura) was 4000 *li* (or 667 miles) and its capital above 30 *li* (or just 5 miles) in circuit.[564] His evidence attests to the fact that the ancient name of the city remained in use till the first half of the seventh century. A few years after his visit, probably in the middle of that century, it was invaded and captured by brāhmaṇa *rājā* of Sindh named Chach. Subsequently, it was occupied by Muhammad bin Kasim in CE 713. The decline and fall of many towns and cities may be assigned to the Arabs who overran the whole of the lower Punjab.

Arrian not only refers to the cities of the Malloi but also to that of the Oxydrakai[565] (Kṣudrakas of Pāṇini, *Gaṇa-Pāṭha,* IV, 2, 45,[566] Pāli Khuddakas). Their name in the classics appears in various forms.[567] Arrian *(Indika,* pt. 1. ch. IV) places them on the Hydaspes above its confluence with the Akesines, and if this was their real position they must have been situated to the north of the Malloi. The same author places them (in other source, *Anab.,* VI, 4) between the Hydraotes and the Hyphasis. Bunbury has made it clear that a trace of third name may be found in that of Ooch, a principal city situated just below the junction of the Sutlej with the Cenāb.[568] "Very little reliance can be placed on this etymology, but the position thus suggested would accord well with the narrative of Arrian, and on the whole it seems not improbable that the Oxydracae may have occupied the district of Ooch together with the adjoining province of Bahawulpoor".[569]

The capital of the Oxydrakae (one of the free nations or tribes) has been identified with modern Uchh in the southern Punjab. "This old town", says Cunningham, "is situated on the eastern bank of the Panjnad (Pañcanada or confluence of the five rivers), 70 miles to the south-south-west of Multan, and 45 miles to the north-east of the present confluence with the Indus at Mithānkot".[570] "Its favourable position at the old confluence of the Punjab rivers must have made it a place of importance from the earliest times". In the time of Alexander, it must have been a very populous city. There is another Uchh on a mound to the west of the confluence of the Cenāb and Jhelum; and a third Uchh is also situated on a mound. Wilson has identified it with "Ooch, a town on the left bank of the Akesines."[571] In Alexander's time, this river (Cenāb) joined the Indus near this town, but now the point of junction is lower down near Mithānkot,[572] probably at the distance of forty miles. St. Martin has identified it with "Chuchpur" or an ancient fort standing on the eastern bank of the Indus right opposite Mithānkot.[573] According to Burnes, Uchh is formed of three distinct towns, a few hundred yards apart from each other, and each encompassed by a brick wall, now in ruins. The mound was formed of the ruins of houses caused by the inundation of the Cenāb.[574] Masson mentions only two separate towns, and adds that Uchh is chiefly "distinguished by the ruins of the former towns, which are very extensive and attest the pristine prosperity of the locality".[575] Rennell identifies it with "Outch" of the Greek historians.[576] The popular belief and the old tradition also confirm that there were once seven different towns bearing the same name Uchchanagar.

We learn from Arrian *(Anab.,*VI,15, 2) that Alexander ordered a city to be built at the confluence of the two rivers (Cenāb and the Indus), hoping that by the advantage of such a situation it would become a great city and make a name for itself in the world. He also ordered for the construction of dockyards there. The city bore the name of Alexandria Uchh which corresponds with Askaland-Usah, one of its later names.[577] This city was the capital of one of the four principalities of Sindh under Ayand who reigned after Alexander. It was captured by Chach on his expedition against Multān. The "Iskandar" of the *Chach-nāmah* must be the Alexandria Uchh.[578] At a later period, it formed part of the independent kingdom or province of Multan. This ancient city was repeatedly destroyed and rebuilt the details of which do not fall within the purview of the treatment of the subject.

Sankalia's statement, that in the whole Punjab the urban culture flourished,[579] seems to be perfectly correct.

Both Megasthenes and Pliny mention twelve tribes each possessing two cities. The tribes include the Sibarae, Abaortae, Sarabhan, Sarophages, Sorgae, Baraomatae, Umbrittae, Aseni etc. The Aseni had altogether three cities, including the capital Bucephala which was so named because it was built where Alexander's famous horse was buried.[580] The tribes enumerated must have occupied a tract of country lying above the confluence of the Indus with the streams of the combined rivers of the Punjab. The Sibarae represent Sauviras who were not far from the banks of the Indus with their capital Roruka. The Aseni were situated to the east of the river. The Umbrittae are definitely the Abastanoi (Skt. Ambaṣṭhas) of the historians of Alexander who dwelt in the neighbourhood of the lower Akesines. The other obscure tribes cannot be identified with any certainty. The details of their cities are not available either.

Before we proceed further to describe some of the important towns and cities of Sindh in the north-west, it will be quite in the fitness of things to make it clear here that in ancient times it comprised the whole valley of the Indus from the Punjab to the sea, including the Delta and the island of Kacch.

The towns situated in the Indus valley and its neighbourhood numbering about forty-one have been divided by Ptolemy into the following six groups. The towns of the first group (five in number) belonged to the upper part of the valley and were situated near its junction with the Kophes. The towns of the second group are indicated by their relative positions they held. They were successive stages on the great caravan route which ran parallel with the western bank of the river all the way from its junction with the Kophes downwards to the coast. The third group consists of the towns which were the chief marts of commerce in the Delta. The towns of the fourth group were successive stages on another caravan route which on the eastern side of the river traversed the country from the great confluence with the combined rivers of the Punjab downward to Delta. The towns of the fifth group (seven in number) were situated towards the eastern side of the Delta. The towns of the sixth group were included in the territory of the "Khattriaioi" (kṣatriya tribes or warriors) which extended on both sides of the river from the confluence with the Punjab rivers as far as the Delta.[581] St. Martin's statement, that none of them can be identified,[582] is no longer tenable. The towns identified have been placed in the relevant places.

Here we will begin with the towns (called also cities) situated in Upper Sindh. The royal city or the capital of a sovereign called Musikanus or Mousikanos by Strabo,[583] Diodorus[584], Arrian[585] and Julius Valerius,[586] Sousikana or Musikana by Ptolemy"[587], and Musicani by Curtius[588] has been identified with Alor,[589] which remained the metropolis of the rich, powerful and flourishing kingdom of Upper Sindh for many ages. It figures conspicuously in the records of the Macedonian invasion. We learn from

Arrian that this kingdom in Alexander's time was "the richest and most populous throughout all India". Onesikritos, while speaking of its opulence and economic prosperity, noted that "the country produced everything in abundance", as we learn from Strabo.[590] That the territory of its ancient capital Alor or Aror was very rich and fertile is a well ascertained fact. Arrian relates that Alexander "ordered Kraterus to build a castle in the city..." It was no doubt a large fortified city. It was visited by Hiuen Tsang in CE 641.[591] This celebrated city was situated on the west bank of the Indus, near Bhakar, the ruins of which are still traceable five miles to the south-east of modern Rohri or Ruhri in Sukkur district. In ancient times, it was about 150 miles distant from Debal (modern Karachi). The said capital city, Alor, continued to flourish till its destruction by the Indus partly before CE 680 and completely after CE 712. The inundations of the Indus made an Eden of all the lands they overspread. It is also asserted by the Mohammedan chroniclers of the conquest of Sindh that this city was deserted in consequence of the alteration of the course of the Indus.

Both Arrian *(Anab.,* VI, 16) and Curtius *(Hist. of Alex.,* IX, 8, 26) mention those two principal cities, which were situated within the dominion of the king Oxykanus (Portikanos of Strabo, *Geog.,* XV, 1, 33) on the west of the Indus adjoining those of Musikanus or lying to the south-east of Alor. Curtius' description of the two towers of the citadel of the chief city, perhaps the capital, point to the fact that it was the lofty town or *porta-gām.* It was perhaps one of the five towns called *Pentagramma* by Ptolemy. The said capital was captured by Alexander after a siege of three days. Another city also met the same fate. The capital has been identified with Mahorta (Mahāvarddha-grāma or the great lofty city) situated on the bank of the Ghār river, 10 miles north-west of Larkāna.[592] Masson describes it as "the remains of an ancient fortress, on a huge mound, named Maihota".[593] It was "one of the most flourishing places in Sindh". "The site of Mahorta must always have been a position of great importance, both commercially and politically, as it commanded the high road from Sindh, via Kachh-Gandava, to Kandahār".[594] In the time of Alexander, when the Indus flowed down the bed of the Nāra, the nearest point of the stream was Alor, from which Mahorta was distant 45 miles to the south of west, but at present the latter place is within a few miles of the river Indus.

Ptolemy's Binagara, placed on the Indus to the eastward of Oskana (Oxykanus),[595] has been identified by Cunningham with Alor.[596] But more correctly it can be connected with Mahorta. The early Arab geographers also mention a town of identical name, Bania, but they place it in lower Sindh, situated at the distance of a single journey below Mansura.[597]

Ptolemy's "Boudaia"[598] has been identified by Arab geographers or chroniclers of the conquest of Upper Sindh with the town of "Bodhpur" situated between Alor and Mittankot (or Mithānkot) or to the west of the Indus.[599] One of the largest and populous towns to the west of the Indus called by Ptolemy "Banagara", lay on the line of communication between Kābul and the Indus,[600] which was visited by both Fa-hian and Hiuen Tsang.

Ptolemy places a town called "Musarna" on a small affluent of the Indus to the north of the "Askana" rivulet. This town belonged to the people called by him Musarnei (the Massanae of Diodorus or the "Masūrakarṇa" of the *Gaṇa-Pāṭha* on Pāṇini, II, 4, 49; IV, 1, 112) whose name still exists in the district of Muzarka to the west of the Indus below Mithānkot in Upper Sindh. Musarna may be the town of Shahpur.

We learn from Arrian *(Anab.,* VI, 15) and Diodorus *(Bib. Hist.,* XVII, 102) that Alexander founded a city or town in the realm of the people called the Sogdi by the former and the Sodrae by the latter which was named after him Alexandria. This can also be supported by the statement of Curtius *(Hist. of Alex.,* IX, 8). On the basis of Diodorus' testimony it can be established that Alexander "placed 10,000 inhabitants" in the new city, built on the opposite banks of the Indus (probably to the northward of Alor). It is said that he founded this city, "marking out docks again for the commerce which he foresaw under Greek initiative in the new Age".[601] As a matter of fact, the capital city of the Sogdi or the Sodrae, the free tribe of Upper Sindh, had already come into existence before the arrival of Alexader there. The latter might have constructed his own city or erected a citadel near the former one with the settlements of the Greek and native population in conformity with his usual practice. The site might have later developed as one of the urban centres in Sindh. The narrative preserved by Arrian (*Anab.,* VI, 15) is very much in favour of the identification of the old site, Seorai, near Fazilpur with the town of the Sogdi. Here Masson heard that there was formerly a considerable town.[602] "About 8 miles to the north-east of Sabjalkot there is a village named Sirwahi, which may possibly represent the Seorai of Sindhian history. It is 96 miles in a direct line below Uchh, and 85 miles below Alor, or very nearly midway between them".[603] The native historians as well as the early Arab geographers place a strong fort, named Bhatia, between Multān and Alor, which from its position has a good claim to be identified with the city which Alexander is said to have built amongst the Sogdi. However, it is very difficult to say as to how far these identifications are satisfactory. Bhatia, defended by a lofty wall and a deep broad ditch, was taken by assault in CE 1003 by Mahmud of Ghazni.

The ancient city of Sindomana or Sindimana distinctly figures in the accounts of Strabo,[604] Arrian[605] and Plutarch[606] as the capital of the king called Sambos, Sambus or Sabos (Sambhu) whose principality was situated in Middle Sindh. Curtius *(Hist. Alex.,* IX, 8) without naming his (Sabus') capital states that Alexander after having received the "submission of several towns, captured the raja's strongest city by mining", Diodorus *(Bib. Hist.,* XVII, 102) mentions only the name of the king and not his capital. The said capital city has been satisfactorily identified with Sehwan, which stands on a site of very high antiquity that is the vicinity of the Lakki mountains. It preserves many vestiges of antiquity, especially the great mound, which was once the citadel or castle, which, according to Burnes, "is in all probability as old as the ages of the Greeks".[607] Its early occupation is admitted by all inquirers. M'Murdo says "Sehwan is undoubtedly a place of vast antiquity, perhaps more so than either Alor or Bāhmana".[608] It is also stated by Cunningham that "The favourable position of Sehwan, on a lofty isolated rock, near a large lake, with food and water in abundance would certainly have attracted the notice of the first inhabitants of Sindh".[609] In all the old maps, it is placed on a western branch of the Indus. In Alexander's time, however, the river pursued a course from which Sindomana lay at a considerable distance to westward. It is said that "when the river flowed down the eastern channel of the Nara, Sehwan was not less than 65 miles distant from its nearest point at Jakrao".[610] The Greek name Sindomana corresponds with *Saindhava-vanam* or *Saindhuwān* meaning the "abode of the Saindhavas". Wilson is of the opinion that "Sindomana is readily recognisable in a very allowable Sanskrit compound, Sindhu-mān (the possessor of the capital or Rāja of Sindh) with which Sindhu-vān is synonymous, and the latter may have been softened in common speech to the modern Seh-wan".[611] The early Arab geographers mention the capital differently as Sadustān or Sadusān. It is mentioned in native histories of Sindh as one of the towns captured by Muhammad bin Kasim in CE 711. It was again captured by Mahmud of Ghazni in the beginning of the eleventh century. It remained for several centuries as one of the most flourishing urban centre in Sindh. But now it is in a very much decadent position.

Ptolemy's "Pesipeda",[612] which can be identified with little plausibility with "Besmeid" of the early Arab geographers, appears to be a town of considerable importance, which lay to the east of the Indus on the route from Mansura to Multan. Cunningham has identified it with Sehwan,[613] but this identification does not appear to be valid.

Alexander's historians – Arrian,[614] Curtius,[615] Diodorus[616] and Plutarch[617] – have also taken notice of a large city or town of the Brachmans (brāhmaṇas) of the Indus valley. Diodorus in particular calls this city *Harmatelia (Brāhmathala* or Brāhmaṇa-sthala – an honorific denomination) and adds that it was the "last town of the Brāhmaṇas on the river".[618] This town has been placed by them near Sindomana in Middle Sindh, but after having thoroughly investigated the data available to us and carefully analysed them we find that it was situated in the territory of Musikanus. His dominions must have embraced the whole of the valley of the Indus down the head of the Delta (Patala). In fact, it was the capital city which belonged to the whole brāhmaṇa population inhabiting the Upper, Middle and Lower valley of the Indus. It can be certainly identified with the ancient city of Brāhmaṇābād, Bahmanwā or Bahmaṇābād of the early Arab geographers and historians. It was originally called Bāmiwān and afterwards Brāhmaṇābād. It corresponds both in name and position with the city called Brāhmaṇa. According to an age-old tradition of the Sindhians too, it was known as Bāmiwān. The greek historians call the country of the brāhmaṇas Brachmanoi or Brahmaṇoi and its capital Brāhmaṇa. The same place has been called Brāhmaṇaka by both Pāṇini *(Sūtra,* V, 2, 71),[619] and Patañjali *(Mahābhāṣya,* IV, 2, 104).[620] The *Kāśikā* on Pāṇini describes it as "the land of brāhmaṇas" who were *āyudhajīvins* or followers of military art. It is to be noted that even Rājaśekhara in his *Kāvyamīmāṃsā* (ninth century CE) mentions Brāhmanavaha (abode of the brāhmaṇas) as one of the *janapadas* of the west.

The Brāhmaṇic capital appears to have been one of the magnificent cities in Sindh. It was defended by a brick-wall and adorned with gates. It was stormed and captured by Alexander the account of which has been provided by Plutarch on the basis of former's letters. After a gap of several centuries, the city of the brāhmaṇas was occupied by Muhammad bin Kasim in CE 712. According to the native histories and traditions of the people, Brāhmaṇābād was destroyed by an earthquake. Its destruction may be tentatively assigned to the latter half of the tenth century. Several legendary accounts are there about the destruction of all the old cities in the Punjab as well as of those in Sindh. However, it is no use dwelling upon them further. We are very much indebted to M. Bellasis for the discovery of the ruins of a large city at Bambhra-ka-thūl in 1854 which was in the occupation of the brāhmaṇas at the time of Alexander's invasion as well as in the later period. The ruins are situated near an old bed of the

Indus at a distance of 47 miles to the north-east of Haidarabad, 28 miles to the east of Hala, and 20 miles to the west of the eastern Nara. The broken brick tower still stands on the place. His excavations which include even extensive pre-historic remains have proved conclusively that the city was destroyed by some terrible convulsion of nature.[621] It is probable that most of the inhabitants who escaped the great catastrophe would have returned to the ruined city and many of them again reared their houses on the old sites. But the walls of the city were fallen and the place had become decayed so much so that it remained uninhabited for sometime. According to another evidence, it was Bāhmana, 8 miles east of Shehdādpur.[622]

If the city of the brāhmaṇas taken by Alexander was near Sindomana, as indicated by his historians, we may rather look for it in the position of Amree, eighteen miles below Sehwan, which, although now an insignificant village, is said to have been once a large city and the favourite residence of former kings.[623]

The Delta of the Indus (Lower Indus Valley) called Patalene or Pattalene (resembling the Delta in Egypt) received its name from the city of Patala or Pattala, which was its capital. Strabo has very categorically stated that Patalene contained "a considerable city Patala", which gave its name to the island.[624] The light of history first falls upon it in the writings of the historians of Alexander's Indian expedition. *Arrian* says that in the time of Alexander it was not only fortified but also the greatest city in the parts of the country about the mouths of the Indus.[625] Diodorus calls it "a city of great note".[626] Nearkhos in his *Journal of Voyage* has also described it as a town of considerable importance.[627] It also figures in Ptolemy's *Geography* (VII, 1, 59).[628] Arrian, on the authority of Nearkhos, says, "this river also forms a delta by its two mouths, no way inferior to that Egypt, which, in the Indian language, is called Pattala".[629] Dionysios periegetes also supports the view that it was "called in the tongue of the natives, Patalene".[630] Pliny, quoting Onesikritos and Nearkhos as his two chief authorities, clearly mentions "Patala, a celebrated port".[631] He further says that it lies at the mouth of the Indus triangular in shape 220 miles in breadth.[632] Nonnos also makes a passing reference to it.[633] In his life of Apollonius of Tyana, Philostratus records that Apollonius in the course of his visit to India saw with his own eyes the city of Patala. (*AICL*, p. 195; *CAI*, p. 408).

The ancient city of Patala in Lower Sindh also known as Pāṭalpur or Potalpurī seems to have derived its name from the Sanskrit word Poṭala, i.e., the "harbour" or "a station for ships". It was obviously a port town. (*AICL*, p. 188, and note 2). It is definitely Pāṭṭana of the *Gaṇa-Pāṭha* on

Pāṇini (IV, 1, 14) and Pāṭṭanaprastha of Patañjali (V, 2, 104) and Patasila or Pitasila of Hiuen Tsang. It is curious to note that the name "Poṭala" has been consistenly applied to a city in the Delta of the Indus in the Buddhist writings of Tibet.

The absence of any concrete evidence in the classics about the geographical position of the city of Patala sparked off different kinds of speculation about its identification. The only clue which we can draw from the narratives of Arrian *(Anab.,* VI, 17) and Curtius *(Hist. of Alex.,* IX, 8) is that it was not very far from Brāhmaṇa, the city of the brāhmaṇas. This very indication provided solid ground for some writers to identify it with Brāhmaṇābād or modern Bāhmaṇābād, four miles south-west from Thaṭha, or with the latter itself.[634] But this does not appear to be very much convincing because of the fact that the city of Patala was either at or near the head of the Delta which may not be the position of either of them. This city in Alexander's time stood where the river Indus bifurcated. And hence the supposition of M.R. Haig (the chief authority on the Indus Delta country) that it was not far from a spot which lies 35 miles south-east of Haidarabad[635] may be taken as tenable to some extent. Its identification with ancient Pāṭalpur is absolutely correct, but its identification with modern Haidarabad (the native capital of Sind), 47 miles to the south-west of the ruined city of Brāhmaṇābād, and 85 miles from Laribandar (or ancient Debal, a site between Karachi and Thatha)[636] is not beyond question. The identity of Haidarabad and Nirankot of the Arab historians and geographers is a well-established fact. In fact, the city of Patala in Alexander's time was the capital of Lower Sindh. It was at a distance of 30 miles from Haidarabad or near the very ancient site of Brāhmaṇa or Brāhmaṇābād. The distance between the two ancient cities, Brāhmana and Patala, was about 17 miles. Thomas Holdich (*The Gates of India Being an Historical Narrative*, p. 148) has categorically stated that Patala was neither Hyderabad as suggested by A. Cunningham nor Thatta as upheld by other authorities, but about 30 miles south-east of the former and 60 miles north-east of the latter in which locality, indeed, there are ruins enough to prove it.

In support of the identification of Patala with the site near Brāhmaṇābād we feel necessary to add that the base of the Delta was reckoned by Aristoboulos at 1000 stadia (or 115 miles), by Nearkhos at 1800 stadia and by Onesikritos at 2000 stadia, as quoted by Strabo.[637] Onesikritos mistakenly compares it in size with the Egyptian Delta, which has a base of 1300 stadia or 160 miles. The distance of Patala from the sea may be taken at from 1000 stadia or 115 miles up to 125 miles. Now, the distance of Haidarabad from the Ghāra, or western mouth of the Indus is 110 miles, and from the Kori or eastern mouth 135 miles. Thus, this city can unhesitatingly be identified with the site at some distance from present Haidarabad.

The local tradition recorded in the Sanskrit books of the *brāhmaṇas* of Sehwan also confirms it that the ancient name of Patala city near the city of the brāhmaṇas quite far from Haidarabad was Pāṭalipurī, of Kābul Chichapālapur, and of Multān Prahlādapur.[638] Strabo records that Patalene was reduced by Alexander.[639] Most of the ancient towns and cities in Sindh were re-designated by the brāhmaṇas as well as the Mohammedans.

It has been rightly observed that "…the Punjab and Sindh republics were studded with numerous and prosperous cities".[640]

In the time of the author of the *Periplus* (the last quarter of the first century of the Christian era), the capital of Lower Sindh vas Minnagara, "City of the Min", which was the Hindu name for the Indo-Scythians or the Śakas and Yueh-chi. It was called so because of its occupation by the Pārthians (Dahae Scythians from the Oxus) who gave the name of Indo-Scythia (Śakasthāna) to the lower valley of the Indus.That is why this city has been mentioned as "the metropolis of Scythia".[641] In the list of Isidor of Charax (or Kharax) also it figures as one of the cities of Śakastene, or Sejistan. Mr. Schoff, the translator and annotator of the text- *Periplus,*- says: "Minnagara was a name given temporarily to several cities in India during the period of the occupation by the Scyths. After the collapse of the Indo-Scythian power these cities resumed their former names with their autonomy".[642]

Schoff has identified Minnagara with Patala – "the capital of the delta country".[643] The author of the text himself saw here some of the antiquities such as "ancient shrines, walls of forts", etc. of Alexander's time.[644] It was a market-town where the foreign merchants reached by ascending the river from another port-town in the maritime region to the north of Patala. This port-town has been called Barbaricum in the *Periplus,"*[645] which is Barbarei of Ptolemy's *Geography* (VII, 1, 59)[646] and perhaps the Barce of Justin.[647] It stood at the mouth of the Indus river, and was a famous emporium of coral trade. It was an entrepot (a centre for import and export). From the *Periplus* it appears that both Minnagara and Barbaricum were well-connected with each other through trade. It is said that the merchant vessels anchored at Barbaricum, where all their cargos were unloaded and carried up to metropolis (Minnagara) by the river, to the king.[648] The former place has been distinctly mentioned by the author as the "market-town". It is said that Barbaricum is the Hellenised form of the Hindu word – "Bandar, port or possibly some name such as Bahardipur, which survives in the modern Delta".[649] It may be Shah-bander (Royal port) which now lies far inland to the east of the present main channel of the Indus. The frequent references to this place in the *Periplus* as an important centre of trade and commerce creates an impression that it must have been one of the flourishing urban centres in the Lower Indus Valley during the period concerned. Both the towns (Patala and Barbarikon or Barbaricum) were abandoned at a much later period.

Cunningham has judiciously identified Minnagara with the city of Thatha, situated at the distance of 3 miles from the western bank of the Indus, or 2 days' journey from Laribandar. Minnagara, according to him, is Manhābari of the Arab geographers, which is placed on the western bank of the Indus at 2 days' journey from Debal. In modern times, the ships anchored at Laribandar from where the merchants carried their goods to Thatha either by land or by water.[650] This reminds us of position of Minnagara and Barbaricum in the first century of the Christian era. Vincent has wrongly placed the former at the distance of about 60 miles above Thatha.[651] M'Murdo places it on the Lohāna river, not far from the city, Brāhmaṇa, and he identifies it with Bi-nagara or Agri-nagara of Ptolemy.[652] But this proposition is very confusing. Bi-nagara, as mentioned earlier, appears to be completely different city from Minnagara position wise. Agri-nagar was, of course, the later appellation of Minnagara. It was in the possession of a chief by caste an Agri, which is believed to have descended from Alexander. It is compatible with our supposition that it must have been a city bearing this name in the first half of the second century of the Christian era. Barbaricum is generally identified with the "ruined town of Bhampura, situated at the head of the Ghāra creck, which is supposed by the natives to be the site of the most ancient seaport in Sindh".[653] The importance of Minnagara and Barbaricum as two chief centres of trade and commerce in the lower valley of the Indus has been acknowledged by all those scholars who made little investigation into the subject.

Curtius *(Hist. of Alex.,* IX, 10) says that Alexander himself founded several towns during his long stay in Lower Sindh. The contribution he made to the urban growth of the northwest before his departure from India in October 325 BCE is well reflected in the classical accounts of the subject.

Pliny, quoting Megasthenes, makes a mention of 300 cities that belonged to the people adjoining the island of Patale.[654] There seems to be palpable exaggeration in his statement with regard to the number of cities. These cities in all probability include the villages also. However, the people who are said to be in possession of the cities belonged to different areas. They include the tribes who occupied the territories between Śikārpur and Mithānkoṭ on the western bank of the Indus. The other tribes to whom the cities belonged are Syrieni or Suriyanis occupying the territories near the Indus in the neighbourhood of Bhakar or Bakkar, Jhadejas of Kacch, Kokaris now settled on the banks of lower Sutlej, Nharonis of Baluchistan with ancestral seat in regions to the east of the Indus, and Godiarei, Nereae, Olostae, etc. of Baluchisatan.[655]

The towns situated to the west of the lower Indus within the geographical limits of India are also worthy of our notice. One of the famous port towns of ancient times has been called by Nearkhos Krokala or Krokola, where he himself stayed for twenty-four-days in the course of the voyage. He found its harbour so large and commodious that he dignified it with the great conqueror's name, as stated by Arrian.[656] This town, which is identical with the Kolaka of Ptolemy, can undountedly be identified with modern Karachi.[657] This identification does not rest on the slender ground. It is rather confirmed by the fact that "the district in which Karachi is situated is called Karkalla to this day".[658] According to Nearkhos, this island town was situated oppostie the river Arbis at a distance of 70 stadia. This is the river on the eastern bank of which the territory of the people of the maritime region immediately adjoining the Indus called Arabitae (the tribesmen of the Dravidian stock, popularly known as Arava), was situated. The said town was "150 stadia, or 17¼ miles, from the western mouth of the Indus, which agrees exactly with the relative position of Karachi and the mouth of the Ghara river".[659] Pliny, quoting from the *Journal of the Voyage* of Onesikritos and Nearkhos, states that "the town of Arbis" was founded by the latter in the course of the voyage. He further adds on their authorities that a city, "Xylenopolis" was founded by Alexander.[660] The town of Arbis perhaps corresponds in position with that of Aroba or Arba at the mouth of the river of the said name, which belonged to the Arabitae.[661] Pliny's statement, that it was built by Nearkhos, is purely based on the information supplied by the latter. It is not sufficiently explained where and near what river Xylenopolis was founded. It is perhaps a Greek compound meaning either "Timber-town" or "Wooden-town", which was situated, no doubt, on the western bank of the western arm of the Indus, and probably near the island of Krokola.

The Oritae or Horitae (another Draviḍian tribe repesented by the modern Brahui) occupied an extensive territory on the western bank of the Arbis. The region inhabited by them was known as Ora. Their capital called Rhambakia, according to an unanimous testimony of Arrian,[662] Curtius[663] and Diodorus,[664] was originally a large village, but later it was converted by Alexander into a city. He, hoping that it would rise to be a rich and populous city, got it colonised and provided all necessary infrastructure required for the purpose concerned. The foundation of the city was laid by Alexander and its superstructure was later raised by Leonnatus, who was left behind to complete it. The latter was entrusted with the responsibility to look after the peopling of the new city. Its new population comprised largerly the people from the Pashtu country (Arachosians), which has been hinted at by Curtius.[665] The native people and the Greeks had already occupied the place which rose to be a city of great importance. Diodorus reveals that "it was built on a very favourable site near the sea but above the reach of the highest tides". There was gradual increase in the urban population. The new city was named after Alexander as Alexandria. This is recorded not only by the former's historians, but also by his two famous companions, Onesikritos and Nearkhos, whom quoting, Pliny says: "Alexandria was built by Leonnatus by Alexander's order in the territories of this people (Horitae)".[666] Pliny himself describes it as a "fine city defended by marshes.[667] It appears in the *Periplus* as "Rhambacia",[668] and in Ptolemy's *Geography* as "Rhambakia", the capital city of the Rhamnai (the Ramaṇas of the *Mahābhārata* and the Ramaṭhas of the Purāṇas) whose early seat was in the land of the "Oreitai" before they settled in Gedrosia (Baluchistan),[669] west of modern Karachi. It is said to have been at no great distance from the modern Las Bela. According to Holdich, its whole neighbourhood is full of evidences of early occupation,[670] but the exact site is undetermined. Cunningham has placed it at the western boundary of the Oritae at a place called Malana "to the east of Rās Mālān or Cape Mālān of the prsent day, about twenty miles to the west of the Aghor river".[671] But his identification of the city with "Rāmbāgh"[672] seems to be a mere deduction or fanciful notion.

The city, Rhambakia, has been described by Stephanus of Byzantium in his *In Voce Alexandria* as the "sixteenth Alexandria", near the bay of Melane. It is worthy of remark that Alexander during his nineteen months' stay in India built new cities, ports, and roads on the lines of his marches, which became radiating points of Hellenism. It has been correctly stated that his military and non-military colonies, both large and small, in India were far numerous. They were in the occupation of the urban communities of the Greek type, and some of them were large and important towns. Many cities were founded by him with native population, and Greek population, including his disabled soldiers, in oriental environment. The colonization during his time marked the opening of a new era in the economic life of the ancient world. The new and momentous feature of it was the transformation of the oriental marts into business centres of a type hitherto unknown to the East. Most of his colonies were undoubtedly Greek city-states not only from the political and social but also from the economic point of view.[673]

Some authorities are of the view that in all the newly built towns or cities Alexander established Greek colonies and/or garrisons, and they became centres of Greek culture and of inter-communication between India and Greece.[674] M.I. Finley says that everywhere Alexander and his successors founded new cities modelled on the Greek.[675] Greek influence on Indian Urban culture in northwest India in the Hellenistic age can hardly be denied.

Alexander not only built cities in India, but also fortified his newly acquired dominions, by the establishments, from distance to distance, of permanent camps or stations, termed by his historians cities, which were intended to hold the neighbouring tribes in check.

The towns or cities founded in Afghanistan, the Punjab and the lower valley of the Indus by Alexander were named after him Alexandria or Alexandreia, which finds mention in ancient Indian literature in variant forms. It has been called Yavanapur in the *Mahābharāta*[676] and the *Yuga Purāṇa* (a section in the *Gārgī Saṃhitā*), Ālakandaka or Alakṣandraka in the *Arthaśāstra* of Kautilya,[677] Alasanda in the three Pāli texts, *Apadāna*,[678] *Milindapañha* (III, 7, 5)[679] and *Mahāniddesa*,[680] and in the Ceylonese Pāli chronicle *Mahavāṃsa* (XXIX, 39),[681] and Ālisamdaya in the Jaina canonical texts (ascribed to Śvetāmbara Jains)- *Bhagavatī Sūtra* (6,7) and *Sthānāṅga* (5,3,459).[682]

"Alasanda, of the Yonas" (=Macedonian Greeks = Skt. Yavanas) mentioned in the said Buddhist works, according to H.G. Rawlinson, is none other than the town Alexandria built by Alexander at the confluence of the rivers Indus and Alesines,[683] recorded by Arrian in his *Anabasis* (VI, 15, 2). The town was built close to modern town of Ucch (also called Uchh), as noted before. Rawlinson has rightly pointed out that it survived the overthrow of the Macedonian powers in the Punjab for many years and became famous under the rule of the Baktrian kings as a great Graeco-Buddhist centre.[684] B.C. Law has identified Alasanda mentioned in the

Milindapañha with the town of Alexandria founded by Alexander on the Indus.[685]

Sylvain Levi[686] and M. Pelliot[687] have identified Alasanda with the town Alexandria built by Alexander in Egypt (after its conquest in 332 BCE), which is not valid at all. In fact, this particular town does not figure in Indian literature. This is the reason why W.W. Tarn[688] has rejected the identification proposed by these two French scholars.

The towns or cities of ancient Gedrosia (Baluchistan), a dependency of Sindh, also received the notices of classical writers. Arrian, on the authority of Aristoboulus, calls the capital of Gedrosia "Poura."[689] Strabo refers to it as the "royal city of the Gedrosioi", visited by Alexander.[690] It is identified with a town called Puhra, which is probably Bānpur (in western Baluchistan) of the present day.[691] Ammianus Marcellinus says, "Gedrosia too has its cities… The cities which are considered superior to the others are Sedratyra and Gynaeconlimen".[692] But these two unfortunately have not yet been identified. The "Killouta" of Onesikritos and Nearkhos corresponds as nearly as possible with the town of Kilāt or Kalāt in modern Baluchistan.

The existence of towns and cities in different parts of northern and north-western India testifies to the material prosperity of the people concerned. We find that several factors were responsible for decay of the towns and cities in those parts of the country. It is undeniable that in pre-Alexandrian period some cities in eastern Afghanistan were razed to the ground by the Persians. But the greater responsibility for their destruction can undoubtedly be assigned to Alexander and his mercenaries. In the course of their campaigns, a large number of tribal people were put to sword and their towns and cities were assaulted, stormed, captured, damaged and destroyed. The survivors, including the populace and potentates, fled away to seek refuge in nearby safer places. Some towns and cities were set ablaze by their inhabitants themselves having lost all hopes to defend them. Some towns were deserted by the people out of fear and sheer frustration. A large section of the tribal people abandoned their respective original place, dispersed in different groups and took refuge in the neighbouring as well as far distant areas which resulted in the decrease of the urban population and decline of the towns and cities. More or less the same story was repeated in the Punjab. This particular fact is well attested by the statements of the classical authors themselves. Both Julius Valerius[693] and Aelian[694] have attributed the destruction of the tribal cities in general to the Macedonians. The brāhmaṇic cities in the Punjab and Sindh met the same fate. Most of the towns and cities in Afghanistan, the Punjab, Sindh and other parts of northern and north-western India were destroyed in the course of Alexander's invasion as appears from the classical accounts of the subject. Here this fact should not be lost sight of that Alexander not only destroyed but also built the cities especially in the Punjab and Sindh. Some were re-built by his successors as well as by the indigenous population. However, some towns in the Punjab in particular were demolished by the White Hūṇas in the early part of the sixth century of the Christian era. An evidence to this effect has been furnished particularly by Kosmas Indikopleustes. An indication given by him shows that they sacked and captured some Indian cities including "one that was surrounded by water and was thus protected from assault".[695]

The inundation of the areas inhabited by the urban communities in the Punjab which may be attributed to the flood waters of its rivers, particularly the Hydraotes and Akesines, also resulted in the decline and decay of some towns there. And so is the case with some towns of Sindh which were devastated by the river Indus. It has been remarked that "for ages the Indus has been pushing its bed across the valley from east to west, generally by the gradual process of erosion, which effectually wipes out every trace of town and village on its banks; but at times also by a more or less sudden shifting of its water into entirely new channel; leaving large tracts of country to go to waste, and forcing the inhabitants of many a populous place to abandon their old homes, and follow the river in search of new settlements".[696]

Both Nearkhos and Aristoboulos, as quoted by Strabo, speak of the rising of the rivers in the Punjab and Sindh and the following inundations of the plains. They also concur in stating that "the cities built upon mounds become islands, as in Egypt and Ethiopia and that the inundation ceases after the setting of Arcturus when the waters subside",[697] Aristoboulus says that "when he was sent on some business, he saw a tract of land deserted which contained more than a thousand cities with their villages, for the Indus, having forsaken its proper channel, turned itself into another on the left much deeper into which it burst like a cataract ... for this had been raised by the inundations..."[698]

The convulsion of the nature, particularly the earthquakes, also resulted in the destruction of some cities. The remains of the ancient cities in the Punjab and Sindh constitute the mute evidence to the urban settlements there. Most of the towns and cities in general had eclipsed by the seventh century of the Christian era. However, some towns in Sindh fell under the occupation of the Arabs between CE 711 and 713. The glory and glamour of the old cities thereafter diminished. Some continued to exist even beyond that period. Some in spite of being occupied by the rulers of several dynasties continued to flourish for centuries, and they are still found in excellent state of preservation. The extensive ruins of ancient cities (described in classical literature) found in different parts of northern and north-western India constitute the distinguishing hallmark of the past urban life of the people concerned.

Notes and References

1. Cf. Herodotus, *History,* Bk. IV, 44; tr. G. Rawlinson, Vol. III, pp. 589-91; see also *AICL,* p. 4; *AIMA,* Introd. p. 5, note; A.V.W. Jackson, "The Persian Dominion in Northern India Down to the Time of Alexander's Invasion", in E.J. Rapson (ed.), *CHI,* Vol. I, *Ancient India,* p. 301; B.N. Puri, *India as Described by Early Greek Writers,* pp. 4-5 and 49.
2. *CHI,* 1, p. 301.
3. *MAGK,* p. 12, fn. 2.
4. See *AICL,* pp. 4-5, fn. 2; *CHI,* I, p. 301, fn. 1.
5. Fragm. 179 in C. Müller(ed.), *Frag. Hist. Graec.* (Paris, 1841), I.p. 12cf. *CHI*, Vol, I, p. 301; *AICL,* p. 2, fn. 2; *AIMA,* Introd. p. 5, note and pp. 152-53, note; E.R. Bevan, "India in Early Greek and Latin Literature", in *CHI,* Vol. 1, pp. 354-55.
6. *History,* Bk. III, 102 and also IV, 44; *AICL,* p. 2; see also V. De. St. Martin, *Ĕtude,* pp. 364, 376-78; *Memories de l'cademie des Inscriptions, Sav. e'trang, Ire S'erie, t.v.* pp. 17f, 81-86.
7. *The Geographical System of Herodotus,* Vol. I, p. 309.
8. *MAGK,* p. 11.
9. *Periplus*, 48, p. 189, note.
10. *Geog*., VII, I, 42 and 49, *AIT*, pp. 105,108-09, 125, see also pp. 128 and 360, note.
11. St. Martin, *E'tude*, p. 226; *AICL*, p. 199, note 5; and CASE, p. 28.
12. *Various Journeys,* Vol. III, p. 164, ef. *ibid.*
13. *Ind. Alt.,* II, p. 898.
14. *Memories de L'Acade'mie des Inscriptions, Sav. e' trang, Ire S'erie, t.v.,* p. 330.
15. *AICL,* pp. 2-3, fn. 2, p. 199, fn. 5; *IIA,* p. 194, note 1; *AIMA*, pp. 152-53, note; *AIT,* pp. 108-09.

16. Cf. *AIT,* p. 108.
17. *Antiquite Geographique de l' Inde,* pp. 21f, 40f.
18. Cf. *MAGK,* p. 11; H.H. Wilson, *HHK,* App. V111, p. 114.
19. *HGAI,* p. 97.
20. *Tribes in Ancient India,* pp. 9-17.
21. *Geog*., VI, 16, 6, AIT, p. 299.
22. *History,* Bk XXIII.
23. *E'tude,* p. 414,
24. Cf. *MAGK,* p. 10.
25. *AICL,* p. 199.
26. *HAG,* Vol. I, p. 142.
27. *Historical Researches*, Vol. I, *Asiatic Nations,* 280, 293; see also p. 189.
28. Cf. H.H. Wilson, *Ar. Ant.,* p. 136.
29. *MMH*, p. 146.
30. Cf. Troyer's *Rāja-Taraṅgini,* Vol. II, p. 305.
31. Cf. *Ar. Ant.,* p. 136.
32. *Ar. Ant.,* pp. 136-37, *HHK,* App. VIII, pp. 114-16; *Miscellaneous Essay,* p. 117; see also *AIT,* p. 108.
33. *CASE*, p. 29; W. Smith (ed), DGRG.
34. E.C. Sachau, *Alberuni's India*, I, p. 298.
35. *L'ancienne Route de l'Inde*, Vol. I, pp. 94, 190-94; Vol. 2, pp. 195-98, cf. Motichandra, *Sārthvāha*, pp. 47-48.
36. *CNAIO,* I, p. 12.
37. *Co. Anc. Ind*., p. 32; *CAGI*, p. 199; CASE, pp. 28-29.
38. *Ind. Alt.* Vol. I, p. 142; Vol. II, pp. 63, 631, 635.
39. *Asie Centrale*, I, p. 102.
40. *EHI*, 4th rev. edn. by S.M. Ewards, pp. 32, 37-38.
41. *MAGK*, pp. 12-13.
42. See Lassen, *Ind. Alt.,* I, p. 142: II, p. 631.
43. GTCP, I, p. 27, note 1.
44. *The Geography of Herodotus*, pp. 198-99, and 299.

45. *Intercourse Between India and the Western World from the Earliest Times to the Fall of Rome,* p. 16, note 2, and p. 17.

46. *Op. cit.,* p. 281

47. *Hist. Anct. Geog*., p. 74.

48. *Ĕtude*, pp. 376-78.

49. Rawlinson, *op.cit.,* p. 16.

50. *The Pathans*, p. 32.

51. *Hist. Nat*., VI, 23 (25); AIMA, p. 108, note.

52. Thomas Watters, *YCTI,* Vol. I, p. 122.

53. Thomas, *JRAS,* 1906, pp. 191, note 1, 460-61; E.J. Rapson, *JRAS.* 1905. pp. 783-S4: see also R C. Jain (ed.), *MAIMA,* p. xxxvi.

54. *Geog.,* VI, 18, 4.

55. *Ĕtude,* p. 14 f.

56. *Op. cit.,* Vol. I, p. 52 cf. Motichandra, *op. cit.,* p. 11.

57. *PAHI,* p. 74.

58. *Op. cit.*

59. See *Old Persian Inscriptions* in general, ed. and tr. F.H. Weissbach (Leipzig, 1911), *Bahistān Inscription,* 3, 61; *Bahistān Inscription,* ed. and tr. L.W. King and R.C. Thompson (London, 1907); S. Sen, *Old Persian Inscriptions,* pp. 2 ff; *JAOS,* Vol. 72, No. 1 (Jan. - March, 1952), p. 9 f.

60. Thomas, *JRAS,* 1906, p. 191, note 1.

61. Sten Konow, *Ep. Ind.,* Vol. XXII (1933), p. 111.

62. *JASB,* Vol. V, (Jan. 1836), pp. 1-6.

63. See V.A. Smith, "The Itinerary of Yuan-Chwang", in Thomas Watters, *op. cit.,* Vol. II, pp. 333-35.

64. *CAGI,* p. 17.

65. *Travels, iii,* p. 126. cf. *CAGI.* pp. 17-18.

66. *Ibid., iii,* p. 161, cf. *CAGI,* p. 18.

67. *Ibid., iii, p. 159, cf. CAGI,* p. 25.

68. Hekataeus, *Geog.,* Frag., 174-79, Fragm, 175 in C. Müller (ed.), *Frag. Hist. Graec* (Paris, 1841), I, 12; see also *AICL,* p. xiv.

69. *Op cit.,* p. 5.

70. R. Girshamana, *Le Kuṣāṇs* (Paris, 1946), p. 145; *YCTI,* Vol. 1, p. 124.

71. *YCTI*, Vol. I; pp. 122-29; Vol. II, p. 266.
72. *Geog*. Bk. XV, Ch. II, sec. 10, *AICL*, p. 90.
73. *Hist. Nat.*, VI. 21, 23.
74. *Anabasis of Alexander and Indica,* Eng. tr. by E.J. Chinnock, *Anab.*, Bk. III. Ch. XXVIII; Bk. IV. Ch. XXII; IIA, pp. 58 and 331-32, note A.
75. *Hist. Alex.,* Bk.VII, Ch. 3.
76. *Itin. Alex.,* Ch. 104, *AICL*, p. 150.
77. *AICL*, pp. 87, fn. 4, 90, fn. 2, 150, fn. 1; E.H. Bunbury, *HAG*, Vol. I, p. 142, V.A. Smith, *EHI,* pp. 52-53; *CAGI*, p. 19.
78. Lord, "Account of Koh-daman", *JASB*, Vol. VII, p. 521.
79. *Hist. Nat.,* VI. 17.
80. Cf. *CAGI*, p. 18, fn. 3.
81. *In Voce Alexandria*, Cf. *CAGI*, p. 18.
82. *Hist. Nat.* VI. 17 (21).
83. *GBI,* p. 462.
84. *JASB.* Vol. III (April, 1834), p. 153 f; *JASB,* Vol. V (Jan., 1836), pp. 1f, 5-6; *Travels,* III, pp. 155-65.
85. *Travels in Punjab, Bokhara,* etc., Vol. 1, p. 184.
86. *Visit to Ghazni, Kābul and Afghanistan,* p. 198 cf. H.H. Wilson, *Ar. Ant.,* p. 180.
87. Quoted by H.H. Wilson, *op. cit.,* p. 180.
88. *JASB*, Vol. V, p. 390.
89. *EHI*, p. 52, note 3.
90. CASE, p. 25.
91. *History of India*, App. III, "On the Greek Accounts of India", p. 232.
92. JASB, Vol. V, p. 1. Concerning the precise site of *Alexandria and Caucasum* or *Alexandria Opiane* see E.H. Bunbury, HAGI, I, Note X, pp. 490-91.
93. *HAG*, I, p. 464.
94. *Hist. Nat.,* VI, 23.
95. *CAGI,* p. 23. In his CASE (p. 25), Cunningham identifies the town Cartana with the famous ruins of Begrām, 27 miles to the north of Kābul, of which details have been provided by Masson (*Travels in Baluchistan*…, III, pp. 155-59.

96. *CAGI,* pp. 24-25.

97. Pliny, *Hist. Nat.*, VI, 25; Solinus, *Coll, Rer. Memo*, LVII.

98. Cf. *CAGI*, p. 27.

99. Cellarius, III, 22, p. 514, cf. *CAGI*, pp. 26-27.

100. *CAGI*, p. 27.

101. Masson, *Travels,* II, p. 166 cf. *CAGI,* p. 27.

102. *Hist. of Alex.,* VII, 3, 23.

103. *Bib. Hist.* XVII, 83.

104. *Oration,* I 5, *AICL,* p. 207 and fn. 2.

105. *Geog.,* VI, 18, 4, *AIT,* pp. 311-13.

106. *Ibid.*

107. *CAGI,* p. 27.

108. *AIMA,* 1st edn. pp. 45-49; Pliny. *Hist, Nat., VI, 23.*

109. Strabo, *Geog.,* Bk. XV. Ch.II, Sec. 9. *AICl,* p. 89; Ptolemy, *Geog.,* VI, 17, Sec. I. *AIT,* pp. 305-6.

110. Every 10 Stadia = approximately 11/6 miles.

111. *Ar. Ant.* p 150; Rawlison. *Ind. Ant.,* Vol. V, pp. 329-30. The distance from Meshed to Herāt is about 232 miles, according to Conolly, *Travels,* Vol. 1, p. 414; by a different route it is 279 miles, cf. Ar. *Ant.*, p. 150, fn. 3. According to Fraser, it is either 221 or 238 miles, *Travels in Khorasan,* App. p. 118 Cf. *ibid.,* pp. 171-72, fn. 5.

112. *Geog.*, VI, 17, 4-7, *AIT*, pp. 307-10.

113. *Ar. Ant.*, p. 151.

114. *Ibid.,* p. 151 and fn. 4.

115. Letters from Mohun Lall, *JASB,* Jan. 1834, p. 9, cited in *Ar. Ant.,* p. 151 and fn. 5.

116. *Geog.,* XI, 10, p. 516; see also *AIT,* p. 309; *Ar. Ant.,* p. 151.

117. *Anab.,* III. XXVI; see also Cunningham, CASE, pp. 20-21.

118. *Geog.,* XV, ii, 8, *AICL,* p. 87.

119. Cf. *Ar. Ant.,* p. 151.

120. *Mans. Parth.,* 15.

121. *AIT,* pp. 307-10.

122. *History,* Bk. XXIII, Ch. VI, *AICL* p. 93 and *AIT,* p. 328.

123. *Geog*.. XV, i, 26; XV, ii, 8, *AICL,* pp. 31 and note 1, 87 and note 3.

124. *AICL,* p. 87, note 3.

125. Bunbury, *HAG,* Vol. I, pp. 486-87.

126. *AICL,* pp. 88, note 2, 100 and note 2 (culled from Falconer's Version); see Eng. tr. of Strabo's *Geographica* by H.C. Hamilton and W. Falconer, Vol. III; see also Pliny *Hist. Nat.,* VI, 17; VI, 21.

127. *Ar. Ant.,* p. 149, see also p. 171. Alexandria founded by Alexander in Aria probably occupied the site of the ancient capital of Artakoana or the site of the modern Herāt and its neighbourhood. See Bunbury. *HAG*., I, p. 464, and also Note R. pp. 485-86.Wilson (Ar. Ant., p. 152) is of the opinion that Artakaona, Alexandria and Aria are aggregated in Herāt.

128. *Ar. Ant.,* p. 150.

129. *Ar. Ant.,* p. 150.

130. *AIT,* pp. 307-10.

131. Notes by M. Jacquet on M. Court's *Conjectures Sur les Marches d'Alexandre, JA,* October 1837.

132. *Historical Researches*., Vol. I (*Asiatic Nations*), p. 256.

133. *Ar. Ant*.. p. 152.

134. *Geog.* XV. ii. 9. *AICL*, p. 89.

Drangiane of ancients corresponds in general with the province now called Seistan on the frontier of Afghanistan. It was actually adjacent to southern Afghanistan. Some parts of the Drangiana are included in modern Baluchistan and some in northern part of Iran. In ancient times, some portion of it formed part of India, as it transpires from the accounts of classical scholars. It was well known for its urban culture. The inhabitants were called variously Drangai, Zarangae and Sarangaei (of Herodotus). Its another name Zarang, according to Burnout, was derived from the Zend word, Zarayo, a lake, a word still retained in the name of the lake in Seistan Zarah. In fact, Śakasthāna (abode of the Śakas), which formed southern part of Baluchistan, was later called Seistan (Drangiana of classical writers).

135. *Geog.,* XV, ii, *8, AICL,* p. 87.

136. *Hist.Nat.,* VI, 21.

137. *History*, XXIII, vi, *AICL*, p. 94.

138. *Mansiones Parthicae,* ed. C. Müller, *Geog. Graec. Mino.* (Paris, 1855), I, 244-56; ed. and tr., W.H. Schoff, *Parthian Stations of Isidore of Charax* (Phildelphia, 1914), Section 16; also *AIT,* pp. 307-10.

139. *AICL*, p. 87, note 6, p. 100, note 3; *Ar. Ant.*, pp. 153-54; *AIT,* pp. 307-10.

140. *HAG,* Vol. I. pp. 486-87; *AICL,* p. 87, note 6.

141. *Oration,* 1.5, *AICL,* p. 207.

142. *AICL,* p. 88, note 2, p. 100.

143. *Hist. Nat.,* VI, 25.

144. *Anab.,* III, xxviii.

145. *Ar. Ant.,* p. 154.

146. *Ar. Ant.*, p. 154.

147. *Hist.*, XXIII, vi, *AICL*, p. 94.

148. *Ar. Ant.,* pp. 155, 177.

149. Quoted by Starbo, *Geog.*, XI, viii, 9; *AICL*, p. 88, note 2, and p. 100.

150. *Geog.*, XV, ii, 8-9, 10, *AICL*, pp. 88-89.

151. *Hist. Nat.*, VI, 23; also VI, 21, 8-23 inserted in *AIMA*, 1st edn. Frag. LVI, p. 151. Pliny borrowed or derived his information from Megasthenes' *Indika*. See also *AIMA*, p. 108, note.

152. *Anab.*, III, xxviii; VI, 15.

153. *Hist. Alex.,* VII, 3.

154. *Orb. Des.*, vv. 1080-1165, *AICL*, p. 188.

155. *History*, XI, 34, *AICL*, p. 210.

156. *History*, XXVIII, vi, *AICL*, p. 94.

157. *Geog.*, VI, 24, *AICL.*, p. 212.

158. Fragments of the *Indika* of Megasthenes, ed. E.A. Schwanbeck (Bonn, 1846), Bk. 1, Fragms. III and IV, pp. 12, no. 6, 29-30, no. 24; AIMA, 1st edn. p. 108, note, and Frag. LVI, p. 151, and note.

159 *Dionysiaka,* XXVI, pp. 206-9; *AICL,* p. 199; see also G.P. Singh, "*The Dionysiaka:* A Classical (Greek) Source of History of Ancient India", *Shodhak,* JHR, Vol. XXVIII, pt. A, sr. 82, 1999, p. 1.

160. *Geog.*, VII, I, *AIT*, pp. 33-34.

161. Strabo, *Geog.,* XV, ii, 9; *AICL,* pp. 88 and note 1, 89. 199, note 2; *AIT,* pp. 341-42. note.

162. See *Avesta,* Eng. tr. J. Darmesteter, SBE, Vol. IV, (Oxford, 1887, rept. Delhi, 1974), p. 2f.

163. See *Behistun, Persepolis and Naqsh-i-Rustam Inscriptions* of Darius (522-486 BCE) and Persepolis Insc. of Xerxes (486-465 BCE) in D.C. Sircar (ed.), SI, Vol. I, pp. 5-14; also JAOS, Vol. 72, no. I (Jan-March, 1952), pp. 9 ff (the Word has been called variously Haraquaiti, Harakhuvati, etc.)

164. *Geog.*, VI, 12, 4, *AIT*, p. 276, see also p. 281; Bunbury, HAG, Vol. II, pp. 641-42. Ptolemy has distinguished Kandaroi or Kandahār (VI, 12, 4) from Gāndhārai or Gāndhāra (VII, 1, 44). But he has erroneously placed the former in Sogdiana. Such mistakes are found in his work. The tribe of Sogdiana has been separately mentioned by him as Kandari, who cannot be confounded with that of modern Kandahār.

165. Cf. *Ar. Ant.*, p. 151.

166. *Periplus*, 47, p. 183.

167. *AIMA*, 1st edn. pp. 151-52, note; *AIT*, p. 34; *CHI*, Vol. I, pp. 388, 489; V.A. Smith, *EHI*, Append. F, pp. 158-60.

168. *Ar. Ant.*, p. 175.

169. Starbo, *Geog.*, XI, viii, 9, *AICL*, p. 100.

170. *JRGS*, XII, p. 113; see also *AICL*, p. 100, fn.4.

171. Starbo, XI, viii, 9, *AICL*. p. 100.

172. *Ar. Ant.*, p. 175.

173. *Ibid.*

174. *CHI*, Vol.I, p. 490.

175. *Op.cit.*, p. 175.

176. Pliny, *Hist. Nat.*, VI, 25.

177. Cf. *Ar. Ant.*, p. 157.

178. *Ibid; AIT,* p. 34; H. Rawlinson, *JRGS*, XII, p. 113.

179. MMH (London, 1793), p. 169; D'Anville, *Geographie Anc. tom.*, ii. p. 291.

180. *Ind. Ant.*, Vol. V, pp. 329-30.

181. *As. Res.,* Vol. VIII, p. 336.

182. Ouseley, *Oriental Geography*, pp. 209, 210 cf. *Ar. Ant*. p. 174.

183. *Geography of Al-Edrisi*; Preface to Ibn Haukil, p. xvii, cf. *Ibid.*

184. *Op. cit.* 174.

185. *Op. cit.* 178.

186. *CAGI*. pp. 33-35.

187. *E'tude*, pp. 14ff.cf. *AIMA*,1st edn. p. 108, note.

188. *Ibid.*

189. *CAGI*, p. 34.

190. Quoted in *ibid.*, p. 35.

191. *Dionysiaka*, XXVI. 30.

192. Cf. A. Cunningham, *CISSK,* pp. 32-33; *Geog. Jour.,* Vol. XII p. 13.

193. *History,* XXIII, 6, 72; see also *AICL,* p. 94.

194. H.H. Wilson, *op. cit.* p. 157; *CHI,* Vol. I, p. 311; Paul Masson Oursel *et. al., AIIC,* p. 30.

195. *CHI,* Vol. I, p. 311.

196. Strabo, *Geog.,* XV, i, 8; XV, ii, 8, 9, 10; *AICL,* pp. 14, note 3, 87-89; *AIT,* VI, 18, 4, pp. 310-12; A. Marcellinus, *Hist.,XX*III, vi, *AICL,* p. 93.

197. *Hist. Nat.,* VI. 23.

198. *Geog.,* VI, 24 cf. *AICL,.* p. 212.

199. *Geog.,* VI,18, 5, *AIT*, pp. 34 and 311 -12; see also *IIA*, p. 58, note 4; *Ar. Ant*., pp. 160, 176.

200. *Ibid.*

201. *Geog.,* XV, ii, 8, *AICL,* p. 87.

202. *Hist. Nat.,* VI, 17, 21.

203. Cf. Strabo, XI, viii, 9, *AICL,* P. 100 and note 5.

204. *Op. cit.*

205. *CAGI,* pp. 19, 30; see also his *CASE,* pp. 24-25.

206. *Op. cit.,* p. 176.

207. *Op. cit.,* Vol. 2, pp. 213-14, cf. Motichandra, *op. cit.,* p. 91.

208. *YCTI*, Vol. II, pp. 266-267.

209. "The Itinerary of Yuan-Chwang", in *ibid*., pp. 342-43.

210. *CAGI*, p. 30.

211. *AIT*, pp. 311-12.

212. *Op cit.*

213. *Op cit.*

214. *AIT*, pp. 311-12.

215. *AICL*, Introd., xiv, Bunbury, *HAG*, Vol. I, p. 142.

216. *CAGI*, p. 32; M. Elphinstone, *An Account of the Kingdom of Kābul,* Vol. 1, p. 160.

217. *Geog.,* XV, ii, 10.

218. For details see Strabo *Geog*., XV, i. 10; XV, ii, 9; *Pliny Hist. Nat*., VI, 20; Plutarch *Vit. Alex.,(Life of Alexander*) Ch. LXII; Justin, *Hist. Phil*., XV, 4;

Periplus; p. 189; R.C Jain (ed.).*MAIMA*, pp. xii-xiii; V.A. Smith, *EHI*, App. F. pp. 158-60; Lassen, *Pent. Ind.*, p. 42.

219. Cf. Strabo, *Geog.*, XI, xi, 1, *AICL*, pp. 100-1.

220. *Ibid*, XV, ii, 9, *AICL*, p. 89.

221. *Hist. Nat.,* VI, 16(18).

222. *Geog.*, VI, 11, 1-9, *AIT*, pp. 267-74.

223. *Ibid.*

224. *RTGEA*, p. 40, note 3.

225. *Geog.*, XI, 11, 3.

226. *Anab.*, III, 29.

227. *Geog.*, VI, 11, 9.

228. *Hist, Alex.*, VII, 4.

229. *History*, Bk. XXIII.

230. *AIT*, p. 271.

231. *Historical Researches*, Vol. I. *Asiatic Nations*, p. 424.

232. *Bactria from the Earliest Times to the Extinction of Bactrio-Greek Rule in the Punjab*, p. 18.

233. *Ibid.*, p. 23.

234. *Ibid.*, p. 10.

235. *Intercourse Between India and the Western World from the Earliest Times to the fall of Rome*, p. 69.

236. *Bactria* (*op.cit.*), p. 10.

237. *Caravan Journeys,* p. 206, cf. *Ibid.*, p. 10, note 3.

238. *A History of Greece to the Death of Alexander the Great*, p. 789.

239. *Geog.*, XI, xi, 2; XV, ii, 10; see also Bunbury *HAG*, Vol. I., pp 425ff.

240. *Hist. Nat.*, VI. 18.

241. *Anab.*, III, 29; IV, I,7, 15.

242. *AIT*, pp. 268-69.

243. *AICL.*, p. 90, note 4.

244. *YCTI*, Vol. I, p. 108.

245. *Anab.*, IV, 22, 6; *IIA,* p. 59.

246. *Itin. Alex.,*Ch. 104, *AICL,* pp. 150-51.

247. *Ar. Ant.,* p. 183.

248. *IIA,* Appendices, Note B, pp. 332-33.

249. *NAB,* pp. 48-51.

250. *Op. cit.,* Vol. III, pp. 186-90.

251. *EHI,* p. 53.

252. *History of the Panjab Hill States,* Vol. II, p. 666.

253. *Op. cit.,* p. 183.

254. *HAG,* Vol. I, p. 439, note 7.

255. *History of Greece,* Vol. VII, p. 5.

256. *CAGI,* p. 30; see also HAG, I, p. 491, note X.

257. *IIA,* Note B, pp. 332-33.

258. *The Gates of India.* pp. 85-88; see also *CHI,* Vol. I, p. 312, note 3.

259. JA, October 1837, p. 379, note.

260. *Op. cit.* Vol. II, p. 205.

261. *Indika, Bk.* IV, Fragm. XLVI, and Fragm. LVI, cf. *AIMA*, 1st edn, pp. 110 and 152; *Ind. Ant*., Vol. V. p. 89.

262. *Hist.Nat.* VI, 21. 8; VI, 23, 11.

263. *Geog.,* XV, i, 8 and 27, *AICL,* pp. 12-13, 32-33; see also Hamilton and Falconer, *op, cit.,* Vol. IIII, P 76; *AIMA,* p. 110.

264. *Anab.,* Bk. V, Ch. I, *IIA*, pp. 79-80; *Indika,* pt. I, Chs. I & V, cf. *A1MA,* 1st edn, pp. 179-80 and 195; see also Chinnock, *op. cit.,* p. 399.

265. Hist. Alex., VIII, 10, *IIA*, pp. 192-94.

266. *Hist. Phil.,* XII. 7, *IIA*, p. 321.

267. *Vit. Alex. (Life of Aexander),* Ch. LVIII, *IIA*, p. 305.

268. *AIMA*, 1st edn. p. 110.

269. *Ibid.,* pp. 179-80.

270. *AIMA.*, p. 195.

271. *Bib. Hist.,* III, 63 and 72.

272. *Geog.,* XV, I, 8, *AICL,* p. 13.

273. *Bib. Hist.,* tr. by Booth, Bk. I. ii, 12, *AICL,* p. 204.

274. *AICL,* p. 192.

275. See J.E. Schwartzberg (ed.), *HASA*, pp. 169 ff; Heeren, *Historical Researches,* Vol. I, p. 294.

276. Cf. *IIA,* Note G. p. 339; *AIMA*, p. 180, note.

277. *Ethnography of Afghanistan,* pp. 64-76.

278. *The Indian Borderland*, pp. 270-342; *The Gates of India,* pp. 122-24; see also Ar. *Ant.,* p. 193; W.W. Tarn, *Alexander the Great*, II. pp. 45ff.

279. *EHI,* pp. 56-57. R.C. Jain (*MAIMA*, XXXVII, App. 3) has mistakenly placed the city between the Kaukasos and the Pamir or Meru mountain.

280. *AICL*, p. 13, note 1; *IIA,* Note G, p. 338; *CAGI,* p. 39; *AIT*, pp. 113-14; *JRAS,* Vol. XIII, pp. 183- 207. Many places bore the name of Nysa. The Indian Nysa did not become known to the Greeks till Alexander's expedition. In the cosmogonic geography of the *Zend-Avesta* it figures as a part of Ancient Iran. See A.D. Humboldt (ed.), *Central Asia* (1843), I, pp. 116 ff.

281. Cf. M. Julien. *Hiouen Thsang, iii,* p. 305; see also *IIA,* p. 338, note; *AIT,* p. 113.

282. *CAGI,* pp. 38-39.

283. H.A. Giles. *RBK,* pp. 12, 15.

284. *YCTI,* Vol. I, pp. 182-89.

285. *Geog., XV,* i, 26, *AICL,* p. 31.

286. *AICL,* p. 31, note 3.

287. Thirlwall's *History of Greece,* Vol. VII, p. 7.

288. *Anab.,* IV, 24, *IIA,* p. 64.

289. *Indika,* tr. Chinnock, *op. cit.,* pp. 230-31.

290. *The Itinerary of Alex.,* Ch. 105, *AICL,* p. 151, and note 3.

291. *IIA* p. 64, note 1; Ar. *Ant.,* p. 189; B.C. Sinha, *Studies in Alexander's Campaigns,* p. 26; J.F.C. Fuller, *The Generalship of Alexander the Great,* pp. 126, 245.

292. *IIA,* p. 64, note 1; Fuller, *op. cit.,* p. 126.

293. M. Court, "Alexander's Exploits on the West of the Indus", in *JASB*, April 1839, pp. 307-9.

294. *Ar. Ant.*, p. 189.

295. *IP.,* p. 457.

296. *CHI,* Vol. I, p. 317.

297. Arrian (*Anab*., IV, 24-25) and Ourtius (*Hist. Alex*. VIII, 10) mention them as Aspasians, whereas, on the other hand, Aristoboulos (quoted by Starbo,

Geog., XV, I, 17, *AICL*, p. 22) refers to them as Aspasioi. Strabo mentions them both as Aspasioi and Hippasii or Hippasioi (*Geog.* XV, I, 27, AICL, p. 33; also MSS, XV, 691, 698, cf CHI, Vol. I, p. 316, note 1).

298. *IP*, pp. 456-57.

299. Arrian, *Anab.*, IV, 24-25, *IIA*, pp. 63-66; Valerius, *The Itinerary of Alex.*, Ch. 105, *AICL*, p. 151.

300. Arrian, *Anab.*, IV, 25, *IIA*, pp. 65-66.

301. *Anab.*, IV, 23, *IIA*, pp. 60-62; *Indika*, tr. Chinnock, *op.cit.*, pp. 230-31.

302. *Hist. Alex.*, VIII, 10, *IIA*, pp. 192-93, also p. 64, note 1.

303. *Ar. Ant.*, p. 187.

304. Arian, *Anab*, IV, 26, *IIA*, pp. 66-68; *Indika*, pt. I, ch. I, *AIMA*, Ist edn. p. 180 and note; Chinnock, *op. cit.*, pp. 230-31; Curtius, *Hist. Alex.*, VIII, 10, 22-5, *IIA*, pp. 191-94; Diodoros, *Bib. Hist.*, XVII, 84, IIA, pp. 269-70; Justin, *Hist. Phil.* XII , 7, *IIA*, p. 322 and note 2; Plutarch, *Lif. Alex.*, Ch. 58, IIA, p. 305; Strabo, *Geog.*, XV, i, 27, *AICL*, p. 33; J. Valerius, *The Itin. of Alex.*, ch. 106, AICL, p. 151; see also CAI, pp. 11-13, 162, 215; B.N. Puri, *op.cit.*, p. 54; Bunbury, HAG, Vol. I, pp. 425-29, 442-43; Heeren, *Historical Researches*, Vol. I, pp. 294-95; HASA, pp. 169ff; Duncker, HA, Vol. IV, Ch. IV; "The Nations and Princes of the Land of the Indus", p. 393; J.T Wheeler, *India from the Earliest Ages,* Vol. III, pp. 156, 160-61; "Greek and Roman India", in *The History of India from the Earliest Ages*, 1st edn.(London, 1881), rept, in *Ancient India* (Delhi, 1983), pp. 99, 102-3; W.W. Tarn, *Alexander the Great*, Vol. I, p. 89; Holdich, *The Gates of India Being an Historical Narrative*, p. 128; Raverty, *NAB,* pp. 200, 234; Enriquez, *The Pathana Borderland,* p. 37; Deane, *JRAS,* 1896, p. 655; Aurel Stein, *On Alexander's Track to the Indus,* pp. 43-44; "Alexander's Campaign on the Indian North-West Frontier", *Geog. Journ, JRGS,* no. 70 (1927), pp. 417-39; "An Archaeological Tour in Upper Swāt and Adjacent Hill Tracts", MASI, no. 42 (Calcutta, 1930); *Archaeological Tour in Buner* (Lahore, 1898), p. 53.

305. *Geog.,* XV, I, 27, *AICL,* p. 33, and note 2.

306. *Hist. Alex,* V111, 10, 22-5, see also *IIA*, pp. 194-95; CAI, pp. 109-10.

307. *Itin. Alex.,* Ch. 106, *AICL*, p. 151.

308. See also Arrian's *Anab.*, tr. by E.J. Chinnock, pp. 233-34, and by E.J. Robson, Vol. I, pp. 427-28.

309. *Hist. Alex.*, VIII, 10.

310. Cf. *IIA,* Note D, pp. 334-35.

311. MMH, pp. 120-21.

312. On the Alexander's exploits on the West of the Indus", *JASB*. April 1839; also *IIA*, Note D, pp 334-35; *AICL,* p. 33, note. 2; *Ar. Ant.,* pp. 189-90; Holdich, *op.cit.*, p. 105.

313. *Ar. Ant.,* pp. 189-90

314. *IP,* pp. 43, 75, 456-57, 489; also *Bh. Sāv.*, Vol. I, p. 207; Lassen, *Ind. Alt.,* Vol. 11, pp. 136-38; St. Martin, *E'tude,* pp. 35-36.

315. *On Ālexander's Track to the Indus,* p. 44.

316. Cf. *AICL,* p. 33, note 2.

317. *Bhīśma Parva*, 12, 33-34; see also *Bh. Sāv.,* Vol. 2, pp. 130-31; *Mbh. Ko.,* pp. 667, also 512.

In the aforesaid Parvan of the *Mbh.,* the town has been confounded with the people of the same name inhabiting the Śaka-dvīpa or Śakasthān called by the ancient historians of Greece Massagetae who had ethnic affinities with the Śakas or Indo-Scythians.

The Hanskāyana of the *Mbh.* (*Sabhā Parva*, 48, 13) in all probability represents the Aśvakāyana or Assakenoi because it finds mention along with other tribes of the north-west.

318. *The History of India,* ed. E.B. Cowell, 9th edn.. pp. 331, 36.

319. *The Pathans,* p. 53.

320. *East and West* (New Series). Vol. XIV, nos. 1-2. p. 27.

321. *Op. cit.,* p. 128 and Map facing p. 94; see also *EHI,* p. 57: L.J. Trotter and W.H. Hutton, *History of India from the Earliest times to the present day*, p. 29.

322. R.C. Jain, *MAIMA*, App. 3.

323. *Oration* I. *Concerning the Fortune of Alexander,* 2, *AICL.* p. 206, note 1.

324. For details about the Aspasians and Assakenians with special reference to the Aśvakas see *AIMA,* 1st edn, pp. 152-53, note; *IIA,* Note C, pp. 333-34; *AICL,* p. 22, note 1; *CHI,* p. 316, note 1: St. Martin, *Ĕtude;* pp. 376-78; A.A. Macdonell. *HSL* (Oxford. 1936), pp. 412 ff; Lassen. *Ind. Alt.* Vol. II, p. 129; *HA,* Vol. IV, Ch. IV, p. 386; *IP,* pp. 456-57; Tucci, "The tombs of the Asvakayana Assakenoi", in *East and West,* Vol. XIV, Nos. 1-2, pp. 27-28; R.N. Saletore, *EIC,* Vol. I, pp. 126, 128. 139; B.C. Law, *HGAI,* pp. 66-67; *Tribes in Ancient India,* p. 180; *IETBJ,* p. 107; S.M. Ali, *The Geography of the Purainas,* pp. 171-72; Varāhamihira's *Br. Sam.,* XIV, 22 (described as Aśmaka).

325. S.B. Cbaudhan, *ESAI.* p. 52.

326. *Arrian, Anab.,* IV, 26, 27, IIA, pp. 66-70; Curtius, *Hist. Alex.*, VIII, 10, *IIA*, pp. 194-96; Valerius, *Itin, Alex.*, Chs. 106 and 109, *AICL*, pp. 151-52.

327. *Co. Anc. Ind.,* p. 61, Pl. 11, 17.

328. *CCIM,* Vol. I, pp. 147, 157.

329. *Indian Studies* (Wien, 1895), No. III, p. 46.

330. *Op. cit.,* p. 147 (In p. 157 he has suggested third century BCE).

331. Indian Coins, p. 14.

332. *CCBM,* pp. cxlvi-cxlvii.

333. See the views of C. Silvi Antonini and G. Tucci, *East and West,* Vol. XIV, nos. 1-2, pp. 16-17, 27- 28.

334. *Anab.,* IV, 27, 28, *IIA,* pp. 68-71; see also *Anab.*, tr, E.I. Robson, Vol. I, pp. 431-33.

335. *Hist. Alex,* VIII, 10, *ibid.,* p. 194.

336. *Itin. Alex.*, Ch. 107, *AICL*, p. 152; See also Smith, *EHI*, pp. 59-60; *HASA*, pp. 169 ff; Bunbury. *HAG*, Vol. I, pp. 442-43; *HA*, Vol. IV, Ch. IV, p. 395; *CAI*, pp. 13-15; B.C. Sinha, *op.cit.*, pp. 27-28; Fuller, *op.cit.*, pp. 126, 246-247; Heeren, *Historical Researches*, Vol. I, pp. 294-295.

337. *Ep. Ind.,* Vol. XXI, p. 301.

338. *On Alexander's Track to the Indus,* pp. 46-48, 59-60.

339. Cf. *Ar. Ant.,* p. 191.

340. *CAGI,* p. 56.

341. *Ibid; IIA,* Note E, p. 335; *Ar. Ant.,* p. 191.

342. *MMH* (Section III, corrected and enlarged in 1791), p. 121.

343. *Op.cit.,* pp. 59-60; see also W.W. Tarn, *Alexander the Great*, Vol. I, p. 90.

344. *JASB.* April, 1839, p. 309.

345. *Anab.*, IV., 27-28, *IIA,* pp. 68-71.

346. *Itin. Alex.,* Ch. 107. *AICL.*, p. 152.

347. *Ibid.*, Ch. 108, *AICL*, p. 152.

348. *Anab.*, IV. 28-30, *IIA*, pp. 70-76.

349. *Geog.,* XV, I, 8, *AICL,* p. 13.

350. *Bib. Hist.,* XVII. 85, *IIA,* pp. 271-72.

351. *Hist. Phil.,* XII.7, *ibid*, p. 322.

352. *Vit. Apollo.* (*The Life of Apollonius of Tyana)* ii, 10.

353. *Itin. Alex.,* Ch. 108, *AICL,* p. 152.

354. *Geog.,* XV, i, 8, *AICL, pp.* 13-14; see also Curtius, *Hist. Alex.,* VIII, 11, *IIA,* pp. 197-200.

355. *JASB,* 1836, p. 395.

356. *CAGI,* pp. 51-52, *JASB,* 1848, p. 103.

357. *JASB,* 1854, p. 309; 1863, p. 409; see also *IIA*, Note F, pp. 335-37; *AICL,* p. 13, note 2; Grote's *History of India,* Vol. VIII, pp. 437-38, cf. *AIMA,* 1st edn. pp. 110-11.

358. *Anab.,* IV, 28.

359. *AICL.,* p. 13, note 2.

360. *Geog. Jour.,* no. 70 (1927), pp. 417-39; *Alexander's Track to the Indus,* pp, 118-19, 143-48, 154.

361. *Itin. Alex.*, Ch. 108; *AIMA,* p. 152.

362. Arrian, *Anab.,* IV, 29, *IIA,* pp. 73-74; Strabo, *Geog*., XV, i, 8, *AICL.* p. 13.

363. *Anab.,* IV, 30; *IIA,* pp. 75-76.

364. *Ibid.,* IV, 29.

365. Arrian, *Anab.,* IV, 30; *IIA*, p. 76 and note 3.

366. *Ar. Ant.,* p. 192.

367. *Anab.,* IV. 28: *IIA,* p. 72.

368. *Geog.,* VII, I, 57, *AIT,* pp. 142-43.

369. *Hist. Alex.,* VIII, 12; *IIA*, p. 200.

370. *Anab.,* IV, 28; *IIA,* pp. 72-73.

371. VIII, 12.

372. *AIT,* pp. 142-43.

373. *JASB.* 1854. p. 309; also *IIA,* pp. 72, notes 3 and 5, 337, Note F.

374. *CAGI,* p, 48; see also his *CASE*, p. 27.

375. Cf. *Ar. Ant.*, p. 191.

376. *IIA*, p. *72,* note 5; George MacMunn, *MRI,* pp. 22-23; *AIT.* pp. 142-43.

377. *Ibid.*

378. *AIT,* pp. 142-43.

379. *IIA,* p. 72, note 1; *EHI* p. 60.

380. *An Account of Kābul,* Vol. 1, p. 328, cf. Ar. *Ant.,* p. 188.

381. *Geog.,* XV, i. 27, *AICL,* p. 33, and note 3.

382. *Hist. Nat.,* VI, XXI, 23.

383. *Anab*., IV, 22; and 28, *IIA*, pp. 59 and 72; *Indika*, I, I, *AIMA*, 1st edn., p. 180 and note; Chinnock, *op.cit*., pp. 228, 403; also Lassen, *Ind. Alt*., Vol. II, p. 858.

384. *Geog.,* VII, I, 44, AIT, pp. 115-17, and 362, note.

385. *Periplus,* Sec. 47,p. 41, and pp. 183-84, note.

386. *CNES,* p. 121.

387. *Orb. Des*., vv. 1080-1165, *AICL,* p. 189.

388. *Indika,* I, I; *IIA,* p. 180.

389. *Periplus,* p. 183; note; *IIA,* p. 59, note 5.

390. Arrian, *Anab.,* IV, 22; *IIA,* p. 60.

391. Arrian, *Anab*., IV, 22; *IIA*, p. 60, note 1; also Curtius *Hist. Alex*., VIII, 12, 13; *HA*, Vol. IV, Ch. IV, pp. 392-93.

392. Strabo, *Geog*., XV, I, 27, *AICL*, p. 33 note 1.

393. *IP*, p. 456.

394. *Indika,* I, I; *AIMA,* 1st edn. p. 180.

395. *Geog.,* XV. i, 27.

396. *AIT,* pp. 115-17.

397. *CASR,* Vol.II (1871), pp. 90 ff; Vol. XIX (1885), pp. 96-110; *ASIAR,* 1902-3 (by John Marshall), pp. 41 ff, 140-54; *AIMA,* pp. 180-81, note; *Periplus,* p. 184, note; *IIA,* pp. 59, note 5, 72, note 3; see also St. Martin, *Ĕtude*, p. 37; Bunbury, HAG, I, pp. 440, and 498-99, note Cc; *CASE*, p. 26; Holdich, *op.cit.,* p. 99; B.C.Law, *Geographical Aspect of Kālidāsa's Works,* p. 5.

398. A Foucher, "Notes Sur La geographie ancienne du Gāndhāra", in *Bulletin de L'Ecole francaise d' Extreme-Oreint,* Hanoi, October 1901, tr. into English by H. Hargreaves, *Notes on the Ancient Geography of Gāndhāra* (Vārāṇasī, 1974), pp. 10-11; *CAGI,* pp. 42-43; see also Cunningham, *Co. Anc. Ind.,* p. 32; B.N. Puri, *op. cit.* p. 55; *IIA*, p. 59, note 5, 181, note.

399. *JASB*, 1836, p. 479.

400. *JASB,* 1836, p. 394.

401. M. Wheeler, *Charasada,* Summary facing p. 1; *EIP,* p. 172 and Pl. 54; see also John Marshall, *Taxila,* Vol. 1, p. 4.

402. *YCTI,* Vol. I, p. 214.

403. *Ibid*., p. 199.

404. Arrian, *Anab.,* IV, 28.

405. A.E. Anspach, *De Alexandri Magni Expeditione Indica* (London, 1903), p. 65, note 200, cf. *CHI,* p. 319, note 1.

406. Obtained by Roberts, deciphered by J. Downson, *JRAS*, Vol. XX, p. 221; see also notes on the same inscription in *JASB,* 1863, p. 139.

407. W.W. Hunter, "The Greeks in India", in *The Indian Empire: Its peoples, History of Products*, 3rd edn. (London, 1882), rept. in *Ancient India* (Delhi, 1983), p. 87, note 6; see also *JRAS*, Vol. XX. p. 343.

408. Quoted by Strabo, *Geog.,* XV. i, 17, *AICL,* p. 22.

409. *Geog.,* XV, i, 28, *AICL,* pp. 33-34; also Hamilton and Falconer's tr. *The Geography of Strabo*, Vol. III, p. 90; H.L. Jones' tr. *The Geography of Strabo,* Vol. VII, p. 25.

410. Anab., V, 3 and 8; *IIA,* pp. 83 and 92; see also Henry Baveridge, *Com. Hist. Ind.,* Vol. I, p. 31; F. Annie Steel, *IPPH,* p. 37; Holdich, *Gates of India,* pp. 114, 179, 185.

411. *Vit. Alex.* (Life of Alexander), Ch. 59, *IIA,* p. 305.

412. *Geog.,* XV, i, 28, *AICL*, p. 34; see also AICL, p. 22, note 2.

413. *Hist. Nat.,* VI, XXI, 23.

414. *Bib. Hist*., XVIII, *6, AICL,* p. 201.

415. *Itin. Alex.,* Ch. 104, *ibid.,* p. 150, and note 4.

416. *Orb. Des*., vv. 1080-1165, *AICL,* p. 189.

417. *Geog.,* VII, I, 45; see also *AIT*, pp. 118-21.

418. *Hist. Nat.,* VI, 21; *AIMA,* 1st edn. Frag, LVI, p. 150, note; *AICL,* pp. 17-18, note 1. Taxila has been described as one of the greatest cities of the east and as the principal seat of learning in northern India. See V.A. Smith, *EHI*, p. 65; and F.A. Steel, *IPPH*, p. 37.

419. For details see *CASE*, p. 27; *CASR*. Vol. 11(1871), pp. 112, 125; Vol. V(1875). p. 66; *CAGI,* pp. 88-89,94 f; A. Foucher, *op. cit.,* p. 38 note 4; see also Delmerick's "Notes on the Archaeological Remains at Shah-Ki-Dheri and the site of Taxila". *JASB,* 1870. p. 89; *ASIAR* (by John Marshall), 1912-13, Pt. I, pp. 1-5, 8-16; 1915-16, pt. I, pp. 10-12; Aurel Stein, *ARNWI*, p. 11; Robert Shafer, *EAI,* p. 129; N.L. Dey, *GDAMI,* pp. 200-2; V.A. Smith, *The Oxford History of India,* rev. by H.G. Rawlinson, p. 49; *AIMA,* pp. 150-51, note; *IIA*, p. 342, note 1; *AICL*, pp. 22, notes 2, and 33, note 4; Burnes, *Travels*, II, p. 58; St. Marti, *Ĕtude*, pp. 92-98; Wilson, *Ar.Ant.*, p. 196; Burnbury, *HAG*, I, pp. 443, and 499, note Dd; V.A. Smith, *EHI*, p. 65.

420. *CAGI,* pp. 94-95.

421. *Taxila,* Vol. I, p. 20; see also M. Wheeler, *EIP,* pp. 173-74, pls. 50, 51.

422. *Taxila,* Vol. I, p. 89.

423. *Taxila,* pp. 92 f.

424. *Ibid.,* pp. 3, 12 f, 20.

425. *Hist. Alex.,* VIII, 12, 14, *IIA,* pp. 200-3.

426. *Bib. Hist.,* XVII. 86, *ibid.,* pp. 272-73; see also Sylvain Levi, *JA,* Vol. XV, Series, 8, 1890, p. 234.

427. *Hist. Alex., VIII.* 12, *AICL,* p. 34, note 1.

428. *Anab.,* V. 3, *IIA,* p. 83.

429. Wheeler, EIP, p. 174. pl. 53; Allan, *CCBM,* pp. xvi, 1, 2, pl. 1; Smith, *CCIM.* p. 136; *MASI,* no. 59 (Delhi, 1939), pp. 1, 3,100, pl. vi; G.M. Young, " A New Hoard from Taxila (Bhir Mound)", *AI,* no. 1(1946), pp. 27-36; see also *IPPH,* p. 37; *JNSI*, Vol. IV, pt. 1, p. 61.

430. *Op. cit.,* p. xvii.

431. *IIA,* pp. 342-43, note I.

432. *History,* XI, 34 (2), *AICL,* p. 209.

433. Lassen, *Ind. Alt.,* Vol. II, p. 273.

434. *JIH,* Vol. LVI, pt. I, (1978), p. 48.

435. W.W. Tam, *GBI,* p. 130, and note 2; *JASB,* 1920, pp. 305, 310.

436. p. 270, note.

437. Marshall, *op.cit.,*Vol. I, pp. 4, 12 f, 21 f, 113; *CAGI,* pp. 97-98; also W.W. Tarn, *The Greeks in Bactria and India*, pp. 359-60.

438. E.J. Rapson, *Indian Coins,* pp. 5-6, 14.

439. Sten Konow, *CII,* Vol. II, pt. I, no. XIII, pp. 23-29; see aslo *JIH,* Vol. XIV (1935), pp. 328-38.

440. Rapson, *op. cit.,* pp. 7-8, 14; Cunningham, Co. *Anc. Ind.* p. 60, pl. II, III; *CASR,* XIV, p. 16, pl. x.

441. *Vit. Apollo*., II, 12, 20,22, 23-25, tr. by F.C. Conybeare, *The life of Apollonius of Tyana,* Vol. I, pp. 147, 167-83, and 185; also Priaulx, *The Indian Travels of Apollonius of Tyana...,* pp. 13-15; *AICL*, pp. 191-93; *CAI*, pp. 387-89; B.N. Puri, *India as described by Early Greek Writers,* pp. 146-49; IIA, p. 344, note I; *CAGI*, p. 91; G.P. Singh, " Early History of North-West India as described by the Greek and Assyrian Travellers," JIH (Paltinum Jubilee Volume), pp. 45-48.

442. *Taxila*, Vol. I, pp. 140-41, also pp. 12, 63-64, 198, pl. 24; also his *Guide to Taxila,* pp. 15, 91; *ASIAR*, 1912-13. pp. 8, 30, 34 and 37; see also *AIHA*, pp. 242-43; S. Piggott, *Some cities of Ancient India* (Oxford, 1945). G. Woodcock (*The Greeks in India,* p. 130) has rightly pointed out that the archeological discoveries at the ancient site of Taxila are in agreement with the description of the city given in Philostratus' *Life of Apollonius of Tyana.*

443. *CAGI,* p. 100.

444. M.A. Court, "Memoir of a Map of the Provinces of Peucelaotis and Taxila", *JASB,* Vol. V (1836). p. 468.

445. H.A. Giles, *The Travels of Fa-hien* or *RBK,* p. 12.

446. *YCTI,* Vol. I, pp. 240-41.

447. *Akhaṇḍa Bhārata Mein Saṁskṛtī Kā Uṣāḥ Kāla,* p. 9.

448. *CASR,* Vol. 5, 1875 (report for the year 1872-73). pp. 4-5.

449. Quoted by Strabo, *Geog*., XV, i, 3. *AICL,* pp. 8-9.

450. *Hist. Phil.,* XIL, 6.

451. *Hist. Alex.,* IX, I; *IIA,* p. 217.

452. *Anab.,* V. 22, 4; *ibid.,* p. 115.

453. *Bib. Hist.,* XVII, 91.3; *IIA,* pp. 279-80.

454. *Geog.,* XV, 1, 30; *AICL,* pp. 36, 37, note 1; see also Hamilton and Falconer, *op. cit.,* Vol. III, p. 92.

455. *IGI,* Vol. XII, p. 393; V.A. Smith, *JRAS,* 1903, P. 687: *EHI,* p. 81.

456. CHI, Vol. I, p. 332, note 7.

457. For details see Rennell, *MMH*, sec. iii, pp. 122-23; HA, Vol. IV, Ch, IV, pp. 400-2; H. Baveridge, *Com. Hist. Ind*., Vol. I. pp. 35-36; A. Steel, *IPPH*, p. 40; Bunbury, *HAG*, Vol. I, pp. 444-45 and 505, note Hh; Heeren, *MAHA*, p. 218f; R.D. Banerji, *PAHI.* p. 79: J.T. Wheeler, *India from the Earliest Ages,* Vol. III, p. 165; "Greek and Roman India" in *op. cit.,* p. 105. W.W. Hunter. "The Greeks in India" in *op, cit.,* p. 88: Burnes, *op. cit.,* Vol. III, p. 182; J.B. Bury, *A History of Greece to the Death of Alexander the Great,* p. 807; see also AIIC, p. 32.

458. "Extracts from Notes of a journey from Lahore to Kerachee", JASB, Vol, VI, p. 57.

459. *Anab.,* V, 23; V, 24, 5; *IIA,* pp. 117-21; see also *CAI,* pp. 47-51.

460. *IP,* p. 73.

461. Sylvain Levi, *JA,* Vol. XV, Series 8 (1890), pp. 237-39; *AIT,* p. 365, note.

462. *AIT,* pp. 122-24, 157, 169 and also 365-66, note; see also M.R. Singh, GDEP, pp. 155-56.

463. *Ĕtude*, p. 326.

464. See Lassen, *Pent. Ind*., p. 65, v. 16; *AIT*, p. 365, note.

465. *Ibid.,* p. 20: *AIT.* p. 365, note.

466. Wilson, *Ar. Ant.,* pp. 196-97: see also *As. Res..* Vol. XV, p. 108; Bunbury, *HAG,* Vol. 1, pp. 444-45.

467. *CAGI,* p. 151.

468. *CAGI,* pp. 153-55, 160; also Wilford, *As. Res.,* vols. V, p. 282: VI, p. 520; IX, p. 53.

469. *IIA.* note M, pp. 347-48: *AICL,* p. 37, note 1; see also C.J. Rodgers, *Report on Sangala Tibba,* News Press, Lahore, 1906; *PASB,* 1896.

470. *AICL,* p. 200, note 2; B.C. Law, *HGAI,* pp. 105, 122; *AIT,* pp. 365-66, note; Fleet, *PIOC,* 14th Session (Algiers, 1905), I, pp. 164 ff; see also *CASR,* XIV, pp. 44-46.

471. *Dionysiaka,* Bk. XXVI, *AICL,* p. 200, and note 2.

472. Saint Martin, *Ĕtude;* pp. 103-8; *Ind. Ant.,* 1884, p. 350: *AICL,* p. 200, note 2.

473. *GBI,* pp. 247-48, 486-87.

474. B.C. Law, *HPL,* Vol. II, p. 356; Rāhula Sāṅkṛtyāyana, *Pāli Sāhityu Kā Itihāsa,* p. 183.

475. *Milinda-pañha,* ed. V. Trenckner, pp. 1-3; Rāhula Sāṅkṛtyāyana, *op. cit.,* pp. 183-84.

476. *YCTI,* Vol. I, 288-90.

477. *Anab.,* V, 2; *IIA*, pp. 115, 116, and note.

478. *Bib. Hist.,* XVII, 91; *ibid.,* pp. 279-80.

479. *Hist. Phil.,* XII, 8; *ibid.,* p. 323; see also Orosius, *History,* III, 19 (for Adraestae); B.C. Law, *HGAI,* p. 63 (for identification of Adraistai).

480. *AIT,* p. 377, note.

481. *Geog.,* XV, 1, 29, *AICL,* p. 35; Hamilton and Falconer, *op. cit.,* Vol. III, p. 91.

482. *CAGI,* pp. 135-36.

483. *CAGI,* p. 137.

484. *Ibid.,* p. 138.

485. Burnes, *op. cit.,* Vol. II, p. 51; Court, *JASB.* 1836, pp. 472-73.

486. *Op. cit.*

487. *CAGI,* p. 136.

488. *Op. cit*

489. *CAGI,* p. 137.

490. *Geog.,* XV, I, 29, *AICL,* pp. 35-36 and note 4.

491. *Anab.*, V, 19; *IIA*, p. 110; Chinnock, *op. cit.*, p. 296, note 4.

492. *Hist.Nat.*, VI, 21,23, cf. *AIMA* 1st edn.. Frag. LVI, pp. 149-50.

493. *Bib. Hist.,* XVII, 89; *IIA*, pp. 276-77.

494. *Hist. Phil.,* XII, 8; *IIA,* p. 323.

495. *Life of Alexander*, Ch. LXI, *IIA,* P. 309: also *Oration,* I, 5, *AICL,* p. 207.

496. For details see *CAGI,* pp. 149-50; *CASR,* vols. II, pp. 174-75; XIV, pp. 41-42; *AICL,* pp. 35-36, note 4; *IIA,* p. 110, note 3; *AIMA, p. 150,* note; Aurel Stein, *ARNWI,* p. 32; "The Site of Alexander's passage of the Hydaspes and the battle with Porus", *Geog. Jour.* (JRGS), LXXX,1. (1932), pp. 31-46; Baveridge, *Comp. Hist. Ind.,* Vol. I. pp. 34-35; A.K. Majumdar, *EHIDS* (1st pub. Dacca, 1917, rept. Delhi, 1981), Vol. II, p. 508; J.T. Wheeler, *India from the Earliest Ages,* Vol. III, p. 163; W.W. Hunter, "The Greeks in India", in *op. cit.,* pp. 88, 90; Elphinstone, *Kābul,* Vol. I, p. 109; Burnes, *op. cit.,* Vol. II, pp. 49-51; Court, *JASB,* 1836, pp. 472-73; Abbott, *JASB,* Pt. 2 (1848), p. 619; *AIT,* pp. 124, 366, note; Bunbury, HAG, I, pp. 499-500, note Ee; St. Martin, Etude, pp. 99-102.

497. *Periplus;* p. 184, note; see also *CNES,* p. 121 and comm.

498. *Dionysiaka,* Bk. XXVI, *AICL,* p. 198 and note 5.

499. *IIA,* p. 129, note 2; Lassen, *Ind. Alt.,* Vol. II, p. 165, note.

500. *Anab.*, V, 20; *11A,* p. 112; Chinnock, *op. cit.,* p. 276; see also *HA*, Vol. IV, p. 400; *Comp. Hist. Ind.* Vol. 1, p. 35.

501. *IP,* pp. 75-76, 496.

502. *IIA*, pp. 111, note 2, 112, also 113-15.

503. *Geog.,* XV, I, 3; XV, I, 33; *AICL,* pp. 9 and 39- 40 (respectively).

504. *Geog.,* XV, I, 33; *ibid.* p. 40.

505. *Hist. Nat.,* VI, 17 (21), *AICL*, p. 108.

506. Cf. M. Elphinstone, 'The Greek Accoounts of India", in his *The History of India,* ed. by E.B. Cowell, 9th edn. (London, 1911), rept. in *Ancient India* (Delhi, 1983), Ch. III, p. 28.

507. *Anab.,* VI, 2; *IIA,* p. 133.

508. *EHI,* p. 93.

509. *Lif. Alex.,* Ch. LX, *IIA.* p. 309.

510. *IIA,* p. 112, note 1.

511. *HAG*, Vol. 1, p. 453.

512. *Anab.*, VI, 2, 2; IIA, p. 133; see also *AICL*, p. 37, note 1.

513. *CAGI*, pp. 130-31, 142.

514. *Geog*., XV, I, 30, *AICL,* pp. 36-37; Hamilton and Falconer, *op.cit*., Vol. III; p. 93.

515. *Hist. Alex*., IX,I, *IIA*, p. 219; see also *AICL,* pp. 37, note 1, 46, note 3; *IIA,* pp. 133, note 2, 411; Bunbury, *HAG,* Vol. 1, p. 455; *MMH,* p. 123 (for different views about the locations).

516. *Bib. Hist*. XVII, 91, 92; *IIA*, pp. 279-80.

517. *Hist. Alex*., IX, I; *IIA*, pp. 219-20; see also *AICL*, p. 57, note 3.

518. V.A. Smith, *CCIM,* Vol. I, pp. *7,* 8, pl. I. 1; Rapson, *Indian Coins,* p. 3, pl. I, 8; also his Remarks in *Num. Chron*., 1904, p. 323; D.C. Sircar, *SI,* Vol. I, p. 83 and note 2; *CHI,* Vol. I, p. 348 and pl. I, 17; *AICL,* p. 37. note 1.

519. *Num. Chron.,* 1943, pp. 60-72 cf. *JNSI*, Vol. VII, pp. 23-26. Sylvain Levi (*JA*, XV, 8, 1890, p. 237 f) has correctly identified Sophytes with Saubhūti.

520. *Geog*., VII, I, 48, *AIT*, pp. 125-27.

521. *Ind. Alt.,* Vol. III, p. 152; see also Ar. *Ant.,* p. 99.

522. *CAGI*, pp. 164, 166; see also *AIT,* p. 127.

523. *AIMA*, 1st edn., p. 111, and note.

524. *AIT,* p. 290.

525. *Indika*, pt. I, V (12); *AIMA*, p. 196; see also R.C. Jain (ed.) *MAIMA*, p. XV.

526. *Geog.,* XV, I, 8 and 33, *AICL,* p. 14, and note 2, and p. 40 (respectively).

527. *Orb. Des*., vv. 1080-1165, *AICL,* p. 189.

528. *Dionysiaka,* Bk. XXVI, *AICL,* pp. 199-200, note 11.

529. *Hist. Alex.,* IX. 4, *IIA,* pp. 232-33.

530. *Bib. Hist.,* XVII. 96, *ibid.,* pp. 285-86.

531. *Hist. Phil.,* XII. 9, *ibid.,* p. 324.

532. *IIA,* note Ee, p. 366.

533. "Shorkot Inscriptions", in J. Ph. Vogel, *Ep. Ind.,* Vol. XVI (1921), p. 16; see also B.C. Law, *HGAI,* pp. 66, 127-28.

534. *IP,* p. 73, also pp. 54, 66.

535. *Op. cit.,* Vol. I, p. 113.

536. *JASB,* 1840, p. 913.

537. For details see Arrian. *Anab.,*V1, 4-9; *Indika*, pt. I, ch. IV; also *IIA*, pp. 137-46; *AIMA*, 1st edn., pp. 190-91, note; Curtius. *Hist. Alex.,*IX, 4-7, *IIA,* pp. 234-46; Diodorus, *Bib. His.,*XVII, 98-99, *IIA,* pp. 287-89; Plutarch, *Lif. Alex.,* Ch. 63, *IIA,* pp. 311-12; Justin, *Hist. Phil.,* XII, *9,IIA,* pp. 324-25; *IIA,* note P, pp. 350-51, note Q. pp. 351-52; Smith, *EHI,* pp. 98-100; Raverty, *op. cit.,* p. 364; *Ind. Ant.,* Vol. V, pp. 87-96, 333; also the views of R.L. Raikes and R.H. Dyson, *Ancient Cities of the Indus,* ed. by G.L. Possehl, pp. 225 f, 230 f; B.C. Law, *HGAI,* pp. 110-11; *HA,* Vol. IV, p. 403 f; *Comp. Hist. Ind.,* Vol. I, p. 37; J.T. Wheeler, *India from the Earliest Ages,* Vol. III, p. 165; *AIIC,* p. 33; *AICL,* p. 40, note 1; Gerini *(RTGEA,* p. 535) calls the people 'Malla".

538. *Anab.,* VI, 7, *IIA,* pp. 142-44.

539. *CAGI,* p. 175; *IIA,* p. 141, note 1.

540. Anab.,VI, 6, *IIA,* pp. 140-41.

541. *CAGI,* p. 177; *IIA.,* pp. 141-42, note 2.

542. *CAGI,* p. 178.

543. *Op. cit.,* Vol. 1, p. 117.

544. *Travels,* Vol. I, p. 453: *JASB,* Vol. V1, p. 57.

545. Cf. *IIA,* note Q, pp. 351-52.

546. *MMH,* Sec. III, p. 128.

547. *CAGI*, pp. 189-90; se also *IIA,* p. 142, note 1.

548. *Travels,* Vol. I, p. 456.

549. Rennell, *MMH,* Sec. III, pp. 126-27; Orme's *Indostan*, Vol. II, *p. 225. cf. ibid*., p, 127, fn.

550. *CAGI,* pp. 192-93; *IIA,* p. 143, note 1, and note Q, p. 352. For the cities of Malloi see also Bunbury, *HAG*, I, pp. 514-15, note Ss.

551. *Anab.,* VI, 8, IIA, pp. 144-45.

552. *Ibid.,* VI, 4, *ibid.,* p. 137.

553. *Itin. Alex.,* 115 and 116, *AICL,* p. 154, and note 4, and p. 155.

554. *Geog.*, XV, I, 33, *AICL,* p. 40.

555. *Anab,* VI. 11, *IIA,* p. 149.

556. *Oration*, 1,2; II, 9; *AICL*., pp. 206-7.

557. *Voy. Near*., p. 171, and note 13.

558. For details see *AICL,* pp. 40, note 1, 154, note *4,* 206, note 1; *IIA,* note Q, p. 352; *Voy. Near*., P. 171, note 13; Rennell, *MMH,* Sec. III, pp. 123, 125-26; Baveridge, *Comp. Hist. Ind.,* Vol. I, p. 37. Bunbury, *HAG,* Vol. I, pp. 450-511, and 514, note Ss; Robertson, *HDAI,* p. 20; Burnes, *op. cit.,* Vol. III, p. 114; Gustav Oppert, *O1B* (Delhi, 1972), pp. 20, 82; W.W. Hunter, "The Greeks in India", in *op. cit.,* pp. 88-89; *CAGI,* pp. 186, 198-201; Wilson, *Ar. Ant*., p. 199.

559. *Op. cit.*

560. *EHI*, p. 100.

561. *CAGI,* pp. 194-95. The city of Multān situated to the southward of the Hydraotes is considered to be as one of the oldest in India. It had a citadel, and a brick wall covering an area of four miles. See W. Vincent, CNAIO, Vol.I, *The Voyage of Nearchus from the Indus to the Euphrates,* pp. 116-17.

562. *History of Greece,* Vol. VII. Ch. 54.

563. Arrian, *Anab*., VI, 9-11, *IIA,* pp. 146-49: Curtius, *Hist. Alex.,* IX, 4-6, *ibid.,* pp. 234-44: Diodorus, *Bib.Hist*., XVII, 98-99, *ibid.,* pp. 287-89; Justin, *Hist. Phil*., XII, 9. *ibid.,* pp. 324-25; Plutarch, *Vit. Alex.* or *Life of Alexander*, Ch. 63, *ibid*, pp. 311-12; Julius Valerius, *The Itinerarium Alexandri*, Ch. 115; *Pseudo-Kallisthenes*, III, IV.

564. *YCTI*, Vol. II, p. 254; Julien, *Hiouen Thsang*, Vol. III, p. 410.

565. *Anab*., VI, 14, *IIA*, p. 154.

566. *IP,* pp. 76, 455.

567. Arrian informs us that Megasthenes' Oxydrakai *(AIMA,* 1st edn. pp. 110 and 190) is absolutely correct form. Strabo calls them both Hydrakai *(Geog*.. XV, I, *6, AICL,* p. 12) and Oxydrakai *(ibid.,* XV, I, 8 and 33, *AICL,* pp. 13, 40); they are called by Diodorus Syrakousai *(Bib. Hist.,* XV11, 98, *IIA,* pp. 287-88), by Curtius Sudracae *(Hist. Alex.,* IX, 4, *ibid*., p. 234) and by Pliny Sydracae *(Hist. Nat.,* V1, X11, 6); in the *Romance History of Alexander,* falsely ascribed to Kallisthenes ("Pseudo Kallisthenes") they are also called Oxydrakai; in the Latin version of Julius valerius it is recorded that Alexander lived in their country with brāhmaṇas (AICL, pp. 177-78); see also *Ancient Cities of the Indus,* p. 230: *IIA,* note P, pp. 350-51.

568. *HAG,* I, p. 451.

569. *AICL,* p. 12, note 1; *IIA*, Note P, pp. 350-51.

570. *CAGI,* p. 204; see N.I. Dey, *GDAMI*, p. 195; also *IIA,* p. 156, note 3.

571. *Ar. Ant.,* pp. 200-1.

572. *AICL,* p. 23, note 2.

573. *E'tude,* pp. 124-25 cf. *IIA,* p. 156, note 3.

574. *Op. cit.,* Vol. I, p. 79.

575. *Travels,* Vol. I, p. 22.

576. *MMH,* p. 123.

577. W.W. Hunter, *op, cit.,* pp. 89-90. The city built by the order of Alexander was located at or in the vicinity of Uchh, an old city lying about forty miles to the north-east of Mithānkot, as indicated by McCrindle (IIA, p. 156, note 3). "Uchh is chiefly distinguished", says Masson, "by the ruins of the former towns which are very extensive, and attest the primitive prosperity of the locality". St. Martin (*Ĕtude*, pp. 124-25) identifies the city more precisely with Chuchpur an ancient fort standing on the eastern bank of the Indus opposite Mithānkot. The fort bore formerly the names of Askelanda, Askelend and Sikander, which are but variant forms of Alexandria.

578. JASB, 1838, p. 94.

579. *Op. cit.,* p. 9.

580. *AIMA,* 1st edn. p. 149 and note; Pliny, *Hist. Nat.,* V1, 21 (23), cf. *ibid.*

581. *AIT*, pp. 136-58.

582. *Étude*, pp. 234ff.

583. *Geog.,* XV, I, 21, 22, 33 and 34, *AICL,* pp. 26-27, 40-41; Hamilton and Falconer, *op.cit*., Vol. III, p. 96.

584. *Bib. Hist.,* XVII, 102, IIA, pp. 292-93.

585. *Anab.,* VI, 15, *ibid.,* pp. 157-58.

586. *Itin. Alex.,* Ch. 112, *AICL,* p. 153.

587. *AIT,* p. 145.

588. *Hist. Alex*., IX, 8.

589. *AICL,* p. 26, note 4, p. 41, note 2; M'Murdo, *JRAS,* Vol. I, p. 33; *CAGI,* pp. 216-18; Raverty, *op. cit.,* pp. 566-70, 663.

590. *Geog.,* XV, I, 34, *AICL,* p. 41.

591. *YCTI,* Vol. II, p. 253.

592. *CAGI,* pp. 219-20; see also *IIA,* p. 158, note 1.

593. *Travels,* Vol. I, p. 461.

594. *CAGI,* p. 220.

595. *AIT,* p. 152.

596. *CAGI,* p. 218.

597. *AIT,* p. 145.

598. *Ibid.,* p. 151.

599. *Ibid.*

600. *Ibid.,* pp. 140-41.

601. *CHI*, I, p. 338.

602. *Travels*, Vol. I, p. 382.

603. *CAGI,* p. 215; see also *IIA,* Note R. p. 354.

604. *Geog.,* XV. I, 33, *AICL,* p. 40, and note 2.

605. *Anab.,* V1, 16, *IIA,* p. 159.

606. *Vit. Alex. (Life of Alexander),* Ch. 64, *ibid.,* pp. 313-14.

607. *Op. cit.,* Vol. III, p. 37.

608. *JRAS,* Vol. I, p. 30.

609. *CAGI,* pp. 223-24.

610. *Ibid.,* p. 223.

611. *Ar. Ant.,* p. 205; also *IIA*, note S, p. 355.

612. *AIT*, pp. 142-44.

613. *CAGI,* p. 224.

614. *Anab.,* VI, 16, 5; also *IIA,* p. 159.

615. *Hist. Alex.,* IX, 8.

616. *Bib. Hist.,* XVII, 102 and 103; also *IIA.,* pp. 293-94.

617. *Vit. Alex., (Life of Alexander)* Ch. 59; also II A, p. 306.

618. *Bib. Hist.,* XVII, 103; *IIA,* p. 294, and Note T, pp. 355-56; see also Vincent, *The Voyage of Nearchus,* p. 136.

619. *IP,* p. 51; also *Bh. Sāv.,* Vol. I, pp. 169-72.

620. B. N. Puri, *India in the Time of Patañjali.* p. 74.

621. For detail see JBBRAS, Vol. V. pp. 413-17; *IIA*, note T, p. 355; *CAGI*, pp. 225-32; and CASE p. 29 for correct identification of Brāhmana city.

622. R.D. Banerji, *PAHI,* p. 81.

623. Burnes, *op. cit.,* Vol. III, p. 59.

624. *Geog.,* XV, I. 33, *AICL*, p. 40; see also XV, I, 13, *ibid.,* p. 19, and note, 6. Strabo says (Geog., XV, I, 32) "Many nations and cities lie all around Patalene".

625. *Anab.,* V1,17, 18 and 20, *IIA,* pp. 160-62, 165; see also his *Indika,* pt. I, ch. 2, *AIMA,* 1st edn., p. 183 and note 1. Alexander, as we learn from Arrian (*Anab.*, VI, 20, 5) found at Patala the citadel fortified. He then ordered Hephaistion to make preparations required for the fortification of the harbour, and the construction of a dockyard at the city of Patala which stood where the river Indus bifurcates. The measures taken by Alexander gave fillip to the growth of Patala as a port city. It gradually developed as a centre of commerce.

626. *Bib, Hist.,* XVII, 104, IIA, p. 296.

627. Cf. Arrian, *Indika,* pt. II.

628. *AIT,* pp. 146-48; see also J. Ph. Vogel, "Notes on Ptolemy", in *BSOAS,* Vol. XIV, pt. I, p. 84; Law, *HGAI,* p. 117.

629. *Indika,* Pt. II; see also Bunbury, *HAG*, I, pp. 447, 449-50.

630. *Orb. Des*., vv. 1080-1165, *AICL*. p. 188.

631. *Hist. Nat.,* Bk. II. Ch. 73 (75); *AICL,* p. 109.

632. *Ibid.,* VI, 21 (23); Megasthenes, *Indika,* Frag. LVI, *AIMA,* 1st edn. p. 153, see also p. 141, and note.

633. *Dionysiaka,* Bk. XXVI, *AICL*, p. 198.

634. Bunbury, *HAG*, I, pp. 449-50, and 513, note Rr; St. Martin, *E'tude*, pp. 169-72; AIIC, p. 33; Rawlinson, *Intercourse Between India and the Western World…*, p. 34; McCrindle in his Introduction to *Voy. Near*. (p. 156) has identified it with "Thatha, a town near to where the western arm of the Indus bifurcates…"; Rennell, *MMH,* pp. 129-31; Vincent, *Voyage of Nearchus,* pp. 144 ff; Burnes, *op. cit.* Vols. 1, p. 7 and III, p. 81; M'Murdo, *JRAS,* Vol. I, p. 24; Wilson, *Ar. Ant.,* pp. 207-8; *HA*, p. 406; Beveridge, *Comp. Hist. Ind.,* Vol. I, pp. 37-38; *AIIC,* p. 33; see also C. Speir, *Phases of Indian Civilization,* pp. 211-12.

635. See his *The Indus Delta Country –A Memoir chiefely on its Ancient Geography and History,* p. 19.

636. For detail's see *CAGI,* pp. 235-40; St, Martin, *E'tude,* pp. 180 ff; *IIA,* note U, pp. 356-57; W.W. Hunter, *op. cit.,* pp. 89-90; *AIT,* pp. 146-47, 369-70, note.

637. *Geog.,* XV, I, 33, *AICL,* p. 40.

638. J. Wilson, *JBBRAS,* Vol. III (1850), p. 77.

639. *Geog.,* XV, I, 33.

640. A.S. Altekar, *State and Government in Ancient India,* p. 136.

641. *Periplus*, sec. 38, p. 37.

642. *Ibid.,* p. 165, note.

643. *Ibid.,* p. 166, note.

644. *Ibid.,* Sec. 41, p. 39.

645. Secs. 38-39, p. 37, and p. 165, note.

646. *AIT,* p. 146. Ptolemy (*Geog*., VII, I, 59) distinctly refers to Patala and Barbarei as two towns which stood on the islands in the lower valley of the Indus. See also V.A. Smith, *EHI*, pp. 110-11; and B.C. Law "Studies in Idnia History and Geogrpahy based on Early Greek Accounts", *JGRI*, XVI, 3-4, 1959, p. 284.

647. *Hist. Phil.,* XII, 10. He Says that the city of Barce (Barbarei of Ptolemy and Barbarike of the author of the *Periplus*) was founded by Alexander on the mouth of the Indus as a monument of his achievements.

648. *Periplus*, Sec. 39, pp. 37-38.

649. *Ibid*, Sec. 38, p. 37, and p. 165, note.

650. *CAG1,* pp. 243-44.

651. *Periplus,* p. 349.

652. *JRAS,* Vol. I, p. 31; see also *AIT,* pp. 152, 156, 372, note.

653. *CAGI,* p. 247.

654. *Hist. Nat.,* V1, 21 (23); Megasthenes, Fragm, LVI, *AIMA,* 1st edn., pp. 147-48, and note.

655. See AIMA, pp. 147-48, note; James Tod, *AAR,* Vol. I, p. 86.

656. *Indika,* pt. II, ch. 21.

657. See M'Murdo, *JRAS,* Vol. I, p. 42.

658. Burnes, *op. cit.,* Vol. I, p. 10.

659. *CAGI,* p. 258.

660. *Hist. Nat.,* VI, 23 (26); also *AICL,* pp. 110-11.

661. See Heeren, *Historical Researches,* Vol. I, p. 297.

662. *Arab.,*VI, 21, 22; *Indika.* Pt. II, Ch. 23.

663. *Hist, Alex.,* IX, 10, 34.

664. *Bib. Hist.,* XVII, 104, 8.

665. *Hist. Alex.,* IX, 10, 7.

666. *Hist. Nat.,* VI, 23 (26); VI, 25; see also AICL, p. 111.

667. *Ibid.,* VI, 20.

668. Sec. 37, p. 37, and pp. 161-63, note.

669. *AIT,* pp. 159, 319-22. 375-76, note; see also Banerji, *PAHI,* pp. 81-82.

670. *Gates of India,* pp. 320, 372.

671. *CAGI*, p. 260.

672. *CAGI*, p. 261.

673. For details see M. Rostovtzeff, *SEHHW*. Vol.1, pp. 131-33; *H.A.* Devies. *An Outline History of the World*, p. 147; W. Robertson, *HDAI*, p. 27.

674. F. Tola and C.Dragonetti, "India and Greece from Alexander to Augustus", in *Graeco-Indica: India's cultural contacts with the Greek World*, ed. U.P. Arora, p. 120.

675. *The Ancient Greeks,* p. 174.

676. *Sabhā Parva*, 28, 49.

677. Ed. by Shāmāśāstrī, p, 78; see also *AIT*, pp. 370-71, note.

678. II, p. 359.

679. Ed. V. Trenckner, pp. 327, 331 and 359; see also its trans (from Pāli) by T.W. Rhys Davids, *The Questions of King Milinda,* in SBE, XXXV, I, p. 127.

680. Ed. by L.D. Law and E.J. Thomas, Vol. I, pp. 154-55; Vol. II, pp. 414-15.

681. Trans. by W. Geiger, p. 194, note 3; also trans. by Turnour, p. 110.

682. Cf. A. Weber, *Ind. Stud.,* XVI, 303.

683. *Bactria*, pp. 119-20; *Intercourse Between India and the Western World…*, p. 34.

684. *Intercourse between India and the Western World…*, p. 34.

685. HPL, Vol. II, p. 367; see also his IETBJ, p. 83.

686. "Alexander and Alexandria in Indian Literature" (originally pub. in French in the *Memoires de L'Institut Francais,* Vol. LXVII, *M'elanges Maspero,* Vol.II), tr. by P.C. Bagchi,IHQ, XII, 1936, p. 126.

687. JA, 1914, pt. II, pp. 413-19.

688. *The Greeks in Bactria and India,* p. 421.

689. *Anab.*, VI, 22 and 24. Holdich (*The Gates of India…,* p. 152) and Cunningham (CASE, p. 24) call it Pura.

690. *Geog.,* XV, II, 7, *AICL,* p. 86.

691. Heeren, *Historical Researches*, Vol. I, p. 270; Bunbury, *HAG*. Vol. I, pp. 519-20, AICL, p. 86, note 3; see also A.Stein. "on Alexander's Route to Gedrossia", *Geog. Jour*., Vol. 102. nos. 5-6 (1943), pp. 193-227; "Notes on Explorations in Makran and other Parts of Southern Baluchistan", *Ind. Ant*., Vol. 58 (1929), pp. 211-12; " An Archaeological Tour in Gedrossia", MASI, no. 43, Calcutta, 1931 (for its ancient boundary); *IIA*, Note V. pp. 357-58.

692. *History*, Bk. XXIII, Ch. 6, *AICL*, p. 94.

693. *Itin, Alex*., chs. 104-16, *AICl*, pp. 151-55.

694. *De Nat. Anim*., Bk. XV, Ch. XXI, *AICL*, p. 145.

695. *Top. Chr*., Bk. XI, *AICL*, pp. 163-64.

696. *JRAS* (New Series), Vol. XVI, p. 281.

697. Strabo, Geog., XV, 1, 18, *AICL*, p. 23; also Hamilton and Falconer's tr. *The Geography of Strabo,* Vol. III, pp. 83-84.

698. Cf. Strabo, *Geog.,* XV, 1, 19, AICL, p. 25.

Book Eleven
Splendour of Art

1

Evolution of Art

The civilization of a nation finds reflection also in its artistic heritage. The ancient Greek and Roman historians did not fail to appreciate the splendour of Indian art. They have transmitted to us trustworthy information regarding the evolution of Indian art. All the main forms of art-architecture, sculpture, iconography, decoration and painting - have received the treatments at their hands. They have the credit of bringing to light some of the important aspects of these forms of art. We learn from their accounts of the subject that the art of constructing building (including the royal palace), temple, shrine, stūpa and other structure or monument of historical importance or interest, the art of making abstract forms, especially by carving stone, wood or metal, the art of casting metal (bronze or copper) or other material to give shape to a picture or design or to produce an object, the art of making an image of god or a person worthy of veneration, the art of making a representative or visual symbol, the art of carving or casting a statue to commemorate a notable person or event, the art of engraving on a hard surface or substance, and the art of decoration and painting gradually developed in India.

"Ancient Indian Art differs from arts in most countries of the West. Predominantly symbolic in character, it aims at giving concrete shape to human feelings and sentiments, concepts and ideals of beauty and of the ultimate reality… The ancient Indians, like the ancient Greeks, were great lovers of beauty. But the latter loved beauty for its own sake and found joy as well as truth in it. But the Indians, lovers of beauty as they were, 'sought to put some deeper significance in their work, some vision of the inner truth as they saw it'. Indian art, by and large, is, therefore, expressive. It is wholly different from the representative art of concrete objects or the creative art of beautiful things..."[1]

We wonder but not so much at the skill, talent, taste, genius and imagination of the ancient Indian artists which they have displayed in the structure they erected and the artistic objects they produced.

The statement of Mrs. C. Speir that "The Greeks mention no temples, palaces, or other large buildings..."[2] can be falsified in the light of the evidence thereof furnished by the Greek writers themselves.

M. Elphinstone says, "From the silence of the Greeks respecting Indian architecture we may infer that the part of the country which they visited was as destitute of fine temples as it is now".[3] This is just an inference and not a reality. And hence we do not take any cognizance of it.

There were several stages of the growth and development of Indian art.

On the testimony of classical writers it can conclusively be proved that the art of constructing buildings including those of architectural importance by employing wood commenced in India as early as the fourth century before the Christian era. The earliest use of wood as building material in northwestern part of the country in the time of Alexander can be testified to by an evidence that Curtius[4] has adduced. The eastern Indian architecture during that century was also more or less wooden. Megasthenes was the first Greek historian to give an account of the wooden architecture of Candragupta Maurya's time. The Indian art in the Maurya age has been described here subsequently. It is worthwhile to mention here that stone also became the material *par-excellence* to be used for constructing buildings, temples etc.

The hitherto existing beliefs, that the history of Indian art begins with the advent of the Mauryas, that no architectural monument of pre-Maurya age is worth-mentioning, and that before the time of Aśoka stone was not used for architectural purpose, can be dispelled in the light of the facts discovered by the Greeks writers relating to the art and architecture that flourished at Taxila in northern India. The famous temple of stone at Taxila that was built during the rule of Porus belonged to the pre-Maurya age. When architecture reached its formative and creative stage, there emerged the conception of temples. The use of stone masonry in temple - architecture dates back to the last quarter of the fourth century before the

Christian era. V.A. Smith's statement, that "... no Indian example of stone either of architecture or sculpture earlier than the reign of Aśoka has yet been discovered",[5] can only partly be accepted in view of the facts that the temple built of stone at Taxila was an architectural monument of pre-Aśoka's days, as noted before, and that the stone was not used for sculptural purpose before his time. The sculptural or carving works anterior to his time were mostly on metals.

The Indian artists of Taxila attained a high degree of perfection in all the branches of art- architecture, sculpture, iconography, decoration and painting. The temples and shrines built at Taxila constitute monumental evidence of their attainment of high skill in the art of architecture. Some of their sculptural works in the temple built of stone excited the admiration of the Greek traveller Apollonius and his Assyrian companion Damis who visited the place in the first century of the Christian era. The exquisite carvings, engravings, representation of various objects, etc which were found in the temples there bespeak the artistic glory of the past ages.

Giving an account of the evolution of Indian art at Taxila, Philostratus has thrown a good deal of light on the architectural style of the royal palace, temple-architecture, some splendid structures of artistic beauty, sculptural works, iconographic objects, decoration and painting, and other works of art. He also speaks of the statues of Alexander and Porus - representing two historical monuments - found by the said two travellers in the plain area of the Punjab.[6] The artistic objects of the Indian artists of Taxila of Alexander's time were placed by king Porus in the temple he got built after the death of Alexander (323 BCE). The said statues were carved or cast by the Indian artists and erected in the memory of those two great kings and events of their times.

The progress of Indian art in northern India in pre-Maurya age can fairly be attested to by the foregoing Greek account of the subject.

It was only the sculptural works of the Indian artists of Taxila which bore the stamp of the influence of Greek artists of Alexander's time. There were some reflections of the Greek influence on the productions of the Indian artists found on the walls of a shrine in the temple built of shell-like stone or red marble at Taxila, as stated by Philostratus.[7]

Placing his reliance on the statements of the classical authors, G.N. Banerjee has also pointed out that the area which came under the Greek influence in the Punjab was situated between the Indus and Hydespes, and that in Taxila, where Alexander reached after crossing the Indus and which was visited by the Greek traveller Apollonius, the Greek influence on Indian art was perceptible.[8] He has correctly stated that Indian architecture is of native origin.[9] The "classical culture had acted as a ferment to revive the native qualities of the Indian artists, without robbing them of their originality and subtlety", says he.[10] His description of temple plan of Taxila similar to that of Athens, and that of Taxila temple with columns and pillars setting the example of Indo-Hellenic architecture[11] is completely different from the temple witnessed by Apollonius and his fellow-traveller Damis and described by Philostratus. "The impress of Greek influence on Indian art", observes D.Th. Vassiliades, "becomes evident in the post-Alexandrian age but there is nothing to mitigate against the supposition that Greek artists could have been employed in India from a much earlier date".[12] It is true that Taxila was a meeting place of Indian, Persian and Greek cultural influence,[13] but we cannot deny that there was a local tradition of art without being much influenced by the Greek art. W.W. Hunter has categorically stated that the Indian sculpture in northern India was possibly influenced by the Greek artists who came to India along with Alexander the Great. The Graeco-Bactrians were the practical masters of Greek sculpture. The Indian sculptural art directly came under their influence during their rule in the Punjab.[14] The influence of the Greek art on Indian sculptural art at Taxila in Alexander's time cannot be denied. The other forms of Indian art in his time remained unaffected.

The art of building temple, shrine and other monument had flourished in Lower Sindh as early as the time of Alexander's Indian expedition as appears from the *Periplus*.[15]

The Maurya age was no doubt a great landmark in the history of Indian art. It has been rightly said by J.H. Marshall that "from the Mauryas' time onwards we are able to trace step by step and with relative precision the evolution both of architecture and of the formative arts. The history of Indian art is one of continuous forward progress."[16]

The Maurya emperors were marvellous builders. They erected magnificent buildings and other artistic monuments. They deserve to be included among the finest specimens of ancient architectural art. The buildings, palaces and monuments of Emperor Candragupta Maurya were mostly made of wood. Generally the buildings were large and imposing. Their grandeur, architectural beauty, decorative richness, and ornamentation have been brought to light by the classical writers. In the Maurya age, both architectural and sculptural arts were in a highly developed stage. The Maurya kings patronized arts, and consequently, architecture and sculpture attained a very high level of excellence.

Aelian, perhaps on the authority of Megasthenes, has given an account of the royal palace of Sandrakottus (Candragupta). He has specifically described its architectural splendour.[17] The progress of the decorative art in the time of Sandrakottus is proved by the testimony of Curtius.[18]

From Aśoka's time onwards stone as a material was used for both architectural and sculptural purposes. V.A. Smith, quoting Fergusson, a well-known authority on Indian art and architecture, states that "the sudden introduction of the use of stone instead of wood for the purpose both of architecture and sculpture in India was the result of communication between the empire of Alexander and his successors, and that of Maurya dynasty of Candragupta and Aśoka".[19] But this statement is not tenable.

The truth contained in the account of the royal palace of Sandrakottus at Pāṭaliputra given by Aelian and in that of the royal palace at Taxila given by Philostratus is respectively confirmed by the archaeological excavations carried out by the D.B. Spooner in 1912 and by John Marshall between 1913 and 1934. The value of their accounts of the subject can be judged in the light of the modern discoveries.

On the basis of parallelism between the architectural design of the multi-pillared hall of the Maurya imperial palace and the pillared hall of the Achaemenid emperor Darius at Persepolis, some scholars have strongly advocated the Persian influence on Maurya art and architecture.[20] Spooner, who discovered that said hall of the Maurya palace in the course of the archaeological excavations at Kumharār in 1912, went to the extent of saying that hall was "probably the work of Persian masons".[21] Equally wrong is the statement of M. Wheeler that the Persian artists and craftsmen contributed to the growth of masonry architecture of the Maurya age.[22] Such statements are nothing more than a far-fetched imagination. The fact remains that the Maurya age had its own artistic tradition. The resemblance between the Persian and Mauryan architectural styles was due to common traditions which does not necessarily indicate the influence of one on the other or imitation of one by the other. It has been correctly stated by N.R. Ray that the similarity between the two royal palaces does not mean that the Achaemenian pillar-type and form were adopted by the Mauryan court artists.[23] V.A. Smith's statement, that Persian style of architecture derived from that employed in the Achaemenian palaces of Susa and Persepolis was extensively used throughout northern India,[24] can unhesitatingly be disposed of.

The Hellenistic influence on Indian architecture and sculpture in the post-Maurya age cannot be denied. The transmission of Hellenistic art and culture into northern India during the Greek rule in the second century before the Christian era has been acknowledged by a number of scholars.[25] It must, however, be admitted that Hellenic and Indian conceptions of art differed fundamentally and that Hellenic art never took a real and lasting hold upon India. J.H. Marshall is also of the view that Hellenistic art inspite of its diffusion in north-west India never dominated the Indian art.[26]

Some modern authorities have also tried to prove that there was Roman influence on the development of Indian arts of architecture and sculpture.[27]

E.B. Havell, one of the noted authorities on Indian art, repudiates the idea that Indian art owes anything to Graeco-Roman influence.[28]

We do not find in the classical sources any evidence of Persian influence on Maurya art and architecture. There are, of course, some evidence therein of the Greek influence on Indian sculpture in the time of Alexander, as noted before. The Hellenistic influence on Indian art in the post-Alexandrian age is historically a proven fact. But the Roman influence on Indian art is doubtful.

The monuments erected at Taxila and in its neighbourhood during the Parthian rule in the first century of the Christian era were of classical type. Though the decorative feature in the Parthian architecture of classical style had become almost Indianized, the Hellenistic elements in them were still in complete preponderance over the oriental.[29]

There is a classical evidence of the growth of the art of sculpture and iconography in western India. Bardesanes' account of the sculptured image of Śiva in the cave temple in the Deccan, of iconography, etc is preserved by Stobaeus.[30]

Mounds or tombs, generally regarded as the earliest specimens of Indian art being erected mainly for the preservation of relics or bones of the dead, were the precursor of the stūpa – an architectural monument of the Buddhist. Megasthenes,[31] as we learn from Strabo,[32] says that the tombs of the Indians were plain (of simple type), and the mounds raised over the dead small. But, on the other hand, Arrian says that the Indians did not rear monuments to the dead, but considered the virtues which men had displayed in life, and the songs in which their praises were celebrated, sufficient to preserve their memory after death.[33] His statement appears as an exception and not as a rule. A Buddhist ascetic from Bargosa (Broach), who had accompanied an Indian embassy from the Pāndyan king (according to Strabo)[34] or from king Porus (according to Nikolaos Damaskenos, as quoted by Strabo[35]) to the Roman Emperor Augustus, immolated himself at Athens to get rid of the anxieties and sufferings of life. On his tomb was an inscription, "*Zarmanochegas* (incorrect transliteration of *Śramanācārya*), an Indian from Bargosa, having immortalized himself according to the custom of his country, lies here". The erection of a tomb or mound was a religious practice which was followed in almost all parts of the country. The stūpa was also originally a funerary monument to hold the ashes of the Buddha. The tombs or mounds gave place to Buddhist stūpas which were solid domical structures of brick or stone on a round base. The main purpose of erecting them was to enshrine the relics (ashes, bones, or tooth) of the Buddha's body or of a great Buddhist ascetic, saint or teacher as an object of adoration or veneration, or to commemorate some sacred place or site or important event of the life of Buddha or in the history of Buddhism. The stūpas formed an important part of the architectural inheritance and achievement of Mauryan India.

One of the classical writers, Clemens of Alexandria, speaks of the Buddhist stūpas as sacred structures and object of worship. He also refers to the structural similarity between a stūpa and a pyramid.[36] The Buddhists were also familiar with the art of erecting monasteries, as we learn from Pliny,[37] and temples, as we are told by Porphyrios[38] and Stobaeus.[39] The information available in the classical sources about the Buddhist art and architecture is meagre but valuable.

On the testimony of the classical writers it can be proved beyond doubt that the Indians had developed considerable proficiency in the science of art and architecture. The artistic tradition that evolved in ancient India was by and large indigenous one. Indian art, on its side without losing any of its original character, absorbed some Greek elements in Alexandrian and post-Alexandrian age only in northern part of the country.

Notes and References

1. S.B. Mookherji, *India's Empire of Mind*, p. 104.
2. *Phases of India Civilization: A Historical and Cultural Outline*, p. 219.
3. *The History of India*, App. III. "On the Greek Accounts of India", p. 240.
4. *Hist. Alex.,* VIII, 10.
5. "Graeco- Roman Influence on the Civilization of Ancient India", JASB, LVIII,I, 1889, p. 108.
6. *The Life of Apollonius of Tyana*, II, 20, 22, 24, 25 and 42.
7. *Ibid*., II, 20; see also Priaulx, *The Indian Travels of Apollonius of Tyana*, p. 14.
8. *Hellenism in Ancient India*, pp. 39f.

9. *Ibid.*, p. 31.
10. *Ibid.*, p. 26.
11. *Ibid.*, p. 44.
12. *The Greeks in India*, p. 55.
13. NEB, XVII (Chicago, 1980), p. 1082.
14. "The Greeks in India (327-161BCE)", reptd. from his *The Indian Empire: Its peoples, History and Products* (London, 1882), in *Ancient India* (Delhi, 1983), pp. 94-95.
15. Sec. 41.
16. "The Monuments of Ancient India", in CHI, I, p. 560.
17. *Nat. Anim.,* XIII, 18.
18. *Hist. Alex.*, VIII, 9.
19. "Graeco-Roman Influence on the Civilization of Ancient India", JASB, LVIII, I, 1889, p. 108.
20. Spooner, JRAS, 1915, pp. 63-89, 283ff, 405-55; R.A. Jairazbhoy, *Foreign Influence in Ancient India*, pp. 44-45; J.H. Marshall, "The Monuments of Ancient India", in HI, I, p. 563.
21. JRAS, 1915, p. 63.
22. EIP, pp. 176-77.
23. "Mauryan Art" in R.C. Majumdar and A.D. Pusalker (ed), *History and Culture of the Indian people,* Vol. II, *The Age of Imperial Unity*, p. 509; see also K.C. Sagar, *Foreign Influence on Ancient India*, pp. 40-41, 279.
24. "Graeco-Roman Influence on the Civilization of Ancient India", JASB, LVIII, I, 1889, p. 109.
25. R.A. Jairazbhoy, *op.cit.,* p. 109; Smith, *op. cit.*, pp. 108-09; G.N. Banerjee, *Hellenism in Ancient India*, pp. 37-38; Marshall, *Taxila*, I, p. 19; "The Monuments of Ancient India", in CHI, I, pp. 563, 584; H.G. Rawlinson, *A Concise History of the Indian People*, p. 58.
26. "The Monuments of Ancient India", in *op. cit.*, p. 588.
27. See V.A. Smith, *op. cit.*, pp. 108 ff, 159ff; R.A. Jairazbhoy, *op. cit.,* p. 109.
28. See Review of his book, *Indian Sculpture and Painting* (Murray, 1908), in JRAS, April 1909, pp. 541ff.
29. See Marshall, "The Monuments of Ancient India", in CHI, I, p. 585; G.N. Banerjee, *Hellenism in Ancient India*, p. 44.
30. *Physica*, I. 56.
31. *Indika*, Bk II, Fragm. XXVII, AIMA, p. 70.
32. *Geog.*, XV, I, 54.

33. *Indika*, I, 10, AIMA, p. 204; see also U.P. Arora, "Classical Accounts on India-some Observation", in *Graeco-Indica: India's Cultural Contacts with the Greek World,* ed. by himself, p. 96.
34. *Geog*., XV, I, 4.
35. *Ibid*., XV,I, 73.
36. *Strṅmateis*, III, 194.
37. *Nat. Hist.,* VII, 21-30.
38. *De Abstinentia,* IV, 16-17.
39. AICL, p. 168.

2

Architecture, Sculpture, Iconography and Painting

The Maurya age witnessed spectacular progress in the field of art, as noted before. In the time of Sandrakottus (Candragupta), the great Maurya emperor, the art of architecture and sculpture was in a highly developed stage as appears from the classical accounts of the subject. His royal palace at the imperial capital at Pālibothra (Pāṭaliputra) was a splendid and impressive monument from both historical and architectural points of view. It excelled in splendour and magnificence the Persian palaces of Susa and Ekbatana which can best be qualified in what Aelian says, "In the Indian royal palace where the greatest of all the kings of the country resides, besides much else which is calculated to excite admiration, there are wonders with which neither Memnonian Susa with all its glory and splendour, nor Ekabatana with all its magnificence can hope to vie; indeed, only the well-known vanity of the Persians could imagine such a comparison; there are other wonders besides, which he cannot undertake to describe in his treatise".[1]

S.B. Mookherji, while dwelling upon ancient Indian architecture and sculpture, correctly stated that the Greek writers regarded the Maurya palaces as the magnificent and "the largest and finest in the whole world".[2]

But his view, that "... no architectural monument of the Maurya period has been discovered ...",[3] is unworthy of credence. Highly praising the architectural beauty of the Maurya palace, D.B. Spooner, who discovered its remains in 1912, observed that a structure of this type did not exist anywhere in ancient India.[4] It was, according to him, unparalleled in ancient India. He, however, found, according to him, some similarity between its architectural design and that of the Persian palace of Darius at Persepolis the details of which have been furnished here subsequently separately. R.A. Jairazbhoy states that Aelian makes a direct comparison between the Maurya palace and the said two Persian palaces,[5] but it is just not a comparison. In fact, comparing them he has shown that the former was more magnificent than the latter, as is evident from his account thereof.

It is Curtius who informs us about the sculptural and decorative work in the palace of Sandrakottus. "The palace", he says, "is adorned (decorated) with gilded pillars clasped all round by a vine embossed (carved design) in gold, while silver images of those birds which most charm the eye diversify the workmanship."[6] The elegant sculpture and exquisite carving were of such a high order as they really bear testimony to superhuman workmanship.

Excavations conducted at Kumharār by Spooner in 1912 resulted in the discovery of the remains of the Maurya Hall of a hundred columns (pillars).[7] The wooden columns of the palace were of Candragupta's time which were replaced by stone ones in Aśoka's time. In the time of the former, there was a wooden architecture but looking sumptuous. The Maurya palace and other buildings, according to Spooner, were modelled on the palace of the Achaemenid king Darius at Persepolis, and were probably the work of Persian masons,[8] which do not appear to be reliable, and hence cannot be accepted. M. Wheeler's statements, that Aelian's whole description of the Maurya palace is reminiscent of a Persian paradise, and that the former was the work of Persian artists and craftsmen,[9] can also be dismissed as unworthy of faith. Such statements are actually nothing more than a far-fetched imagination. Some authorities have pointed out that the Maurya palace was the prototype of the said palace at Persepolis, and that there was resemblance between the two.[10] Spooner's view about Achaemenian influence on Mauryan India is not acceptable to some scholars. Dealing with Indian art and architecture. K.C. Sagar reasonably concluded that the parallelism between the Maurya pillared hall and the pillared hall of Darius at Persepolis cannot altogether be denied, though the former "might not necessarily have been copied from Persia".[11]

Apollonius and his fellow-traveller Damis, in the course of their visit to Taxila city where they had sojourned for three days in CE 44, witnessed with their own eyes some specimens of architecture, sculpture, iconography and painting. Their eye-witness accounts thereof are recorded in Philostratus' *Vita Apollonii (Life of Apollonius of Tyana).*

The said two travellers saw the royal palace at Taxila which was large and well built. It had several entrances and outer fortifications. It was decorated with gates. It had courts, halls, waiting and inner rooms, etc. They say that "they admired this arrangement more than they did the pompous splendour of Babylon, and their esteem was enhanced when they went within. For the men's chambers and the porticoes and the whole of the vestibule were in a very chaste style".[12] It was, however, not distinguished by any superior splendour or extraordinary magnificence[13] from architectural point of view. The palace had, in fact, only few architectural features. The Greek account of the subject that is given in Philostratus' work can partly be corroborated and supplemented by an archaeological evidence. John Marshall, in the course of the excavations he conducted at the site between the years 1913 and 1934, discovered some remains of almost identical nature. The royal palace, according to him, was planned on a bigger scale and with more spacious courts and rooms. Its gates had decorative designs.[14] He himself says that Philostratus' observation on Taxilla city and its buildings correspond with the facts disclosed by the excavations conducted by him.[15] He rightly pointed out that Taxilla was adorned with temples, shrines and various other religious structures, and monuments.

The travellers saw a beautiful temple in front of the wall of Taxila city which was not far short of 100 feet in size (length). It was built of porphyry (fine polished granite stone, shell-like stone, or red marble[16]). They also saw within the temple a well constructed shrine, somewhat small as compared with the great size of the temple and its peristyle, but nevertheless worthy of admiration. It was surrounded with many columns which were very attractive. Round the shrine (on each of its walls) were hung pictures engraved on copper or bronze tablets representing the feats, and deeds or exploits of Alexander and Porus. The various figures- elephants, horses, soldiers, helmets and shields- were portrayed or carved in a mosaic of orichalcum, silver, gold, and oxidized copper, but the weapons-spears, javelins and swords- in iron, "in a respectable style of art". The metals were worked into one another (or blended "in the design, melted in like so many colours") so ingeniously and "with so nice a gradation of tints", that the pictures which they formed, "in corrections of drawing, vivacity of expression, and truthfulness of perspectives", were comparable to the productions of the most famous Greek artists, Zeuxis, Polygnotus and Euphranor, who "infused life into their designs, as well as a sense of depth and relief". The character of the said pictures was pleasing in itself. It was not till after the death of Alexander, the Macedonian, that Porus placed them in the temple, though they represented the former as a conqueror, and the latter as conquered and wounded, and receiving from the former the kingdom of "India" (i.e., Taxila) as a gift.[17]

Philostratus' reference to "Greek reliefs (reliefs showing the Greek method or style of carving) in temple at Taxila"[18] bears testimony to the influence of the Greek artists (sculptors) on the productions of the Indian artists. The Indian artists of Taxila might have borrowed some ideas from the Greek artists of Alexander's time relating to the art of sculpture without losing the originality of their art. Philostratus' statement, that the metals were worked so ingeniously that the figures which they formed closely resembled to the productions of the Greek artists, "shows", says B.N. Puri, "the ingenuity of Indian art which was unaffected by Hellenistic influences... The Indian objects were so garbed in Greek costumes that it was difficult for a visitor to discriminate whether it was a Greek object or an Indian one. The fact, that they were found in Hindu temples, was the only clue for discrimination. This shows the highest achievement of the Indians in the field of art."[19]

The said travellers speak of Painting of pictures in the temple at Taxila they visited. Philostratus has given an interesting account of the discussion held between the two travellers regarding the art of painting, works of painting, etc while they were in the temple. Apollonius asked: "O Damis, is there such a thing as painting?" "And what does this art do?" "It mixes together", replied Damis, "all the colours there are, blue with green, and white with black, and red with yellow." Apollonius said, painting cannot be confined to the mere use of colours. As the art advanced, its form underwent changes. He told Damis that "the elaborate works of Porus cannot be regarded as works of brass founding alone, for they resemble regular pictures, nor as works of painting alone, for they are cast in brass; they can be regarded as the *chefs d'oeuvre* of a man who is both painter and brass-founder, and as similar to the work of Hephaestus"[20].

The temple seen by the travellers and described by Philostratus has been identified by some authorities with a temple at Jaṇḍiāl but not with absolute certainty as appears from the style of their expression. This temple was unearthed in the course of archaeological excavations carried out at Taxila between 1913 and 1915 under the direction and supervision of John Marshall.[21] The Jaṇḍiāl temple, according to him, occupied a commanding position on an artificial mound some 700 yards north of north gateway of the city then called Sirkap. It had resemblance to the classical temples of Greece. Its Ionic columns and pilasters were composed of massive blocks of grey sandstone. On the basis of the Greek character of its plan and the design of its Ionic pillars, he suggested that it was erected under the rule of the Bactrian Greek kings who built and occupied the Sirkap city during the second century BCE. The Hellenistic architecture had long been a familiar site at Taxila, as asserted by him.[22] In order to justify the identification of Jaṇḍiāl temple with the temple made of porphyry, visited by the travellers, and to defend his arguments in favour of it, he relates that Philostratus' account of the temple shows the position of the Jaṇḍiāl temple. "As to the picture panels on the walls of the sanctum, there is nothing inherently impossible in Philostratus' account. Works of art handed down from bygone ages were commonly preserved in Greek temples and the practice may well have been followed at Jaṇḍiāl."[23]

"The Taxilian temples with Ionic pillars were like all the known examples of Indo-Hellenic architecture", observes V.A. Smith.[24]

W.W. Tarn states that the temple described by Philostratus is a little Ionic temple that was discovered at Jaṇḍiāl, and that it belonged to the Parthian period (first century CE) but in form was like a Greek temple. It was covered with the common shell stucco. It was built by a Greek architect.[25] At Taxila, he says, a few pieces of Greek sculpture and various small objects of art of Parthian period were found.[26]

The said Jaṇḍiāl temple, according to another contradictory evidence, was built in the "Scythio-Parthian period".[27] None of the authorities concerned seems to be certain about the period of the construction of the said temple.

The identification of the temple described by Philostratus with Jaṇḍiāl temple is not justified particularly from the point of view of their antiquity. The former was built in post-Alexandrian period during the rule of Porus over the kingdom of Taxila and the latter in the second century BCE during the Greek rule or in the first century of the Christian era during the Parthian rule over Taxila.

Apollonius and Damis also saw the temple of the Sun, which stood outside the walls of Taxila city, and in it statues of Alexander and Porus, the one of gold and the other of bronze. Its walls were of red marble, but glittering with gold, and the image of the god was of pearls arranged in the symbolic manner, as found in other Indian shrines.[28] The artistic objects including the iconographic one were purely the creations of the Indian artists. Their beauty excited the admiration of the travellers.

Both the travellers left Taxila, and marched to the Hyphasis. After two days' journey they reached the plain in the Punjab where Porus had been defeated by Alexander. There they saw the place adorned with a triumphal arch on which there was a statue of the great conqueror (Alexander) standing in a four-horse chariot as he appeared in the battle with the Satraps of Darius at Issus. A little further on, they came upon two other arches, on one of which was the statue of Alexander, and on the other that of Porus, reconciled to one another after the battle, the one saluting or greeting another, and the other in an attitude of submission.[29] These statues taken together constitute an excellent specimen of art. They were erected or established by the Indian artists as memorials or monuments to commemorate the two mighty potentates or great kings and the historic events of their times. It has been rightly observed by Priaulx that "Apollonius found many monuments of Alexander's invasion and considerable traces of Greek influence".[30]

Philostratus' descriptions of the temples, shrines and other monuments, and the artistic objects, based on the observations of the Greek traveller Apollonius and his Assyrian companion Damis, show that the Indian artists had attained perfection in all the branches of art-architecture, sculpture, iconography and painting. The originality of Indian art and the artistic talent of the Indians are well reflected in the objects produced. The deities, or images, and the objects contrived exhibit the ingenuity of the Indian artists. The antiquity of the temples and shrines at Taxila and that of all the specimens of art preserved in them and of all the monuments in the Punjab plain that were witnessed by the travellers goes back to the last quarter of the fourth century before the Christian era. All of them remained in excellent state of preservation till the time of their visit.

The statement of Thomas McEvilley, that "The entire Taxila region has yielded an abundance of Graeco-Roman objects, including ..., metalwork, and bronze and stone sculpture...",[31] cannot be connected with the Indian artistic objects Philostratus speaks of.

In the regions adjoining the Indus mouth, there were preserved even to the time of the author of the *Periplus*, old temples, memorials of the expedition of Alexander, etc. In Minnagara, called metropolis (i.e. Patala, the capital of the Lower Indus valley), he saw some of the antiquities such as ancient shrines, walls of forts, etc of Alexander's time, as recorded by himself.[32]

There is an evidence in one of the classical works about the sculpture and iconography in the cave temple in western part of India. We learn from Bardesanes' account of India preserved by Stobaeus in his work, *Physica*,[33] that there was a large natural cave on a very high mountain almost in the middle of the country, wherein there was a statue ten or twelve cubits high, standing upright with its hands folded crosswise, and the right half of its face was that of a man, and the left half that of woman. This androgynous or hermaphroditic image was no doubt Arddhanārīśvara (half man, half woman). This is represented by the image of God Śiva with his consort Pārvatī in a single human body. This is a unique specimen of sculptural art. Such sculptured images are found in the rock-cut temples of India. We are further informed by Bradesanes that in like manner the right hand and right foot, or the whole right side of the statue was that of male, and the left that of female. The spectator was struck with wonder at the combination, as he saw how the two dissimilar sides coalesced in an indissoluble union in a single body. On the right breast of the statue was engraved the sun, and on the left the moon, while on the two arms was artistically engraved a host of *angels* (devas - gods of secondary rank), the sky, mountains, rivers, oceans, plants, animals etc. The statue thus represented Śiva as the supreme God flanked by titular or tertiary gods with visible representation of natural objects. Here we find one of the finest specimens of the art of engraving as well as that of the visual art. On the head of the statue, it is said, was the image of a god, which probably refers to the goddess Gaṅgā, who is often depicted on the head of Śiva in Indian iconography. Regarding the material the statue was made of Bardesanes informs us that it was neither gold, nor silver, nor brass, nor stone, nor indeed any known substance, but it most resembled something very hard material, quite free from rot. He tells us further that "the Brachmans (Brāhmaṇas) visit the cave to see the statue. At the same time, they examine the sculptures (carvings) on the statue and try to discover their meaning, for it is not easy to attend to the whole representation, the objects being so numerous, such then is the account which the Indians themselves gave of this statue".[34]

The entire information regarding the said cave temple and an image or statue of Śiva in it, and the sculpture, iconography, engravings, etc was transmitted by the members of the Indian embassy led by Sandanes to Bradesanes who met them at Antioch (in Syria) in CE 218. The embassy was on its way to Rome to honour and welcome the emperor Heliogabalus (called Elagabalus) on the occasion of his enthronement in that very year. The information collected by Bradesanes from the Indian ambassadors about the subject under notice was transcribed by him in his own words in Syriac and was recorded by him in his work. The relevant passage from his work, before it was lost, was transcribed in Greek by Stobaeus and was preserved by him in his *Physica* (I.56). Sandanes, the chief of the embassy, probably belonged to the dynasty of the Sātavāhana king Sundra Śātakarṇi called Sandares by the author of the *Periplus* (sec. 52, p. 43) and Sadinon or Sandineis by Ptolemy (*Geog*., VII, I, 6, AIT. p. 39), who had governed Kaliena (Kalyāṇa), 33 miles northeast of Bombay. H.G. Rawlinson had reasonably postulated that Sandanes, the informant of Bardnesanes, came from the Decan.[35]

The cave temple described by Bradesanes has been called by Rawlinson "one of the great Hindu rock-temples of the Decan".[36] It is, in fact the rock-cut Śiva temple at Elephanta[37] near Bombay. Rawlinson has correctly placed it in western India.[38] U.P. Arora says, " it could be somewhere in the region of Mahārāṣṭra".[39] "The great rock-cut Śiva temple on Elephanta Island is one of the best known monuments of its kind in India, by reason partly of the grandeur of its sculptures and partly of its proximity to Bombay".[40]

There are some incidental or fragmentary notices of the Buddhist art and architecture in the classics. One of the most important architectural monuments of the Buddhists is stūpa, a solid dome- like structure of brick or stone resting on a round base. Clemens, a Greek Christian monk of Alexandria, has given a brief account of it. He has described it as a kind of pyramidal structure beneath which, he says, the Buddhists think the bones, one of the relics of the divinity (Buddha, called by him Boutta, generally called Buddas by the classical writers), lie buried or enshrined. He also speaks of Buddhist worship of stūpas which were no less than shrines for them. He appears to have established the structural similarity between a Buddhist stūpa and a pyramid.[41]

Pliny describes the monasteries in India.[42] They were built of brick for the residence of the Buddhist monks. A passage preserved from the lost work of Bardesanes by Porphyrios[43] and from his work by Stobaeus[44] contains a description of Buddhist temples which were founded by the king (called a royal foundation) to provide facilities to the Buddhists.

Besides what we have written above, we do not find any other evidence in the classical treatises about architecture, sculpture, iconography, or painting worthy of the name.

Notes and References

1. *Nat. Anim.*, XIII, 18,1. Aelian's statement, that "... only the well-known vanity of the Persians could imagine such a comparison", "should be remembered by those modern writers who find traces of Persian influence in Maurya architecture", observes H.C. Raychaudhuri (PHAI, p. 275, note 3). Aelian's account of the palace "is most probably copied from Megasthenes", says J.W. McCrindle (AICL, p. 142, note 1). This is contradicted by R.C. Majumdar (CAI, p. 421, note 3) on the ground that no extract or fragment from the *Indika* of Megasthenes relating to the said palace is preserved by Aelian. But there are some authorities, notably, E.R. Bevan ("India in Early Greek and Latin Literature", in CHI, I, p. 369), B.N. Puri (*Indian as described by Early Greek writers*, p. 144), J.T. Wheeler (*The History of India from the Earliest Ages*, ch. IV, "Greek and Roman India", p. 181), P.L. Bhargava (*Chandragupta Maurya: A Gem of Indian History*, pp. 106-07), D.B. Spooner (JRAS, 1915, p. 406) and N.M. Chapekar (*Ancient India and Iran: A study of their cultural contacts*, p. 58), who have admitted that Aelian described the palace of Candragupta Maurya on the authority of Megasthenes. The imperial palace probably stood close to a place now called Kumharār on the outskirts of Patna. The Sugānga palace was the favourite resort of Candragupta (JRAS, 1923, p. 587). Radha Kumud Mookerji (*Chandragupta Maurya and His Times*, p. 64) tells us that "while the exterior and the grounds of the palace are thus described by the Greek writers, more light is thrown on its interior and its design by Kauṭilya (*Arthaśāstra*, I.20-21).
2. *India's Empire of Mind*, p. 106.
3. *Ibid.*
4. JRAS, 1915, p. 88.
5. *Foreign Influence in Ancient India*, pp. 43-44.
6. *Hist. Alex.*, VIII, 9.
7. ASIAR, Eastern Circle, 1912-13, pp. 53-61.
8. JRAS, 1915, pp. 63ff, 405ff; see also P.L. Bhargava, *Chandragupta Maurya*, p. 108.
9. EIP, pp. 176-77.

10. V.A. Smith, EHI, 4th revd. edn. p. 128; R.A. Jairazbhoy, *Foreign Influence in Ancient India*, pp. 43-45; G.N. Banerjee, *Hellenism in Ancient India*, p. 57.
11. *Foreign Influence on Ancient India*, pp. 40-41.
12. Philostratus, *Vit. Apoll.*, tr. F.C. Conybeare, *The Life of Apollonius of Tyana,* Vol. I, II, 25, pp. 182-83; see also Priaulx, *The Indian travels of Apollonius of Tyana …*, p. 15; CAI, pp. 388-89.
13. AICL, p. 192; Priaulx, *op.cit.*
14. *Taxila*, Vol.I, pp. 140-141.
15. *Ibid.*, p. 64.
16. The temple, Marshall says (*Ibid.*, p. 227), was made of "stone covered with stucco, powdered shell having been used in India from time immemorial for the making of fine stucco".
17. Philostratus, *Vit. Apoll.*, tr. Conybeare, *The life of Apollonius of Tyana,* Vol. I, II, 20, pp. 168-71; AICL, p. 192; Priaulx, *The Indian Travels of Apollonius of Tyana…*, pp. 13-14; CAI, p. 388; B.N. Puri, *India as described by Early Greek writers*, p. 147; G.P. Singh, "Early History of North-west India as described by the Greek and Assyrian Travellers", JIH, (Platinum Jubilee Volume), 2001, pp. 46-47; "North-west India as described by the Greek and Assyrian Travellers of the First Century", JASM(New series), Vols. 77-78, 2002-2003, p. 176; J. Marshall, *Taxila*, I, p. 227. The sculptured or carved objects and other works of art of Alexander's time were placed by Porus in the temple (containing a shrine) he got constructed during his rule over the kingdom of Taxila which he received from Alexander shortly before his departure from India in October 325 BCE in recognition of the valour he displayed in the battle he fought with him and the worth he proved as a ruler. Alexander had full faith in the ability of king Porus to govern that kingdom.
18. *Vit. Apoll.,* tr. Conybeare, *op. cit.,* II, 20, p. 169.
19. *Op. cit.,* p. 150.
20. *Vit. Apoll.* tr. Conybeare., *op. cit.*, II, 22, pp. 172-73, 176-79.
21. For Excavations' reports about Jaṇḍiāl temple see ASIAR, 1912-13, pp. 35-39; 1913-14, pt. I, pp. 16-17; 1914-15, pt. I, p. 14.
22. *Taxila,* I, pp. 43, 222-23, 225 and 229; see also B.N. Puri, *op. cit.*, pp. 147-48; G.N. Banerjee, *Hellenism in Ancient India*, p. 44.
23. *Taxila*, I, p. 227.
24. "Graeco-Roman Influence on the Civilization of Ancient India", JASB, LVIII, I, 1889, p. 115.
25. *The Greeks in Bactria and India*, pp. 359-60.
26. *Ibid*, p. 361.

27. NEB, XVII (Chicago, 1980), p. 1083.
28. Philostratus, *Vit. Apoll.*, tr. Conybeare, *op. cit.*, II, 24, pp. 180-81; Priaulx, *op. cit.*, p. 15; CAI, p. 388.
29. Philostratus, *Vit. Apoll.,* tr. Conyubeare, *op. cit.*, II, 42, pp. 226-27; Priaulx, *op. cit.,* p. 25; AICL, p. 193.
30. *Op. cit.*, pp. 11-12; also H.A. Rose, GTCP, I, p. 33.
31. *The Shape of Ancient Thought: Comparative Studies in Greek and Indian Philosophies*, p. 362.
32. *Periplus*, sec. 41, p. 39; see also IIA, p. 162, note 1.
33. I, 56.
34. See AICL, p. 173, and note 1, and p. 174; D. Th. Vassiliades, *The Greeks in India,* pp. 80-82, and p. 101, ref. no. 205, note.
35. *Intercourse Between India and the Western World from the Earliest Times to the Fall of Rome*, p. 146.
36. *Ibid.*
37. Burgess, *Elephanta* (1871 edn.), p. 20; Thomas McEvilley, *The Shape of Ancient Thought*, p. 391.
38. "India in European Literature and Thought", in *The Legacy of India*, ed. G. T. Garratt, p. 18.
39. "Ancient India and Ancient Greece", in HIC, Vol. I, pt. 2, *Life, Thought and Culture in India* (from c. 600 BC to c. AD 300), p. 1064.
40. See S. Kramrisch, "The Image of Mahādeva in the cave-Temple on Elephanta Island", AI, no. 2, July 1946, p. 4, also pl. I, facing p. 6.
41. *Strómateis*, III, 194; see also H.G. Rawlinson, *"India in European Literature and Thought,"* in *The Legacy of India*, ed. G.T. Garratt, p. 19; D. Th. Vassiliades, *The Greeks in India*, p. 57; Thomas McEvilley, *The Shape of Ancient Thought*, p. 391; R.A. Jairzabhoy, *Foreign Influence in Ancient India*, p. 88 (for *Strom.*, IV, 4, para 17); U.P. Arora, "Ancient India and Ancient Greece", in HIC, Vol. I, pt. 2, *Life, thought and Culture in India* (from c. 600BC to c. AD 300), p. 1064 (for *Strom.*, I, 15, 71-72;III, 7, 60).
42. *Nat. Hist.*, VII, 21-30.
43. *De Abstinentia,* IV, 16-17.
44. See AICL, p. 168.

Book Twelve
Education, Palaeography and Chronology

1

Education and Learning

The brāhmanical and Buddhist system of education and learning in ancient India received the attention of classical writers to the extent they deserved.

Megasthenes attributed education to the Brachmanes (Brāhmaṇas), who formed a separate class, and were held in high esteem in the contemporary society by virtue of their learning and wisdom.

Megasthenes' description of the system of education is analogous to *Gurūkula* system that was introduced in post-Vedic times. That system was prevalent in India in his time too.

Under the *Gurūkula* system of education, the child after his initiation ceremony and attaining boyhood used to leave his parents' house and reside in the *Gurūkula* - the House of the Gurū, preceptor or teacher - which was no less than an educational institution. The initiation of the boy into the studentship by the teacher was regarded as his second birth. In the *Gurūkula*, the education was imparted under strict rules and discipline.

Megasthenes,[1] as we learn from Strabo,[2] says that after their birth the children (in brāhmaṇa family) were under the care of one person after another, and as they advanced in age each succeeding master was more accomplished than his predecessor. The philosophers (brāhmaṇas intending to study) had their abode in a grove in front of the city within a moderate-sized enclosure. They lived in a simple style, and slept on beds of rushes or (deer) skins. They abstained from animal food, material comforts, and sexual pleasures, and spent their time in listening to serious discourse. The brāhmaṇa teachers imparted knowledge to their pupils or disciples. They listened to their instructors maintaining silence and showing respect to them. They were not allowed to speak or cough or even to spit in the course of learning lesson. The offender was cast out from the society that very day, as being a man without self-control. We are further told that the pupils or students lived with their Gurū under his care and guidance. They received education from him for a period of thirty-seven years. After having completed the austerities of the first period (of the fourfold division of a brāhmaṇa's life), that is, the period of *brahmacarya* (celibacy), they left the *Gurūkula*, returned to common life, got married and became the householder. They lived for the rest of their days in ease and security.[3]

The *Gurūkula* system of education was followed also at Taxila. The Greek traveller Apollonius and his Assyrian companion Damis were informed by king Phraotes of Taxila in the course of their visit to the place (in CE 44) that the brāhmaṇas before admitting any one into his house as his student used to inquire into his character, and pretence or antecedents. After getting fully satisfied, he undertook the task of educating his pupils or students. We are also told that the most important subject of study was philosophy.[4]

Megasthenes[5] states, as recorded in Strabo's *Geography*,[6] that the Brachmanes did not "communicate a knowledge of philosophy to their wives, lest they should divulge any of the forbidden mysteries to the profane if they became depraved, or lest they should desert them if they became good philosophers." The Greek authors had a high impression of the learning and wisdom of the Hindus and of some particulars of their philosophy.

The Greek writers have produced the evidence of also women education. The ancient Indian women enjoyed complete liberty in the realm of education. No restriction was ever imposed upon their education. Like learned brāhmaṇas, they also belonged to the learned class.

Strabo, citing Nearchus (one of the companions of Alexander, and one of the trustworthy Greek historical writers) as his authority, tells us that women studied philosophy along with the Brachmanes, and led an ascetic life.[7] Megasthenes[8] also writes to the same effect, as we learn from Strabo.[9] Philosophy was the main subject of study for both men and women among the brāhmaṇas, as appears from the Greek accounts of the subject.

We are told by Strabo that apart from philosophy, the Brachmanes studied physiology and astronomy.[10]

We learn from both Nearchus[11] and Megasthenes[12] that among the Brachmanes the Physicians were engaged in the study of the nature of man.

In accordance with the prevailing system of education in India, students could specialize in any branch of learning according to their capacity, ability and interest. They had the freedom of choosing the subject of study.

In his account of the kingdom of Mousikanos (in Upper Sindh), Onesikritus, one of the companions and historians of Alexander, notices those characteristics which its inhabitants shared with other Indians. Strabo, on his authority, informs us that they studied the science of medicine with much attention.[13]

The Indians' knowledge of medical, astronomical and astrological sciences can very well be proved by the testimony of the classical authors.

Strabo records Indians' knowledge of medicines for curing eye-diseases and for healing up the wounds.[14]

Strabo[15] relates, on the authority of Aristoboulus, the companion and historian of Alexander, that as per law of the land a person, who discovered anything deadly, was put to death unless he also discovered its antidote (a cure for it), and if that person succeeded in discovering it he received a reward from the king. This shows that the study of medical science in ancient India received all encouragement and support from the state government.

We learn from Diodorus Siculus that the midwives had specialized in the field of embryology.[16]

J. Filliozat commented that "the Greeks and Indians were having scientific communication in the filed of medicine".[17]

The other two important subjects of study were astronomy and astrology. Curtius records that Indian philosophers (brāhmaṇas) observe the motions of heavenly bodies and predict future events on scientific principles. He also refers to the calculation of time by the Indians. The division of time, according to him, was marked by the course of the moon.[18] Strabo also states that the brāhmaṇas studied different subjects, including the science of astronomy.[19]

"If we are to rely on the classical accounts", observes Vijay Govind, "India achieved a great progress in almost all the branches of science and technology… it would not be incorrect to say that in ancient times India provided the beacon light to other countries of the world in the realm of different branches of scientific knowledge. No other conclusion can be drawn if we are to give credence to the works of the classical writers on India".[20]

We have very little information in the classics regarding Buddhist system of education and learning which was quite different from brāhmanical one.

The Buddhists generally acquired knowledge of philosophical doctrines of life and death. A passage regarding them (called Shamans) from Bardesanes' work (now lost) preserved by Stobaeus from porphyry bears witness to the fact that they were devoted to "the study of divine things".[21]

Notes and References

1. *Indika*, Bk III, Fragm. XLI.
2. *Geog.*, XV, I, 59; see also AIMA, pp. 98, 99, and fn; AICL, pp. 65, and note 2, 66, and note 1.
3. See also M. Elphinstone, "The Greek Accounts of India", reptd., from his *The History of India* (ed. E.B. Cowell, 9th edn. London, 1911), in *Ancient India* (Delhi, 1983), pp. 19-20; W.W. Hunter, "The Greeks in India (327 to 161 BCE)", reptd. from his *The Indian Empire: Its Peoples, History and Products* (London, 1882), in *Ancient India (Supra)*, p. 92; H.F. Tozer, *Hist. Anc. Geog.*, p. 152. Lassen points out (*Ind. Alt.*, II, p. 701) that it was the established custom as well as a prescript of the law that the disciple should always submit himself to but one single guru preceptor, who also during his childhood and youth performed all the ceremonies according to Hindu custom. There must have been exceptions, he says, with regard to more than one guru or preceptor. We are told by Manu (*Manusmṛti*, III. 1; see also V.S. Agrawala, *India as described by*

Manu, p. 11) that sufficient latitude was granted with regard to the period of study in the *Gurūkula*. It continued for 36, 18, or 9 years, or to any length of time depending on the subject of study.

4. Priaulx, *Indian Travels of Apollonius of Tyana*..., in CAI, p. 391.
5. *Indika*, Bk. III, Fragm. XLI.
6. XV, I, 59
7. *Geog*., XV, I, 66.
8. *Indika*, Bk, III, Fragm. XLI.
9. *Geog*., XV, I, 60; see also D.Th. Vassiliades, *The Greeks in India*, p. 54; R.A. Jairzabhoy, *Foreign Influence in Ancient India*, p. 86.
10. *Geog*., XV, I, 70.
11. Cf. Strabo, *Geog*., XV, I, 66.
12. *Indika*, Bk. III, Fragm. XLI, Strabo. *Geog*., XV, I, 60.
13. *Geog*., XV, I, 34; see also Hamilton and Falconer (tr.), *The Geography of Strabo*, III, p. 96.
14. *Geog*., XV, I, 43; see also B.N. Puri, *India in Classical Greek Writings*, pp. 152,156.
15. *Geog*., XV.I, 22; see also Puri, *op. cit*., pp. 145-46.
16. *Bib. Hist*., XIX, 30.
17. *The Classical Doctrine of Indian Medicine*, p. 257.
18. *Hist. Alex*., VII, 9.
19. Geog., XV, I, 17; XV, I, 70; see also Pliny, *Nat. Hist*., VI, 22 (24); VI, 23(26); Nearchus, in Arrian's *Indika*, II, XXV, cf. *Voy. Near*, pp. 185-86.
20. "The Growth of Science and Technology as Gleaned from the Classical Accounts of India", JIH, LIX, 1-3, 1981, pp. 85-86.
21. AICL, p. 167.

2

Evolution of the Art of Writing

The art of writing was known to the Indians much before the time of Alexander. That art further developed in India in his time and later.

The information provided by the classical writers regarding the evolution of the art of writing in India is of exceptional value.

The earliest known historical evidence in the classical writings on India regarding the Indians' knowledge of writing and its antiquity is that which was produced by the Greek writer Nearchus in the early part of the last quarter of the fourth century before the Christian era. He had accompanied Alexander the Great into India. The knowledge of writing in India at the time of the Macedonian invasion (327-325 BCE) can fairly be attested to by his statement that the Indians wrote letters upon cloth very closely woven, as quoted by Strabo.[1] The cloth was, in fact, well-pressed to make it smooth for the purpose of writing. It is significant to add that Strabo invariably quotes Nearchus as his authority. Since Nearchus' account of India (which he wrote shortly after 324 BCE after completing his voyage, begun in 325 BCE) is an eye-witness one, we can give full credence to his statement quoted above. The statement of Nearchus quoted by Strabo, according to H.L. Jones, runs as follows: "they (the Indians) write missives (letters) on linen cloth that is very closely woven" ("*de graphein epistola's en sindosi lian kekrotamenais*").[2]

Curtius also, like Nearchus, did not fail to take notice of the system of writing in India. He writes: "The tender side of the barks of trees receives written characters like paper".[3] Though he belongs to a later period, seems to describe the state of things prevailing in Alexander's time. G. Bühler, the Principal authority on Indian palaeography, says: "The inner bark of the *Bhürja*-tree (*Baetula Bhojapatra*), which the Himālaya produces in great quantity, probably is alluded to by Q. Curtius as a writing material used by the Hindus at the time of Alexander's invasion, and later it is frequently named as such in Northern Buddhist and Brāhmaṇical Sanskrit works."[4]

"Curtius", observes Lallanji Gopal, "generally derived his information from earlier writers. But, his source of information in the present case is not known. None of the other earlier writers, who have recorded the history of Alexander's invasion, mention this fact. It is not unlikely that Curtius received this information from source other than the contemporaries of Alexander. In that case this statement will not be of much use; it cannot be taken to be faithful to the practice in the times of Alexander. But, the possibility cannot be ruled out that this statement also goes back to some writer contemporary of Alexander. In that case Curtius is important in recording another writing material used in those early times".[5]

Here we cannot pass over the observation made by Bühler: "To the last quarter of the fourth century BC refer the statement of Nearchus, according to which the Hindus wrote letters on well-beaten cotton cloth, and the note of Q. Curtius, which mentions the tender inner bark of trees as serving the same purpose, and clearly points to the early utilization of the well known birch-bark. The fact that, according to these two writers, two different indigenous Indian materials were used in 327-325 BC, shows that the art of writing was then generally known and was nothing new."[6]

We learn from Pliny that paper made from the papyrus plant did not come into common use out of Egypt till the time of Alexander the Great. He then goes on to say that for writing on, the leaves of palm-trees were first used, and then the barks (*libri*) of certain trees.[7] This shows that different systems of writing were followed at different periods of history. Before paper, the cloth, leaves of palm-trees and barks of trees were used for writing in India in pre-Alexandrian age. It has been rightly pointed out that the native writing materials were barks of trees in the north and palm-leaves in the south.[8]

The Indians, says McCrindle, were "acquainted with writing for some centuries before Alexander's time, but whence they got their alphabet is a question not yet quite settled, though the weight of opinion inclines to assign it a Himyaritic origin."[9] From Nearchus' time when letters were written on cloth, we come to Pliny's time when they were written on different other materials. Thus, within four centuries a considerable progress was achieved in the field of writing. The introduction of paper for writing in India was a later development whose exact date cannot be ascertained.

The absence of written laws led Megasthenes to believe that the Indians were ignorant of the art of writing, and regulated everything by memory.[10] It is true that laws were uncodified or unwritten in his time, but it does not mean that the writing was not in vogue. Nearchus, as we learn from Strabo,[11] also says that the Indians had no written laws, but does not deny that they possessed the art of writing in Alexander's time,[12] as noted before. The writing of laws and knowledge of writing are two different subjects to be treated of. "Megasthenes", says McCrindle, "could not possibly have been ignorant of the fact that the art of writing was known to the Indians. What he said must have been that the Indians in their judiciary transactions did not employ written laws because the judges knew the laws by heart."[13] Lallanji Gopal is absolutely right in stating that Megasthenes "did not personally see the use of writing".[14] Megasthenes' statement, according to J.T. Wheeler, "must be accepted with some reservation". "The Brāhmaṇs", he observes, "certainly possessed sacred literature, but they would never have produced their books to the Greek ambassador ..."[15]

It is striking that Megasthenes himself says that among the Indian philosophers (brāhmaṇas) there were some who used to commit the useful suggestion to writing to pass it on to the king in whose service they were employed,[16] as recorded by Strabo.[17] This statement of the former credits the Indians with a knowledge of writing. The familiarity of the Indians with writing also gets proved thereby. The writing was in common use not only for literary purpose but also in public business.

The Indians, no doubt, possessed the knowledge of writing in the time of Candragupta Maurya generally called by the ancient Greek writers Sandrakottus. The Indians' knowledge of writing in his time or in the time of Megasthenes can also be corroborated by the statements of Lallanji Gopal.[18]

"There is ... hardly any doubt that the art of writing was known to the Indians at the time of Megasthenes, and even much earlier. This is proved by inscriptions engraved on rocks and pillars during the reign of Aśoka, about half a century later. These letters are so well formed that there must have been an anterior period of development of writing extending over centuries", says R.C. Majumdar.[19]

We have another evidence of knowledge of writing in India. Strabo,[20] quoting Nikolaus of Damascus as his authority, informs us that Nikolaus personally read the letter sent by the Indian king Porus (probably one of the descendants of king Porus of Alexander's time) through his ambassadors (in 22 BCE) to Roman Emperor Augustus. Nikolaus met the Indian ambassadors at Antioch (in Syria) and read the letter written by king Porus. Nikolaus says that "the letter was written in Greek on parchment and that king Porus was the writer". Parchment, a stiff material made from the prepared skin of a sheep or goat, or a kind of translucent paper, was formerly used for writing. Herodotus[21] also affirms that parchment was a writing material. That it was used for writing on in India can be supported by the statements of Heeren[22] and Priaulx[23]. Some authorities are of the opinion that the letter written by Porus in Greek on skin contained the names or credentials of the ambassadors who were sent to Augustus.[24] The letter, according to H.G. Rawlinson,[25] was written on Vellum (fine parchment made originally from the skin of a calf). The Greeks, says R.A. Jairzabhoy, may have imported parchment (writing material) into India, for it had been manufactured from pergamum, and exported in great quantities by Eumenes II in the early second century before the Christian era.[26] We are informed by Isidore of Charax that the Parthians used to write on parchments.[27]

That, the letter was written by king Porus in Greek, shows the use of that language in northern India in the first century before the Christian era. The statement of E.J. Rapson, that a system of writing developed from the Greek alphabet during the Greek rule (200-25 BCE) in northern and northwestern parts of India,[28] is not incredible.

We are told by Philostratus that Phraotes, an Indian prince of Taxila, had given to Apollonius, the Greek traveller who has sojourned with him for three days during his visit to the place in CE 44, a guide to accompany him on his onward march to meet the brāhmaṇas, whose seat lay between the Hyphasis and the Ganges, and also a letter of introduction (written in Greek) requesting the chief of the brāhmaṇas to let the Greek philosophers know all that he himself knew.[29]

There were several stages in the evolution of writing in ancient India. The classical accounts of Indian palaeography covers the period from the fourth century BCE to the first century CE. Different systems of writing evolved during the period. The writing was, no doubt, introduced in pre-

Alexandrian age. But, according to classical testimony, the fourth century BCE was the blooming period for its growth and development. It further continued to flourish down to the first century of the Christian era. The period under notice saw the regular use of writing.

Notes and References

1. Geog., XV, I, 67; see also Hamilton and Falconer (tr), *The Geography of Strabo*, III, pp. 115-16; FGH, Nearchus, No. 133, Fragm. 33; U.P. Arora, "Classical Accounts on India-Some Observation", in *Graeco-Indica: India's Cultural Contacts with the Greek World,* ed. by him, p. 95. G.N. Banerjee (*Hellenism in Ancient India*, p. 209) says that the art of writing was certainly known to the Indians anterior to the time of Alexander's conquest of India as testified to by Nearchus who himself ascribes the knowledge of the art of writing to the Indians. H.G. Rawlinson's statement, that the Indians first acquired the art of writing through the officials of the Persians who ruled in the Punjab for nearly two centuries (*A Concise History of the Indian People,* p. 58), is a mere supposition. We do not have any such evidence in the classical sources of the history of India.
2. *The Geography of Strabo* (tr. by him), VII, p. 117.
3. *Hist. Alex.*, VIII, 9; see also *Frag. Hist. Graec.*, 2, p. 421.
4. *Indian Paleography*, p. 139.
5. "Early Greek writers on Writing in India", PIHC, 37th session (Calicut, 1976), pp. 544-45.
6. *Op.cit.,* p. 23.
7. *Nat. Hist.*, XIII, 21.
8. Reinaud, *Memoire sur I' Inde*, p. 305.
9. IIA, p. 186, note 2. In Pāṇini's time, script was used in northwestern part of India for writing which is evidenced by his allusion to *lipīkāra* (writer of script) in his *Aṣṭādhyāyī.*
10. *Indika*, Bk. II. Fragm. XXVII, cf. Strabo, *Geog*., XV, I, 53; see also H.L. Jones, *The Geography of Strabo*, VII, pp. 87-88. Strabo's remark, that the other writers affirm that the Indians had no knowledge of written letters (XV, I, 67), applies to no other than Megasthenes.
11. *Geog*., XV, I, 66.
12. *Ibid*., XV, I, 67.
13. AICL, p. 56, note 1.
14. *Op. cit*., p. 549.
15. *The History of India from the Earliest Ages* ch. IV, "Greek and Roman India", p. 200. M. Elphinstone ("The Greek Accounts of India", reptd. from his *The History of India*, ed. E.B. Cowell, London, 1911, in *Ancient India*, Delhi,

1983, p. 28) has rightly pointed out that Megasthenes maintains that the Indians were ignorant of writing, while other Greek writers praise the beauty of their writing.

16. *Indika*, Bk. III, Fragm. XXXIII.
17. *Geog.*, XV, I, 39. Of all the works of early Greek writers that have come down to us, it is only Megasthenes' work in which we find some contradictory statements.
18. *Op.cit.*, pp. 546, 549.
19. CAI, Introduction, xx.
20. *Geog.*, XV, I, 73. The concerned passage was preserved by Strabo from the Universal History of Nikolaus.
21. History, V, 58.
22. *Historical Researches*, II, p. 107.
23. *The Indian Travels of Apollonius of Tyana…*, p. 65, note 3.
24. J.T. Wheeler, "Greek and Roman India", reptd. from his *The History of India from the Earliest Ages* (London, 1881), in *Ancient India* (Delhi, 1983), pp. 138-39; W.W. Hunter, The Greeks in India", in *Ancient India* (supra), p. 96.
25. "India in European Literature and Thought", in *The Legacy of India,* ed. G.T. Garratt, p. 15.
26. *Foreign Influence in Ancient India*, p. 91.
27. *Mans. Parth.*, tr. W.H. Schoff, *The Parthian Stations of Isidore of Charax*, p. 40.
28. *Ancient India from the Earliest Times to the First Century AD,* p. 71. The Greek script, called by Pānini *Yavanani lipi,* was known to the Indians in his time. They might have acquired its knowledge through the Persians.
29. *The Life of Apollonius of Tyana*, in AICL, p. 193.

3

Systems of Chronology

Some of the systems of chronology followed in ancient India also attracted the notices of some of the ancient Greek and Roman historians. The information supplied by them regarding the chronological system of the Indians in the fourth century before the Christian era first deserves our notice. It was the Greek historian Megasthenes who first recorded in his *Indika* the chronological system that prevailed in those days in India. Some of the Greek and Roman writers of the subsequent period derived the information about that system from the said work of Megasthenes.

During his five years' stay (303-298 BCE) at the imperial court of Sandrakottus (Candragupta) in Pāṭaliputra as a Greek ambassador, Megasthenes gathered information from various sources regarding the ancient history of the Indians and their chronological system. He was given at the court of the said Maurya emperor a list of Indian kings who had preceded him on the throne, 153 in number, covering by their reigns a period of over 6000 years.

Megasthenes' statement, that the reigns of 154 Indian kings down to the time of Alexander the Great extended over 6451 years and 3 months,[1] was recorded by Pliny,[2] the Roman geographer and historians of the first century, and by Solinus,[3] the Roman historian, who flourished in the first half of the third century. He actually copied it from Pliny's *Naturalis Historia* (Natural History).

The famous Greek historian, Arrian (second century), informs us that from the time of Dionysus (identical with the first Āryan king Manu of the Purāṇas) to Sandrakottus, the Indians counted 153 kings, and a period of 6042 years, and that Dionysus was earlier than Heracles by fifteen generations.[4] The said 153 kings, who had preceded Candragupta Maurya, are said to have reigned for a period of 6042 years, which is at variance with the period recorded by Megasthenes, Pliny and Solinus. The actual number of kings from Manu to Candragupta in the present Purāṇas is 135 which is very close to the number mentioned by the classical authors. The Purāṇic genealogies and chronology of pre-Candragupta period are, no doubt, supported by the classical evidence to some extent.[5]

"It is not known from what sources Megasthenes derived these figures, which are extremely modest when compared with those of Indian chronology", observes McCrindle.[6] He also states that Pliny and Arrian were indebted for the chronological details to Megasthenes, "who evidently endeavoured to bring the chronology of the Brāhmaṇs into some degree of correspondence with that of his countrymen."[7] He has aptly remarked that Megasthenes' estimate of the number of the kings is much higher than of any of the lists which now exists.

Dealing with traditional Indian chronology, R.C. Jain mentions the chronological data of the classical writers. He also asserts that Megasthenes knew the Indian tradition of chronology. He says: "… the traditional history began to take some shape in the third century BC".[8]

The historicity of Dionysus may be doubted, but it cannot be denied that Heracles, mentioned by Arrian as possessor of two large cities, Methora and Cleisobora (Mathurā, and Kṛṣṇapura or Vrindāvana), was no other than Hari or Śrī Kṛṣṇa. C.V. Vaidya has correctly stated that "Since there were 153 generations from Dionysus to Candragupta and Dionysus was 15 generations earlier than Heracles (as recorded by Arrian), it follows that Heracles preceded Chandragupta by 138 generations of kings… Such was the tradition prevalent in India in 312 BC (Candragupta's time), i.e., at a time when European scholars are agreed that the Indians had not learnt or discovered the methods of calculating the position of planets. That the inquisitive Greek ambassador at the court of Chandragupta has left carefully sifted information about India without exaggeration or fabrication has also been admitted. The only possible way in which the above tradition may be impeached is by supposing that the Indians themselves had exaggerated notions about their antiquity".[9]

The natives of the Indus region informed the Greek traveller Apollonius at the time of his visit to the place that, according to their chronological computation, roughly 350 years had elapsed since the battle of Porus with Alexander (fought in 326 BCE), as recorded by Philostratus.[10]

Notes and References

1. *Indika*, Bk. IV, Fragm. LC.
2. *Nat. Hist.*, VI, 17 (21); VI, 21, 4-5; see also AICL, p. 108; CAI, p. 340.
3. *Coll. Rer, Memo.*, 52, 5; also CAI, p. 457; AIMA, p. 115.
4. *Indika*, I, IX; see also AIMA, pp. 203-04; *Indika*, tr. Chinnock, in Godolphin's *The Greek Historians*, II, pp. 738-39; B.C. Law, "Studies in Indian History and Geography Based on Early Greek Accounts", JGRI, XVI, 3-4, 1959, p. 266.
5. See also F. Wilford, "Chronology of the Hindus", *As. Res.*, V (Delhi, 1979) pp. 291-2.
6. AIMA, p. 203, fn.
7. AICL, p. 108, note 1.
8. EAB, p. 203.
9. *The Mahābhārata: A Criticism*, p. 58.
10. *Vit. Apoll.,* tr. F.C. Conybeare, *The Life of Apollonius of Tyana*, II, 12, pp. 146-47.

General Conclusions and Observations

The contributions made by the ancient Greeks and Roman to the discovery of geography, history, culture and civilization of India are of inestimable value.

The name of this country – India – was derived either from one of the Greek words, *Indika*, Indies, and Indus, or from one of the Latin words, Inde, and Indica. And the Indians were first called by the Greeks Indoi. From the classical accounts of India it appears that this country was the "largest of the four parts into which southern Asia was divided", and the most populous in the world.

The geographical boundaries of northern and north-western India time to time underwent transformation due to the historical changes. Anterior to the sixth century before the Christian era, the great mountain ranges of the Hindukush in Afghanistan, designated both Paropamisus and Paropanisus by the classical writers, was the northern boundary of India. From the sixth to the fifth centuries BCE, almost the whole of Afghanistan, to the west of the Indus, was under the rule of the Persians. After Persian occupation of the Indus valley, the river Indus formed the western boundary of India. At the time of Alexander's invasion, and even after his departure from India, the Indus remained the western boundary of this country for sometime. After Seleukus Nikator ceded to Sandrakottus (Candragupta, the Maurya emperor) the four provinces west of the Indus-Aria (Herāt), Arachosia (Kandahār), Paropanisadae (Kābul valley) and Gedrosia (the modern Baluchistan) – in accordance with the provisions of the treaty concluded between the two in 303 BCE, India attained its pre-sixth century BCE geographical position, and the Hindukush once again became its northern boundary. The Indus was no longer its western boundary, as the territories to its west now formed parts of this country. In the time of Candragupta Maurya, India no doubt extended to the Hindūkush mountain. India from the Himalayas (Hemodus) in the north to Cape Comorin (cape of Komari of the author of the *Periplus*, and Komaria of Ptolemy) in the south was known to the classical geographers and historians.

Ariana, which comprised Bactria or Bactriana, Aria, Arachosia, Paropanisadae and Gedrosia on the west and Sindh on the east, was the land of the Āryans. They were the original inhabitants of the Ariana region which was within the geographical limits of India. This country was inhabited not only by the Āryans but also by various non-Āryans. Both geography and ethnography of India received the notices of the classical authors.

The people of ancient India were very fortunate, and gifted with many virtues. They were just, honest, truth-loving, sober, moderate, kind-hearted, industrious, brave, healthy and wealthy. They led happy and peaceful life.

The Indian society, in the time of Megasthenes, was divided into classes and castes. The philosophers, the farmers or agriculturist called husbandmen, and the soldiers or warriors formed the castes. These three corresponded to the brāhmaṇas, vaiśyas and kṣatriyas respectively. The shepherds (herdsmen) and hunters, handicraftsmen or artizans, overseers, superintendents or inspectors, and councillors and assessors represented the classes. The underlying principle of this social division or stratification was the professions and duties of the people.

The life-style of the Indians varied from person to person. The persons of high social rank, or of great wealth led luxurious life in contrast to the general simplicity of the life-style. The social status was determined by their dresses and ornaments. There were different social customs, practices, traditions and institutions.

The position and status of women in the Indian society varied from time to time. The women were looked at from different perspectives. They neither enjoyed the freedom nor did they occupy any respectable place in the contemporary society. They had to perform different types of duties. They were put under several social restrictions. They did not exercise their own choice or freedom in the matters of marriage. As per ancient Indian law, it was binding on their part to be sati after the demise of their husbands. They had to burn themselves alive along with their dead husbands on the funeral pyre. Those women who became Sati of their own accord were held in high esteem. In the domain of education, the Indian women from both brāhmaṇa and Buddhist families enjoyed some freedom. The women in the tribal society occupied very honourable position.

There was no uniformity in ancient Indian agrarian system. Land in India was the property of the crown, and no private person was permitted to own land. The cultivators of land (ryots) paid a land-rent to the king. Among some tribes, there was common ownership of the land. There was agrarian economy (the practice of cultivation of land), as appears from the classical accounts of agrarian and agricultural system of the Indians. Irrigation was practised in India to increase the fertility of the lands. Agricultural works were carried out extensively. The agricultural production was very high. There were various agricultural crops and products. India was gifted with various natural, mineral and commercial products. Various arts, crafts and indigenous industries flourished in the country.

The internal trade was carried on not only by overland routes but also by river and sea-routes. There existed many routes which linked up the principal centres of trade in various parts of the country. The external trade was carried on by sea, and overland routes. India had commercial intercourse not only with the western world – the Roman Empire, including Egypt, and Greece – but also with other countries – China in East Asia, Malaya Peninsula in southeast Asia, Ceylon in South Asia, Persia in West Asia, and Arabia and Africa.

On the basis of his indepth study of the Greek accounts of India, B.N. Puri observes : "The economic life of the people was well-advanced, and it was confined not to one particular branch, namely agriculture, but embraced multifarious forms of human endeavours such as agriculture, trade and industries, which goes to prove that Indian economic life was of an advanced type... This highly developed economic life was manifested through the process of production, consumption, distribution and exchange of wealth. Even money and credit was in use, which shows that it was a full-fledged and developed economic life." *(India as described by Early Greek Writers,* p. 154*)*.

The two prevailing forms of government in India at the time of its invasion by Alexander the Great were monarchy and republic, as gleaned from the accounts of his Indian campaign given by his own historians. The monarchies and republics existed side by side in Afghanistan, the

Punjab and Sindh. In Baluchistan, only the republics flourished, as some tribes there followed the republican system of government.

Various factors were responsible for the decline and downfall of Indian republics. In the course of Alexander's invasion of India, all the republican institutions in the Punjab and Sindh were destroyed. These two places were the main seats of republics in northwestern part of India. Most of the republican tribes who fought against him and his troops were put to death. Those who survived moved from one place to another in Alexander's time and after. The Nysaeans, who were the republican community in Afghanistan, were allowed by him to maintain their republican tradition, as they did not raise their voice against him and surrendered to his authority. There was a general tendency on the part of the rulers of monarchical states to capture the neighbouring republican states and annex them to their respective kingdoms. The fifteen republics in the neighbourhood of the kingdom of great Porus of the Punjab were under his sway. They lost their independence. Monarchy was the greatest barrier in the way of the growth and prosperity of the republics. Samudragupta, the great champion of monarchy, forced all the republican tribes of his time, including the descendants of those of Alexander's time, to acknowledge him as their overlord. They lost their freedom which was the soul of Indian republics. By the end of the fourth century of the Christian era, the republics disappeared from the pages of Indian history. The monarchies, however, continued to survive.

As regards the system of administration, in monarchical set-up the king was the supreme head of the state; and in republican states the power was vested in the whole community or in a small or fairly bigger body. In a confederate state, the political power was shared jointly by two independent tribes who formed a confederation. The chiefs of the provinces were the governors. Decentralisation of power in the sphere of local government constitutes one of the notable features of the Maurya system of administration in the time of Candragupta. Villages, towns and cities were self-governed. State officials were appointed in his time to look after the administration of public affairs. The municipal administration of the capital city Pāṭaliputra in his time was witnessed by Megasthenes during his stay at the imperial court there and recorded by him in his *Indika*. Military department was well organised. Justice was administered in India in accordance with the laws established. Revenue system was well maintained. The espionage system–the system of employing spies to watch or observe secretly the conduct or activities of the government officials and others to collect information and report to the concerned authorities –

formed one of the important elements in the Indian administrative system. The classical writers, no doubt, made immense contribution to the discovery of facts relating to ancient Indian political system.

India's religions and philosophies, for which she is still famous in the west, did not fail to attract the attention of Greek historians and philosophers. The three popular religions of India described by them were Brāhmaṇism, Buddhism and Jainism. The Brāhma was called Brachmans or Brachmanes, the Buddhists, designated Sarmanes and Jains, who constituted some sections of the Sramanai, had different religious beliefs and practices, modes of life, and philosophical doctrines. The Brāhmaṇas, Buddhists and Jains were divided into various sects.

It was the first century that marked the introduction of Christianity in India. The progress of Christianity in South India was witnessed during the first two centuries of the Christian era. By the year CE 535, Christianity had spread in a number of places in India, especially in southern and western India.

The Assyrians were the first to undertake an expedition against the Indians in the beginning of the ninth century before Christ or in 808 BCE. In the first chapter of the first part of his *Indika*, the Greek historian Arrian records that the regions beyond the river Indus on the west were inhabited, upto the river Kophen (Kābul), by two Indian tribes, the Astakenoi and the Assakenoi, who were in old times subject to the Assyrians, before they submitted to the persians. The Assyrians subjugated some parts of Afghanistan, and established their hold over the regions between the Indus and the Kābul. The portion of India lying along the west bank of the Indus formed part of the Assyrian empire which was later overthrown by Cyrus the Great, the founder of the Achaemenian empire of Persia. The pre-Persian Assyrians' Indian expedition is yet to be recorded in the ancient history of India.

During the period from the sixth to the fifth centuries BCE, the Persians conquered Bactria, Aria (Herāt) Arachosia (Kandahār) and Paropanisadae (Kābul valley) – all parts of Ariana – the city of Kāpiśī in the upper region of the Kophes (upper Kābul valley), Gāndhāra (west of the Indus), the Indus valley and a considerable portion of the Punjab east of the Indus. The Persian domination in northern India continued up to the time of Darius III (336-330 BCE), the last Persian ruler of the Achaemenid dynasty. After the Persians, the Macedonians invaded India.

The invasion of India by Alexander the Great of Macedonia was one of the epoch-making events not only in the political history of India but also in the history of the world.

Most of the kings or rulers, and the tribes, who raised the banner of revolt against Alexander and entered into battles with him and his forces were put to sword. Those rulers who tendered their submission to him were reinstated in their sovereignty by his clemency. Of the independent, autonomous or republican tribes, those who resisted the attempt of Alexander to conquer their territories were either subdued or subjugated, and those who surrendered to him were allowed to maintain their freedom.

In the Punjab, the Great Porus and the Mālavas fought more bravely than others against the Macedonian invader and his troops, and displayed exemplary courage and valour in the course of their fight with them. Porus did not surrender to Alexander, rather fought against him till he was badly injured and fully exhausted. Being highly impressed by the bravery of Porus, Alexander treated him well, and returned not only his territories he conquered, but also added to them the territories of others he occupied to be governed by him. Porus eventually became his faithful ally and trustworthy friend. Through the persuasion of Alexander, king Āmbhi of Taxila and Porus of the Punjab, who were earlier hostile to each other, now joined hands with each other, which constitutes one of the examples of magnanimity or greatness of Alexander.

Of all the Indians who fought against Alexander, the Brāhmaṇas of Sindh gave a historic fight to him. They kindled the spark of patriotism in the hearts of the populace and potentates of Sindh and stirred them up to expel the foreign invader from the country. The Brāhmaṇas themselves fought against the invader with swords in their hands. Many of them were mercilessly butchered; and some of them were hanged. The sacrifices they made for the defence of the country will always be remembered by the posterity.

The Indians could not fight unitedly (with few exceptions) against common enemy-Alexander. Moreover, there were some traitors amongst them who were loyal to Alexander and extended all possible help and co-operation to him against their fellow-countrymen.

During the period from 327 BCE to 325 BCE, Alexander conquered some parts of Afghanistan, the Punjab, Sindh and Baluchistan. The Punjab and Sindh passed under the Macedonian rule.

Alexander's dream of conquering the Gangetic kingdom of Magadha with its capital Pāṭaliputra and making it a part of his Asiatic Empire was not fulfilled because of the refusal of his army to advance beyond the river Hyphasis, as they were scared of facing the formidable forces of the reigning king of that kingdom, Dhananand, called Xandrames and also

Agrammes. The altars erected or set-up on the banks of that river marked the eastern limits of Alexander's empire.

The Persian and Macedonian invasions of India changed its geography and history.

Alexander's invasion of India proved to be a boon for the country from the commercial, political, historical and cultural points of view to a considerable degree.

It was Alexander who broke down the barrier between the East and the West and thereby paved the way for the establishment of trade contacts between the two. His invasion promoted the political unification of India. After his invasion, the Indians realised their mistakes of not fighting unitedly against him, and felt the necessity of maintaining unity at the time of foreign invasion of the country.

Alexander's invasion opened up communication between Greece and India and paved the way for a more intimate intercourse between the two. A new era of cultural interaction between the Greeks the Indians began. They mutually borrowed ideas and principles from each other. A close contact was established between the two great civilization – Eastern and Western. His invasion brought a vast increase in the knowledge of the Europeans about India. The writings of his companions and historians in their respective works about contemporary history, culture and civilization of India contributed to the enrichment of their knowledge about this country. Alexander was not only an invader but also a discoverer. He also made some contribution to the discovery of India. His Epistles, in which he recorded all that he witnessed with his eyes while in India and learnt from his companions and historians about the Indians, became one of the sources of information about India and the Indians for his successors and later Greek and Roman writers.

The Indians were influenced to some extent by Hellenistic culture that saw its efflorescence in the post-Alexandrian period.

After liberating the Punjab and Sindh from the Greek rule in 317 BCE, Sandrakottus rose to power. He returned from the Punjab with a powerful force to Magadha. On reaching its capital Pāṭaliputra (called both Pālibothra and Pālimbothra) in 315 BCE, he entered into a battle with the last Nanda monarch Dhananand and his forces and defeated them. The Nanda dynasty was uprooted. He ascended the throne of Magadha and founded the Maurya dynasty.

The accession of Sandrakottus to the throne of Magadha took place in 315 BCE, eight years after Alexander the Great had passed away. Some historians of ancient India, presuming that the expulsion of the Greeks from the Punjab and Sindh and the overthrow of the Nanda rule in Magadha by Sandrakottus took place within two years of Alexander's death, place his accession in 321 BCE, which in the light of the testimony of some ancient Greek and Roman writers and the evidences of some modern authorities does not appear to be worthy of faith. Of all the available dates of his accession, 315 BCE appears to be the most reliable.

Seleukus Nikator, the Greek king of Syria, along with his army led an expedition into India in 303 BCE, and not in or about 306 or 305 BCE as held by some authorities, with a view to recover the territories conquered by Alexander in north western India and to rule over them. In pursuit of his object, he crossed the Indus which marked the western boundary of the Maurya empire at that time. He entered into a war with Sandrakottus, "the king of the Indians". The war between the forces of the two potentates took place in 303 BCE on this side of the Indus or on its banks in which Seleukus was defeated or accepted the defeat and submitted to Sandrakottus, and then entered into a treaty with him.

In 303 BCE itself, a treaty of peace and friendship was concluded between the Syrian monarch Seleukus and the Indian sovereign Sandrakottus. In accordance with the provisions of the treaty, the former ceded to the latter the satrapies of Aria, Arachosia, Paropanisadae and Gedrosia, and received in return a present of five hundred elephants from him. The four provinces west of the Indus, which Sandrakottus received from Seleukus, formed parts of the Maurya empire. As a mark of friendship and amity Seleukus entered into matrimonial alliance with Sandrakottus according to which he gave him his daughter in marriage. The friendly relations seem to have subsisted ever afterwards between the two sovereigns.

All the territories between the Indus and Paropamisus, which were formerly under the sway of the Macedonians, were ceded by Seleukus to Sandrakottus.

Sandrakottus extended his conquests far beyond the eastern limits of Magadha. After the conclusion of the treaty, he ruled an empire extending westward from the river Indus to the southern slopes of the Hindukush.

The celebrated Candragupta Maurya built up an empire such as no Indian king had ever possessed. It was the greatest empire India had ever produced. His empire extended from the mouths of the Ganges to the regions beyond the Indus. He liberated the Punjab and Sindh from the Macedonian rule. The political unification of northern India was the greatest of his all achievements.

There were several kingdoms and principalities in India. Of all the ancient Indian kingdoms, Gāndhāra was of the highest antiquity. The classical writers have provided very valuable information regarding the Sātavāhana kingdom in the Deccan. The three kingdoms of South India-Coḷa, Cera and Pāṇḍya – that existed from a fairly remote antiquity were also known to them, as appears from their descriptions of Indian Kingdoms. They have also thrown light on the principalities that existed in north western India in the time of Alexander.

The Greeks established their rule in Bactriana, Ariana, the north-western frontier province, Gāndhāra, Taxila, the Punjab, Sindh and other parts of India as a whole from about the middle of the third century before the Christian era till about the second quarter of the first century of the Christian era. There were various factors that led to the fall of the power of the Indo-Greek kings and the extinction of Greek rule in the East. One of the important factors was the rise of two new rival powers, the Śakas and the Parthians.

The Śakas first occupied Bactria (north Afghanistan) in or about 135 BCE after driving out the Indo-Greek king. Heliocles from there. In the first century, the Indo-Greek rulers had been dispossessed of Lower Sindh by the Śakas. The Śakas ruled the lower valley of the Indus from about 25 BCE till they were dislodged by the Indo-Parthians about CE 60. The Śakas who ruled in north-western parts of India were from eastern Iran. They extended the Śaka rule to the eastern part of the Punjab. There was expansion of the Śaka rule in other parts of India. The Śaka Kṣatrapas, who ruled in Gujarat and Mahārāṣṭra in western India and in west Mālavā region in Central India, were independent rulers. The Śaka rule in western and central India finally came to an end towards the close of the fourth century.

The Parthians ruled northwest India from about the middle of the third century BCE to CE 64. The Parthian power began to decline from CE 64 onwards. It appears that by CE 79 the Parthians were overthrown by the Kuṣāṇas about whom nothing is written in the classics.

The ancient Greeks and Indians were mutually influenced by each other in various fields through their contacts and interactions. The influence of Greek town-planning ideas in India, the Greek influence on Indian art, coinage, language and literature, influence of Indian religions – Buddhism and Hinduism – on the Greeks in India, influence of Indian philosophical ideas on the thought of the Greek philosophers of both pre-and post-Alexandrian age, and the influence of Indian science of medicine on the Greek medicine can very well be proved on the testimony of the classical writers. There was also some Roman influence on the art of the Gāndhāra School. The ancient Greeks and Romans, no doubt, made great discovery in the field of Graeco-Roman influence on the civilization of India, and in the field of Indian influence on western culture and thought.

India's political relations with Persia in West Asia were maintained during the period from the sixth to the fourth centuries BCE. There were diplomatic and friendly relations between the Maurya Empire of Northern India and the Hellenic kingdoms of Syria (in Western Asia) and Egypt in the fourth and third centuries BCE. Diplomatic relations between India and the Roman Empire were maintained from the time of Augustus down to the time of Justinian which covers the period from the first century BCE to the sixth century CE. Indian embassies were frequently sent to the courts of the Roman Emperors either at Rome or at Constantinople.

The urban culture flourished in India as early as the epic age. Towns and cities existed in almost all parts of India in ancient times, as appears from the ancient Greek and Roman accounts of the subject. The urban decay commenced from the fourth century onwards, and by the end of the sixth century most of the towns and cities lost their existence which may be attributed to several factors, including the decline of trade and commerce, and the foreign invasions.

Ancient India had rich artistic tradition. All the main forms of art-architecture, sculpture, iconography, engraving, decoration and painting – had evolved. The Maurya age witnessed a spectacular progress in the field of art. In that age, architecture, sculpture, and also decorative art were in a highly developed stage. In Taxila city, some specimens of architecture, sculpture, iconography and painting were witnessed by the Greek traveller Apollonius and his Assyrian companion Damis in the first century of the Christian era. There they saw with their own eyes the royal palace, temples, shrines and other monuments and the artistic objects. There was some influence of Greek art on the productions of Indian artists of Taxila. These two travellers reached the plains of the Punjab where they saw some monuments of historical importance. All artistic objects, which they saw there, were the productions of Indian artists.

The sculpture, iconography, engravings, etc in the Hindu rock-temples of the Deccan also attracted the notices of the Greek writers.

The Indian artists had attained perfection in all the branches of art. The originality of Indian art and the artistic talent of the Indians are well reflected in the objects produced. However, the foreign influence on the Indian art to a considerable extent is an admissible fact.

The classical writers also speak of Buddhist art and architecture. Stūpa, one of the most important architectural monuments of the Buddhists, received the notices of especially the Greek historians and philosophers. The worship of Stūpas was widely prevalent among the Buddhists. The Buddhist temples and monasteries also find mention in the classical treatises on India.

The ancient Greeks and Romans will always be remembered for exploring the wonders and marvels of India.

The brāhmanical and Buddhist system of education and learning in ancient India also attracted the attention of the classical writers. In both the systems of education, women had the freedom to study philosophy.

The ancient Greeks and Romans made a wonderful discovery in the field of palaeography. They brought many valuable facts to light regarding the writing system in India. There were different stages of the evolution of the art of writing in the country. The art of writing was known to the Indians much before the time of Alexander the Great.

The Indian tradition of Chronology was another area of interest for the classical writers. There were different systems of chronology in ancient India. The chronological system, that was followed in Indian in the time of Sandrakottus, was first noticed by Megasthenes, and then by Pliny and Arrian. That the ancient Indians had the sense of Chronology can also be proved by the testimony of ancient Greek and Roman historians.

The ancient Greeks and Romans made the greatest contributions in the field of discovery of India. They made many new discoveries, both geographical and historical, regarding that country. They have their own place in the history of the discovery of culture and civilization of Asia.

General Bibliography

Original Sources : Greek and Latin Texts, Translations and Annotations

Ammianus Marcellinus, *Rerum Gestarum*, 3 Vols. London, 1935-39.

Apollodorus, *Parthica* (History of Parthia), Fragments, in C. Müller (ed), *Frag. Hist. Graeco*. Vol. IV, pp. 308ff.

Appian, *Syriake*, ed. L. Mendelsohn, Leipzig, 1879-81.

Arrian, *Anabasis*, ed. A.G. Roos, Leipzig, 1907; Eng. trans. by A. de Selincourt under the title *The Campaigns of Alexander,* with Introd. and Notes by J.R. Hamilton, London, Penguin, 1971.

______*Indika*, ed. R. Hercher 2nd edn. Leipzig, 1885.

______*Anabasis and Indika*, ed. F. Didot, Paris, 1877; Eng. trans. of both by E.I. Robson, 2 Vols. LCL edn. London, 1949, and by E.J. Chinnock, with a copious commentary, London, 1893.

Athenaeus, *Deipnosophistae*, ed. G. Kaibel, Leipzig, 1887-90.

Bios Alexanderou tou Makedonos Kai Práxeis (Romance History of Alexander the Great of Macedon), by an anonymous Greek author, trans. from the Greek into Latin by Julius Valerius under the title *Res Gestae Alexandri Macedonis,* ed. by B. Kübler under the title *Julii Valerii Res Gestae,* Leipzig, 1888; trans. from the Greek into English by W. Kroll, *The Life of Alexander of Macedon by Pseudo – Callisthenes,* New York, 1955.

Clemens Alexandrinus, *Stromateis*, I, ed. Colon, London, 1688.

Curtius (Quintus Curtius Rufus), *Historiae Alexandri Magni*, ed. E. Hedicke, Leipzig, 1908; ed. T. Davison, London, 1826; trans. from the Latin into English by P. Pratt under the title *The History of the Life and Reign of Alexander the Great,* 2 Vols. London, 1809, rept. 1821; Eng. trans. by J. Yardley, *The History of Alexander the Great*, with Introd. and Notes by W. Heekel, London, 1984.

Diodorus Siculus *Bibliotheca Historica,* Books I-XV, ed. F. Vogel, Leipzig, 1888, 1890, 1893; Books XVI-XVIII, ed. C.T. Fischer, Leipzig, 1906; Book XVII, ed. and trans. by G. Booth, 1st edn. London, 1700, new edn. 1814; Complete work, ed., and trans (into English) by C.H. Oldfather, 10 Vols. LCL edn. London, 1912-1933, rept. 1935-1954.

Dion Chrysostom, *Orations,* ed. by Reiske, 2 Vols. Paris, 1784, and by L. Dindorf, Paris, 1857.

Eratosthenes, *Geography,* Fragments collected and ed. by Seidel, and pub. under the title *Eratosthenis Geographicorum Fragmenta,* Goettingae (Gottingen), 1789, and more fully together with the remains of his other works, by Bernhardy, *Eratosthenica,* Berolin, 1822.

Eusebius Pamphilus, *Historia Ecclesiastica,* Eng. trans by Rev. C.F. Cruse, *The Ecclesiastical History,* Philadelphia, 1833.

Frontinus, *Strategematica,* Eng. trans. by E. Benett, I, New York, 1925.

Hekataeus, *Periodos Ges*, Fragments collected and pub. with copious notes and a life of the author, by R.H. Klansenart (Klausen), *Hecataei Milestii Fragmenta,* Berlin, 1831; Fragments of the original work in C. Müller (ed), *Frag. Hist. Graeco,* Vol. I, (pp. 1-31), Paris, 1841.

Herodotus, *Histories*, ed. O. Hude, 2 Vols. 2nd edn., Oxford, 1913-14; Eng. trans. by G. Rawlinson, *History of Herodotus,* 4 Vols. London, 1858-60, also 1862; Eng. trans. G.C. Macaulay, London, 1904; ed. and trans. A.D. Godley, LCL edn., London, 1946-48, rept. 1950.

Isidore of Charax (Isidorus Characensis), *Mansiones Parthicae,* Fragments, in C. Müller (ed), *Geog. Graec. Mino*., Vol. I (pp. 244-56), Paris, 1855; ed. and trans. W.H. Schoff, *Parthian Stations of Isidore of Charax*, Philadelphia, 1914.

Julius Valerius, *Itinerarium Alexandri Magni*, 1st edn., Milan, 1817.

Justinus (Justin), *Epitoma Historiarum Philippicarum (Historiae Philippicae)* ed. F. Ruehl, Leipzig, 1886; ed. Otto Seel, Leipzig, 1935; Complete Eng. trans. by J.S. Watson, BCLS, London, 1853.

Ktésias, *Indika*, Fragments, in C. Müller (ed), *Frag. Hist. Graeco*, pp.79-105, in G. Dindorf's *Herodotus*, Paris, 1844, rept. 1877.

______*Persica* (History of Persia), Fragments, ed. J. Gilmore, London, 1888.

Kosmas, *Topographia Christiana,* Eng. trans. by J.W. McCrindle, *The Christian Topography of Kosmas,* London, 1897.

Megasthenes, *Indika*, Fragments collected and ed. by E.A. Schwanbeck and pub. under the title *Megasthenis Indica*, Bonn, 1846.

Nonnos, *Dionysiaka*, Eng. trans. by O.D.B. Priaulx, Paris, 1874.

Origen, *Contra Celsum*, ed. Delarue, Vol.I, Paris, 1733.

Pausanias, *Hellados Periēgēsis,* ed. L. Dindorf, Paris, 1845; trans. from the Greek into Eng. by W.H.S. Jones, 6 Vols. LCL end. London.

Periplus Maris Erythraei, by an anonymous author, ed. B. Fabricius, Leipzig, 1883.

Philostratus, *Vita Apollonii,* a Greek text, with parallel Eng. trans. by F.C. Conybeare, *The Life of Apollonius of Tyana*, 2 Vols, LCL edn. London, 1912, rept. 1969; Eng. trans. by E. Berwick, London, 1811; trans. from the Greek into Eng. by CH. P. Eels, *Life and Times of Apollonius of Tyana,* Stanford University pub. Vol. II, No.1, California, 1923.

Pliny, *Naturalis Historia,* ed. C. Mayhoff, Leipzig, 1892-1909; ed. and tr. by H. Rackham and others, LCL edn. 10 Vols. rept. London, 1956-63; Eng. trans, by J. Bostock and H.T. Riley, *The Natural History,* London, 1890; Eng. trans. by B. Riley, London, 1962.

Plutarch, *Parallel Lives* (of the famous men of Greece and Rome), ed. K. Sintenis, Vol. III (for author's *Vita Alexanderi – Life of Alexander –* Chaps. 57-67), Leipzig, 1881; *Parallel Lives*, ed. and tr. by B. Perrin, 11 Vols. LCL edn., London, 1914-22 (Vol. VII for *Life of Alexander)*; Eng. trans. by J. Williams London, 1860; two complete Eng. trans of *Parallel Lives,* one by A. Stewart and G. Long, 4 Vols. London, 1880-85, rept. 1908-12, and other in *The Outline of Knowledge* Series, ed. J.A. Richards, New York, 1924.

______*Moralia* (an anthology of his sixty essays, including two *ORATIONS On the Fortune of Alexander*), ed. G.N. Bernardakis, 5 Vols. Leipzig, 1888-96; ed. H.N. Fowler, LCL edn. London, 1936-40.

Polyaenus, *Strategemata,* ed. J. Melber, Leipzig, 1887.

Polybius, *Historiae* (*History)*, ed. Th. Buettner Wobst, Leipzig, 1904; Eng. trans. by W.R. Paton, 6 Vols. LCL end. London, 1922-27.

Ptolemy, *Geographike Huphegesis (Guide to Geography)*, ed. C.F.A. Nobbe, 3 Vols. Leipzig, 1898-1902; Eng. trans. by E.L. Stevenson, *The Geography of Claudius Ptolemy,* New York, 1932.

Skylax, *Ges Periodus,* Fragments, in C. Müller (ed), *Geog. Graec. Mino*, Vol.I (pp. 15-96), Paris, 1855.

Solinus, *Collectanea Rerum Memorabilium,* ed. M. Mommsen, Berolin, 1864.

Strabo, *Geographica*, ed. A. Meineke, Leipzig, 1866-67; Eng. trans. H.C. Hamilton and W. Falconer, *The Geography of Strabo*, 3 Vols. BCLS, London 1854-57; Eng. trans. H.L. Jones, *The Geography of Strabo*, (based in part upon the unfinished version of J.R.S. Sterrett), 8 Vols. LCL end., London, 1917-32.

Xenophon, *Cyropaedia*, ed. and tr. W. Miller, 2 Vols. London, 1914, rept. LCL end., London, 1925.

Conybeare, F.C. *The Life of Apollonius of Tyana, The Epistles of Apollonius, and The Treatise of Eusebius,* trans. from the Greek into English, 2 Vols., London, 1912.

Godolphin, F.R.B. (ed), *The Greek Historians* (The complete and unabridged historical works of Herodotus, tr. by G. Rawlinson, Xenophon, tr. by E.J. Chinnock), 2 Vols., New York, 1942.

Jacoby, F. Von (ed), *Die Fragmente der Griechischen Historiker,* I-II D, Berlin, 1923-30; III A-III C, Leiden, 1954-58 (A Collection of the Fragments of the works of Skylax, Ktésias, Nearchus, Onesikritus, Aristoboulus, Megasthenes, Deimachus, Dionysius, Patrokles, Apollodorus, Alexander Polyhistor, Nikolaus, Bardesanes and other Greek writers on India).

Majumdar, R.C. *The Classical Accounts of India* (a compilation of the English translations of the Greek and Roman Accounts of Ancient India), with introduction, notes, appendices, etc., Calcutta, 1st edn., 1960, rept. 1981.

McCrindle, J.W. *Ancient India as described by Megasthenes and Arrian,* trans. of the Fragments of the *Indika* of Megasthenes collected by E.A. Schwanbeck, and of the first part of the *Indika* of Arrian (from Teubner's end, Leipzig, 1867), with annotations, 1st edn., London, 1877; same ed (with conculturuum, appendices, and notes) by R.C. Jain, Delhi, 1972, rept. 1984; McCrindle's trans. of the Fragments of the *Indika* of Megasthenes also in the *Ind. Ant.*, Vol. VI, 1877.

______*The Commerce and Navigation of the Erythraean sea*, trans. of the *Periplus Maris Erythraei*, by an anonymous author (as given in the *Geog. Graec. Mino.*, Vol. I, pp. 257-305, ed. C. Müller, Paris, 1855), with commentary, 1st edn., London, 1879, rept. Calcutta, 1973, Patna, 1987; McCrindle's trans. of the *Periplus Maris Erythraei,* also in the *Ind. Ant.*, Vol. VIII, 1879, pp. 108-51.

______*The Voyage of Nearkhos* from the mouth of the Indus to the head of the Persian Gulf as described in the second part of the *Indika* of Arrian (copied from the *Journal of the Voyage* written by Nearkhos himself), trans. from C. Müller's edn. as given in the *Geog. Graec. Mino.*, Paris, 1855, with annotations, London, 1879.

McCrindle, J.W. *Ancient India as described by Ktésias the Knidian,* a trans. of the abridgment of his *Indika* by Phótios, and of the fragments of that work preserved in other writers (rept. with additions from the *Ind. Ant.*, Vol. X, 1881), with annotations, 1st edn., London, 1882, rept. Delhi, 1973.

______*Ancient India as described by Ptolemy*, a trans. of the Chapters from the *Geography* of Ptolemy describing India and Central and Eastern Asia (rept. with additions from the *Ind. Ant.* 1884) with commentary, 1st edn., London, 1885; same ed. with Notes by S.N. Majumdar Śāstrī, Calcutta, 1927; same ed. by R.C. Jain (with conculturuum and Appendices), Delhi, 1973-74.

______"Ptolemy's Geography of India and Southern Asia", *Ind. Ant.*, Vol. XIII, 1884, pp. 313-411.

______*The Invasion of India by Alexander the Great* as described by Arrian, Curtius, Diodorus, Plutarch, and Justin (being trans. of such portions of the works of these and other classical authors as describe Alexander's campaign in North West India), with annotations, Westminster, 1893, new edn. 1896, rept. Patna, 1989.

______*Ancient India as described in classical Literature* (a collection of Greek and Latin texts relating to India, translated and annotated), 1st edn., Westminster, 1901, rept. Delhi, 1984.

Müller, C (ed), *Fragmenta Historicorum Graecorum* (a collection of the fragments of the historical works of some Greek authors), 5 Vols. Paris, 1841-70, rept. Paris, 1878-85.

______(ed) *Geographi Graeci Minores* (A collection of the fragments of the geographical works of some Greek authors), 2 Vols. Paris, 1855-61.

Schoff, W.H. *The Periplus of the Erythraean sea* (Travel and Trade in the Indian Ocean), by a Greek merchant (anonymous) of the first century, translated from the Greek and annotated, London, 1912.

Vincent, W. *The Commerce and Navigation of the Ancients in the Indian Ocean,* Vol. I, *The Voyage of Nearchus from the Indus to the Euphrates* (collected from the original *Journal* preserved by Arrian, and illustrated by authorties, ancient and modern, containing an account of the first navigation attempted by the Europeans in the Indian Ocean), London, 1797; Vol.II, *The Periplus of the Erythrean Sea,* London, 1807. Both translated from the Greek and annotated.

MODERN WORKS

Abbott, E. *History of Antiquity,* trans. from the German of Max Duncker, Vol.IV, London, 1880.

Adams, R. *The Evolution of Urban Society,* London, 1966.

Agrawala, P.K. (ed), *Itihāsa – Darsāna* (collection of papers of the late V.S. Agrawala), Vārāṇasī, 1978.

Agrawala, V.S. *India as known to Pāṇini* (A study of the cultural Material in the *Aṣṭādhyāyī*), Vārāṇasī, 1963.

______"Geographical Data in Pāṇini's *Aṣṭādhyāyī*", JUPHS, XVI, I, pp. 18ff.

______*Bhārata Sāvitrī*, Vols, I, and 2, 2nd end., Delhi, 1977, Vol. 3, 1st edn., Delhi, 1968.

______*India as described by Manu*, Vārāṇasī, 1970.

______"An Ancient Reference to Menander's Invasion", IHQ, 1953, pp. 180 ff.

Ali, S.M. *The Geography of the Purāṇas,* Delhi, 1983.

Alleyne, S.F. *History of Greece from the Earliest times to the end of the Persian War,* trans. from the German of Max Duncker, Vol. I, London, 1883.

Altekar, A.S. *State and Government in Ancient India*, Delhi, 1977.

Anspach, A.E. *De Alexand'ri Magni Expeditione Indica,* London, 1903.

Anville, M.D. *Recherches geographiques et historiques sur la serique des Anciens,* Paris, 1768.

______*Antiquite Geographique de L'Inde,* Paris, 1775.

Arora, U.P. *Greeks on India*, Indian Society for Greek and Roman Studies Publication, Bareilly, 1966.

______"Classical Accounts on India – Some observation", in *Graeco – Indica* : *India's Cultural contacts with the Greek world,* ed. by himself, Delhi, 1991, pp. 86-108.

______"Ancient India and Ancient Greece", in G.C. Pande (ed), *Life, Thought and culture in India* (from *c.* 600 BC to *c.* AD 300), Vol.I, pt. 2, of HIC, New Delhi, 2001, pp. 1045-70.

______"Form of State Power in Mauryan India–Megasthenes' Evidence", in *Facets of Indian History, Culture and Archaeology,* eds. S.P. Gupta and K.S. Ramchandran, New Delhi, 1991, pp. 164-72.

Bagchi, P.C. *Pre-Aryan and Pre-Dravidian in India* (Eng. trans. of Original French articles by S. Levi, J. Przyluski and J. Bloch), Calcutta, 1929.

Banerjee, G.N. *Hellenism in Ancient India*, Calcutta, 1920.

______*India as known to the Ancient World, or India's Intercourse in Ancient times with her neighbours, Egypt, Western Asia, Greece, Rome, Central Asia, China, Further India and Indonesia,* Calcutta, 1921.

Banerjee, J.N. "Indian Elements in the coin – devices of the Early Foreign Rulers in India", IHQ, 1938, p. 293f.

Banerjee, R.D. *Pre-historic Ancient and Hindu India*, Calcutta, 1934, rept. 1950.

Basham, A.L. *The Wonder that was India,* London, 1954.

Baveridge, H.A. *Comprehensive History of India*, Vol. I, London, 1862, rept. 4th edn., Delhi, 1982.

Bellew, H.W. *The Races of Afghanistan, Being a Brief Account of the Principal Nations Inhabiting that Country,* Calcutta, 1880.

______*Ethnography of Afghanistan,* Woking, 1891.

Bevan, E.R. "Indian in Early Greek and Latin Literature", in CHI, I, ed. E.J. Rapson, Cambridge, 1922, pp. 351-83.

Bhandarkar, D.R. *Carmichael Lectures on the Ancient History of India,* Calcutta, 1918, Pub. 1919.

Bhandarkar, R.G. *A peep into the Early History of India from the foundation of the Maurya Dynasty to the downfall of the Imperial Gupta Dynasty,* 322 BC – *circa* 500 AC, Delhi, 1978.

Bhargava, P.L. *Chandragupta Maurya : A Gem of Indian History*, Delhi, 2007.

Bigwood, "Ctesias as Historian", *Phoenix,* 32, 1978, pp. 36-39.

Brown, T.S. *Onesicritus : A study in Hellenistic Historiography,* Berkley, 1949.

______The Reliability of Megasthenes", *American Journal of Philology,* 76, 1955, pp. 18-33.

Budge, E.A.W. *The Life and Exploits of Alexander the Great,* Cambridge, 1889.

Bühler, G. *Indian Paleography* (rept. from *Indian Studies : Past and Present*), Calcutta, 1962.

Bunbury, E.H. *A History of Ancient Geography Among the Greeks and Romans from the Earliest Ages till the Fall of the Roman Empire,* 2 Vols. 1st edn. London, 1879, rept. New York, 1959.

Burnes, A. *Travels in Punjab, Bokhara, etc.* Vol. I, London, 1835.

Burn, A.R. *Alexander the Great and the Hellenistic Empire,* London, 1959.

Bury, J.B. *The Ancient Greek Historians,* London, 1909, rept. New York, 1958.

______*A History of Greece to the death of Alexander the Great,* London, 1900, rept. 1959.

Bury, J.B., Cook, S.A. and Adcock, F.E. (ed), *The Cambridge Ancient History,* Vol. III, rept. Cambridge, 1960, Vols. V & VI, Cambridge, 1926-27.

Cady, J.F. *Southeast Asia: Its Historical Development,* New York, 1964.

Cary, E. *History of Rome,* London, 1936.

Cary, M. and Warmington, E.H. *The Ancient Explorers,* London, 1929.

Casson, L. *Travels in the Ancient World*, London, 1974.

______*The Ancient Mariners : Seafarers and Seafighters of the Mediterranean in Ancient Times*, Princeton, 1991.

Chakraberti, C. *Classical Studies in Ancient Races and Myths*, Delhi, 1979.

Chakraborty, S.K. *A Study of Ancient Indian Numismatics,* Mymensingh, 1931.

______"The Seleukidan Emperors, their coins and coin-imitations in India", IHQ, 1935, p. 241f.

Chapekar, N.M. *Ancient India and Iran - A study of their cultural contacts,* Delhi, 1982.

______*Ancient India and Greece – A study of their cultural contacts*, Delhi, 1977.

Charlesworth, M.P. *Trade – Routes and commerce of the Roman Empire,* Cambridge, 1924.

______"Roman Trade with India, a Resurvey", in *Studies in Roman Economic and Social History*, ed. P.R. Coleman – Norton, Princeton, 1951.

Charpentier, J. *The Indian Travels of Apollonius of Tyana,* Uppsala – Leipzig, 1934.

Chatterji, S.K. *Kirāta – Jana – Kṛti,* ASB, Calcutta, 1974.

Chattopadhyaya, S. *Racial Affinities of Early North Indian Tribes,* Delhi, 1973.

______*Early History of North India,* Calcutta, 1958.

Chaudhuri, S.B. *Ethnic Settlements in Ancient India*, Calcutta, 1955.

Chwostow, M. *History of the Eastern Trade of Graeco-Roman Egypt,* London, 1907.

Cunningham, A. *The Ancient Geography of India,* London, 1871, rept. Vārāṇasī, 1979.

Das, D.R. *Economic History of the Deccan from the first to the Sixth century AD,* Delhi, 1969.

Dasgupta, K.K. *A Tribal History of Ancient India,* Calcutta, 1974.

Devies, H.A. *An Outline History of the World*, Oxford, 1964.

Dey, N.L. *Civilization in Ancient India*, Delhi, 1972.

Dodge, T.A. *History of Alexander and His Art of War,* 2 Vols. Delhi, 1995.

Dorey, T.A. (ed), *Latin Historians,* London, 1966.

Doshi, S (ed), *Indian and Greece – Connections and Parallels,* Bombay, 1985.

Douie, J. *The Punjab, North-West Frontier Province, and Kashmir,* Cambridge, 1916, rept. Delhi, 2003.

Eliot, Charles, *Hinduism and Buddhism : An Historical Sketch,* Vol. II, London, 1921, rept. 1957.

Elphinstone, M. *The History of India* (App. III, "On the Greek Accounts of India", pp. 229-42), Allahabad, 1966.

______"The Greek Accounts of India", rept. from his *The History of India* (London, 1911), in *Ancient India* (a collection of articles, rept. from the works of various oriental scholars), Delhi, 1983, pp. 11- 33.

______*An Account of the Kingdom of Kābul*, Vol. I, 2nd edn., London, 1839.

Farrington, B. *Diodorus Siculus : Universal Historian*, University of Wales, 1937.

Fick, R. *The Social Organisation in North-East India in Buddha's time,* trans. by S.K. Maitra, Calcutta, 1920, rept. Vārāṇasī, 1972.

Filliozat, J. *The Classical Doctrine of Indian Medicine,* trans. by D.R. Channa from the French, 1949, rept. Delhi, 1964.

Finley, M.I. *The Ancient Greeks,* London, 1963.

______(ed), *The Greek Historians : The Essence of Herodotus, Thucydides, Xenophon, and Polybius,* London, 1959.

______(ed), *The Legacy of Greece – A New Appraisal,* Oxford, 1981.

Fuller, J.F.C. *The Generalship of Alexander the Great*, Dehradun, 1977.

Gait, E. *A History of Assam,* Calcutta, 1926, rept. 1964.

Garbe, R. *The Philosophy of Ancient India,* Chicago, 1897.

Gerini, G.E. *Researches on Ptolemy's Geography of Eastern Asia,* London, 1909, rept. Delhi, 1974.

Gomperz, *Greek Thinkers,* Vol. I, London, 1969.

Gopal, L. "Early Greek Writers on Writing in India", PIHC, 37th session, Calicut, 1976, pp. 544-52.

Govind, V. "The Growth of Science and Technology as Gleaned from the classical Accounts of India", JIH, LIX, 1-3, 1981, pp. 51-86.

Grote, G. *History of Greece,* Vols. X and XII, London, 1906-10.

Gupta, P. *Geographical Names in Ancient Indian Inscriptions* (up to AD 650), Delhi, 1977.

Gupta, S.P. and Ramachandran, K.S. (ed), *Aspects of Indian History and Archaeology* (a collection of thirty-three papers of H.D. Sankalia, Delhi, 1977.

Hadas, M. *Hellenistic Culture : Fusion and Diffusion,* New York, 1972.

Haig, M.R. *The Indus Delta Country – A Memoir Chiefly on its Ancient Geography and History,* London, 1894, rept. Gurgaon, 1974.

Heeren, A.H.L. *Historical Researches into the Politics, Intercourse and Trade of the Principal Nations of Antiquity,* Vol. I, *Asiatic Nations,* Oxford, 1833.

______*Manual of Ancient History : The constitutions, the commerce and the colonies of the states of antiquity,* Oxford, 1833.

Holdich, Thomas, *The Indian Borderland,* London, 1901.

______*The Gates of India being an historical Narrative,* London, 1910.

______"The Greek Retreat from India", JRSA, XLIX, 1901, pp. 417ff.

Hunter, W.W. "The Greeks in India (327-161 BC)", rept. from his *The Indian Empire : Its Peoples, History and Products* (London, 1882), in *Ancient India* (Delhi, 1983), pp. 86-96.

Hutchison, J. and Vogel, J. ph. *History of the Panjab Hill States,* 2 Vols. Lahore, 1933, rept. Shimla, 1982.

Iyengar, P.T. Srinivas, *History of the Tamils from the earliest times to 600 AD,* Madras, 1929.

Jackson, A.V.W. (ed), *History of India*, Vol. II, *From the sixth century BC to the Mohammedan conquest including the invasion of Alexander the Great,* by V.A. Smith, Delhi, 1987.

Jain, R.C. *Ethnology of Ancient Bhārata,* Vārāṇasī, 1970.

Jairzabhoy, R.A. *Foreign Influence in Ancient India,* Bombay, 1963.

Jayaswal, K.P. *Hindu Polity : A Constitutional History of India in Hindu Times,* Bangalore, 1981.

Kagan, D (ed), *Yale classical studies,* Vol. XXIV, *Studies in the Greek Historians,* Cambridge, 1975.

Karttunen, K. "The reliability of the *Indica* of Ktésias", *Studia Orientalia,* Helsinki, 50, 1981, pp. 105-7.

______*India in Early Greek Literature,* Helsinki, 1989.

Keith, A.B. *History of Sanskrit Literature,* Oxford, 1920, rept. Delhi, 1973.

Kennedy, J. "Some Notes on the *periplus* of the Erythraean Sea", JRAS, 1916.

Laistner, M.L.W. *A History of the Greek World from 479 to 323 BC,* London, 1936, 2nd edn. 1947.

______*The Greater Roman Historians,* Berkeley, 1947, rept. 1977.

Lamotte, E. "Early Relations between India and the West", pt.I, *Buddhist Studies Review*, no.2, 1988, pp. 117ff.

______"Early Relations between India and the West Conclusion", *Buddhist Studies Review,* 6, No.1, 1989, pp. 5-16.

Lassen, Chr. *Indische Alterthumskunde,* Vols. I and II, Leipzig, 1847 and 1852, 2nd edn., Leipzig, 1867 and 1874.

______*De Pentapotamia Indica*, Bonn, 1827.

Law, B.C. "Studies in Indian History and Geography Based on Early Greek Accounts", JGRI, XVI, 3-4, 1959, pp. 265-306.

______"India as known to the Early Greeks", JGRI, XVII, 1-2, 1960-61, pp. 1-41.

______*Some Kṣatriya Tribes of Ancient India*, Calcutta, 1923, rept. Delhi, 1979.

______*Ancient Indian Tribes*, Research Series pub., Vol. II, London, 1934.

______"Countries and peoples of India", ABORI, XVII, 3, 1936, pp. 225ff.

______*"Tribes in Ancient India,* Bhandarkar Oriental series, no. 4, Poona, 1943.

______*Historical Geography of Ancient India,* Paris, 1954, rept. Delhi, 1976, also 2nd revd. Edn., Paris, 1967.

______*Geographical Essays Relating to Ancient Geography of India,* Delhi, 1976.

______*A History of Pāli Literature,* 2 Vols. Delhi, 1983.

Levi, S. "Alexander and Alexandria in Indian Literature" (trans. from the French, by P.C. Bagchi), IHQ, XII, 1936, pp. 121-33.

Luckenbill, D.D. (ed), *Ancient Records of Assyria and Babylon*, Vol. I, New York, 1927.

Macdonell, A.A. *History of Sanskrit Literature,* Oxford, 1936.

Macdonell, A.A. and Keith, A.B. *Vedic Index of Names and Subjects,* 2 Vols. London, 1912, rept. Delhi, 1967.

MacMunn, G. *Martial Races of India*, Delhi, 1979.

Major, R.H. (ed), *India in the Fifteenth century Being a collection of Narratives of Voyages to India* (with an introd. by him), London, 1857, rept. Delhi, 1974.

Majumdar, A.K. *The Early Hindu India: A Dynastic Study*, Vol. I, Dhaka, 1917, rept. Delhi, 1981.

Majumdar, R.C. "The *Indika* of Megasthenes", JAOS, Vol. 78, no. 4, 1958, pp. 273-76.

______*Ancient India,* Delhi, 1977.

______*Corporate Life in Ancient India*: Calcutta, 1920.

Maria, R (ed), *Ancient Rome and India : Commercial and Cultural contacts between the Roman World and India,* Delhi, 1995.

Marincola, J. *Authority and Tradition in Ancient Historiography* (Study of ancient Greek and Roman Historians based on Greek and Latin Literature), pub. In CSS, Cambridge, 1997.

Marshall, J. *Taxila* (An Illustrated Account of Archaeological excavations carried out at Taxila between the years – 1913 and 1934), Vol. I, Cambridge, 1951, 1st Indian rept. Vārāṇasī, 1975.

Martin, M. V. de Saint, *E'tude Sur La Geographie Grecque et Latine del'Inde*, Paris, 1858.

______*Histoire de La Geographie et des decouvertes geographiques,* Paris, 1873.

Martin, R.M. *The History of the Indian Empire,* Vol.I, Delhi, 1983.

Masson – Oursel, P. and others, *Ancient India and Indian Civilization,* trans. from the French by M.R. Dobie, London, 1934, rept. 1951.

Maurice, Thomas, *Indian Antiquities or Dissertations of Hindustan,* Vol.I, London, 1806, rept. Delhi, 1984.

Max Müller, F. *A History of Ancient Sanskrit Literature,* London, 1859, revd. and ed. by S.N. Śāstrī, Vārāṇasī, 1968.

______*India – What can it teach us* ?, London, 1899.

May, R. Le, *The Culture of Southeast Asia,* London, 1964.

McEvilley, Thomas, *The Shape of Ancient Thought : Comparative Studies in Greek and Indian Philosophies,* Delhi, 2008.

Mead, G.R.S. *Apollonius of Tyana : Philosopher – Reformer of the First Century AD,* London, 1901, rept. New York, 1966.

Miller, J.J. *The Spice Trade of the Roman Empire,* Oxford, 1969.

Mitra, R.L. *Indo-Aryans,* Vol. II, Calcutta, 1881, rept. Delhi, 1969.

Mommsen, T. *Provinces of the Roman Empire from Caesar to Diocletian,* trns. W.P. Dickinson, 2 Vols. London, 1909.

Motichandra, *Sārthavāha,* Patna, 1966.

Mookerji, Radha Kumud, *Indian Shipping : A History of the Seaborne Trade and Maritime Activity of the Indians from the Earliest times,* 1st edn., London, 1912, with an introductory Note by B.N. Seal, 2nd revd. edn., Calcutta, 1957.

______*Chandragupta Maurya and His Times*, Delhi, 1999.

Mookherji, S.B. *India's Empire of Mind*, Agra, 1973.

Mure, W. *A critical History of the Language and Literature of Ancient Greece,* Vols. IV & V, London, 1853 and 1857.

Narain, A.K. *The Indo-Greeks,* Oxford, 1962.

Oppert, G. *On the Original Inhabitants of Bhāratavarṣa or India,* Delhi, 1972.

Pande, S.N. *Geographical Horizon of the Mahābhārata,* Vārāṇasī, 1980.

Pandey, R.B. *Bhāratīya Itihāsa Kā Paricaya,* Vārāṇasī, 1963.

Pargiter, F.E. *Ancient Indian Historical Tradition,* London, 1922, rept. Delhi, 1972.

Pearson, C. "Alexander, Porus and the Panjab". *Ind. Ant.*, XXXIV, 1905, pp. 253 ff.

Pearson, L. *The Lost Histories of Alexander the Great,* New York, 1960.

Phillimore, J.S. (tr.), *Philostratus in Honour of Apollonius of Tyana,* Vol. I, Oxford, 1912.

Pococke, E. *India in Greece,* London, 1852.

Powell, J.E. *The History of Herodotus,* Oxford, 1939.

Prasad, Beni, *The State of Ancient India*, Allahabad, 1928.

Priaulx, O. de Beauvoir, *The Indian Travels of Apollonius of Tyana and the Indian Embassies to Rome from the Reign of Augustus to the Death of Justinian,* London, 1873.

______"Indian Travellers, Life of Apollonius of Tyana, and Indian Embassies to Rome", JRAS, XIX, pp. 294ff.

Prinsep, H.T. *Historical Results from Bactrian Coins : Discoveries in Afghanistan*, Vārāṇasī, 1973.

Prinsep, J. *Essays on Indian Antiquities*, ed. by E. Thomas, London, 1858.

Przyluski, J. "Indian Influence on Western Thought before and during the 3rd century AD", JGIS, Jan. 1934, pp. 1-10.

Puri, B.N. *India as described by Early Greek Writers,* Lucknow, 1939, rept. Vārāṇasī, 1971.

______*India in Classical Greek Writings,* Delhi, 1963.

______ *India in the Time of Patanjali,* Bombay, 1968.

______"Greek Bias in Indian Historiography", in *Bias in Indian Historiography,* ed. by Devahuti, Delhi, 1980, pp. 84-89.

Pushkas, Ildiko, "Myth or Reality : Apollonius of Tyana in India", JIH (Platinum Jubilee Volume), 2001, pp. 29-40.

Radhakrishnan, S. *Eastern Religion and Western Thought*, Oxford, 1939.

Rai, R.K. *Mahābhārata Kośa* (A Descriptive Index to the Names and Subjects in the Mahābhārata), Vārāṇasī, 1982.

Rapson, E.J. *Ancient India from the earliest times to the first century AD,* Cambridge, 1914, rept. Vārāṇasī, 1981.

______(ed), *The Cambridge History of India,* Vol. I, *Ancient India*, Cambridge, 1922, rept. Delhi, 1962.

Raverty, H.G. *Notes on Afghanistan and part of Baluchistan: Geographical, Ethnographical and Historical,* London, 1880.

Rawlinson, H.G. "Foreign Influence in the Civilization of Ancient India, 900 BC-400 AD", JRAS, 1908-1913, pp. 217-38.

______*Bactria, the History of a Forgotten Empire,* London, 1912.

______*Intercourse Between India and the Western World from the earliest times to the Fall of Rome,* Cambridge, 1916, rept. Delhi, 1977.

______*India : A short Cultural History*, London, 1937, rept. 1965.

______"India in European Literature and Thought", in *The Legacy of India,* ed. G.T. Garratt, Oxford, 1938, pp. 1-37.

______*A Concise History of the Indian People,* London, 1938, rept. 1956.

______*Bactria from the earliest times to the Extinction of Bactria-Greek Rule in the Punjab,* Delhi, 1978.

Ray, A. *Maritime India :Ports and Shipping,* Calcutta, 1993.

Raychaudhuri, H.C. *Political History of Ancient India*, 6th edn., Calcutta, 1953.

Rennell, J. *Memoir of a Map of Hindoostan* (based on M.D. Anville's Maps of Asia and India pub. in 1751-52), London, 1788, with section III corrected and enlarged in 1791 and then Pub., London, 1793, 1798.

______*The Geographical System of Herodotus, examined and explained,* 2 Vols. London, 1830.

Renou, L (ed), *La Geographie de Ptolemee L' Inde,* Paris, 1925.

Robertson, W. *An Historical Disquisition concerning Ancient India,* Edinburgh, 1818, rept. Delhi, 1981.

______*An Historical Disquisition Concerning the knowledge which the Ancients had of India,* Calcutta, 1904.

Rose, H.A. *A Glossary of the Tribes and Castes of the Punjab and North-West Frontier Province,* 3 Vols (bound in 2), Lahore, 1919, rept., Delhi, 2008.

Rostovtzeff, M. *Social and Economic History of the Roman Empire,* London, 1951.

______*Social and Economic History of the Hellenistic World*, Vol. I, Oxford, 1972.

Roy, B.P. *Political Ideas and Institutions in the Mahābhārata,* Calcutta, 1975.

Sagar, K.C. *Foreign Influence on Ancient India,* Delhi, 1992.

Saletore, B.A. *India's Diplomatic Relations with the West,* London, 1958.

______*The Wild Tribes in Indian History,* Lahore, 1935.

Sarkar, S.S. *Ancient Races of Baluchistan, Punjab and Sind,* Calcutta, 1962.

Śāstrī, K.A.N (ed), *Foreign Notices of South India,* Madras, 1939.

Schoff, W.H. "Isidore of Charax", JAOS, XXXIII, I, 1913.

______"The Name of the Erythraean Sea", JAOS, XXXIII, IV, 1913, pp. 349-62.

Schroeder, L. Von, *Pythagoras und die Inder,* Leipzig, 1884.

Schwartzberg, J.E. (ed), *A Historical Atlas of South Asia,* Chicago, 1978.

Sedlar, J.W. *India and the Greek World : A study in Transmission of Culture,* Totowa, New Jersey, 1980.

Selincourt, A. de, *The World of Herodotus,* London, 1954, rept. Baltimore, Penguin Books (classics), 1964.

Sen, Chitrabhanu, *Ancient Peoples of the Punjab* (Eng. trans. of two articles of J. Przyluski, pub. in French in the JA, Paris, 1926, and 1929, rept. from *Indian Studies : Past and Present,* Calcutta 1960), Calcutta, 1962.

Shafer, R. *Ethanography of Ancient India*, Wiesbaden, 1954.

Sharma, R.P. *Paurāṇic Kośa,* Vārāṇasī, VS. 2028.

Sharma, R.S. *Aspects of Political Ideas and Institutions in Ancient India,* Delhi, 2001.

______*India's Ancient Past*, Delhi, 2008.

Shastri, A.M. *India as seen in the Bṛhat Saṁhitā of Varāhamihira,* Vārāṇasī, 1969.

______"The Kṣaharatas of Western India : Fresh Light", IHR, XXVI, 1999, pp. 23-59.

Singh, G.P. *The Kirātas in Ancient India : A Historical Study of their Life, Culture and Civilization,* Delhi, 1990.

______*Political Thought in Ancient India,* Delhi, 1993.

______*Early Indian Historical Tradition and Archaeology,* Delhi, 1994.

______*Republics, Kingdoms, Towns and Cities in Ancient India,* Delhi, 2003.

______*Facets of Ancient Indian History and Culture New Perception,* Delhi, 2003.

______*Ancient Indian Historiography : Sources and Interpretations*, Delhi, 2003.

______"The North East Indian Tribal Races as described in Literary and Classical Sources", PNEIHA, Shillong, 1980, pp. 14-23.

______"The Paurāṇic Account of the Ancient Kingdom of Prāgjyotisha and the Kirātas in North East India", PNEIHA, Barapani, 1983, pp. 16-23.

______"An Analytical and Critical Study of the Classical Accounts of Foreign Expeditions of North-Western India before the time of Cyrus (*c.* 558-530 BC) of Persia", *Research Journal, Humanities and Social Sciences,* Manipur University, Imphal, IV, 1, 1987, pp. 1-8.

______"India from Ariana to the Gaṅgā Valley", *Adhyayan,* JBIAS, II, 2, 1992, pp. 1-21.

______"Was Herodotus of Greece the Father of History?" *Adhyanan,* JBIAS, III, 1 & 2, 1993, pp. 1-10.

______"The Origin, Antiquity and Identification of the Cinas as depicted in Ancient Indian Literature and Inscriptions", *Adhyayan,* JBIAS, V, 1 & 2, 1995, pp. 1-17.

______"The Role of the Brāhmaṇas in Anti-Alexander Movement in North-West India 326-325 BC", SHC, III, 1, 1995, pp. 1-7.

______"Trade and Commerce in Ancient India in the Light of Jain and Buddhist Traditions Bearing on its Economic and Cultural Contacts with the Asian Countries", SHC, IV, 1, 1996, pp. 1-13.

______"The Dionysiaka : A classical (Greek) Source of History of Ancient India", *Shodhak,* JHR, XXVIII, A, 82, 1999, pp. 1-3.

______"Early History of North-West India as described by the Greek and Assyrian Travellers", JIH (Platinum Jubilee Volume), 2001, pp. 41-52.

______"North-West India as described by the Greek and Assyrian Travellers of the First Century", JASM, LXXVII-LXXVIII, 2002-3, pp. 171-81.

Singh, M.R. *A Critical Study of the Geographical Data in the Early Purāṇas,* Calcutta, 1972.

Singhal, D.P. *India and the World Civilization,* 2 Vols. Michigan, 1969.

Sinha, B.C. *Studies in Alexander's Campaigns,* Vārāṇasī, 1973.

Sircar, D.C. *Studies in the Geography of Ancient and Medieval India,* Delhi, 1971.

Smith, V.A. "Graeco-Roman Influence on the Civilization of Ancient India", JASB, LVIII, I, 1889, pp. 107-97, LXI, I, 1892, pp. 50-76, and LXII, I, 1893, pp. 84 -87 (supplementary note).

______"The position of the Autonomous Tribes of the Punjab conquered by Alexander the Great", JRAS, 1903, pp. 685 ff.

______*The Early History of India from 600 BC to the Muhammadan Conquest including the Invasion of Alexander the Great,* revd. by S.M. Edwards, 4th edn. Oxford, 1924, rept. London, 1967.

______*The Oxford History of India*, revd. by H.G. Rawlinson, Oxford, 1908, 3rd Indian rept. Delhi, 1981.

Speir, C (Mrs), *Phases of Indian Civilization : A Historical and Cultural Outline,* Delhi, 1973.

Srivastava, B. *Trade and Commerce in Ancient India* (from the earliest times to *c.* AD 300), Vārāṇasī, 1968.

Steel, F.A. *India Through the Ages: A popular and picturesque History of Hindustan,* Delhi, 1976.

Stein, Aurel, *On Alexander's Track to the Indus-Personal Narrative of Explorations on the North-West Frontier of India,* London, 1929.

______*Alexander's campaign on the Indian North West Frontier,* rept. from the *Geog. Jour.,* no. 70, 1927, pp. 417-39.

______*The Site of Alexander's Passage of the Hydaspes and the Battle with Porus*, rept. from the *Geog. Jour.*, LXXX, 1, 1932, pp. 32-46.

______*Archaeological Tour in Upper Swat and Adjacent Hill Tracts, rept.* from MASI, no. 42, 1930.

______*Archaeological Reconnaissances in North-Western India and South-Eastern Iran,* London, 1937.

Stein, M.A. *Memoir on Maps Illustrating the Ancient Geography of Kashmir,* ASB, Calcutta, 1899 (rept. from JASB, LXVIII, I, 2, 1899), rept. Patna, 1977.

Stunkel, K.R. *Relations of Indian, Greek and Christian Thought in Antiquity*, Washington, 1979.

Sykes, P. *A History of Afghanistan,* 2 Vols., London, 1940.

Tarn, W.W. "Hellenism in Bactria and India", *Journal of the Hellenic Society,* 1902.

______*Hellenistic Civilization*, London, 1930.

______*The Greeks in Bactria and India*, Cambridge, 1938.

______*Alexander the Great,* 2 Vols. Cambridge, 1948.

Taylor, J. "Remarks on the sequal to the *Periplus of the Erythrean sea,* and on the country of the Seres, as described by Ammianus Marcellinus," JASB, XVI, I, 1847, pp. 1-78.

Thapar, R. *A History of India,* Vol.I, Penguin Books, Harmondsworth, 1966.

______"Epigraphic Evidence and some Indo-Hellenistic contracts during the Mauryan Period", in *Indological Studies : Professor D.C. Sircar commemoration volume,* ed. S.K. Maity and Upendra Thakur, New Delhi, 1987, pp. 15-20.

Thirlwall, *History of Greece,* London, 1852.

Thomas, F.W. "Śakastana, Where dwelt the Śakas named by Darius and Herodotus", JRAS, 1906, pp. 181-216, and 460-64.

Thompson, E.A. *The Historical work of Ammianus Marcellinus,* Cambridge, 1947.

Thompson, J.O. *History of Ancient Geography,* New York, 1965.

Tozer, H.F. *A History of Ancient Geography,* Oxford, 1897, rept. (with additional Notes by J.D. Akhtar), Delhi, 1975.

Tripathi, R.S. *History of Ancient India,* Delhi, 1985.

Trotter, L.J. and Hutton, W.H. *History of India from the Earliest Times to the Present Day,* Delhi, 1975.

Usher, Stephen, *The Historians of Greece and Rome,* London, 1969.

Vaidya, C.V. *The Mahābhārata : A Criticism,* Delhi, 1966.

Vassiliades, D. *The Greeks in India : A Survey in Philosophical Understanding,* Delhi, 2000.

Vogel, J.Ph. "Notes on Ptolemy", BSOAS, XIV, I, pp. 80-84.

Warmington, E.H. *The Commerce Between the Roman Empire and India,* Cambridge, 1928, revd. edn. London, 1974, 1st Indian edn., Delhi, 1995.

Watt, G. *The Commercial Products of India,* London, 1908, rept. Delhi, 1966.

Wheeler, J.T. *The Geography of Herodotus,* London, 1854.

______"Greek and Roman India", in his *The History of India from the Earliest Ages,* London, 1881, rept. Delhi. 1973, pp. 153-208; the same "Greek and Roman India", reptd. From his said work, in *Ancient India* (*supra*), Delhi, 1983, pp. 97-139.

Wheeler, M. "Arikamedu : An Indo-Roman Trading Station on the East Coast of India", AI, 2, 1947, pp. 17-124.

______*Rome Beyond the Imperial Frontier,* London, 1954.

______*Early India and Pakistan to Ashoka,* London, 1968.

______*Charasada,* Oxford, 1962.

Wilcken, U. *Alexander the Great,* New York, 1932.

Williams, H.S. (ed), *The Historians' History of the World* (A Comprehensive Narrative of the Rise and Development of Nations as recorded by the Great Writers of all Ages), Vol. I, Oxford, 1907.

Williams, J. *Two Essays on the Geography of Ancient Indian Intended Partly to Illustrate the Campaign of Alexander and the Anabasis of Xenophon,* London, 1829.

Wilson, H.H. *Ariana Antiqua : A Descriptive Account of the Antiquities and Coins of Afghanistan,* London, 1841, rept., Delhi, 1971.

______*Notes on the Indika of Ctēsias,* Oxford, 1836.

Wilson, J. *India Three Thousand Years Ago : The social state of the Aryans on the Banks of the Indus in the Times of the Vedas,* Bombay, 1858.

Winternitz, M. *History of Indian Literature,* eng. trans. from the German, by Mrs. S. Ketkar, Vol. I, Calcutta, 1927, rept. Delhi, 1977.

Woodcock, G. *The Greeks in India,* London, 1966.

Yate, C.E. *Northern Afghanistan,* Edinburgh, 1888.

Coins and Inscriptions

Allan, J., *A Catalogue of the Indian coins in the British Museum, Coins of Ancient India,* London, 1936.

Banerji, R.D. "A New Type of Audumbara Coinage", *Numismatic Supplement* (to the JRASB), XXIII.

Cunningham, *A Coins of Alexander's Successors in the East*, 1st edn. London, 1873, rept. Delhi, 1970.

______*Coins of the Indo-Scythians, Śakas and Kushans*, London, 1888, rept. Vārāṇasī, 1971.

______*Coins of Ancient India from the Earliest Times Down to the Seventh Century* AD, London, 1891, rept. Vārāṇasī, 1971.

______"Coins of the Indian prince Sophytes, a Contemporary of Alexander the Great", *Num. Chron.* 1866, pp. 220ff.

Douglas, R.O. "On some Malava Coins", *Numismatic Supplement* (to the JRASB), XXXVII.

Fleet, J.F. *Corpus Inscriptionum Indicarum, III, Inscriptions of the Early Gupta Kings and their Successors,* Calcutta, 1888, rept. Delhi, 1971.

Gardner, P. *A Catalogue of Greek Coins in the British Museum, Seleucid Kings,* London, 1878.

______*ACatalogue of the Coins of the Greek and Scythic Kings of Bactria and India in the British Museum,* London, 1886.

Kala, S.C. "Some Interesting Coins of the Yaudheyas", JNSI, XVIII.

King, L.W. and Thompson, R.C. (ed. & tr.). *The Sculptures and Inscriptions of Darius the Great on the Rock of Behistūn in Persia,* London, 1907.

Rapson, E.J. *Indian Coins,* Vārāṇasī, 1969.

Samar, R.L. "Coins of the Śibi Republic", JNSI, IX.

Sen, S. "Old Persian Inscriptions", JAOS, LXXII, 1, Jan-March 1952, pp. 9ff.

Sircar, D.C. (ed), *Select Inscriptions Bearing on Indian History and Civilization,* I (from the sixth century BC to the sixth century AD), Calcutta, 1965. (This work also contains old Persian Inscriptions : Behistun, Persepolis and Naqsh-i-Rustum inscriptions of Darius, *c.* 522-486 BCE, pp. 4-11).

______*Inscriptions of Aśoka*, Delhi, 1957.

Smith, V.A. *Catalogue of the Coins in the Indian Museum, Calcutta, I, Coins of Ancient India,* Oxford, 1906, rept. Vārāṇasī, 1972.

Vogel, J. Ph. "Shorkot Inscription of the year 83" *EP. Ind.*, XVI, 1921, p.16.

Weissbach, F.H. (ed. & tr.), *Old Persian Inscriptions* (in general), Leipzig, 1911.

Whitehead, R.B. *Catalogue of Coins in the Punjab Museum, Lahore, I, Indo-Greek Coins,* Oxford, 1914, rept. Vārāṇasī, 1971.

Wroth, W.*A Catalogue of the Greek Coins in the British Museum, Coins of Parthia,* London, 1903.

General works

Sanskrit works

Arthaśāstra of Kauṭilya, ed. by R. Shamasastri, Mysore, 1909; trans. by him, Bangalore, 1915.

Asṭādhyāyī of Pāṇini (*Sūtrapāṭha with Gaṇas and Vārttikas)*, ed. by S.C. Śāstri, Trichinopoly, 1112; ed. with Eng. trans by S.C. Vasu, 7 Vols. Allahabad, 1891-98; ed. with comm. by Brahmadatta Jijñāsu, pt. I, 1st edn. Amrtisar Vs. 2021, pt. II., 2nd edn. Amritsar, Vs. 2031.

Atharvaveda Saṁhitā, ed. with Sāyana's comm. by S.P. Pandit, Bombay, 1895-98; trans. with comm. by R.T.H. Griffith, *The Hymns of the Atharvaveda,* 2 Vols. Vārāṇasī, 1896-97.

Bṛhat Saṁhitā of Varāhamihira, ed. by H. Kern, BIS, ASB, Calcutta, 1865; ed. with Hindi trans. and comm. by B.P. Mishra, Bombay, 1952.

Mahābhārata, ed. with Hindi trans. by S. Dāmodar Sātavalekar and Śrutiśila Śarmā, Pāradi (Gujarat), 1968-82.

Mahābhāṣya of Patañjali, ed. by F. Kielhorn, 3 Vols. Bombay Skt. Series, Bombay, 1880-85.

Manu Smṛti, ed. with Hindi trans. and the *Manvartha-Muktāvali* comm. of Kullūka Bhatta and the *Maniprabhā* Hindi comm. of H.G. Śāśtri by Gopāla. Śāśtri Nene, Vārāṇasī, 1970.

Mudrārāksasa of Viśākhadatta, ed. with the *Śaśikalā* Sanskrit and Hindi comms. by S.V. Singh, Vārāṇasī, 1973.

Purāṇas: *Brāhmaṇda*, Veṅkateśvara Press, Bombay, 1913; ed. with Hindi trans. by R. Sharma Ācārya, 2 Vols. Bareli, 1988; *Markandeya*, ed. by

K.M. Banerjee, BIS, ASB, Calcutta, 1862; ed. with Hindi trans. by Dharmendra Nāth Śāśtri, Meerut, 1983; Eng. trans by F.E. Pargiter, BIS, ASB, Calcutta, 1904; *Matsya,* Ānandāśrama Skt. Series, Poona, 1907; text with Hindi trans. 2 Vols. Gorakhpur, 1985; ed. with trans. of various oriental scholars and notes of B.C. Majumdar, S.C. Vasu, H.H. Wilson, Bentley, Wilford and others, by J.D. Akhtar, Vol. I, SBA, Delhi, 1972; *Padma,* ed. by V.N. Mandalika, Ānandāśrama Skt. Series, Poona, 1893-94; *Vāyu,* Ānandāśrama. Skt. Series, Poona, 1905; ed. by R.L. Mitra, 2 Vols. BIS, ASB, Calcutta, 1880-88; text with Hindi trans. of R.P. Tripāthi Śāśtrī, Prayag, 1987; Viṣṇu, ed. by J. Vidyāsāgara, Calcutta, 1882; text with Hindi trans. of Muni Lal Gupta, 9th edn. Gorakhpur, Samvat, 2041; Eng. trans. by M.N. Dutt, Calcutta, 1894, and by H.H. Wilson, Calcutta, 1961.

Rājataraṅgini of Kalhaṇa, ed by Durga Prasad Bombay, 1892; tr. by M.A. Stein, 3 Vols. Westminster, 1900, rept. Delhi, 1961; tr. by R.S. Pandit, Allahabad, 1935.

Ṛgveda Saṁhitā, ed. with Sāyaṇa's comm. by F. Max Müller, London, 1890-92; tr. by R.T. H. Griffith, Benares, 1896-97.

Buddhist Works

Dīgha Nikāya, ed. by T.W. Rhys Davids and J.E. Carpenter, 3 Vols. PTS, London, 1890-1911, rept. 1947-60; trans by T.W. and C.A.F. Rhys Davids, *The Dialogues of the Buddha,* 3 Vols. PTS, London, 1899-1921, rept. 1959.

Mahāparinibbāṇ, Suttam, Pāli text with parallel Hindi trans. ed. by S.G. Prajñānand, Lucknow, 1981.

Milindapānha, ed. by V. Trenckner, London, 1880; ed. R.D. Vadekar, Bombay, 1940; Trans. from Pāli by T.W. Rhys Davids, *The Questions of King Milinda,* in SBE, Vols. XXXV, pt. I, Oxford, 1890, rept. Delhi, 1969, XXXVI, pt. II, Oxford, 1894, rept. Delhi, 1969.

Arabic Work

Tahqiq-i-Hind of Al-Biruni, Eng. trans. of the Arabic text by E.C. Sachau, *Alberuni's India*, 2 Vols. Berlin, 1888, rept. Delhi, 1964, 1989.

Chinese Works

Fa-hien, *Foe–Kue–ki*, Eng. trans. *A Record of the Buddhistic kingdoms* (an account of the travels of Fa-hien), by J. Legge, Oxford, 1886, rept. Delhi, 1972, and by H.A. Giles, Cambridge, 1923, rept. Vārāṇasī, 1972.

Hiuen Tsang. *Si-Yu-Ki,* Eng. trans by Samuel Beal under the title *Buddhist Records of the Western World* (Chinese Accounts of India), 2 Vols. London, 1884, rept. 1906.

Thomas Watters, *On Yuan Chwang's Travels in India* (CE 629-45), RAS, London, 1904-5, rept. Delhi, 1973.

Oriental Works

Avesta, Part I, the *Vendidad,* Eng. trans by James Darmesteter, SBE, Vol. IV, Oxford, 1887, rept. Delhi, 1974.

The Sikandar Nama E Bara (On Alexander the Great, relating to his adventures and Conquest), by Shaikh Nizami, trans from the Persian Manuscipt into Eng. by H.W. Clarke, Calcutta, 1880, reptd. Delhi, 1995.

Other Work

Rājamālā (Royal Chronicle of Tripura), ed. K.P. Sen, Vol.I, Agartala, 1926.

Journals and Periodicals

Ancient India–Bulletin of the Archaeological Survey of India, New Delhi.

Annals of the Bhandarkar Oriental Research Institute, Poona.

Asiatic Researches, Calcutta, now rept. Delhi.

Bulletin of the School of Oriental and African Studies, London.

Calcutta Review, Calcutta.

East and West, Rome.

Epigraphia Indica, Delhi.

Geographical Journal, London.

Indian Antiquary, Journal of the Oriental Research, Bombay.

Indian Culture, Journal of the Indian Research Institute, Calcutta.

Indian Historical Quarterly, Calcutta, new reprint, Delhi.

Indian Historical Review, Journal of the Indian Council of Historical Research, New Delhi.

Journal of the American Oriental Society, New Haven, Connecticut, USA.

Journal Asiatique, Paris.

Journal of the Asiatic Society, Calcutta.

Journal of the Asiatic Society of Bengal, Calcutta.

Journal of the Asiatic Society of Mumbai (Bombay).

Journal of the Bhāratiya Itihāsa Adhyayan Saṁsthān, Allahabad.

Journal of the Bihar and Orissa Research Society, Patna.

Journal of the Bombay Branch of the Royal Asiatic Society, Bombay.

Journal of the Economic and Social History of the Orient.

Journal of the Gaṅgānatha Jha Research Institute, Allahabad.

Journal of the Greater India Society, Calcutta.

Journal of Historical Research, Jaipur.

Journal of Indian History, Trivandrum.

Journal of the Indian Society of Oriental Art, Calcutta.

Journal of the Numismatic Society of India, Bombay, now from Vārāṇasī.

Journal of the Oriental Research, Madras.

Journal and Proceedings of the Asiatic Society of Bengal, Calcutta.

Journal of the Royal Asiatic Society of Bengal, Calcutta.

Journal of the Royal Asiatic Society of Great Britain and Ireland, London.

Journal of the Royal Asiatic Society, Malayan Branch, Singapore.

Journal of the Royal Geographical Society, London.

Journal of the Royal Society of Arts, London.

Journal of the UP Historical Society, Lucknow.

Memoirs of the Archaeological Survey of India, Calcutta.

Modern Review, Calcutta.

Numismatic Chronicle and Journal of the Numismatic Society, London.

Studies in History and Culture, Journal of the Post-Graduate Department of History, Berhampur University (Orissa).

Proceedings and Reports

Archaeological Survey of India, *Annual Reports*

Archaeological Survey of India Reports, by A. Cunningham and others.

Proceedings of the Asiatic Society of Bengal, Calcutta

Proceedings of the Indian History Congress.

Proceedings of the Indian Oriental Conference.

Proceedings of the International Oriental Congress.

Reports of Archaeological Survey in North-Western India.

Dictionaries, Encyclopaedias and Gazetteers

A Classical Dictionary of Greek and Roman Biography, Mythology and Geography, by W. Smith, revd. throughout and in part rewritten by G.E. Marindin, London, 1st edn. 1848, 23rd, impression, 1925.

A Dictionary of Greek and Roman Biography and Mythology, by various writers, ed. by W. Smith, 3 Vols. London, 1890.

A Dictionary of Greek and Roman Geography, by various writers, ed. by W. Smith, 2 Vols. London, 1873, 1878.

A Smaller Classical Dictionary of Biography, Mythology and Geography, a new edn. of W. Smith's larger dictionary thoroughly revd. and in part rewritten by G.E. Marindin, London, 1898, new impression, 1949.

Classical Dictionary of Hindu Mythology and Religion, Geography, History and Literature, by J. Dowson, London, 1950.

Geographical Dictionary of Ancient and Medieval India, by N.L. Dey, Calcutta, 1927, rept. Delhi, 1971.

Encyclopaedia Britannica, Vols. 1-23, Chicago and London, 1768, rept. 1971.

The New Encyclopaedia Britannica, Vol. XVII, Chicago, 1768, 15th edn. rept. 1980.

Encyclopaedia of Indian culture, by R.N. Saletore, 2 Vols. Delhi, 1981-83.

The Himalayan Gazetteer, by E.T. Atkinson, Vol.I, pt.I, and Vol. II, pt. I, Delhi, 1973.

The Imperial Gazetteer of India, Vols II & III (The Indian Empire), new revd. Edn, Oxford, 1907-9.

Index

A

A. Cunningham,588, 645.
A. Garrison,408.
A.A. Macdonell, 443.
A.B. Keith, 511.
A.H.L. Heeren, 367, 510, 587.
A.K. Majumdar, 368, 443
A.N. Marlowe, 510.
A.V. Williams Jackson, 585.
A.V.W. Jackson, 376.
Abaortae, 638.
Abastanoi, 407, 639.
Abhisâra, 395, 461, 463, 615.
Abhisara, 395, 461, 463, 615 .
Abydos, 365.
Accae (Assakenian), 610.
Achaemenian emper, 377, 524, 589.
Achaemenian Empire, 375, 378, 523, 731.
Achaemenid dynasty, 379, 525, 731.
Acta Thomae (Acts of Thomas), 355, 375.
Adraistai, 396, 413, 627.
Adris (Râvî), 463, 586.
Aelian, 333, 393, 449, 465, 479, 507, 549, 567, 651, 691, 697, 698.
Afghanistan (Kandahâr region),497.
Agenor, 441.
Agrammes, 399, 437, 438, 733, .
Ahicchatra, 560, 56.
Akadera, 609.
Akbar, 627.
Akesines, 333, 398, 401, 042, 403, 404, 406, 407, 418, 441, 461, 505, 553, 624, 625, 627, 629, 631, 632, 633, 634, 636, 637, 638, 639, 652.
Akesines-a tract, 391.
Akhaia, 595.
Alasanda, 650, 651.
Alberuni, 588.
Al-Edrisi, 599.
Alexander Polyhistor, 337, 341, 510, 530.
Alexandria, 333, 341, 356, 357, 361, 376, 418, 441, 460, 462, 501, 502, 507, 512, 513, 532, 540, 590, 561,592, 593, 594, 595, 596, 597, 600, 604, 605, 629, 638, 641, 649, 650, 651, 651, 690, 692, 693 .

Alkexander attacked, 387.
Amanda (Gândhâra), 617.
Amarâvâtî Stupa, 465, 572,.
Amarâvatî, 465, 572, 577,
Ambar-Ohind, 614.
Amb-Balimah, 614.
Âmbhi, 389, 390, 391, 441, 442, 620, 732.
Amitrochates (Bindusâra), 532.
Ammaianus Marcellinus, 601.
Ammianus Marcellinus, 464, 542, 549, 587, 595, 596, 697, 600, 602, 603, 651.
Amritsar, 624.
Amyntas, 482.
Andaka, 385, 609, 650.
Ândhra coins, 574.
Ândhradeœa, 464, 465, 575, 57.
Androkottos (Candragupta), 439.
Antioch, 376, 479, 493, 494, 531, 532, 538, 541, 704, 720.
Aœoka, 449, 450, 508, 529, 532, 570, 590, 620, 688, 689, 691, 698.
Aomos, 614.
Aonla town, 560.
Aornos, 385, 388, 389, 613, 614.
Arabian sea, 363.
Arachosia (Kandahâr), 377, 453, 478, 525, 721, 731.
Arachosia, 368, 377, 453, 478, 479, 480, 481, 482, 488, 495, 496, 525, 530, 594, 597, 598, 599, 530, 594, 597, 588, 599, 600, 602, 624, 727, 728, 731, 734,
Arachosians, 599, 649.
Arachotia, 380, 453, 597.
Arachotus, 368, 597, 598, 599, 601
Arakhosia, 377, 380, 598,598, 600, 602.
Arbaca, 600.
River Arbaios, 411.
Archelaos, 346, 509.
Ardekoun, 596.
Argacum, 608.
Argaru, 466, 575.
Arghasan river, 396, 599.
Argolic Gulf, 576.
Arhat (Buddhist ascetic), 508.
Aria (Herât), 377, 453, 454, 478, 597, 721, 731.
Ariaca, 489.
Ariana Paropamisadai (Kâbul), 453.
Ariana region, 453, 482, 728.
Ariana, 362, 369, 377, 453, 454, 473, 497, 481, 482, 495, 589, 593, 594, 595, 602, 624, 633, 728, 731, 735.
Ariane (Ariana), 453.
Ariaspa, 597.
Arigacum, 608.
Aristoboulus, 342, 385, 391, 394, 651, 713
Arkandab, 598.
Arrian Arigaion, 598, 599.
Arrian Bazira, 612.
Arrian Dyrta, 614.
Arrian, 332, 338, 342, 349, 362, 364, 368, 390, 441, 449, 460, 514, 525, 549, 559, 566, 589, 604, 613, 625.
Arriya, 595.
Arsaces, 493.
Artakakana, 595.
Artakaudna (Artakoana), 595.
Artakoana, 595.
Aseni, 609, 638.
Asia, 364, 376, 400, 487, 603.
Asiatic Empire, 83, 400.
Asini, 629.
Askaland-Usah, 638.

Asmirae, 464.
Asmiraia, 587.
Aspasians, 385.
Aspasioi (Aspasians), 385.
Aspasioi, 385.
Assakenians, 385, 395, 412, 555, 609.
Assakenoi (Assakenians), 368, 385.
Assakenoi, 368, 385.
Assyria, 331, 362.
Assyrian companion Damis, 401.
Assyrian empire, 731.
Assyrian, 331, 362, 401.
Assyrians, 362, 376.
Assyro, 367.
Astakenoi (Astakenians), 368.
Astakenoi, 368, 376.
Astes, 385.
Astravad of Iran, 493.
Atari, 414, 635.
Athens, 690.
Attalas, 388.
Aurangabad district, 464, 572.
Aurel Stein, 610.
Automela, 571.
Avesta, 595.
Avestan Upâirisaena, 600.
Avestan US-Hindava, 600.

B

B.C. Sinha, 419.
B.N. Puri, 332, 337, 344, 590, 700, 729.
Babylon, 383, 406, 451, 622.
Babylonia, 451.
Bacchi fashion, 333.
Bactra (Bactria), 481.
Bactria, 367, 375, 451, 477, 478, 488.
Bactrian empire, 483.
Bactrian Greeks, 479, 501.
Bactrian, 479, 494, 501.
Bactriana, 477, 525.
Bagawar, 608.
Bahardipur, 647.
Bahistân, 377.
Bâhlika, 602.
Bahman, 595.
Baithana (Paithana), 572.
Bajour valley, 609.
Bajour, 607, 613.
Bakkar, 648.
Baktra, 366, 389, 591, 603.
Baktria, 366.
Baktrian, 366.
Baktriana, 366, 375, 595.
Bala Hisar, 601, 616.
Baleokouros, 574.
Balkh region, 366.
Baluchisatan, 648.
Baluchistan, 648.
Bamanpur, 623.
Bamian, 592, 623.
Banaouasei, 577.
Banavâsî, 577.
Bankipur, 569.
Baraca (Cutch), 489.
Baraomatae, 638.
Barbaricum, 646.
Bareilly district, 560.
Bargosa (Broach), 692.
Barman, 601.
Bartholomew, 357.
Barugaza, 571.
Barygaza (Broach), 481, 540.
Barygaza, 464, 481, 540, 571.
Barzaura, 594.
Bassarika, 464, 587.
Bazarak, 594.

Baziphara (Bazira), 388.
Bazira, 388, 412.
Begrâm, 590, 606.
Behistun Rock Inscription, 377, 589.
Behistun, 377, 589.
Beira (Bazira), 388.
Bengal, 565.
Besnagar, 509.
Beveridge, 365.
Bezwada, 577.
Bhâgavata, 509.
Bhâgavata, 509.
Bhagvanlal Indraji, 574.
Bhandarkar, 574.
Bhâratavarša, 605.
Bharukaccha, 571.
Bhavanagar, 571.
Bhimber, 630.
Bhir Mound, 619, 623.
Bidaspes (Jhelum), 586.
Bihar, 565.
Binagara, 489.
Bishop, 357.
Bitana, 595.
Bocage, 596.
Bodhpur, 641.
Boukephala, 394, 628.
Boukephosalos, 394.
Boutta (Buddha), 346.
Boutta, 346.
Brachmanai, 337.
Brachmanas, 341.
Brachmanes (Brâhmaòas), 332, 512.
Brachmanes abstain, 342.
Brachmanes, 332, 337, 342, 512, 711.
Brachmanoi, 414.
Brachmans (Brâhmaòas), 332, 338, 405, 414, 635.
Brachmans, 333, 337, 405, 414, 635, 643, 703, 731.
Brâhmanic, 509.
Brâhmaòa philosophers (Gymnosophists), 344.
Brâhmaòa philosophers, 338, 344,
Brâhmaòas, 331, 340, 574, 574, 731.
Brâhmaòism, 337, 340, 574.
Brâhmaòs, 340, 416.
Brahmaputra, 570.
Brahmi, 509.
Brihatphalayana dynasty, 577.
British Museum, 365.
Broach region, 481.
Bucephala, 638.
Buddha, 335, 346, 505.
Buddhism, 332, 337, 340, 348, 501, 508, 532, 560, 615, 693, 731.
Buddhist art, 505, 693.
Buddhist doctrine, 346.
Buddhist families, 729.
Buddhist king Kaniška, 622.
Buddhist robe, 347.
Buddhist system, 711, 714.
Buddhist temples, 705.
Buddhist, 443, 559, 693.
Buddhists, 332, 337, 346, 508, 559, 693.
Bulandibag, 569.
Busheng, 596.
Byzantium, 332, 342, 459, 488, 574, 577, 587, 590, 597, 600, 649.

C

C. Masson, 624.
C. Ritter, 592.
C.V. Vaidya, 724.
Calliena (Kalliena), 572.
Candragputa, 439.
Candragupta maintained, 451.

Candragupta Maurya, 449, 529, 566, 602, 688, 690, 719.
Candragupta, 380, 437, 443, 449, 530, 565, 697, 698, 723.
Canon Chronicon, 538.
Câòakya, 439.
Caphusa, 589.
Carabaga, 606.
Cartana (Kartana), 593.
Caspeiri, 587.
Caucasus Standeth, 593.
Cenâb, 586.
Central Hindukush, 591.
Central Punjab, 508.
Ceylon, 540, 729.
Chach-nâmah, 638.
Chandragupta, 442, 454.
Charax Phra, 596.
Charikar, 590, 601.
Chariots, 363, 450.
Charles Eliot, 332.
Charles Masson, 590.
Charorai, 614.
Chenab, 630.
Chichapâlapur, 646.
China, 729.
Chinese pilgrim, 568.
Chinese, 550.
Chinnock, 415.
Choaspa, 600.
Christ, 355, 365, 488.
Christian Church, 355.
Christian doctrine, 356.
Christian era, 355, 356, 366, 401, 416, 478, 482, 490, 495, 505, 512, 524, 530, 537, 540, 549, 556, 568, 571, 573, 588, 601, 607, 621, 628, 632, 646, 688, 701, 717, 720, 723, 727, 730.
Christian missionaries, 355.
Christian, 355.
Christianity, 355, 357.
Christians, 357.
Chrysostom met, 507.
Chrysostom, 507.
Chuchpur, 638.
Chumla valley, 614.
Churches, 355.
Classical culture, 504.
Clemens, 333, 337, 512, 530.
Clisobora, 560.
Coenon (Coenus), 388.
Coimbatore, 466.
Colebrooke, 332.
Constantinople, 538.
Cophen (Kâbul) river, 585.
Cosmas, 356.
Critobulus, 406.
Cunningham, 404, 410, 443, 462, 494, 559, 588, 599, 607, 619, 631, 635, 647.
Curtius Beira, 612.
Curtius, 339, 384, 386, 388, 392, 409, 437, 450, 551.
Cynic philosophers, 342.
Cynic, 344.
Cypriot sailors, 366.
Cyrus, 361, 369, 375, 523.

D

D.B. Spooner, 569, 691.
D.C. Sircar, 577.
Dachinabades, 464, 572.
Dakhinabades, 572.
Damis, 401.
Damma, 507.
Dandaguda, 570.
Dandagula, 570.

Dandamis, 342, 512.
Danish invasion, 418.
Dantapura, 570.
Darapur, 628.
Darius, 362, 377.
Deccan, 334, 464, 541, 572, 692, 735.
Deity (God), 349.
Delta, 410, 639.
Demetrius, 357.
Depâlpur, 632.
Dhanananda, 399, 400, 437, 438, 439, 440, 441.
Dhânyakaþaka, 464.
Dharma-Chakra, 508.
Dhârwâd district, 576.
Digambara Jains, 349.
Dilâwar (Udinagar), 628.
Dilâwar, 628.
Diodorus Siculus, 343, 363, 366, 387, 549.
Dion Cassius, 538.
Dion Chrysostom, 507.
Dionysiaka, 464, 587.
Dionysios, 587.
Dionysius Periegetes, 489.
Dionysos, 407, 550.
Dionysus, 333, 362, 724.
Diya (Dion), 509.
Drachma, 507.
Drangai, 596.
Drangiana, 595, 598.
Drangiane, 596.
Drapsaca, 604.
Drastoka, 594.
Drepsa, 594, 604.
Drepsiani, 594.
Droysen, 606.
Dynasty, 365.
Dytra, 389.

E

E.A. Schwanbeck, 331.
E.B. Havell, 692.
E.H. Bunbury, 346, 587, 593.
E.H. Warmington, 539.
E.I. Railway, 569.
E.J. Rapson, 362, 377, 494, 720.
E.R. Bevan, 348.
East Asia, 729.
Eastern Afghanistan, 598.
Eastern Asia, 603.
Egypt, 341, 362, 377, 383, 390, 418, 451, 507, 511, 529, 607, 617, 644.
Egyptian Delta, 645.
Egyptian Rameses, 365.
Egyptian Sesostris, 364.
Egyptian, 363, 507.
Egyptians, 363, 509, 511.
Ekabatana, 697.
Ekbatana, 567, 697.
Elagabalus, 541.
Elder Porus, 399.
Elphinstone, 605.
Embolima, 389, 614.
Emperor Aurelian, 541.
Emperor Candragupta Maurya, 690.
Emperor Claudius, 540.
Emperor Hadrian, 540.
Emperor Julian, 542.
Emperor Justinianus (Justinian), 542.
England, 418.
English Cardamom, 514.
Erannoboas (Son), 566.
Eratosthenes, 362.
Erod Yirodu, 576.
Erythraean sea, 376, 573.
Erythraean, 373.
Ethiopia, 357, 363.

Eucratides, 479.
Eudemus, 441.
Euphranor, 700.
Europeans, 416, 419, 733.
Eusebius Pamphili, 356, 357.
Eusebius Pamphilus (Pamphili), 355.
Eusebius, 355, 357.
Euthydemia, 626.
Euthydemus, 478.

F

Farah, 596.
Farrukhâbâd district, 561.
Farzah, 594.
Fazilpur, 641.
French, 463.
Frumentius, 357.
Furrah, 596.
Fusheng, 596.

G

G. Macdonald, 478, 494.
G. Tucci, 611.
G.N. Banerjee, 501, 689.
Gadârâ (Gândhâra), 377.
Gandaraeans (Gândhârians), 589.
Gandaridai, 396.
Gândhâra country, 585.
Gândhâra region, 377, 497, 555, 588.
Gândhâra, 368, 375, 459, 460, 478, 482, 496, 505, 524, 555, 585, 602, 611, 616, 731.
Gândhârians (Gandarioi), 379.
Gândhâric territory, 460.
Ganges (Gaógâ), 565.
Gangetic Doâb, 559.
Gangetic kingdom, 398, 400, 437, 732.
Gangetic Magadha kingdom, 439.
Gangetic region, 383, 399, 438, 559, 566.
Gangetic valley, 555.
Gaógâridai, 399.
Gaógâ-Yamunâ valley, 559.
Garuda, 509.
Gaza, 464.
Gedrosia (Baluchistan), 370, 376, 411, 453, 479, 649, 651.
Gedrosian, 411, 441.
Gedrosoi (Gedrosians), 411.
General Ferrier, 604.
Ghâr river, 640.
Ghazni, 599, 608, 642.
Ghor, 589.
Ghorband rivers, 591, 593.
Ghorband valley, 601.
Ghorband, 589.
Glauganikai, 630.
Glaukanikoi, 394, 630.
Glausai, 394, 553, 630.
Godâvarî river, 574.
Godiarei, 648.
Gospel, 355, 357.
Graeco-Bactria, 488.
Graeco-Bactrian coins, 629.
Graeco-Bactrian monarchy, 478, 503.
Graeco-Roman, 505, 692, 702.
Great Porus, 333, 392, 413, 442, 627.
Greater Ariana, 453.
Grecian Sangala, 625.
Greek Christian monk, 704.
Greek Governor, 442.
Greek imperialism, 441.
Greek rule, 441.
Greeks Muziris, 355.
Gujarât peninsula, 571.
Gujarat, 481, 489, 570, 735.
Gulf of Kutch, 571.
Gurûkula system, 711.

Gushtasp, 595.
Guzaristan, 599.
Gymnetai, 349.
Gymnosophists, 409.
Gymnosophists, 337.

H

H. Cousens, 572.
H. G. Rawlinson, 338, 364, 419.
H.C. Ray Chaudhri, 418.
H.D. Sankalia, 623.
H.F. Tozer, 531.
H.G. Rawlinson, 338, 364, 419, 443, 454, 502, 507, 523, 530, 589, 603, 650, 704, 720.
H.H. Wilson, 348, 367, 462, 587, 595, 601, 761.
H.J. Mackinder, 370.
H.L. Jones, 365, 717.
H.T. Prinsep, 494.
Haidarabad, 410, 644.
Hajiyak, 601.
Hara, 334.
Haraivâ, 377.
Haraouvati, 377.
Harapa, 404.
Harappâ, 624.
Haro river, 618.
Hasan Abdal, 618.
Hashtnagar, 461, 607, 613, 623.
Hasti, 384, 460.
Hâstinâyana, 385, 461.
Hebrew, 357.
Hecatacus, 587, 589.
Hecataeus, 459, 586.
Heeren, 367, 510, 587, 596, 720.
Hekataeus, 590.
Heliodorus, 509.
Heliogabalus, 541, 704.
Heliopolis, 363.
Hellenic fashion, 401.
Hellenic kingdom, 529, 736.
Hellenic rulers, 531.
Hellenism, 419, 501, 600.
Hellenistic art, 504, 691.
Hellenistic culture, 502, 733.
Hellenistic, 501, 532, 621.
Hellenized, 420, 482.
Helmund, 597.
Henry Beveridge, 365.
Hephaistion, 385, 400.
Herakles, 332.
Herât, 377, 453, 478, 595.
Hermaeus, 482, 496.
Herodotus, 349, 363, 377, 459, 523.
Hierokles, 332, 342.
Himâlayan region, 463.
Himalayas (Hemodus), 728.
Himyaritic origin, 719.
Hinduism, 332, 501, 736.
Hindukush, 377, 384, 453, 454, 479, 487, 591, 727.
Hippokoura, 574.
His Epistles, 733.
Hiuen Tsang, 550, 568, 590, 601, 616, 623, 637, 641.
Hodgson, 560.
Hora (Ora), 388.
Houpian, 591.
Humboldt, 588.
Hydaspes, 333, 390, 398, 460, 495, 552, 617.
Hyderabad, 645.
Hydrakai, 379.
Hydraotes, 396, 404, 461, 624.
Hylobioi, 339.
Hypahsis, 400.
Hypanis (Hyphasis), 394, 400, 481.

I

Ibn Haukil, 596.
Indian Brachmans, 332, 342.
Indian Brâhmaòas, 331.
Indian Caucasus (Hindukush), 591.
Indo-Hellenic architecture, 690, 701.
Indo-Scythia, 487, 605, 621.
Indo-Scythian period, 629.
Indo-Scythian Sus, 621.
Indo-Scythians, 487, 605.
Indus Delta, 410, 645.
Indus Ptolemy, 460.
Indus Valley deserve, 552.
Indus valley, 378, 415, 441, 455, 480, 524, 552, 639, 703.
Isidore, 479, 595, 720.
Island, 574, 639.

J

J. B. Bury, 417.
J. Filliozat, 713.
J. Hutchinson, 606.
J. Rennell, 586, 599.
J.B. Bury, 604.
J.F. Fleet, 572.
J.F.C. Fuller, 406.
J.H. Marshall, 690, 692.
J.Ph. Vogel, 606.
J.T. Wheeler, 347, 589, 719.
J.W. McCirndle, 376.
J.W. Mccrindle, 334, 362, 419, 494, 502, 510, 529, 587.
J.W. Sedlar, 510.
Jabalpur, 575.
Jahangira, 585.
Jainism, 337, 731.
Jains, 337, 731.
Jalâlâbâd, 384, 606.
Jalâlpur, 627.
Jalalpur, 627.
James Douie, 378.
Jayapur, 605.
Jesus, 355.
Jhadejas, 648.
Jhang district, 625.
Jhang districts, 634.
Jhelum (Bidespes), 629.
River Jhelum, 628.
Jhelum, 463, 554, 586, 615, 626, 630.
John Marshall, 494, 618, 691, 699.
Jomanes, 370, 481.
Julius Valerius Pecanus, 462.
Julius Valerius, 384, 394, 408, 462, 549, 591, 605, 636, 651.
Jupiter Pluvius, 334.
Justin, 368, 383, 396, 411, 417, 440, 454, 477, 493, 537, 549, 606, 624, 646.
Justinian, 537, 736.

K

K.C. Sagar, 698.
Kabolitae, 594, 601.
Kâbul mission, 605.
Kâbul river, 333, 384, 389, 459, 461, 585, 589, 600, 605, 608, 614.
Kâbul valley (Paropanisadae), 601.
Kâbul valley, 375, 384, 442, 453, 460, 478, 586.
Kâbul, 368, 371, 375, 384, 442, 453, 459.
Kâbulistan, 600.
Kâbul-Rûda, 602.
Kabura (Kâbul), 594, 608.
Kacch, 639, 648.
Kachh-Gandava, 640.
Kadambas, 577.
Kafiristan, 589.
Kalanos, 343.

Kalinipaxa, 561.
Kalisapura, 560.
Kalliena, 464.
Kallisthenes, 418.
Kalyana, 541.
Kanagora, 561.
Kânârâ district, 577.
Kanara, 577.
Kanauj, 561.
Kandahâr region, 496.
Kandahâr, 368, 453, 478, 595, 640.
Kandake, 598.
Kânyakubja, 561.
Kaoemîr, 461, 463, 630.
Kaoeyapamira, 587.
Kaoeyapapura (Kashmir), 588.
Kaoeyapapura, 587.
Kapioea, 589, 593, 608, 624.
Kapisene, 589.
Karachi, 640.
Kardamomum, 514.
Karmania, 441.
Karòâþadeoea, 575.
Karoura, 466, 578.
Karsana, 593.
Karura (Karoura), 601.
Karyanda, 377, 585.
Kashabpur, 587.
Kashmir, 462, 586.
Kaspapyros, 586.
Kaspapyrus, 587.
Kaspatyros, 585.
Kaspeira, 586.
Kaspeiria (Kaoemîr), 464.
Kaspeiria, 463, 586.
Kaspeiroi, 464, 587.
Kaspian Gates, 596.
Kathaia (Kathaians), 398.
Kathaia, 396, 555.
Kathaians (Kšatriyas), 413.
Kathaians, 397, 398, 413, 555.
Kathaioi, 631.
Kathiawar, 571.
Kedrenus, 342.
Kerala, 356, 466.
Kerobothros, 466.
Kharošþhi, 506.
Khattriaioi, 639.
Khuddakas, 637.
King Âmbhi, 391, 441.
King Kaoeiputra Bhagabhadra, 509.
King Ninus, 366.
King Pandion, 539.
King Seleukus, 452.
King Porus, 442.
Kirrhadae, 333.
Kirrhadia, 333.
Kleitarchus, 367.
Kodungalur, 355.
Koh-Daman, 591.
Kohistan, 591.
Kohistan-Kafiristan, 589.
Koimbatur district, 466.
Koimbatur gap, 467, 576.
Kokaris, 648.
Kokkamangalam, 355.
Kolhapur, 574.
Kolkhoi, 467.
Kollam, 355.
Komaria, 728.
Kophen (Kâbul), 368, 376.
Kophen, 384, 459.
Kophes (Kâbul), 368, 385.
Korkai (Kolkai), 467.
Koroungkala, 577.
Kos Meropis, 630.

Kosmas, 380, 571.
Kot-Kamâlia, 404.
Kottakkayal, 355.
Kottayam, 355.
Kranganur (Cranganore), 355.
Krokola, 648.
Kšatriyas, 412, 626.
Kshudrakas, 379.
Kunâr river, 385, 609.
Kunâr valley, 385, 412.
Kunduz, 604.
Kušâòa empire, 590.
Kushan valley, 601.

L

L.A. Waddell, 569.
L.J. Trotter, 365.
Labokla, 632.
Laddakh region, 463.
Lahor, 624.
Lahore, 624, 632.
Lallanji Gopal, 718.
Landai, 608.
Laribandar, 645.
Libya, 377.
Logarh river, 601.
Logarh valley, 602.
Logarh, 593.
Lohawar, 632.
Lohrasp, 595.
Lokharna, 593, 601.
London, 593.
Lord Curzon, 555.
Lord Krishna, 332.
Lower Himâlayan region, 463.
Lower Hydraotes, 403.
Lower Indus region, 488, 495.
Lower Indus Valley, 441, 462, 480, 489, 497, 644, 703.
Lower Indus, 411.
Lower Kophen, 389.
Lower Sindh, 410, 416, 481, 498, 555, 640.
Lower Swât valley, 610.
Lysimachos, 392.

M

M. Court, 368, 592.
M. Elphinstone, 338, 348, 415, 593.
M. Ghosh, 569.
M. Jacquet, 596.
M.A. Stein, 585.
M.L.W. Laistner, 418.
M.R. Haig, 645.
Macedon, 333, 361, 384.
Macedonains, 403, 442.
Macedonia, 333, 361, 400.
Macedonian attack, 385.
Macedonian empire, 383.
Macedonian Greeks, 592.
Macedonian invaders, 552.
Macedonian king, 440.
Macedonian power, 650.
Macedonian rule, 732.
Macedonian soldiers, 385, 406.
Macedonian storm, 420.
Macedonians, 333, 361, 383, 394, 405, 412, 453, 479, 552, 600, 651,731.
Madura, 467, 539.
Madurâ, 540.
Madurai, 467.
Magadha kingdom, 565.
Magadhan king, 399.
Magadhan, 399, 439.
Mahâbhârata, 368, 575.
Mahâpadma Nanda, 437.
Mahârâšþra, 464, 489, 541, 572, 704.

Mahmud, 642.
Mahorta, 462, 640.
Maihota, 640.
Maisolia, 577.
Maisoloi, 577.
Majumdar, 338, 368, 540.
Malabar region, 355.
Malabar, 356, 466.
Malana, 649.
Malanga, 577.
Mâlavas, 732.
Malaya Peninsula, 729.
Malloi (Mâlavas), 413, 633.
Malloi, 397, 404, 406, 553, 633.
Mandalai, 570.
Mandanis, 342, 512.
Mandaravara, 606.
Manetho, 365.
Mangal-De hill, 627.
Mannert, 587.
Mansura, 640.
St. Martin, 369, 462, 560, 610, 638.
Mashkine, 610.
Massanoi, 408.
Masulipatam regions, 577.
Materia Medica (Herbal), 514.
Maurya (Sandrakottus), 529.
Maurya art, 691, 692.
Maurya dynasty, 437, 443, 691, 733.
Maurya emperor, 449, 530, 565, 690, 697, 723, 727.
Maurya Empire, 380, 452, 529, 565, 602.
Maurya Hall, 698.
Maurya period, 567.
Maurya system, 730.
Mauryas, 530, 565, 620, 688.
Max Duncker, 340, 368, 463, 554.
Max Müller, 369, 443.
Mazaga, 387, 609.
McCrindle, 334, 362, 369, 419, 443.
Medes, 376, 482, 524.
Megasthenes Arrian, 550.
Megasthenes, 332, 337, 340, 345, 362, 369, 400, 449, 467, 511.
Mekran-barren, 370.
Memnonian Susa, 697.
Memphis, 363.
Menander, 480, 508, 626.
Menandrum (Menander), 481.
Menandrus, 480.
Menephthah, 365.
Mihirakula, 626.
Milinda, 508, 626.
Minnagara, 488, 490, 646, 703.
Mithânkot, 638.
Modern Furrah, 596.
Modern Peshawar, 460, 589.
Modura, 467, 576.
Montgomery Martin, 365.
Mophis, 391.
Mousikanus, 408, 414.
Mr. Masson, 590, 593.
Mr. Schoff, 646.
Mr. Vigne, 592.
Mrs. C. Speir, 443.
Muchiri, 355.
Muhammad bin Kasim, 637, 642.
Muhammedan ruins, 604.
Multan district, 634.
Multân Prahlâdapur, 646.
Multan, 405, 586.
Multân, 634.
Musarna, 641.
Musarnei, 641.
Musicani, 639.

Musikana, 639.
Musikanus, 639, 642.
Mysore, 577.

N

N.M. Chapekar, 378.
N.R. Ray, 691.
Nagara, 347, 488, 497, 593.
Nagarahâra, 607.
Nâgârjunakoṇḍa, 577.
Nâgasena, 508.
Nahapana, 490.
Nammadus, 571.
Nanda dynasty, 399, 437, 733.
Nanda king, 438.
Nanda Monarch (Dhananananda), 441.
Nanda monarch, 437, 733.
Nangnihar, 606.
Naqsh-i-Rustam, 377.
River Narmadâ, 490, 539.
Nâsik, 465.
Naulibis, 594, 602.
Naulibus, 602.
Nearchus, 340, 369, 376, 418.
Nearkhos Krokala, 648.
Nearkhos, 636, 644, 651.
Nellore, 466.
Nereae, 466, 648.
Nestorian Christians, 357.
Nharonis, 648.
Nicaea, 605, 624.
Nihar Ranjan Ray, 567.
Nikaea, 605, 628.
Nikaia, 394, 605, 628.
Nikolaos Damaskenos, 571.
Nilab, 594.
Niphanda, 593.
Nirankot, 645.
Nisa, 375, 442, 478.
Nisibis, 595.
North West Frontier Province, 480, 555.
Nysa, 333, 368, 384, 606.
Nysaeans, 384, 606, 730.
Nysaeons, 333.
Nysaioi, 606.
Nysatta village, 607.
Nyssa, 606.

O

Odisha, 565.
Oeconomicus, 332, 342.
Olostae, 648.
Omphis (Âmbhi), 390, 442.
Omphis, 390.
Onesikritos, 631.
Onesikritus, 342, 418, 512.
Ora, 332, 344, 378.
Oreitai, 411, 469.
Orissa, 565, 570.
Oritai, 411.
Orrhotha, 571.
Orthospanum, 601.
Ortospana, 591, 598, 606.
Osmanabad, 572.
Ossadioi, 407.
Oxydrakai, 379, 397, 553, 637.
Oxykanus, 408.
Ozene (Ujjayini), 490.
Ozene, 490.

P

P.L. Bhargava, 443.
Paethana, 464.
Pahalavas, 621.
Paithan, 464.
Paithana, 572.
Pakistan, 555.
Paktyike, 586.

Palayoor, 355.
Pâlibothra (Pâþaliputra), 530, 568, 697.
Pâlibothra, 383, 399, 437, 530.
Pâlimbothra, 437, 565.
Palladius, 332, 400.
Pandian, 466.
Pândyan king, 692.
Panjab, 389, 413, 463, 554.
Panjhir, 594.
Panjkora river, 609.
Panjkora valley, 609.
Panjkora, 386.
Panjshir river, 594.
Panjshir Valley, 594.
Panjshir, 589, 601.
Pantaenus, 356.
Pâõini, 368.
Paropamisadai (Kâbul), 453, 591.
Paropamisadai, 453, 591.
Paropamisus range (Hindukush), 453.
Paropamisus, 377, 453.
Paropanisadae (Kâbul valley), 375, 378, 453.
Paropanisadae, 375, 453, 478, 592.
Paropanisadai (Kâbul Valley), 442.
Paropanisos (Hindukush), 603.
Paropanisus, 480.
Parthia, 483, 493.
Parthian emperor Vardanes, 497.
Parthian empire, 495.
Parthian king, 493.
Parthian kingdom, 493.
Parthian rule, 489.
Parthians, 482.
Patala, 410, 480, 489.
Pâþaliputra city, 566.
Pâþaliputra, 383, 399, 437, 452.
Pâþalpur, 644.
Patna, 567.
Pauravas, 559.
Pedukotta, 466.
Peithon, 408, 441.
Pentagramma, 640.
Perdikkas, 389, 404.
Peringkarei, 576.
Periodos Ges, 459.
Periplus Maris Erythraei, 464.
Periplus, 411, 459, 552, 649.
Persia, 343, 375, 453, 513.
Persian empire, 367, 524.
Persian Gulf, 418.
Persian Monarch Cyrus, 361.
Persians, 362, 453.
Persic empire, 367.
Peshawar District, 586.
Peshawar, 385, 460, 507.
Peukelaitis, 460.
Peukelaotis (Puškalâvatî), 388.
Peukelaotis, 384, 460.
Peukolaitis, 460.
Phegeus, 398.
Philemon Holland, 591.
Philip, 383, 441.
Philosophical Doctrines, 338.
Philostratus, 332, 346, 497, 555.
Phoenician, 366.
Phoenicians, 377.
Photius, 356.
Phraates, 496.
Pimprama, 396.
Pir-sae, 614.
Pityndra, 577.
Pliny Capisa, 589.
Pliny Modura, 467.
Pliny, 342, 400, 452, 628.

Vellâru (Vellar), 466.
Vijayadurga, 574.
Vijayapurî, 577.
Vijayawâdâ, 577.
Vikramâditya, 574.
Vilivâyakura, 574.
Vindhyas, 455.
Virasena, 620.

W

W. Robertson, 364.
W. Vincent, 370, 588.
W.H. Hutton, 365.
W.H. Schoff, 464, 488, 497, 586.
W.W. Hunter, 443, 690.
W.W. Tarn, 333, 378, 418, 481, 502, 591, 651, 701.
Warangal, 577.
Wazîrâbâd, 629.
Wessex, 418.
West Asia, 729.
West Mâlavâ region, 489.
Western Asia, 477, 523, 736.
Western Punjab, 439, 525.
Western Roman Empire, 542.
Westminster, 561, 593.
Wilkinson, 365.
William Ouseley, 599.
Wilson, 348, 367, 462, 588.

X

Xathroi, 407.

Y

Yamunâ river, 481.
Yamunâ Valley, 481.
Yasamatika, 490.
Yavanas, 600.
Yellapur, 576.
Ysâmotika, 490.
Yuan Chwang, 589.
Yueh-Chi tribe, 487.
Yusuf-Zai tribe, 615.

Z

Zaradros (Sutlej), 586.
Zaranj, 597.
Zariaspa, 597.
Zarmanus, 539.
Zarmaros, 539.
Zend, 598.
Zeus (Jupiter), 343.
Zeus Ombrios, 334.
Zeuxis, 700.

Plutarch, 344, 384, 393, 415, 440, 481, 549, 594, 606.
Polybius, 478.
Polygnotus, 700.
Porouaroi (Pauravas), 559.
Porouaroi, 559.
Portikanus, 408, 462.
Porus, 333, 391, 398, 401, 413, 438, 442, 461, 497, 504, 531, 627, 631, 688.
Porvaroi, 559.
Poura (Bâmpur), 412, 441.
Prâkrit, 507, 572.
Pramnai, 347.
Prasii, 438.
Prophthasia, 596.
Pseudo-Kallisthenes, 345.
Pseudo-Origen, 341.
Ptolemy Kandaroi, 598.
Punjab Government, 625.
Punjab, 333, 378, 439, 442, 454, 479, 489, 497, 525, 550, 552, 588, 619, 624, 626, 632, 652, 689, 730, 733.
Purali, 411.
Purušapura, 385, 460, 555.
Pushkarasarin, 523.
Puškalâvatî, 384, 412, 460.
Pyramid (Stûpa), 348.
Pythagoras, 344, 346, 509.
Pythagorean philosophy, 510.
Pythagoreans, 510.

Q

Queen Cleophis, 387.
Queen Semiramis, 366.
Quintus Curtius Rufuš, 549.

R

R.A. Jairazbhoy, 698.
R.C. Jain, 338, 724.
R.C. Majumdar, 540, 720.
R.D. Banerji, 589.
R.S. Sharma, 630.
R.S. Tripathi, 416, 443, 494.
Radha Kumud Mookerji, 442, 450.
Raja Amba, 632.
Raja Hodi, 613.
Rajauri districts, 630.
Rajur, 616.
Râmnagar, 560.
Ram-Shehristan, 597.
Râvî, 405, 463, 586, 624.
Rawalpindi district, 390, 460, 617.
Rawalpindi, 390, 460.
Râwalpiṇḍî district, 555.
Rawlinson, 589, 603, 650, 704, 720.
Reliqua Inde Seleuco Nicatori, 452.
Rennell, 587, 610.
Revenue system, 730.
Rhambacia, 649.
Rhambakia, 649.
Ritter, 592.
Rock Edict, 532.
Rohilkhand, 561.
Roman Emperor, 357, 513, 538, 692.
Roman Empire, 355, 505, 537, 541, 729.

S

S.B. Mookherji, 697.
Sabbas, 409.
Sabjalkot, 641.
Sadenoi, 573.
Sadineis, 465.
Sadinon, 464.
Sagala, 479, 508.
Saidu Sharif region, 612.
Saindhava-vanam, 642.
Saindhuwân, 642.
Saint Martin, 625.

Samanaeans, 347.
Sambalaka, 561.
Sambalpur, 570.
Sambhal, 561.
Sambus, 408, 642.
Sammanaeoi, 337.
Sammuramnat, 369.
Samos, 464, 539.
Sandabal (Cenâb), 586.
Sandabal, 463.
Sandanes, 464, 541.
Sandares, 464.
Sandrakottus (Candragupta), 691, 697, 723.
Sandrakottus, 380, 441, 449, 453, 529, 691, 697, 719, 723.
Sandrocottus (Candragputa), 439.
Sandrokoptos (Candragupta), 530.
Sandrokottos (Candragupta Maurya), 602.
Sandrokottos, 449, 602.
Sangala Hill, 625.
Sangala, 397, 479, 555, 624.
Sangalawala-Tiba, 625.
Sangola, 397.
Sanjay, 385, 615.
Sanskrit Kardama, 514.
Sanskrit Saubhûtu, 398.
Saôhitâ, 577.
Sarabhan, 638.
Sarmanai (Buddhists), 335.
Sarmanes, 337, 731.
Sarmatina, 595.
Sarophages, 638.
Sâtavâhana dynasty, 464, 573.
Sâtavâhana kingdom, 464, 572, 735.
Sâtavâhana kings, 464, 572.
Sâtavâhana period, 577.
Sâtavâhana rulers, 464, 490.
Sâtavâhanas, 464, 572.
Saubhûta, 398, 631.
Scythia, 480, 487, 574.
Scythians, 480, 487, 574, 621.
Scythio-Parthian period, 701.
Sehwan, 462, 633.
Seistan, 488, 597.
Seleucid empire, 477.
Seleucus Nicator, 452, 477, 493.
Seleukus Nikator, 451, 478, 529, 566, 727.
Seleukus, 392, 452, 453, 455, 566.
Semiramis, 362, 367, 599, 603.
Semnoi (holymen), 349.
Semnoi, 337.
Semulla, 573.
Seorai, 641.
Sepulchral, 590.
Shah Jahan, 623.
Shahpur, 641.
Shaikhan, 616.
Shamans, 714.
Shehdâdpur, 644.
Sheikh Mithia Ghari, 568.
Shekohpura, 632.
Shikarpur, 369.
Shirpao, 616.
Sibarae, 638.
Sighan, 592.
Simylla, 573.
Sindh, 377, 407, 410, 441, 454, 488, 497, 554, 609, 633.
Sindhu Valley, 497.
Sindhu, 378.
Sindimana, 408.
Sindomana, 408, 462, 642.
Sir John Marshall, 618, 619.

Sir Mortimer Wheeler, 616.
Siro Polemaios, 465.
Sirsi Taluk, 577.
Sir-Suk, 623.
Sirwahi, 641.
Sisikottos (Œaœigupta), 614.
Sisikottos, 395.
Skiratai, 333.
Skt. Prasthala, 489.
Skylax, 377, 585.
Sodrai, 408.
Sogdoi, 408, 418.
Solinus, 451, 549.
Sonârgâon, 570.
Sopeithes, 398.
Sorath, 571.
Sorgae, 638.
Sotera, 595.
Souanagoura, 569.
Sousa (Susa), 343.
Sousikana, 639.
South Asia, 729.
Southern Ghats, 467, 576.
Spain, 539.
Sramanai, 347, 731.
St. Jerome, 342, 346, 356.
St. Martin, 369, 377, 462, 464, 560, 569, 571, 599, 638.
St. Matthew, 357.
St. Thomas, 355.
St. Zerome, 357.
Starbo Paropamisadai, 600.
Stephanus Byzantinus, 587, 633.
Stephanus, 332, 342, 459, 488, 587, 591, 597, 649.
Sthavarpati, 368.
Stoicism, 356.
Storm, 387.
Strabo Peukolaitis, 615.
Strabo Polyaenus, 384.
Strabo tells, 379.
Strabo, 334, 339, 362, 375, 395, 449, 453, 460, 466, 478, 487, 512, 531.
Subhagasena, 479.
Sukkur district, 640.
Suppara, 572.
Surat, 490, 571.
Suriyanis, 648.
Susa, 343, 412, 567.
Sutlej, 586, 632, 648.
Sûtra, 385.
Suvarœagrâma, 570.
Swât (Souastos), 555.
Swât river, 616.
Swât Valley, 333, 368, 376, 412.
Syria, 451, 477, 493, 514, 529, 538, 704.
Syrian court, 529.
Syrian kingdom, 451.
Syrian kings, 478.
Syrian Monarch Seleukus Nikator, 529.
Syrian monarch Seleukus, 453, 529, 734.
Syrian monarchy, 451.
Syrian, 355
Syrieni, 576.

T

T.H. Holdich, 606.
T.H. Thornton, 632.
Ta-cha-shi-lo, 623.
Tagara, 572.
Tagarapura, 572.
Tainour, 576.
Takkas, 617.
Takšaoeilâ, 460, 617.

Tamilakam, 575.
Tamluk, 569.
Tâmraliptî, 569.
Tâmraparṇî river, 467.
Tangala, 576.
Tangi, 616.
Taprobane (Ceylon), 540.
Taxila city, 332, 503.
Taxila region, 482, 612.
Taxila, 332, 342, 385, 390, 439, 460, 479, 489, 503, 509, 525, 555, 594, 611.
Teliṅgânâ region, 577.
Tewar, 575.
Thane district, 357, 464, 541, 573.
Thatha, 645.
Thatta, 645.
Thebes, 363.
Theodotus, 477.
Thirlwall, 606.
Thomas Maurice, 361.
Thomas McEvilley, 511, 702.
Tibet, 463.
Tibetan portion, 463.
Tinneveli, 576.
Tinnevelley, 467.
Tinnevelly, 467, 576.
Tondiman Râja, 577.
Toulumba, 635.
Travancore, 466.
Trichinopoly, 466, 575.
Tulamba, 405, 635.
Tuṅgabhadra, 577.
Turangzai, 616.
Turanian race, 617.
Tyana, 497.
Tyros (Tyre), 357.

U

Udayanapura, 607.
Umbrittae, 638.
Umrzai, 616.
United Panjshir, 591.
Unnâo district, 561.
Upanishadic age, 509.
Upper Kâbul valley, 376, 480, 496, 586, 731.
Upper Mahânadi, 570.
Upper Sindh Oxykanus, 414.
Upper Sindh, 408, 462, 639, 713.
Upper Swât District, 614.
Upper Syria, 451.
Uragapur, 466.
Uraiyûr, 466, 575.
Uraoea, 461.
River Urghundab, 598.
Usmanzai, 616.
Uttar Pradesh, 560, 561.

V

V.A. Smith, 420, 454, 463, 502, 588, 601, 612, 630, 689, 701.
V.S. Agrawala, 415, 460.
River Vaigai, 467, 576.
Vaijayanti, 574.
Vaijayantipura, 574.
Vaišṇava cult, 509.
Valerius Baziphara, 612.
Valerius, 408, 462.
Vallabhî, 571.
Vallabhîpura, 571.
River Varadâ, 577.
Varâhamihir, 577.
Vasai (Bassein), 573.
Vasudeva (Vishnu), 509.
Vasudeva Sharana Agrawala, 554.

Vellâru (Vellar), 466.
Vijayadurga, 574.
Vijayapurî, 577.
Vijayawâdâ, 577.
Vikramâditya, 574.
Vilivâyakura, 574.
Vindhyas, 455.
Virasena, 620.

W

W. Robertson, 364.
W. Vincent, 370, 588.
W.H. Hutton, 365.
W.H. Schoff, 464, 488, 497, 586.
W.W. Hunter, 443, 690.
W.W. Tarn, 333, 378, 418, 481, 502, 591, 651, 701.
Warangal, 577.
Wazîrâbâd, 629.
Wessex, 418.
West Asia, 729.
West Mâlavâ region, 489.
Western Asia, 477, 523, 736.
Western Punjab, 439, 525.
Western Roman Empire, 542.
Westminster, 561, 593.
Wilkinson, 365.
William Ouseley, 599.
Wilson, 348, 367, 462, 588.

X

Xathroi, 407.

Y

Yamunâ river, 481.
Yamunâ Valley, 481.
Yasamatika, 490.
Yavanas, 600.
Yellapur, 576.
Ysâmotika, 490.
Yuan Chwang, 589.
Yueh-Chi tribe, 487.
Yusuf-Zai tribe, 615.

Z

Zaradros (Sutlej), 586.
Zaranj, 597.
Zariaspa, 597.
Zarmanus, 539.
Zarmaros, 539.
Zend, 598.
Zeus (Jupiter), 343.
Zeus Ombrios, 334.
Zeuxis, 700.